The Geography
of Public Finance

Welfare under Fiscal Federalism and
Local Government Finance

The Geography of Public Finance

Welfare under Fiscal Federalism and Local Government Finance

R. J. BENNETT

METHUEN
London and New York

First published in 1980 by
Methuen & Co. Ltd
11 New Fetter Lane, London EC4P 4EE

Published in the USA by
Methuen & Co.
in association with Methuen, Inc.
733 Third Avenue, New York, NY 10017

British Library Cataloguing in Publication Data

Bennett, Robert John
    The geography of public finance.
    1. Finance, Public
    2. Geography, Economic
    I. Title
    336   HJ192   79 — 41792

ISBN 0-416-73090-6

Contents

Acknowledgements

In writing a book such as this it is inevitable that I have become deeply indebted to a large number of individuals and institutions. The stimulus of Gerald Manners and Bill Mead at University College, London, and the catholic atmosphere of that institution, provided the initial impetus for the work, but the material took its present shape during visits to the United States and Canada. This was initially made possible by the generous financial support of the Houblon-Norman Fund and the William Waldorf Astor Foundation. In addition, the support of the Brookings Institution, where I was privileged to be a Guest Scholar in 1978, proved a turning point in the thinking behind the book. I owe a great debt to Joe Pechman, Dick Nathan, Paul Dommel, Jim Sunquist, Martha Derthick, Kathy Bradbury, Tony Downs and many others at Brookings who gave generously of their time in meetings and helped by providing an atmosphere which was totally stimulating to the work. Outside Brookings, other friends and contacts in Washington also gave me their help generously and I would especially like to thank Bob Reischauer, Peggy Cuciti, Kent Halstead, Phil Dearborn, Janet Pack and Tom Muller. As well as similar discussions, Gary and Carolyn Hufbauer and Bob and Janice Burns also provided much-needed accommodation in Washington. In addition friends in Berkeley, Toronto, Buffalo, McMaster, Boston, Minnesota, Princeton and New York contributed in various ways to the formulation of the ideas in this book and I am very grateful for their tolerance and help. Finally, I must thank my wife Elizabeth for her continual help and support: a true galley slave.

The figures were drawn by Pamela Morgan-Lucas, Arthur Sheldon, Roy Versey and Mike Young, and photographs were provided by Bob Coe. The manuscript was typed mostly by Mrs Claudette John.

In addition to this help, I am grateful to the following individuals, editors and publishers for permission to reproduce copyright material:

Urban Institute, Washington D. C., for tables 4.3, 5.5, 6.3 and 8.5.

Directorate-General for Economic and Financial Affairs, Commission of the European Communities, Luxembourg, for tables 4.4, 11.2, 13.4, 13.21, 14.8 and Appendix 1, and figures 13.1–13.3.

North Holland Publishing Co., Amsterdam, for table 5.3, and figure 3.1 and Professor W. W. Snyder for figure 3.1.

Department of the Environment (Crown Copyright reserved) for tables 6.4, 6.7, 6.8 and 6.9, and figures 6.1, 6.3–6.8 and 10.5.

Cambridge University Press for table 6.10, and figure 6.2.

Canadian Tax Foundation, Toronto, for tables 7.6 and 13.8–13.11.

Tax Institute of America, Columbus, Ohio, and Mr T. F. Pogue for table 8.3, and figure 12.5.

Lexington Books, D. C. Heath, Lexington, Mass., for tables 8.7, 8.8, 11.5, 13.4, 14.5 and 14.6 and figures 8.7 and 9.7.

US Advisory Commission on Intergovernmental Relations, Washington D. C., for table 8.10, and figures 4.2, 8.9, 9.6 and 11.5.

Praeger Publishers, Inc., for table 9.3.

Brookings Institution, Washington D. C., for tables 9.4, 9.5 and 13.15.

Wesleyan University Press, Middletown, Conn., for table 10.1.

The Director of Her Majesty's Stationery Office (Crown Copyright reserved) for table 10.2, and figure 10.3.

American Economic Association, Nashville, Tenn., and Mr E. M. Gramlich for table 10.4.

Martinus Nijhoff, The Hague, for table 11.1.

R. Honey, Department of Geography, University of Iowa, for table 11.7.

The European Economic Community, Brussels, for table 13.22.

Institute of Public Affairs, University of California, Los Angeles, Calif., for table 14.7.

Ohio State University for table 15.1.

Regional Studies Association, London, and Regional Science Research Institute, University of Pennsylvania, P.O. Box 8776 Philadelphia, Pa 19101, for figure 4.1.

Dr R. D. Reischauer, Assistant Director, Congressional Budget Office. Washington D. C., for figure 7.3.

Wayne State University Press, Detroit, for figure 8.1.

Sage Publications, Inc., for figures 8.3 and 9.4.

National Institute of Education, Department of Health, Education and Welfare, Washington D. C., for figure 8.10.

Oxford University Press, Nairobi, for figure 9.3 and Oxford University Press, Oxford, for figure 10.1.

R. Peiser, Dallas, Texas, for figure 10.6.

Preface

Public finance is a dominating influence in all modern societies. The turning of the tax screw fundamentally affects the relative burdens of different individuals, whilst the eligibility criteria for benefits and public goods modifies both the level of the social wage that people receive and the level of industrial externalities. After first gaining significance in the funding of nineteenth century urban services, followed in the 1920s and 1930s by attempts at economic renewal and the 'New Deal', the role of public finance has assumed major importance since the late 1940s and 1950s with the rapid expansion of the 'welfare state'.

The geography of public finance, as defined in this book, concerns the provision of public services in different locations emphasizing the imbalance between, on the one hand, the spatial pattern of revenue raising and tax exporting, and, on the other hand, the geographical distribution of public expenditure benefits. Whereas the traditional concern of public finance has been with who derives what benefits under the public fisc, the geography of public finance is concerned with additional issues of how burdens and expenditure incidence vary as a function of geographical location. Who gets what benefits, and bears what burdens as a function of where they live: *who gets what, where, at what cost?*

The discussion of these issues is particularly important and topical because of increasing fiscal problems that are concentrated spatially, and because of the increasing political fragmentation of western society. Particular attention is focused in this book on the fiscal crisis of cities, on the resources-needs gap in local governments, on the massive investments required in renewal of infrastructure in declining regions, on the devolution and separatist movements in western countries, on the tax cutting issue, and on the realignment of major intergovernmental grant programmes such as the UK Rate Support Grant and US Revenue-Sharing.

Traditionally there has been considerable dispute as to the degree to which a geographical point of view on public finance can be upheld. The classic wisdom apportions major responsibility for most functions, except price determination, to national governments that normally pursue, or claim to pursue, spatially uniform policies. It is argued in this book that although the functions of distribution, stabilization and the stimulation of economic growth are indeed primarily national, nevertheless a high degree of spatial differentiation of public finance is required.

To develop this argument, Part 1 of this book seeks to clarify the concept of a public good, its relationship to political economy, and the degree to which the functions of public finance must be tackled at a geographical as well as at a personal level. Part 2 of this book (chapters 5 to 10) treats the problem of fiscal equity over space through each of its aspects: of needs, revenue burdens, revenue incidence, benefit incidence, and the capital account. Part 3 analyses the forms of intergovernmental co-ordination required to achieve fiscal equity over space; especially important is the consideration of tax separation, grants and revenue-sharing. Chapter 14 draws each of these elements of the argument together and yields assessments of the final impact of fiscal incidence on the individual or firm. This discussion includes treatment of regional industrial policy and regional balance of payments accounts. Chapter 15 combines these conclusions with consideration of the influence of the political pork-barrel and log-rolling. The discussion employs extensive example material from the UK, the USA, Canada, Australia and Germany. The end product of the discussion is a general methodology for the geography of public finance which follows six stages: need assessment, cost measurement, determination of revenue capacity, measurement of revenue burden, assessment of benefit incidence, and determination of the appropriate levels of intergovernmental transfers.

R. J. BENNETT
Fitzwilliam College, Cambridge

1

Public finance geography

"Taxes milk dry, but, neighbor, you'll allow
Thet havin' things onsettled kills the cow".

J. R. Lowell, *The Biglow Papers* (1862)

1.1 Introduction

Public finance can be defined in the most general terms as being concerned with the manner in which public services are provided. The geography of public finance concerns the provision of public services in different locations. The analysis of public finance is involved essentially with three questions: first, how is revenue raised; second, how is public expenditure allocated to finance public goods and services; and third, what is the balance between revenue and expenditure? The geographical analysis of public finance is involved with the same three essential questions but places the emphasis on the *spatial* pattern of revenue-raising, the *spatial* pattern of public expenditure, and the *spatial* balance between revenue and expenditure. The central concern of most studies in public finance has been the relative burden of revenue sources (especially taxes) between different groups of people (usually income groups), and the relative differences of expenditure between different groups of people either in terms of direct receipts, or in terms of 'benefits received'. This relation of burden and expenditure is frequently termed fiscal incidence, or 'who gets what' benefits from public finance. The geography of public finance does not lose sight of the question of distribution between people, but asks a second set of questions concerned with how burden and expenditure incidence vary as a function of geographical location: *who gets what benefits* from public finance as a function of *where* the individual lives and *where* the industrial enterprise is located. The degree to which these geographical questions are subsidiary to those relating to incidence of benefits between people, or vice versa, depends upon the character of each public finance decision, upon the nature of the public service considered, and upon the nature of the state in which decisions are made. It has often been assumed in writings on public finance that the geographical component is very much subsidiary. Certainly in many important instances it is, but in other important cases the geographical factor is pre-eminent. In general, the geographical component forms a distinctive factor to be considered, together with inter-group components in questions of public-finance. Indeed it has been recognized as such by many economists in studies

1

of 'fiscal federalism' (e.g. Musgrave 1959, 1969; Oates 1972, 1977), and by geographers in their studies of 'social well-being' (Harvey 1973; Smith 1977).

Decisions relating to public finance have always been surrounded by great controversy and debate, but at present in almost all western countries increasing attention is being directed to modification of the existing systems of public finance. This has been reflected both in academic debate and within government and institutional policy documents. This new interest has been brought into focus by four main factors: the increasing fiscal problems of urban areas; the fiscal imbalance within metropolitan and megalopolitan communities, especially between poor suburbs, still poorer central cities, and the richer suburbs and satellites; the conflict of national and subnational interests consequent upon eroded community ties and in regional devolution and separatist movements; and finally, attempts by supra-national organizations, such as the EEC, World Bank and IMF to create a better fiscal harmony in international financial relations. The suggested solutions to these problems all involve important geographical questions of fiscal balance. Such suggestions range from consolidation of small local government units, through increased co-operation between governments, to the reorientation of public expenditure and the separation of fiscal powers into new governments. This book is concerned in various ways with these issues.

Traditionally there has been considerable dispute as to the degree to which a geographical view of public finance can be upheld. Many writers have claimed that geographical factors are only an expression of deeper social forces. Such views are discussed at length in subsequent chapters. But to travel from downtown New York, Buffalo, Oakland or Washington's riot corridors to the suburbs of Amherst, Marin, or Chevy Chase, or from London's Docklands or central Merseyside to London's Hampstead or to Cheshire's Cheadle-Hulme; or to journey from the rural poverty in the US Southern States, Spain's Las Hurdas, Italy's Mezzorgiorno, or Wales' mining valleys to the vigorous economies of the US West coast and Texas, to Barcelona, to Turin and Milan, or South-East England; to see in every country highly marked concentrations of wealth and of poverty makes it difficult to accept that the geographical focus of such inequalities is also often not the best focus through which to attack problems of distribution.

The geographical focus of attention gives rise to a number of important questions which it is necessary to resolve. First, when is it appropriate to tax or make public expenditure at a personal level, local government level, some intermediate level (State, region, Länder), or nationally? Second, when should intergovernmental transfers (grants, revenue-sharing, credits) be used, and how far should they be earmarked for achievement of spatial equalization? Third, what is the extent of geographical tax exporting and benefit spillover between jurisdictions in any country, how important are these effects, and how might they be reduced? Fourth, what functions of public finance (with respect to price determination, social redistribution, economic stabilization, and encouragement to economic growth) should be adopted at each level of government? Finally, how are new policies and changes to the system of public finance constrained by existing constitutional structures? The answers to these questions are the focus for violent historical and current debate. Where we choose to live, where we educate our children, where we seek leisure facilities, how we travel, the general level of our wages and prosperity; these are all the issues which are fundamentally affected by the geographical impact of public finance. Indeed, it is usually the geographical features of public finance that are most central to the 'man in the street': local politics, the organization of local services, and the allocation of local resources are usually the primary areas for awareness and conflict; it is at the local level that the public fisc impinges on everyday life, and it is in the often violent divisions and inequalities of local life that geographical features of public finance emerge and dominate attention.

This book is concerned with analysing these factors. In Part I the interface between geography and political economy is explored. In Part II the character of individual jurisdictions is examined and each element of public finance discussed in turn (from needs, costs, revenues to benefits and the capital account). In Part III intergovernmental arrangements are explored, final fiscal incidence studies assessed, and the political elements of pork-barrel and log-rolling of public finance examined.

Each of the issues discussed involves the general geographical problem of balancing local needs and preferences against greater national and international imperatives. Whilst the current issues of fiscal imbalance are kept always in mind, it is hoped that this book offers a general approach which is not too specific to the policy questions of the present. Towards this end, important lineages from early writings are drawn. The fiscal problems of the present, although often more extreme, accord closely with many recurring problems of public finance and political economy; problems which have challenged the minds of classical, 17th, 18th, and especially 19th-century scholars. Certainly the geographical problems underlying current fiscal imbalance seem to be endemic to human society as it adjusts to changing technology and social values; they will not be completely solved now, any more than they have been in the past, or are likely to be in the future. But this should not discourage us from the challenge of attempting to improve and redirect the public fisc to achieve a better social and economic distribution in the future.

1.2 The role of public finance

The central issue of public finance is how the 'national cake' is divided: how resources are allocated between industries, individuals and programmes; how investments are balanced between long and short term goals; and how resources are distributed so as to increase or decrease the attraction of different locations. The 'national cake' is usually measured in terms of the

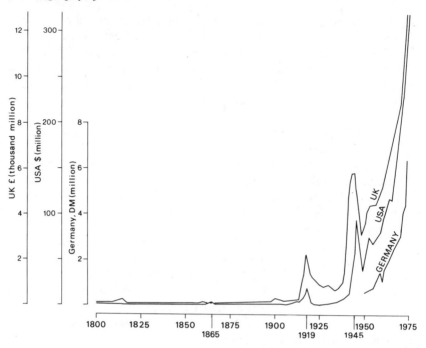

Figure 1.1 Level of total public expenditure at current prices in various western countries, 1800–1975. (*Sources*: US Treasury *Annual Reports*; Peacock and Wiseman 1961; *Statesman's Yearbook*.)

Gross National Product (GNP) or national income. In all western countries as the size of the national income or GNP has steadily risen, so the level of public expenditure has expanded rapidly, as shown in figure 1.1. As national resources rise, the capacity of the state to take on new spending responsibilities has increased and public finance has shifted from purely regulatory roles in the early part of this century, through the acquisition of stabilization functions in the post-Keynesian period of the 1930s and 1940s, to form the basis of the welfare state of the late 1940s and present time.

The increasing awareness of the ability of public finance to counteract the free workings of the economic system has been coupled with a rapid increase in the desires of people of most states for a higher degree of intervention by the state. Hence in most western countries the share of economic resources that is either directly controlled, or influenced, by elements of public finance has tended to increase steadily as shown in figure 1.1.

Linked with the general increase in the magnitude of public finance has been an increasing awareness of specifically geographical factors which has led to increasing emphasis on five new features in public finance. First, many public finance programmes have been oriented towards specific spatial problems. In the US, for example, there are programmes of counter-cyclical assistance,

4

regional development, community development, Indian and Alaskan settlements and so forth, which have directed public finance and assistance towards some locations and have not been available at others. In the UK, there are similar programmes of regional policy, inner city development, and General Improvement Areas. A second feature, which is linked to increasing spatial segmentation of public finance, has been the increased awareness by elected representatives of their power to win votes by preferential disbursement of aid or government contracts. This so-called 'pork-barrel' or 'log-rolling' feature of public finance is usually a detrimental feature, but has undoubtedly coloured the allocation of defence contracts in both the US and UK, and also affects the investment patterns of nationalized industries, e.g. in the UK steel, railways, and power generation. Indeed it can be argued that these spatial political factors are often much more crucial than economic or inter-personal ones in determining many decisions in public finance (see, for example, Taylor and Johnston 1978). A third feature has been the more direct assessment of differences in the geographical pattern of need for public expenditure at a given level, measurement of its spatially variable costs, and attempts to equalize the pattern of expenditure needs and costs with the local ability to support those needs. In the US this has given rise to various federal grant and aid programmes, especially of Revenue-Sharing since 1972 and Community Development since 1976, whilst in the UK especially since 1974/5 there have been refinements in the methods of assessing needs and resources in allocating grants to local authorities under the Rate Support Grant. A fourth feature of greater geographical awareness has been increasingly pointed demands for information on public finance rendered on a spatial basis. This has been more marked in unitary states such as the UK than in federal countries such as the US or Germany. But in most countries there have been increasing demands to reveal the distribution of the public budget between regions and other geographical jurisdictions, i.e. to see who gets what, where. In the UK, for example, there have been demands in many Regional Planning Strategies for such regional income accounts with the result that the Northern Regional Strategy (1976) was for the first time in the country's history able to obtain a breakdown of public expenditure by UK Economic Planning Region. This feature of geographical awareness has been linked to a fifth feature: demands for greater geographical autonomy in public finance allocation. In the UK this has been seen in the debate over the devolution of power to Scotland, Wales and the English Regions and in the problems of Northern Ireland. In other countries it has been linked with demands for separatism: for example of Quebec from Canada; of Catalans and Basques from Spain, of Friesland from Holland; of Corsica from France; of the break-up of Pakistan; of tribal rivalry and even civil war in Africa; and the demands for sovereignty by Moluccans and Banabans. In most cases there are also cultural, ethnic, religious or tribal differences. Coupled with a rise in the role of public finance, there have been demands for increased accountability to local needs, increasing awareness of geographical susceptibility to pork-barrelling, attempts better to assess local needs, and demands for better information. The increasing importance of these geographical features underlines each of the components and functions of public finance which will be developed in this book.

1.3 Conclusion

This book is concerned with the essential elements of the geographical distribution of public expenditure benefits, the areal variation of revenue burdens, and the spatial balance between the two. In some situations this gives rise to purely local models of public finance in which no spatial balance exists or is required. In other situations, there is an overriding national interest in the equity of the public fisc. Much of the book is concerned with the issue of equity. Whilst the detailed meaning of this term will be developed later (pp. 56–7), it is useful at this stage to summarize just what is, and what is not, meant by equity. Primarily, we are concerned with equality within the system of public finance, but this does not necessarily mean equal shares of public goods for all, nor the equal burden of taxation for all. Rather, public finance is oriented towards the supply of goods which are required in variable proportions by different individuals, client-groups or locations, as different needs. The need for public goods, however, is not geographically uniform, since some needs are more heavily concentrated in one set of locations, and the costs of providing for different needs also varies between individuals and locations. Hence, we must consider the variation in costs for unit needs. Finally, those groups or locations which are the most needy are frequently the ones which are the least able to support the expenditures required to satisfy their needs. This is almost definitional: individual, group and geographical needs exist because people cannot afford to provide for their needs themselves. Hence the burdens placed by taxation cannot vary with the need to spend, but instead must be based on some alternative principle; that most usually chosen is the apportionment of burdens in proportion to the ability to bear them.

Equity in public finance, then, concerns first, the distribution of expenditures to maintain equal service levels to those in equal need, taking account of variations in service costs, and second, the distribution of revenue burdens in proportion to ability, with equal levels of tax burden exacted from those with equal ability to pay. Geographical equity in public finance also concerns the equal treatment of those in equal need or with equal ability, but adds the dimension of requiring equal treatment of equals irrespective of location.

Against this background, the following chapters seek to refine the definition of terms. In chapter 2 a more precise definition is given to the term public goods, and the interrelation between public goods and the role of the state is examined as an issue of political economy. Chapter 3 examines in more detail the four main functions of public finance, namely allocation, distribution, stabilization and growth, in order to define more clearly which functions

6

should be tackled at a personal, and which at a geographical level. Chapter 4 then focuses on a number of specific aspects of public finance where geographical components are important or decisive. This leads, in chapters 5 to 10 (Part II) to the treatment of respectively: needs, costs, revenue burdens, revenue incidence, benefit incidence and the capital account. Thus the equity issue is attacked through each of its elements. However, important aspects of the equity issue require methods of intergovernmental organization which divide expenditure functions and revenue burdens between local, intermediate, and national level governments. These issues are discussed in Part III, where chapter 11 reviews the forms of government organization, chapter 12 discusses methods of intergovernmental co-ordination, and chapter 13 examines the practice of co-ordination in a range of western countries. In chapter 14 each of these strands is drawn together to yield a resolution of the overall question of the pattern of total fiscal incidence at an individual or a geographical level. Finally, in chapter 15, the assessments of earlier chapters are compared with the political elements of reality, and this leads to a review of the relatively new areas of research concerned with fiscal politics.

Part 1

Geography
and public economy

2

Public goods and public economy

Catherine the Great: 'Sir, can you tell me the best way to govern a state?'
Mercier de La Rivière: 'There is only one way, Madame. Be just, that is to
say, uphold the constitution and observe the laws.'
C: 'But on what basis should laws be made?'
M: 'On one basis only, Your Majesty, on the nature of things and of men.'
C: 'Most certainly. But when one wishes to make these laws what rules
should be observed?'
M: 'Madame, to give laws to mankind is God's prerogative. How can mere
man venture on such a task? By what right would he dictate to those
whom God has not placed in his hands?'
C: 'To what then do you reduce the science of government?'
M: 'To the study of laws which God has so manifestly engraven in human
society from the time of its creation. To seek to go beyond this would be
a great mistake and a disastrous undertaking.'
C: 'Sir, it has been a great pleasure to meet you. I wish you good day.'

Reported by Thiebault, *Souvenirs de Berlin* (1805). quoted in
L. Robbins (1952) *The Theory of Economic Policy.*

2.1 Introduction

Public finance raises a range of important issues concerned with social values
and the organization of the state, the views of the Physiocrat Mercier de La
Rivière quoted above, that the organization of the state should be left to
nature and to God, being one of the more unusual. Generally government, and
the system of public finance which supports it, can be seen as a means of
organizing the provision of some goods and services collectively rather than
individually. But there are, as we shall see, no absolute criteria of how public
finance, or indeed of how government, should be organized.

Since public finance concerns the financing and provision of public services,
a major initial question is what constitutes a public service; what is more
frequently termed a 'public good' or 'social good'. This topic is introduced in
section 2.2. However, all public finance decisions are constrained by the
structure, organization and constitution of the state within which they take
place; indeed any discussion of public goods must conclude that the choice of
those goods which are provided, and those which are not, is largely a political,
or even an ideological, decision. Hence public finance, its size, what services it
finances, how it is financed, and who benefits from its operation, is

11

fundamentally constrained by the *polity* or *political economy* of the state within which finance is organized. The dimension of political economy is discussed in sections 2.3. and 2.4. However, even, or especially, within the state (within a particular polity) the questions of the size, what, how, who, and where of public finance are far from determined. Indeed it is within the state, as discussed in section 2.5, that most of the interesting questions concerning the geography of public finance arise. Geographical space is not uniform and consideration of its partitioning and frictional effects on movement introduce the economic arguments of fiscal federalism. Especially important are the effects of tapering and spillover of benefits, and disbenefits from one location or jurisdiction to another.

2.2 The nature of public goods

The distinction between public and private goods has chief relevance in market and mixed economies. Public goods are those economic functions which cannot be performed by private market action, or can be more efficiently provided by public action. Included in this group are usually such functions as national defence, police, fire and health services, street lighting, some transport services, some industrial and employment policies, education and welfare policies.

Economists normally treat the origin of public goods as largely a technical issue: public goods are required where the market will otherwise fail. This technical hypothesis of market failure derives from Samuelson (1954) and Musgrave (1959). In their terminology, a pure public good has three main characteristics:

(1) *joint supply*: the supply to any one person allows the supply of an identical quality good to all people at no extra cost;

(2) *impossibility of exclusion (non-excludeability)*: the supply to any one person prevents the good being withheld from any other person wishing access to it, and people who do not pay for a service cannot be excluded from its benefits (the free-rider problem);

(3) *impossibility of rejecting (non-rejectability)*: once a service is supplied, it must be fully and equally consumed by all, even those who might not wish to do so.

The classic example of a good with each of these characteristics is national defence. Other examples are the maintenance of laws, the stability of money values, and many regulatory procedures such as safety standards of medicines, roads or buildings. However, few goods possess the Musgrave—Samuelson characteristics completely and these conditions must be seen as specifying an extreme theoretical case. Moreover, often the most important factors which undermine these conditions are geographical components resulting from political divisions of space excluding access to public goods.

Despite its problems, the pure public good concept is a useful yardstick against which to judge goods. The technical hypothesis, from which the pure public good concept derives, adduces purity or impurity to the character of the good itself. A degree of purity exists wherever the market mechanism will fail, and this depends on two technical characteristics. First, that the good possesses externalities: benefits (or disbenefits) are available to one individual by the action of other individuals; for example the general public benefits derived from a single individual act of pollution control. In this case 'free-riders' who benefit from the expenditure of others cannot be excluded. A second origin of non-excludeability, which is related to the 'free-rider' problem, is preference revelation: that individuals will not indicate their true preferences if their contribution towards costs is in any way related to this revelation. In each case the rational, self-interested individual has no incentive to pay for a good: due to non-excludeability, the market, as a system linking consumer and supplier through price, fails. Thus the technical hypothesis splits economic goods into two classes: those which can be organized mainly through the private mechanism of market bargaining, and those which must be organized mainly through a political or voting process which gives preference to particular assemblages of social goods. The degree to which a good must be provided publicly, as opposed to privately, will depend upon the degree of its externalities, jointness and non-rejectability, but most important of all, the degree to which there is a collective desire that the goods should be provided.

In practice, a division between public and private goods based on the nature of the good itself runs into a number of difficulties. First, most goods possess a degree of externality, and the distinction between them becomes one of recognizing the appropriate level at which the external effects of a given good merits its provision by public as opposed to private action. This throws up a second difficulty, that in many circumstances the choice of which public goods to provide must be based on ideological rather than technical grounds. In many circumstances the public sector is the only sector which will provide a particular good, e.g. unemployment benefits, pollution control, and increasingly, mass-transit facilities. The decision to supply these public goods cannot, therefore, be based on a purely technical distinction since this will not define which of the infinite range of possible public goods should be provided. Instead a decision is needed at some stage which defines what public goods are *needed*. As we shall see in chapter 5 and elsewhere, need has fundamentally ideological components which necessarily involve initial value judgements. A third difficulty with the technical hypothesis is that in some cases, although private action may be feasible, it may be desirable to organize the good publicly to achieve other social goals. Thus many public service programmes are not aimed purely at providing the service, but have goals of redistribution and other social goals which private action would undermine.

However we define public goods, they have two distinct sets of impacts.

13

First, to the entrepreneur or industrial enterprise, public goods represent a set of *externalities* from which benefits will be gained without any specific contributions being made. Especially important are services such as fire and police protection, education of its workforce, and infrastructure such as transport facilities. A second impact of public goods is upon the individual for whom they perform the function of a *social wage*. This is the element of income received in terms of benefits from services and facilities, plus transfer payments and subsidies, which give an individual a base level of welfare by virtue of the fact that he lives in a particular state or area.

2.3 The dimension of political economy

The discussion of public goods has already raised the spectre of political and ideological dimensions as crucial underpinnings of public finance. The decision as to which goods will be publicly organized, which private, and which not provided at all, can be treated as either a revelation of a collective preference or an ideological desideratum. Hence the underpinning of public finance which is sought is the polity: the overall collective organization or sense of community which defines the aims of the state, or smaller-scale political jurisdictions, and which traditionally defines the dimension of political economy. This element determines the size, the what, the how, the who, and the where of public finance. Before dealing with these issues, however, let us first explore the notion of political economy itself.

Political economy involves the study of the *ethical* rules which underlie economic relations. Traditionally these have been approached by economists as an exploration of the two extremes of the market and the planned system. Others have variously seen political economy as a search for justice and the good life (Plato and Aristotle); as a means of securing society against life which is poor, nasty, brutish and short (Hobbes); as a means of organizing consensus for the supply of public goods through a social contract expressing the general will (Locke, Leibnitz and Montesquieu); as a means of promoting private and collective interest to the greatest happiness by 'felicific calculus' (Bentham, J. S. Mill, and the Utilitarians); as a 'social contract' which renders certain claims legitimate (Rousseau); as an instrument by which a class of exploiters maintain their monopoly and exploitation (Marx); as an abstract entity claiming duty and allegiance (Hegel); or, as the modern scientific school suggests, as a bureaucratic regulator and decision mechanism (Eulau and March 1969). Despite the variety of these approaches, there is an overall and more fundamental dichotomy which relates to the differences between those scholars, on the one hand, who take a positive or normative approach and require the form of political economy to be 'revealed' by evolution of institutions and preferences, and those, on the other hand, who believe that questions concerning the size and nature of the public sector can be resolved only at the level of either scientific or of ideological debate, and then, once decided, the polity remains relatively fixed. This dichotomy can be characterized in relatively crude terms as the differences between 'evolved' and 'designed' economies: what Keynes characterized as the difference between knitting wool, and carving in stone.

Those who advocate 'evolved' economies draw their main stimulus from Adam Smith and *The Wealth of Nations*. Smith was concerned with the scientific study of the economic system in order to determine how it worked. His analysis is in essence, therefore, descriptive and exploratory. Smith is thus a spectator who attempts to view the system objectively. To this view he adds the concept of evolution of society through a series of stages: first from the 'lowest and rudest' to a second pastoral stage; third, the emergence of property, feudal land tenure and the origins of commerce; finally, the full economic market system. The argument is one which is fundamentally evolutionary. In its most extreme form as stated by the 18th-century Physiocrats such as Quesnay or Mercier de La Rivière, or by the 19th-century Darwinians, Herbert Spencer and Burke, society is a product of natural history; it is a complex equilibrium of changeable parts which is suited to the people who possess it, but which cannot be transferred. Recent discussions by anthropologists continue to emphasize this view; that values are not inborn, but evolve from communication within the family or social group to give rank ordering of human conduct which becomes dogmatized and abstracted within society. These values answer the need for moral laws, but because of their evolutionary origin, each set of values is specific to the society or group in which the values are formed. Moreover, there is no predictable end-point to their evolution. Each of these approaches derives from a market approach to political economy in which choice and preference is extended to the public sector of goods and services.

The alternative view, that economies should be the outcome of conscious decisions on their design, finds two areas of support. On the one hand are the arguments of Marxist and radical economists who believe that society should be organized on the basis of a clearly stated ideological position. On the other hand are the scientific schools represented in the 19th century by Bentham, James Mill, Wicksell, Lindahl, and the Utilitarians, and in the 20th century by such writers as Gulick, Fayol, March and Simon, and Dror. These workers believe that government and the economy result from the invention of man to solve specific problems. Both approaches are quite distinctly opposed to the 'emergent' philosophy of social evolution discussed above.

For the radical school of economists, in contrast to the unpredictable evolution of norms there is a necessary economic progression from primitive economies, through slavery, feudalism, bourgeois revolution with capitalism, proletarian revolution with socialism, to communism. This is a necessary historical progression because it is inbuilt into society by the location of vested power lying within it. The progression is usually coupled with the aim of making things go in the direction desired: consciousness of historical progression is the stimulus to change. Thus Marx (1888, p. 30) states that

"The philosophers have only *interpreted* the world, in various ways; the point, however, is to change it". When re-interpreted by Lenin (see Lenin 1960) Marx's stimulus to change becomes one of directing the behaviour of the economy to conform to overall planned goals: neither the description nor observation of other mechanisms by which economic goals might be achieved is in any sense relevant. Marxist political economy in practice, therefore, is often prescriptive.

For the scientific school there are clearly specified goals or objectives towards which it is sought to direct social development. In the writings of the early welfare economists these objectives are formulated into abstract measures of the overall social happiness of society (Bentham), the minimization of subjective sacrifice (J. S. Mill), or the maximization of social welfare or utility (Wicksell, Pigou, Marshall, Common and Sidgwick). Later writers, such as Sax, Lindahl and von Wieser, and particularly thinkers of the Swedish school, emphasize instead of total social welfare or happiness, the marginal concept. Rather than attempt to achieve a maximization of total social welfare, Lindahl (1919) Wicksell (1896) and especially Pareto (1966) argue that governments should instead attempt to achieve a relative improvement both in general happiness and more especially in the justice of its distribution. This whole lineage of approach is often referred to as that of welfare economics. There has been a considerable and growing criticism as to the value of welfare economics, but despite these criticisms, recent developments in management science and planning have extended the general characteristics of the approach into new areas of application. The concept of scientific administration of Fayol (1925), Gulick and Urwick (1937), and March and Simon (1961), for example, or the control system approach of Dror (1971), emphasize the measurement of public decisions according to rational and clearly defined objectives. The influence of this new welfare school has been particularly influential in physical and land-use planning both in the US and especially in the UK.

There is clearly a conflict between economies based on design and those which are not made, but grow. A polity built to design suffers from the crucial criticism that we need an abstract ethical code to decide on design and to order decisions; it "creates a situation in which it is necessary for us to agree on a much larger number of topics than we have been used to, and . . . we cannot confine collective action to the tasks on which we agree, but are forced to produce agreement on everything in order that any action can be taken at all", (Hayek 1944, p. 46). The concept of an ethical code is usually defined in terms of achieving the greater *common good*, social good, and general welfare. However, the difficulties in this approach are well recognized by Hayek (1944, pp. 42–3):

'The welfare and happiness of millions cannot be measured on a single scale of less or more. . . . It cannot be adequately expressed as a single end, but only as a hierarchy of ends, a comprehensive scale of value in which every need of every person is given its place. To direct all our activities according to a single plan presupposes that every one of our needs is given its rank in an order of values which must be complete enough to make it possible to decide between all the different courses which the planner has to choose.'

In rejecting abstractly framed ethical codes, Hayek and the evolutionary school are reaffirming the stance of Smith: as scientists the best we can do is to spectate on the evolution of cultural norms and political economy; albeit implementing public services where necessary. We cannot answer the ethical question of how society should be organized but instead must allow its organization to evolve or emerge through political and collective development. Hence the public finance of the state "has its origin in, and depends for its continuance upon the desires of individuals to fulfil a certain portion of their wants collectively. The state has no ends other than those of its individual members and is not a separate decision-making unit. State decisions are, in the final analysis, the collectivity decisions of individuals" (Buchanan 1960, pp. 11–12).

In contrast to the evolutionary school the design approach can argue equally forcefully that a policy based on natural evolution is in a paralysis of inaction, the structure is constant and unadaptable to new forces which may be put upon it. It is clear, however, that there is no simple solution to the conflict between these two extremes. One resolution to the problem, suggested by Alexis de Tocqueville, and by John Stuart Mill in opposition to both the Utilitarian views of his father James Mill and to Burke's view of natural history, is that the polity is the product of man, is managed by man, but is subject to a series of constraints. These constraints govern the willingness of the people to accept a given polity, the willingness to maintain it, and the willingness to comply with it (Mill 1848, p. 177). Within these constraints, institutions can be a matter of choice or design: the constraints define the scope of ideological or scientific possibilities for development. The determination of a resolution to this conflict is not our direct concern here, but we should be aware of the complex underpinnings of ideology and political economy which affect the treatment of public finance. For the purposes of this book, we may accept Mill's concept of the constrained possibilities for development as a useful framework from which to approach the geography of public finance (although we need not accept the rest of Mill's political philosophy).

2.4 The impact of political economy on public finance

Turning to the specific implications of political economy for public finance, we become involved in the much more concrete issues of the *size* of the public sector, the delimitation of *which* are public and which are private goods, *how* these goods are financed, and *who* benefits from their provision. Although more concrete, however, these questions may be no easier to answer.

With respect to the size of the public sector, few would now dispute the necessity for a large provision of public goods in modern economies. The expectation of the common man (usually taken for granted) is of a large base of public utilities, public services, welfare programmes, public education and important influences on industrial investment and employment. Few, if any, western economists now advocate the unfettered rule of 'free market' forces without the constraint of a degree of public participation giving some form of so-called 'mixed economy'. More radical economists too have now readily incorporated the role of the public sector into their models of capitalist accumulation giving forms of so-called 'state capitalism'. For the common man, the organization and size of the public sector governs not only his access to, and the size of his social wage, but also the degree to which he may decide how to spend his income and the degree to which it has already been allocated for him. To the economist, choices between various degrees of pervasiveness of the public sector represent various categories of 'comparative economic systems' which he may categorize as a dichotomy between 'market' and 'planned' systems or, more commonly now, as a continuum between these two idealized types. To the political scientist and to the sociologist, as we have seen above, the questions of interplay between public and private elements within society present a set of ethical questions the answers to which can be found only in analysis of our values, our moral polity, and our ideology.

When the questions are raised of which goods should be publicly organized, how they should be financed, and who should benefit from their provision, there are three distinct schools of approach to deriving solutions which accord fairly closely with the 'evolutionary' and 'designed' schools of political economy discussed above.

(i) *The market-surrogate school.* This advocates that the public sector should be organized as closely as possible along the lines of market principles. It should satisfy individual and collective preferences as revealed and expressed, but not as defined by any *a priori* forces (e.g. by ideology). Public goods should be allocated according to the willingness of people to pay for them, and the costs of the goods should be distributed in relation to the benefits received. This approach is often closely related to the evolutionary explanation of the origin of political economy, and is often termed the *public choice* approach.

(ii) *Ideology-appeasement school.* This suggests that the public sector is provided by a dominating class in order to appease the interests of a repressed class. Hence public goods absorb those areas of concern to repressed groups which will not be provided by a private capitalist investment, but which are necessary to maintain acquiescence in class domination. This approach is usually associated with the radical economists' explanation of political economy.

18

(iii) *Needs-assessment school*. This suggests that public goods should be allocated between beneficiaries on the basis of their needs. There is no necessary or direct relation between the benefits received from public goods and tax payments, and costs are instead based on the ability to pay. Although related to the appeasement school ((ii) above), needs-assessment does not adduce the organization of public goods to a mechanism of class oppression, but is instead related more closely to the scientific allocation of public benefits to achieve the greater utility or welfare of society as a whole.

THE MARKET-SURROGATE SCHOOL

The most distinguished definition of the tenets of the market-surrogate school is provided by Adam Smith. The choice of which goods are provided publicly is made on the technical criterion of those areas in which desirable public works do not possess the rate of profit to repay the expense of private investment (Smith 1776, Book V, iii). Desirable public works are defined by three main duties of the public sector (Smith 1776, Book IV, ix, p. 687–8):

> 'First, the duty of protecting society from the violence and invasion of other independent societies; secondly, the duty of protecting, as far as possible, every member of society from the injustice or oppression of every other member of it, or the duty of establishing an exact administration of justice; and, thirdly, the duty of erecting and maintaining certain publick works and certain publick institutions, which it can never be for the interest of any individual, or small number of individuals, to erect and maintain; because the profits could never repay the expense . . . though it may frequently do much more than repay it to a great society.'

Extending Smith's argument, J. S. Mill (1848) defines private goods as those parts of life which have no strong effect on the interests of others; public goods are defined, firstly, as the residual element from private action and, secondly, as those on which it is possible to reach agreement. Mill lists four main objections to the unbounded extension of government agency and the public sector (Mill 1848, Book V, Chapter 2): first, that there is a limit to state interference defined by that part of personal life that does not affect the interests of others; second, continuous extension of government power restricts individual freedom, but has its own natural momentum: "the public collectively is abundantly ready to impose, not only its generally narrow views of its interests, but its abstract opinions, and even its taste, as laws binding upon individuals", (Mill 1848, p. 550); third, the extension of government control results in increasing bureaucratic division of labour and tends to increase inefficiency because government tends to have "the one great disadvantage of an inferior interest in the result" (Mill 1848, p. 553); finally, the extension of government chokes individual motivation and willingness to take risks. As a result of these perceived limits, Mill suggests that a public good

19

should be provided only when there is a strong necessity to justify it. Extending this concept Jeremy Bentham (1952), and to a lesser extent Mill, believed that public goods should be financed as 'collateral aids' which private enterprise would not provide but which would create improved economic or social conditions permitting 'the greatest good to the greatest number', but which would also permit the *laissez-faire* pursuance by one individual of his enlightened self-interest. Like Smith, the chief public functions were seen by Bentham and Mill to be education and justice, but health provision was also advocated (especially water supply, sewerage and refuse disposal). A similar but alternative definition of public goods provided by Hobson (1938) uses the possibilities of standardization as a criterion to delimit public from private goods. Where standardization of goods or services is possible (or desired), then public control is not only possible but also essential to assure uniformity and equality of treatment. Modern developments of this approach divide public and private goods between those where a collective agreement exists on their type, nature and standard, and those where agreement does not exist. This approach delimits areas of private and collective action (Buchanan 1965; Buchanan and Tullock 1969). For private action each individual is governed by the mechanisms of the market and when confronted by choices, is considered to execute actions based on Lerner's rule (Lerner, 1946): that the alternative marginal products of each action will be weighed and a choice made on that which yields the greatest return. Collective action, in contrast, will only be entered into when there is an expectation of increased benefits to be derived from participation, i.e. where the costs to the individual resulting from the action of others and from his participation in collective actions gives a greater return than can be derived by individual action (Buchanan and Tullock 1969, pp. 30–60). These conditions yield what Buchanan and Tullock term a 'calculus of consent'. An extreme statement of this view by Milton Friedman (1962) leaves to the market all functions except a residual which has large scale externalities or spillover. Although less extreme, some form of division between individual and state action now finds commonplace acceptance, perhaps stimulated most by the influential works of Keynes. Certainly Keynes remained close to the classical view:

> 'The most important *Agenda* of the state relate not to those activities which private individuals are already fulfilling, but to those functions which fall outside the sphere of the individual, to those decisions which are made by *no one* if the state does not make them. The important thing for government is not to do things which individuals are doing already', (Keynes 1926, pp. 46–7).

In Keynes' belief, such functions related most closely to those of the aggregate (to aggregates such as consumption, investment and production), but the lineage of his thought from classical economic writings is clearly traceable.

There are a number of important areas of criticism of the market surrogate school. Firstly, it is difficult to determine preferences, willingness to pay or the beneficiaries of a given policy. The revelation of preferences by the mechanism of the market does not allow the implementation of policies of redistribution, and expression by voting as suggested by Buchanan is patently incapable of revealing the total ranking of all goods. With respect to willingness to pay, there are advantages to be gained by not revealing preferences in the hope that the action of someone else will yield external benefits without costs. Measurement of the incidence of benefits is complicated by different patterns of benefit being received by different people, by the presence of many indirect benefits, and by the spatial tapering, spillover and spillin of benefits to be discussed in the next section. A second criticism of the market-surrogate school is that it is of no help in deciding on the pricing policy for more *pure* public goods such as defence, police and fire protection, and freedom from pollution. From these goods everyone benefits, but there may be variable patterns of preferences. But the third and major criticism of this school is that it offers no way of defining those specific goods which Adam Smith recognizes repay investments to a greater society, but which do not repay individual investment. The chief limitation of the market-surrogate school, therefore, arises from its basis in the 'evolutionary' view of political economy discussed earlier (p. 15). Since we must await the emergence of goals, we cannot change the present operations of the market. When interpreted by Mill, Ricardo and other classical economists, capital and profit were seen as the prerequisites for the improvement of the working-class and hence reforms and limitations of capitalism were resisted. In the extreme form of Spencer's neo-classical Darwinianism, there should be stringent limits to government interference in order to assure a healthy economy by the survival only of the 'fittest'. Adherents of the market-surrogate school would not now take such an extreme position, but would suggest necessary limits on government activity to ensure a sufficient degree of personal freedom of action and civil liberty. A final criticism of the market-surrogate school is that it assumes that public choice, or revealed preferences, can effectively arbitrate in all areas. Many public goods have the characteristic that individuals acting alone are incapable of assessing society's need for them. We are instead dependent upon expert advice. As Abel-Smith and Titmuss (1956, pp. 68–9) note:

'Free choice works admirably for a housewife buying vegetables. . . . But can you really conclude anything from the choice between a cabbage and a one-in-a-million chance of contracting polio, between a cauliflower today and a cauliflower in the year 2000? How many people know the exact chances of getting ill, or surviving to old age, of breeding a backward child? If they don't know, what conclusions can you draw from the fact that people choose to save or pre-insure? When there is delay or risk, free choice proves nothing.'

21

THE IDEOLOGY-APPEASEMENT SCHOOL

Arising out of the criticisms of the market-surrogate school, the second school of ideology-appeasement adduces the origin of public goods, their finance, and the distribution of their benefits, as determined by the specific interests of capital itself. Like Smith, this school argues that goods are provided publicly when the profit rate is low relative to alternative investments, but unlike Smith, it is argued that public goods also emerge when the state must have a monopoly of a particular service in order, first, to assure the continuation of a higher rate of private profits, and second, to ensure the continuation of the domination of a particular class group. Thus for O'Connor (1973) and Poulantzas (1975) the purpose of public finance and of the state itself is to maintain a degree of cohesion by absorbing public goods, thus allowing increases in private profit in other sectors, thence appeasing dominated groups, and so sanctioning and legitimizing a process of repression. The modern state with its large and growing public sector is, therefore, controlled by what Gramsci (1975) had earlier termed a mechanism of *hegemony*, of the consent of the masses in class rule, in order to maintain class dominance. Thus the answer to Rousseau's paradox that men choose willingly to give up their liberty to rulers and are defrauded of their guardianship by oppression (that "man is born free, and everywhere he is in chains"), is adduced to a process of fraud by a class group to legitimize its dominance.

According to these radical interpretations the public sector is composed of two distinct but overlapping categories, of social capital and social expenses, which are related to the two public roles of increasing accumulation of private profit and of legitimation. *Social capital* is organized to improve the rate of profit (or surplus value) in private industry and is composed of two subcategories. First, social investment, termed 'constant capital' by Marx, is composed of projects and services aimed at achieving increased private profit by increasing the productivity of labour through provision of physical facilities such as transport, infrastructure and industrial estates. Social consumption, the second category of social capital, termed 'social variable capital' by Marx, is composed of projects and services that improve the quality and hence lower the costs of labour, through, for example, social insurance, education and urban renewal. *Social expenses* comprise a second group of public finance components organized to maintain harmony and cohesion, and hence may not be directly productive. Major examples are adduced in welfare payments, health services and support for arts and sport. The Marxian explanation of public finance therefore adduces the public sector as indispensable to the expansion of private industry (O'Connor 1973). But inbuilt into this explanation is a model of a fiscal crisis of the state. Increasing profits and labour productivity lead to a growing redundant labour force of unemployed and unemployables, what Marx terms an 'industrial reserve army'. This, in turn, leads to increasing inequality and greater demands for

public expenditure as social expenditure in terms of both transfer payments, and maintenance of law and order. But since the radicals would argue that the bulk of profitable enterprise remains in private hands, a fiscal crisis results in which intervention leads to an increasing burden of public costs whilst profits remain private: so-called 'socialization of costs and privatization of profits'. Thus the fiscal crisis of the state is evidenced by the increasing difficulty in matching expenditure needs and revenue resources.

The above explanation suggests that arising out of the ideology-appeasement school is the concept that, as time progresses, public expenditure and the range of public goods must expand to absorb those sectors in which the rate of profit is low. An important stimulus to this view is given by Wagner (1890) and Adams (1898). Both argued that there is a law which explains increases in public expenditure as a result of economic growth and development; i.e. progress in material wealth leads necessarily to increases in public expenditure. "The law is the result of empirical observation in progressive countries, at least in Western European civilization; its explanation, justification and cause is the pressure of social progress and the resulting changes in the relative spheres of private and public economy, especially compulsory public economy" (Wagner 1890, p. 16). Although based on a set of empirical observations, *Wagner's law* was justified by arguing that in three areas of public activity, expenditure necessarily increases (Peacock and Wiseman 1961). For the first group of activities, the maintenance of law and order (*Rechtzweck und Machtzweck*), growth of public involvement is necessitated by both increasing division of labour which increases internal friction, and by desires for an expanding quality of public services. The second group of activities, material production, is subject to growth of state participation because the state increasingly provides the only means to finance many new services and indivisible collective goods, and because of the inferior performance of private industry, especially its mis-management of capital and enhancement of the effect of business cycles by speculative endeavours. In a third group of activities, the provision of economic and social services, Wagner argues that increased public expenditure arises from the increasing need to counteract the effect of private monopolies and from the need for many services that do not repay simple economic investment criteria, e.g. education.

There is obviously a great deal of evidence to support Wagner's law at an empirical level (see, for example, Fabricant 1952); but when we turn to the factors which he and other radical economists have adduced to explain the origin of the growth in public expenditure, there are important areas of criticism. First, it is difficult to confirm that increases in the general level of wealth resulting from increases in productivity lead directly either to increases in demand or to increases in the costs of providing public goods. As national income grows, the nature of public expenditure will undoubtedly change, but there are no *general* arguments which apply over all stages of development in

23

all economies which suggest that these changes in structure will always result in increases in the quantity or cost of public goods; indeed in some cases the contrary can be argued. In a second area, national income can increase without changes in productivity if the population is growing, and some writers have adduced population pressures as a primary stimulus to growth in public expenditure. Whilst population growth can be an important factor, here again there is no simple or general relationship. More important than population numbers is often the composition of the population which controls its pattern of expenditure need (see chapter 5), e.g. the mix of old, young, disabled and other groups. A third criticism is that with respect to prices, there is no conclusive evidence to suggest that the prices of public goods should or do rise as time progresses. There are obviously many short-term fluctuations and these may affect the taxation and expenditure patterns of the public sector, but there are usually no long-term trends which can be separated from other factors. Finally, with respect to employment, there will be a fairly direct relation between unemployment levels and the level of public expenditure because of resultant increases in transfer payments; but the extent of unemployment and transfer payments will depend more upon political and ideological decisions as such, rather than inbuilt tendencies of capitalism. It can be argued that continuing innovation in production leading to increased output per man can lead to increasing unemployed labour reserves (as an industrial reserve army in Marx's terms), but productivity changes can also be absorbed in other ways such as increased leisure, earlier retirement, job-sharing, and so forth. These result more from the way in which increases in income are distributed, and affect the form rather than the magnitude of the public sector.

Despite these criticisms, however, there are a number of factors which do lend support to Wagner's law and indeed to some of the radicals' views. Firstly, Peacock and Wiseman (1961) argue that major social upheavals, especially war, can give a major stimulus to concentration in the public sector. Although giving isolated peaks in public spending, war expenditure, for example, has usually separated plateaux of public spending in which later magnitudes of public expenditure never return to pre-war levels. This results from the *displacement effects* of public expenditure: people will accept, in a period of crisis, a higher level of state involvement and taxation than would be supported in more 'normal' times, and as the disturbance subsides, a level of acceptance remains. Since such social disturbances are often fairly common and regular in occurrence, it can be argued that they provide an important mechanism to support Wagner's arguments. Keynesian economic management and deficit spending is an important example of this process over the period of the economic cycle. A second factor which also suggests these views is the so-called *concentration process*. It is argued, for example by Peacock and Wiseman (1961), Myrdal (1958), and others (see chapter 3) that, as economies grow or become developed, then public expenditure tends to shift from lower

to higher levels of government. This is a function of demands for improved and uniform standards of public services, of the need for improved transport and social infrastructure, and of the impact of scale economies which allow larger production and service units to operate at lower unit costs (see chapter 6). While such pressures should lead to economies in organization and scale, they almost invariably also lead to demands for increased local involvement and participation. Concentration, therefore, rather than lowering the total costs of public services, instead often leads to proliferation of government activity. A third factor is the influence of inflation. During periods of inflation at high rates many taxes tend to rise at a comparable or higher rate, as in the case of income tax (especially when this is progressive: see chapter 7). Hence under the influence of inflation, public taxation often rises as a proportion of national income without any conscious decision or intention that this should happen: so-called '*fiscal drag*'. It is rare that governments in this position decide to re-cycle all of the increases in tax receipts they have received. Moreover, the fiscal drag effect of inflation tends to encourage the displacement and concentration processes.

THE NEEDS-ASSESSMENT SCHOOL

This school has some elements in common with that of radical economists. Needs must be defined on some basis of values, and hence a moral or ideological judgement may be required at some stage, but most advocates of needs-assessment have adduced mechanisms neither of class hegemony or repression nor of the inbuilt tendencies of capitalism. Instead, the assessment of the needs is based on a complex interplay between the scientific schools of social design and efficiency, and the organization of public goods within the context of constraints. As specified by J. S. Mill, these constraints ensure the acceptability to, maintenance by, and compliance of the polity in provision of a specific mix of public goods. The origins of this school of approach can thus be drawn from two factors: first, the nature of agreed social needs; and second, the technical nature of the goods themselves.

The extent and nature of accepted needs is a highly charged ethical question, and it has been approached from two opposing standpoints: as an absolute and as a relative concept. As an absolute concept need assessment has found support from both Marxist and welfare economists. In the former case, need is defined on the basis of an abstract notion of social justice, whilst in the latter case concepts such as the greatest happiness to all, minimum sacrifice and general good have been formulated. In general, both definitions of need are largely metaphysical and are somewhat devoid of meaning (see chapter 5): the absolute and unassailable definition of what constitutes utility, happiness or justice represents an unanswerable question except against the background of a particular value or ideological position. Hence, many writers have sought instead to define need as a relative concept: to improve the social distribution of the status quo. For example, Kaldor, Hicks and Scitovsky have

25

proposed a *compensation principle* to evaluate changes resulting from public policy. Alternatively, Samuelson, Bergson and Graaff have proposed the use of social welfare functions upon which all possible states of society are ordered and the best possible policy selected using Pareto or other criteria. Whilst an improvement on the definition of need in absolute terms, however, the relative (or marginal) school of needs-assessment does not overcome the basic problems of valuation since the balancing of relative need still requires a measurement yardstick (or need indicator) against which to make assessments. Moreover, as we shall see in the discussion of later chapters, need is inextricably linked with how we attempt to measure benefits, to raise taxes, and hence to balance burden and benefits. Thus the objective assessment of need, apart from being difficult and arguably impossible, is also totally interlinked with other elements of public economy and cannot be decided apart from them. An alternative approach to needs-assessment has therefore emerged through the technical character of the public goods themselves.

The technical character of public goods determines first, their costs and organization of their provision, and second, their elasticity and redistribution properties with income. With respect to costs and organization, we have already seen that economies of scale and concentration are one factor which lends support to Wagner's law of the ideology-appeasement school. The scale and concentration factors also influence the needs-assessment school. Economic efficiency and reduced costs allow the satisfaction of a greater proportion of human wants for a given level of expenditure and have implications for optimal sizes of public units to provide them (chapter 6). *Income elasticity* describes the degree to which consumption of a good rises with increases in income. Thus for some goods, e.g. consumer durables (electrical appliances and so on), leisure and housing, consumption rises as income levels rise: the wealthy have a higher consumption than the poor. Such goods are said to be income elastic. For other goods, however, consumption does not rise as income levels rise and consumption stays roughly equal over all income groups. Such goods are said to be income inelastic or neutral. Important examples are many public goods such as refuse disposal and street lighting, and to a lesser extent food consumption. It has been argued by Pigou (1928) and Wicksell (1896) that the public sector should be confined to those goods which are neutral, or at least are relatively inelastic with income. For these goods, the level of need does not change with income and hence objective measures of need can be used to determine the correct equation to make supply approximately equal the distribution of demand. For goods which are income elastic, however, attempts to relate supply and demand at any given level through measures of needs will break down. The quantities demanded by the aggregate will be larger and qualitatively different from that demanded if the quantity and quality are set by price. Because price does not restrict demand, regulation is achieved instead by a deterioration of the quality of service or by its overcrowding. In the case of the National Health Service in the

UK for example, Buchanan and Tollison (1972) argue that inefficiency in resource allocation results from the provision of a health service which does not coincide with collective demands. Consumption of health facilities is elastic with income and since there is no price relation to demand, the incorrect mix of services has been provided. This can be replaced, Buchanan suggests, either by introducing a price system to regulate demand, or by improved administration to measure more accurately real needs and demands.

A large number of goods which are usually publicly provided are income elastic. For example, consumption of highways, education and health all rise with income. Hence their provision by private means is regressive with income, i.e. benefits are larger as incomes rise. This suggests that if we look at the redistribution properties of goods we come to a different conclusion as to which goods should be provided publicly than that reached by Pigou and Wicksell. If we have a deliberate aim of improving the benefits of lower income groups, then the public provision of income-elastic goods provides the best method of improving the social wage. Moreover, the finance of such goods should be progressive with income, and the access to benefits should be regressive with income. Thus there will be no direct relationship between benefits received and tax payments; the costs instead will be based on the ability to pay. The problem implicit in this approach to defining public goods is that recognized by Pigou, Wicksell and Buchanan, that there will usually be inefficiency in organization and supply of income-elastic public goods because supply is set arbitrarily with respect to demands. Thus it behoves the advocates of the needs-assessment school to provide an adequate replacement of the market as a means of allocating economic resources. It is this problem which has occupied most attention within the needs-assessment school, and which occupies much attention in this book: to determine the most appropriate relation of public finance benefits to needs and of revenue burdens to ability to pay.

Although the distinction between the approaches to public finance of the three major schools of political economy are in many instances arbitrary in nature, they demonstrate the distinctiveness of style which underlies the approach of many writers on public finance, and begin to raise some of the deeper issues which arise in the study of public finance. The question which each school raises, of how public goods are organized and who benefits from their provision, is the central issue of public finance and is also the central concern of this book. As we shall see, the organization of public goods may on some occasions be deliberately structured so as to limit the access of some groups, for example, the selective direction of infrastructure investment or welfare spending to inner cities. On other occasions, access to public goods may be limited unintentionally by the way in which they are organized. As later chapters will show, geographical factors are often the most important in determining both the deliberate and unintentional exclusion of some people from services.

27

2.5 Geographical components of public finance

Despite an increasing general awareness of the question of public finance and political economy, there have been few attempts, as yet, to analyse the distinctively *geographical* questions which relate to the public sector and its finance. Such geographical questions concern who gets what, where, how this spatial distribution of public goods has emerged; and how it can be altered. Since it is rarely, if ever, possible to provide public services on a uniform or ubiquitous basis, then the relative size and standard of services and access to them will vary from place to place as a function of location. Thus the size of the social wage, the impact on industrial externalities, and the degree to which individuals are free to decide on allocation of their incomes and the degree to which their choice is constrained, is geographically variable. That there is obviously a high degree of variation in the form of public services from state to state is recognized by the economists' concern with comparative economic systems. However, geographical factors often emerge most strongly *within* states, i.e. within a given polity, and have a greater impact than is often realized. The three main geographical components are the effects of tapering, jurisdictional partitioning, and spillover.

Tapering describes the commonly observed pattern by which the benefits from a public good diminish, or taper-off, with distance from the point at which they are supplied. This is sometimes referred to as the 'neighbourhood effect'. Important examples of public goods affected in this way are fire protection, police and health services, and recreational facilities. Because the ease of access to these goods decreases, or the time and cost involved in gaining access rises, with distance, they do not satisfy the Musgrave – Samuelson first and second conditions, of joint supply and non-excludeability characteristics. Since the distance of travel to gain access to a public good may become preclusively expensive or difficult, supply to one person does not allow supply to all who wish to have access. In addition, it is extremely common to find cases of rejection of public goods, thus violating the Musgrave–Samuelson third condition. For example, it is well known that some public goods generate disbenefits to those living in close proximity to them. Important examples are urban blight, proximity to pollution and noise, as with power stations, disruption through street parking and disturbance adjacent to recreational and school facilities, disturbance from ambulance noise near a hospital, and so forth. Although each such factor may be minor, its effect on residential location, and hence on house prices, can be very great and undermines the Musgrave–Samuelson third condition of non-rejectability. Thus the effect of tapering of benefits for public goods with geographical distance is sufficient to undermine each of the Musgrave–Samuelson conditions. Because tapering has significant effects on most public goods, this factor alone is sufficient to introduce an important geographical component into public finance. It also gives rise to the subsidiary question: if benefits vary as a function of distance from the point of provision of the good, should the level of taxation also vary as a function of distance and thence be related to the level of benefit received? This leads to the principle of benefit taxation which will occupy a great deal of attention in later chapters (see p. 163).

Jurisdictional partitioning is a second major geographical component which undermines the universality of public goods required by the Musgrave–Samuelson conditions. Geographic space is not uniform physically, nor is it economically, nor politically. Most important, it is divided into sets of jurisdictions corresponding to the bounds of local, intermediate and national-level governments. Hence public goods are not usually provided on a uniform basis within a given state. There are many reasons for this which result from the political, economic and technological factors discussed in later chapters. The consequence, however, is that for those public goods which are organized at a sub-national level, we have to consider the effects of different local political juridisdictions. Each of these will have variable financial resources, variable expenditure needs, and variable preferences for particular bundles of public goods. Also since each jurisdiction will usually differ in the way it levies taxation or provides benefits, there will be a lack of uniformity of treatment between people in different locations. The possibility of such variability in resources and needs underlies a series of economic models which describe the emergence of patterns of geographical disparity in social well-being. These are determined by three processes. First, differences in income and wealth of people and industry in different jurisdictions give a geographically variable taxable base: an equal tax rate across different jurisdictions will give different *per capita* yields (usually irrespective of whether this is a sales, income or property tax). This gives a *resource-disparity hypothesis*. This effect is often reinforced by cumulative cycles of growth or poverty which tend to exacerbate geographical differences in resources and well-being (see chapter 3). Second, the collective and political decision-making of the people in different jurisdictions allows the formation of 'service clubs': the bundle of public goods which accords most closely with local collective preferences–the so-called *Buchanan hypothesis*. Third, there is the tendency of the people to migrate from one jurisdiction to another in order to gain the pattern of public goods which most closely accords with their individual preferences and which gives them the lowest tax rate for a given level of service provision–the so-called *Tiebout hypothesis* of fiscal migration.

These three hypotheses will be explained at length in later chapters (see Buchanan 1965, 1967; Tiebout 1956, 1961). For the present, it is sufficient to note four main consequences for public finance. First, the benefits available from public goods are affected by spatial exclusion and are not available to all groups uniformly. This may accord well with some 'liberal' views of political economy which interpret the most desirable pattern of public goods as emerging from collective decisions of the polity (in this case the local jurisdiction), but accords badly with 'radical' interpretations of political economy which seek equality of treatment of all individuals wherever they may live. The radical interpretation will be particularly critical of the Tiebout hypothesis, for example, since the mobility required to choose one's preferred jurisdiction can often be argued to be specific to certain income groups, and is not usually available to the poor. A second consequence, resulting especially from the Buchanan hypothesis, is that this strongly implies that public finance should be organized and paid for by those people within the jurisdiction who decide on its size and benefit from it. This implies a third consequence, that public goods should be divided into classes dependent upon the jurisdiction or level at which they are most efficiently supplied or can be agreed upon. Hence public goods, their finance, and the jurisdiction organized towards their supply, should be divided into local, regional (or, in federal countries, state), national, and perhaps even international levels. But a fourth consequence which results from the disparity of resources between jurisdictions, is that a measure of co-ordinated local action, or indeed national action, on public finance may be necessary in order to ensure a reasonably equal treatment of people. This may be particularly important in overcoming the effects of extreme poverty which is often very localized in geographical occurrence. As we shall see in chapter 4, many of the most pressing consequences of taking a geographical view of public finance result from the resource disparity hypothesis, the city versus suburbs issue and regional disparity issue being the two most important cases.

Spillover is the third major geographical component of public finance and is a consequence of jurisdictional partitioning. It describes the mismatching of the area which bears the costs of a given public good and the area which receives the benefit. Benefit spillovers occur when the benefits of a given good are available to those living outside a given jurisdiction. The alternative, of cost spillovers (or spillin), occurs when a given jurisdiction has access to benefits from other jurisdictions. In the case of spillovers, the jurisdiction exports externalities and bears the costs of providing benefits to others, whereas spillings (cost spillovers) allow the jurisdiction to import externalities and enjoy the benefits of the expenditure by others. Spillovers arise as the inevitable consequence of jurisdictional partitioning: it is not possible completely to separate the 'service club' of one jurisdiction from another, not only because of tapering effects, but also because of the general mobility of people in modern economies who will often live in one jurisdiction, work in another, and seek leisure and shopping outlets in yet others. In addition, migration allows individuals to realize benefit spillovers arising from long-term capital investment (schools and infrastructure) for which they have not paid. Migration also represents the import and export of 'human capital' externalities, i.e. the benefits and costs derived from education and training investment obtained in other jurisdictions. Finally, jurisdictions are subject to temporal constraints since it is not possible continuously to redraw jurisdictional boundaries to cope with the impact of changing commuting and transport patterns, the influence of population growth (or decline), and technological innovations. Various theoretical solutions to resolve the problems resulting from spillover have been suggested in terms of inducing 'fiscal equivalence' (Olson 1969), 'perfect mapping' (Breton 1965), and 'matching grants' (Lea 1978; Musgrave 1959; Pigou 1947). Fiscal equivalence and perfect mapping require a one-to-one mapping of jurisdictions to benefit areas, and this is achieved by restructuring local government to correspond to the areas of '*local public goods*': goods which have a uniform distribution of benefits within a given jurisdiction, and for which benefits fall to zero at the boundary, (see p. 222). This approach is subject to two difficulties: first, few goods possess such properties; second, a different jurisdictional arrangement is required for each good. The use of matching grants, suggested initially by Pigou, provides a more practical soultion which is discussed further in chapters 11 and 12. Payment is exacted from jurisdictions receiving benefit spillover, or grants are used to equalize benefit spillover and costs.

The combination of tapering, jurisdictional partitioning and spillover induce marked, but subtle, effects on the distribution of personal income (through the social wage) and private profit (through externalities). It is these effects which form the central problem of the geography of public finance which is the motivation for this book. As stated by Netzer (1968, p. 438) the problem is as follows:

> 'distribution policies or consequences ultimately concern individual consumer units. One dimension, the usual measure in incidence studies, is the approximate dimension of incidence by income *class*. Another dimension, important in a metropolitan context, is that of *geographic* redistribution within large urban areas. The fragmentation of tax bases among a large number of political jurisdictions of extremely disparate character, their highly uneven geographical distribution of expenditure needs (notably, residences of the poor) and the possibility of exporting some tax burdens across jurisdictional lines, together suggest that the metropolitan fisc might have redistributive consequences among communities. The usual variant of this is the 'suburban exploitation of the central city' hypothesis'.

Although directing attention specifically at metropolitan and urban questions of public finance in the US, this statement has general relevance for the geography of public finance and neatly summarizes its central problem: the question of who gets what, *where* as a result of the means of organizing the provision of public goods.

2.6 Conclusion

The interplay between tapering, jurisdictional partitioning and spillover has profound influences on public finance which are specifically geographical.

These influences have only been indicated in the discussion above and will be extended in the following chapters. Despite the importance of these effects, however, comparatively little attention has been given to them, until recent studies of fiscal federalism and urban finance. Smith (1977, p. 113) adduces this to the covert nature of spatial redistribution in the public sector, and quotes the United States' experience of Shoup (1964, p. 383):

> 'Little is known about the distribution of government services by location, race, religion, income class, or other categories. Usually no record is made, no estimate attempted. . . . This silence reflects in part a social propensity to discriminate covertly in ways that are not tolerable in taxation, where the pattern of impact is more obvious. For example; education has been distributed unequally, by social class, race or colour, in communities (i.e. local 'service clubs') that would not think of distributing the tax bill by those indicia'.

In Britain, the debate over devolution has thrown up specifically spatial questions about the present distribution of public expenditure in order to determine who gets what, where. But attempts to answer these questions have been systematically obstructed, the justification by the UK Royal Commission for the Constitution (1973, p. 181) being clearly indicative of the policy:

> 'Much more detailed studies would be a necessary preliminary to de- volutionary reform. But it seems that a system of financial devolution would necessarily start and probably continue with wide differences and expenditure per head between Scotland and Wales on the one hand and the English regions on the other . . . . That in essence is the position now. But technical difficulties would inevitably arise in attempting to formalise what is now informal; and *political difficulties could be expected to arise from revealing year by year what is now not merely undisclosed but largely unrecorded'* (italics added).

This is precisely the central problem of the geography of public finance: a decision on the appropriate degree of spatial variability of public expenditure per head and its related benefits, which is necessarily political. But the difficulties, which are inevitable, must be overcome in order to make overt what is now covert. It is towards the publicizing of this view, and its attendant implications, that the following chapters of this book are directed.

3

The geographical functions of public finance

"Wealthy men go where wealthy men are. . . . Poor men try to go where wealthy men are, and the wealthy try to keep them out . . . geographical fragmentation is . . . only an expression of the desire of the well-to-do to operate under something as close to a market pricing system as possible."

Carl Shoup, 1969, *Public Finance*, p. 633.

3.1 Introduction

Public finance, as we have seen in the previous chapter, is intimately involved with the nature of the social polity and its underlying political ideology. As such, public finance bears both on the level and distribution of personal incomes, through the social wage, and on private profit, through externalities to the firm. The geography of public finance involves the variable level and distribution of public goods which results from the effects of tapering over space, jurisdictional partitioning over space, and spillovers of benefits and costs of public goods from one location to another. Although questions of ideology are raised by questions of public finance, as we have seen, the discussion in this book is concerned largely with the revenue and expenditure side of the public budget. Adopting this view, it is sought in this chapter to explore the major functions of the revenue and expenditure sides of the geography of public finance. This then clears the ground for the consideration in later chapters of the economics of revenue and expenditure as separate elements, and their relationships in determining the geography of fiscal incidence.

One of the most useful and workable approaches to the functions of public finance is given by Musgrave (1959) and Musgrave and Musgrave (1976) who divide these functions into three classes, now almost hallowed as a 'trinity' in economic studies of public finance:

(1) *Allocation function (the price mechanism).* This is the process by which the total financial and real resources of a state are divided between public and private goods, and by which a particular mix of public goods is chosen. In the public sector there is no necessary link between the price of a given public good and its cost, reflecting its relative scarcity. Hence, the allocation of public goods often depends more upon a decision of whether and how a public good should be provided rather than its relative scarcity.

33

(2) *Distribution function (social policy)*. The use of the public sector is the primary way, in a capitalist system, by which income, profit and social well-being can be redistributed amongst its members without violent social disruption or revolution. The natural drive in capitalist economies is towards the selfish maximization of personal income and private profit, the deleterious effects of which can only be overcome by a force greater than that of the capitalist drive itself. Such a force can be provided by a government which chooses to organize public finance as an element of social policy to achieve a desired income distribution. This necessitates policies which now form the basis of the 'welfare state' which seek to redistribute resources between income groups.

(3) *Stabilization function (economic policy)*. Public finance is also used to effect certain elements of general economic policy. Particularly important are those policies deriving from Keynes (1936) which aim at either stabilizing an economy, or at achieving economic growth. Stabilization is concerned with maintaining an even level of employment and prices by reducing the effects of economic cycles of boom and slump. Economic growth determines the overall level of unemployment, prices and social well-being. In a perfect market, booms and slumps will be self-equilibrating in that price and wage levels will adjust automatically: excess demand is damped by decreases in wages and increases in prices; deficient demand is stimulated by increases in wages and decreases in prices. Recognition that these self-equilibrating forces do not usually work, due to institutional and other rigidity, is due mainly to Keynes who proposed a method of expansionary policies of public spending to raise deficient demand during recessions, and deflationary policies of heavier taxation and credit restrictions in times of boom. At the same time, it is hoped by such policies of public finance to direct the economy as a whole along a long-term trajectory of economic growth. Such policy is normally achieved through *fiscal measures*: taxation or expenditure decisions will have selective effects on one sector of an economy rather than another.

The three functions of public finance – namely allocation, distribution and stabilization – have been discussed here solely in the macro-economic terms familiar to the economist, but it should already be clear that each of these functions has very significant geographical impacts which should be taken into account in any discussion of public finance. It is these geographical impacts which are analysed in the rest of this chapter, but because of the geographical significance of both cyclic stabilization, and economic growth, these are given separate treatment in sections 3.4 and 3.5, respectively.

3.2 Geographical allocation or price function of public finance

The allocation function determines price, which in turn is determined by relative supply and demand. For public goods the theory of price derives from Lindahl (1919) and Wicksell (1896) for *pure* public goods. For *impure* public goods, Ellickson (1973) has shown that the Lindahl theory will hold good under certain conditions. In each case, price is determined via neoclassical analysis applied to the consumption of each individual. This is dependent upon the *Lindahl optimality condition:*

> 'each person will be charged or taxed that price per unit of good consumed equal to his marginal evaluation. The marginal evaluation is given as the marginal rate of substitution between the public good and a so-called *numeraire private good* which represents the alternative consumption possibilities. Under this condition output will be increased to the point at which the sum of taxes or charges just equals the marginal cost of the public good.'

Hence price determination for public goods is assumed to evolve in the same way as for private goods, and in competition with them. Such a solution is also Pareto optimal, but as shown by Lea (1978) there are many Pareto optima, whereas there is only one Lindahl optimum.

In the presence of geographical factors, very few public goods can be considered pure: the influence of space induces non-joint supply, exclusion and rejectability. These arise from the effects of transport costs, congestion, indivisibilities, and difficulties of designing revenue and expenditure systems which permit total jointness. It has been suggested by Lea (1978) and others that the use of marginal prices overcomes many of these problems, but as we shall see in many cases there is no necessary link between the price of a public good and the costs of providing it, and hence there is no reason to expect that marginal prices will be any better related to marginal costs as between those who pay and those who receive a public good. Hence, the allocation of public goods and services between users cannot, and probably should not, be assumed to reflect the relative scarcity or price of these goods.

The classical approach to the allocation aspects of public finance (see Groves 1964; Shoup 1969; Musgrave and Musgrave 1976) involves analysis of the effects of different modes of public finance (revenue, expenditure and capital) on the price, quality, and quantity of both public and private goods. These studies provide an important set of theoretical and empirical results which will be drawn upon in many places. Their results can be briefly summarized as follows. On the revenue side, taxes can be expected to have a direct price effect, but the extent of any price increase will vary with the degree to which the final incidence of revenue burdens can be shifted. Considerable analysis is usually required to determine who bears the final burden after shifting between people and jurisdictions has been taken into account (see chapter 8). On the expenditure side, public expenditures usually reduce the costs of goods to the consumer and hence increase the demand. This frequently requires the limitation of supply by regulation, congestion, or other means. Intergovernmental transfers can frequently be used to even out differences in price, quantity or quality and supply constraints, but such transfers also have impact on price and supply which underprice goods and further modify the allocation problem (see chapter 12).

Despite the importance of the traditional emphasis on price, quantity, quality and supply aspects of finance, many elements of the geography of public finance allocation relate more to the political and administrative aspects of the public economy. These lead us to two opposed views on the way in which decisions on the allocation of the public fisc can be made. On the one hand there are 'localist' or 'public choice' models which suggest that the public sector should be organized around various spatial scales of collective preferences. On the other hand are 'centralist' models which suggest that public goods should be allocated geographically on the basis of the measured 'needs' of each spatial location. The distinction between the localist and centralist models, though somewhat artificial, provides a starting point for the discussion below.

The localist model is grounded in the two hypotheses, due respectively to Buchanan and to Tiebout, introduced in the previous chapter. Buchanan (1965, 1967) suggests that given a geographical pattern of separate political jurisdictions, individuals will join together in 'service clubs' within each jurisdiction. The result will be an allocation of public goods which varies from place to place in accordance with the collective preferences of the people living within each jurisdiction. The decision as to whether a specific public good is available in any jurisdiction is based on whether the benefits received by each individual from the public organization of that good outweigh the benefits to each individual from the non-provision or private provision of that good. Thus geographical allocation is rooted in the liberal economic principles of Smith, Mill and Bentham: that a public good is provided only when collectively desired by the local community, otherwise it is organized on a private basis. Since the area of collective agreement will usually be fairly limited, the resultant local polity will satisfy Mill's condition as the residual element from private action, where it is possible to reach agreement. In such models, when an individual finds himself in a local polity in which he does not agree with the overall decision on the nature and extent of public goods, he has three possible courses of action. First, he may actively participate in public decision-making and attempt to influence decisions, i.e. by becoming a local councillor or representative. Second, he may lobby his representatives either personally or through a pressure group. Finally, he may 'vote with his feet' and migrate from one local jurisdiction in favour of another which has a mix of public goods which accords better with his preferences, or has a lower tax rate, or both. This final response accords with the Tiebout (1956, 1961) hypothesis of a fiscal stimulus to migration.

At its face value the localist model for geographical allocation of public finance seems eminently reasonable. Some jurisdictions will have a large public sector whilst others will have a small one, "each community will do its own thing and everyone will be satisfied" (Musgrave and Musgrave 1976,

p. 619). Thus Scott (1964) has argued that geographical inequalities in wealth and public benefits between locations should be accepted as inevitable in any state in which a measure of local autonomy is allowed. Musgrave (1961, p. 133) has argued even more extremely that the essence of location is determined by differences in preferences and income which constitute a datum for location: like the distribution of natural resources, they are part of the economic map. Moreover, a polity which interferes with such regional differentials will be much less efficient when viewed against non-public sector criteria of efficiency: allocation of resources relating supply and demand through price to scarcity. Thus both Tiebout migration, and geographical variation of public services, are essential to allow market principles to determine the allocation of public goods. Hence "efficient location planning (in the absence of other overriding considerations) will encourage co-residency of people with similar tastes" (Musgrave 1969, p. 299). Indeed Tiebout (1961, p. 93) argues that it should be the primary purpose of planning to provide a variety of different public services at different locations and allow people with similar tastes to move together.

However, the localist model as formulated by Tiebout and Buchanan contains a number of inadequacies that limit its application in practice. First, the model ignores the effects of both the tapering of benefits and costs, and of spillovers into adjacent jurisdictions. The theory assumes that a pure local good exists for which the benefits are uniform everywhere within the jurisdiction and drop to zero outside the boundaries: a characteristic which is rarely attained. Second, differences in income between jurisdictions limit the ability of some areas to purchase social goods. A third limitation, induced by differences in income, is that in two communities with identical mixes of public goods, the wealthier community, because of its larger tax base, can choose to finance its public goods by lower rates of income tax or property tax. Hence there will be an inequality between areas: different areas will tax the same people differently but provide the same range of public goods. A fourth limitation in the localist model induced by differences in tax rates is that the operation of Tiebout immigration into a jurisdiction with lower tax rates is frequently countered by land-use zoning and other restrictions which limit access of migrants to richer communities; limitations which are usually particularly stringent against the poorer migrant. The effect of each of these factors is to lead to increased spatial polarization between income groups resulting in rich and poor areas. This effect may be combined with social and ethnic factors to lead also to increased polarization between racial, religious and cultural groups. A fifth and central dilemma in the localist model, however, is represented by the effect of collective decisions on minority groups. Buchanan and Tullock (1969) argue that an optimum community size will be at that size at which the marginal gains of the majority who agree to a collective decision just offset the marginal losses which derive from violating the wishes of minority groups. But this resolution is possible only if homogeneity of preference increases as the group size gets smaller. As Margolis (1961) suggests, it is more common for homogeneity to decrease with smaller groups since the effect of merging of views to obtain consensus is removed; thus smaller groups tend to polarize into extremes thence increasing faction and sectionalism.

Because of these and other limitations of the localist model, it is generally accepted that the allocation of public goods cannot be left entirely to local collective action. The unfettered collective and locational decisions of individuals will lead to increasing faction and polarization between classes, ethnic and cultural groups, and increasing fragmentation of jurisdictions between extreme minority views. Hence some role at least is usually accorded to the alternative *centralist* model which suggests a measure of equalization between locations on the basis of measures of standards and needs. The aims of such centralist models, which are related to those of the needs-assessment school of political economy, are to promote at least a degree of equity in the local level and cost of public goods by spreading out the geographical differences in costs over the community at large, and evening out geographical differences in the ability to pay. Such considerations overlap with the geographical distribution and stabilization functions of public finance to be discussed in the next sections. It is argued that a degree of centralization allows a degree of equalization of local taxes and local benefits. However, since incomes and benefits differ greatly between people, and hence between locations, it becomes necessary to measure the differences in local income and benefits. Moreover, since local benefits will differ, often on a purely arbitrary basis, it is also necessary to define and to measure differences from a desired 'norm' of local benefits. Such *benefit norms* again vary between individuals, and are often referred to as measures of local *needs*. Once local needs have been identified, the centralist model proceeds by attempting to delimit the areas of political responsibility in relation to those needs, i.e. a decision is required as to whether a given need can be satisfied by organizing the allocation of public finance at a national, a local, or at an intermediate level. This style of approach has characterized some of the discussion in the UK on the appropriate forms of local finance, where the Layfield Report (*UK Committee of Enquiry into Local Government Finance*, 1976), for example, has attempted to make clear delimitation between local and central responsibility and accountability.

There are a number of criticisms of the centralist approach. The most important of these is that it tends to lead to the development of rather general and average pricing rules which are inappropriate for those regions and jurisdictions which diverge from the average. As Newman (1978, p. 2) notes for the US, "general rules for average situations will lead to multitudes of examples to fill the scrapbooks of collectors of public administration horror tales". A second criticism of the centralist approach is that the rigid dividing lines of government responsibility which are suggested are usually irrelevant.

What is required instead is a definition of certain minimum standards of needs which should be financed at a national level, usually by grants, with variations above this level financed on a local basis. This allows a compromise between the more rigid centralist definition of areas of accountability, and a totally localist model (Day, p. 306 in Layfield Report, *op cit.*), and leads to methods of deficiency payments.

Perhaps the earliest discussion of the relation between the localist and centralist models of determining the allocation of public finance is for the US, in *The Federalist* (1788) papers by Hamilton, Madison and Jay. These authors argue that the greatest danger of the localist model is the encouragement it gives to faction and to polarization where "a number of citizens . . . are united and actuated by a common impulse of passion, or of interest adverse to the rights of other citizens, or to the permanent and aggregate interests of the community" (Madison, *The Federalist*, No. 10, p. 130). But *The Federalist* writers believed, like Hobbes, and Rousseau, that the causes of faction cannot be removed, since these emerge as part of both a natural competitiveness of man and of the workings of the economic system; or even if they could be removed, then the method of removing faction was even more unacceptable as it relied on two methods "the one, by destroying the liberty which was essential to its existence; the other, by giving to every citizen the same opinions, the same passions, and the same interests" (*op cit.* p. 130). But if the causes of faction could not be removed, the consequences can, and *The Federalist* suggestion (e.g. nos. 10 and 39) is the control of *minority faction* by the creation of a union or republic, and the control of *majority faction* by the division of the union into a federation of states. The republican union enlarges the public view which can be brought to bear on any issue, thus limiting the possible effects of narrow sectionalist interests; but a federation of states safeguards minorities from what de Tocqueville termed the 'tyranny of the majority', thus preventing local interests being overridden. A similar balance of local and overall interests was less successful in the devolved government of Northern Ireland to the Stormont Parliament in the 1960s.

Certainly the issue of the correct balance of local and central control in taxation, expenditure programmes and decisions on public goods is not an easy one to resolve, nor is it an issue for which there is a general solution which can be applied to all countries. A multitude of different mixed central and local fiscal structures have evolved. Recent history in North America, in Australia, and in the EEC shows a continuing debate between the merits of alternative centralist and localist arrangements which has given rise to new public finance programmes such as the US Revenue-Sharing and Community Development Programmes, Australian income tax base sharing, UK devolution and inner cities proposals, and EEC public finance integration proposals.

3.3 Geographical distribution of public finance

Consideration of the geographical allocation function of public finance has already raised the questions of social distribution, and indeed the two issues of allocation and distribution are intimately related. The social distribution question is one which involves the introduction of public sector forces to counter the natural workings of the economic market. If incomes are unequally distributed this will require the use of a taxation policy which relates payment for public goods to the ability to pay, i.e. taxation will usually be *progressive*: higher on higher incomes. Similarly public expenditure policy, as we have seen, will involve the allocation of services to those in most need. On a geographical basis, redistribution of incomes requires the disparate raising of taxation as progressive over different spatial ranges of wealth, and re-distributive over different spatial configurations of need.

The concept of raising and expending taxation on a variable spatial basis has not, however, met with universal support as a measure for implementing distribution policies. There are two issues involved. First, the degree to which local jurisdictions should undertake autonomous redistribution programmes. Second, the degree to which national and higher level governments should implement spatially differentiated redistribution programmes between in-dividuals in different locations. The criticisms of both forms of geographical variation in distribution policies comes from three sources: the free market view, the classical public finance view, and the Marxist social critique. Each of these views is discussed in turn below.

THE FREE MARKET VIEW

This states that local autonomy in taxation and expenditures, or national level differentiation of revenue and expenditure policies, distorts location costs and induces inefficiency away from the optimum locations which would obtain if there were uniform revenue and expenditure policies. A uniform public fisc, on the other hand, will exert no spatial influences: the location of both industries and of people will accord with the minimum cost location (as in for example, Losch 1941; Weber 1909). The market view, therefore, credits geographical differentiation of the public fisc with inefficient pricing and allocation, the propping up of old and inefficient locations, and creating barriers to new and more efficient locations (see Bish 1971; Musgrave and Musgrave 1976; Scott 1952). For example, in Britain it has been suggested that regional industrial policy has been instrumental in reducing economic growth in South East England, and in the UK as a whole.

THE CLASSICAL PUBLIC FINANCE VIEW

This is best stated by Musgrave (1969, p. 312) who argues that income distribution is fundamentally an inter-personal problem: it "relates to people and the family unit. It does not relate to differentials in average *per capita* income between regions". The main support for this view is the fact that inter-regional differences in wealth usually conceal intra-regional differences in wealth which are often of much greater extent and importance. Thus a policy to equalize regional *per capita* incomes may do nothing to equalize personal incomes. In another context Self (1972) has argued that the organization of public services on an areal basis does nothing to solve the distribution problem, it merely removes it to a lower level. Moreover the classical view contends that there may be nothing inherently inequitable in regional income differences. As Musgrave (1969, p. 312) notes "after a proper state of inter-personal distribution has been secured by central action . . . there is no objection to such differential in regional averages as remain . . . these, like differences in the average consumption of private goods, are merely a reflection of what inter-individual distribution policy considers a tolerable level of inequality". Thus regional income differences can be expected if personal incomes overall are inequitable and if the wealthier and poorer live in separate areas. The classical view further states that it is inevitable that there should be a considerable demand for income distribution at a local level, since this is not only the most visible level of inequality, but also the level at which higher income groups gain most from raising the incomes of poorer families. In particular, if these income supplements are received as grants or payments from a national level government, the rich gain considerable externalities from reduced blight, increased local turnover, and better local facilities at a lower total cost.

On the basis of these arguments Musgrave and others (see Oates 1972; 1977) have argued that redistribution is best approached as a national policy. Thus local taxes should not be progressive with income, nor should there be local welfare and transfer payments. Any progression in local taxation and benefits will tend to exacerbate fiscal migration which, as suggested by the Tiebout model, will lead to increased spatial polarization. Local level redistribution gives incentives to immigration by low income families and emigration by high income families.

THE MARXIST SOCIAL CRITIQUE

This states that the distribution of wealth and opportunity between people arises from the mode of production which determines the division of labour, and this in turns gives the division of society into classes. The extreme Marxist point of view then contends that since social relations determine the distribution of wealth, redistribution (or rather the restructuring of society as a whole) should be attacked at the social level. In this case the spatial component is irrelevant. As stated in most extreme form by Castells (1976, p. 443): "there is no space but only . . . social relations, of course, there is the 'site', the 'geographical' conditions, but they concern analysis only as the support of a certain web of social relations . . . . But not *qua* 'space' – rather as a certain efficacy of the social activity expressed in a certain spatial form". Similar views are expressed to a greater or lesser extent by Anderson (1974) and Lee (1976a, b). In contrast, Levebvre (1972) and Harvey (1973) follow a more tenable line in which spatial components together with class and other factors are argued to be valid foci for social study. Certainly an argument

41

which emphasizes social differences in wealth, but which ignores geographical variation in the division of labour and processes of production must be far off the mark.

THE CASE FOR GEOGRAPHICAL REDISTRIBUTION

Despite the strength of many of the arguments suggesting that distribution policies should be undertaken only at national level and with no degree of geographical differentiation, there are a number of strong counter-arguments, the three most important of which are discussed below.

The first and primary argument is that the needs, costs, and preferences for public goods, and the ability to pay for them, vary as a function of geographical location. Many *needs* are specific to an area and are not specific to the people as individuals. For example, housing, infrastructure, industry, prevention of crime, and health-care are all to some extent area-specific local goods. Similarly the costs of providing public goods varies with location as a function of climate, subsoil, physiography, elevation and economic size of the government unit. In addition, *preferences* vary to reflect a degree of local cohesion in rural communites, in urban social areas, and in regional identity. Moreover each of these locational characteristics is significant, even in fairly small countries such as the UK, Denmark, Holland, Belgium or Switzerland. Geographical variation in *fiscal ability* is also as specific to an area as it is to an individual. Concentrations of the poor and of the rich arise from the historical and constitutional evolution of the economic structure of each location, its interlinkage with the rest of the national economy, and mechanisms of social and economic exclusion. Of course it is not usually possible to separate the areally specific features of need, cost, preferences and ability from those which are individually specific. For example, crime is as much the result of individual poverty as it is of an impoverished environment; industrial performance varies as much due to individual entrepreneurial behaviour and labour relations as local conditions, and economic multipliers; preferences are certainly more highly variable within areas than between them such that regional or local community identity is often a small residual element; and revenue ability is undoubtedly as much a function of the nature of individuals and of the national economic health as it is a function of historical and local factors. Nevertheless, a large component of area-specific variation, perhaps impossible to separate from other factors, is present in most components of public finance and can often be tackled at a geographical level.

A second argument for geographical redistribution, which derives from the area-specific components discussed above, is that *local governments* differ as to the nature of their fiscal needs, costs and capacities. Since local needs and capacities will rarely be in accord, a needs-resources disparity frequently arises at the local level which, without a level of geographical differentiation of public finance, cannot be corrected. Even within narrowly constrained patterns of national income distribution, it is possible to have differences in the areal distribution of wealth. In general of course, the distribution of wealth over space can be as great as (but no greater than) the personal distribution. But although there may be some strong arguments for variations in personal income levels, such as provision of incentive and reward, and variations in personal needs, in accord with individual preferences, differences in spatial needs and incomes pose a number of important dilemmas. Although personal income differences may be justifiable in terms of individual career structures, as incentives to undertake unpleasant employment and so forth, spatial differences in wealth, because they have no other justification than that different income groups choose to live apart, tend to offer polar comparisons divorced from the personal factors which underlie their generation. Thus, as we shall see in chapter 4, spatial factors lend themselves to ready interpretation in class terms: as urban–rural, city–suburbs, or centre–periphery. Moreover, it is these geographical differences that may often be most visible. The spatial concentration of wealth in Los Angeles' Beverley Hills, or in Hampstead's Bishops Avenue, present extreme contrasts to downtown Baltimore or London Docklands. The problems of the redundant and unemployed, of old people, of the young, and of dilapidated housing stock are often concentrated in particular areas by the very nature of the economic conditions which are their cause. The decline of traditional industries, and the decay of neighbourhoods and of housing are each specific to the areas and periods in which the problems are located. Hence the US Community Development programme Title II and Title V authorities, and the UK Regional and Inner City Policies, represent highly suitable adjustments of public finance to problems which are convenient to identify and are particularly well-defined in spatial terms. Such concentrations of social problems cannot be left to be treated solely as an exogeneous factor apart from questions of the determination of what constitutes a proper distribution of incomes.

A third argument for geographical differentiation of redistribution policies is the *cumulative* nature of interjurisdictional imbalances. This is related to the economic growth and stabilization functions of public finance to be discussed in the next sections. Since the distribution of wealth in capitalist economies unfettered by public interference will tend towards increasing the income differences between the wealthy and the poor, an initial spatial concentration of wealth or poverty will engender a pattern of increasing spatial imbalance between areas. It is now widely accepted that initial patterns of regional income inequality contain the seeds of continued growth in disparities in the future, as capital and labour resources are attracted to the wealthy areas at the expense of the poorer in a continuing and cumulative process. In the face of such intensifying pressures which exacerbate spatial differences, the exclusion from distribution policies of spatial aspects allows the writing-off of the social and the human infrastructure of urban tracts and whole regions. Hence most countries have implemented various redistribution policies among regions and jurisdictions to equalize fiscal capacity. In Canada, Australia, the United

States and Western Europe various unconditional grants and forms of revenue-sharing (see p. 313) have been used as specific income redistribution measures to improve the level of local services and hence of the social wage in poorer areas.

A series of other arguments for an element of geographical redistribution policies obtain in different countries. In the US and elsewhere, instruments of individual redistribution (transfer and social security payments) have become saturated such that jurisdictional redistribution may be a more pragmatic and feasible solution. In other cases it is possible to attack personal distribution problems by geographical transfers where personal transfers have failed, e.g. local in-kind transfers in the form of free or subsidized school meals, hospital treatment or public transport, community health centres, recreation areas and urban renewal grants. In still other cases, geographical differentiation of national policies may be required to assure a range of local choice. When either local resources or the scale of local demand is insufficient to stimulate local provision, then area-specific higher level government action may provide a useful alternative. For example, geographical differentiation of public finance may also be required to balance out the distribution effects of tapering and spillover. Finally, geographical intergovernmental transfers oriented towards the variable pattern of need may be undertaken so as to provide a base level of public services, as in the case of the frequently used national minimum standards of 'merit goods' (see chapter 5).

Certainly it is not sought to argue here that redistribution should be based totally on geographical criteria. It will never be possible to discriminate taxes, at either a central or local level, so as to equalize the total tax payment of individuals for the same level of service benefits and to relate this to the variable ability to pay. This would involve an impossibly complex calculus for measuring all needs, burdens, benefits and incomes, and for rationalizing between national, local and intermediate level effects. Nor will it be possible to attain total equality of services and fiscal burdens over a whole economy: it will never be possible to provide for the Mezzorgiorno, or the Scottish Highlands, the same level of amenities and public services as for Rome, or Edinburgh. Nor is it necessarily desirable that equality of public services obtains uniformly. This is inconsistent with allowing variation to suit local preferences. And finally, nor should major and insuperable barriers to geographical mobility of labour and capital seek to erode the basis of incentive and local self-reliance, offer more to the unemployed in one jurisdiction than those at work in another, or undermine the viability of local community feeling. For these and other reasons, the search for total geographical equality of the public fisc must be doomed to failure.

Nevertheless, it is possible, and it is certainly desirable, that as high a degree as possible of equalization in public finances should be achieved. But this will be achievable only by mixed patterns of nationally uniform, nationally variable, and locally autonomous organization of the public fisc. Such a desire is stated well by Matthews (in EEC 1977, pp. 403–4): the purpose of geographical equalization is

> 'to permit or encourage governments to equalise the fiscal burdens and benefits accruing to individuals in the different jurisdictions subject to equalisation. ... to make it possible ... for governments within the equalisation system to provide a standard range and quality of administrative, social and economic services for their citizens, whilst maintaining comparable fiscal efforts in the form of standard rates of taxation and other charges. The purpose (and the effect) of redistributing financial resources among governments rather than individuals is to decentralise the responsibility for resource allocation decisions ... whilst leaving citizens in the different jurisdictions ... equally well off in terms of their governments' capacity, and effectiveness in, service provision.'

As we shall see in later chapters, only in this way it is possible to achieve equal treatment of equals, and unequal treatment of unequals under the public fisc; and hence at least to neutralize the impact of the public economy on distribution. To ignore these geographical factors will exacerbate both spatial and personal inequities, rather than diminish them.

3.4 Geographical stabilization function of public finance

Public finance may be used as an instrument of economic stabilization to achieve two main aims: first, smoothing out of the economic cycle, and second, achievement of the overall goal of economic growth. Because of the geographic significance of these two functions, they are treated separately in this chapter, stabilization of the economic cycle being discussed in this section, and the geography of growth being discussed in the next section 3.5.

There are undoubtedly strong geographical components in the stabilization function of public finance but, as in the case of the distribution function, many economists have argued that stabilization policy is best undertaken at the national level; little or no geographical variation in the policy measures of fiscal, monetary, or balance of payments manipulation can or should be contemplated (see, for example, Hansen and Perloff 1944; Musgrave and Musgrave 1976; Oates 1972). For monetary and for balance of payments policies there is obviously limited scope for geographical variation. Certainly different currencies and direct adjustments to the exchange rate between separate political jurisdictions in the same state will never be consistent with the orderly development of economic interdependence within a state. But some geographical variation in stabilization policy can be effected through selective taxation, expenditure, credit and protection measures as outcomes of fiscal policy. Moreover, geographical variation in fiscal policy can be achieved in practice and can be used both for cyclical stabilization and for stimulating growth.

The reservation of the stabilization function to national governments is based on three arguments: the problems of local debt management, the openness of local economies, and the supposed perversity of local finances. Local debt management based on Keynesian fiscal policies requires the management of budget deficits to coincide with periods of recession, and surpluses to coincide with periods of excessive demand. This is indeed difficult to achieve at the local level. Local areas are less able to raise loans abroad and indeed must be limited in national economic management of the balance of payments. Moreover since local debt will usually be held on a national capital market external to the local jurisdiction, this gives a lack of local control and freedom to move in a pattern contrary to that of other jurisdictions. Moreover any debt finance burdens are transferred on to future generations (see chapter 10). Because of the high degree of 'openness' of local economies, and of mobility between them, it is impossible to balance the burden of debt between generations, and hence local debt financing serves merely as an important further stimulus to fiscal migration.

The 'openness' of local economies results from the strong interlinkage and interdependence between industries and public services in different locations. Indeed it has been the central tenet of export-base models, for example, that the economic health of urban jurisdictions depends upon the high degree of openness of these economies to external influences of demand. Indeed North (1955) describes the export base as "the primary control of the level of economic activity and economic health for the region". But if one jurisdiction is very open to the effects of external demand, so usually are most others. Hence any local fiscal measures have strong 'import leakages'; that is, any local expansionary or restrictive measures which change local income per head will also adjust imports. Thus local deficit spending will usually have small local multipliers and will instead leak largely into other jurisdictions improving the demand for their goods and services at the expense of the local area. Conversely, spending restrictions, although having deflationary leakage effects, will have limited impacts if the demand for the local goods and services is not restricted in other jurisdictions. These effects tend to lead to strong co-ordinative stimuli between the economic policies of different jurisdictions which limit the degree to which local fiscal stabilization measures are possible. This effect is further compounded by the increasing importance in western economies of large and multinational companies such that Musgrave and Musgrave (1976) and Oates (1977, p. 3) argue that fiscal policy can be implemented most effectively only at a national level; the 'littleness' of local economies give them little scope for independent action.

Other commentators have argued that local financial management is *fiscally perverse* and undermines national stabilization policies. The classic statement of this view by Hansen and Perloff (1944, p. 49):

'The taxation, borrowing, and spending activities of the state and local governments collectively have typically run counter to an economically sound fiscal policy. These governmental units have usually followed the swings of the business cycle, from crest through trough, spending and building in prosperity periods and contracting their activities during depression'.

Such fiscal perversity results, on the expenditure side, from local spending placing large demand pressures on the national economy when it has already reached capacity limits. On the taxation side, local taxation, because it is usually concentrated on property taxes, is relatively inelastic to changes in income, but the effect of highly elastic changes of expenditure with inflation tends to make local finance de-stabilizing, i.e. excess demand is not immediately absorbed by local taxes, and deficit demand is not matched by freeing resources from the local public sector.

Certainly the openness of local economies and the difficulties of local loan finance prevent autonomous stabilization policies. However, recent analysis demonstrates that local finances have usually been more stabilizing than national ones, i.e. fiscal perversity, if it exists, is a national rather than a local phenomenon. Thus Maxwell (1952, 1958), Rafuse (1965) and Hansen (1969) have shown that US State and local finances expanded during cyclic downturns in the period since 1945. Further analysis by Balopoulos (1967, chapters 6 to 8), Robinson and Courchene (1969), Snyder (1970, 1973), and Pommerehne (1977) confirm these results from a range of other countries. It would seem, therefore, that Hansen and Perloff's results overemphasize the role of certain expenditures (especially construction), are specific to the period of the 1930s when the recession involved was extremely steep and long in duration, and relate to a period in which Keynesian countercyclical deficit financing was poorly understood. This can be appreciated from figure 3.1 taken from the results of Snyder (1970a). This shows that for a range of six western economies local and state-local finances are usually stabilizing rather than the reverse. The stabilizing effects tend to be greater in those countries, like the US and France, in which there is a large component of local social security payments. Stabilization is weakest in countries such as Germany where the local finances are dominated by the construction sector (Knott, 1977). As Maxwell (1952) and Robinson and Courchene (1969) cogently note, the most perverse revenue effects derive at the local level, not from the exercise of local discretion, but from the national level policies with respect to grants and transfers. Thus the modern theory of local government finance places little, if any, emphasis on fiscal perversity and accepts that the local sector is usually stabilizing.

An additional issue in stabilization policy derives from geographical variation in the timing of the economic cycle. There is now a considerable amount of evidence which suggests that cyclical instability in national economies has an important degree of spatial differentiation. Studies in North America by Vining (1945), Thompson (1965), King *et al* (1969) and Weissbrod (1976), and in the UK by Brechling (1967), Haggett (1971), Sant (1973),

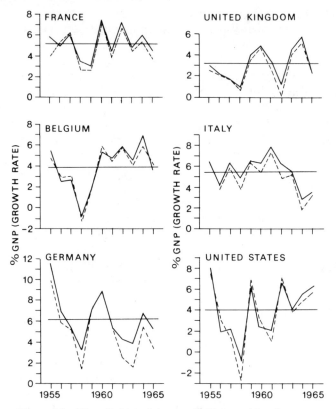

Figure 3.1 The relation of changes in State and local revenues to fiscal perversity. Solid line is actual change in GNP, dotted line is the level of GNP with the effect of State and local changes in revenues removed, horizontal line is average change in GNP. (*Source*: Snyder 1973.)

Bennett (1975), and Hepple (1975) have shown that in both these countries there are significant leads and lags between indicators of instability in different locations. These studies demonstrate that the movement of unemployment levels and wage rates registers first in some jurisdictions, often those at the top of the urban hierarchy, and then over successive months or years affects other jurisdictions as a form of the economic diffusion process. As recognized by Borts (1966), "The cycle spreads among the states through the impact of changes in national demand upon each state's industry-mix. The cycle spreads within each state through the impact of the contractions of each state's key industries and the demand for products of its other industries". Such patterns have been regarded by some as necessary to stimulate the mobility of resources within the national economy (see, for example, Brazer 1964), but these patterns also lead to important criticisms of the treatment of patterns of instability by policies based on national aggregate statistics of cyclical changes, or on aggregate relationships such as the Phillips curve which vary spatially. As Netzer (1968) concludes, national aggregates do not reflect the impact of society's choice among alternative scales and mixes of local expenditure, nor do they reflect the variation in employment structure. It is frequently the case that national economic indicators may show an economy close to full employment capacity, when significant undercapacity exists in some regions.

Hence geographical variation in the timing of the economic cycle clearly suggests the need for a degree of variation in interjurisdictional fiscal policy. For example, there have been bitter criticisms in Scotland of the implementation of counter-cyclical policies for the UK as a whole. Deflationary policies advocated on the basis of overheating of the English economy have usually been implemented on a national basis when the Scottish economy has been far from any ceiling of full employment of its resources. Again in West Germany, procyclical, perverse fiscal behaviour has been greatest in the richest regions which have reached full employment ceilings earliest (Knott 1977). Since national stabilization policies never allow the economies of lagging regions to run at full capacity, they have depressed the wage and productivity rates of these areas and have been important in reinforcing natural inbuilt tendencies towards interregional imbalance.

These problems are discussed further below as part of the public finance function of encouraging growth. It is sufficient here to note three points. First, local discretion in fiscal policy is usually stabilizing and rarely perverse. Second, a major component of any fiscal perversity which does occur at local level is national level perversity in intergovernmental tranfers. Third, there are strong arguments for suggesting that a degree of spatial differentiation in national stabilization policy is essential. Taken together these points suggest that the classical public finance orthodoxy must be modified to allow some degree of local discretion, but most important, that national policies of stabilization should be applied with variable intensity in different locations.

3.5 The geography of growth and economic balance

Economic growth describes changes in the overall level of employment, prices and social well-being. The geographical component of economic growth is crucial since levels of well-being often differ markedly between jurisdictions. Most important, however, because most patterns of disparity in social well-being tend to be self-reinforcing, differences in the past and present levels of employment, prices and well-being often reflect stages in a progression towards increasing polarization between rich and poor jurisdictions. The implications for public finance are two-fold. First, it is necessary to determine the effect that public finance decisions can have in fuelling this process. Second, it is crucial to determine how systems of public finance can be designed to counteract the inbuilt tendencies towards polarization. This problem leads us to the central concern of this book: that of balancing needs, resources and expenditure in different jurisdictions.

Despite the crucial role accorded to the geographical components of economic growth, the spatially differentiated manipulation of fiscal instruments to counteract imbalance in the growth rates between jurisdictions has again been subject to severe criticism. Musgrave and Musgrave (1976), for example, argue that overall growth is generated most reliably through uniform national policies without distorting patterns of inter-regional trade. They accept that certainly it is possible and necessary to implement a limited policy of attracting new industries to jurisdictions which are beset by employment problems, but they argue that such policies must be based on the unique and special nature of such problems which make them in every instance special cases for the provision of aid or assistance, as for example, in development planning, inner city, or regional policies. The general use of local fiscal policies to stimulate growth in a local economy through improved investment or industrial movement leads, they argue, to a 'beggar-thy-neighbour' approach which accentuates inter-jurisdictional differences and competition, and may lead to inefficient location of investments and of resources in the economy as a whole.

The counter-arguments to this case can be stated very strongly and were touched on in the earlier discussion of redistribution policy. Stated very crudely, consideration of the geographical component in public finance allows the recognition of the 'lumpiness' of economic growth and development both between and within countries. Since it is impossible for economic growth to begin everywhere simultaneously, its initiation is specific to certain regions and political jurisdictions. But once initiated, economic growth tends to become concentrated in those regions where growth has already occurred and which already possess a degree of infrastructure and fixed capital investment assets. The reasons for this are three-fold. First, internal economies of scale encourage increasing concentration of industrial production in single and existing plants. Second, the presence of existing physical stock and infrastructure usually encourages industrial expansion in existing locations. Third, external economies of scale encourage further concentration either because many existing industries make similar demands for public services and infrastructure, or because linkage between component suppliers and market demand encourages the close location of firms, i.e. there are agglomeration economies. Thus the growth process is an uneven one which cumulatively concentrates investment and accentuates the imbalance between regions and political jurisdictions. A system of public finance which ignores this fact, and waits for the imbalance to reach such an extreme that it can be termed a special case, ignores the process which creates increasing inequality of opportunities, income and life-chances between jurisdictions. Moreover, public finance itself plays an important role in this process. Since jurisdictions with large industrial bases and high *per capita* incomes will be able to provide a larger range of public investments, they will be able to increase the size of potential externalities to the firm and the magnitude of the personal social wage, and thus will encourage Tiebout-type fiscal migration. Thus systems of public finance which ignore the process of cumulative spatial imbalance will usually reinforce rather than counteract the in-built tendencies for imbalance to arise.

The mechanisms which underlie such patterns of cumulative imbalance can be approached from at least two points of view. First, neo-classical and Keynesian economics (see, for example, Harrod 1948) suggest, through the use of equilibrium models, the direction in which adjustment mechanisms must work in order to cancel imbalance. Taking the case of two sets of jurisdictions with the same overall growth rates and capacity constraints, but different initial income levels, equilibrium theory suggests that labour flows should occur from low income to high income jurisdictions (to equilibrate labour demand and supply in the two sets of areas), but capital should flow from high income to low income regions (to equilibrate capital supply and demand since the lower income region will have the under-used investment opportunities). The two sets of labour and capital flows should continue until an equilibrium of incomes, labour and capital supply is reached (see Richardson 1969). In fact, such an equilibrium pattern does not occur since an equilibrium requires the marginal productivity of capital to change in favour of the lower income jurisdictions. Instead it is more usual for the effect of actual and potential internal and external economies to favour capital flows to the higher income jurisdictions. In addition there may be higher risks associated with capital investments in lower income regions, and certainly their investment opportunities are often less clearly perceived. Hence although labour flows are equilibrating, capital flows generally are not.

The inadequacy of the predictions of equilibrium economics has led to a second set of models based on mechanisms of imbalance which represent the pattern of disequilibrating labour and capital flows (see, for example, Brookfield 1975; Myrdal 1958). Probably the most famous of these is the Myrdal model of *circular and cumulative causation*. This suggests that since economic growth is always initially locationally lumpy or uneven, subsequent capital flows are attracted because of the potential external economies and higher perceived or real rates of return for continued investment in the same location. The process then continues as investment is attracted through the momentum of the internal economies possessed by existing plants, by further external and agglomeration economies, and by the inertia of entrepreneurial predisposition. Spatial *spread* effects deriving from returns to investors in different jurisdictions, journey-to-work, and industrial linkage flows, may diffuse development to some extent. Hirschman (1958) for example, suggests that in some cases such 'trickle-down' effects may absorb the unemployed labour resources in the poorer jurisdictions. Generally, however, these spread effects are far outweighed by *backwash* effects by which continued growth is generally at the expense of the jurisdictions which are the donors of the factors

51

of labour and capital (Myrdal 1944, 1958). In this way a vicious circle of *immiserization* is set off by which some jurisdictions become poorer whilst others become richer and richer, the so-called *poverty cycle* or *poverty trap* (Bhagwati 1958; Nurske 1961). Other writers have emphasized the role of specific industrial sectors acting as important sectoral or spatial *growth poles* in this process (Moseley 1974; Perroux 1955).

The role and effect of this process on public finance can be understood from figure 3.2. An increase or decrease in the demand for goods produced in one jurisdiction leads to an increase or decrease in its number of jobs. This in turn leads to changes in patterns of journey-to-work, but most important in the

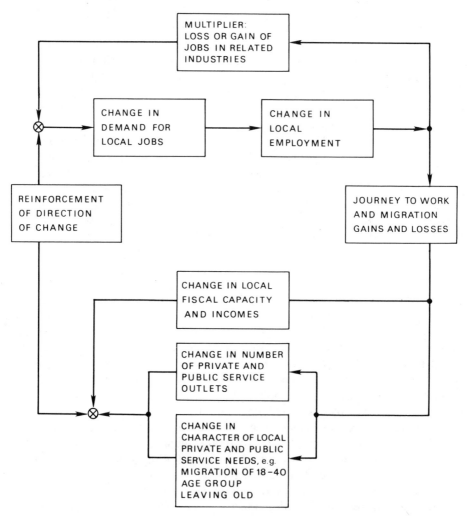

Figure 3.2 Process of circular and cumulative causation as it affects public finance.

long term, it stimulates migration. Migration has both a quantitative and qualitative impact. Net gains or losses of population require adjustments to the scale of public services, but because migration is selective and has the highest impact in the 18 to 40 year age groups, net losses and gains have a more than proportionate impact. Net migration losses tend to increase the proportion of old, young and infirm in a given jurisdiction: the groups which make the greatest demands on public finance. Net migration gains tend to give a larger proportion of the self-supporting, and often the more able, talented and enthusiastic. Thus, on the one hand, migration changes give an overall quantitative and qualitative change in the demands placed on the public sector. On the other hand, migration leads to changes in the financial capacity to provide public goods: declining areas have a smaller tax capacity whilst growing areas have a larger one. If we relate the changes in demands to the change in capacity it can be seen that they are in opposite directions and this is the key to the cumulative causation process. Net migration *gains* give an increase in overall tax capacity, but a less than proportionate increase in the needs for public goods leading to lower tax rates. Net migration *losses*, however, give a decrease in overall tax capacity, with a more than pro-portionate increase in needs for public goods which leads to higher local tax rates. Differences between the rate of local taxation, therefore, increase and reinforce the initial direction of change as a 'poverty cycle'. Lower local tax rates, through the Tiebout hypothesis, encourage a higher degree of immigration, whilst higher local tax rates encourage a higher degree of emigration; and both processes are further reinforced by local inter-industry linkage and multipliers, the related effects on capital, and the effect of increasing or decreasing scale on both internal and external economies of the public sectors.

Of course the processes of cumulative imbalance discussed here have lent themselves very readily to a Marxist interpretation. Marx himself saw imbalance as the outcome of competition to obtain economies of scale, the cheapest production and hence the largest market and profit going to that enterprise which is able to concentrate production to the greatest extent. Luxemburg (1913) and Lenin (1960), on the other hand, saw international imbalance as due to the needs of an ever-expanding market to permit capitalism to continue the accumulation process. This led to the imperialist-colonial invasion of primitive economies in order to open up new markets. Within a given state, more recent Marxist writers have attempted to identify mechanisms of *internal colonialism*. Frank (1973), Harvey (1973), Hechter (1975) and Holland (1976), for example, have argued that imbalance results from the monopoly of credit and capital in the wealthy jurisdictions which is reinforced by selective recruitment, discrimination on the basis of language, race or religion, the control of political decision making, the concentration of research and innovation at the centre, and the use of land-use and zoning restrictions. Such mechanisms are not symmetric with class domination since

53

internal colonialism gives the domination of whole populations which are themselves sub-divided into classes. In the UK, examples of the operation of such processes are provided by so-called chauvinism of London and the South-East towards the Northern periphery (Campaign for the North 1978), a degree of racial repression of Wales (Hechter 1975), and a commercial exploitation of the peripheral North of England or South Wales based on single commodity raw material economies (Carney *et al.* 1976). With respect to Italy and France, Tarrow (1977) argues that economic forces of market concentration have been reinforced both by an undermining of local solidarity (giving a nominal local community in which people share only each other's misery), and by bureaucratic and institutional features. Government bureaucracy in particular is argued in many cases to be in a state of malaise and disorder, stratified like a large-scale industrial enterprise, often very elitist and with a lack of communication and disorder between strata; what has been termed by Lamennais "apoplexy at the centre and anaemia at the periphery".

The evidence for such views is extremely contentious, but we do not need to posit a mechanism of exploitation or regional hegemony to see why imbalance should occur. The Marxists add a teleological drive to a process which we can understand quite adequately from the Myrdal concept of cumulative causation, but as we shall see in later chapters, the role of jurisdictional dominance and exploitation by one area of another has concentrated considerable attention on some of the fundamental features of public finance which are focused at a geographical level.

3.6 Conclusion

This chapter has initiated the detailed discussion of the geography of public finance through consideration of its four functions of allocation, distribution, stabilization and growth. Whilst most previous writers have accorded an important role to geographical factors in the allocation decisions of public finance, they have often been sharply critical of developing a geographical component for policies of distribution, stabilization and growth. These criticisms, as we have seen, are five-fold: first, that they insulate a region from economic changes the overall effects of which will increase the level of national efficiency and growth; second, that they promote interjurisdictional competition; third, that they breed provincialism which is detrimental to the overall national good; fourth, that they undermine attempts to redistribute incomes at a national level; and finally, that they are fiscally perverse. Unfortunately, these arguments ignore the imperfections of the economic assumptions upon which they are based. Hence despite these five criticisms, the argument of this chapter has brought us to the point at which we are drawn to accept a significant degree of variation in the spatial impact of distribution, stabilization and growth functions, as well as in the allocation function. This shift from the orthodox views of public finance is based on three theses. The first of these, with respect to distribution, is that spatial factors frequently lead to a polarization of income differences between jurisdictions which leads both to a greater degree of visibility of inequality of distribution, and also to a greater degree of ease in tackling many problems of distributional inequity. Second, with respect to stabilization, significant geographical variations in the timing, extent and nature of the economic cycle require that counter-cyclical and other assistance should normally be spatially differentiated. The third thesis is that economic growth is never based on national uniformity but is instead rooted in patterns of imbalance between regions. Moreover, because of the effect of internal economies of scale and external economies of agglomeration, spatial imbalances tend to be cumulative and self-reinforcing. To ignore these latent tendencies until a time at which they can be accorded the status of special cases greatly undermines our ability to tackle them.

4

Major issues in public finance geography

"Financial systems make venal souls; and where profit is the only goal, it is always more profitable to be a rascal than to be an honest man . . ., since the circulation of money is secret, it is still a better means of making pilferers and traitors, and of putting freedom and the public good on the auction block."

J. J. Rousseau (1772, pp. 226–7) *Considerations on the Government of Poland.*

4.1 Introduction

The crucial issue of public finance geography is whether the fiscal pattern obtaining in any situation agrees with accepted norms of how the incidence of revenue burdens and expenditure benefits should be distributed spatially, and how far spatial factors detract from the achievement of these accepted norms of individual incidence. Such norms are underlain by accepted relationships between people and places and correspond to some loose concept of the degree of justice in the distribution of benefits and burdens in any situation. Three generalized norms have been evolved to become accepted sets of social beliefs of what constitutes a 'just' distribution (Miller 1976): norms based on rights, or deserts, and on needs.

Rights express a legalistic definition of norms which contains principles derived from previously accepted behaviour. Such rights often accord with generalized ideals of 'natural rights' such as civil liberty and free speech. They also accord with particular categories of individual rights (the rights of lessees, tenants, or contracting parties) or particular groups of people (the old, the young, the sick). In both cases spatial factors play an important role. For example, the right to compensation consequent upon planning or highway decisions; redress against nuisance from neighbours; or claims for noise, air or water pollution.

Deserts correspond to the benefits allocated to individuals on the basis of personal attributes that they possess. "Desert . . . denotes a relationship between an individual and his conduct. . . . When we make a judgement of desert, we are judging the appropriateness of this particular individual, with his qualities and past behaviour, receiving a given benefit or harm" (Miller 1976, p. 92). We may identify many attributes that society has used to allocate benefits. Rescher (1966) notes five main approaches that have been used. The first, *equity*, takes no account of claims, desires, capacities or talents, and

56

provides only for equal treatment of equals. It does not, however, provide for unequal treatment of unequals. Allocation of benefit in accordance with *ability* represents a second criterion, espoused by Aristotle, Jefferson and Adam Smith. Modern interpretations, associate ability with purely material elements of income and wealth (chapter 8 *q.v.*). A third criterion for allocating deserts is by *effort* or *work*. This criterion derives especially from puritanism. For Edmund Burke and Rousseau, for example, this criterion is interpreted as giving help to those who help themselves. Marx extended this to become the whole basis of socialism through the concept of labour-power. A fourth criterion deriving from that of work is *productivity*, allocating deserts to those whose efforts are most productive or who render the most service. A fifth criterion for allocation of benefits is that of *scarcity*, deserts are allocated via the market mechanism of equating supply and demand through price. Price then reflects the collective view of merit within the society as a whole.

Needs represent a third norm. Needs are a form of moral claim, first thrust to prominence by Marx in *The Gotha Programme* (1875), in which needs are equated to a mixture of desire and capacity, but where other elements of need (kinship, consensus) are ignored. Needs are essentially intrinsic, they are important to the person who does not have what is needed, and as a consequence he suffers harm. It is harm which interferes with aspirations and life-chances.

When we seek some rational rule for organizing public finance, bearing in mind rights, deserts and needs, we seek not an equality of individuals in all their complex attributes, but an equalizing of the effects of society itself. As Tawney (1952, p. 39) in his great work on *Equality* comments: the inequality which is deplored is "not inequality of personal gifts, but of social and economic environment". Public finance in general and in its geographical components in particular, is aimed at eliminating, or at least reducing, the unequal treatment of individuals in society. In so doing it seeks to redistribute economic and social benefits not personal attributes. As a consequence, then, its focus is upon economic and social characteristics. Hence, it is natural to measure the deserts provided by society to individuals or to places in terms of ability, measures of income, wealth or expenditures, and to measure needs of individuals or locations in terms of the lack of particular social and economic goods which are available within society as a whole. It is the mismatch of material benefits and abilities (deserts) with material needs which is the concern, not a search for the will-of-a-wisp of equality of all personal and geographical attributes.

To answer the question of public finance geography as posed, to determine whether a particular fiscal pattern accords with accepted norms of spatial incidence, two major steps are required. First, the construction of measures of revenue burdens, expenditure benefits, or fiscal needs; and second, the comparison of these measures with each other. This comparison then allows us to determine the degree of match or mismatch of benefits and abilities on the one hand, with material needs on the other, and thus to determine the degree of accord of the incidence of public finance with accepted individual and geographical norms.

In the present chapter it is possible to give only a preliminary sketch of these concepts by indicating, first in section 4.2, how benefits, abilities and needs should be compared by the use of social or public accounting, and then, in subsequent sections, indicating some of the conditions in which accepted norms of the geographical incidence of public finance are not achieved. In section 4.3 the major causes of geographical inequalities in the public fisc are explored; in the section 4.4 the dilemmas which arise from the competition between spatially and politically separated jurisdictions are examined, and in section 4.5 the urban and regional foci of geographical inequities are discussed.

4.2 The geography of public finance revenue and expenditure accounts

The answers to the crucial question of public finance geography, the degree of accordance of the distribution of the public fisc with accepted norms, can be determined only by comparing measures of fiscal need, benefit and ability expressed in standardized terms. This requires a means of tracing flows of revenues, expenditures, and benefits between people and between places, and between levels of governments. It is, then, necessary to determine the overall match of these flows with assessed individual and jurisdictional need. To accomplish this, we require a set of accounts for the public fisc, expressed simultaneously in individual and in jurisdictional terms, which permits tracing of the flows of revenues and expenditures between people and places.

The concept of income accounts derives mainly from William Petty (1687) and Gregory King (1804) in England, and Pierre Bois-Guillebent (1840) and Sebastien Vauban (1707) in France. It has been greatly extended, on the one hand, through the work of Adam Smith to the familiar national income accounts of Western countries deriving from Marshall (1920) and Keynes (1936), and on the other hand, from Rousseau and Marx to state planning systems of Eastern economies (Kornai 1967; Lenin 1960). However, the concept of geographical income accounts is much more recent. Although foreshadowed by earlier writers, especially in the concern of Rousseau and Marx with the urban–rural dichotomy and colonialism, and even in Plato's concept of the state, the disaggregation of national income accounts into regional or spatial components is due mainly to the initial work of Ohlin (1933), which has been developed by Isard (1956), Ingram (1957), Stone (1961), Czmanski (1966, 1973) and Stolper and Tiebout (1978). Regional accounts, like national accounts and normal business accounts, consist of two basic components: first, a component measuring flow over an accounting period, and second, a component measuring stocks or capital assets. The first account is a profit and loss account, and the second is a balance sheet.

In questions of the geography of price, flow-of-funds accounts are often the most useful, whilst for stabilization policy, income and product accounts are of most utility. In questions of growth, balance of payments, and wealth accounts, are more useful. Distribution questions can be approached through each form of accounting depending upon whether short or long term impacts are emphasized. But the formal accounting applicable to most questions of the geographical distribution of the public fisc is a form of flow-of-funds account with the addition of components permitting balance of payments and welfare aspects to be assessed. Input–output accounts reflect a desire for sectoral disaggregation. They can be applied to each form of social accounting and can be used in industrial, price, employment, and policy impact studies.

Two highly simplified forms of account are shown in tables 4.1 and 4.2 for the respective revenue and expenditure sides of the public fisc. It should be emphasized that these two accounts are simplified for expository purposes

Table 4.1   Regional revenue account by jurisdiction and income group.

Revenues to	*Revenues from*										
	Jurisdiction 1				...	*Jurisdiction N*				*Total revenue from*	
	Income groups					*Income groups*				*Income groups*	
	1	*2*	*...*	*m*		*1*	*2*	*...*	*m*	*1*	*2*	*...*	*m*
Jurisdiction 1											
Income group *1*	.	.		.		.	.		.	.	.		.
2	.	.		.		.	.		.	.	.		.
.											
.											
.											
m	.		.			.		.		.	.		.
Jurisdiction N											
Income group *1*	.	.		.		.	.		.	.	.		.
2	.	.		.		.	.		.	.	.		.
.											
.											
.											
m	.	.		.		.	.		.	.	.		.
Total revenues to											
Income group *1*	.	.		.		.	.		.	.	.		.
2	.	.		.		.	.		.	.	.		.
.											
.											
.											
m	.	.		.		.	.		.	.	.		.

Table 4.2 Regional expenditure account by jurisdiction and income group.

Benefits to	Benefits from								Total benefits to		
	Jurisdiction 1				. . .	Jurisdiction N					
	Income groups					Income groups				Income groups	
	1	2	. . .	m		1	2	. . .	m	1	2	. . .	m
Jurisdiction 1												
Income group 1	.	.		.		.	.		.	.	.	.	
2	.	.		.		.	.		.	.	.	.	
.												
.												
m	.	.		.		.	.		.	.	.	.	
Jurisdiction N												
Income groups 1	.	.		.		.	.		.	.	.	.	
2	.	.		.		.	.		.	.	.	.	
.												
.												
m	.	.		.		.	.		.	.	.	.	
Total benefits to												
Income groups 1	.	.		.		.	.		.	.	.	.	
2	.	.		.		.	.		.	.	.	.	
.												
.												
m	.	.		.		.	.		.	.	.	.	

only; complete discussion of regional income and expenditure accounts requires financial effects of the public sector to be set against those arising from private and institutional flows. However, the revenue and expenditure accounts shown in table 4.1 and 4.2 do capture most of the features of the public fisc in which we are interested in this book.

With respect to the revenue accounts, table 4.1 displays the extent to which revenue is raised and spent internally, the degree to which transfers take place to and from other levels of government, and the magnitude of the revenue imports and exports (revenue spillovers) which occur with other regions. Furthermore, each of these effects is disaggregated by the income group concerned. As we shall see in chapters 7 and 8, the determination of degree of impact of taxes, user charges, debt charges and other revenue sources on individual income groups and different geographical locations involves a complex analysis of tax shifting, not only between groups of people in the same jurisdiction, but also between people in different locations.

With respect to the expenditure accounts, table 4.2 displays the movement of benefits deriving from the supply of public goods and services for income groups in each jurisdiction, the extent to which these benefits spillover to other jurisdictions, and the extent to which expenditure benefits are transferred to other jurisdictions by transfers through higher level government. The nature of these benefit movements is discussed further in chapter 9 where it is shown that the extent of benefit spillover and transfer is often very large, but very difficult to estimate.

Both the revenue and expenditure accounts displayed here can be totalled across rows and down columns and the net revenue and expenditure balance for each individual, income group, or jurisdiction determined. In addition, the net revenue balance of any income group of jurisdiction can be compared with the net expenditure balance in order to determine how far its revenue burden is in line with the expenditure benefits it derives from the public fisc. Such comparisons may allow comment on the extent of individual and geographical redistribution. However, such direct comparisons are not necessarily meaningful. Two additional factors have yet to be taken into consideration in the social accounts: revenue ability, and expenditure needs. In order to determine the extent to which the apportionment of the public fisc between income groups and locations accords to accepted norms of incidence, we need to adjust expenditure benefits to relative need, and revenue burden to relative ability. Distributional norms will have been satisfied when each income group and geographical component of the revenue account in table 4.1 shows a ratio of revenue burden to ability, of one, and when each income group and geographical component of the expenditure account in table 4.2 also shows the ratio of expenditure benefits to need, of one. If these conditions are satisfied in each case, then revenue has been apportioned in accordance with ability, and benefits in accordance with need.

4.3 Geographical inequities arising from jurisdictional partitioning

The distribution of the public fisc in accordance with accepted norms of equalization between needs and benefits, on the one hand, and revenue burdens and abilities, on the other, requires similar individuals or firms to be treated equally by the public economy wherever they are located. Moreover this must apply to both revenue-raising and the public service benefits. This fiscal norm can be achieved in completely centralized systems of public finance, but in countries which possess mixed levels of government with local and intermediate (regional, state or province) autonomy in revenue-raising or expenditure, a number of problems arise which make the achievement of fiscal equity more complex.

In countries with a decentralized or federal structure each jurisdiction will behave differently in accordance with the local political and fiscal pressures, and in accordance with local preferences. Each jurisdiction may treat equals equally, and unequals unequally, in accordance with accepted principles of

61

equity (p. 56 *q.v.*), but there is no guarantee that equals living in different jurisdictions will be treated equally, nor that unequals in one jurisdiction will be treated equally unequally with those in other jurisdictions, i.e. that taxation will be equally progressive, and expenditures oriented equally to the same needs. Hence equity in decentralized and federal countries requires assessment of the joint fiscal impact at all levels of government.

Differences between jurisdictions in the treatment of individuals and firms result from the five modes of jurisdictional behaviour: local clubs of service preferences, interjurisdictional competition, fiscal prudence, the 'State's dilemma', and the 'Samaritan's dilemma'. Each of these is discussed in turn below.

Local service clubs result from the Tiebout and Buchanan models of fiscal migration. In the Tiebout model, migration replaces consumer choice as a market mechanism for public goods. By moving to a jurisdiction offering a bundle of goods in accord with an individual's preference pattern, the market is introduced into public finance. "The consumer-voter may be viewed as picking that community which best satisfies his preference pattern for public goods. ... The greater the number of communities, and the greater the variance among them, the closer the consumer will come to realizing his preference position" (Tiebout 1956, p. 418). Hence citizens in areas of fragmented jurisdictions are able to maximize their utility subject to income and price constraints, and a neoclassical optimum results. The optimum pattern of public services will be supplied in accordance with what Buchanan (1960) terms the local service clubs of demand, and each individual will maximize his service benefits and minimize his costs by locating in that area which provides the best fit to his desired preferences for public goods and taxes. A number of studies suggest that Tiebout-type fiscal migration does occur (Aronson and Schwartz 1973; Brazer 1964; Haskell and Leshinski 1969; Mills and Oates 1975; Muller 1976; Oates 1969; Pollakowski 1973) and is encouraged by local fiscal and zoning practices. Thus a major consequence of the reasoning behind the Tiebout model is that the political fragmentation of urban areas is natural and desirable in order to allow the expression of different preferences, choices, and demands for public goods. This has profound implications since it encourages the maintenance of many small jurisdictions in accordance with preference patterns, or even suggests an increase in their number.

Interjurisdictional competition results from the scarcity of finance available for physical infrastructure and local public services, and from the shortage of industry, retail and commercial activities providing local economic growth. In a very real sense, interjurisdictional competition for finance and for economic resources represents the entry of the rationale of the market place into a geographical space dissected by political boundaries. Often the competition is most evident between jurisdictions which are close together and especially when they abut each other. The competition between such near-neighbours is nowhere more evident than in urban areas, especially in the fragmented urban governments of the US. But competition between political tracts is not confined to urban areas nor to close neighbours. It is also evident in the regional competition of the North and South ('sunbelt'–'frostbelt') in the United States, in interregional competition between Scotland, Wales and the English regions in the UK, in the Canadian, German, Swiss and Australian federations, and elsewhere.

There may, of course, be useful outcomes resulting from the market-like stimuli of competition between jurisdictions. For example, efficiency and economy in public fisc may be encouraged, local independence and community involvement may be fostered, there may be a greater chance to vary public expenditures to fit in with the pattern of local needs and preferences, and a greater range and mix of bundles of public goods should be available from which individuals, commercial enterprises or industrialists can choose in making a locational decision (see chapter 14). Certainly there is nothing inherently illogical in having different mixes of public goods performed by different agencies and jurisdictions.

However, the competition and rivalry more frequently result in less desirable outcomes. On the revenue side, the effects of competition are two-fold. First, different jurisdictions may compete for the same tax base which limits the capacity of each jurisdiction to determine its taxes at the rate it would individually desire. For example, water authorities and general purpose city governments compete for the property tax base in both Britain and the United States and this results in a form of close interdependence between different jurisdictions. Secondly, jurisdictions which are either close neighbours of each other, or abut, must keep taxes low in order to retain desired industry or residents (recognizing the problems arising from the Tiebout fiscal migration hypothesis); certainly their freedom of action is much reduced. On the expenditure side, the effects of competition mainly modify the range of public services available. Jurisdictions which are close neighbours have strong stimuli to provide the same range of public services, again, in order to reduce the impact of Tiebout-type migration of population and industry. Competition also makes itself felt through the effect of spillovers of costs and benefits. Successful competition by a jurisdiction can be recognized by its ability to shift revenue burdens onto other jurisdictions whilst maximizing the spillovers of benefits it receives from other areas. Such competitive shifts of costs and benefits have frequently given rise in most Western countries to cries of interjurisdictional exploitation: of central cities by their suburbs; of poor suburbs by richer city tracts; of rural areas by urban areas; of peripheral areas by the centres of economic activity; and of older industrial zones by those which are presently faster growing.

Fiscal prudence characterizes fiscal behaviour in those situations in which actions are relatively cheap for one set of jurisdictions but are relatively expensive for others. In such cases there is much to be gained in the high cost location by co-operation, but much to be lost by such co-operation in the low cost locations. Hence, if we are reliant on voluntary effort alone, co-operation will not usually result. Unfortunately, situations of fiscal prudence are frequent in occurrence. Important cases arise in the resistance of rich city tracts to sharing the burdens of urban renewal and welfare programmes with poor urban areas; in the lack of local mechanisms for expanding the economic area to share the burdens of renewing outdated infrastructure and production facilities in declining regions; and in the lack of incentive for developed industrial and urban areas to share the proceeds of economic growth by diffusing the facilities and services to less developed rural areas or regions on the economic periphery. Fiscal prudence, then, results in the well-off geographical regions maintaining an autonomy of local action which allows them to be free of commitments to bear the burden of raising the economic and social welfare of less well-off regions. Such independence of action often results in unsavoury activities to protect the local community (Mills and Oates 1975): by planning, zoning, building codes, transport rates, and discrimination in housing sales, and encouragement to industry to locate in a given area.

In the urban context Curran (1973), in a study of Milwaukee, finds four types of behaviour patterns influenced by fiscal prudence:

(i) middle-income jurisdictions in search of industries to share tax bases (West Milwaukee village and Glendale city);

(ii) middle-income jurisdictions in search of a public utility to promote income by shared taxes and sale of the products to other jurisdictions (the town of Lake);

(iii) high-income jurisdictions using large lot and other forms of zoning to exclude both industry and poorer residencies (River Hill, Fox Point, Bayside);

(iv) middle-income jurisdictions imitating the behaviour of the previous set of jurisdictions (iii), hoping for increases of property values; the hopefuls (Midtown Milwaukee).

Imprudence, on the other hand, could be recognized in Curran's study in those jurisdictions where a small amount of industry was allowed to locate. This reduces that jurisdiction's residential desirability with little fiscal gain. Alternatively fiscal imprudence is exhibited in those areas with small lot sizes: giving high densities, a large number of families with children giving a high school cost, and vulnerability to invasion by low income groups.

The State's dilemma derives from the game theory concept of the 'prisoner's dilemma', and has been proposed in the context of urban renewal by Davis and Whinston (1961). For example, two jurisdictions may both invest jointly in a needed public facility with the result that the facility will be provided, and any economies of scale attained in this investment will make it cheaper for each jurisdiction. However, if one area invests independently it can attain the facility, but at a higher cost. The dilemma enters in that, without the collusion or co-operation between jurisdictions, the individually rational action for each government is to invest independently. The same logic applies also to tax competition. Two jurisdictions may both have strong incentives to raise local taxes, but this action undertaken by either jurisdiction independently will favour the other jurisdiction by encouraging Tiebout-type migration. Again, without collusion, either the services of each jurisdiction will tend to deteriorate, or both jurisdictions will fall increasingly into debt. Each jurisdiction, in seeking an individual solution to its problems, sacrifices a greater joint good of the larger area. This 'State's dilemma' applies, as we shall see later, particularly effectively to the urban context in which large numbers of jurisdictions abut each other. The State's dilemma results in a stimulus to co-operation between jurisdictions in which each will gain by co-ordination. Hence the solution to the dilemma is often to induce co-operation by higher level government action.

The Samaritan's dilemma, suggested by Buchanan (1975), applies to decisions in which one jurisdiction makes contributions to another, usually through intergovernmental transfers or external benefit spillovers. The dilemma is, for the 'Samaritan' jurisdictions to decide how they should treat the 'parasite' jurisdictions receiving the transfers or spillovers. When a one-off effect is involved, probably no action is taken, but when the transfers or spillovers are recurrent, the dilemma is stated as follows. Should the Samaritan jurisdictions contribute to the welfare of the poorer parasite jurisdictions in the cause of equality and greater national good, or should a jurisdiction follow a course of local sectional self-interest and fiscal prudence? In the horizontal payment of equalizing financial transfers between rich and poor Länder in the German Federation, it is clear that there is a considerable spirit of liberalism, or Samaritanism. Similarly, the substantial contribution of the North-East United States, especially New York, to the 1930s New Deal has been described as a spirit of cosmopolitan liberalism by Moynihan (1978). But such liberalism is not present in other cases, nor necessarily met by reciprocity when fortunes turn. The deficiency payments element of the UK Rate Support Grant (see p. 355), contains no such altruistic element of transfer from rich to poor jurisdictions; and Moynihan (1978) and Gifford (1978) would claim that New York's liberalism in the New Deal era is not being met by similar attitudes from the Gulf and Southern States now the tide of economic prosperity is reversing. Indeed Buchanan argues that fiscally Samaritan behaviour is now much less frequent than fiscally prudent behaviour, and this results from an ethic of self-interest deriving from both increasing affluence and reduction of community ties.

Given these five modes of jurisdictional fiscal behaviour, it is not surprising that geographical inequities in the treatment of individuals and firms should arise, and should have a natural tendency to increase. In order to overcome these inequites, a number of policy responses are possible and will be discussed in later chapters: voluntary co-operation and co-ordination induced by outside agency or higher level government, together with reorganization and amalgamation of jurisdictions (see chapter 11); improvements to the local

65

revenue base (see chapters 8 and 12), and the use of equalizing grants and other intergovernmental transfers (see chapters 12 and 13). As will become apparent in these later chapters, it is intergovernmental transfers which offer the greatest potential for achieving equality of revenue burdens and expenditure benefits between equals. Such transfers are not subsidies, they

> 'do not represent charitable contributions from the rich to the poor, and are not analogous to ability to pay in any inter-personal sense. The principle (of equity) establishes a firm basis for the claim that citizens of the low income states within a national economy possess the 'right' that their states receive sums sufficient to enable these citizens to be placed in a position of fiscal equality with their equals in other states' (Buchanan 1950 p. 596).

Instead these transfers are means of eliminating the inequity produced by fiscal federalism and decentralized government: so that individuals and firms are penalized neither by the inequities resulting from the overlapping of political jurisdictions and constitutions nor by the geographical distribution of economic factors over space. The aim, then, is to achieve equity in which total local resources are invariant to geographical variations in the need to spend. This equity argument is similar to that of Buchanan (1950) which states that in each jurisdiction the *fiscal residuum*, the difference between contributions made and the value of public services received, should be equalized for similar individuals and be independent of geographical location.

The argument for equalization should not, however, be mistaken for one emphasizing either uniformity or increased central control. Uniformity is avoided by seeking transfer programmes, which permit local independence and autonomy in ordering preferences for expenditures and service provision, and which seek to equalize the capacity of each jurisdiction to make the same choices, should they wish; and hence, to eliminate fiscal disparities which restrict choice in some jurisdictions as opposed to others. As we shall see in chapters 12 and 13, this requires transfers in the form of revenue sharing, tax credits or block grants with 'no strings'. Such transfers permit resource equalization, but leave to local discretion which services are provided in what quantity.

However, jurisdictional inequities cannot always be so easily eliminated. As noted in the conclusion to chapter 2, the effect of inequities has often been heightened by the fact that the areas involved do not correspond to true jurisdictions in the political or legal sense: hence no intergovernmental transfer system can be easily implemented, often no statistical or other information is available to validate the arguments of imbalance, and no representative government or democratic arrangement is available to articulate any grievances (e.g. *ad hoc* and other unrepresentative bodies are employed such as TVA, the English Regional Water Boards, and the French prefect). This has given rise, as discussed in chapter 11, to demands for new information and statistics, to demands for adaptation of institutions which can represent local views, to the growth of popular regional movements, to the emergence of new groupings of local bodies, and to the development of new separatist and federalist movements in many countries.

4.4 Geographical inequities arising from market imperfection

Whilst mixed levels of government present a constitutional impediment to the achievement of an equity norm in the distribution of the public fisc, as discussed in the previous section, imperfections in the market mechanism present a second impediment to the achievement of full geographical equalization through the public economy. Classical and neoclassical economics suggest that capital and labour flows between economically developed and less developed regions should be mutually equalizing (see p. 51): capital should move from economically advanced to less advanced regions in search of new investment opportunities, and labour should move from economically lagging to more advanced regions in search of employment opportunities. That these equalizing flows do not occur is due in part to inadequacies in neoclassical theories, but is mainly due to imperfections in the nature of the market which undermine all of the assumptions of neoclassical theory.

Market imperfections lead to preferential economic growth in some jurisdictions as opposed to others. Thus economic growth increases local personal and corporate incomes in both absolute terms, and relative to other jurisdictions. As personal and corporate incomes rise, so the resources available to taxation by local jurisdictions increase, and this gives rise to higher levels of public service benefits and/or to lower local tax rates than are possible in the less economically developed jurisdictions. These tax and expenditure benefits give unequal treatment of equals in different locations and this undermines the equity norm. Moreover, these inequities in public service externalities and the social wage act as an attraction for further economic growth of the more advanced jurisdictions in a cumulative process. Hence, the organization of public finance must take account of these inequities. Those arguments that suggest that individual income redistribution, economic stabilization, and economic growth can all best be achieved by uniform, national-level organization of public finance, ignore the realities of the actual markets, i.e. that there are market imperfections. These market imperfections arise from eight main factors which are discussed in turn below.

(i) *Unequal access of locations both to natural resources and to markets.* The physiographic, environmental and geological factors which determine variation in soil quality, water supply, vegetation, climatic yields of crops, minerals, fossil fuels, harbours, waterways, and other natural resources, just do not give a uniform distribution of potential for economic development across the globe, within a country, within a region, or even within an urban area. The possession of such resources, of course, does not always confer economic advantages since other factors (especially institutional controls of price and access to markets) come into play. But natural resources do confer the necessary conditions for economic growth even if they are not the sufficient conditions. In addition, unequal distance to markets is another feature of differential access. Figure. 4.1 shows the map of the market potential of North America and of Western Europe. Potential here is represented by contours which display the aggregate accessibility of any one location to the location of people and their consumption power in all other locations within each economy. No one can argue that every location on these maps is endowed with equal opportunities for development. As a consequence of these differences in access, both to markets and to natural resources, differences in levels and types of economic activity arise inevitably, and just as inevitably, these give rise to differences in levels of population distribution, social characteristics related to the different needs of the workforce, and different income levels resulting from differential rewards for different categories of work. Each of these factors in turn gives rise to differences in the development ability of different locations and causes imperfections in the market.

(ii) *Technological change.* Changing technological demands or discoveries shift and reverse previous geographical development patterns. It is argued that such shifts abound. In the UK, the shift of wool textiles from 14th-century East Anglia to the 19th-century Yorkshire, or the iron industry from 15th-century Kent to the 18th- and 19th-century Midlands and North of England are only precursors of the shifts of growth stimuli from these 19th-century locations to the consumer goods and service industry belts of the Midlands and South-East noted since the 1920s and 1930s. In the US, similar shifts are the decline of gold-mining communities in the Basin-and-Range Province, the movement away from the older textile, shipbuilding and heavy industry base of the North-East and Mid-West, the rapid growth of the aerospace industry in the West Coast, Seattle and California, and the expansion of the South-West Gulf cities based on oil and natural gas. Further impacts of technology, however, have been the shift in personal residential locations that have occurred. From the 19th-century streetcar tram suburbs, to the 20th-century automobile suburb, the capacity of people to move away from declining urban areas has accelerated the pace of both suburban development and urban decline, and the emergence of geographical inequalities in well-being.

Figure 4.1 *(on facing page)* Spatial variation of economic potential in the US and Western Europe.

a A potential surface for income in the US (*Source:* Warntz, 1956).

b Potential surface of income for EEC (*Source:* Clark, et al., 1969).

Potential of any location i is calculated for all locations M as:

$$\frac{Regional\ income\ (i)}{minimum\ cost} \sum_{j=1}^{M} \frac{income\ of\ region\ (j)}{\underset{i\ to\ j}{min.\ +\ travel\ +\ tariff\atop cost\ \ \ \ \ cost}}$$

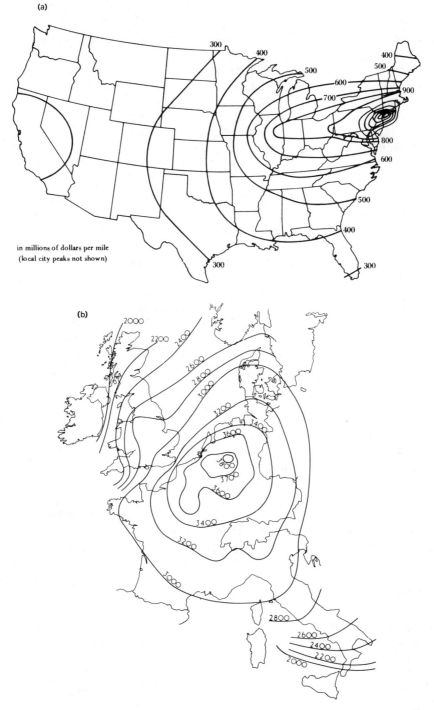

(a)

in millions of dollars per mile
(local city peaks not shown)

(b)

(iii) *Increasing indivisibility of production.* Many investment decisions in both the private and public sectors, especially with increasingly large plants under the impact of economies of scale, give a smaller and smaller number of locations which can partake in growth stimuli.

(iv) *Institutional barriers.* These undermine the idealized model of competition and mobility. On the one hand, large companies and financial institutions hold considerable monopoly power which allows them privileged entry into the market at inflated prices, and on the other hand, organized labour, through the mechanism of the unions, is able to impede capital mobility by preventing closure of unproductive plants encouraging, via a government coercion process, the diversion of capital to unproductive locations, and through national wage bargaining, placing wage levels on a nationally uniform basis. Each of these factors is real to the practical world but does not exist inside a neoclassical model which predicts labour and capital flows to equalize regional growth rates. Institutional barriers also induce market imperfections through local government preventing free mobility especially of the poor into higher income jurisdictions through zoning and other controls.

(v) *Information constraints.* Lack of perfect information limits the capacity of both the public and private decision makers to respond to spatial factors. These may arise because of imperfect perception of the economic advantages of other new and often more peripheral locations. Alternatively, they may result from imperfections in the attempts of an overloaded public sector to cope adequately with the personal distribution problem. A combination of local government information sources and central government financial resources may cope adequately in many cases in targeting aid to people and locations of severe need, but in significant areas it is becoming clear that the apparatus and policy instruments available to the public sector planner are unable to cope with the strong inbuilt tendencies of both industry and individual to seek out the individually economically prudent location at the expense of a greater overall public good.

(vi) *Purity of public goods.* Many features of market imperfections contribute to undermining of the joint supply, non-rejectability, non-excludeability conditions which characterize pure public goods (see p. 12): but in addition there are the effects of geographical space and of a tapering of spillover of costs and benefits of public goods which more than any other factors undermine the pure public good concept. It is these features which create a complex accounting problem in order to equalize burdens and benefits and prevent a perfect equalization being ever achieved. They also permit what some authorities have called an exploitation process: of the city by the suburbs, of the lagging by the growing regions, of the rural areas by the urban, and so forth.

(vii) *Political and preference constraints.* As discussed in the previous

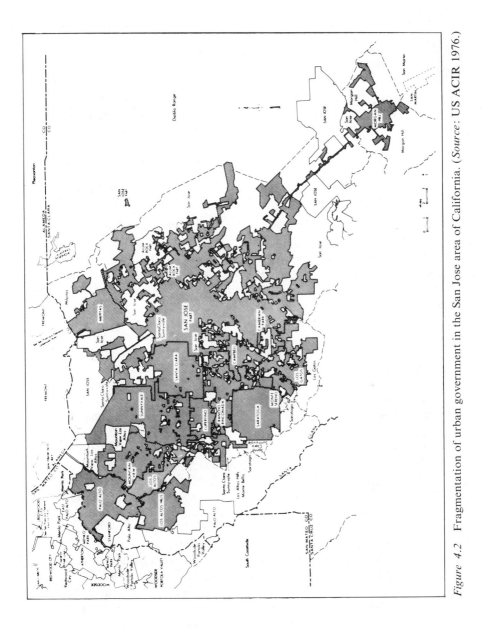

Figure 4.2 Fragmentation of urban government in the San Jose area of California. (*Source*: US ACIR 1976.)

71

section, non-uniformity of preferences encourages, according to the Buchanan hypothesis, the formation of different service clubs for the provision of public goods. Since it is the local 'community' of contact which frequently gives rise to some accordance between preferences, a high degree of geographical variation results. Such differences, together with those caused by other inequalities in economic wealth and social factors, provide stimuli to migration. These features become combined with political actions of fiscal prudence and interjurisdictional competition which serve to place impediments on the levels of social labour mobility required by neo-classical theory. In the UK and France in particular, most public housing finance is directed at maintaining the status quo of social mix in a jurisdiction in order to maintain a safe local electorate. This also affects selective preference for industry in which the employment structure accords with existing local patterns.

(viii) *Fragmentation of government.*   A final feature, which derives in part from variation in local preferences, is the 'littleness' and fragmentation of government in many urban areas. Nowhere are urban administrative tracts smaller or more fragmented than in the US. As figure 4.2 demonstrates for the California area of San Jose, the metropolitan area is split between a multitude of different governments which can act autonomously of each other, and San Jose itself is split into a number of spatially separated units. When this smallness is combined with prudence, the State's and Samaritan's dilemmas, and zoning controls, it is possible for great barriers to the free movement of people and industry to emerge which severely undermine the neoclassical model, and generate great disparities in wealth and service levels between jurisdictions.

Because of the impact of these eight factors, and because of the impact of other factors, the geographical distribution of wealth and income can never be uniform either in its initiation or its development. As long as the process of unequal development occurs only within one region, the capital and labour made redundant in the declining sectors can often be re-employed in the growing sectors and non-uniform development creates relatively few problems. But when growth and decline characterize different political jurisdictions, fiscal and other disparities are bound to arise through the process of cumulative causation (see p. 51). On the one hand, public and private facilities take advantage of increasing internal or external economies of scale in areas achieving rapid economic growth, and this raises local earnings which in turn allows reduction of tax rates or improvements in services. On the other hand, slow growth or declining areas require higher tax rates or lower standards of services (either in relative or in absolute terms). Hence, equity of treatment of individuals and firms under the public fisc requires fiscal transfers between jurisdictions. Moreover, since the total income of jurisdictions is bound to diverge with time, as economic growth rates diverge, further intergovernmental transfers are required and, since inequities in public spending also rise with economic growth, then transfers must also increase with time, both in their absolute size, and as a proportion of public finance. This is necessary if inequity is to be at all reduced.

No modern economy (either Western or Communist) is free from the impact of wide differences in the geographical distribution of wealth, of opportunity and of income. This is evident at all levels and scales from national, through regional, to local levels. Urban fiscal disparities have been a major focus of much research, but regional imbalances are often no less marked between the zones with rapid industrial growth and those with static or declining economies. This imbalance has recently been a source of considerable debate in the US over the imbalance of the 'sunbelt' and 'frostbelt', and the older imbalances of the north and south. In Canada it has been focused by the issue of Quebec's separatism. In Western Europe similar imbalances are represented in extreme form by the development problems of southern Italy, rural France or Germany, of Wales and of Scotland, and of Spain, Portugal or Greece. Hence as disparities in regional growth have increased, so have regional incomes diverged, and thus have the revenues and benefits of public finance been thrown into conflict with norms of equity of distribution which have been overcome only by dependence upon ever larger fiscal transfers between governments.

4.5 Urban and regional issues and fiscal crises

There are many dimensions and scales to the impact of public finance geography on the achievement of norms of equity under the public fisc. In economics the emphasis has been at the national scale: the price, distribution, stabilization and growth dimensions as discussed in the previous chapter. In political science, the concern has been with dimensions of decision-making: the organization and expression of opinion and preferences, with access to, and participation in decision-making, with models of coalition formation, and with bureaucratic goals affecting log-rolling and pork-barrelling of decisions. In public administration the emphasis has been on the dimensions of bureaucratic structure, management efficiency and responsiveness. In sociology, especially in the formulation of Talcott Parsons, the concern has been with dimensions of mutual adjustment and adaptation of groups and individuals forming groupings and communities of collective views and preferences. Finally, in geography, emphasis is given to the role of spatial components of man–environment interrelationships within a specific area or region, and this is adduced to give rise to area as 'community': a humanistic concern with economic and social relationships within places. A general approach to equity under the public fisc, as discussed in this book, requires each of the dimensions and scales of interest to be considered. But, frequently certain issues become focused more clearly at one scale rather than another, and it is the purpose of this section to discuss briefly the specific urban and regional issues which affect equity under the public fisc.

Nowhere is the departure from accepted norms in the distribution of public goods thrown into more immediate or higher relief than in urban areas. This is in part a result of the density and close abuttal of rich and poor within the city, but it is also a result of the greater development of the extremes of wealth and poverty which have arisen in cities. There are three aspects in which urban issues are particularly focused. First, it is in urban areas that there is the greatest disparity of expenditure needs and benefits, of revenue burdens and abilities, and of financial needs and revenue resources; and hence it is in the city where most concern is focused on the equity of the public fisc. These inequities are a natural result of fiscal prudence and interjurisdictional competition: the benefits to be gained by richer jurisdictions are all in favour of individual action to economize on their level of expenditure by not sharing their resources with poorer jurisdictions which are in dire fiscal need. Second, urban areas frequently have the most marked inequalities in levels of public service provision between jurisdictions. This results partly from differences in preferences and partly from fiscal disparities, but it also arises from mere lack of co-ordination. This can affect the economics of transport systems which become unco-ordinated across jurisdictional boundaries. For water supply, recreation provision, health care, schooling, and the disposal of waste and pollution, individual jurisdictional action may pre-empt more efficient developments for larger scale developments, or for co-ordinated treatment. Urban areas, more than any others, suffer from the adverse effects of prudence and the State's dilemma in public finance. In a third area, urban jurisdictions are frequently the focus for what some have termed the disintegration of political control over social and economic development (Wood 1961). This may be a result of spillovers, externalities and economic independencies which generate economic dependence without direct electoral representation. At the urban level, this is the frequent consequence of the complexity of fragmentation of local government.

In contrast to the urban level, the regional level has been a less vigorous and marked orientation of research. Nevertheless, fiscal disparity, unequal service levels, and the disintegration of political control are no less marked at this scale. These effects are frequently most marked between urban and rural regions, and between economically growing and lagging regions. Each of these effects, of fiscal disparities, unequal service levels, and the disintegration of political control, is discussed in turn below.

FISCAL DISPARITIES

At the urban level the fiscal disparity problem is nowhere better developed than in the United States. Table 4.3 gives *per capita* expenditures and revenues for a sample of US cities in 1973 experiencing either population growth or

Table 4.3 Expenditures and revenues in a sample of large US cities in 1973. (*Source:* Peterson 1976.)

		Large growing cities	Large declining cities
(1) *Expenditures* ($)			
expenditure *per capita* in main functions		15.2	26.5
per capita service costs	police	27.7	68.7
	housing and urban renewal	8.75	20.3
	fire	17.8	29.7
	sewers	14.4	13.3
	parks and recreation	17.5	16.0
average monthly wage of main function workers		812	958
(2) *Revenues* (%)			
mean property tax rate	1962	1.85	2.05
	1972	1.33	2.54
total tax effort (as % of family income)	1962	3.5	5.1
	1972	4.0	6.7

decline. Although highly simplified, it can be seen that declining cities have *per capita* expenditures which are 70% higher overall than growing cities, largely due to higher levels of expenditures for fire and police protection, and for housing and urban renewal. The wage costs of providing public services are also higher. Against these higher expenditure costs, the revenue side reveals that both tax rates and tax effort (see p. 207) are higher in declining cities and are increasing. US cities exhibit the classic fiscal disparity problem: growing expenditure demands and declining revenue resources. The growing imbalance can be matched either by further increases in local taxes absorbing a still greater percentage of local income, and encouraging further population decline through migration, or by increased dependence on fiscal transfers from higher level government. Although these features are more highly developed in the US than elsewhere, fiscal disparities of a similar form are present in all modern economies. For example in a controversial study of the NW region of England, SPNW (1973) suggested that the mechanism of intergovernmental transfers in the form of the Rate Support Grant was far from equalizing in its effect and encouraged poverty cycles of increasing fiscal disparity (see also Godley and Rhodes 1973).

At the regional level fiscal disparities are often not quite as pronounced, mainly because of the greater scale of the regions in comparison to urban jurisdictions which gives a greater averaging-out of internal differences in

Table 4.4 Per capita income by region for eight Western countries. National average per capita income = 100. (Source: EEC 1977)

Country	Year	Poorest region	Level of per capita income	Richest region	Level of per capita income	Min/max ratio	Inequality (Gini) coefficient
Australia	1973/4	Tasmania	87	NSW	105	1.2	0.03
Canada	1973	Newfoundland	54	Ontario	117	2.2	0.09
US	1975	Mississippi	60	D.C.	125	1.4	0.06
UK	1964	N. Ireland	69	South East	119	1.7	0.06
Switzerland	1967	Oswalden	72	Basel Stadt	143	2.0	0.07
Germany	1970	Saarland	81	Hamburg	133	1.6	0.05
France	1970	Midi-Pyrenee	80	Paris	139	1.7	0.09
Italy	1973	Calabria	60	Liguria	134	2.2	0.14

revenue ability and expenditure levels. Despite these effects, however, marked disparities still do exist. Table 4.4 shows the *per capita* income differences between regions in eight Western countries (where regions are defined as Economic Planning Regions, or administrative units such as States, Provinces, Länder, Départements, or Cantons). It can be seen that considerable ranges of *per capita* incomes affect regions in many countries. These disparities may be mitigated by fiscal flows between regions. In order to satisfy the norm of fiscal equity, for expenditure to individuals and firms in relation to their needs, and fiscal burdens in relation to their abilities, the income differences shown in table 4.4 should lead to higher transfers to the lowest income regions and the lower flows to higher income regions. This pattern does in fact obtain but, as further analysis in chapters 12 to 14 will show, it is extremely debatable whether these flows are sufficiently large to achieve full equalization.

The major cause of both urban and regional fiscal disparities is selective migration of industry and people. There are various dimensions to this phenomenon. That emphasized in most urban research has been the migration from inner central cities to their suburbs. However, it is clear that the city–suburbs dichotomy is only one dimension of the fiscal disparity issue in most cases. Important migration flows also occur between cities, between suburbs, and into gentrifying areas of inner cities. At the regional level, the emphasis has been on the centre and periphery, growing and lagging regions, or on urban and rural differences. In each case fiscal disparities arise because of differences in fiscal treatment in different jurisdictions and other factors. Migration on the one hand places demands on the local public sector in one direction, and on the other hand changes the local revenue capacity and tax base for providing the public goods in the other direction. As Wood (1961, p. 199) notes for the United States: "If in a given part of the region, public service levels fall too low, or conditions of blight and obsolesence become too severe for our taste, many of us simply move out further into the suburbs. This is in the great American pioneering tradition of abandoning settlements we have despoiled".

UNEQUAL PUBLIC SERVICE LEVELS

There are obviously important components of unequal service levels which result from both the fiscal disparity issue and from difference in preferences. These certainly give a greater or lesser capacity or desire to fund services, but there are also more specific effects. It is simply not possible to organize equal levels of service provision everywhere: fragmentation of urban and regional government increases local disparities, and it is not possible totally to match local service levels to local preferences. Thus in Milwaukee, Curran (1973, pp. 157–8) ascribes increasing metropolitan disparities mainly to the lack of adaptation of local government structures to changes in transport technology: "local governments in Milwaukee County are expected to perform as

77

though they were still geographically isolated and economically independent entities".

In both urban and regional systems in which each jurisdiction is increasingly interdependent with other tracts, the difficulties of achieving equal service levels affect each form of public service. In education, the tendency of different social groups to live in different jurisdictions gives what Coleman (1970) terms the 'group externalities of schooling'. The education resources of a school include the group externalities of the educational backgrounds of other children in the school which come from a specific catchment area. Since these external effects will vary as a function of the social structure of a catchment area, it is not possible to achieve full equalization of service levels. In the case of transport, mass transit facilities tend to cluster along high density routeways giving minimum services to interstitial areas. The development of highways, conservation zones free of traffic, regulation of traffic signals, and so forth, when remaining in the control of local units who are very reasonably attempting to use them to improve the local environment, tend to undermine the ability to develop an integrated transport system. In addition, suburbs often wait on central city initiatives for projects in the knowledge that the former is obliged to invest in new transport facilities to permit, via commuting, the maintenance of its employment centre and workforce. In the case of water supply, competition between jurisdictions for reservoir sites has often produced extremely sub-optimal results: there has been a tendency to employ small scale expedients, using pumping, which compete for the water table, or development of small reservoir sites where a large reservoir would be cheaper for the whole community. Disposal of sewage and industrial waste by one jurisdiction has often been to the detriment of the water supply, ground-water, air quality standards, and recreational facilities of adjacent jurisdictions. Much early suburban development, for example, was accompanied by the use of septic tanks which discharged into the ground, or into the sea. With local police forces, fire brigades and health care, the problems are often connected with economies of scale and lack of co-ordination. In the US, there is a multiplicity of overlapping health care jurisdictions, the fire brigades have radically different equipment and manning levels in adjacent areas, whilst the distribution of police forces has little relation to that of need as measured by crime rates, and so forth. In the UK and other Western European countries, these problems are less marked and are often restricted, but nevertheless occur.

In each case inequalities in service levels arise as a result not only of fiscal disparities and preferences, but also of specific geographical factors which limit the access of some individuals or jurisdictions to the service levels available to others.

THE DISINTEGRATION OF POLITICAL CONTROL

This results in urban areas from the multiplicity of local governments which diffuse citizen control of governments. This is especially marked in the US.

Lineberry (1971) for example, quotes the case of the Minneapolis suburb of Fridley where residents are expected to exercise informed control over nine separate local governments as well as the state and national governments. Each of the local governments, covering the city, a school district, a sanitary sewer district, a sanitation district, a hospital district, a soil conservation district, a county government, an airport commission, and a mosquito control district, has different and overlapping boundaries, possesses different aims, and behaves as an independent fiscal entity operating under totally different criteria of costs and efficiency. Moreover, because of the effect of spillover and externalities, many areas affected by the voters, and many areas which affect the voters, in a given location allow those voters no representative voice. For example, the suburban dweller has no electoral representation in central city affairs, just as the central city dweller has no representation in suburban government.

At the regional level, the disintegration of political control has been marked by similar overlapping and confused jurisdiction, e.g. in the United States Water Basin Commissions, TVA, the Appalachian Regional Commission, EDA areas, and State boundaries. But in most countries the regional disintegration of political control has resulted from features deriving from the lack of any representative government available at regional level. The region, almost by definition, has always been a diffuse and changing concept reflecting more administrative than political consciousness. In the UK, the regional level is marked by a range of *ad hoc* bodies such as the Regional Water Boards, Regional Health Authorities, Economic Planning Boards, Gas and Electricity Boards each resulting from administrative decentralization. Similar bodies are present in most countries, but in few cases is there any democratic representation on such bodies.

A particular feature of loss of political control is the so-called exploitation hypothesis. This hypothesis is espoused especially but not exclusively by Marxist economists (see Castells 1976; Harvey 1973; Hill 1976; Lojkine 1977; O'Connor 1973). It is most frequently applied in urban areas to central city and suburbs as the so-called 'suburban exploitation' hypothesis. The claimed exploitation relates to the fiscal disparity issue discussed above, but is focused specifically at the political level. Under the influence of autonomous modes of behaviour dictated by prudence, competition and the Samaritan's dilemma, no one jurisdiction can solve the disparity problem independently. Instead local jurisdictions respond by attempts to reduce local residential tax burdens by attracting industry and using short-term tax concessions, and the suburbs usually adopt building code definitions and zoning restrictions to maintain what Eckstein (1973) has termed 'tax havens' for the higher and middle income groups who are already in residence. Hence, where the Tiebout model explains that fiscal stimulus to migration, zoning procedures permit the maintenance by existing groups of low tax rates, low incidence of welfare benefits, and high environmental access. Hence they provide a mechanism for heightening the spatial inequalities between jurisdictions. In addition, more covert discrimination by house sellers, real estate agents, and financial and loan institutions may reinforce the process.

Such practices give the most valid basis for charges that the suburbs and higher income tracts exploit other areas. According to one Marxist writer (Castells 1976) this process leads to "the socialization of costs and the privatization of gains", i.e. the higher income groups are able to maintain insulated environments of higher property values and lower fiscal burdens whilst passing on to the community at large, and to the lower income jurisdictions in particular, the welfare and other costs associated with lower income groups. As evidence of this exploitation, many studies have shown that central city expenditures rise as the size of the suburban population increases (see, for example, Hawley 1957; Margolis 1968). The rise in such expenditures results especially from the need to support a large transport infrastructure for the commuting population and commercial market centre of the city, but may also result from particular forms of intergovernmental relations in the finance of water supply, waste and sewerage disposal. But the strongest argument to support the exploitation hypothesis is that, since the central city must bear the higher costs of serving the needs of the poor and disadvantaged left behind by the suburban filtering process, their public needs are inflated by a more subtle 'exploitation': the natural workings of the economic system, which favours the mobility of the more wealthy and able, work to produce the same exploitation effects.

However, the suburbs may not present the increased burden on central cities that these results imply. In many cases, the extra cost to the central city may be offset by larger industrial and commercial tax base, together with retail receipts and taxes. The suburbs also increase the city's tax capacity by maintaining industrial productivity and by a supportive effect on property values. A number of studies of the relative subsidy and exploitation effects between the city and the suburbs leave us, as yet, with conflicting and uncertain conclusions (see chapters 9 and 14).

At the regional level, the exploitation thesis has a lineage deriving from both Rousseau and Marx. Both link exploitation to the role of the money economy. For example, Rousseau (1765, pp. 297–8) sees the origin of regional imbalance as due to the establishment of an exchange economy:

'poverty did not make itself felt in Switzerland until money began to circulate there; money created inequalities both in resources and in fortunes; it became a great instrument of acquisition which was inaccessible to those who had nothing. Commercial and manufacturing establishments were multiplied; the arts and crafts diverted a multitude of hands from agriculture. Men multiplied and, no longer distributed evenly throughout the country, concentrated in regions whose location was comparatively favourable and whose resources were comparatively rich.

Some deserted their fatherland; others became parasites upon it, consuming without producing anything; large numbers of children became a burden'.

An additional feature affecting the level of local political control is the role of party politics. As Downs (1967) and Margolis (1968) have demonstrated, the local political system often functions more to maintain a party or coalition in office and not to attain the best decision on public administration and finance (see chapter 15). Thus in many declining city areas political leaders have often resisted the courses of action which would cure the inner city problems. In London's Docklands for example, the five local boroughs concerned have all resisted development of office employment, middle income housing and transport facilities, such as extension of the London Underground, which would change the local jurisdiction from socialist-dominated boroughs to more marginal electorates. Again, many much needed investments have not been undertaken even when the tax capacity has been available because this would require rises in taxes which might cause a loss of support at an election. At the regional level the specific interests of regional units have often been subsumed either to local constituency interests, or to national party concern. Hence the frustration, in Quebec, Scotland, Wales, Catalonia, Friesland, or the Swiss canton of Jura, with national parties which have caused them to form regional 'national' parties often strongly separatist in aims.

4.6 Conclusion

The aims of public finance geography as posed in this chapter are three-fold. First, to determine whether particular fiscal patterns agree with the accepted norms of spatial equalization under the public fisc; second, to determine how far geographical factors detract from the achievement of accepted norms of incidence; and third, to comment on policies which seek to create a better achievement of these accepted norms. As we have seen above, there is a set of strong forces inbuilt into economic relationships which undermine the possibilities of achieving the desired equalization of fiscal burdens and benefits in relation to abilities and needs, and these are strongly focused at both urban and regional levels in most modern economies. Nevertheless, it must be the aim of any public finance system at least to be neutral to distribution questions, if not to improve the individual and geographical distribution of resources. A methodology of social accounting has been suggested which enables assessments to be made of how far the present public fisc is achieving or undermining goals of redistribution, allocation, stabilization, and growth. This methodology is explored in detail in chapters 5 to 10 where the problems of measuring the individual components of need, cost, benefit, and revenue burden are each discussed in turn. The elements of intergovernmental transfers and policy tools aimed at improving the allocation of the public fisc are then discussed in chapters 11 to 14.

Part   2

Individual fiscal jurisdictions

5

The geography of expenditure need

"The poor man has always a precise view of his problem and its remedy: he hasn't enough and he needs more. The rich man can assume or imagine a much greater variety of ills and he will be correspondingly less certain of their remedy.

As with individuals so with nations. And the experience of nations with well-being is exceedingly brief. Nearly all throughout all history have been very poor. The exception, almost insignificant in the whole span of human existence, has been the last few generations in the comparatively small corner of the world populated by Europeans."

J. K. Galbraith (1958) *The Affluent Society*, p. 1.

5.1 Introduction: the geography of needs and wants

The geography of expenditure needs concerns the variable distribution of individual wants and demands, and hence of revenue requirements between locations: between less and more needy individuals and between less and more needy locations. Need, like most concepts in public finance, is a relative concept. The geography of expenditure need, defining the size of public finances (revenue resources) required to support a given mix of public goods at any location, is no less so.

Two distinct approaches to the definition of need have emerged. The first recognizes that most of the public expenditure which we now take for granted in Western society is no longer catering for what we might term real need. It is not absolutely necessary for survival. It is more in the nature of wants or demands: things we desire because other people have them. Moreover, such wants or demands often do not become less urgent the more we are supplied with the means to satisfy them. Or as Galbraith would argue, production to satisfy wants also creates those wants: wants and needs are dependent on production, on what is available, or what other people have; needs are not an independently measurable entity. The second approach to the definition of needs is evidenced in the recent writings in political science, e.g. the Caucus for a New Political Science within the American Political Science Association. These writers have attempted to separate needs from wants, and in particular have tried to distinguish true human needs from false and artificial needs (see, for example, Fitzgerald 1977). However, it is far from clear that 'needs' can be separated from 'wants', 'desires', or 'demands'. Traditional liberal theory has stressed the latter, relying on revealed preference to define need. Radical

85

scholars, such as Marx, Marcuse, Bay and Maslow, on the other hand, have attempted to distinguish 'human need', a deep unalienated need, which is not superimposed on individuals by particular social interests to perpetuate work or injustice, but instead derives from a sense of excellence, ideal health, and the fulfilment of human possibilities.

In this chapter we neither agree totally with Galbraith as to the validity of the dependence hypothesis (that the higher the level of production, the higher the level of need creation), nor with the New Political Science 'human needs' school. Instead, needs are interpreted as the revenue requirements in different locations. Relative wants, demands and revenue requirements differ between locations because of the variable distribution of population and economic activity, because of the variable concentration of different people or different types of economic activity, because of differences in physical and cultural environments, and a host of other factors. Hence, the geography of fiscal need can specify the relative priority to be given to sectors of public activity. Alternatively it can define the characteristics of certain persons who should be eligible for a given public service and those who should not. Again, it can delimit a level of minimum standards, of type and amount of public service, that should be available everywhere irrespective of location. Yet again, it can specify locational priorities for community development, the spreading of economic welfare, or the tackling of pressing problems that are concentrated spatially. Whatever the area of definition, needs specify the relative revenue requirements for public expenditure in one form rather than another. Hence relative need can be measured by indicators such as population size, (*per capita* equality), personal incomes (distribution equality), a person's age, or the costs of public service provision. Thus, need requires a judgement on the relative importance of large as against small population groups, the poor versus the wealthy, the young as opposed to the old, the low versus the high cost location for production, and so forth.

Need is a quantity measure: the number of different units of public good or service required in a given jurisdiction. Unit needs are interrelated with the cost per unit of providing those needs, and the total measure of expenditure need of a jurisdiction is the sum of needs, weighted by their unit cost. However, in this chapter needs are treated independently of their unit costs. The costing problem is discussed in detail in the next chapter.

In this chapter, the concept of need is further developed in section 5.2, and in section 5.3 the relation of geographical need to individual need is considered. Section 5.4 summarizes the various methods that have been adopted for measuring expenditure need and section 5.5 discusses various patterns of geographical incidence of expenditure need that have been analysed in a number of practical cases.

5.2 The definition of need

The concept of 'need' for public goods has, as we have already seen, considerable semantic ambiguities such that we must approach it as a purely relative concept: needs defined relative to a standard, and relative to other needs measured in comparable terms. This indicates the two essential problems surrounding needs discussed in this chapter: how is the standard of needs to be judged, and how are needs to be measured against this standard? In this section, standards of needs are discussed, whilst in the next chapter we are concerned with their measurement. There have been six main approaches to defining standards of needs: *a priori* or philosophical, physiological, expert opinion, revealed preferences, political, and economic. Each of these is discussed in turn below.

A PRIORI OR PHILOSOPHICAL DEFINITION OF NEEDS

Philosophy, religion, ethics, and political sociology, have all been concerned to establish the existence of abstract norms against which to order society. As we have seen in chapter 4, such norms have generally converged on three criteria: rights, deserts, and needs. Rights concern the general ideals of 'natural rights', whilst deserts concern allocation of the benefits of society against such criteria as equity, ability, work, productivity, or scarcity. Needs, in contrast, are a form of moral claim specific to the individual only in comparison with other individuals: wants for certain goods created because other people have them. As Galbraith notes, needs exist only because supply is available. Hence, need has a metaphysical circularity. Paraphrasing Joan Robinson's (1969) definition of utility, need is the quality of people (or locations) that makes people want certain public and private goods; because goods have a certain variable pattern of wants, this shows that people have needs. However, not only is need metaphysical, it also has a highly ambiguous and degraded meaning. As a consequence, Culyer *et al.* (1972, p. 114), conclude that

> 'the word "need" ought to be banished from discussion of public policy, partly because of its ambiguity but also because . . . the word is frequently used in . . . "arbitrary" senses . . . . Indeed . . . in many public discussions it is difficult to tell, when someone says that "society needs . . .", whether he means that *he* needs it, whether he means society ought to get it in *his* opinion, whether a *majority* of the members of society want it, or *all* of them want it. Nor is it clear whether it is "needed" *regardless* of the cost to society'.

Because of its metaphysical circularity and ambiguity, need can be judged not against an abstract norm, but only against a specific set of values, and relative to other needs measured in comparable terms. Each such judgement of relative need involves a valuation, and hence, as discussed in chapter 2, is a decision which is ideological in nature. The ideology of valuation of need will vary, and may emerge as a set of collective preferences of a given jurisdiction; it may reflect the judgement of elected representatives; it may be entrenched in a

Constitution or Bill of Rights; or it may be produced, as the Marxists suggest, by acquiescence in a hegemony of class rule. But whatever its origin, with the rejection of abstract norms of need, beyond the minimum physiological requirements discussed below, the definition of need must be accepted as specific to each time, place and person and can be assessed only in terms which attempt to relate individual or geographical wants to the benefits available to other individuals and locations over any specific time period.

PHYSIOLOGICAL DEFINITION OF NEEDS

There are certain fundamental needs of individuals which are in essence physiological. Primary among these are food and shelter, limitation of stress, freedom from disease, and so forth. However, the costs of providing the minimum level of food and shelter required for subsistence leaves most of the 'needs' of modern society undefined, even if such needs have tended to rise with time (Stigler 1945; Thurow 1973). Hence at any level above subsistence, the physiological definition of need is of little help: as Reischauer (1974) points out, the conditions of human need concern elements far in excess of physiological needs, and are thus fundamentally different from those of plants and animals where physiological needs are pre-eminent.

EXPERT OPINION

It is eminently reasonable that for many public services expert opinion should be an important, or even dominating criterion of need assessment: for example, who is better able to judge the medical needs of a patient than a doctor, or the sewerage disposal needs of a community than an engineer, or the educational needs of a pupil than a teacher. On the basis of this argument, many studies of need definition have been made, especially in the US, using opinions of groups of experts in order to gain a consensus on services needed. For example, the American Library Association (1967) have used techniques similar to Delphi analysis. Expert opinion is also crucial to the definition of highway needs (DOT 1972), levels of police force (Vosel 1974), fire prevention (IAFF 1970), and health needs (Boulding 1966; Culyer 1974). Expert opinion is much less liable to be stinting of provision of public goods and in many instances must be the best judge of standards. However, there are two drawbacks to total reliance on this approach to need definition. First, there is an inbuilt tendency of expert opinion consistently to over-estimate needs. This is partly a function of professional 'empire building', but also derives from the insufficient weight given to the associated factors of the costs and political trade-offs which impinge upon any need decision: it is very easy to specify needs in the absence of the direct constraints of a budget. A second drawback is the operation of what Bleddyn Davies (1968) terms the 'policy paradigm': frequently those services are provided which are perceived by a technocratic elite to be those which are needed, rather than those which are desired. Hence Davies (1968, p. 37) states that in the UK social services, 'because of imperfect perception of needs by untrained and overworked staff, misplaced departmental loyalties, imbalance in the development of services, and other factors, people tend not to get the combination of services most appropriate to their needs . . . (and) it is the least well informed and least independent who are most likely to suffer'.

REVEALED PREFERENCE DEFINITION OF NEEDS

Rather than resort to abstract norms or to expert opinion, the individual may define his needs directly. This can be through either what Bradshaw (1972) terms 'felt need', or 'expressed need'. Felt need can be determined by questionnaire or direct consultation of individuals for their preference among a range of public goods. Expressed needs, in contrast, use criteria derived from the present system of public goods to indicate preferences. For example, waiting lists in public health services, number of users of public transport, telephone or postal services, or the level of actual expenditures in any service, each give a good indication of need as expressed through preferences. Unfortunately, such preferences are not independent of the system of public goods which is at present provided, its quality, its cost (if any), the alternatives available by non-public provision, and the socio-economic characteristics of the individual himself, especially income. For example, the present usage of public health will be increased by the ease of access, its perceived quality, alternative private health treatment available, the presence of any charges, and the income of the individual which controls his ability to seek alternatives outside the public health service. The revealed preference approach has been the basis of the public choice school of public finance which seeks to apportion needs, public benefits, and burdens in accordance with optimality criteria which are the same for public as for private goods (see Buchanan 1960; Bish and Ostrom 1973; Lindahl 1919; Sax 1924). The individual acts, then, on the basis of his individual ranking of needs or preferences, to achieve the provision of public goods which best accords with his personal ranking. The ranking of goods by each individual then becomes the ranking of goods by the collective of society as a whole. As stated by Sax (1924, pp. 194–5), "collective decision implies a value judgement: that it is justified to use the goods which the individual has to give up as his tax, to pay the cost of the collective purposes which assure the nature of an essential need for each individual". This leads us to the relation of need assessment to benefit theory of taxation (chapter 7 *q.v.*) and benefit incidence (chapter 9 *q.v.*).

POLITICAL DEFINITION OF NEEDS

With the political definition of need we are brought back to the essential problem of need definition: who assesses needs? Ideas as to the existence, non-existence and extent of needs will vary according to the political party or group that holds office. There is some dispute as to the extent of influence the political factors have on need determination, Fried (1972), Newton and

Sharpe (1976) and others claiming that such factors are very much subsidiary to the technical, social and economic ones. Certainly the extent to which expenditures and public good provision vary as a function of political party is often small, but the distribution of goods between people, the burdens of revenue payments they bear, and the priorities for change in use of finances are all significantly affected by politics, and this element in need definition often becomes very significant when the length of time a party has been in office is taken into account. Certainly, as the discussion in chapters 11 and 15 serves to emphasize, political factors, especially in the apportionment of intergovern-mental grants, are often of considerable significance both for the way in which need is assessed, and the degree to which it is satisfied.

Need as defined by the political process will often differ from need defined by philosophical, individual or expert opinion. Using the degree of accor-dance of individual, political (or social), and expert opinion, Spek (1972) classifies need into five categories:

(i) *'justified' need*: in which individual, expert, and political opinion are all in accord, e.g. education, old age pensions;

(ii) *latent need (1)*: in which individuals do not recognize needs but political and expert opinion is in agreement as to the existence of a need. This may often be the case in unpopular health treatment, e.g. vaccination programmes, and in costly public sewerage, defence, or infrastructure expenditures, and perhaps in wage and price controls;

(iii) *latent need (2)*: in which the individual and either political or expert opinion do not recognize the need, but the other party of political or expert opinion does. This often characterizes stabilization policies through wage and price controls;

(iv) *'unjustified' need*: individuals desire a certain need to be satisfied, but political and expert opinion agree that it should not be: e.g. medical care in the US prior to the institution of Medicaid;

(v) *irresolvable need*: political, expert and individual opinion all differ, but individuals want a particular service.

Of these needs, 'unjustified' needs accord most closely with the results of revealed preference or public choice schools where, as Ritschl (1931, p. 235) states, "needs are subjectively felt by the competent public authorities and by individuals, insofar as they think, feel and act as members of the community". Latent needs, however, accord most closely with expert opinion.

ECONOMIC DEFINITION OF NEEDS

The economic approach is concerned primarily with the allocation of scarce resources between competing wants in order to achieve maximum satisfac-tion, utility, or efficiency. As such, many of the classical developments of economics are of little help in assessing expenditure needs. On the one hand, the supply of public goods does not regulate price, since need exists only because the supply of public goods is available. On the other hand, demand for public goods does not result from individual decisions of consumer sovereignty, nor is it related to price; instead demand is regulated by wants. As we have seen above, allocation decisions result not from the interrelation of supply and demand, but instead from the interplay of individual wants with political and expert opinion, the degree of support for abstract norms and, to a limited extent, physiological drive. Nevertheless, two approaches to definition of needs based on classical economics are of considerable importance: the consumption function approach, developed especially by Auten (1972a, 1972b, 1974); and the production function approach of Wood (1961), Adams (1965), Bradford *et al.* (1969), and others. In the case of the consumption function approach, observed differences in expenditures and service levels for each public good are related to hypothesized determining variables of income, cost, preferences, prices and efficiency, thus relating the economic definition of needs to that of revealed preferences. In the production function approach, service levels and expenditures are related to the costs of determining inputs such as socio-economic and physical environment, individual, institutional and political factors. Both of these approaches are discussed extensively in section 5.4.

Economic definitions of need must also be distinguished between individual and industrial, commercial, and entrepreneurial interests. Whilst the level of wants may be a major regulator of the supply of public goods to individuals as a social wage, such wants are much less significant in determining the level of externalities available to firms. Industrial and entrepreneurial needs concern four main areas; firstly, general economic and monetary stability; second, stable international and political relations; third, efficient transport, supply, distribution services and infrastructure; fourth, public policy influences deriving from revenue, expenditure and regulatory functions which have fairly minor impact on efficiency and profit formation. It should be noted that the economic needs of industry are frequently in conflict with those of individuals. One source of such conflict is the fact that much social expenditure to satisfy individual wants is derived from the growth in industrial output, hence greater social contol of industry to provide greater social benefits (e.g. through higher corporate taxes) may impair industrial performance. Again, the cheapest forms of industrial expansion may seriously impair the physical and social environment through the presence of excessive air, water, and noise pollution, the use of extensive green field sites, and the expansion of urban freeways. At the spatial level, the impetus for industrial growth in some regions is frequently at odds with the social needs for employment in other areas. The resulting policy problem of aiding either capital or labour mobility, when resolved in favour of moving jobs to workers tends to erode economic efficiency by distorting location away from the most economically efficient sites, and when resolved in favour of moving workers to jobs, undermines social cohesion and individual want satisfaction.

There are not only conflicts in satisfying economic needs. Each of the

91

definitions of needs discussed here, philosophical, physiological, expert opinion, revealed preferences, political and economic, frequently conflicts with each of the other need definitions. Again, as we shall see in the following chapters, in the definition of revenue burdens and in expenditure benefits, no unambiguous criterion of assessment under the public fisc is available. Hence, needs, as one element of the public fisc, must usually be assessed relative to the *present* values of society and are specific to *present* wants.

5.3 Geographical need and individual needs

Need can be defined only against a standard, relative to other wants or needs measured in comparable terms. Individual need concerns the distribution of wants, demands or revenue requirements between people, whilst geographical need concerns the distribution of these wants, demands or revenue requirements between locations. As stressed in chapter 3, however, an important, complex and new dimension of fiscal relations emerges when geographical components of public finance are considered together with individual wants. With respect to needs, the definition of geographical needs which will be used throughout the ensuing discussion will be *the revenue requirements or costs incurred in providing a given level of public service to a particular individual at a particular location.*

Need is a measure of inequality between individuals, firms and locations. Just as ability can be used as a measure of the degree of inequality between unequals and revenue raising apportioned progressively in accordance with that ability (see chapter 7), so need can also be adopted as a criterion of inequality with the aim that expenditure benefits can be apportioned on a progressive basis in accordance with needs. Hence, need and ability are analogous concepts for the respective expenditure and revenue sides of the public economy. The relation between these two measures and their respective degrees of progression is examined in chapters 12 and 14. Here we are concerned with need only as an indicator of relative equality and inequality in satisfaction of wants. These wants may be purely for public goods and services where the major issue involved is that of fiscal equality raised in chapter 4, or may be for private goods and hence involve issues of the degree to which it is desirable to achieve equity in the distribution of these goods as well. Recalling Tawney (1952, p. 38): "the equality which all these thinkers emphasized as desirable is not equality of capacity or attainment, but of circumstances, institutions, and manner of life. The inequality which they deplore is not inequality of personal gifts, but of social and economic environment". A search for equality in manner of life and socio-economic environment will require not only fiscal equity, but also an equity imposed on the distribution of private goods. Hence individual and geographical needs assessment must be concerned in addition to the equity of public good distribution also with the assessment of private needs. Of these latter, transport payments, insurance settlements, in-kind transfers, and other public finance remedies can be given for the operation of the market for private goods.

The issue of equality returns us to the central argument of chapter 3: the degree to which the allocation, stabilization, growth, and especially distribution functions of public finance should be tackled at an individual or a geographical level. As the discussion of that chapter has already argued, spatial factors induce unequal access to resources and markets due to transport costs and institutional barriers. Further, spatial elements give indivisibilities, underlie the variable impact of technological change, and are affected by differences in preferences and costs between locations. This leads in turn to a polarization in disparities of wealth which undermines fiscal equity, and which tends to be cumulative and self-reinforcing through the influences of internal economies of scale and external economies of agglomeration. As so vividly expressed by Galbraith (1958, p. 257), "poverty is self-perpetuating because the poorest communities are poorest in the services which would eliminate it". These effects lead, then, to marked differences in needs, which although affecting the individual or firm, are nevertheless fundamentally geographical in origin and in character.

Some commentators have disputed the degree to which geographical needs exist independently of individual needs as we have seen in chapter 3. For example, Davies has formulated a principle of so-called *territorial justice* of needs. This is stated as assigning "to each area according to the needs of the population of that area" which is achieved when there is "a high correlation between indices of resource-use, or standards of provision, and an index measuring relative needs of an area's population for a service" (Davies 1968, p. 16). Territorial justice is then, a matching of needs and standards of services on an individual by individual basis, but summed over the whole of each jurisdiction to determine how far there are local matches or mismatches in concentrations of need or wants. Territorial justice is then identical to individual justice in assignment of the benefits of the public fisc.

However, whilst one can agree with Davies that his principle of territorial justice gives one criterion for the existence of geographical needs, on two grounds we must dispute that such needs can arise only as the sum of individual needs. First, as we shall see in the next section, it is often not possible in assessing geographical need to retain an individual-by-individual assessment and more gross indicators of needs have to be adopted. The aim then is to seek equality of needs between jurisdictions such that their local resources (either through local taxes or intergovernmental grants) are invariant to geographical variation in need to spend between jurisdictions. Second, and most important, there is the very real distinction to be drawn between "geographical need" and "individual need", which arises from externalities and indivisibilities of needs, and draws us back to the differences between public and private goods discussed in chapter 2. Individual need is appropriate to the assessment of wants for private goods, but geographical need is appropriate to the assessment of public goods which possess an important degree of joint externality and indivisibility between individuals, but where the extent of 'publicness' is not infinite. In fact, Davies has been mainly concerned in his principle of territorial justice with personal social services, personal health services and other services directly available to an individual. In contrast to these personal services there are four main components which lead to the emergence of geographical needs.

(i) *The existence of local public goods:* goods possessing jointness, non-excludeability, and non-rejectability, but only over limited spatial extent.

(ii) *Externalities:* where private needs differ from social needs.

(a) *Production to production externalities:* e.g. river basin development where flood control aids hydro-electric power development, transport infrastructure aids industry.

(b) *Production to consumption externalities:* industry impinges on individuals, e.g. air, noise, and water pollution.

(c) *Consumption to consumption externalities:* actions of individuals impinge upon each other, e.g. joint demands for utilities and local public goods (i) above, crowding in shopping centres, traffic delays, conflicts of cars, pedestrians and public transport.

(d) *Consumption to production externalities:* actions of individuals affect industry, e.g. recreation and urban development affect farming, traffic congestion reduces industrial efficiency.

(iii) *Indivisibilities:* where joint needs cannot be disaggregated as in large investment projects, e.g. mass transit, electricity generation, etc.

(iv) *Public welfare:* where joint social needs cannot be meaningfully divided between people, e.g. law and order, transfer payments, and income subsidies. Especially important are:

(a) *needs for deferred consumption:* where the needs of individuals and society as a whole differ over time, e.g. deferment of present consumption of resources, educational investment:

(b) *the public interest:* where the rate of return on group need satisfaction greatly exceeds that on individual need satisfaction.

One of the most important of these components is that of local public goods. It is possible in a very general sense to recognize a hierarchy of public needs which correspond to a hierarchy of public goods. The reasons for the emergence of such a hierarchy of public goods, which range from purely private, through neighbourhood, local, metropolitan, regional, to national goods, are discussed in detail in chapter 11. The effect is to produce a hierarchy of needs which correspond to this hierarchy of public goods.

For purely private needs, Davies' (1968) principle of territorial justice is quite appropriate: the sum of individual needs equals geographical needs. But geographical needs may not be disaggregated into individual elements of need. Thus, there is little meaning in assigning to individuals the need for a proportion of a power station, sewerage plant, refuse disposal dump, water supply system, fire or police service, and so forth. Whilst geographical needs are a sum of individual needs, they cannot be easily satisfied, or they exist, independently of one another. At the extreme of pure public goods, the level of national needs is frequently termed that at which exist 'merit' goods or national 'minimum' or 'average' standards. Such goods will conform to Hobson's criterion as characterizing those goods where standardization is possible or desired, but Auten (1972a) has emphasized the importance of adequate rather than minimum standards. The existence of merit goods has been an important motivation for the allocation of grants to jurisdictions: to maintain a given national standard of service which is organized locally, taking into account differences in local resource capacity (Hansen and Perloff 1944). As stated in the UK in the *Green Paper on Local Government Finance* (UK Government 1971, p. 3) such grants should be distributed "in such a way that the cost of providing a standard level of service should be a standard amount per head". Indeed, Adam Smith (1776, Book V, I, p. 815) recognizes the difference between local and national merit goods and, as we shall see in chapter 11, uses this as the basis for a proposal of separation of revenue sources: "those local or provincial expenses of which the benefit is local or provincial . . . ought to be defrayed by local or provincial revenue . . . . It is unjust that the whole society should contribute towards an expense of which the benefit is confined to a part of society". This also draws us towards the issues of benefit incidence which, as we shall see in chapter 9, also have considerable and inescapable geographical components.

As a result of these two features discussed above – namely the lack of ability to identify individual needs, and the indivisibility of geographical needs leading to the emergence of local and regional public goods – individual and territorial need will often not be in accord. Hence any assignment of public revenues or expenditures to equalize territorial needs may not achieve an equality of individual needs, and vice versa. This is an important motivation for the examination of geographical need indicators and becomes an especially important issue when intergovernmental transfers are concerned (see chapters 12 and 13).

One final issue should also be raised. Attempts to differentiate the public fisc in order to achieve redistribution in the cause of greater equality must result in the unequal treatment of unequals. Where there are more needy, these are accorded greater service benefits, greater service qualities, or lower service costs. Where there are less needy, these are forced to accept lesser benefits and service quality, or to pay higher service costs. The more unequal are the needs of society, and the more it is attempted to redress these imbalances in needs, the more unequal must be the operation of the public fisc. As Tawney (1952, p. 39) notes: "the more anxiously, indeed, a society endeavours to secure equality of consideration for all its members, the greater will be the differentiation of treatment which, when once their common human needs

95

have been met, it accords to the special needs of different groups and individuals among them". Hence the more unequal the spatial organization of the public fisc also tends to become.

5.4 The measurement of geographical needs

We have seen in the preceding discussion that need can be defined only against a standard and relative to other needs or wants measured in comparable terms on a geographical basis. Moreover, the standard of needs cannot be defined abstractly, but derives instead from the preferences revealed within society, from political and economic elements, and from technological and physiological bases. The measurement of geographical need admits no easy solution. Cuciti (1978) recognizes six difficulties.

(i) Which definition of geographical area should be adopted: should whole cities or neighbourhoods be assessed for needs; how are regional needs to be offset against those which are local or national?

(ii) What summary statistics are to be used: the mean, median and mode, as measures of an area's need, may each suffer from definitional inadequacies; additionally, when should distribution measures of variation be used instead of average measures?

(iii) Is the current level, or the trend in needs the most important?

(iv) How are needs to be assessed differentially: e.g. how much worse is an unemployment rate of 10% than one of 9%?

(v) How are different needs to be compared and combined: e.g. how much worse is a crime rate of x break-ins per thousand population, than y% of families below the poverty level?

(vi) What procedure should be adopted where need is recognizable but no data, or no adequate data, are available for its measurement?

Because of these difficulties need measurement cannot be divorced from the values and decisions of individuals within society at a particular point in time. Generally, therefore, analysts have sought to look at the present organization of public goods as a yardstick to indicate the fiscal needs of different peoples and locations. In so doing, however, considerable difficulties arise because of the interplay of 'real need' with differences in jurisdictional responsibilities, differences in local preferences, differences in local service quality, and especially differences in local income. It is no easy task to differentiate from these various features, geographical need. The most direct measurements of needs require the determination of the costs or revenue requirements of providing services to the assessed 'population at risk', work load, or need for each service. This gives a direct assessment of revenue requirements, but its use in practice has been limited by the lack of available data on cost variation, and lack of consensus on its use in the assessment of expenditure needs. This approach forms the background to the discussion here, but is not expanded in detail until chapter 6.

Because of the limitations and indeterminacy in measuring the unit cost of expenditure needs, a wide variety of other approaches have been developed for the measurement of geographical needs and the five most important of these are discussed below: individual indicators; composite measures; representative needs indices; standard service input indices; and standard service output indices.

INDIVIDUAL INDICATORS

These are used to generate individual measures of cost, availability, extent and quality of single services. Individual need indicators are most appropriate for limited, specific programmes where the recipients of the benefits of public expenditure are easily identifiable. Hence they are commonly associated with specific grants as opposed to general block grants (see chapter 12). Indeed they are most useful when a highly specific and clearly defined location or group of people can be determined for the receipt of specific and targeted aid. Individual indicators usually consist of simple ratios expressing the needs of individuals in a jurisdiction relative to the size of the total population, or to the size of the client group concerned.

The most frequently used measures of need rank the relative priority of given locations with respect to the character of the persons eligible and the amount and type of service they should receive. Examples for the UK are provided for the social services by Davies (1968, 1971a, 1974), health services by Culyer (1974) and DHSS (1976), and for planning, control and investment by DSPSE (1976). In the US general need indicators have been developed by Johnson (1947) and Maxwell (1946), for poverty by HEW (1976), for education by a number of State Governments, especially Florida. Other useful studies of needs are by OECD (1962), Boulding (1966), Boaden (1971), Davies (1971b), Culyer *et al* (1972) and Williams (1974).

The aim of the individual need indicator approach is probably most easily stated with respect to health care: "to secure, through resource allocation, that there should eventually be equal opportunity of access to health care for people at equal risk" (DHSS 1976, p. 7). Special health-care needs can be readily measured for the old, young, women in maternity, for special diseases such as tuberculosis, polio, venereal disease, or cancer, and for specific geographical variation in birth and death rates. Hence the 'population at risk' or workload factor can usually be readily assessed from demographic data on age structure and past patterns of incidence of disease. For example, the total size of a population is usually a very adequate indicator of the use of out-patient, community, ambulance, and family planning services, and also services such as mental, blind, and handicapped needs, and special disease incidence. Johnson (1947) and DHSS (1976), for example, state that population is usually a totally adequate individual index of geographical health needs unless jurisdictions are very small, the demographic structure is very perverse, there is an exceptionally high concentration of medical schools (as in London), or there is a wide variety of different ages and qualities of capital stock (as in the antiquated hospital buildings of Northern England, or in the North-East United States cities).

For personal social services, education and other public goods, individual indicators of need are often less successful. Even for health care, labour costs vary, and morbidity rates may vary considerably as a result of climatic, occupational categories, water supply, sanitation facilities, insect life, and age of economic infrastructure; and for other services the demographic structure and income levels of different individuals and locations have a much more marked impact. This has occasioned the use of 'education unit' and other complex indicators of education needs in the UK Rate Support Grant and US State Grants. In each case these aim at assessing the total number of children in each level of education from nursery, through primary and secondary to post-secondary level; each of which has very different manpower, equipment, cost and hence expenditure, needs. Similarly in social services the size of family, family income, extent of disabilities and costs of living all impact on the local revenue requirements, as for example Davies' (1968) family care index for provision of social service homes for the aged. Such indices for the ratio of local to national needs can be constructed for each social service need. Moreover, since the need for social service benefits is linked to income level, this has occasioned proposals in many countries for linking social service systems to the income tax system at an individual level. This directly recognizes the interdependence of personal needs and personal fiscal ability; in fact, need is often measured as inverse fiscal ability (see chapter 7). Such proposals have often been linked to negative income tax proposals, where individuals below a poverty level of income receive income deficit payments, and those above that level pay a proportional income tax burden. The negative income tax proposal is discussed further in chapter 12. Here it is sufficient to note the close interdependence of need and revenue ability.

COMPOSITE INDICES

These combine two or more individual need indicators and are the most frequently used approach to need assessment. Whereas individual need indicators are most appropriate for restricted programmes with clearly identifiable recipients of public benefits, composite need indices are more useful for diffuse programmes, where beneficiaries are not clearly identifiable, where government responsibilities are not clearly delimited, and where general rather than specific benefits are intended. Hence, when used in grant programmes, composite need indicators have been used most frequently in the allocation of general block grants, as in the case of the UK Rate Support Grant, German Equalization Grants, and US Community Development (see chapters 12 and 13). Moreover, composite indicators are usually more flexible

Table 5.1 The Orshansky index of poverty levels in the US. Weighted average poverty cut-offs in 1974 by size of family, sex, and area of residence. (Source: US Bureau of the Census, *Current Population Reports*, Series P-60, No. 102)

Size of family unit	Total	Non-farm			Farm		
		Total	Male head	Female head	Total	Male head	Female head
1 person (unrelated individual)	$2,487	$2,495	$2,610	$2,413	$2,092	$2,158	$2,029
14 to 64 years	2,557	2,562	2,658	2,458	2,197	2,258	2,089
65 years and over	2,352	2,364	2,387	2,357	2,013	2,030	2,002
2 persons	3,191	3,211	3,220	3,167	2,707	2,711	2,632
Head 14 to 64 years	3,294	3,312	3,329	3,230	2,819	2,824	2,706
Head 65 years and over	2,958	2,982	2,984	2,966	2,535	2,535	2,533
3 persons	3,910	3,936	3,957	3,822	3,331	3,345	3,133
4 persons	5,008	5,038	5,040	5,014	4,302	4,303	4,262
5 persons	5,912	5,950	5,957	5,882	5,057	5,057	5,072
6 persons	6,651	6,699	6,706	6,642	5,700	5,700	5,702
7 or more persons	8,165	8,253	8,278	8,079	7,018	7,017	7,066

and adaptable, and do not tend to perpetuate the special treatment of the segment of population for which the aid was originally given.

One of the most complex indicators of need is the US Poverty Measure deriving from Orshansky (1963, 1965). The resulting Social Security Administration Index (Orshansky Index) provides a range of income cut-offs adjusted by such factors as family size, age and sex of family head, number of children under 18 years old, and farm–nonfarm residence. Families and other related individuals are then classified in relation to this poverty level by the extent of their income shortfall. When these cut-offs are calculated for each cross-qualification of need groups, 124 poverty lines result, termed the Orshansky Matrix. Because of the information demands of this index, a set of weighted average cut-offs are more usually adopted as shown in table 5.1. The Orshansky Index is used for a number of US federal intergovernmental grants and also for individual income supplement programmes, e.g. by the Community Services Administration for income supplements, by HEW in the Elementary and Secondary Education Act, and in modified form in the Comprehensive Employment and Training Act (CETA). However, it is an index based on individual rather than geographical needs (although geographical needs can be reconstructed from it by summing the individuals at each location).

A major example of the use of a composite set of indicators based on geographical assessment of needs is the set of need indicators which have been adopted in the allocation of UK Rate Support Grants since 1974/1975. These are shown in table 5.2 and are discussed more fully in chapter 13, but from the table it can be seen that the social, economic, cost, unemployment, and density factors are all being included at various times. The weighting given to each indicator is determined by a regression analysis of past expenditure levels on the range of chosen lead indicators. Similar composite need indicators have been used in a large number of US grant programmes as discussed in chapter 13.

An important set of composite need indicators which have been receiving increasing attention are those relating to geographical 'fiscal distress'. Such indicators have importance to two types of communities. On the one hand, expanding communities, cities and new towns have had to bear heavy fiscal burdens of investment in schools, water, sewerage, housing and transport infrastructure (DSPSE 1976). On the other hand, declining communities have had to bear the high costs of environmental renewal, pollution, renewal of housing and other facilities, clearance of derelict land, and (in the US) welfare programmes (CBO 1977; Dommel *et al.* 1978; Downs 1978; GAO 1977; Gramlich 1976; Nathan and Adams 1976; Peterson 1976; SPNW 1973). A third set of problems, which is frequently neglected, is the fiscal distress of rural and agricultural communities requiring extensive resources for improvement of rural roads and distribution of services to enable comparable service standards with urban communities (Sunquist and Davis 1969). Indicators of need for each of these three categories of fiscal distress have centred around two issues (Bradbury 1978): first, the fiscal problems of a jurisdiction's government; second, the quality of services available to the people in a given jurisdiction. The fiscal problems of a jurisdiction's government depend on the extent of its debt, liquidity, and balance of revenues and expenditures (together with intergovernmental transfers and debt management). Dearborn (1977) and Bradbury (1978) suggest that the three primary measures of governmental distress are as follows:

(i) debt-burden measure (Aronson and King, undated; Bahl 1971)

$$\text{fiscal distress} = (LR + I + SO)/RO$$

(ii) relative liquidity measure (Adams 1977)

$$\text{fiscal distress} = (CU + SO)/EO$$

(iii) current account surplus or deficit measure (Adams 1977)

$$\text{fiscal distress} = \frac{[(RT + RU) - (EO + EU + LR + PG)]}{(EO + EU + LR + PG)}$$

where RO, RU and RT are the respective locally raised, utility and total revenues, LR and SR are the respective long-term and short-term debt returned during the year, I is interest expenditures, EO and EU are the year's respective general and utility operating expenditures (excluding capital outlays), SO is short-term debt outstanding, CU cash and securities not earmarked as sinking funds or bond issues, and PG is the city's contribution to old-age retirement schemes. The first index indicates the extent of a jurisdiction's current revenues which is used in debt servicing whilst the second index displays the proportion of jurisdictional operating expenditures which can be financed by local revenues. The third index gives the total difference in resources and expenditures excluding capital outlay. A second set of fiscal distress indices falls into four groups concerned with tax burdens, tax resources, fiscal performance, and composite measures of the three elements. As such these indices of fiscal need overlap, or are inverses of, the indices of tax effort, tax capacity and tax severity to be discussed in chapters 7 and 8. Figure 5.1 displays the range of need variation in the metropolitan areas of the United States. Other studies have concentrated on the degree of variation in spatial needs between city and suburbs, or between suburbs (e.g. Caputo and Cole 1976; Nathan and Adams 1976; Petersen 1976).

A major drawback to the use of composite need indicators is the difficulty of knowing the extent to which each indicator should be weighted relative to the other indicators. Most of the examples discussed above have made either arbitrary decisions, or have based the choice of weights on regression analysis between needs and past expenditure levels. The former approach suffers from the defect of being based on a value judgement, and the latter approach has a circularity of argument which perpetuates past trends of need satisfaction.

Table 5.2 Needs indicators used in the UK Rate Support Grant up to 1979/80. Note that education and social service units are simplified, and that London and Scotland have separate schemes. (*Source*: UK Government, *Statutory Instruments, Rate Support Grant Orders and Regulations*, various years.)

Indicator	Year						
	Pre-1974	1974/75	1975/76[1]	1976/77[2]	1977/78	1978/79	1979/80
1. Education units							
Nursery school pupils	X	X	X	X			
Primary school pupils	X	X	X	X	X	X	X
Secondary and Special School pupils	X	X	X	X	X	X	X
Higher education students	X	X	X	X	X	X	X
School meals served	X	X	X				
2. Social service units							
DHSS units		X					
Children in care		X					
Population over 65 or 60	X	X	X	X	X	X	X
Persons without basic facilities				X	X	X	X
Lone parent families				X	X	X	X
Multi-occupied households					X	X	X
Children under 5	X						
Children under 15	X						
Persons over 65 or 60 living alone			X	X	X	X	X
High density households				X	X	X	X
3. Population growth or decline							
Rates of change of population	X		X	X	X	X	X
Total population	X		X	X	X	X	X
4. Area and density							
Acreage	X		X	X	X	X	X
High density population	X		X	X	X	X	X
Low density population	X	X	X	X	X	X	X
Road mileage	X						

5. *Regional weights*
   West Midlands
   Outer South East[3]
   Special areas
   Separate treatment of London
   Metropolitan–non-Metropolitan weight[4]

6. *Miscellaneous*
   Unemployment levels
   New dwelling starts
   Wage rates

Notes: [1]Includes 71.3% hold-harmless from 1974/75.
        [2]Includes 83.86% hold-harmless from 1975/76.
        [3]Absorbed in wage rate differentials 1975/76 onwards.
        [4]Absorbed in density weights from 1978/79.

103

Moreover, it is not clear that the variables used in composite indicators are independent of each other. This has important collinearity effects when regression analysis is used, but may also produce non-linear interactions. For example, Davies (1968, p. 304) notes that "in education, the relationship between relative 'need' for the service in individual social conditions indices could well be defined as being non-linear, because interaction might take place between various aspects of bad conditions so that 'needs' might be increased by more than the sum of the effects of individual factors or need". In such cases, the simple summation of the effects of each individual indicator will not offer a valid criterion for the assessment of jurisdictional needs. A final problem arises when the need indicators are derived from a sample survey. In this case, Jabine (1977) notes that the sampling theorems of statistics (law of large numbers and central limit theorem) require that the samples should be independently drawn and of sufficient size or otherwise differences in assessed needs may be purely the result of sampling error.

REPRESENTATIVE NEEDS INDICES

The representative needs index is a special case of composite need indices and corresponds to the representative tax base index to be discussed in chapters 7 and 8; however, it has been used to a much smaller extent. Representative needs attempt to allow for the fact that different jurisdictions follow different expenditure programmes and offer different qualities of services. Such needs are assessed as the cost of supplying average service levels for the existing mix of all local government expenditure programmes, if each local jurisdiction were able to provide the same services at the same unit cost. The representative needs for each expenditure function of each jurisdiction is determined by multiplying a standard weighting term for that function with the jurisdiction's share of the population group needing that expenditure function (e.g. school-age children for school expenditure, prison population for prison expenditure, etc.) and summing the result for all functions. Need is assessed, therefore, on the basis of the actual level of demand relative to actual expenditure levels, i.e.

$$\text{Need (in jurisdiction } j) = \sum_{\substack{\text{all functions} \\ i}} \text{workloads} \left\{ \begin{array}{c} \text{for functions } i \text{ in} \\ \text{jurisdiction } j \end{array} \right\} \times \text{weight.}$$

The standard weighting term can be chosen to equal the national average *per capita* expenditures in each function, the highest *per capita* expenditure in any jurisdiction, or any other form. If the national average is used, as adopted by Musgrave and Polinsky (1970), then the needs assessment is a local deficiency one only. But if the expenditure in the largest spending jurisdiction is used, full equalization of needs is possible. This accords with the principles governing grant payments to be discussed in chapter 12. The workload terms can be adjusted to take account of different mixes and qualities of services in different jurisdictions, the effects of benefit spillovers to other jurisdictions, and the composition of the population (age-specific, or population-at-risk). Hence, representative needs provide a considerable advance over other composite need indicators.

There are a number of problems with the representative needs approach. First, where different levels of government are responsible for different mixes of public services in different areas, as in the US, it becomes difficult to make reliable comparisons of service needs in different locations since competition between some needs, or between public needs and non-public substitutes is ignored. Second, in the division between public and non-public provision it becomes difficult to decide which services to include and which to exclude from the representative needs index. Finally, there is the difficult problem of determining the standard of weighting which determines the degree of need-equalization which can be achieved.

STANDARD SERVICE INPUT INDICES

This fourth method of need assessment attempts to relate actual public service outputs to the inputs that generate them. Hence if needs are defined in terms of given service output levels, e.g. pupil–teacher ratio, hospital beds per jurisdiction, population levels, and so forth, the policy changes required to inputs to achieve given output levels can be readily determined. This approach derives from the production function of economics and has been used in a number of studies in the US, for example Brazer (1959), Hawley (1957), Hirsch (1959), Wood (1961), Hansen (1965) and Adams (1965) and also in the UK, for example *Royal Commission on Local Government in England* (1968a, b), Oliver and Stanyer (1969), Nicholson and Topham (1971, 1972), Davies *et al.* (1971a, b), Boaden (1971), Alt (1971), Ashford (1974), and Danziger (1974). Typical results derived from Adams' (1965) study are reproduced in table 5.3. This shows the partial correlation coefficient relating seven expenditure functions to each of eleven input variables for 478 counties in the US with a population density greater than 100 people per square mile. As can be seen from the table, density and degree of urbanization are particularly important in affecting the levels of need for police, fire and sanitation expenditure, whilst the degree of dependence on tourism affects expenditure needs for fire, police and recreation facilities. The regional dummy variable mainly affects street maintenance needs through the effect of size of snowfall. Need for greater fire expenditures is created by larger percentages of older and multiple occupancy housing, whilst income, number of foreign born inhabitants, and number of jurisdictions have most important impact on police expenditure needs.

The main problem with these input indices is that they are very difficult to relate to output levels of expenditure: equal levels of expenditure do not necessarily mean that the quantity and quality of services are equal since cost and other factors have not been taken into account. Moreover, the aim of

Table 5.3 The relation of expenditure levels to various indicators of need. Coefficients of multiple and partial determination grouped by expenditure functions for the US in 1963. (*Source*: Adams 1965)

Demand Factors		Expenditure functions R^2						
		Police 0.750	Fire 0.647	Sewage 0.281	Sanitation 0.546	Recreation 0.563	General Control 0.576	Street maintenance 0.419
(1) Socioeconomic environment	Density	0.577	0.290	0.215	0.277	0.140	—	—
	Urbanization	0.172	0.120	0.096	0.116	0.078	0.107	0.062
	Transients	0.298	0.179	0.036	0.116	0.252	0.179	—
(2) Physical environment	Region	0.059	0.094	0.070	0.081	0.208	0.169	0.296
	Older housing	—	0.051	—	—	—	—	0.043
	Multi-unit housing	—	0.064	—	—	0.090	—	—
	Average annual snowfall	—	—	—	—	—	—	0.023
(3) Income and wealth	Level and distribution of income	0.066	0.042	0.029	0.035	0.049	0.041	0.033
(4) Individual differences	% Non-white	0.119	—	—	0.037	—	—	—
	% Foreign-born	0.221	0.141	—	0.049	0.106	—	—
(5) Institutional and political factors	Number of jurisdictions	0.128	0.053	0.040	0.025	0.038	0.021	—
	% In-migrant	0.082	0.069	—	0.024	0.069	0.037	0.047
	Per capita police expenditures	—	—	—	—	—	0.313	—
	Employees *per capita*	—	—	—	—	—	0.144	—

equality of service outputs may be unobtainable given technical and environmental limitations: as noted in chapter 3, it is not feasible to give the same level of service to everyone everywhere.

STANDARD SERVICE OUTPUT INDICES

Service output indices are related to the input indices discussed above, but tackle the needs question from the other end. Instead of asking what public inputs produce a given level of output, the output approach is concerned with asking what outputs best satisfy measured needs. This approach derives from the consumption function of economics and has been used in a relatively small number of studies most notably by Horowitz (1968), Henderson (1968), Auten (1971, 1972, 1974) and Reischauer (1974, chapter 4) for the United States. The method of estimation, as with input indices, is by means of regression analysis. Auten (1974), for example, suggests that the consumption function $C_{jk} = f(Y_j, C_k, t_j)$ can be transformed into a needs estimation term and estimated by a regression equation as follows:

$$C_{Njk} = a + b\bar{A}_j + cN_j + t_j,$$

Where C_{Njk} is public expenditure need. $\bar{A}_j$ is the average value of tax capacity (as used in the discussion of chapter 7), N_j is a vector of need variables in jurisdiction j for function k, C_{jk} is consumption in jurisdiction j for function k, Y_j is jurisdictional income, and t_j is the taste variation in jurisdiction j. Auten's (1974) analysis of 24 need variables for New York State uses indicators of economic health, population character, area, density, crime rate, income and property values. The resulting estimates of the coefficient b and c give the average expenditure response to ability and need, with any differences ascribed to the error term t_j of differences in local taste for average need preferences.

The main contribution of Auten's studies is to emphasize the relationship between local expenditure needs and local tax capacity, otherwise the regression equation and resulting estimates do not differ substantially from the input (production function) studies discussed in the preceding paragraphs. Differences in tax capacity, which affect variation in the propensity to consume, are controlled for in assessing needs, and hence need measurement is reduced to a common level of tax capacity.

In the study by Horowitz (1968) the level of US local government employment and the level of federal aid are added to income capacity as endogenous variables. Both of these variables are affected by need and are not independent of it, as the Auten and other studies assume. Controlling for the effects of *per capita* income, tax effort, and income distribution, Horowitz finds that local *per capita* expenditure is increased by $1.26 for every $1 in *per capita* revenue from federal government, and local employment is increased by 8 to 10 employees for every 100,000 of local population. In a similar study, Henderson (1968) allows for the effect of personal income, intergovernmental aid, level of urbanization, and population. An explicit welfare function is introduced to represent the effect of budget constraints. After controlling for income and population, Henderson found that each $1 of intergovernmental revenue increased local expenditures by $1.42 in metropolitan counties, and by $1.04 in rural counties.

In each of these studies the dependence of revenue requirements on income is removed and this permits a very considerable step forward in need assessment. The logical next step of this approach is simultaneous equation estimation of both expenditure needs and tax capacity, i.e. a combination of the need indices discussed in this section with the ability indices discussed in chapters 7 and 8. The aim is assessment of the two equations:

(I) Need $= f$(need indicators + controls + fiscal ability + intergovernmental transfers)

(II) Ability $= f$(ability indicators + controls + fiscal need + intergovernmental transfers).

The first equation represents the concern of this chapter with need assessment, and attempts to determine the level of jurisdictional needs controlling for the effects of differences in fiscal ability and other factors. The second equation represents the concern of chapters 7 and 8 with assessment of ability and attempts to determine the levels of jurisdictional ability controlling for the effects of differences of fiscal needs and other factors. From the theory of multivariate statistics and econometrics we know that it is possible to estimate these two equations jointly by simultaneous equation methods. Alternatively, each equation can be estimated independently using reduced form estimators such as 2SLS (Bennett 1979). Auten's approach discussed above adopts the second approach, and no study has yet attempted simultaneous need and ability assessment.

5.5 The geographical incidence of expenditure needs

The measurement of expenditure need aims at capturing, in some simple or composite index, a measure of the total expenditure requirements of the individuals and firms at a given location. The geographical incidence of expenditure need reflects the distribution of a population, or the distribution of eligible population in a country, weighted by geographical cost factors, and other components reflecting the economics of size of given government units, differences in fiscal distress and hardship, preferences for public goods, and local political imperatives.

Where needs are measured in direct *per capita* terms, geographical incidence of needs will be symmetrical with the distribution of population. Where needs are measured in terms of the proportion of population eligible (i.e. formerly within a given client group), then needs reflect the distribution of the client group in the population. Where geographical criteria of needs such as sparsity, density of population, and costs of servicing population, are measured, then need will reflect these additional factors as well. Each of these components is used in assessing local authority needs for distribution of the Rate Support Grant in the UK, and separate indices of needs for total population, eligible population, density, and cost terms. As might be expected, considerable differences in the areal instance of needs result, depending upon the definition of need adopted (see chapter 13).

A number of recent analyses of fiscal distress measures of need for the US have been made, e.g. Aronson and King (undated), Bahl (1971), Adams (1977) and Bradbury (1978). In particular, Cuciti (1978) combines a large number of need indicators: using three groupings based on social, economic and fiscal criteria, she groups cities by size categories and regions. Social needs are most severe in the cities of the South, where poverty is the major problem. Large cities in the North-East and Mid-West, and some of the smaller North-East cities, also have severe social needs. Economic needs are concentrated in North-East cities which are characterized by absolute population decline, a large proportion of old housing, high densities, and low rates of income growth. Fiscal needs are more diffuse. Debt is high in the South, in the North-East, and in the large Mid-Western cities, whilst high tax effort and low liquidity are characteristic of the largest cities of all regions, especially those in the North-East. However, the impact of these fiscal needs differs by region: high tax effort and low level of debt in the South and West being partly the result of high rates of growth, whilst in the North-East and Mid-West the same fiscal pattern is the result of population decline and the high costs of urban renewal. Hence, when the dimensions of need are taken together, the concentration of US urban needs is in the North-East and Mid-West. This

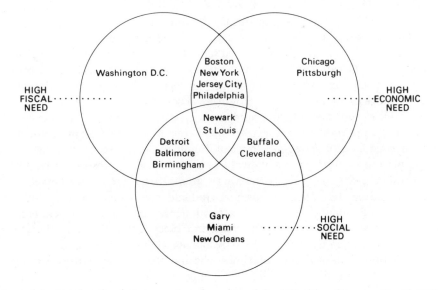

Figure 5.1 Overlapping between categories of need for US cities, (*Source*: Cuciti 1978.)

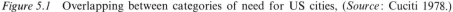

109

pattern of interrelated needs is displayed for the highest ranking cities on each indicator in figure 5.1.

The use of measures such as fiscal distress draws us back to the fundamentals of need assessment: the determination of the revenue requirements incurred in providing the given level of service to a particular individual or jurisdiction. Hence, where, on the one hand, there is high distress (low *per capita* expenditures, high tax rates, or both) there is a clearly defined revenue requirement, but an inability of the local level to satisfy that need. Where, on the other hand, there is a low level of distress (high *per capita* expenditure, low tax rate or both) there is a low level of revenue requirements, but a surplus of funds to meet that requirement. Need assessment leads, then, to a direct comparison of revenue requirements with distribution of both fiscal ability and expenditure benefits, to the inevitability of intergovernmental fiscal transfers between locations of low and high expenditure need, and hence to the issues discussed in the following chapters.

5.6 Conclusion

Expenditure need is a fundamental element in the allocation and distribution of public goods. In the absence of supply constraints and without the limitation of demand by price, need determines the degree to which the individual, collective and geographical wants of people and government units can be satisfied. Despite its importance, need assessment has until recently been little used in many governmental programmes. However, the use of need measures is becoming increasingly common. Examples of the use of such need indicators are discussed in chapter 13 for the cases of US Revenue-Sharing, AFDC, Medicaid and food stamps, UK Rate Support Grant and housing grants, and West German Equalization Grants.

The increasing use of need indicators has been stimulated by both the scientific design and needs-assessment schools of public finance: to determine a standard for rationalization of competing wants which can be uniformly applied. Such standards can then be stated in legislation and are not subject to arbitrary discretionary criteria. However, in some situations it may be more desirable to allow considerable administrative discretion in the determination of needs. Important cases arise when there are few or no reliable indicators of need available and in this case 'rules of thumb' and past precedent often take the place of statutory need indicators. Important examples in the case of individual needs are the discretionary grants for some higher education courses in the UK (especially for post-graduate, law, accountancy and other professional qualifications). For general needs discretion is often more common: especially in the case of general block grants (such as the UK Rate Support Grant), deployment of resources is left to the discretion of local jurisdictions within general guidelines. The aim, then, is to equalize the range of discretion available in different geographical locations. Within any government unit, however, it is a generally accepted principle that where the need permits legal or statutory definition, this is preferred to discretionary procedures, since the latter are more open to arbitrariness, personal prejudice, and political influences.

The increasing concern with fiscal requirements has concentrated attention on ways of measuring needs which are independent of the present distribution of government responsibilities and choices of particular qualities or quantities of service. At the individual level the unit cost approach based on the costs of providing similar standards of service to similar groups of people, taking into account the special characteristics of each jurisdiction, offers one possibility which is discussed further in the next chapter. At the jurisdictional level, the simultaneous estimation of local fiscal ability and local fiscal need offers a great deal of potential but has not yet been used. This requires the combination of Auten's consumption function for need assessment discussed in this chapter, with the methods of assessing fiscal ability to be discussed in chapters 7 and 8. As with each element of public finance, needs cannot be assessed in isolation from other elements. Needs, costs, abilities, and benefits are all intimately interrelated and final comments on need assessment must await the consideration of these other factors in the following chapters.

6

Service costs

> "For which of you, intending to build a tower,
> Sitteth not down first and counteth the cost,
> Whether he have sufficient to finish it?"
>
> Luke, **Xiv**, 28.

6.1 Introduction: unit costs and geographical costs

When the question, discussed in the previous chapter, of what constitutes needs, has been answered, the question of revenue requirements still remains open. The same needs and standards of service will usually require different levels of expenditure in different locations. Since both needs and costs vary geographically, a final assessment of revenue requirements requires some combination of the two.

The question of cost determination is, however, a complex one. Even if needs can be unambiguously determined, it is difficult to differentiate the degree to which differences in costs of servicing those needs in different jurisdictions results, on the one hand, from local preferences for higher cost services or inefficient organization, or on the other hand, derive from real differences in costs beyond the control of local jurisdictions. As in the case of need measurement, considerable attention has been directed at measuring variation in costs by analysing present expenditure patterns (see, for example, Boaden 1971; Brazer 1959; Davies 1971; Fisher 1961; Hirsch 1957; Maxwell 1969; Newton and Sharpe 1976; Nicholson and Topham 1971; Sacks 1961; Thring 1975; Wood 1961). But even if differences in needs, quantity, quality and preferences for services can be allowed for, it is still extremely difficult to separate cost components. Despite these difficulties, this chapter seeks to differentiate the various factors which create cost difference for public goods between jurisdictions. Two main approaches have evolved for tackling the costing problem: one based on unit costs, and a second based on geographical costs. The former corresponds to individual needs and the principle of territorial justice discussed in chapter 5, whilst the latter corresponds to the joint needs of any location which cannot be meaningfully expressed at the individual level.

THE UNIT COST APPROACH

This derives from need assessment at the individual level. The basic assumption is that similar individuals need similar standards of service

112

irrespective of where they live. But the same needs will have different costs in different locations so that final assessment of local needs as a revenue requirement must be a combination of need with their cost at a given level of quality, intensity or extensiveness. Hence, the unit cost approach defines needs as the solution of the following equation:

(revenue requirements) = (workload) × (price) × (scope and quality).
  (needs)

The workload is concerned with needs for a given population, eligible population, 'population at risk', or client group. The scope and quality factor determines the level of services and in what proportion they are provided to different members of the client group. Workload, scope and quality determine the overall needs discussed in chapter 5. The price element is the subject of this chapter and gives the final revenue requirement.

The unit cost approach requires measurement of each jurisdiction's inputs, outputs, number of clients, the ways in which factor inputs are translated to become service outputs, the level of quality and scope, and finally the costs. Clearly this approach is complex, requiring a great deal of quantitative information, and a detailed understanding of the economics of public service provision. It is these factors which have limited the application of the approach in practice since the quantitative information on client needs is seldom accurately available, the knowledge of costs is poor, and the extent of understanding of the relation of factor inputs to public service outputs is very limited. Moreover, for the small scale of local jurisdictions, the costs of assembling such information are extremely high, and at small scales the needs change very quickly.

GEOGRAPHICAL COSTS APPROACH

The motivation for this approach derives from both the practical difficulties of the unit cost approach, and the existence of distinct geographical components of costs independent of individual needs. The complexity of unit costing has led to the use of surrogates for costs such as inverse *per capita* incomes, city size, costs of living, or just total population levels. The usefulness of these surrogates is greatly enhanced by their relation to geographical costs. Because of the extent of jointness in many local public goods, their degree of externality, and indivisibility, they possess cost characteristics which do not admit meaningful disaggregation into individual unit costs. They exist instead as a result of a given geographical environment, economic structure, location, technical layout, or density and size. Despite these differences, however, geographical costs are clearly closely related to unit costs, and in practice the two approaches tend to merge together.

Geographical costs throw emphasis on jointly received local benefits resulting from the effect of four main factors: environmental, technical, locational and historical. The physical environment affects the costs of fuel, production, morbidity, flooding, weather damage, and so forth. Technical features of settlement size, layout, shape, density and age also have very significant cost effects. Finally, the locational features of the level of development, degree of urbanization, level of income, cost of housing, population change, and transport impedence again affect the cost of providing public goods. Historical factors affect costs through the legacy of past levels and patterns of development. They are those costs which are 'sunk' into the pre-existing infrastructure, housing, and human capital of any location and which affect the costs of subsequent development by providing renewal costs, maintenance costs, surplus capacity, social capital, and inherited debt.

The combined effect of these geographical factors generates cost variation which is specific to place, or to groups of people in a place, rather to individuals *qua* individuals. Moreover, these geographical costs raise a number of complex and contentious issues such as the degree to which the fiscal burdens of costly growth, or renewal in decline should be shared by wider populations than those presently resident in place; the degree to which cost burdens should be shared between present and future generations; and the degree to which in-place benefits of social capital should be maintained, rehabilitated, or moved to new locations.

Despite their jointness, the impact of geographical costs can still be represented by workload, price and quality factors, as with the unit cost approach, but now these characteristics reflect the nature of locations as a whole rather than client groups. What is required is an accounting matrix of the form discussed in chapter 4, expressing the revenue requirements of needs displayed in terms of costs. For each jurisdiction such a table will have the form shown in table 6.1, giving the total revenue requirements of each jurisdiction. There are three main approaches to determining the cost elements in this table:

(i) *expert opinion*: as in need assessment, to give the costs of servicing given workloads;

(ii) *cost indicators*: either individual or composite indicators, e.g. density, shape, size and other objectively measurable variables;

(iii) *Statistical cross-section studies*: based on either single or multiple services and using either the consumption function or production function approaches.

Hence cost assessment can be based on the same simultaneous equation assessment used for needs: controlling for differences in service quality and quantity of inputs, and especially of income capacity, whilst estimating the specific local factors contributing to cost variation. Towards this end the following sections of this chapter deal with the respective environmental, technical, locational, and 'sunk' factors that contribute to geographical cost variation in the supply of public goods.

Table 6.1 Calculation of revenue requirements for any jurisdiction *i* using estimates of client population, costs, scope and quality

Expenditure programme	Client group	Client population (workload)	Cost or price per client in jurisdiction *i*	Scope and quality of service in jurisdiction *i*	Total revenue requirement
Education	{ Elementary Secondary Higher	·	·	·	·
Health and hospitals	{ ages 0–4 5–14 15–24 25–44 45–64 > 64	·	·	·	·
Welfare assistance	{ Old age Medical Disabled Blind Family supplements Unemployment	·	·	·	·
Special locational services		·	·	·	·
Transport and highways		·	·	·	·
Capital repayments		·	·	·	·
Total revenue requirements over all programmes		·	·	·	·

6.2 Environmental costs

Most social scientists have tended to ignore the effect of the physical environment from their consideration of economic relationships and public goods. We might not agree with the extreme views of Huntingdon (1945) or Mills (1942) that the whole pattern of human history derives from environmental controls, especially those of climate, but certainly there are important and often dominant effects of the environment on both the possibilities and especially the costs of different human activities. Moreover, these effects often have their chief impact on the public rather than the private economy. These impacts range from the effects of extreme natural events, through recurrent and often fairly minor impacts on production costs, to effects on health, morbidity and living habits. They have impacts on the public economy both through their influence on the costs of factor inputs, and in their influence in creating new needs for public goods. New need creation may be in the form of compensation for extreme disasters, flood or famine as relief aid, or may be in the form of continuous maintenance of services for weather forecasting, pollution control, and environmental modifications.

The influence of climate on public costs is well summarized by Taylor (1970) and Maunder (1970). Climate has an important influence in controlling the level of economic activity and industrial development in a region. This affects the level of *per capita* incomes and income produced, and hence both the local ability to pay for public goods, and the costs of providing them. It determines the level of agricultural production, and has important influences on the costs of production in the fishing, manufacturing, construction, transport, sport, recreation and power utility industries. One of the most important of these production costs is that associated with control of temperature and humidity through heating and air conditioning. Roads and transport facilities are other public goods which are particularly sensitive to climatic effects on costs. Road surface maintenance and snow clearance costs, for example, were found by Adams (1965) to be the major cause of different levels of local expenditures on street maintenance (see table 5.3). The influence of climate on health, disease, morbidity, and insect infestation, also has important impacts on health care and social service costs, and these in turn may affect residential choice and hence produce disparities in local and regional levels of *per capita* incomes and income produced. For example, the combined effects of living environment and health has had important influences on the growth of retirement centres such as Florida, Southern France, South Portugal, or the English South Coast, which again has important impacts on the public economy through its effect on geographical differences in need for care for the aged.

Extreme natural events such as hurricanes, tornadoes, lightning, blizzards, hail, fog, floods, and drought also have significant effects both on the indirect costs of factor inputs, especially through the insurance industry, and directly on the public fisc through the payment of disaster relief. Table 6.2 gives the estimated range of insured property losses from a number of these extreme events in the United States in the mid 1960s. In each case the total costs are high, and much of this is borne by federal aid subsequent to the designation of Disaster Areas. Attempts at climatic control and modification to alleviate disasters is also a further public cost. For example, hurricane reconnaissance and protection measures cost $9.55 million in the United States and Canada in 1964 (Sugg 1967), and weather forecasting represents a more continuous and long-term commitment. Most of these finances are borne at national level. Indeed it is an important function of public finance that the costs of disasters are shared over the widest possible population, rather than being a burden on the local population involved. Some climatic effects are locally borne, however, and where these involve the spillover of goods or bads on to other

Table 6.2 The costs of extreme natural events in the US and Canada. (*Sources:* Hendrick and Friedman 1966; Maunder 1970)

Event	Range of annual insured property losses and other costs ($m)
Hurricanes	250–500
Tornadoes	100–200
Hail, thunderstorm and wind damage	125–250
Extra-tropical windstorms	25–50
Lightning	11–19

areas, there may be important intergovernmental implications. For example, the costs of pollution control are often borne locally, but the benefits spillover to other areas. Similarly, flood control may produce benefits for some jurisdictions or, as in the case of the Thames Barrage at Woolwich, may be a disbenefit spillover by producing increased flood hazards elsewhere.

The influence of natural resources also has important impacts on public cost. Their existence or non-existence locally has the effect of making cheaper or more expensive the factor inputs to both the public and private sector, and also influences the local income produced and balance of payments with other regions (see chapter 14). Moreover, a cleverly designed mix of local taxes on natural resource products, or on localized industry, can be extremely effective in exporting the burdens of taxation away from local taxpayers onto the national market (see chapter 8). For example, the advantages of climate and natural resources, combined with the technological innovation of air conditioning, have been substantially responsible for the rapid recent growth of the 'sunbelt' States of the United States. Additionally, it is claimed by North-Eastern lobbies, that these states have also been successful in shifting a substantial burden of their taxes elsewhere by the extensive use of severance tax on oil and natural gas production (especially important for Texas and Louisiana). Natural resource endowments also affect the costs and availability of materials in the construction industry. For example, the shortage of building aggregates in South-East England is likely to necessitate expensive transport from the Mendips and Wales, plus substantial investment in new railway terminal facilities (DSPSE 1976), as discussed in the next section.

6.3 Technical factors and costs

A range of technical factors affects the cost of public good provision. These range from engineering components, through the density, shape, productivity, and layout of settlements, to the influence of economies and diseconomies of scale.

117

DENSITY

The relationship between density and cost is well-established: the costs of capital installation, maintenance, and running costs are usually much lower with all services that require extensive land assembly, or where a substantial distribution network is needed; for example water, electricity, gas, sewerage, and roads (Downing 1969a, b; Harvard Regional Planning Department 1955; Isard and Coughlin 1957; Jones 1969; Ludlow 1953; Real Estate Research Corporation 1974; Stone 1970; Thring 1975). Figure 6.1, for example, shows the effect of density on the decline in distribution cost per head for these

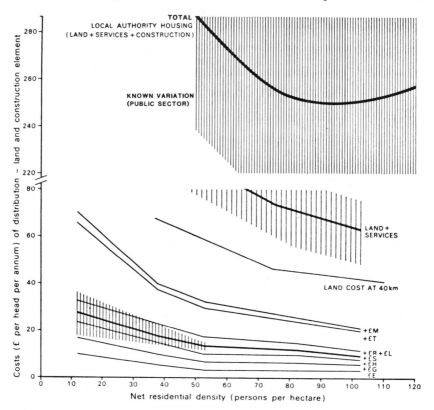

Figure 6.1 Variation in distribution costs associated with various densities of development. (*Source*: DSPSE 1976.)

 £M = postal deliveries
 £L = telephone costs
 £T = public heating costs
 £R = refuse disposal costs
 £E = electricity
 £G = gas
 £S = sewerage

Shaded areas show the range of presently available estimates.

services in the UK. The reduction in costs with rising density is greatest in absolute terms for postal, telephone, public heating, and the costs of land assembly, but the greatest percentage reduction of the costs is obtained from water, sewerage, and gas services, although the effect of density economies begins to decline after about 50 to 70 persons per hectare.

The cost savings of high population densities have led to highly contentious conclusions as to the relative merits of concentrated urban development as opposed to dispersed suburban expansion, especially of the suburban 'sprawl' in isolated developments (leap-frogging, or sprawl-and-skip suburbs) so characteristic in the United States. The Real Estate Research Corporation (1974) for example, made detailed costing analysis of six types of neighbourhood development patterns and six types of community development patterns derived from mixtures of the six neighbourhood types typical of high standard, new suburban construction. The main conclusions of this study are that unplanned 'sprawl' is the most expensive form of residential development in terms of economic costs, environmental costs, natural resource consumption, and many personal costs (such as travel time, accident rates, and aesthetic features of development). But the alternative of high densities has significant impacts on overall personal costs by inducing alienation, as now recognized with high-rise apartments. Hence, the short-term economic savings may often be far outweighed by the longer term increases in crime, personal isolation, and alienation. The Real Estate Research Corporation study is based on hypothetical settlement patterns. Other studies based on real cities have disputed the importance of density components. For example, Brazer (1959), Bahl (1971), Hirsch (1970) and Hufbauer and Severn (1975), find relatively little evidence to support density as an important influence on costs in comparison with other components. Hufbauer and Severn suggest that this is due to the inclusion of much undeveloped land not needing services in low density cities, and the requirements for duplication of service lines in high density cities. Moreover high densities lead to very expensive forms of special buildings. For example, an elevated shopping area in a high-density development costs about five times as much as a ground level shopping area in a low-density development (Stone 1973). Similarly, elevated freeway, cut-and-cover motorways, and bored tunnels, cost respectively, 8 to 9, 15 and 50 times the cost of a normal ground level road (Stone 1970b). Again, high densities impose greater costs in use, Stone (1970a) noting that high-rise housing is 50% more costly than separate housing units, and a seven-storey factory is 25% more costly than a single-floor one. Again, Stone (1973) suggests that a 25% increase in density reduces road development costs by only 2% and journey costs by only 4%. Hence, on cost grounds alone, the evidence for the high costs of suburban development as opposed to that in central cities is far from conclusive.

SHAPE

The influence of community shape and layout has also been used to account

119

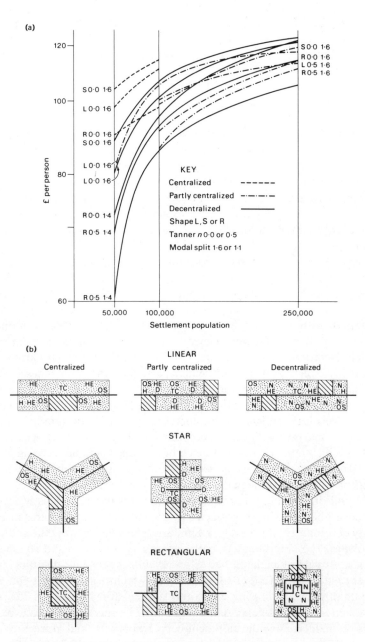

Figure 6.2 Costs for various settlement shapes and layouts. (*Source:* Stone 1973.) HE higher education; OS open space; H hospital; D district; N neighbourhood; TC town centre; industry shaded; residences stippled.

    a Travel costs for different distance exponents

    b Different road systems.

120

for differences in public service costs. This feature is obviously related to density as discussed above, and is certainly an element in the cost differences found in the Real Estate Research Corporation study quoted. But there are additional components which suggests that in some situations a relatively long and narrow settlement form is the most cost-efficient, whilst in other situations a relatively circular and compact shape may be better. The linear form draws on economies in the cost of distribution of services such as electricity, water and power which can be most cheaply distributed along a central major supply line, with short, less important, feeders branching off this. The more compact form is more efficient for services requiring extensive movement and ready access over a wide area, as with street cleaning, fire and police protection, and access to central facilities where the consumer bears the costs of travel (as is the case of education and hospitals). These two different shape features are brought out well in Barlow's (1978) study of jurisdictions in the Montreal Metropolitan area. Jurisdictions with compact shapes have low fire and police protection costs, but high public works and administrative costs. These results are also confirmed in Stone's (1970a, b, 1973b) studies of the sum of travel-to-work and road construction costs. For the various hypothetical settlement shapes shown in figure 6.2b costs are significantly lower for linear and rectangular settlements than for more compact star forms (figure 6.2a). Costs are also lower for decentralized as opposed to centralized forms.

PRODUCTIVITY

This concerns the relative efficiency with which public services are provided in different jurisdictions. Productivity should differ as a result of technical factors such as community size, reflecting economies of scale and density. But in addition to technical factors, there are differences which result from the different degrees of effectiveness with which jurisdictions combine factor inputs to produce a given level or quality of public service outputs. This results partly from differences in incentives for governments to be more efficient through local political pressures as discussed in chapter 15 (see Ross and Burkhead 1974). For example, in the UK, Liverpool City Council with a slim electoral majority has been far more effective in keeping down the costs of public goods under Liberal Party control than under previous councils and in comparison with national trends. Productivity differences also derive from differences in preferences for service organization, more extensive public participation being more expensive, different choices of capital and current finance shifting the cost burdens between generations, and so forth. Some of these differences will, of course, reflect patterns as to particular service quality. Again, productivity also differs through bad organization. Often simple procedures for re-routing refuse collection or school buses, re-scheduling police, fire and other manpower shifts, streamlining training and adminis- trative procedures, can produce considerable savings in cost (Garland and Weddle 1974; Reischaeur 1974). For example, a study by the Comptroller

General of the United States (1972) estimates considerable savings in hospital service costs by adopting convenience foods, unit dose pharmacy, compacted forms of waste disposal, and contract laundry services. Groves (1964) suggests that the likelihood of inefficiency and inappropriate organization increases with the size of government: unnecessary procedures proliferate, delays increase, and co-ordination breaks down the larger the size of the government unit. However, normal cost–efficiency criteria cannot be applied to the public sector in every respect since sometimes inefficiency is produced by compromising quality to political expedience, and in other cases the public service has a social as well as an economic function. Thus Reischauer (1974) notes that the high wages paid to New York City sanitation and other workers can, in part, be evaluated against the level of the refuse service available, but also must be evaluated against criteria such as income maintenance for the labour force, and as an example set to the private sector.

ECONOMIES OF SCALE

The degree to which the provision of public goods attains economies of scale varies with the good considered, but is a contentious question (Richardson 1973, Cameron *et al.* 1973, give reviews of the literature). Hirsch (1959) found that economies of scale are important in reducing administrative costs up to 50 to 100,000 population, and for water and sewerage there was no diseconomy limit to the extent of such economies. However, he detected no economies of scale for police, fire, education, or refuse disposal. Similarly no economies of scale were found for police by Schmandt (1961), for garbage collection by Hirsch (1965) or education by Kiesling (1966), Dawson (1972) and Thring (1976). Indeed, personal services display the least effects of economies of scale while construction and utilities show the greatest effects. Thus economies of scale are usually accepted in gas, water and electricity, sewerage, transport and telephone services, and in construction (Isard and Coughlin 1957; Johnston 1960; Lomax 1951; Nerlove 1961; Thring 1975).

Hirsch (1970) accounts for these differences by distinguishing scale economies in horizontally and vertically integrated services. In the former, many studies have shown that average cost curves are U-shaped with diseconomies setting in at between 100 and 300, 000 population, but for the latter, vertical integration, average cost curves are steadily declining. The distinction between horizontal and vertical integration depends on the type of service: horizontal integration allowing only co-ordination of different units, as in schooling, police and fire protection, refuse collection and hospitals, for which administration costs increase rapidly with large numbers of units; whilst vertical integration allows internal economies of scale to be obtained within one plant, as in electricity, gas, sewerage and water supply, such that no diseconomies of scale occur.

On the basis of the vertical integration economies, some writers have concluded that a jurisdiction can never be so large that the marginal external diseconomies outweigh the marginal economies. For example, Barwent (1968) suggests that all evidence points in the direction that as city sizes increase, *per capita* incomes, manufacture input activity, wholesale trade, and most other economic measures, all rise without apparent limit. Indeed, Hirsch (1965) claims that no study to date shows that the social costs of urban areas outweigh the benefits accruing to society; nor is there any reason to claim *a priori* that urban sprawl or balance is socially desirable or undesirable. However, as Hansen (1970) points out, such arguments are generally based only on considerations of private cost and benefits, where the economies tend to become internalized but the diseconomies tend to be placed external to the firm on the local public economy. Traffic congestion and improvements to transport infrastructure, air pollution and its control, urban renewal and housing, provision of open space and recreation facilities, are all external effects to firms in large cities which put increasing fiscal burdens on the city governments. Taking these and other factors into account, most analysts argue that economies of scale obtain only up to a certain level after which diseconomies set in (see, for example, Svimez, 1967; Stone, 1973 Townsend, 1960). These latter authors produce European results which show that economies of scale are exhausted, even for vertically integrated services, for cities exceeding 50,000 in population, and after that level diseconomies lead to increases in unit costs. The combined effects of economies of scale offset by diseconomies at large scales of production gives a familiar U-shaped cost curve. Such cost curves were found by the Royal Commission on Local Government (1968) to characterize hospital services, housing management in urban areas, and bus systems (see figure 6.3). These results are supported for total expenditures on all city services in United States cities over 50,000 population, for which Muller (1976) gives the results shown in table 6.3. From this it can be seen that city expenditures rise with city size, and have increased

Table 6.3 Variation of per capita expenditure and debt with city size in the US 1965–1973. (*Source:* Muller 1976, table 5)

City population	$ *per capita expenditure all services*		% change 1965–1973	Per capita interest on debt		% change 1965–1973
	1964–5	1972–3		1964–5	1972–3	
1 million	117	281	140	11	33	200
500,000–1m	96	233	143	7	16	129
300–500,000	76	176	132	6	18	200
200–300,000	78	180	131	6	15	150
100–200,000	77	159	106	5	12	140
50–100,000	77	135	75	4	9	125
50,000	53	100	89	3	7	133
Total	72	155	115	5	13	160

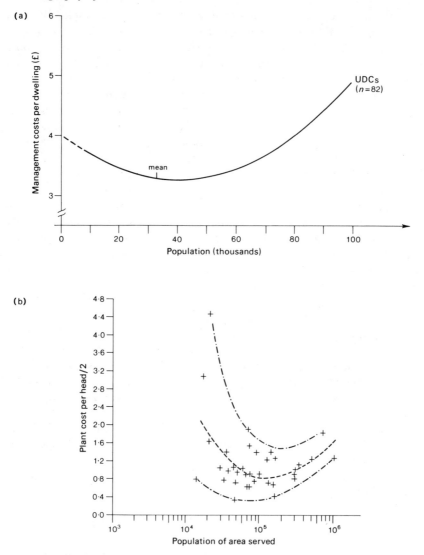

Figure 6.3 Variations in the costs of
 a management of public housing in urban district councils, and
 b central plant and equipment from bus systems in UK.
(*Source*: Thring 1975.)

in recent years. In addition, the table also shows that it is the larger cities that
have the highest level of debt, and have the highest rate of increase in debt.
There is an important interplay between city size and the quality of services.
As city sizes rise, so do expenditures, but so also does the range and quality of
services available. But even with this factor taken into account most analysts

now agree that diseconomies lead to greatly increased costs by the level of about 300,000 population, if not before.

OPTIMAL COMMUNITY SIZE

The interrelationship of density, shape, and diseconomies of scale, has led some analysts to suggest that there is an optimum community size. This has

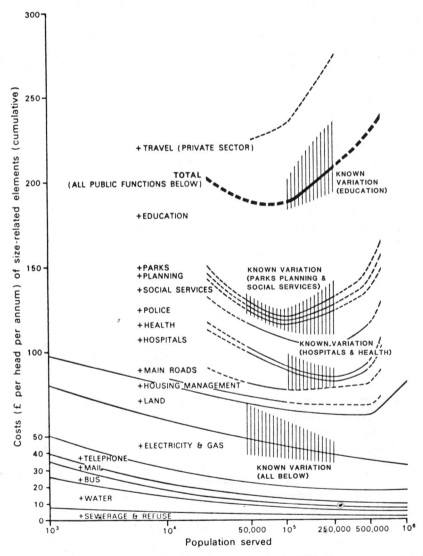

Figure 6.4 Aggregate economies of settlement size in the UK. Costs are cumulated with shaded areas showing the range of variation from the average. (*Source*: DSPSE 1976.)

125

stimulated, as we shall see in chapter 11, arguments for the amalgamation of small jurisdictions, and has underlain the reorganization of local government in the United Kingdom. For example, DSPSE (1976, Annex 7) and Stone (1970, 1973a) have produced a general model for the economies of urban size based on a synthesis of the existing literature for the British case. The cost estimates for various services based on this model, shown in figure 6.4, demonstrate the different scale economies of vertically integrated services for which economies of scale are largely undiminishing, and for horizontally integrated services for which U-shaped cost curves result. From the point of view of economies of scale this and other studies suggest that an optimum community size would appear to lie somewhere between 50,000 and 300,000 population.

Other criteria also point to some optimum community size. For example, there are considerable grounds for believing that whilst the costs resulting from internalizing the external costs of decision-making increase as group size increases, administrative and participation costs increase with group size indicating an optimum cut-off size of group for making collective decisions. This has underlain concepts of optimal governments and constitutions suggested by Buchanan and Tullock (1969) and is discussed further in chapter 11. A further stimulus to seek an optimum community size is provided by fiscal effects. With increases in jurisdictional size, a wider variety of revenue sources becomes available (such as local income tax). It then becomes easier to raise loans, minority services become more viable as service thresholds are crossed, and since larger units enclose a wider variety of groups of incomes, it is possible to implement a wider range of policies aimed at equalization and redistribution. However, the scope for implementing new revenue sources, expenditures, or equalization is limited by the constraints on participation, with excessively larger units becoming divorced and alienated from the local electorate and unable to command group solidarity or any sense of local community. This then leads, as discussed in later chapters, to extensive resistance both to paying taxes, and to policies aimed at redistribution to social groups or locations which have no apparent relevance to those who have to bear the greater burdens.

From this discussion one thing is certain, that whilst there may be an optimum community for any service or any one community, there is no general optimum size for all services in all communities, since the economies of administration, distribution, economic activity, and personal contacts differ widely for different functions and different areas dependent on the different environments, divergent patterns of historical development and settlement, and differences in the range of local preferences for services. Hence, to search for an optimum community size for a country as a whole, as intended in the UK reorganization of local government in 1974, may be somewhat misguided and inefficient.

6.4 Location costs

Apart from the influence of size, density, shape, and other attributes of specific settlements, other components of costs for public and private goods vary spatially. Such location costs concern three components of variation in the overheads of providing public goods: on-site costs, assembly costs, and distribution costs. First, the on-site costs of producing a good or providing a service vary as a result of environmental factors, especially construction costs, and interplay between the public and private sectors in competition for various factors of production reflected in variable labour costs, costs of living and in the extent of non-public service provision. On-site costs also vary as a result of the public finance decisions within each jurisdiction since different policies of apportioning taxation, charges and benefits critically affect the costs of production and the level of demand. A second cause of variation in the overheads of public good provision is the variable costs of assembling the factors required to produce a given good. Since most public services are labour-intensive, assembly costs are often less significant for the public than for the private sector, but do have important impacts on the location of utilities for which bulky raw materials must be transported. More significant effects of transport costs are reflected in a third cause of variation in the overhead costs of providing public goods that of the variable costs of distributing the final good or service. Unlike the private sector, the costs of distributing a large number of products in the public sector are borne by the producer, although they are passed on through taxation and charges. For example, water supply, sewerage, police, fire, ambulance, refuse collection and disposal, street lighting, day-care places, and school transportation costs, are frequently all borne in the first instance by the producers.

The costs of assembling factors of production in the private industrial sector are emphasized in Weber's (1909) theory of industrial location, subsequently extended and generalized by Isard (1956) and others. The relative importance of each factor of production, expressed through its transport costs, suggests that the final location of a firm is determined as that point at which the transportation costs of all inputs are minimized. Particularly important are the differential costs of labour, land, and raw materials, the availability of transport facilities, and closeness to markets. For the individual, a similarly large body of theory attempts to account for residential location in terms of the costs of travel and access to the supply of public and private goods and services, the costs of land and housing, and the costs of other goods (Alonso 1964; Lösch 1941; Richardson 1969). As with the individual and industrial sectors, so with the public sector, costs of public service provision vary significantly over space. Local characteristics, the costs of land, labour costs, the cost of living, and the distance away from the source of supply are all important factors and are discussed in turn below. A further component, the geographical variation in costs of capital, is discussed in chapter 10.

LOCAL CHARACTERISTICS

These are especially important in construction costs and often reflect particular environmental effects which require more or less costly styles of building, heating or air conditioning, different forms of foundations, different forms of road surfacing, and investment in particular equipment (snow clearing, flood control, special fire fighting, etc.). For public housing construction costs in South-East England, table 6.4 displays the percentage cost increase above the national yardstick which is allowed in various locations dependent upon the design, building materials, and form of foundations required. Rehabilitation schemes are more costly in central London and decrease outward, usually because of the high cost of land assembly and conversion; but new schemes do not vary a great deal in costs

Table 6.4 Percentage costs above national level yardstick for housing construction and renewal costs. Data for South-East England. (*Source:* DSPSE 1976)

Type of scheme	% above yardstick				
	Inner London	Outer London	London periphery	Outer South-East	South-East (all)
Redevelopment schemes					
Special foundations	0.2	1.9	2.2	0.4	1.5
Special materials	—	—	0.3	—	0.1
Special design	0.3	0.8	3.5	0.0	1.1
Redevelopment allowance	4.9	4.1	1.5	4.1	3.8
Total	5.4	6.8	7.5	4.5	6.5
Non-redevelopment schemes					
Special foundations	12.6	3.5	2.0	2.4	3.5
Special materials	1.4	1.0	0.3	0.6	0.6
Special design	2.1	2.4	2.8	0.9	2.2
Total	16.1	6.9	5.1	3.9	6.3
Average	9.3	5.7	7.2	5.0	
All schemes					
Special foundations	6.5	2.3	2.0	2.2	2.8
Special materials	0.7	0.3	0.3	0.6	0.4
Special design	1.2	1.3	2.9	0.8	1.8
Redevelopment allowance	2.4	2.9	0.2	0.4	1.3
Total	10.8	6.8	5.4	4.0	6.3
All schemes average	7.2	5.5	4.6	3.4	

with location. In a study of health facility construction costs by the Comptroller General of the United States (1972) it was found that costs varied as a result of geographical differences in the type and size of facility needed, type of materials used, wage rates, and equipment installed. For example, hospital construction cost per square foot in 1970 varied from $28 in Mississippi, to $78 in the Far West, and cost per bed varied from $14,000 in Mississippi, to $72,000 in the Far West.

THE COST OF LAND AND LABOUR

These both vary as a result of competition between demands in the private and in the public sectors, and as a result of institutional decisions on investment and sale of land by pension funds, insurance companies and loan institutions. Both cost components are significant for public service provision since many public services are land and labour intensive. For example, water supply, infrastructure, hospitals, schools, public housing, parks and recreation areas all make considerable demands for land. Again, police, fire, health-care, personal social services, education, street cleaning, and many other services are highly labour-intensive. Hence variation in local government salaries is

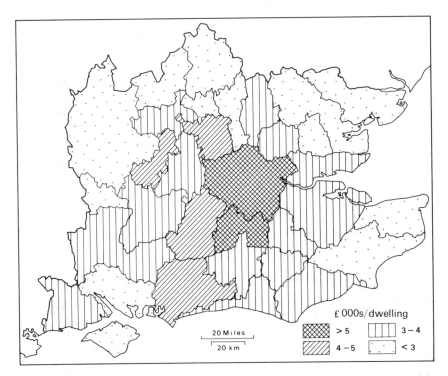

Figure 6.5 Variation in land prices (£000s per dwelling) in South-East England in 1975/6. (*Source*: DSPSE 1976.)

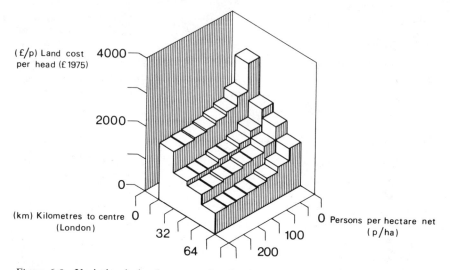

Figure 6.6 Variation in land costs per head, taking account of density and distance from London. (*Source*: Stone 1970.)

often an important determinant of cost differences (Schnenner 1973). Even in the UK, where salary scales are agreed on a national basis, rates of promotion and appointment level within the salary scale can often be significant in changing labour costs geographically. In both the case of land and of labour costs, the public sector must compete with non-public demands. As a result of the dominance of public services by high land and labour costs the rise in production costs in this sector has been extremely rapid in recent years. Figure 6.5 shows the variation in land prices per dwelling in South-East England in 1975. This map is confused by variation in occupancy, plot size and density effects, but displays the clear dominance of higher land costs in London and in the sector south and west of London. Taking both density and distance from London into account, figure 6.6 shows the clear relationship of land cost per head with distance from London.

COSTS OF LIVING

Costs of living reflect the overall effect of demand in all sectors of the economy in a given area. Costs of living vary significantly in different geographical areas and are most important in their impact on public finance for income supplements, transfer payments and unemployment and other personal benefits. Hence, such benefits frequently take into account variable rents and mortgages; but less frequently are the variable costs of private goods such as food and clothes taken into account. Assessment of the variation in costs of living has considerable definitional problems. Geographical differences in prices of public and private goods might be assessed by costing a fixed 'market basket' of goods and services in different areas, but if tastes and preferences

130

also vary spatially, the market basket will be inappropriate, and some components of price differences will quite legitimately reflect differences in demand for different goods. Moreover, needs vary, as we have seen in chapter 5, with climate, and the economies and diseconomies of sparse population. This effects the costs of heating, housing, transportation, and food, especially between farming and non-farming areas. Table 6.5 gives an index of comparative costs of living in 44 US urban areas for a low income family of four in 1974, with adjustments to the market basket in line with consumption patterns. Apart from the two exceptional cases of Honoloulu and Anchorage, the range of variation in living costs is relatively small: from 88 to 108 for total budget; 89 to 112 for food; 84 to 123 for transport; and 84 to 122 for medical care (where the United States average equals 100). There are, however, major differences in transportation costs between metropolitan and non-metropolitan areas, and in personal income taxes (this latter ranging from 66 to 131). If differences in consumption patterns are no longer taken into account (i.e. a standard market basket is used) and differences in climate and availability of transport are ignored, the range of variation is somewhat reduced. Eliminating each of these factors, as shown in table 6.6, results in total consumption being reduced to a range of only 91 to 113. Comparison of tables 6.5 and 6.6 reveals the important fact that, for the US, the differences which arise from geographical effects are less than differences in the budget level between areas.

DISTANCE FROM SOURCE OF SUPPLY

The component of distance, as reflected in the transport cost of assembly factors of production, or distribution costs of a good or service, is the basis of the location theories of Weber, Lösch and Isard. Where the costs of factor assembly or service distribution are borne by the public producer these costs are passed on in taxation or user charges, and the incidence of costs then depends on the incidence of tax burdens in the economy as a whole. Some locations, usually the areas of greater remoteness or with difficult terrain or climate, are extremely costly relative to others: for example, water supply in Los Angeles, power generation in the North-Eastern United States, or rural service provision in the Prairies, Scotland, or Southern Italy. For example, the costs of school busing vary considerably as a function of the type of location. As shown in table 6.7, for school busing in the UK, these costs are smallest in large conurbations and largest in rural areas. However, when the costs of service distribution are borne by the consumer of public goods, the effect of transport costs is the same in the public as in the private sector: an increase in the level of price gives a decrease in the level of demand, with distance from point of supply. This tapering of benefits and costs, together with the suggestion of Tiebout (1961) for a spatial tapering of taxation to reflect benefit tapering, is discussed further in chapter 9. However, it is clear that it is not possible to provide the same level of service to everyone, everywhere,

131

Table 6.5 Indexes of comparative costs for 44 US urban areas in 1974. Based on a low income, four-person family, with US average cost = 100. (*Sources*: US Bureau of Labour Statistics, *Monthly Labour Review* (June 1975); US Department of Health, Education and Welfare 1976)

Area	Total budget	Total consumption	Food		Housing		Transportation		Cloth-ing	Personal care	Medical care	Other family consumption	Personal income taxes
			Total	Food at home	Total	Renter	Total	Automobile owners					
Urban United States	100	100	100	100	100	100	100	100	100	100	100	100	100
Metropolitan areas	101	101	101	101	101	102	95	103	101	103	103	104	103
Nonmetropolitan areas	94	95	94	96	93	89	123	92	94	87	87	81	87
Northeast													
Boston, Mass	108	106	104	105	119	125	97	118	98	101	96	106	131
Buffalo, N.Y.	101	101	101	101	99	97	104	106	111	101	88	106	106
Hartford, Conn	107	108	105	105	119	125	102	105	107	121	96	112	96
Lancaster, Pa	100	98	102	103	98	100	93	94	103	96	85	92	116
New York-Northeastern, N.J.	107	106	112	111	104	105	84	107	100	101	110	114	118
Philadelphia, Pa.N.J.	103	100	108	107	91	90	91	111	95	100	101	105	128
Pittsburgh, Pa	97	96	101	100	89	87	95	95	95	101	87	101	109
Portland, Maine	103	104	102	102	115	117	94	97	101	100	95	108	94
Nonmetropolitan areas	98	98	100	102	96	96	126	95	95	82	89	81	99
North Central													
Cedar Rapids, Iowa	96	95	91	90	99	100	86	89	111	106	88	101	105
Champaign-Urbana, Ill	103	103	98	99	114	119	91	94	115	99	98	99	106
Chicago, Ill-Northwestern Ind.	104	104	103	104	107	110	101	120	100	108	105	108	107
Cincinnati, Ohio-Ky.-Ind	94	95	102	103	85	84	91	95	99	95	87	104	91
Cleveland, Ohio	99	100	100	97	94	93	104	102	106	119	98	105	94

Dayton, Ohio	95	96	101	102	90	87	92	93	99	98	88	108	86
Detroit, Mich	99	99	103	102	90	91	98	99	101	108	103	104	101
Green Bay, Wis	96	95	91	92	99	97	89	93	107	104	84	98	112
Indianapolis, Ind	98	99	97	98	97	98	102	101	97	101	102	107	94
Kansas City, Mo.-Kans	98	99	102	102	90	89	101	99	101	112	97	102	97
Milwaukee, Wis	101	99	94	94	104	107	97	94	106	106	94	103	122
Minneapolis-St. Paul, Minn	102	99	98	98	98	99	94	97	109	107	93	104	128
St. Louis, Mo.-Ill	96	97	102	103	90	89	101	105	94	105	88	99	93
Wichita, Kans	95	96	97	97	95	94	93	95	99	104	95	101	88
Nonmetropolitan areas	97	97	95	98	100	100	120	90	99	89	83	83	96

South

Atlanta, Ga	94	95	96	96	92	89	92	94	96	104	95	100	80
Austin, Tex	88	91	89	88	83	77	93	97	100	102	95	102	66
Baltimore, Md	103	100	95	94	107	108	97	100	97	101	110	101	128
Baton Rouge, La	90	93	96	97	84	78	92	96	96	104	87	103	71
Dallas, Tex	91	94	90	87	87	84	96	98	93	103	114	104	71
Durham, N.C.	97	97	94	95	99	98	87	92	93	107	106	103	102
Houston, Tex	92	95	95	93	86	80	96	96	94	106	105	99	73
Nashville, Tenn	91	94	91	91	93	88	93	95	103	98	89	104	71
Orlando, Fla	96	98	91	90	110	113	94	95	90	91	106	103	78
Washington, D.C.-Md-Va	106	104	102	101	115	120	99	102	93	96	104	107	123
Nonmetropolitan areas	89	91	91	92	87	78	121	91	89	87	86	81	74

West

Bakersfield, Calif	95	96	94	94	92	91	97	102	97	102	110	91	74
Denver, Colo	97	98	98	98	91	87	95	97	117	98	94	98	97
Los Angeles-Long Beach, Calif	104	104	98	97	109	114	103	107	104	98	122	96	91
San Diego, Calif	101	102	97	95	103	107	102	106	106	99	118	95	87
San Francisco-Oakland, Calif	108	108	102	102	120	127	103	110	112	112	111	103	101
Seattle-Everett, Wash	105	107	104	104	113	115	99	104	113	106	106	103	92
Honolulu, Hawaii	124	120	120	124	143	153	108	115	101	113	105	106	160
Nonmetropolitan areas	98	98	95	97	101	98	124	93	105	91	91	79	100

Anchorage, Alaska	149	143	122	127	189	209	159	119	122	123	157	100	202

133

Table 6.6 Indexes of comparative costs for 44 US urban areas in 1974 taking account of differences in consumption patterns of standard 'market basket' and differences in climate. Index 1 takes account of different local tax requirements excluded from Table 6.5. Index 2 includes effect of personal income tax and social security. Index 3 removes region, transport and city size effects (i.e. gives average climate and price levels). Index 4 is same as 3 but excludes climatic costs. (*Sources:* US Bureau of Labor Statistics, *Monthly Labor Review* (June 1975); US Department of Health, Education and Welfare HEW 1976)

Area	Family budget indexes	Fixed weight indexes		
	Index 1 — Total costs (including income and social security taxes)	Index 2 — Consumption costs	Index 3 — Consumption costs adjusted for climate	Index 4 — Consumption costs not adjusted for climate
US urban average costs	$14,333	$10,781	$10,880	$10,915
Urban United States	100	100	100	100
Metropolitan areas	102	102	102	102
Nonmetropolitan areas	90	91	92	92
Northeast				
Boston, Mass	117	114	113	113
Buffalo, N.Y.	107	105	103	102
Hartford, Conn	108	111	109	109
Lancaster, Pa	99	98	95	95
New York-Northeastern N.J.	116	114	113	113
Philadelphia, Pa-N.J.	103	101	100	100
Pittsburgh, Pa	97	96	94	94
Portland, Maine	103	104	101	102
Nonmetropolitan areas	99	99	97	98
Minneapolis-St. Paul, Minn	104	98	98	97
St. Louis, Mo.-Ill	97	97	97	96
Wichita, Kans	93	94	93	94
Nonmetropolitan areas	92	92	93	92
South				
Atlanta, Ga	91	93	94	95
Austin, Tex	86	90	91	92
Baltimore, Md	100	97	99	99
Baton Rouge, La	90	93	95	95
Dallas, Tex	90	93	95	95
Durham, N.C.	97	96	98	98
Houston, Tex	90	93	94	95
Nashville, Tenn	91	94	95	95
Orlando, Fla	89	92	94	97
Washington, D.C.-Md-Va	105	103	102	102
Nonmetropolitan areas	86	88	90	90

North Central

Cedar Rapids, Iowa	98	97	96	95
Champaign-Urbana, Ill	102	102	102	101
Chicago, Ill-Northwestern Ind	103	104	104	104
Cincinnati, Ohio-Ky-Ind	96	97	96	95
Cleveland, Ohio	102	103	103	102
Dayton, Ohio	93	95	94	94
Detroit, Mich	100	101	101	101
Green Bay, Wis	99	96	95	94
Indianapolis, Ind	99	100	99	98
Kansas City, Mo-Kans	97	98	97	96
Milwaukee, Wis	105	101	100	99

West

Bakersfield, Calif	91	92	91	92
Denver, Colo	95	95	95	94
Los Angeles-Long Beach, Calif	98	99	99	100
San Diego, Calif	98	98	98	99
San Francisco-Oakland, Calif	106	106	106	106
Seattle-Everett, Wash	101	104	104	105
Nonmetropolitan areas	90	90	91	91
Honolulu Hawaii	119	115	115	116
Archorage, Alaska	133	130	132	131

Table 6.7 Variation in school bus costs with location in England and Wales in 1975. (*Source:* UK Department of Education and Science, quoted in Thring 1976, table 3.6.1)

Location	Cost per pupil (£)	Cost per person in jurisdiction (£)
Large conurbation (London)	2.1	0.35
Town (Metropolitan Districts)	7.7	0.54
Rural areas (Non-Metropolitan Counties)	9.7	1.80
Average	6.4	1.20

irrespective of cost. The calculus of costs and benefits is impossibly complex to allow the achievement of such equality, and it is not altogether clear that such an equality is desirable.

COMPOSITE COSTS

The combined effect of various location costs gives rise to particular geographical cost environments. For example, *inner city costs* are a combination of high labour costs, high land prices, complex underground services giving high civil engineering costs, high costs of debt, and low rates of return on investment. *Suburban costs*, on the other hand, are made up of high distribution and travel costs, the high costs of servicing low density dispersed settlements, and lower labour and land costs. *Urbanization costs* combine the low costs of high density and agglomeration, low costs of travel, high levels of demand for services, and high sunk costs of pre-existing capital investment. *Large city costs* combine agglomeration economies with high labour and floor space costs, and low costs of public services. *Rural costs* are a combination of high distribution costs, low labour costs, low costs of living, and low levels of externalities from other services. Different locations may also reflect attributes of administration or political costs, urban areas having large or fragmented bureaucracies with a high degree of interdependence and relatively high economies of scale, rural areas having smaller interdependence and often less efficient governments.

Table 6.8 displays the variation in composite costs of public housing cost yardsticks used by the UK government in allocating housing grants to local authorities in England and Wales. A national cost yardstick is varied to take account of the differing total construction costs of the various regions, which, in order of increasing costs, vary from 0% over the national yardstick in Wales, to nearly 50% in central London.

6.5 Sunk costs

Sunk costs are those resources spent in the past which cannot be diverted to present use. The capital invested in a road, a school, a hospital, or in housing, for example, cannot be diverted to other uses; apart from costly conversion, it is sunk forever in its existing use. Sunk costs are thus the corollary of opportunity costs (Netzer 1974, p 19): they are costs incurred in the past, whilst opportunity costs are those that are foregone in the future. Such sunk costs affect public finance in adjusting the relative costs in some areas rather than others by the availability of existing infrastructure and the debt charges which derive from it. These are absolute constraints on local finances. As Davies (1968, p. 291) notes:

> 'The inheritance of bricks and mortar and the location of these not only limit the possibility for reorganizing the structure of secondary education, but also are a very important determinant of costs and standards which are not under the control of the local authorities in the short run'. (For example) 'The inheritance of workhouses is still an important determinant of standards of provision of old people's homes, and will probably remain so for some time. The inheritance of manpower ... softened the impact of the new ideals of 1948, and made a continuous ... open dialogue about aims and techniques between the Ministry and individual local authorities unlikely.'

Sunk costs have three main impacts on public finance: by providing surplus capacity, social capital, or affecting interest charges. First, the existence of the under-used or spare capacity of an existing facility suggests that it can satisfy a high level of demand with little or no extra cost. Such spare capacity can act as an economic stimulus to growth. For example, the under-used capacity of a road linkage can be used as a strong economic argument for further developments of the transport network incorporating this link, or as a stimulus to industrial location along the linkage. A second impact of sunk costs is through their performance as elements of social capital. In many instances under-used capacity may result from a shift in locational patterns. Thus surplus school or hospital capacity may be the result of migration of population to other areas. The use of this capacity would require either transport of pupils and patients to the existing facilities, or resettlement of the area by new groups of people. Frequently it has been argued that the social capital sunk into existing settlements represents a strong incentive to orientate future development towards these settlements rather than allow development instead on new sites. Hence, the sunk costs of social capital focus the conflict between growing and declining areas. A third impact of sunk costs is on the level of inherited debt from past investments. Although undertaken in the past, the debt created by investments must be serviced in the future until the capital is amortized. Considerable variation in present levels of revenue

137

Table 6.8 Regional variation in cost yardsticks for public housing in England and Wales, 1975. (*Sources*: DOE 1975b, *Housing Cost Yardstick*, Circular 61/75; Thring 1976, table 2.1)

Economic planning region	Counties and Metropolitan Counties	Yardstick plus	
		Variation of price contracts	Firm price contracts
Northern	Cleveland, Cumbria, Durham, Northumberland and Tyne and Wear.		
North West	Cheshire, Greater Manchester, Lancashire and Merseyside (excluding Metropolitan District of Liverpool).	Nil	6%
South West	Avon, Cornwall, Devon, Dorset, Gloucestershire, Somerset and Wiltshire.		
Yorkshire and Humberside	Humberside, North Yorkshire, South Yorkshire and West Yorkshire.		
North West	Metropolitan District of Liverpool.	2½%	8½%

South East (continued)

Variation of price contracts — Yardstick plus 15%
Firm price contracts — Yardstick plus 22%
District Authorities wholly within 35 miles (56.327 km) of Charing Cross:

Basildon	Gillingham	Spelthorne
Beaconsfield	Gravesham	Stevenage
Bracknell	Guildford	Surrey Heath
Brentwood	Harlow	Tandridge
Broxbourne	Hertsmere	Three Rivers
Castle Point	Luton	Thurrock
Chiltern	Mole Valley	Tonbridge and Malling
Crawley	Reigate and Banstead	Watford
Dartford	Runnymede	Welwyn Hatfield
East Hertfordshire	Rushmoor	Windsor and Maidenhead
Elmbridge	St Albans	Woking
Epping Forest	Sevenoaks	
Epsom and Ewell	Slough	

South East (continued)

Variation of price contracts – Yardstick plus 15%
Firm price contracts – Yardstick plus 22%
Any housing sites wholly or partly within 35 miles (56.327 km) of Charing Cross in the following District Authorities:

Aylesbury Vale	Maldon	South Oxfordshire
Braintree	Medway	Swale
Chelmsford	Mid Bedfordshire	Tunbridge Wells
Chichester	Mid Sussex	Uttlesford
Dacorum	North Hertfordshire	Waverley
Hart	Rochford	Wealden
Horsham	South Bedfordshire	Wokingham
Maidstone	Southend-on-Sea	Wycombe

Variation of price contracts — Yardstick plus 25%
Firm price contracts — Yardstick plus 32½%

The London Boroughs of:

Barking	Enfield	Merton
Barnet	Haringey	Newham
Bexley	Harrow	Redbridge
Brent	Havering	Richmond-upon-Thames
Bromley	Hillingdon	Sutton
Croydon	Hounslow	
Ealing	Kingston-upon-Thames	Waltham Forest

Variation of price contracts — Yardstick plus 40%
Firm price contracts — Yardstick plus 48½%

The City of London and the London Boroughs of:

Camden	Islington	Southwark
Greenwich	Kensington and Chelsea	Tower Hamlets
Hackney	Lambeth	Wandsworth
Hammersmith	Lewisham	City of Westminster

Region	Area	%
East Anglia	Cambridgeshire, Norfolk and Suffolk	5%
East Midlands	Derbyshire, Leicestershire, Lincolnshire, Northampton-shire and Nottinghamshire.	11½%
South East	Bedfordshire, Berkshire, Buckinghamshire, East Sussex, Essex, Hampshire, Hertfordshire, Isle of Wight, Kent, Oxfordshire, Surrey, West Sussex (excluding the Districts and any Housing Sites set out in Schedules A & B).	10%
Wales		16½%
West Midlands	Hereford and Worcester, Salop, Staffordshire, Warwickshire and West Midlands.	15%
South East	District Authorities wholly within 35 miles of Charing Cross as Schedule A. Any housing site wholly or partly within 35 miles of Charing Cross in the District Authorities as Schedule B.	22%
	London Boroughs as Schedule C.	25%
		32½%
	City of London and London Boroughs as Schedule D.	40%
		48½%

burden and need in both North American and European cities results from variable patterns of past investments: for example, the legacy of Victorian infrastructure and the cost of its replacement in cities like New York or London, the costs of meeting the political expediency of the past where bond issues have been used in preference to rises in taxation, and numerous other historical legacies. The inheritance of debt and interest charges is discussed further in chapter 10 as part of the general issues of the public capital account: however, surplus capacity and social capital are discussed further below.

SPARE CAPACITY

This is a measure of the under-used resources available in any location. It may be defined in physical terms as the difference between the number of people that an existing element of public service investment can supply at a given standard of service, and the present number of people served. Alternatively, spare capacity can be defined in economic terms as the cost of supplying services to a small increment in demand, i.e. the marginal cost, which will be low where there is surplus capacity, but high if new investment is required. Two points stand out from either definition (DSPSE 1976). First, each definition implies a service standard or quality. There is only surplus capacity in an existing service if the resources exist to supply additional service demands without a decrease in the quality below a given standard. Spare capacity does not exist where the additional demands are satisfied by lowering quality or congesting the service. Second, capacity can be considered only in relation to the time and qualitative pattern of demand. Thus road, public transit, electricity, gas, and sewerage facilities may all have surplus capacity, but this may be available only at certain times of day or at certain times of the year, e.g. with transport facilities in period of slack demand away from rush hours, with utilities, in periods outside of peak demand such as those for winter heating.

Spare capacity may arise from four main causes. First, there may have been errors in the anticipation of changes in demand and hence investments in new capacity made when they are not required: so called *excess design capacity*. Frequently, however, errors in demand forecasting are offset by reductions in price which result in increased consumption. Alternatively, surplus capacity is used as an argument for increased investments in other sectors which then stimulate demand. In fact, in some cases errors in demand forecasting are deliberately made in order to justify a case for other investment, and the extent to which we believe surplus capacity to be due to errors in demand forecasting depends on the degree to which we subscribe to a conspiracy or incompetence theory of public administration, the building of the under-used M11 London–Stansted–Cambridge motorway close to the stalled projected Third London Airport being perhaps one case in point.

A second cause of surplus capacity is the installation of plant in excess of current levels of demand because of the economies of investment sizes and phasing. For example, extra investments may be undertaken to allow larger plant and the achievement of economies of scale where long-term future growth in demand is expected (advance capacity); and larger investments may allow for emergency situations (emergency capacity), or for predictable changes such as seasonal or diurnal patterns of demand (seasonal capacity). Each of these situations provides for the existence of *marginal capacity*: the difference between actual demand and maximum demand capable of being satisfied without additional expenditure at existing standards. Such forms of excess capacity are particularly common in the electricity, gas, sewerage, water supply, fire, and police services. In order to limit the excess design capacity and hence surplus costs of a particular investments, sophisticated techniques of demand forecasting are required, further discussion of which is given by Thring (1975) and DSPSE (1976).

A third source of excess capacity is changes in technology which permit better use of existing assets. For example, natural gas has permitted twice the calorific value to be obtained from the same volume as a manufactured gas, hence greatly increasing the capacity of existing distribution networks and reducing the need for new ones. Again, obsolete investments are often kept available for use in special or emergency circumstances, as with many small and outdated coal- and oil-fired electricity generation stations and manufactured gas installations in uneconomic sites (DSPSE 1976; Manners 1964).

A final and major cause of excess capacity is locational shifts in demand with their effect on social capital. Existing, although perhaps old, infrastructure facilities are left under-used when population migrates elsewhere. This affects roads, schools, utilities, and manpower and local services. For example, in 1976 inner London had 35% spare capacity in primary education as a result of the combined effect of errors in investment, population migration, and declines in birth rates (DSPSE 1976). The pattern of surplus capacity in electricity, water, sewerage and gas services, and in total spare capacity of all services, for South-East England in 1976, is shown in figure 6.7. This demonstrates that London, especially inner London, has the highest level of spare capacity estimated to be worth £3.7 million per year. On the basis of these results DSPSE (1976), whilst recommending growth outside of London, also strongly advocated the concentration of population growth in the inner city in order to obtain the benefits of the lower costs of the surplus existing capacity available there.

SOCIAL CAPITAL

The role of social capital derives from the existence of under-used or excess capacity resulting from locational shifts in demand following population migration and demographic changes. But there are also the wider implications which derive from private and human investments in property, manpower and skills. Hence, social capital is more than the investment in the public facilities of the location. In its widest sense it includes the whole of society within a given

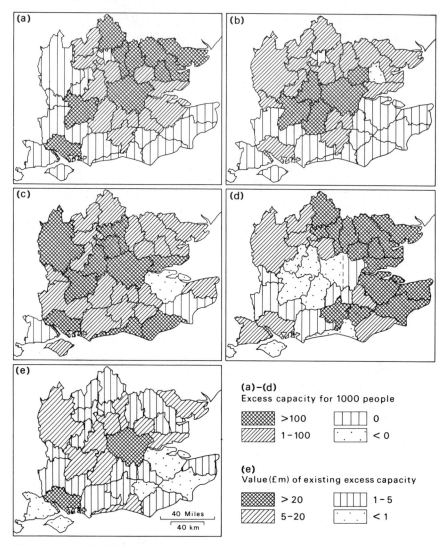

Figure 6.7 Variation in spare capacity for various public utilities in South-East England, 1975. (*Source*: Thring 1976.)

a Gas bulk supply
b Sewerage treatment
c Water supply
d Electricity bulk supply
e Total spare capacity

area: the combination of the fixed costs of capital, plant and infrastructure, with the variable costs of population, labour force, and so forth. Thus, the existence of social capital has much to do with the existence of needs and wants in their widest sense (see chapter 5), and thus of aspirations and hopes within society as a whole. The discussion of social capital has thrown up two controversies; first, that of the relative costs of growth and decline, and second, that of the relative costs of rehabilitation and redevelopment of settlements. In neither case, however, is a general conclusion possible at this stage.

There has been considerable controversy, as we have seen in the earlier technical discussions of the effects of density on costs, concerning the relative costs of population *growth* and of *decline*. On the one hand, it is argued that growth is usually associated with high costs of land purchase and assembly, high labour costs, costly new infrastructure, utilities, and public service provision including new schools, hospitals, police and fire stations. In addition, both population growth and economic growth are usually associated with quantitative and qualitative changes in demand for public goods, as discussed in chapter 2 as one aspect of Wagner's Law. Population decline, it is argued, on the other hand, leads to declining morale, increases in costs per head resulting from loss of economies of scale, amalgamation of services (schools, hospitals, police stations) resulting in unused resources elsewhere, overmanning, and under-use of capital equipment. For example, USCRS (1977, p. 19) state with respect to central cities in the US that their abandonment

> 'would represent a sizable economic loss not merely to the owners of the lost capital including financial institutions holding bonds, but to society as a whole. To the extent that the infrastructure has a useful remaining life, it represents a form of in-place wealth. Its replacement elsewhere requires duplication of existing facilities and needless waste of scarce resources'.

The volume of capital tied up in cities is enormous, Goldsmith *et al.* (1973) estimating this for the United States in 1971 at $87,000 million. Hence abandonment places considerable costs on the community at large, both because new investment is required elsewhere, and because of the loss of in-place social capital.

But the issues are far from clear-cut. Population growth produces spin-offs in increased local incomes which may leak elsewhere, new facilities and standards are created rather than maintaining old and outdated ones, and extensive multipliers further enhance local incomes and encourage further cumulative national economic growth. Decline in population in an area may be balanced by increases in demand resulting from growth in the incomes of its population, and increases in local export incomes. Thus, it has been claimed that in some parts of inner cities declines in levels of population have been offset by the gentrifying downtown, as in London's Islington or New York's Greenwich Village; or increased income is obtained from the non-resident population either through increased retail and commercial turnover, or through exported taxation (see chapter 8) by commuter taxes or increased tourism. Population decline may also be offset by changes in service needs or quality per head. Thus population decline may save the need for costly new investments in hospitals, schools, infrastructure or personnel. Again, population decline may be concentrated in areas where the physical capital stock is nearing the end of its useful life and needs replacement, or where conversion to other use can be achieved at low or reasonable costs. Thus GLDP (1968), for example, argues that considerable savings could be achieved in construction and other capital expenditure by reducing London's population from 7 million to 6.5 million, although this has since been hotly contested on the grounds that no assumption for changes in living space requirements were made.

Despite these caveats, which indicate that there is no simple and general relationship between population decline and increases in public costs, it is clear that population decline is more often detrimental than alleviative, especially when great in magnitude and highly concentrated spatially. The general magnitude of the investment needs of many declining areas, especially of the relatively small areas in inner cities, is enormous. For example, the London Docklands Joint Planning Team (1976) estimate that the capital investment required to rejuvenate 5,500 acres of London's Docklands is £2,043 million of which 56% is required from the public sector. Again, a number of regression analyses have demonstrated a statistical relationship between population decline and levels of public costs. For example, using UK data for 1964–74, Salathiel (1975) has demonstrated a very strong positive relationship between levels of population decline and local authority expenditure, and a rather weaker, but statistically significant, negative relationship between population growth and expenditure (see table 6.9). Moreover, this relationship is generally stronger for London than for non-London authorities. Hence, it is now generally concluded that the combined effect of wasted manpower, the encouragement of inflation, the underutilization of existing facilities, and the imbalance of opportunity within society implied by the existence of social capital in declining areas, leads to increases in total service costs overall and discriminates within society on a spatial basis which cannot be accepted.

The controversy over the relative costs of growth and decline is no more

Table 6.9 Correlation of local expenditure per head with population growth and population decline per head for selected periods in 115 England and Wales local authorities. (*Source:* Salathiel 1975; see Thring 1976)

Variable		London authorities	Non-London authorities	Total
Population decline per head	1964–74	0.882	0.509	0.843
	1969–74	0.883	0.525	0.861
Population growth per head	1964–74	− 0.281	− 0.540	− 0.537
	1969–74	− 0.175	− 0.496	− 0.502
	1972–74	N/A	− 0.412	− 0.466

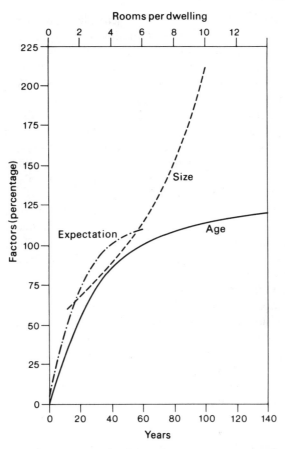

Figure 6.8 Variation of costs of rehabilitation with age, size and expectation of increase in value of dwelling. (*Source*: Thring 1976.)

complex than a second controversy involving the relative costs of *re-habilitation* or *redevelopment* of settlements. The general costs of re-habilitation rise with size of dwelling, to some extent with age (see figure 6.8), and with the condition of local services, especially sewers. But density, urban-rural differences, and locational differences have little effect (Thring 1976). The major determinants of rehabilitation costs, in any specific case, are usually the standard to which it is sought to rehabilitate, and the very specific character of each property. Hence cost assessment depends on a case by case evaluation from which it is difficult to draw generalizations. For South-East England, Thring (1976) for example, concludes that rehabilitation is usually cheaper than new development, by up to 47%, but in the case of the worst initial fabric and highest quality of renewal, rehabilitation costs exceed new development costs by 100%.

Despite these difficulties in making generalizations, a number of studies have attempted to compare rehabilitation costs (especially those in inner cities) with the costs of development in green field sites, and with the expansion of the urban fringe (see, for example, Real Estate Research Corporation 1974; DSPSE 1976; Stone 1970a, b, 1973; Thring 1975, 1976; Wheaton and Schussheim 1956). Most detailed costing studies show rehabilitation to be considerably cheaper than redevelopment for *neighbourhood* units in cities. But the reduced costs of rehabilitation are achieved by maintaining population at high densities, or by increasing density through multiple occupancy. It is not altogether clear that these short-term costs are sufficiently lower than the longer-term costs of additional crime, health care, alienation and other costs which are not taken into account.

When we turn to the relative costs of rehabilitation and redevelopment on a large scale, the differences are often reversed. For example, the British New Towns are cheaper in all categories of expenditure than comparable development in the inner city areas of London's Docklands. However, comparison of New Town costs with the development costs at the urban fringe demonstrate that fringe development may be more expensive than other New Town development schemes. For the case of peripheral expansion of towns in England, Stone (1973), Thring (1975) and others have demonstrated that such expansions often have higher costs than redevelopment on green field sites. For example, table 6.10 shows a comparison of the cost per head for expansion of a number of British new and expanded towns. The range of variation is quite large, only £4,000 to £8,000 per head, and varies inversely with the size of the expansion.

From these various tables and other published results it is clear that

Table 6.10   Costs of various forms of urban expansion in 1975. (*Source:* Stone 1970a)

Towns	Expansion as % of original population	Costs per additional person (£ per person)
(1) Fringe		
Worcester	50	8,000
Peterborough	100	5,000
(2) New Towns		
Skelmersdale	700	4,240
Washington	260	4,010
Runcorn	230	4,700
Telford	200	4,880
Redditch	180	5,310
Northampton	80	4,430
Warrington	70	5,270

generalizations as to the most economic form of development (growth on new sites, or rehabilitation of existing sites taking advantage of sunk costs) is by no means clear. To reach a final assessment of the relative costs of each strategy, requires a detailed assessment of the costs of conversion of existing fabric compared to those of new building, plus an assessment of all local multipliers and allowance for quality and environmental factors. This is no easy task, and cannot lead to hard and fast general conclusions since a great deal depends upon local conditions, the specific characteristics of the existing units, and the financial costs of obtaining capital which reflect private and public assessment of the risks involved. Moreover, care must be taken both to include all costs (economic and non-economic) and to avoid the unrealistic romanticism that has frequently surrounded some Victorian city tenements and terraced housings.

6.6 Conclusion

The discussion of the costs of public goods in this chapter completes the definition of revenue requirements begun in chapter 5. The combination of needs with unit cost then allows assessment of total expenditure needs in any jurisdiction. The discussion has also focused on a number of complex issues: the conflict of new developments with rehabilitation of existing capacity; the conflict of settlement in low density, isolated settlements close to the country, with the decline of the inner city; the role of sunk costs and the extent to which costs should be shared by larger populations and other generations. Each of these issues throws into relief the conflict of public and private costs which is not possible readily to disentangle. Where, on the one hand, sunk costs and the lower costs of rehabilitation suggest the encouragement of industry to move to lagging and declining areas with restraint on economic growth elsewhere, on the other hand, economic efficiency and competitive efficiency suggest that economic development should not be shackled, but allowed to move to those developable locations where it has a natural momentum. Where again the lower economic costs of high density and multiple occupancy housing suggest concentrated urban development, such residential development often leads to oppressive environments, high rates of crime, mental disorder and alienation, and is contrary to the living conditions which most people would prefer. For both growing and declining regions heavy burdens are placed on the public fisc and on the private sector: on the one hand, to create new industrial, social and residential infrastructure, and on the other hand, to rehabilitate the old. Which of these relative costs, of growth or decline, is the higher is, as we have seen, a complex issue for which simple generalizations are not usually readily available. In any case, the degree to which costs vary is only one issue, since differences in costs and their attendant needs, can be offset by fiscal transfers. Hence the degree to which a particular pattern of costs favours rehabilitation of old locations or relocation to new ones depends not only upon criteria of economic efficiency, but also upon social goals and the degree to which the locational benefits and living conditions of some locations are balanced by realistic bearing of the burdens of the public fisc. Hence the discussion of public service costs draws us back to the central issues of the geography of public finance: the relation of local burden to benefits received, and hence the pattern of total fiscal incidence. This leads us towards the issues of the following chapters: the determination of revenue burdens, discussed in chapters 7 and 8, the phasing of costs over different generations of people discussed in chapter 10, the relation of burden to benefits received at unit costs in relation to need discussed in chapter 9, and the equalization of geographical inequity by intergovernmental transfers discussed in later chapters.

7

Revenue ability: the geography of payment for public goods

"The art of taxation consists in so plucking the goose as to obtain the largest possible amount of feathers with the smallest amount of hissing".

Daniel Rogers, *Naaman,* Dd 2 (1642).

"The inequalities and anomalies of the income tax have this advantage: namely that they are understood. The back learns to adapt itself to the burden."

Lord Gladstone,
Speech in House of Commons (1863).

7.1 The philosophy of revenue apportionment

The revenue element of public finance consists of four components, three of which may be either nationally or locally based: (taxation, charges for services, and receipts of savings or loans), and the fourth relates only to local governments (the receipts of grants and other fiscal transfers from higher level governments). The principles of revenue organization, often termed the *canons* of taxation, are outlined in Section 7.2 and the behaviour of taxes and user charges is discussed in Section 7.3. In Section 7.4 methods of assessing ability to bear revenue burdens are discussed, and in Section 7.5 these methods are generalized to specifically geographical measures of revenue ability. In the following chapter the relationship of revenue ability to revenue burden is discussed and this raises issues of tax effort, tax shifting, geographical tax exporting, and final revenue incidence.

The geography of taxes and charges raises the crucial issue of how the payment for public goods is apportioned: who pays what proportion of government revenue as a function of where they live. Revenue incidence can be divided into two major components (Musgrave 1959). First, specific incidence, is concerned with revenue effects in isolation; second, the budget-balance incidence is concerned with the relationship of revenues to expenditures. This chapter is concerned only with specific incidence; the balance of burdens and benefits is treated separately as fiscal incidence in chapter 14.

Over the last 2,000 years, or more, the number of taxes and charges have increased immensely. The following list classifies the main forms in current use.

(i) *Taxes on income*
Personal income tax
Corporate income tax
Severance tax
(ii) *Taxes on capital and wealth*
Death tax
Estate duty
Property tax

(iii) *Taxes on wealth increases and transfers*
Capital gains tax
Capital transfer tax
Gifts tax
Inheritance tax
Taxes on interest
(iv) *Taxes on consumption*
Sales tax
Value-added tax
Excise tax
Cigarette and alcohol taxes
User charges

Taxes on wealth have been historically the major means of measuring ability, for example, in medieval Europe this was based on property acreage. In England this was the land use *hideage* which was later replaced by the 11th-century carucage. To these were added Elizabethan property taxes on the user of land, and in the 17th century so-called presumptive taxes on windows, carriages and hearths (Groves 1964). In each case, an indicator was sought of an individual's ability to pay based on his accumulated stock of wealth in terms of land, head of cattle, or size of property. In contrast to this earlier emphasis on the stock of resources or wealth, more modern taxes have tended to attack *flows* of both *wealth and income*. The income tax was first introduced in England in 1799, followed in Prussia in 1851, and France in 1917. A progressive element was first used in Prussia in 1851, followed in England in 1907 (Seligman 1913). Other taxes on flows have a much longer history, however. Taxes on farm rents were used in ancient Egypt, inheritance taxes derive mainly from Classical Rome, whilst medieval Europe used a form of corporate income tax based on the yield of farm produce (Groves 1964). *Taxes on expenditure* are interrelated with taxation according to benefits. Such taxes were used in Classical Greece and Rome, but were more extensively developed in medieval Europe. A sales tax was used by the Emperor Augustus as 1% upon all articles sold in the market by auction, but in its modern form was initiated in England in 1918, and in the United States, in West Virginia, in 1921 (Groves 1964).

7.2 The canons of revenue raising

In the face of the very different properties of different revenue sources, it has frequently been suggested that both the choice between the employment of one revenue source and another, and the design of the revenue system as a whole, should be based on so-called *canons* of public finance. As originally proposed by Adam Smith in 1776, there are four such canons. Equity, certainty, convenience and economy, and to these it is now normal to add a fifth, that of adequacy.

EQUITY

In simple terms this requires the tax system to be fair or just, but beyond this idea of fairness, it is often very difficult to be precise in detail. Justice in taxation can be defined as treating like people alike, i.e. being impartial in treatment of people with the same relevant characteristics: being neutral. This is often referred to as the principle of *horizontal equity*. But what distinctions and similarities between people should be used to make this comparison? Adam Smith defines the relevant characteristics in terms of 'ability': "The subjects of every state ought to contribute towards the support of the government, as nearly as possible, in proportion to their respective abilities; that is, in proportion to the revenue which they respectively enjoy under the protection of the state"; this determines the 'equality or inequality of taxation', (Smith 1776, V, p. 825). However, Smith's definition in many respects begs the question. Income is the measure of difference and similarity in individual ability to pay taxation. The treatment of equity in relation to ability raises a second principle, that of *vertical equity*: the satisfactorily unequal treatment of unequals (the scaling of different burdens to different abilities). There are many criteria of ability: e.g. wealth, net income, expenditure, or any combination of these, such that now it is usually wished to extend definitions of income to cover accumulated wealth, interest, inheritance, expenditure, and also of fringe benefits such as company cars, meals, etc. Despite these additions and despite the considerable amount of 'rough justice' that often results, Smith's criterion of ability still survives as the major one employed in most countries and we will reserve for later discussion the more complex question of how ability should be scaled with income as some form of progression (see sections 7.4 and 7.5). However we will not be concerned here with the interrelation of ability and benefit which involves more general problems of fiscal incidence, discussed in chapter 14. Shoup (1969) sums up the necessary conditions for equity under six criteria:

(i) relevance of distinctions between groups of like interests;
(ii) impersonality of treatment of each individual;
(iii) certainty of treatment;
(iv) continuity and lack of abrupt changes between groups and individuals;
(v) uniformity of apportionment of any errors in tax assessment;
(vi) cost of complying with a tax measure should be equal for all persons.

CERTAINTY

The organization of any tax should be such that each individual or business knows precisely what his tax liabilities are in the time, manner, and quantity of payments that he has to make so that he may plan ahead accordingly. Tax uncertainty favours arbitrary discretion and corruption of administration. Certainty is essentially the principle that taxes should be intelligible. This is not a fixed criterion, since the experience of society over many centuries has educated people to increasingly complex tax assessment procedures. Nor is total intelligibility of taxation necessarily desirable. As the state has taken on an increased role in shaping and managing the economy, it has become accepted that the uncertainties in national economic conditions must be to some extent reflected in uncertainties of government behaviour. We are now accustomed to violent switches in government tax policies, 'mini-budgets' and special aid to attack financial crises as they arise.

CONVENIENCE

Taxation should be as easy to raise and to pay as possible. From the point of view of the taxpayer who does not usually like paying taxes, payment should cause as little trouble and notice as possible. "Every tax ought to be levied at the time, or in the manner in which it is most likely to be convenient to the contributor to pay it" (Smith 1776, V, p. 826). Thus taxes on purchases should be paid at the time of purchase, taxes on rent at the time rent is due, taxes on income at the time salaries are paid. For example the invention of the PAYE (pay-as-you-earn) system of tax with-holding by the employer has been the great success of achieving convenience in income tax payments.

ECONOMY

This canon derives from the belief that the public economy should minimize the obstacles to the working of the private economy. As stated by Smith (1776, V, pp. 826–7): "Every tax ought to be so contrived as both to take out and to keep out of the pockets of the people as little as possible, over and above what it brings into the publick treasury of the state". Smith held that badly designed taxes would require costly administration, would obstruct industry and investment, would discourage endeavour through the necessity for widespread avoidance, and would require oppressive and odious checking. Hence the premise of the canon of economy is that, on the one hand, efficient resource allocation can be determined only through the mechanism of price determination in the market, and on the other hand, the production of wealth and economic growth is possible only in the private sector, or as stated by von Stein (1885), should be reproductive of capital through benefit to the individual.

ADEQUACY

This additional canon is usually added to Smith's original four in response to the increasing size and dependence of modern society on public intervention. As public expenditures and services have expanded it has become increasingly difficult to find tax sources which are adequate to keep pace with the demand for services and at the same time satisfy the previous four principles. From the point of view of the tax raiser, a tax should be productive in comparison both to expenditure needs and costs of administration, and it should also be flexible to changing economic conditions. In modern times the most important characteristic of flexibility has been that of elasticity to income changes during the economic cycle and during inflation. An ideal tax will *automatically* increase its yield as income and inflation rises, and will decrease its yield as incomes and inflation falls. Such a tax is said to be income-elastic, and the taxes with the most favourable behaviour in this respect are usually progressive personal and corporate income taxes (but see a further discussion of this elasticity concept in section 7.3). Automatic flexibility also possesses the benefits of certainty and economy since increased yields are obtained without changes to tax structure. However, automatic increases may have undesirable distributional effects on equity; fiscal drag, for example, shifts many burdens onto income tax payers in the lower and middle income bands.

Against the background of these canons the discussion of the rest of this chapter is concerned with explaining the characteristics of revenue sources, the ability to pay revenues, and how the burdens of revenues are distributed both at the personal and geographical level.

7.3 Revenue sources and behaviour

Different revenue sources have different characteristics which affect the ability of the people to pay the revenues, and the way in which the incidence of the revenue is diffused to become burdens elsewhere. The most important revenue sources have already been listed on page 150. For each of these sources we explore below their behaviour in relation to the canons of taxation discussed above. This behaviour is addressed through assessment of revenue elasticity and inflation elasticity, both of which affect the canon of revenue adequacy, the redistributional effects of revenues, which affects the canon of equity, and the administration costs of revenue raising, which affects the canons of economy, convenience and certainty.

REVENUE ELASTICITY

This is a measure of the rate of increase (or decrease) in revenues that occurs *automatically* with changes in the revenue base. Hence it has important consequences in relation to the fifth canon of taxation, that of revenue adequacy. Usually elasticity is measured against the revenue base of income, i.e. we measure the income elasticity of revenue. This has strong theoretical justification since income, particularly at national level as measured by GNP, is a measure of the increase and growth of total resources. However, measures of elasticity, like the measures of tax capacity, effort, and severity to be discussed later, can also be measured against the bases from which taxes are derived: expenditure, wealth, and so forth. Nevertheless, it is income elasticity which is normally adopted since it is this which represents the fundamental element of net change in tax resources. The higher the income elasticity of a given revenue source, the larger the automatic increase in revenues that will result, and the greater the adequacy of the revenue to meet existing and new expenditure demands.

153

Table 7.1 Revenue elasticity to changes in income measured by GNP for major revenue sources in the US. (Sources: as listed at head of columns.)

Revenue source	ACIR (1965)	Groves and Bish (1973)	Netzer (1968)	Tax foundation (1966)	Mushkin and Lupo (1967)	CED: Kegan and Roningen (1968)
(1) Taxes						
Property tax	0.7–1.1	0.8	1.0	0.9	1.0	1.0
Income tax: personal	1.5–1.8	1.65	1.7	1.7	1.7	1.7
corporate	1.1–1.3	1.2	1.1	1.2	1.3	1.2
Sales tax: general	0.8–1.05	1.0	0.92	1.1	1.0	1.0
motor fuel	0.4–0.6	0.5	—			
alcohol	0.4–0.6	0.5	0.19			
tobacco	0.3–0.4	0.35	0.62			
public utilities	0.9–1.0	0.95	—	0.7	0.7	0.7
other	0.9–1.1	1.0	1.45			
Motor licences and registration	0.2–0.4	—	—			
Death and gifts taxes	1.0–1.2	—	1.98			
Severance tax	0.9–1.1	—	—			
Other	0.6–0.7	—	1.09			
(2) User charges						
Higher education fees	1.6–1.8	—	—	0.7	0.7	0.7
Hospital fees	1.3–1.5	—	—			
Other	0.6–0.8	—	—			

Mathematically, income elasticity is defined with respect to the income and revenue changes over a given period from a defined base year, i.e.

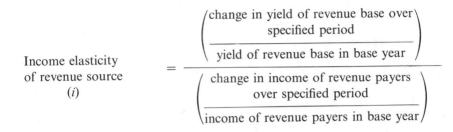

Income elasticity
of revenue source
(i)

$$= \frac{\left(\dfrac{\text{change in yield of revenue base over specified period}}{\text{yield of revenue base in base year}}\right)}{\left(\dfrac{\text{change in income of revenue payers over specified period}}{\text{income of revenue payers in base year}}\right)}$$

Results of estimating this elasticity term by regression analysis give national average elasticities. For the US economy such estimates are given in table 7.1. It can be seen from this table that there is general agreement between the estimates for different authors, although there is some variance in the results. An elasticity of 1 indicates that the revenue source is neutral, it does not change with income changes; elasticity values less than 1 indicate that the revenue source is relatively inelastic and increases more slowly than does income; elasticity greater than 1 indicates an elastic revenue source, since revenue increases faster than increases in income. These results also work in reverse: an elastic revenue decreases faster than decreases in income, and an inelastic revenue decreases more slowly than decreases in income. From the table it can be seen that income taxes, especially on personal income, and user charges, are the most elastic revenue sources. For personal income tax this arises because most additions to income are taxed, and are taxed at high marginal rates. In contrast, relatively inelastic taxes are most specific sales taxes and licences: expenditure on motor fuels, alcohol, tobacco, and so forth, which do not increase as rapidly as do incomes. In between these two extremes are property tax and general sales taxes which are both fairly neutral to income changes: expenditure on property and general goods rises in line with increases in incomes.

These estimates are national aggregates and it can be expected that elasticities will vary with geographical differences, economic structure and individual preferences in different locations. Estimates of revenue elasticities for different locations require revenue and income to be disaggregated by geographical jurisdiction, but this is not attempted here.

INFLATION ELASTICITY

A property of revenue sources closely related to revenue elasticity is that of inflation elasticity. This measures how rapidly the revenue base increases as a result of inflation in prices. This is often of most relevance for property and sales taxes which are most immediately affected by changes in prices. Table 7.2 reproduces estimates of inflation-induced changes in these two tax bases for

Table 7.2 Inflation elasticity of property and sales taxes for six local governments in the US. (*Source:* Maxwell School 1975)

Local government	% gain in tax base from inflation 1971–74	
	Property tax	Sales tax
New York City	22.1	17.5
Atlanta, Georgia	22.3	N/A
Lexington, Virginia	17.8	21.4
Erie County (NY)	22.5	18.4
Orange County (Cal)	21.8	13.4
Snohomish County (Wash)	22.8	18.9
US total (1967–72)	142.6	129.8

the US as a whole and for a small sample of US local governments. This table shows that property taxes are better able to maintain their values against inflationary influences than are all other taxes, even personal income taxes. This is chiefly due to the concentration of inflation in property values over the early 1970s period used, and does not confirm the normal conclusion that property taxes are relatively unresponsive to changes in overall economic conditions. Nor is it likely that these results will hold true for other countries than the United States in which property tax rates are not linked to market values.

THE REDISTRIBUTIONAL EFFECTS OF REVENUE SOURCES

Revenue effects on redistribution relate to the canon of equity and require consideration of five features of the revenue system: first the sources of revenues, or the *revenue base* (who pays the revenue); secondly, the *weighting* of that base in terms of the tax rate or level of user charges, and its distribution between types of user (how much does each person or enterprise pay); third, the *response* of those taxed, their degree of support or assent in the pattern of revenue raising adopted, and the effect of the taxes and charges on motivation and incentive (how acceptable is the redistributional ethic); fourth, what is the degree of *shifting* of payment onto other individuals or geographical locations for different revenue sources (who finally bears the revenue burden); finally, there is the *function* of the revenues to be considered (how are they spent and who benefits from public expenditure). The relationship of the revenue base to weighting of different groups concerns the issue of progression in the tax base, and the relation of shifting of burdens to the balance of benefits raises the issue of fiscal incidence to be discussed in chapter 14. The issue of the response of people and enterprises to different revenue structures is often a crucial feature. For example, progressivity is a far more acceptable ethic in Sweden or the UK, each of which has a wide range of redistributional revenue elements, than it is in the United States or the Netherlands where taxes are far from redistribu-

Table 7.3 Redistribution effects of various revenue sources. A definition of the terms progressive, regressive and neutral is given on page 160.

Revenue source	Redistribution effect on payer and/or incidence effect of final burden
(1) Taxes	
Property tax	Regressive because of low income elasticity of demand for housing
Income tax: personal	Progressive
corporate	Progressive, but can be very regressive when taxes are shifted on to commodities which have a low income elasticity
Sales tax: general	Progressive or regressive depending upon whether good is a luxury or necessity.

motor fuel ⎱
        alcohol   ⎬
        tobacco ⎰
	Fairly neutral

public utilities	Regressive since most utilities involve supply of basic services with low income elasticities of demand.
Motor licences and registration	Fairly neutral
Death and gifts taxes	Progressive
Severance tax	Often progressive, but depends upon nature of goods affected.
(2) User charges	
Education and hospital fees	Regressive
Other	Usually regressive if public services contribute basic necessities with low income elasticity.

tive, and where there is an underlying ethic that people can always better themselves if they make the effort.

Against the background of differential weighting of revenue bases, differential receipt of benefits, and highly variable responses in different societies to different redistributional forms of revenue raising, it is difficult to generalize as to the effect of specific revenue sources on income distribution. However, table 7.3 gives a summary of such effects based on the consensus of various authors. From this table it can be seen that some revenue resources, mainly income taxes on the current base of ability and death and gift taxes on a cumulative base of wealth, can be highly progressive in their incidence. However, other revenues are highly regressive, for example, user charges and property taxes. The progressivity of many revenues depends on the income elasticity of demand for the item in the revenue base being taxed. Hence property taxes, and taxes on food and basic necessities, are usually very regressive. Since all income groups must consume these items, the impact of the taxes on the lower income groups is usually a much larger percentage of their incomes. Hence, food, children's clothing, some utilities, and other basic necessities are often exempted from sales tax in many countries. This is often extended to taxes on cars and motor fuel when they are also considered basic necessities. Muth (1975) and others have criticized the conception that property taxes are regressive arguing that the consumption of housing is highly income elastic, and hence property tax is progressive and not regressive with income. This argument may hold good to some extent in the US where property tax burdens are moderately progressive and are related to property market values, but for most countries the degree of progression in property tax rates is very slight, and assessment or updating of the property tax liability is often arbitrary and infrequently undertaken. Property or sales tax exacted at high rates on luxury items, however, is progressive and related to the expenditure base as a measure of revenue-raising ability. Some revenues such as taxes on motor fuel, motor licences, alcohol, tobacco, and cigarettes, and employment payrolls, are fairly neutral in their effects. The degree of neutrality often varies with each base and this has led, for example, to relatively low tax rates on beer as opposed to spirits in the UK, the argument in this case being that the lower income groups drink more beer than spirits.

Given these differences in individual tax effects it can be concluded that although there are redistributional effects of sales and other indirect taxes, redistribution is best approached through the use of income tax and other direct taxes. These identify individuals directly and can be related directly to burdens and to ability. Although some progressivity of burdens in indirect sales tax is possible, for example, such mechanisms are usually very unsuccessful at redistribution. As Simon notes, luxuries can often be defined as those items which poor people should do without, but will not. Progression in expenditure taxes is poorly related to ability, and requires a social judgement on the division between luxury goods and basic necessities, which usually cannot be easily sustained. Moreover, there can be no differentiation of whether expenditures are derived from savings, earnings, credit, social security, unemployment benefits, charity, or other sources.

Whatever the individual revenue effects, the redistributional consequences of revenue raising and incidence, between either geographical locations or income groups, can be appraised only by studying the whole pattern of tax burdens on individuals, not merely the effect of one tax at a time. Whilst one tax may be regressive, another may be highly progressive so that the total effect is progressive. Estimates of the total tax burden by income groups are given in the next chapter.

THE COSTS OF ADMINISTERING REVENUE SOURCES

This relates to the revenue canons of convenience and efficiency, and is an important factor in influencing the choice of the most appropriate revenues to adopt at any given level of government. Various estimates of administrative

Table 7.4 Costs of administration of various taxes in the US in 1933–34. (*Source:* Reynolds 1935)

Revenue source	Estimate of administration costs as % of revenue yield
Property tax	0.5–2.5
Income tax: personal	2–3
personal and corporate	1–1.5
Sales tax: General	2–4
motor fuel	0.3–0.7
alcohol	3–6
Motor licences and registration	5.5–7
Estate taxes	0.9–2

costs of state and local taxes for the United States are given in table 7.4. It can be seen from this table that there is a great variation in administrative costs between governments. This may reflect relative government efficiency, the density and physical characteristics of their jurisdictions, or differences in economic structure. On the basis of cost alone, liquor and beverage taxes and State motor vehicle licences might never be chosen as revenue sources for local areas, especially since they are usually relatively low in yield. In each case, however, there are social and regulatory functions attached to these taxes, in addition to their value as revenue sources. It should also be noted that although personal income and general sales taxes are relatively easy to administer, they are also relatively expensive to administer. In both cases this is usually deemed tolerable because of their higher yields.

Other factors to be considered in comparing revenue sources are the degree of non-payment or delinquency to which they are subject, the costs of compliance, and the costs and appropriateness of administration at different levels of government.

7.4 The apportionment of revenue burdens

Three main approaches to the apportionment of revenue burdens have been proposed: first, according to ability, as suggested originally by Adam Smith; second, according to benefit or interest, as suggested originally by Hobbes, Grotius, and Pufendorf, and implied to some extent by Smith; and third, according to a strategy of hegemony of class exploitation as suggested originally by Rousseau and Marx. Each of these approaches is discussed in turn below.

TAXATION ACCORDING TO ABILITY

This suffers from the initial problem of how we define ability. Ability must be measured against the base from which it flows. Income has as its base the

159

current flow of resources to the individual or firm. Corporate or personal income taxes have been particularly favoured in modern times because of their redistributive strength and because they are continuous, stable and flexible sources of revenue (see Pechman 1977). Wealth is a measure of ability based on the stock of resources, and is relevant when considering property and estate duty taxes. It must be considered together with current incomes in any measure of ability since purchasing power, welfare, and other forms of well-being all depend as much on capital as current flows of resources. The expenditure measure of ability is relevant when considering user charges, sales tax and value added tax. These are generally imprecise measures of ability and tend to be employed when income and wealth taxes are becoming ineffective in raising sufficient revenues. They do, however, have the advantage of measuring the total flow of benefits as a result of differences in ability, and enter into the definitions of ability which yields a 'total income base' definition (see for example, Kaldor 1955). Such expenditure measures are also important in relation to the benefit principle of apportioning tax burdens, and will be discussed also in that context (see chapter 9). Figure 7.1 compares the various tax bases of income, wealth and expenditure for the United States and shows that, even at the aggregate level of States, considerable differences occur.

Measures of ability attempt to differentiate groups of like people in purely material terms, but the major problem is that, given these groups of like people, how is the tax burden to be apportioned between these groups on a personal or a geographical basis – how do we relate a given level of ability to a given payment of tax? There are three principles upon which such apportionments are made.

(i) *The proportional tax principle*: the rate of taxation with respect to ability is constant over all groups.

(ii) *The progressive tax principle*: the rate of tax increases as the level of ability increases (a special case of this principle is that in which the rate of increase of tax rate with ability is constant, i.e. there is a constant rate of acceleration, this is termed the *degressive* tax principle).

(iii) *The regressive tax principle*: The rate of tax decreases as the level of ability increases.

Graphs of each of these tax principles are shown in figure 7.2. There is no totally objective criterion on how we should choose the form of tax progression and its rate of progress, or regress. In addition it may be that whilst one tax has a characteristic of progression, another is regressive, so that in evaluating or comparing tax systems we must, as Marshall (1920) points out, assess the *total* progressivity or regressivity of all taxes. Any tax structure will have effects on the functions of allocation, stabilization, and economic growth, but usually the choice between proportional, progressive and regressive tax structures is based on the public financial function of distribution. Progressive taxes take resources from those with higher abilities. Since public expenditures derived from revenue resources are

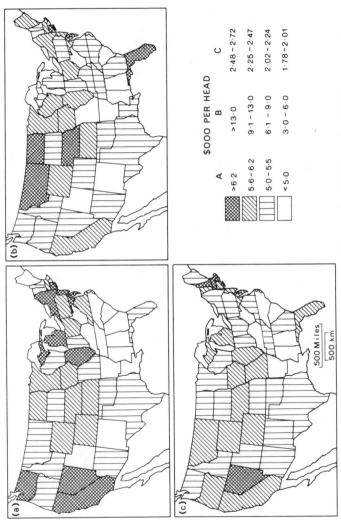

Figure 7.1 Per capita measures of revenue ability of the US States in 1976 in terms of
a   personal income
b   personal wealth
c   personal expenditure.
(Source: Yearbook of the States 1976)

161

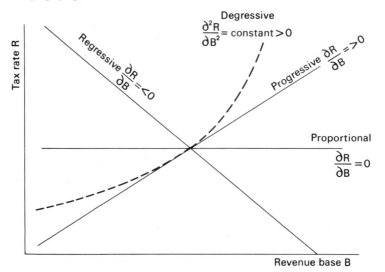

Figure 7.2 Various tax principles of apportioning burden according to the size of the revenue base.

allocated primarily either on a uniform basis, or on the basis of need which is concentrated on those groups with lower abilities, progressive taxes are, in general, highly redistributive. If taxation is indeed robbery, progression works on the 'Robin Hood' principle of robbing the rich to give to the poor. Regressive taxes, on the other hand, exact a higher payment from the poor, whilst proportional taxes are neutral to poverty – or maintain the status quo of income distribution and wealth.

Although there is no objective criterion of the way in which tax burdens should be apportioned between ability groups, there have been a number of attempts to scale progression using various theories of sacrifice. Three main approaches have been adopted. First, the theory of *minimum sacrifice*, which arises from Jeremy Bentham, and the utilitarians, who suggest that those taxes should be chosen which yield the least inconvenience and loss to people as a whole. Since utility decreases as the level of income or wealth increases, the utilitarians argue that a progressive structure will give the least loss of utility to society as a whole. Hence the greatest equality of fortunes is produced with minimum sacrifice when taxes are paid by *only* the wealthy income groups. A second principle, that of *proportional and equal sacrifice*, suggests that all income groups make payments, but that the contribution of the poorer groups should be smaller than that of the wealthier groups, in proportion to the equality of the sacrifice of each group (Carver 1895; Edgeworth 1897). Sacrifice is, then, equalized by using a rate of tax progression equal to that of the loss in utility with incomes. The *marginal utility of sacrifice*, is a third theory suggested mainly by the Swedish school of Wicksell (1934), Lindahl (1919), Sax (1924), and von Wieser (1898). This is concerned with how the existing distribution of income and wealth can be modified to produce a more just distribution. It assumes that a just distribution can be defined and then evaluates each tax structure to determine that which will be best in correcting existing injustices.

The problem with each of these approaches is that they require measurement of the immeasurable entities: utility or justice. Moreover, it is questionable that marginal utility does decline with income; especially with wealth assets, such as property, there is no evidence that utility for space has any limits. There is also the problem that different people have different preferences and abilities so that it is doubtful how far equal incomes should be the only measure of human welfare. Hence, modern approaches to taxation have largely abandoned the utility approach to measurement of ability and concentrate instead on determining a more general ordering of social interests, the items discussed in chapter 5, as elements of national and local merit goods, and private needs. Within these defined needs it is then possible to come to some general social or political ranking, e.g. by which health care ranks higher than greater consumption of cars.

TAXATION ACCORDING TO BENEFITS

This theory states that each individual or business should be taxed in proportion to the benefits received, i.e. there is a *quid pro quo* between people and governments. This derives from Hobbes' concept of the state as the social contract into which all enter because each seeks to obtain a particular set of collective benefits which cannot be obtained individually. This concept has recently been extended by Buchanan and Tullock. As viewed by Montesquieu (1777, bk. 13, chapter 1, p. 273): "Taxes are a payment of part of one's property in order to enjoy the remainder in security". The principle has also been strongly supported in the 1880s by Pantaleoni, Sax, and de Viti de Marco (Buchanan 1960). The benefit theory of taxation is appealing as it limits consumption by bringing into play the price rules of the market. It is especially applicable to public services provided in lieu of private services where there is an important social role requiring public involvement, e.g. postal services, utilities, and transport. It is applicable to most user charges, and to tax sources such as sales tax, motor licence fees, and motor fuel taxes, highway taxes, and to some extent to property tax, where the charge is fairly clearly related to the service benefits received. Property tax, for example, has strong relation to property services such as sewerage and refuse disposal, street provision, cleaning and lighting, police and fire protection.

Benefit taxation is confused, however, with ability taxation discussed above. Since the benefits obtained from society as a whole increase with income, then benefit theory can also be used as a justification for progressive taxation. As stated by Smith (1776, V, p. 825), and noted above, abilities are "proportional to revenues (i.e. benefits) which they collectively enjoy under the protection of the state". Modern interpretations of this theory are the

163

public choice approaches of Buchanan (1960), and Bish and Ostrom (1973). Many of conclusions of the benefit theory of taxation are identical to the ability theory, except that now income, wealth and expenditure are interpreted as benefit derived from society rather than the innate abilities of the individuals themselves. Indeed, Kaldor's expenditure theory of taxation would make ready application as a benefit theory. However, there are two important differences in the conclusions that can be drawn from the two theories; these relate first, to differences of benefits and costs, and second to the geography of benefit incidence.

The benefit theory assumes that the benefits of taxation received by individuals can be accounted for, and can be measured and summed to give the total benefits of public revenue to society as a whole. However, this requires not only that individual benefits can be imputed from the share of common benefits, but also that values can be set on indefinite things. How can the benefits of services like public libraries, recreation facilities and pollution controls be assessed and divided between people; how do we value indirect benefits such as education; how do we value the benefits of those who cannot afford to pay for the benefits they receive; and how do we value the different benefits received by people with different preferences for public services? Because of the impossibility of answering most of these questions, most modern interpretations of benefit theory tend to accord with the view of Say (1855), that the value paid to government by taxpayers is given without the expectation of any necessary equivalent or return.

The geography of benefit incidence is the feature of benefit theory which is an exception to Say's point of view, and it is here where the weight of argument in the modern benefit theory of Buchanan, Bish and Ostrom is often placed. Benefit incidence is discussed in more detail in chapter 9. However, the main geographical feature of this theory is that, because of non-jointness and exclusion, there exists a range of *local* public goods for which benefits are limited in geographical extent. In taking account in the revenue system of these local public goods, we must find some way of relating the benefit region to that in which the revenue is raised. Hence, with many public goods, there is a strong motive to organize a multi-level tax system in which revenues for national merit goods are raised at a national level, and revenues for local and intermediate goods are raised at those respective levels.

TAX STRATEGIES OF HEGEMONY

According to Marx (1967) and Lenin (1960), tax struggle is the oldest form of class struggle, the purpose of which is to protect and enrich one economic group at the expense of another. Hence, tax systems are viewed as a particular form of class system. 'Tax fairness', 'equity' and 'improvement of incentives' are all interpreted as convenient strategies to maintain mass support for this class rule. According to O'Connor (1973, p. 203) "The state must attempt to establish an equitable focus of taxation in order to conceal the inequitable intent of the tax structure and the exploitative process". Usually indirect taxes are particularly castigated as concealing the nature of exploitation. Direct taxes, which may indeed be progressive and hence redistributive in intent, are interpreted as in fact serving the interests primarily of monopoly capital. This argument rests on the interpretation of the bulk of public expenditure in defence and in education as being solely oriented towards improving the rate of capital accumulation. Defence is not interpreted as a national public good (perhaps the only pure public good) available to all on an equal basis, but instead is an allocation of spending to a class of industrialists and employers. Education is not interpreted as a public good contributing to the overall welfare and culture of society, but is a means of increasing labour productivity and hence the rate of capital accumulation. Furthermore, the tenet of Smith and others that equals are treated equally, whilst in theory very reasonable, in practice reinforces inequality since society is not made up of equals; in particular, the *present* state of society, from which both the ability and benefit theory begin, is argued to have in no sense an expression of equal distribution of resources or power between people.

The degree to which we accept these views must be very limited. Whilst it is obvious that defence industries, for example, do aid the employers in those industries, and education certainly does increase productivity, the Marxist critique concentrates solely on these features. It also ignores the considerable and growing proportions of social welfare expenditure. In the US and UK budgets for example, this accounts for nearly one-third of all public expenditure. Defence industries generate employment and wages, and education generates other more intangible but important gains in individual welfare and culture. The Marxists are presumably not suggesting that we should not have defence industries and education, but they are suggesting that no significant redistribution is occurring under the present tax programmes. There may still be insufficient redistribution in many countries and in emphasizing the inequalities of present income distribution, the Marxists are of course, correct. But it seems to most commentators that we have better chances of success in working to improve redistribution within the present system of public finance, rather than attempt to replace this by an idealized alternative which is ill-defined, and which, where it has been employed, has usually led to oppressive, odious and inefficient forms of public finance and intervention.

7.5 Revenue capacity: geographical measures of fiscal ability

Revenue capacity is a measure of the geographical variation in tax ability: the resources which each jurisdiction can draw upon to raise taxes and other revenues. This is determined by variations in income, wealth, expenditure, business activity, and other supply variables which compose the local revenue base. As such it is a difficult and even impossible concept within public finance to quantify in absolute terms, but it is usually possible to obtain adequate

165

measures of *relative* capacity in different jurisdictions. There are two fundamental problems in defining local revenue capacity: first, an adequate indicator of fiscal differences must be found, and second, it must be possible to phrase the definition of that indicator in terms which create clear legal liabilities and can be framed in legislation.

Various definitions of revenue ability have been used at different times, but in each case the aim has been to find the most appropriate measures of ability with respect to the revenue base being considered. They have been developed to a much greater extent in those countries, like the United States, where the local tax system is very complex, than in unitary states like Britain and France where limited revenue-raising powers based on a single local tax are available. Measures of local capacity can be divided into two groups: one based on statistical indicators, and the other based on the uniform (or representative) tax approach. In addition the approach using statistical indicators can be sub-divided into five categories based on measures of income, expenditures, wealth, income produced, and composite indices. Each of these approaches is discussed in turn below.

STATISTICAL INCOME INDICATORS

The use of statistical income indicators of local revenue capacity draws from income taxation at national level. Personal income has the advantage of being simple to measure, having good estimates available, and is obviously a very valid indicator of current resources in a local community since most taxes are paid out of income. Moreover, income is closely related to most other statistical indicators that can be envisaged; especially expenditure and wealth. Mushkin and Crowther (1954), for example, suggest that the use of the single income series yields good statistical estimates since it is, in effect, an additive combination of many other statistical series. Indeed a number of writers, for example Gerig *et al.* (1938), NBER (1939), Studenski (1943), Mushkin and Crowther (1954), and Maxwell (1946), amongst many others, have supported the use of this single series. However, there are a number of criticisms of the single income measure of local capacity. The most important of these is that income is only a satisfactory measure of the ability to pay income taxes. Since local jurisdictions in most countries rely heavily on taxes other than income taxes (mainly property and sales taxes), the income measure is often a very poor indicator of the capacity of local jurisdictions to obtain their funds, even if it is a good indicator of the real assets of an area. Thus Curran (1973, p. 52) notes that

'one might think that the income level of the community should be listed as a resource . . . . Although there is much truth in the statement at the macro or national level, the relationship between public resources and income becomes somewhat strained at the state level, and thinner still at the local level of government. Thus, the use of income as a measure of resources is often worse than uninformative'.

A second problem is what measure of income should be adopted: personal or family income, money income, earnings, disposable income, personal income including in-kind payments (total income), or taxable income. A third problem is the time frame of income. Income is a flow. With most personal and corporate income flows it may be valid to tax on a year-by-year basis, but it is extremely difficult to assess how the limited and depleting stock of natural resources of such areas as Alaska, Texas or Alberta in North America, should be assessed in measures of ability. A fourth important criticism of single income measures is that allowances should be made for the effect of central government taxation withdrawn from local income, and local spending which supplements local incomes. Mushkin and Crowther (1954) showed that allowance for federal grants in the US has little impact on measures of local capacity, but it is likely that greater effects will be produced by allowances for the effect of payments of corporate income taxes and capital gains, and receipts of military spending, government payrolls and income transfers. Finally, simple income measures also give no measure of distribution of income within local areas: total income, median income and other gross measures, describe significant differences in local revenue capacities with respect to different tax bases. The method of overcoming this problem suggested by Reischauer (1974) is to remove from the taxable income of each jurisdiction an initial *per capita* allowance corresponding to the poverty level of income. The residual after this calculation can then be used as a better capacity measure. In addition, each level of income can be weighted differentially in a more complex capacity measure, but there is then the problem of obtaining the most appropriate set of weights for each income band. It must be emphasized, however, that the most important of these criticisms is that income is not a valid indicator of the revenue base from which most local taxation is derived.

STATISTICAL INDICATORS OF WEALTH

These can include all wealth assets. Such indicators have been little used at local level, but have been evaluated in a number of studies. For example, Harris (1905) has suggested that all personal and real property can be used as a wealth indicator, Norton (1926) has suggested tangible wealth plus personal income, and Blough (1935) has examined taxable wealth and income. This last definition of Blough is the most crucial since with wealth, as with all measures of revenue capacity, the assessment must be against the relevant tax base. In the US, UK, and most other countries, the only indicators of wealth available are measures of assessed property tax base through gross market and nominal rental values.

STATISTICAL INDICATORS OF EXPENDITURE

These are obviously related to those of income and are of most relevance when considering sales tax capacity. However, expenditure indicators have an advantage over both single income and wealth indicators in that they combine the effects of both sources into one measure of consumption. Greater emphasis on taxation relative to this measure of capacity would result in a realization of Kaldor's expenditure theory of taxation discussed earlier (p. 160) and would also help to relate tax burdens and tax benefits. However, it is very difficult to determine, at a local level, the degree to which expenditure is locally, or non-locally derived, since there are very considerable spillovers of purchasing between jurisdictions.

STATISTICAL INDICATORS OF INCOME PRODUCED

This measure allows the assessment of the economic capacity of an area *in toto*: its productivity, and the capacity of the economic base to generate local incomes; that is the money income imputed to residents and to businesses for their labour and ownership of assets. Thus, this measure is similar to measures of regional production or value added. There is usually a marked difference in where income is received and where it is produced. This is indicated by the different locations of personal incomes and wealth, and hence has been urged as a basis of special aid policies in the United States by Hansen and Perloff (1944). Economic capacity, as an indicator of the distribution of the production of wealth, is usually measured as a revenue base by the gross output and value added due to the localization of industry. Differences in the geographical pattern of economic growth creates lumpy development and it is the system of investments and savings flows which determine whether the net effect of this lumpiness generates Myrdalian spread or backwash effects. For example, estimates of this ability base for the USA by US ACIR (1962) show great differences between estimates of geographical incomes and economic capacity (income produced). These estimates are derived from the value added in each area for each industry with deductions to payrolls, employee compensation, and non-corporate business incomes. On the one hand, personal incomes are higher than industrial production in Delaware, Maryland, Oregon, and all New England States. These States are the net receivers of income produced in other states through the receipt of dividends and interest payments. On the other hand, Nevada, Arizona, New Mexico, and the South-West States show the effects of absentee ownership of minerals: these areas give out income which flows to other states.

COMPOSITE STATISTICAL INDICATORS

These indicators of revenue capacity have been used both in the US and in Europe. Composite measures combine two or more statistical indicators and have the advantage of being simple whilst giving a broader indication of different elements of revenue raising ability. Early indices given by Cubberly (1905), Strayer and Haig (1925), and Cornel (1936), were developed by Mort (1936) and Norton (1937) who suggest a composite index based on ten indicators from various US census data. This procedure is refined by Gerig *et al.* (1938) by selection of the seven most valid indicators for local capacity: value of farm property per farm, *per capita* bank deposits, *per capita* income, *per capita* retail sales, *per capita* postal receipts, *per capita* state and local tax revenues, and number of federal individual income tax returns per thousand population. This combined index allows some influence from each individual element of income, wealth, expenditure, and income produced. The inclusion of State and local tax revenues also foreshadows some of the effects of the representative tax system to be discussed below. In the UK, the statistical indicators used in the Rate Support Grant needs element, like most needs indicators, in many senses represent inverse measures of local revenue capacity based on the statistical indicator approach.

The major problem in all composite indexes is how to weight the contribution of each component in the general sum. The most rational procedure is to weight each source by the proportion of the tax levied from that source. If this approach is chosen, the composite indicator approach comes close to that of the representative tax system, but without the same comprehensiveness of treatment. A similar quasi-representative system approach often adopted is to weight different components of capacity by the use of multiple regression estimates derived from least-squares or some other statistical estimation technique (see Akin 1973, and Reischauer 1974). Johnston (1972) gives a discussion of such least-squares estimation methods. The aim is to determine the contribution of each of a range of statistical *per capita* indicators of ability to local *per capita* revenue. The result is a set of equations as follows:

Per capita revenue source (1) = for each jurisdiction, the sum of:
per capita taxes + *per capita* special taxes + *per capita* interest payments + *per capita* earnings + *per capita* local government earnings from charges and other sources.

Per capita revenue source (2) =   „   „   „

Per capita revenue source (*m*) =   „   „   „

Thus there are *m* equations, one for each revenue source. This statistical method allows the weights in the composite measure to be determined from past levels of revenue raised. Each jurisdiction's revenue ability is determined by the sum contribution of each of the various indicators of ability to revenue raised in the past from each revenue source. An alternative regression-based capacity measure has been proposed by Morgan (1974) to take account of interdependence (multi-collinearity) between capacity indicators and differences in elasticity of capacity with income.

THE UNIFORM TAX BASE APPROACH

This was suggested by Norton (1926) and developed into a concrete practical form by Newcomer (1935) (see also Chism 1936). The concept is based on using an index tax system for each local jurisdiction as an indicator of capacity based on revenue yield. Various choices of the index tax system can be employed. The three most important of these are

(i) *representative tax system*: weight each revenue base in proportion to the revenues derived from them by local government as a whole;

(ii) *modified representative tax system*: weight each revenue base in proportion to the average tax rates employed by governments actually using that tax;

(iii) *hypothetical (model) tax system*: weight each revenue base in proportion to a desired ideal or hypothetical structure (cf. National Tax Association 1933, p. 34).

The representative tax system is the one most usefully employed US ACIR 1962; 1971), although the hypothetical tax system is useful in assessing the effect of changes to tax procedures. Relative revenue capacity is defined under this approach as the amount of revenue each area could raise, relative to all others, if all areas employed an identical tax system to the average of the present local tax system. In countries like the UK where the revenue-raising procedures are almost uniform across geographical areas, a representative system corresponds to the real tax system. In cases such as the US, where a large variety of different revenue-raising procedures are employed, the representative tax system gives an averaged measure of capacity if the average revenue-raising procedures were used in each local area.

The first major studies based on this approach, which most subsequent studies have followed, are those by the US ACIR (1962, 1971) at State level in the US. Fifteen representative revenue sources were adopted together with a representative tax rate associated with each. The procedure then followed three steps. In step one, the revenue base for each revenue source is determined in each State. In step two, representative tax rates are set at levels such that when they are applied to the tax revenue base in all States, they yield the same amount of revenue as the total yields for all States in the study period. In step three, these representative rates are then applied to each State's tax base. This yields final estimates of revenues for a tax system which is uniform between jurisdictions. Differences between the representative yields or the real yields on a tax by tax basis allow a determination of how far each State is using its revenue capacity to the full.

There are a number of criticisms of the representative tax approach. First, the representative system of measuring capacity takes no account of local practicality, political feasibility, and preferences for different revenue mixes. An average or representative system therefore may bear no relation to the real geographical variation in jurisdictional revenue ability. A measure based more closely on the taxes actually used would be more appropriate. Second, abilities measured for many revenues may bear no relation to final burdens and abilities because no account is taken of the effects of tax shifting and

170

exporting as discussed in the next chapter. Third, the revenue bases of each jurisdiction are not independent of past government action. This is a problem of policy feedback: the present geographical distribution of personal incomes, economic activity, property values and retail sales all reflect the impact of past levels of local taxation, regulations, and public expenditure. For example, zoning and exclusion procedures affect the level of economic activity and the social (and hence income mix) of residences. Governmental permission for gambling, horse-racing, petrol stations, and liquor stores have specific effects on different jurisdictional revenue abilities. Different tax rates in the past have influenced the price of local public and non-public goods, have modified the level of local demand, and hence have affected the size of the local revenue base. This has effects on the location of industry and residences, the capital depreciation of land and property values, and local public service levels (Oates 1969; Reischauer 1974). Hence, if a model or representative tax system were actually imposed as a uniform system on jurisdictions, the bases would differ considerably from those now measured. As Reischauer (1974, pp. 3–55) notes: "shopping and consumption patterns would change, and the desirability of various locations for business and housing will be altered. . . . In general the capacity of jurisdictions with tax rates exceeding those of the representative revenue system will be underestimated while those of low tax areas will be overestimated".

COMPARISON OF VARIOUS CAPACITY MEASURES

Various comparisons of different capacity measures have been made: US ACIR (1962, 1971), Lynn (1968), Halstead (1978); however the only systematic comparison of the various measures of geographical ability for the US is that of Reischauer (1974). The results of this study are shown in figure 7.3. There is little consistency of ranking and only half of the States fall consistently above or below the national average. In addition the range of variations is also unstable. Whilst *per capita* incomes and tax liabilities show some consistency in emphasizing the high abilities of the North-Eastern States and low ranking of the plains and southern States, the representative tax systems show considerable variation amongst themselves, but in general give a much wider range of variation than with other measures.

In assessing statistical and representative systems of measuring tax capacity, an important role is played not so much by the absolute or even relative differences that are found in different areas, but more by the political feasibility of implementing different capacity measures and equalization programmes. There are two interrelated problems stated at the outset of this discussion (p. 166): first, that of defining adequate measures of ability; second, that of stating these measures in terms that can be clearly framed in legislation. Whilst most research has been developed on the representative system in the US, especially by the ACIR, this form of capacity measure has never been used in transfer and grant programmes aimed at fiscal equalization

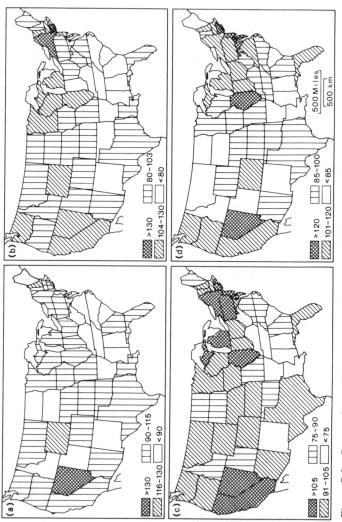

Figure 7.3 Comparison of four measures of tax capacity for the US States. Further discussion of each measure is given on pages 170–1, 173. (*Source:* Reischauer 1974, table 3.8.)

a   Representative tax system (average weights)
b   Representative tax system (regression weights)
c   Representative tax system (regression weights with controls)
d   Federal tax liability of employees and employers

172

in that country. This is due mainly to its complexity and the preference in legislation for the use of the much simpler and more accurate *per capita* income measure. In addition it can be strongly argued that whilst *per capita* incomes might not be related in any meaningful way to the revenues that can be taxed in any jurisdiction, they would usually have a much clearer relationship to ability to pay in a personal sense than does a capacity measure based on the tax system itself. The problem, then, is to resolve between capacity measures based on ability under the actual revenue system, or capacity measures in terms of the general ability conferred by income or wealth.

The only programme where a representative tax system has been consistently implemented is the equalization grant and revenue-sharing structure of the Canadian Federal Government and Provinces. This system will be discussed in more detail in chapter 13. For the present, it is interesting to note the differences, shown in table 7.5, in the tax yields in different jurisdictions based on different revenue sources. The variations in revenue capacity between the various Provinces reflect, not only differences in overall income and prosperity, but also differences in tax mixes. Thus for example, whilst the Atlantic provinces have low capacity overall, they have very high capacity in hospital and medical care insurance premiums, and in mineral revenues.

A major problem with each measure of capacity, is that the resulting estimates of ability reflect as much the geographical pattern of need for revenue raising as they do patterns of ability. Since there is no allowance for the effects of different levels of public service needs, local preferences, differences in present service levels, and costs of financing services in different locations, the various measures of the present tax system, tax rates, and revenues raised are only a broad indicator of ability. As Newcomer (1935, p. 12) notes: "taxpaying ability is significant only in relation to need .... Need is a fundamental factor in the measurement of ability". Hence in attempting to find a truly accurate measure of ability for use in assessing the degree of geographical equity or inequity in the distribution of burdens and benefits, we cannot avoid questions of need, cost, and preference. The attempt to do this, shown in figure 7.3c by Reischauer (1974), draws on the method of Akin (1973). As a first step, a multiple regression equation is estimated in which a series of differential needs are held as controls. As a second step, national average values for the 'control' needs are substituted into the regression equation and geographical capacity variation is determined from the composite of needs and ability variation, i.e. the ability measure is modified for specific differences in need. Thus, figure 7.3c represents fairly closely assessment of ability at State level in the US with need and cost factors controlled out. Alternative methods of accounting for need-cost, and ability interaction are discussed in chapters 5 and 14.

A pervasive problem in choosing between different methods of assessing the revenue ability of jurisdictions is the scale-dependence of the assessment

Table 7.5 Representative tax system for Canadian Provinces. Index of *per capita* yield of each revenue source in the Canadian representative system at average Provincial tax rates. National average *per capita* yield = 100. (*Source*: Carter 1971)

Type of revenue	Nfld.	P.E.I.	N.S.	N.B.	Que.	Ont.	Man.	Sask.	Alta.	B.C.	Total
Corporation income tax	61.9	33.5	45.8	46.4	88.1	128.6	83.9	62.3	94.7	122.6	100.0
Personal income tax	37.1	32.9	53.6	44.1	86.1	132.0	84.5	69.1	89.0	121.9	100.0
Succession duty or share of federal estate tax	18.0	23.1	87.5	61.6	90.8	131.9	74.0	31.9	62.0	139.9	100.0
General sales and tobacco taxes	70.8	88.2	79.5	77.4	86.2	105.6	102.5	120.9	122.5	117.7	100.0
Motor fuel taxes	45.3	95.7	74.3	73.2	88.0	112.0	102.3	115.0	122.9	101.0	100.0
Alcoholic beverage revenues	45.7	73.9	82.2	74.0	87.4	117.0	95.3	87.7	95.3	123.5	100.0
Motion picture theatre admissions tax	40.0	52.0	64.0	56.0	88.0	120.0	84.0	72.0	104.0	124.0	100.0
Hospital and medical care insurance premiums											
Families	83.5	93.9	96.4	91.0	92.5	107.0	101.6	101.6	97.0	107.5	100.0
Individuals	105.9	118.6	124.5	106.9	94.1	92.2	112.7	88.2	127.5	111.8	100.0
Insurance premiums tax	44.4	52.4	68.3	66.1	114.3	112.2	77.8	58.7	88.9	97.9	100.0
Passenger vehicle registration revenues	48.2	85.9	83.7	79.0	77.0	117.7	102.6	105.6	110.3	123.6	100.0
Other motor vehicle registration revenues	52.1	148.4	94.5	78.2	86.5	85.7	126.0	185.6	136.6	126.0	100.0
Drivers and chauffeurs licences	50.0	97.3	86.5	81.1	73.0	108.1	104.1	117.6	135.1	132.4	100.0
Forestry revenues	95.4	29.3	57.3	166.6	86.1	42.7	20.0	21.2	49.0	493.4	100.0
Oil royalties	—	—	—	—	—	1.5	29.8	527.0	910.7	45.1	100.0
Natural gas royalties	—	—	—	2.0	—	12.2	—	32.7	1,149.0	91.8	100.0
Other oil and gas revenues	—	—	—	—	—	0.6	0.3	188.8	1,055.9	130.6	100.0
Metallic and non-metallic mineral revenues	269.8	—	29.5	8.6	112.9	116.5	48.9	117.3	2.2	120.9	100.0
Water power rentals	73.0	—	18.9	37.8	164.9	82.0	91.0	18.9	11.7	153.2	100.0
Other Provincial taxes	58.4	62.2	74.7	66.1	86.7	116.7	97.0	108.2	101.3	114.2	100.0
Miscellaneous Provincial revenues	58.2	62.1	74.5	66.1	86.7	116.6	97.0	108.0	101.1	114.0	100.0
Total	53.6	64.3	66.2	64.2	82.8	107.4	88.3	106.4	159.0	125.2	100.0

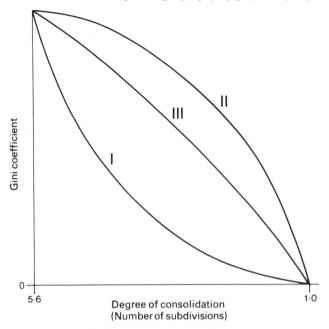

Figure 7.4 The effects of various levels of consolidation of fifty-six jurisdictions in Milwaukee SMSA on incquality in tax capacity as measured by the Gini coefficient.
  I Consolidation reduces inequality rapidly
  II Consolidation reduces inequality slowly
  III Pattern of inequality in Milwaukee SMSA in 1966.
(*Source*: Boelaert 1970, figure 2.)

procedure. The level of ability measured will vary depending upon the size of the jurisdiction and its level in the hierarchy of government. This is due to three factors. First the ecological correlation problem: that the correlation between two aggregate variables may bear no relation to the correlation between the variables based upon individuals within the population. Second, there is the effect of variable spatial averaging. In general, larger areas will include a wider variety of both revenue resources and income groups, and hence representative or average tax capacity measures will be more meaningful at larger scales. This feature has caused many commentators (see Boelaert 1970) to argue that greater fiscal equity can be achieved, especially in urban areas, only by consolidating small, fragmented jurisdictions (chapter 11 *q.v.*). Figure 7.4, for example, shows how the relative levels of inequality in tax capacity are modified by successive levels of consolidation in Milwaukee SMSA. Such is the extent of interjurisdictional equities that consolidation reduces inequality in tax capacity relatively slowly. Third, there is the effect of jurisdictional size on the tax mix problem. Since certain revenue sources, e.g. personal and corporate income tax, are usually reserved to fairly large

175

jurisdictional units such as States and Provinces, it becomes fairly meaningless to use *per capita* incomes as a measure of ability at local level. Indeed, at the local level of the city, where property taxes are most the usual tax levied, it is usually most appropriate to use the property base as the measure of ability. The following results from Reischauer (1974, pp. 3–110) for the correlation between three indicators of ability at local level in Los Angeles county show the danger of adopting a measure of ability which is inappropriate to the local revenue environment:

	(i)	(ii)	(iii)
(i) Money income	1.0	−0.02	−0.03
(ii) Property value		1.0	
(iii) Representative system (based on averages)			1.0

To adopt either the representative or money income ability measures, when it is property tax which is the revenue source, will produce effects which are highly perverse fiscally in that there will be no correlation with true revenue ability under that tax.

7.6 Conclusion

This chapter has been concerned with the way in which revenue is raised to pay for the provision of public goods and services. Various philosophical and practical principles for accomplishing this task have been reviewed and it should already be clear that revenue raising is not a simple task. Evolution of tax and charging systems from at least the period of ancient Egyptian revenue raising has not yet solved the problem of finding revenue sources which satisfy completely each of the canons of revenue raising. With respect especially to one of the most important canons, that of equity, it has been demonstrated that, as in the case of inter-personal comparisons, similarly for geographical comparisons, no unambiguous criterion of equity of treatment is available. The aim of fiscal equity, as discussed in chapter 4, should be equal treatment of equals, and equally unequal treatment of unequals under the public fisc. The precise criterion of individual and geographical ability against which to judge equality is by no means clear. In some situations personal income will be the best determinant of that quality, in others it will be wealth, expenditures or some other criterion.

If the measurement of geographical ability in revenue raising is difficult and complex, the assessment of revenue burdens at their point of fiscal incidence, discussed in the next chapter, is no less difficult to determine. As we shall see, this requires the tracing of the flows of revenue from the point of initial payment to the location of final burdens. When we have determined this location of burdens, it is then possible to assess how far revenue burdens conform with the canons and principles of equity, i.e. how far revenue burdens match revenue ability. This topic is discussed in the next chapter.

8

The revenue burden: the geography of revenue incidence

"a tax laid in any place is like a pebble falling into and making a circle in a lake, till one circle produces and gives motion to another, and the whole circumference is agitated from the centre."

Lord Mansfield *Speech on taxing the colonies* (1766)

8.1 Introduction

Revenue burden measures the geographical variation of the pressure placed on the fiscal resources of individuals, businesses, and governments in different locations. Whereas fiscal capacity discussed in the previous chapter determines the ability of people or jurisdictions to support given levels of taxation, fiscal burden describes the final distribution of incidence of tax payments; i.e. who pays what, where. Moreover, the geography of revenue burdens allows the comparison of fiscal capacity with burden and thus permits questions to be answered on fiscal effort: the relationship of burden to geographical and individual ability, i.e. who makes what effort to pay what taxes.

The major difficulty in assessing revenue burden and effort is the determination of who actually bears the final burden. The taxpayer is frequently not the person who actually loses disposable income to the public fisc. As noted by Lord Mansfield in the quotation above, tax and other revenue burdens, although placed on particular individuals, firms or locations, diffuse so as to affect a much wider range of people. Indeed, in some cases the taxpayer may be able to shift his entire burden onto someone else. Because revenue and money are fungible (that is, they can be shifted between subcategories without ready notice) it is difficult to determine, in accounting terms, who actually bears the fiscal burden.

The revenues raised from any individual or firm located in a particular jurisdiction are shifted in three different directions: first, there are those revenues which go directly to provide services at a given level in a particular jurisdiction; second, there are those revenues which are shifted to higher level governments, largely through personal and corporate income taxation, which is subsequently used to provide national public goods (merit goods) or to redistribute geographical and personal incomes; third, there are those revenue flows which are used to make side payments to other jurisdictions,

177

Table 8.1 Revenue matrix of flows with reference to a specified local political unit.

Revenues to	*Revenues from*		
	Specified jurisdiction	*Higher level government*	*Similar level government*
Specified jurisdiction	Revenues generated and used internally	Grants and intergovernmental transfers	Side payments from other areas for shared services
Higher level government	Transfers to higher level government to pay for merit goods and redistribution	Revenues raised and used at national level	Transfers to higher level government for merit goods and redistribution
Similar level government	Side payments to other areas for shared services	Grants and transfers to other governments	Revenues generated and used internal to other areas

either as tax on benefits spillovers or as payments for shared services. Each local jurisdiction will have a similar three-fold division of revenue destination. In addition, higher level governments raise revenues on a national, state, or regional base. This revenue may be destined ultimately to be spent either at the higher level, to provide national or regional merit goods available to all, irrespective of income or geographical location of residence, or to enter into intergovernment transfers, grant programmes, revenue-sharing and tax credits which aim at equalizing personal and geographical incomes (see chapters 11 to 13). The complete configuration of the revenue flows is shown in table 8.1, as a matrix of accounting flows, the revenue side of the intergovernmental interregional accounts discussed in chapter 4. From this matrix it is possible to determine where the burden of revenue-raising falls on a geographical basis. It is also possible to disaggregate the matrix into income groups for each jurisdiction to determine the interpersonal, intersectoral, and interregional pattern of burden incidence.

From this accounts matrix for revenue burden, three elements of geographical tax burdens can be derived. First, there is the degree to which taxes placed on any individual or jurisdiction shift and diffuse to become burdens on other individuals and locations. Assessment of this effect requires analysis of tax shifting, discussed in section 8.2 and tax exporting discussed in section 8.3. These components have important effects on tax competition and spillover between different jurisdictions. A second component is the assessment of total revenue incidence, by income group and by location, and this is discussed in section 8.4. Third, is the relation of fiscal need to fiscal capacity giving geographical variation in the pattern of tax effort and tax severity, discussed in section 8.5.

8.2 The shifting of burden incidence

The determination of final revenue burdens involves the tracing of revenue effects to their point of final influence or incidence. In most cases the taxpayer is in no sense the bearer of the tax burden, because he is able to shift his payments, in full or in part, onto someone else. Hence it is necessary to differentiate the effects of taxes into three categories:

(i) *revenue impacts*, concerned with the initial stages of who makes the tax payment;

(ii) *revenue effects*, concerned with the changes in prices, incomes, welfare, and the quality and quantity of goods and services produced and received as a result of tax impacts;

(iii) *revenue incidence*, concerned with tracing all these shifts in burdens of taxation to the final bearer of that burden.

The study of tax impacts is quite inadequate in determining revenue burdens. Tax effect studies concentrate on modifications to resource allocation and to price as a result of taxation, for example altering the proportion of labour and capital to change a firm's liability to corporation tax (so-called production shifting; Mair 1975). Hence, it is only from tax incidence studies which concentrate on the modifications to the distribution ensuing from particular tax policies, that it is possible to assess the geography of final tax burdens. It is this latter, incidence, approach which is of primary concern in this chapter.

There are two main types of shifting which affect final incidence: forward and backward. Forward shifting occurs when the owner of a given good or service is able to shift his taxes and revenue burdens forward onto the user of that resource or service. This occurs if corporate income taxes are passed from the producer to the consumer, or when property taxes are passed from the landlord to the tenant. Backward shifting occurs when the user of a given good or service is able to shift his taxes onto the owner or producer of that service. Of course this simple distinction of the impact of shifting of tax measures is somewhat simplified. In practice, a complex set of adjustments occurs in the apportionment of any tax burden. An increase in property tax for example, could be shifted onto the tenant, but he will respond (under the constraint of a fixed budget and under the neo-classical equilibrium theory) by finding cheaper accommodation, thus reducing demand, and thereby shifting a burden back onto the landlord by reducing the market value of the property asset; this in turn will reduce the property tax payable (under most property tax assessment procedures) which will shift some of the burdens back to the government, and if the government must raise a fixed amount of revenue, the burden is then shifted either onto other tax sources and hence other taxpayers, or back onto the landlord and tenant by the need to increase the rate at which property tax is levied. Similar responses occur through the market mechanism in complex shiftings of burdens of corporate income tax and consumer sales taxes. Indeed all tax shifting is subject to a complex interplay of forces producing feedback not only between the actors directly involved, but also between individuals and enterprises in the national economy as a whole. This has led some writers, for example Verri and Carnap, to infer incorrectly that the burden of all taxes is equally borne by all. This view cannot be supported but it serves to emphasize that the assessment of the incidence to tax burdens is no easy task.

A large variety of theoretical approaches to analysing the incidence of tax burdens has been proposed (see Seligman 1927, for an exhaustive review up to that date, and Groves 1964, ch. 6 for a more recent review). These approaches fall into six broad classes. The first of these, due to the *Physiocrats*, especially Quesnay, Mirabeau and Mercier de la Rivière, argues that, since agriculture is the sole source of wealth, this sector must ultimately bear the full burden of taxation. Hence the physiocrats advocated that taxation should be placed only on the purchase of land. This would allow not only the effects of shifting to be eliminated, but also would tie tax increases directly to growth of the national income (believed to be increased only by increases in agricultural output). Whilst incorrect in its basic premises, this theory has the valuable component of linking taxation to national output and had great influence in keeping the French public finances under reasonable control during the time of Louis XIV under the physiocrat Finance Minister Turgot. A related *capitalization* theory propounded in the 17th century by Young, du Puynode, Schaffle and others, holds that all taxes are passed on to the capital value of land; this value is reduced by an equal amount to that of the tax, and then passed on to all subsequent purchasers at that modified value. Hence shifting effects only a loss of value to the initial owner.

In contrast to the theories contending that all incidence falls on agricultural production, a second class of incidence theories, often termed *diffusion theory*, contends that it does not matter where a tax is imposed, all taxes diffuse throughout the body of the economic system and fall on consumption. Prominent figures in this theory are Verri, Hamilton, Carnard, Prittwitz, and Thiers. Verri (1771), for example, holds that the effect of every tax was to raise prices and thence shifted all incidence to the consumer. Carnard (1801) refined this concept and stated that the incidence was not in proportion to the level of final consumption, but in proportion instead to the ratio of individual consumption to aggregate consumption of each commodity. Such a theory has the interesting, but erroneous, implication that incomes can be re-distributed by the rich exercising their purchasing power to achieve higher levels of consumption.

The third class of theory of tax incidence, are the so-called *absolute theories* (Seligman 1927) of Adam Smith and Ricardo. In fact Smith devotes small space to the incidence issue in his the book *The Wealth of Nations,* but believes that since all income was derived from either rent, profit or wages, taxes on these sources could be transferred only onto the social classes of owners, employers and consumers from which these incomes were derived. Ricardo (1817) had similar views about the absolute transferability of tax incidence, but the two authors differ in detail. Smith believed that a tax on rent fell completely on the landlord, and taxes on profit shifted (except for interest payments) onto the consumer. On the other hand, Ricardo held that the rent taxes fall onto the consumer, and profit taxes fall on the employer. On wage taxes they agree that these were always shifted onto the employer.

In contrast to these earlier theories, a fourth school, which Seligman terms the *eclectic and agnostic theories*, contends that the incidence of taxation is so complex that it is impossible to draw any general conclusions about tax incidence. This rather negative approach has been proposed by Say, Sismondi, Mill, von Thunen and Hamilton. For a more practical approach we must rely on two final sets of theories: equilibrium theory and Marxist theory. *Equilibrium theories* allow a fifth approach to tax incidence which is concerned with measuring and tracing out the tax impacts on all flows and transactions of goods, services, and people. This approach is due to Cournot, Walras, Wicksell, Conigliani, Barone, Marshall, Edgeworth, and Hobson. It relates the theory of tax incidence to the general theory of welfare and value and is the basis of most modern theories of incidence. It emphasizes the effect of taxes on prices (i.e. resource allocation) and seeks to determine in what quantity the owner or user (seller or buyer) of a given good or service bears the tax burden. From this determination it is then possible to determine the effects of the tax on the distribution of incomes and welfare. The crucial factor is price determination on the elasticity of demand and supply with price changes induced by taxation. With respect to capital assets, however, there is an income-producting potential, and a tax on these assets will lower the rate of return or income produced. These different effects of taxation on sales and asset values, predicted by equilibrium theory (e.g. see Groves 1964, ch. 6) are summarized as follows:

	Shifting	*Capitalization*
Tax burden	on future owners of commodity	on present owners of income-producing assets
Price effects	price rises to offset levy of tax	price falls to offset levy of tax
Supply elasticity	supply is elastic and is curtailed	supply is inelastic and remains the same

The interrelationship between revenue imposition and price, income and substitution effects is shown in figure 8.1. The major features to note are the complex interplay of taxation with price determination, the distribution of income incentives, and hence with the change and growth in the overall economic wealth.

182

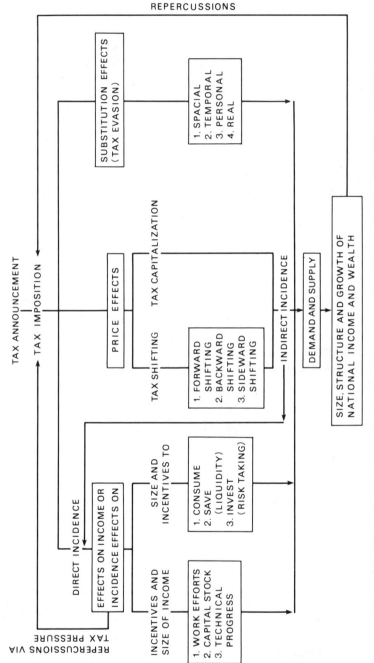

Figure 8.1 Effect of taxation on prices, income and substitution. (*Source:* Rechtenwald 1971, figure II.1.)

The sixth and final set of theories, the *Marxist* and radical approaches, ascribe all taxation policies as aimed at shifting incidence onto the working classes. Due primarily to Rousseau, Proudhon and Marx, this interpretation sees the role of the taxation system, like public finance and the state itself, as primarily designed as a subtle mechanism of exploitation. Thus tax burdens are believed to fall largely on the consumer, shifting incidence either from the employers as the owners of the means of production, or from the landlord, to the purchaser and tenant. Although this shifting is incomplete, in that all consumers irrespective of their wealth will bear some burden, the preponderance of incidence is assumed to fall on working classes creating a surplus for the owners of property and the means of production. Public social programmes and progressive income taxes are then interpreted solely as an exercise in hegemony: a strategy to appease poorer groups and to legitimize the system of class rule.

None of these approaches is entirely satisfactory and the modern theory of fiscal incidence divides shifting effects into two categories: shifting between income groups and economic sectors, and shifting between geographical locations (Musgrave and Musgrave 1976; Rechtenwald 1971). The second element, of geographical shifting, we leave for discussion until the next section. Shifting between economic sectors occurs to some extent with all taxes and revenue sources. Table 8.2 displays a composite picture of incidence of payments and incidence of final burden of taxation as now generally credited in a large number of studies in various countries at different levels of government. The major revenue source subject to virtually no shifting from the payer is personal income tax. Major shifting affects corporate income tax, employment payroll taxes and severance taxes. Major shifting also affects sales taxes and user charges when these are levied on businesses. Shifting of corporate taxes is dependent on four factors which determine the degree of monopoly of local production. First, there is the nature of the tax, forward shifting being total for VAT-I and consumption taxes, but only partial for taxes levied on the production stage. Second, forward shifting increases the higher the degree of local monopoly of production by one geographical location on production. Third, there is the taxing area share in the supply of the taxed goods to other markets: forward shifting increases the greater the dominance of supply. Finally, there is more forward shifting the smaller the degree of competition from other products. The extent of shifting of corporate income taxes has resulted in a number of formulae which are used to assess the share of fiscal burdens that a given business will bear in any jurisdiction. These formulae are frequently used in assessing the extent of federal offset (or tax credit) allowed to reduce the degree of multiple taxation in federal countries. The most common formula used in the US for such assessment is the 'Massachusetts formula'. This gives equal weight to each of three elements measuring the relative concentration of a firm's activities in a particular jurisdiction, given as follows:

Table 8.2 Extent of revenue shifting for various revenue sources. (*Sources*: Gillespie 1975; Musgrave and Musgrave 1976; Musgrave *et al.* 1951, 1974; Newcomer 1935; Shoup 1969; US Treasury 1943; Pechman and Okner 1974)

Revenue	Incidence of payment	Incidence of burden
(1) Taxes		
Property tax	owner of property	(a) owner in owner-occupied housing (b) mainly tenant in rented housing (c) consumer of business or farm products
Income tax: personal corporate	income receiver	not shifted: income receiver partial or full shifting onto (a) consumers (b) holders of capital
Sales tax: general motor fuel alcohol tobacco public utilities	(a) consumer (b) producer	(a) little shifting: sometimes significant if vendor chooses to absorb tax as promotional incentives (b) up to 30% shifted mostly onto consumer; perhaps onto other producers when on stages of production process
Value-added tax VAT-I	various producers at various production stages, with deductions for producers of capital goods.	almost entirely onto consumer
VAT-II	various stages of production with deductions for capital depreciation: burden directly proportional to income	shifted 60 to 70% onto consumer
VAT-III	various stages of production process with no deductions allowed: burden directly proportional to production	shifted about 60% onto consumer
Motor licences	(a) private vehicle owners (b) commercial vehicle owners	(a) consumer; no shifting (b) consumer, mostly shifted
Death and gifts tax	donor	donor, but may be partially shifted to receiver sometimes
Employment and payroll taxes	employer	30 to 40% shifted onto consumer
Severance taxes	producer	largely onto consumer
Customs duties	consumer	consumer; no shifting
(2) User charges	(a) private consumer (b) commercial consumer	(a) consumer; no shifting (b) other producers, mostly onto consumer

$$\text{jurisdictional} \atop \text{tax burden} = \tfrac{1}{3} \left(\frac{\begin{array}{l}\text{Average values}\\ \text{of taxable}\\ \text{property in}\\ \text{jurisdiction}\end{array}}{\begin{array}{l}\text{Average value}\\ \text{of company's}\\ \text{total taxable}\\ \text{property}\end{array}} + \frac{\begin{array}{l}\text{wages, salaries}\\ \text{and other pay-}\\ \text{ments to the}\\ \text{jurisdiction's}\\ \text{employees}\end{array}}{\begin{array}{l}\text{Total wages,}\\ \text{salaries and}\\ \text{payments to}\\ \text{employees}\end{array}} + \frac{\begin{array}{l}\text{gross receipts}\\ \text{within}\\ \text{jurisdiction}\end{array}}{\begin{array}{l}\text{Total gross}\\ \text{receipts}\end{array}} \right)$$

Other elements which may also be considered in such formulae are manufacturing costs, 'business done', purchases of goods and services, cost value of capital assets, accounts received, stocks and inventories, and net sales (see, for example, Hansen and Perloff 1944). The use of different formulae in different jurisdictions can result in tax being levied on greater than the 100% of total company income, but this may be offset by tax exports, as discussed in the next section.

8.3 Revenue exporting

The shifting of revenue burdens between jurisdictions which are pursuing independent taxing policies produces variable geographical incidence and is usually referred to as tax exporting or tax spillover. It is the converse of benefit spillover to be discussed in chapter 9. Tax exporting, like benefit spillover, can form a major element in interjurisdictional competition and fiscal prudence discussed in chapter 4. Hogan and Shelton (1974), for example, have produced a model which examines the strategies which a jurisdiction must follow to maximize the exported revenue burdens and a number of studies have found such strategies important in the organization of US school finance (see, for example, Bowman 1974).

Two important cases of tax exporting are with taxes on various stages of the production process, and taxes on transport. Taxes on any stage of the production process cause a rise in the price of the finished or semi-finished product which is then passed on to the purchaser. If the purchaser is outside the original taxing area, a shift in tax incidence has occurred. Obviously taxes on value-added at the production stage tend to lower the competitive ability of local industry and so these taxes cannot be widely adopted. However, they can be applied when an area has considerable competitive edge or monopoly on that stage of production. Classic examples in the US are tobacco taxes imposed in the South which are shifted onto the national market, and severance taxes imposed in the jurisdictions producing oil, gas and other natural resources. It has been claimed that exported severance taxes yield 34% of Louisiana's revenues, for example. It has also been claimed that New York City's monopoly of certain branches of finance has been used in the same way. This latter yielded 5 to 15% of New York State's revenues in the 1940s. In each case a spatial zone with a monopoly of resources can exploit its position by passing on taxes elsewhere. Transport taxes can be used in a similar way when there are limited alternative trade routes available. The exploitation of transport monopolies by the medieval Rhine traders, the Hanseatic League, the 17th-century commercial shipping monopolies of first the Dutch and then the English traders, the railway and road taxes exacted by the US mountain States on east–west traffic, are examples of these transport monopolies in which the locally exacted taxes are passed on in increased cost of goods to consumers elsewhere.

Two approaches to assessment of the extent of tax exporting for local jurisdictions have been evolved. First, there is the assessment of gross tax exports, which is sometimes referred to as the *Michigan approach* from its initial use by Musgrave and Daicoff (1958) for that State. This approach assesses the tax exports of each local area in isolation of the tax effects of all other areas. The second approach assesses the net tax exports, and is sometimes referred to as the *Wisconsin approach* from its use in that State by Groves and Knight (1959), although its first use is due to Sundelson and Mushkin (1944). From the results of either approach, a net geographical balance, surplus, or deficit cannot be used to infer the same incidence characteristics for different income groups or firms since imports to one group may balance exports from other groups. Thus tax exporting has complex redistributional consequences which can only be assessed by disaggregating gross or net flows by industrial and income groups.

The relationship of measures of geographical tax capacity to tax exporting has been developed by Pogue (1976). Pogue suggests four indices of fiscal capacity which take account of tax exporting. These indices are compared with simple *per capita* income and the ACIR representative tax system for a sample of 14 US SMSAs in table 8.3. Each new capacity index is based on a modification of the following formula:

$$T_j = Y_j - F_j - M_j - X_j + I_j,$$

where for each jurisdiction j, T_j is the fiscal capacity, Y_j is the total personal income, F_j is the total tax or non-tax payment by individuals to higher level governments, M_j is the net impact of direct taxes, X_j is the aggregate disposable personal income, and I_j is the indirect revenue of each jurisdiction from businesses and individuals as sales tax and charges. The capacity indexes, with exports taken into account, are sub-divided into two classes. First, those which take account of exporting, and those which do not. Second, those which deflate the index to take account of regional differences in the purchasing power of disposable income, and those which do not. Centring attention on the capacity measures which include exports (columns 3 and 4 of table 8.3) the entries can be interpreted as follows. New York is able to import 10.91 times the national *per capita* average of imported revenues. In contrast,

Table 8.3 Relation of tax capacity measures to level of tax exporting; 1973 income series, with US ACIR (1971) representative tax base index; index $3 = 100 \times (T_j/M_j)/T$; index 4, as index 3; indices 5 and 6 calculated as for indices 3 and 4 with $I_j = 1.0$. (*Source:* Pogue 1976, table 1)

			Suggested index			
			Marginal exporting		No marginal exporting	
	Per					
	capita	ACIR	Not		Not	
SMSA	income	index	deflated	Deflated	deflated	Deflated
	1	2	3	4	5	6
New York	142	141	1,091	656	746	487
Chicago	128	121	926	638	518	374
Los Angeles	126	149	980	721	566	437
Philadelphia	111	94	402	271	301	214
Baltimore	103	96	181	131	146	117
Cleveland	119	122	800	543	423	301
St Louis	114	102	587	375	333	232
Boston	114	94	474	78	342	84
San Diego	104	107	365	164	241	140
New Orleans	97	110	47	N/A	62	N/A
Seattle	124	144	880	521	474	302
Pittsburgh	104	93	252	187	198	155
Memphis	85	111	− 214	N/A	− 80	N/A
Columbus	96	96	− 12	N/A	44	N/A
US average	100	100	100	100	100	100

Memphis and Columbus export respective proportions of their own source revenues equal to 2.14 and 0.12 times the national average of imported or exported revenue. Such results indicate contradictory policies that these jurisdictions might follow in inter-jurisdictional competition: New York and most of the SMSAs tabulated can raise increasing proportions of revenues from exports from other areas, whilst Memphis and Columbus might seek alternative revenue sources, the raising of which does not leak into other jurisdictions.

Studies of geographical tax exporting have been few in number, mainly because of their complexity and the difficulty of assessing tax burdens spatially. Table 8.4 summarizes the results of major US studies on tax exporting between States by type of revenue source. In addition comprehensive study of 41 US SMSAs by Muller (1976) demonstrates the differing export and imports of revenue burdens between different categories of cities. Growing cities are exporting less of their revenue burdens than declining cities. Table 8.5 shows comparative figures for seven revenue sources. Exporting of revenue burdens, as in all tax shifting, is highest with respect to commercial taxes, but personal income and residential property taxes are also important. Geographical distribution by State of total tax exports and exports for specific taxes is shown in figure 8.2 using McClure's (1967) estimates.

187

Table 8.4 Estimates of revenue exporting at State level from various studies in the US. (*Sources:* as cited at head of columns). Notes: [1]Long run effects differ from short run effects in McClure's study by the allowance for reimporting of products in the long term which have been affected by local tax exports in the short term. [2]The results of the US Treasury and Sundelson and Mushkin studies are not directly comparable because of the very different tax mixes in the 1940s and 1960s. [3]Includes effect of federal offsets only, with addition of factor to allow for reduction in incomes by shifting onto factors of production (commuting, which is only important in D. C., St Louis, New York, and Kansas City at State level, has been ignored—McClure, personal communication)

Revenue source	Extent of exporting (%) US total			
	US Treasury (1943)[2]	Sundelson and Mushkin (1944)[3]	McClure (1967)[1] Short run	Long run
(1) Taxes				
Property tax				
residential	—	0 }	25.5	17.5
commercial		7.7 }		
Income tax				
personal	—	0	17.7	13.8[3]
corporate	16.0	82.0	73.4	47.3
Sales tax				
general	—	6.2	23.8	23.2
motor fuel	44.0	—		
alcohol	33.0	2.8 }		17.9
tobacco	81.0	—	22.8	
public utilities	16.0	34.1 }		
Motor licences	—	4.3 }		
Employment and payroll taxes	10.0	—	—	—
Severance	—	83.5	—	—
Customs duties	44.0	—	—	—
Total (all taxes)	—	4.6	23.8	0.6
(2) User charges	—	—	—	—

These estimates show that considerable tax exporting occurs equal to about 25% US State and local taxes, or $10.2 billion in 1962. Although specific to the economic location and the fiscal structure of the US economy, these results can be used to give indications of the relative orders of magnitude of tax exporting which affect different revenue sources.

Property tax, although displaying considerable geographical variation, is usually exported to a very considerable extent. This is due in small part to payment of property taxes by external owners of local property, but mainly to the forward shifting of commercial property tax onto the prices of products which are then purchased outside the taxing jurisdiction. The exporting of property taxes on railways, manufacturers and mining is a major component

Table 8.5   Level of tax exporting for growing and declining cities of the US in 1973. (*Source:* Muller 1976, Table C-2)

Revenue source	% revenue paid by non-residents		
	Growing cities	Declining cities	New York City
Property tax			
residential	2.0	2.4	2.7
commercial	0.6	10.6	13.3
Sales tax	2.4	1.5	2.7
Income tax			
personal	1.1	4.3	0.9
corporate	0.5	1.9	2.6
Other local taxes	1.1	0.5	0.2
Other local revenues	4.4	0.4	2.9
Total all revenue sources	118%	25%	

of the shifting effect, and it is the component which leads to much of the inter-area variation of tax export rates. For example, in McClure's (1967) study, Arizona, Indiana, Kentucky, Louisiana, Michigan, Montana, South Carolina, Texas, West Virginia, and Wyoming all have large export rates arising from shifting of property taxes on the manufacturing and mining base. Similarly, in the Sundelson and Mushkin (1944) study of net tax exports, the most marked differences between States occur where the areas are imposing large taxes on large mineral resource outputs which flow to other States. Differences in long and short term rates of exports are also accounted for largely by the effects of property taxes (together with severance taxes) on raw material resources.

Personal local income taxes are affected by fairly limited tax exporting. Exporting arises from five causes all of which are minor. First, there is a relatively small element of individual tax returns made at the place of business rather than domicile. This affects about 3.3% of all the US tax returns (US Treasury 1943) and its effect on exporting across State boundaries is likely to be rather less than this figure. Second, there is the allocation of taxes between residents and non-residents due to commuting. Tax is withheld at the source of employment, but the burden falls on the personal incomes of individuals living in other jurisdictions. This is usually a small percentage at State or regional level, but increases markedly as the size of jurisdictions decreases, rising to 90% in some urban areas. At the US State level the highest rate of commuting is for the District of Columbia with 53.9% in 1962. The next highest is Delaware with 7% showing its relative minor importance at the State level for almost all States. However, it is extremely important in urban areas (see chapter 4). The third cause of exporting of personal income taxes is the

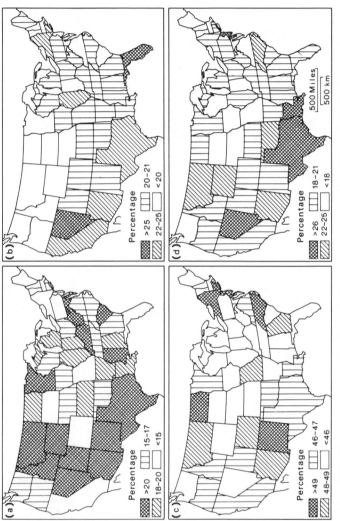

Figure 8.2 Revenue exporting by State and revenue source in the US in 1963. (Data derived from McClure 1967, table 6 and 7; long-term export effects only.)
  a   Property tax
  b   General sales tax
  c   Corporate income tax
  d   Total taxes

effect of central government offsets (often referred to as 'primary offsets'), in those countries in which local taxes are deductible from central tax bills. This shifts the tax burden from local jurisdictions to the nation as a whole. Since local tax-payers receiving this offset are also national tax-payers, the extent of the offset is reduced to an amount depending upon the marginal rates of income tax paid by tax-payers eligible for deductions in each jurisdiction, weighted by the fraction of income in each jurisdiction subject to each marginal rate. The effect of such tax offsets on moving individuals to different marginal tax rates has minor effect and is usually ignored. A fourth factor in exporting personal income taxes is the effect of backward shifting which produces a 'secondary offset'. To the extent that local income taxes reduce income, they reduce demand and hence prices in turn. Thus as local income taxes rise, local gross income falls and there is a secondary offset by which the central government lightens the tax burden of the local area. The respective average US figures for primary and secondary offsets estimated by McClure (1967) are 17.7% and 13.8%. A final feature of income tax shifting is the encouragement that differential tax rates gives to personal migration. At the State and regional level this will be minor, but within metropolitan areas this can be a considerable feature in increasing the export of income tax burdens especially by commuters. Despite this variety of possible means of exporting, however, actual tax exports of personal income taxes are small when personal mobility is ignored.

Corporate income taxes are the major source of tax exports, and are exported in four ways. First, State and local taxes can usually be set against central government tax burdens as deductible allowances (this is true in the United States, Canada, Australia and most of the European countries). The impact of this offset, like that for personal incomes, is determined by the marginal rate of central corporate income tax weighted by the percentage of corporate income subject to each marginal rate. Second, in some countries, notably most of Western Europe, spatially differentiated tax incentives to industrial investment are provided which represent a further offset of local tax to the national tax-payer. The extent of exporting in this case is determined as the reduction in tax payable, firm by firm, depending upon the date and nature of their investment mix of buildings, plant and machinery, research and development costs, and so forth. Third, to the extent that corporate taxation is not offset by tax reduction elsewhere, the tax on products and corporate incomes is usually shifted onto the final consumer. This is the most important source of tax exporting since these products are sold in variable proportions to other jurisdictions. However, if, as in the US, local corporate taxes are allowed as offsets against central taxes, this effect will be greatly diminished, although it is still significant where one jurisdiction has a considerable monopoly on a given stage of the production process, or upon a given product. A fourth source of exporting is that arising from the shifting of burdens relating to corporate taxation of dividends. In this case burdens are shifted out of the local area in proportion to the percentage of non-local residents holding local company shares.

Sales taxes, whether in the form of general, specific, or value-added burdens, are exported in three ways: first, in the ratio of resident to non-resident sales; second, to the extent that federal offsets for local sales tax are allowable against corporate income taxation; and third, to the extent that local producers can shift tax effects to consumers in increased prices depending upon the degree of monopoly in the market. The Groves and Knight (1959) Wisconsin tax study, for example, estimated sales tax exports at 80% of that State's tax imposition, mainly arising from the sale of manufactures to non-residents. In the same study, exports were estimated at 5% of retail sales tax, 50% of sales tax on farm output, and a small proportion of the tax on sales of goods to visitors, students, tourists, salesmen, and others receiving incomes in other areas. In the Michigan tax study of Musgrave and Daicoff, it was estimated that 54.9% of the sales tax burden was exported.

Turning to the remaining taxes shown in table 8.3, it can be expected that death and inheritance taxes will be exported in proportion to the extent to which taxes paid by residents of the taxing area are offset by tax credits from higher level governments. This varies from about 6.9% in Iowa to 85.2% in Florida, with a US average of 36.6%, in McClure's (1967) study. The differences arise from the extent to which different State and local governments employ these taxes.

Severance tax is a very important source of tax exports in those locations which produce a large quantity of basic raw materials. In Louisiana and Texas, McClure found 34% and 32% export rates, respectively (the latter includes also export of property tax on petroleum reserves). Similarly, Brownlee (1960) found iron ore severance tax an important element in exporting from Minnesota. However, the net effect of such tax exports are often reduced by the need to repurchase the manufactured goods which contain in their prices the effect of the severance tax shifting. In Louisiana and Texas, McClure estimates that this reduces the net (long term) exports to 28% and 27% respectively.

Customs duty exporting can be very considerable, but the extent frequently depends upon the supplementary effect of transport rates. If all imported commodities are distributed uniformly across the national economy in relation to demand, then there are no internal exporting effects. However, when heavy or high bulk goods are involved, such as sugar or iron ore, then transport costs from the port of entry often produce two sectors in the national market: one based on local production, and one based on imported goods bearing customs duties. Those areas dependent upon imported goods are subject to a tax export to central government, and hence to people in the nation as a whole.

It is a major conclusion of each of the studies of the US summarized in table 8.4 that, despite high tax export rates, there is a reasonable balance of exports and imports between the various States. Indeed McClure's plot of the export effects using the Lorenz curve (of cumulative percentage of exported taxes against cumulative percentage of all taxes with States ranked in increasing order of export rates) shows only slight departure from the 45° line indicating equality of exports. Hence, at State level, despite very unequal shifting and exporting effects, final incidence patterns are not markedly affected. However, there has been no examination, as yet, of the effects of shifting and exports from the point of view of their effects on particular firms or income groups: it may well be that exports have important distributional effects; and this will be very significant within urban areas, as discussed in chapter 14.

Apart from distributional effects, exporting may also result in inefficiency. Since the real costs of local services are not borne locally, there is no necessary matching of costs and benefits, and local goods may be underpriced. McClure (1967) estimates this underpricing effect as 40% in the US. This may distort both the choice of public and private goods, and the balance of central–local relations: with high tax export areas favouring autonomy, and low tax export areas favouring greater central control and transfer programmes.

The ultimate degree of tax shifting and exporting depends upon the degree of elasticity of supply and demand for the products and services bearing the tax burdens. Differential elasticities between jurisdictions will reduce exported burdens for those areas with high demand elasticity, and increase burdens for areas with low demand elasticity. Between countries, a considerable degree of attention has been given to schemes to harmonize taxation from the point of view of neutralizing tax exports. This has usually resulted in proposals for uniform taxation schemes (see Musgrave and Richman 1964; Rechtenwald 1971: Shoup 1967). The Value-added tax in particular has been seen as a most useful method of neutralizing revenue exports (see, for example, the Tinbergen Report, ECSC 1953, and the Neumark Report, EEC 1963).

CONSTITUTIONAL IMPLICATIONS OF TAX EXPORTING

The different tax export effects of different revenue sources often lead one revenue base to be preferred to another at local level. In particular it has been suggested that tax bases should be aligned with the locations to which benefits accrue. Thus it is usually suggested that personal and corporate income taxes should be primarily national level taxes, property taxes primarily local, and sales tax primarily intermediate (see Musgrave and Musgrave 1976; Thrall 1974). Detailed discussion of these arguments is given in chapter 11.

8.4 The geographical incidence of revenue burden

As the previous discussion demonstrates, the major difficulty in assessing revenue burdens is the determination of who actually bears the final burden once all shifting and exporting effects have been taken into account. The final assessment of burdens is usually referred to as the geographical form of individual fiscal incidence: who pays what amount of taxes as a function of where they live. Few studies have undertaken the task of assessing revenue burdens taking into account the full effect of both shifting and tax exporting. Rather, the emphasis of research has been on assessment of burdens by income group at national level, or by aggregate groups at regional level. The corpus of results in these two areas of research will be summarized briefly below, before a more detailed discussion is made of the very limited number of studies that have given assessments of revenue burdens disaggregated into both income groups and regional or jurisdictional categories.

STUDIES OF REVENUE BURDENS BY INCOME GROUPS

There is a considerable history of research into the issue of the incidence of revenue burdens between income groups at national level. Each of the theories of shifting discussed in section 8.2 has to some extent incorporated this element. Modern research uses the assumptions on shifting detailed in table 8.2, but has been subject to considerable debate as to the definition of income which should be used (see Hall 1938; Musgrave and Frame 1952; Musgrave *et al.* 1948; Newcomer 1937; Pechman 1973; Tarasov 1942; TMEC 1938–9; Tucker 1951). On the basis of these shifting assumptions, the incidence of total revenue burdens at national level between income groups of various countries is shown in figure 8.3. For most countries the aggregate burden of taxes is largely proportional to income. Progression affects only a small number of income receivers in very high tax brackets. The regression of taxation at very low incomes especially for non-central government taxes should be noted. In each case local and intermediate level taxes are regressive, especially at lower incomes, whilst federal and central level taxes are the only level at which an element of progression is present, and this is usually small. In each case broad definitions of income have been used with the effect of non-money income of food and lodging to farmers and domestic servants having been taken into account.

STUDIES OF REVENUE BURDEN BY REGION

Whereas national studies of fiscal incidence by income group give no geographical disaggregation, most studies of geographical fiscal incidence give no disaggregation by income group. Many studies of such geographical tax burdens have been made for the United States and other countries but there has been no attempt to trace fiscal incidence on a geographical basis.

An important set of comparative data on differences in regional tax burdens is provided in a recent EEC study (EEC 1977) the results of which are reproduced in figure 8.4 and table 8.6. The tax rates and final burden in this table includes allowance for shifting of revenue burdens, but not for tax exporting. Apart from this difficulty there are also a number of statistical and definitional problems which require these data to be treated with some care.

194

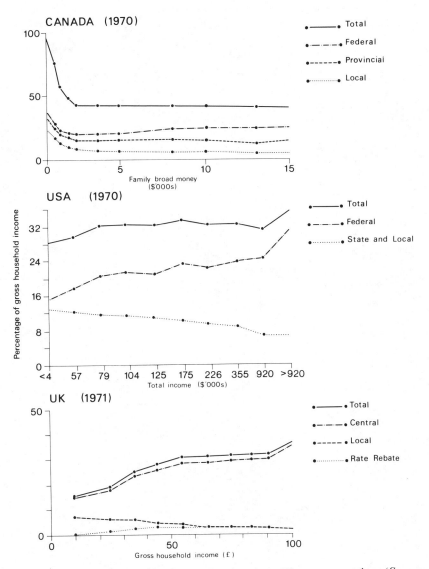

Figure 8.3 Tax burden by income group for three Western countries. (*Source*: *Canada*: Gillespie 1976; *US*: Musgrave *et al.* 1974; *UK*: *UK Committee of Enquiry into Local Government Finance 1976*, table 38.)

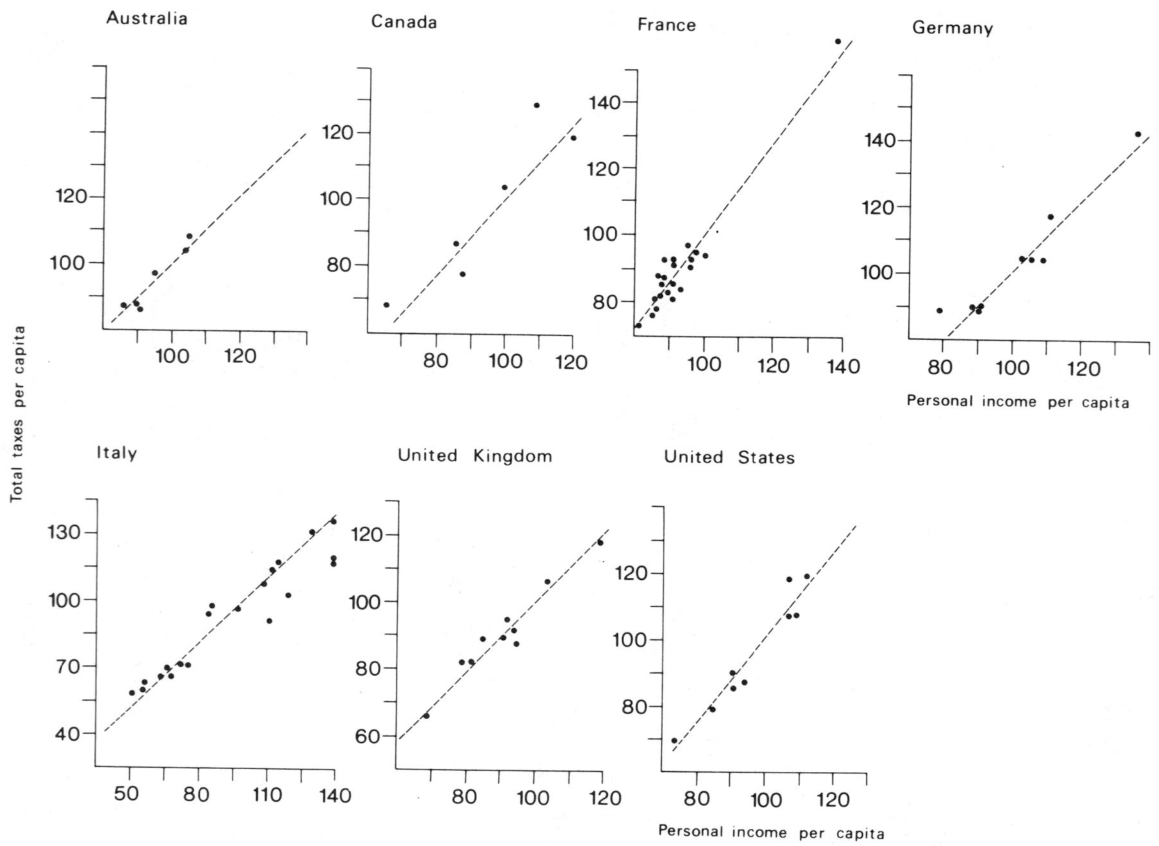

Figure 8.4 The relation of total *per capita* tax burden to total *per capita* personal incomes in the regions of seven countries. (Data derived from EEC 1977, pp. 259–60.)

196

Table 8.6 Elasticity and redistribution effects of various tax sources for redistribution between regions. (*Source:* EEC 1977.) Dates Australia 1971/72, Canada 1969, Germany 1970, USA 1965–71, France 1969, Italy 1973, UK 1964.

Personal income tax

Country and number of regions	Average tax rate	Elasticity with personal income	Redistribution power ratio	Change in Gini coeff.
Australia (6)	14.2	1.44	6.3	9.3
Canada (10)	9.3	1.61	5.7	7.0
Germany (10)	4.2	1.96	4.1	3.0
USA (48)	11.8	1.64	7.5	6.0
France (21)	4.6	2.73	8.0	7.7
Italy (20)	5.0	2.1	5.3	6.2
UK (10)	11.7	1.65	7.6	8.5

General sales tax

	Average tax rate	Elasticity with personal income	Redistribution power ratio	Change in Gini coeff.
Australia	2.5	0.94	−0.2	0.6
Canada	4.4	0.6	−1.6	−1.6
Germany	5.0	0.58	−2.1	−3.0
USA	–	–	–	–
France	12.2	0.53	−5.8	−5.9
Italy	7.0	0.89	−0.8	−1.5
UK	16.3	0.55	−7.2	−8.5

Social security contributions of employers and employees

	Average tax rate	Elasticity with personal income	Redistribution power ratio	Change in Gini coeff.
Australia	–	–	–	–
Canada	3.1	0.68	−1.0	−0.7
Germany	14.8	1.01	−0.1	−1.2
USA	4.7	1.06	0.3	0.3
France	16.6	1.82	13.7	14.0
Italy	15.8	0.61	−6.1	−5.0
UK	5.8	1.06	0.3	−0.3

Corporate income tax

	Average tax rate	Elasticity with personal income	Redistribution power ratio	Change in Gini coeff
Australia (6)	5.6	1.04	0.2	−0.2
Canada (10)	3.5	1.25	0.9	−0.2
Germany (10)	4.3	1.53	−0.4	0.9
USA (48)	4.3	1.5	2.1	1.7
France (21)	3.2	1.79	2.5	2.0
Italy (20)	0.6	0.7	−0.2	−0.2
UK (10)	3.0	0.86	−0.4	−1.4

Excise and import duties

	Average tax rate	Elasticity with personal income	Redistribution power ratio	Change in Gini coeff
Australia	6.2	0.46	−3.4	0.2
Canada	2.9	0.46	−1.6	−1.9
Germany	4.3	0.58	−1.8	−2.6
USA	2.1	0.36	−1.4	−1.6
France	3.2	0.31	−2.2	−2.4
Italy	3.9	0.86	−0.5	−1.3
UK	–	–	–	–

Total

	Average tax rate	Elasticity with personal income	Redistribution power ratio	Change in Gini coeff
Australia	29.5	1.09	2.7	9.4
Canada	23.1	1.11	2.4	2.6
Germany	30.6	1.03	0.8	−3.0
USA	24.7	1.35	8.5	6.6
France	42.8	1.43	18.5	18.6
Italy	40.0	0.96	−1.6	−1.8
UK	36.8	1.0	0.2	−1.8

197

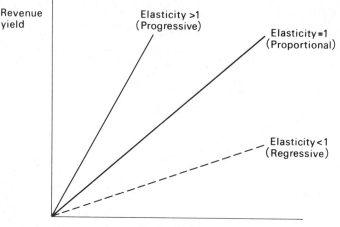

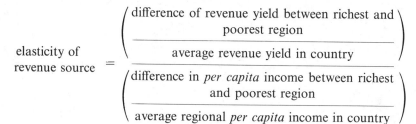

Figure 8.5 Elasticity of revenue yield with *per capita* personal income.

One of the most important elements in this table is the measure of elasticity which is given as follows:

$$\text{elasticity of revenue source} = \frac{\left(\dfrac{\text{difference of revenue yield between richest and poorest region}}{\text{average revenue yield in country}}\right)}{\left(\dfrac{\text{difference in } per \; capita \text{ income between richest and poorest region}}{\text{average regional } per \; capita \text{ income in country}}\right)}$$

Hence, as shown in figure 8.5, an elasticity value greater than 1 indicates a spatially progressive revenue source, whilst a value of less than 1 indicates a spatially regressive one. In each of the seven countries examined in table 8.6, which include four federations and three unitary countries, total revenue burden is either directly proportional to revenue ability as measured by *per capita* personal incomes, or is slightly progressive. But the degree of geographical progressivity is quite variable. Italy, the UK and Germany have relatively less progressive geographical tax burdens than the US and France, although the out-of-date data for the UK and US make firm conclusions questionable. When we look at particular taxes, the degree of progressivity is measured by the elasticity indices in table 8.6. As expected, personal and corporate income taxes are almost universally the most geographically progressive revenue sources, but are more progressive for income tax in centralized states and for corporate tax in federal states. Social Security contributions are fairly neutral regionally, whilst general sales tax and excise duties are highly regressive to geographical differences in *per capita* income with elasticities all less than 1.

We may compare the distribution effects of the revenue burdens by use of the two statistical measures detailed in appendix 1: the change in Gini coefficient, and the redistribution ratio. A positive value of either measure indicates redistribution from high to low income jurisdictions, whilst a negative value of either measure indicates lack of redistribution and the apportionment of revenue incidence so as to place higher burdens on poorer jurisdictions. Table 8.6 shows that personal income tax is uniformly highly redistributive or equalizing between rich and poor jurisdictions reducing pre-tax geographical income differentials by 4 to 9%. On the other hand, general sales tax and excise duties are all regressive with income, placing higher burdens on poorer areas to the extent of between 0.2 and 7%. Corporate income tax is fairly neutral in terms of geographical redistribution. In some countries, it is mildly redistributive whilst in others it is very mildly regressive. Social Security payments, however, vary greatly in their geographical distributional aspect. They are strongly geographically redistributive in France where they reduce pre-tax geographical income differentials by 14%, but in most countries are geographically regressive and are highly regressive in Italy where they increase pre-tax income differentials by 6%. The impact on the total tax burden gives only mild geographical redistribution in most countries of the order of 0.2 to 3%, but in the United States, pre-tax income is equalised by 8.5% and in France by 18.5% (where Social Security payments give a strong geographical redistribution). In Italy interjurisdictional revenue burdens are mildly regressive with regional *per capita* incomes where they increase pre-tax geographical income differentials by 1.6%.

STUDIES OF REVENUE BURDEN BY INCOME GROUP AND REGION

A number of local studies of tax burdens for single jurisdictions have been made, the most well-known being the two seminal tax exporting studies by Musgrave and Daicoff (1958) for Michigan, and by Groves and Knight (1959) for Wisconsin. But the first major studies of revenue burdens which allow assessment of incidence by both geographical location and income group are those by Phares (1973) for the fifty States of the USA and that by Greene *et al.* (1974) for the Washington Metropolitan area. Since these provide the only major studies of the geographical distribution of fiscal incidence, their results will be reported in detail below, whilst the specific relations of burden incidence to benefit incidence and need are introduced in chapter 14.

Phares's (1976) study of tax incidence in the 50 US States is a very detailed study which incorporates detailed personal and corporate shifting assumptions similar to those given in table 8.2. Moreover, inter-State export rates deriving from McClure's (1967) analysis detailed in table 8.4 are used to incorporate geographical shifting. Thus inter-personal, inter-corporate and interjurisdictional shifting of revenue burdens is taken into account. The level

Table 8.7 Average rates of State and local tax by income group for each State using tax in US (*Source:* Phares 1976, table 5.1)

Tax	Income group									No. of States
	$0–1,999	2,000–2,999	3,000–3,999	4,000–4,999	5,000–5,999	6,000–7,499	7,500–9,999	10,000–14,999	Over 15,000	
Corporate income										
All consumption	0.388	0.326	0.310	0.279	0.262	0.250	0.232	0.212	0.153	36
½ consumption, ½ dividends	0.234	0.199	0.221	0.168	0.170	0.157	0.165	0.225	0.566	36
All sales and gross receipts	3.998	3.458	3.495	3.221	2.976	2.794	2.580	2.300	1.505	50
General sales and gross receipts	2.152	1.773	1.690	1.528	1.425	1.363	1.272	1.172	0.861	41
Selective sales and gross receipts	2.233	2.005	2.109	1.969	1.808	1.676	1.557	1.339	0.798	50
Alcohol	0.183	0.163	0.183	0.179	0.158	0.180	0.168	0.193	0.148	50
Tobacco	0.514	0.439	0.404	0.356	0.311	0.280	0.234	0.162	0.087	48
Public utility										
Telephone and telegraph	0.244	0.194	0.177	0.157	0.148	0.143	0.126	0.110	0.074	46
Gas and electric	0.338	0.252	0.202	0.170	0.155	0.138	0.116	0.095	0.061	46
Motor fuel	0.902	0.902	1.081	1.048	0.980	0.881	0.834	0.717	0.377	50
Other selective sales	0.325	0.287	0.271	0.245	0.229	0.219	0.203	0.186	0.134	50
Property										
All housing	6.280	5.143	4.410	3.998	3.750	3.520	3.156	2.820	2.193	50
½ housing, ½ consumption	5.950	4.899	4.370	3.977	3.713	3.520	3.211	2.901	2.176	50
All consumption	5.620	4.655	4.331	3.957	3.675	3.511	3.265	2.982	2.159	50
½ property taxes, ½ consumption	5.412	4.386	3.658	3.370	3.409	3.597	3.368	3.174	2.649	50
Personal income	0.061	0.106	0.221	0.310	0.403	0.540	0.736	1.043	1.821	37
Death and gift	—								0.475	49
All other	1.394	1.152	1.087	0.984	0.010	0.879	0.816	0.744	0.534	50
Imported	2.015	1.677	1.578	1.432	1.337	1.276	1.186	1.083	0.780	50
Total taxes	13.572	11.408	10.853	9.966	9.366	8.977	8.456	7.962	7.214	50
Total taxes net of property tax	7.622	6.508	6.482	5.988	5.654	5.461	5.245	5.061	5.039	50

Table 8.8 Coefficients of variation in effective rates of State and local taxes by income group in US. (*Source*: Phares 1976, table 5.2)

Tax	Income group									Number
	$0–1,999	2,000–2,999	3,000–3,999	4,000–4,999	5,000–5,999	6,000–7,499	7,500–9,999	10,000–14,999	Over 15,000	of States
Corporation income										
All consumption	.446	.454	.450	.451	.452	.451	.451	.455	.468	36
½ consumption, ½ dividends	.462	.468	.503	.468	.467	.429	.434	.480	.546	36
All sales and gross receipts	.420	.361	.360	.342	.346	.359	.350	.363	.388	50
General sales and gross receipts	.598	.540	.548	.537	.530	.542	.529	.516	.507	41
Selective sales and gross receipts	.250	.229	.229	.219	.227	.256	.221	.248	.273	50
Alcohol	.586	.657	.674	.652	.601	.632	.609	.684	.814	50
Tobacco	.362	.362	.343	.340	.340	.335	.330	.343	.358	48
Public utility										
Telephone and telegraph	.967	.949	.944	.938	.938	.943	.942	.940	.949	46
Gas and electric	.966	.961	.957	.963	.962	.955	.956	.953	.952	46
Motor fuel	.353	.287	.278	.257	.268	.303	.248	.254	.239	50
Other selective sales	.886	.836	.844	.836	.828	.847	.835	.827	.830	50
Property										
All housing	.415	.399	.358	.373	.362	.359	.338	.338	.371	50
½ housing, ½ consumption	.400	.386	.352	.368	.355	.356	.345	.347	.368	50
All consumption	.385	.372	.346	.362	.349	.353	.353	.355	.371	50
½ property taxes, ½ consumption	.440	.420	.378	.381	.359	.350	.340	.336	.320	50
Personal income	3.455	1.708	1.082	.863	.791	.698	.654	.609	.526	37
Death and gift	—	—	—	—	—	—	—	—	.811	49
All other	.445	.410	.423	.413	.413	.422	.415	.410	.405	50
Imported	.110	.073	.078	.071	.073	.077	.073	.074	.083	50
Total taxes	.183	.139	.113	.117	.105	.108	.100	.103	.198	50
Total taxes net of property tax	.249	.204	.215	.194	.196	.199	.191	.207	.284	50

201

of resolution chosen is 50 State geographical areas and 9 income groups, and the burdens of 7 taxes are assessed: corporate and personal income taxes, general and selective sales taxes, motor fuel, property, death and gift taxes. The incidence of each of these tax categories for the whole US is shown in table 8.7. Note in particular the progressive incidence of personal income tax and the regressive impact of corporate income, sales and property taxes. It is also significant that the specifically geographical element of shifting (imported tax burdens) is also highly regressive with income. Significant variation of these tax incidence estimates occurs both between income groups and between geographical areas. The taxes which exhibit the highest degree of spatial variation are personal income and general sales tax, but many selective sales taxes also show a high degree of variation (especially alcohol and public utility taxes). Coefficients of variation for each tax and for each income group are given in table 8.8.

As we have noted before, it is not the burden incidence of any specific tax which is important, but the total incidence of all revenues. To test how far the total burden of state and local taxes is regressive or progressive, various methods can be adopted. Phares uses two methods: a regression approach, and the Gini coefficient. Each method and its results is discussed in turn below.

(1) *Regression estimates.* These yield the elasticity of the tax rates R_{ij} with the average income of each State $\bar{Y}_{ij}$. Thus for income group i and State j a regression equation:

$$R_{ij} = a_j + b_j \, \bar{Y}_{ij}$$

can be estimated. In this equation, the b_j terms represent the elasticity (or slope parameter) of tax rate with income. If this term is positive, then state–local taxes are in aggregate progressive, if it is negative they are in aggregate regressive. The tax rates are average aggregate tax rates defined as the average taxes of each income group in each State, divided by the aggregate income of each group in each State. The resulting estimates of income elasticity of total taxation taking account of tax exports are shown in figure 8.6. No States have a tax structure which is progressive over-all. Most States are regressive, and in the case of many Mid-Western and Plains States, are highly regressive. In addition only eleven States have proportional tax structures which are neutral in their distribution effects.

(2) *Gini coefficient.* The method of calculating the Gini coefficient is defined in appendix 1. In the present case the Gini coefficient gives a measure of equality in the distribution of tax incidence between income groups. The Gini ratio does not directly measure the direction of inequality, but since from figure 8.6a it is known that no tax structures are progressive, a high value of this ratio indicates very unequal or regressive burdens, whilst low values of this ratio indicate relatively equal or proportional burdens. A map of the Gini ratio for each State is shown in figure 8.6b from which it can be seen that those States which are most regressive from figure 8.6a are also those with

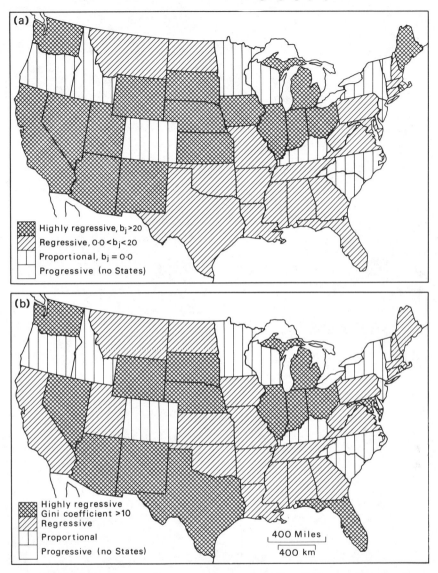

Figure 8.6 Degree of progressivity and regressivity in US State and local taxes as exported.
   a As measured by the regression coefficient b_j
   b As measured by the Gini coefficient
(Data derived from Phares 1976, tables 6.2 and 6.6.)

the highest Gini ratios (e.g. Wyoming, South Dakota and Illinois), whilst those States which have proportional or neutral tax burdens have low Gini ratios (e.g. Delaware, Kentucky, North Carolina, and Wisconsin).

The final study to be discussed here, that by Greene, Neenan and Scott

AFTER OFFSET

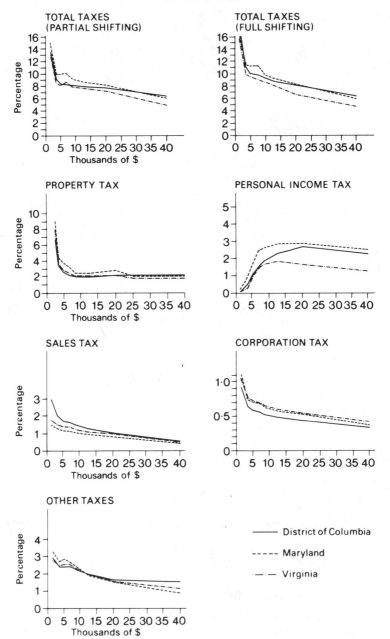

TOTAL TAXES
(PARTIAL SHIFTING)

TOTAL TAXES
(FULL SHIFTING)

PROPERTY TAX

PERSONAL INCOME TAX

SALES TAX

CORPORATION TAX

OTHER TAXES

———— District of Columbia

- - - - Maryland

·—·— Virginia

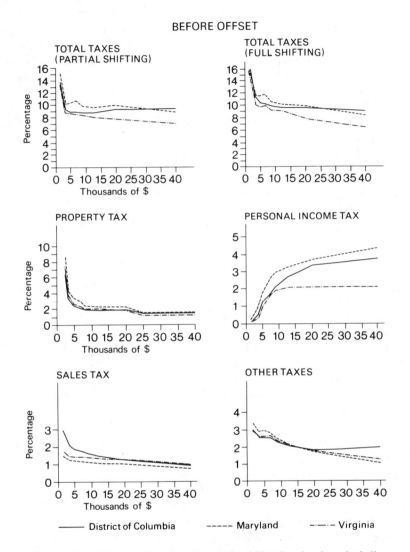

Figure 8.7 Relation of tax burden to tax ability for the three jurisdictions of Maryland, Virginia, and Washington, DC, taking account of different shifting assumptions and different effects of federal offset (tax credits). (Redrawn from Greene *et al*. 1974, figure 6.1 to 6.13.)

205

(1974), concerns the assessment of tax burdens for the three 'state' areas of the District of Columbia, Maryland and Virginia. The results of this study provide estimates of jurisdictional fiscal burdens which, by giving actual estimates of interjurisdictional revenue exporting, accord with the Michigan approach to tax exporting, yielding a tax accounting matrix similar to those discussed in chapter 4. This study, in fact, yields four sets of estimates depending upon whether or not the federal offset (tax credits and deductions available from federal government) is taken into account, and whether partial or full forward shifting of business taxes is assumed. These four accounting tables of jurisdictional burden are shown below.

The total *net* tax exports of each area and for each assumption of incidence are as follows:

Net export ($000)

	Partial forward shifting		Full forward shifting	
	before offset	after offset	before offset	after offset
D. C.	49100	42190	37356	36264
Maryland	− 28411	− 24327	− 20775	− 20254
Virginia	− 16416	− 17863	− 16581	− 16110

Considerable exporting of tax burdens from Washington D. C. to Virginia and Maryland has been achieved. Also there is a small export of tax burdens from Virginia to Maryland. The extent of geographical exporting is less when the effect of federal offsets is taken into account since the revenue burden becomes shared by the US population as a whole. The extent of exporting from D. C. to Virginia and Maryland is also less under the assumption of full forward shifting of all business income and property taxes since this burden is then borne increasingly by the wider US market.

The incidence of burdens from individual taxes is shown in figure 8.7 with and without federal offsets, and for both partial and full forward shifting. The property tax, sales tax, business cost tax and total tax burden are all regressive with income. Only personal income tax is progressive, but even the progression in this tax is greatly reduced when federal offsets are taken into account. The total tax burden is more regressive under assumptions of full forward shifting and after taking offsets into account. Under assumptions of partial shifting and ignoring federal offsets, the tax burden is regressive at low incomes and proportional thereafter. Under each assumption, the Maryland and Virginia taxes are the most regressive and those of the District of Columbia the most proportional (least regressive) with income.

The geography of revenue burdens is complex and requires the tracing of not only interpersonal intersectoral shifting of taxes, but also of interjurisdictional exporting and importing of tax burdens. The results summarized above, of the major studies to date which attempt to estimate inter-personal and geographical incidence of burdens, indicate that this procedure can be undertaken. No doubt other studies will follow suit. In the next section we turn to the relation of revenue burdens to revenue capacity and ability, which requires analysis of tax effort.

8.5 Revenue effort and severity

Revenue burdens vary spatially not only as a result of differences in revenue capacity, but also as a result of the pressure placed upon the financial resources of individuals, industries, and governments, in different jurisdic-tions. Whereas fiscal capacity measures the ability of people to pay a given level of taxes, fiscal burden depends on the distribution of tax payments between people and governments, and the degree to which the fiscal capacity is used to provide services. Two polar cases can be distinguished: first, one in which there is large personal and local fiscal capacity, taxes can be exported to other areas, or there is a relatively small demand or need for public services; second, a case in which there is a small personal or local fiscal capacity, tax burdens are imported, or there is a relatively large demand or need for public services. In the two cases the fiscal burden or effort will differ greatly for the same level of services. In the first case there will be low burden or effort, whilst in the second case there will be high burden or effort.

These two cases are not of just theoretical interest since it is precisely this fiscal dichotomy which divides many suburbs from their central cities, and the economically well-off regions from those which are economically lagging. The interpersonal and spatial differentiation of the incidence of burdens in relation to fiscal ability results in similar people or firms paying significantly different proportions of their incomes for the support of local services. Thus, some individuals or locations make much more fiscal effort than others. Alternatively, some individuals or locations are subject to a higher degree of fiscal severity. The concepts of effort and severity are discussed in turn below.

FISCAL EFFORT

This is a measure of the extent to which a given jurisdiction is using its fiscal capacity, but does not take account of effort between income groups (as given by severity, see p. 210). This concept derives from Newcomer (1935). Shoup *et al.* (1935), Hicks and Hicks (1945), and many other writers. Measures of fiscal effort are based on the ratio of revenue raised to the size or capacity of the revenue base, and hence depend upon the definition of the revenue base which is adopted. Thus it is important to measure both effort and capacity against the most relevent revenue base. For each definition of capacity, effort is defined as the ratio of actual revenue raised to revenue capacity for each area, usually with the terms reduced to become percentages of the national average rates of effort.

In the US, the US ACIR (1962) study has compared four indices of tax

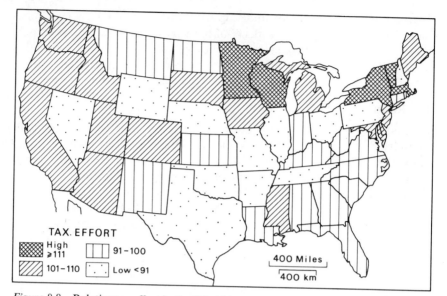

Figure 8.8   Relative tax effort in the US, 1966–7, measured as the percentage ratio of actual revenue to revenue capacity at national average rates under a representative tax system. (Data derived from US ACIR 1971, table g–4.)

effort. Irrespective of which index is chosen, however, high effort is found in the 'frostbelt' areas of the Atlantic Coast and Great Lakes, and also on the Pacific Coast (see figure. 8.8). In contrast, low tax effort characterizes the 'sunbelt' of the South and South West, and also the Plains. A later study by US ACIR (1971) confirms these results, but using a smaller level of spatial aggregation, for SMSAs, and Counties giving a more varied set of conclusions. Many central cities are extremely healthy in a fiscal sense, and there is an important rural division of fiscal effort in the South: the urban areas are characterized by high capacity and low effort, but the rural areas also have some of the lowest capacity levels of the US, and some of the highest effort levels. Similar results, deriving from use of effort as a measure of need, are displayed in the 1978 study by Cuciti given in table 13.18. Although effort is generally higher in the North-East US, Southern cities also have high effort rankings.

FISCAL PRESSURE

Recently, it has been suggested by US ACIR (1977c) that it is not revenue effort as such, but the direction in change in effort which is often most important. Thus, regardless of the fiscal effort at any given point in time, it is suggested that citizens and companies are likely to perceive heavier tax burdens in those areas where taxes are rising, and it is this *perceived pressure* which is most crucial, particularly in its effects on fiscal migration. On this

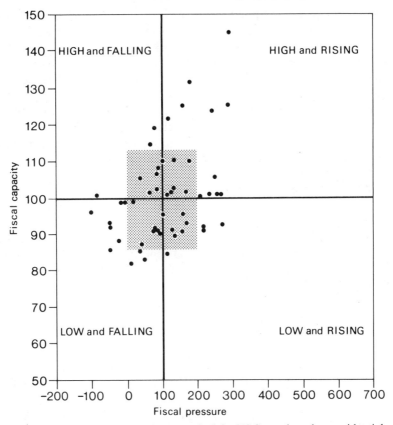

Figure 8.9 The fiscal 'blood pressure' of the US States based on residential income measures of capacity. The central rectangle encloses those States which are less than one standard deviation from the national median. (*Source*: US ACIR 1977c.)

basis, ACIR have constructed an index of 'fiscal blood pressure' which is defined as the ratio of the jurisdiction's fiscal effort in the year of interest, to the change in effort from a base year. This ratio can be used as an index, or alternatively the numerator and denominator terms in the ratio can be plotted separately. As shown in figure 8.9, this gives four categories of jurisdiction for the US: first, those with high fiscal blood pressure (high effort and rising); second, those with low pressure (low effort and falling); third, and fourth, two transitional categories (low effort and rising, high effort and falling). With the exception of Hawaii, California, Nevada and West Virginia, all the States with high pressure are in New England, the Middle Atlantic, and the Great Lakes areas, whilst those with low pressure are States on the Gulf Coast, South, and Prairies.

There are a number of problems to be borne in mind when making inferences with respect to fiscal effort. First, effort covers only the quantitative

209

side of the revenue-expenditure equation: it says nothing of the qualitative pattern of different service levels, differences in costs, the balance of current and debt spending, and differences in preferences. Secondly, if effort is used as a measure of local fiscal need, it may aid the richer areas at the expense of the poorer. Many grant and transfer programmes use effort measures, e.g. US Revenue-Sharing and the UK Rate Support Grant (implicitly). Such grants will simultaneously reward high effort resulting from high levels of need, and high effort resulting from high levels of preference for public goods. A third difficulty with effort indices is that different levels of effort need not reflect different needs, since the efficiency and productivity of local jurisdictions are not allowed for. Finally, different effort levels result from different stages of industrial development, especially the degree to which investments are required for new capital stock or the renewal of old (see chapter 6).

FISCAL SEVERITY

An additional limitation of indices of fiscal effort is that they take no account of differences in the distribution of tax burdens and capacity between people, firms, and places. Tax severity offers an index which measures these important distributional effects. Various such measures have been suggested. One simple measure which allows assessment of relative tax severity *between areas* is given by dividing the local effort index by the local income (Mushkin and Crowther 1954). In this case areas with similar levels of tax effort, but with different *per capita* incomes will have a higher severity index the lower the level of incomes. For example, Halstead (1978) has compared the fiscal effort and fiscal capacity at State level in the US giving levels of severity, as shown in figure 8.10. This figure permits contours of *per capita* revenue collected (as the product of capacity multiplied by effort) to be plotted against respective local effort and capacity. Few States, only Hawaii and California, have high capacity and effort; and this tends to disprove the theory that high income areas raise revenues at high rates to support a larger quantity or quality of services. On the other hand, there are a large number of States with low capacity and low effort. This, Halstead (1978, p. 14) suggests, supports the theory that a poor economy presents a considerable barrier to enlargement of the tax base: families and firms with low or declining incomes are less able to contribute to the public fisc, and their marginal sacrifice is much greater than families or firms with higher incomes. As can be seen from figure 8.10, this affects the Southern and Central States most severely, and is much more marked for property tax than it is for personal income or sales taxes. This reflects the frequently observed phenomenon that property tax is regressive because of the low income elasticity of demand for housing (but see the further discussion of property taxes on pp. 157–8).

Although helpful in assessing relative tax severity, the approaches of both Mushkin and Crowther, and Halstead, take no account of the income distribution within areas. Few studies have attempted empirical assessment of

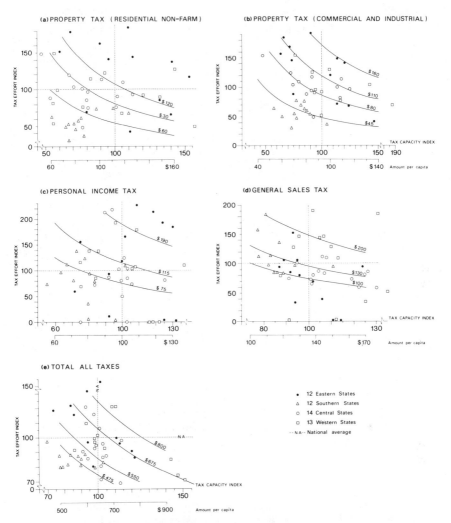

Figure 8.10 Fiscal severity in the US States in 1975. Comparisons of fiscal effort and tax capacity with contours of revenue yield. (*Source*: Halstead 1978, figures 1 and 4–7.)

severity in this form, although it is, in principle, straightforward to disaggregate both capacity and burden by income group, in order to assess effort, and then to relate effort to income capacity as an index of severity. Studies which attempt to relate burden to capacity, allowing assessment of severity by income group, together with the relation of burden to need, benefits, and costs of public goods, are discussed in chapter 14.

8.6 Conclusion

This chapter has been concerned with the assessment of revenue burdens: the

211

different pressures placed by the public fisc on individuals, firms and governments in different locations by the revenue system. A significant feature of burden assessment is the tracing of revenues from the source of payment to the incidence of final burdens. Because revenue and financial burdens are fungible, revenue payments can be shifted to a significant extent between individuals and locations. The magnitude of these flows often has very important effects on the size of revenue burdens, and hence upon the social wage of individuals and the level of externality of firms.

Given the assessment of tax burdens, allowing for shifting and exports, it is then possible to compare the geography of burden incidence with that of revenue capacity. The resulting indices of tax effort show considerable geographical variation, but it must be concluded that such indices must be expanded to allow assessment also of tax severity: the disaggregation of effort not only by geographical location, but also by income group. This complex task is undertaken with great difficulty, and is related to the degree to which we wish to disaggregate by other indicators, such as needs, costs and benefit groups. Hence detailed discussion is left for chapter 14, when final fiscal incidence is introduced.

A further important issue which affects the levels of revenue burdens, but which has been only touched on above, is the interrelation of local revenue bases at different levels of government. With respect to distribution questions, but also to a lesser extent for questions of stabilization and growth, locally autonomous revenue bases have no mechanism by which they can achieve either geographical and individual redistribution, or local stabilization and growth. If the individuals with greater or lesser revenue ability live in different jurisdictions, under autonomous revenue systems, there is no way to exact higher payment from the more able, who live in one jurisdiction, to aid the less able, who live in another. This is often particularly marked for local use of income and sales taxes for which Ecker-Racz (1970, p. 109) observes that "when locally levied and administered, their revenue contribution to individual communities bears no relation to comparative revenue needs". For property taxes, Netzer (1974) quotes the example of the Connecticut School system in 1970–71, which is financed by property tax, and in which the 50 richest towns in the State could spend $989 per pupil using a tax rate of 1.1% (as a percentage of the market value), whereas in the 50 poorest towns the comparable figures were $732 and 1.9%. This and other examples emphasize the impossibility of equalizing burdens by autonomous means alone. Hence in addition to local action, the intergovernmental transfers discussed in chapters 11 to 13, must be undertaken.

9

Benefit incidence: the geography of access to public goods

"A chief source for evils among men are benefits,
  excessive benefits", Menander, *Fragments*, No. 724.

"How bitter it is, when you have sown benefits to reap
  injuries", Plautus, *Epidicus*, 1. 718, (Act V, Sc. 2)

9.1 Introduction

The incidence of the benefits deriving from public finance represents the expenditure element in a complex equation in which the taxes and charges, discussed in the previous chapters, represent the revenue element. The comparison of revenues and expenditure benefits with the other elements of the needs and costs of local jurisdictions allow us in later chapters to determine the answers to the geographical questions of fiscal incidence and fiscal equity: who gets what, where, in relation to their needs for public goods and the cost of providing them.

Much of the classical analysis of public finance in the English language has been concerned solely with tax analysis, e.g. Bentham, Mill, Edgeworth and Marshall. It is only in relatively recent years that the work of continental European writers such as Wicksell, Lindahl, de Viti de Marco, Sax, Mazzola, von Wieser, and Pantaleoni has become better known, most especially through the work of Musgrave and Peacock (1958), Musgrave (1959), and Buchanan (1960). This work has added to the considerations of tax analysis, assessment of the benefit side of the public fisc, and this is the subject of the present chapter.

The geographical incidence of benefits is concerned primarily with the public finance function of distribution. The problem of distributing non-money services has stimulated some writers to call for the general orientation of public finance to achieve income distribution through benefit distribution of in-kind transfers. Dalton (1936, p. 229), for example, states that "that system of public expenditure is most desirable, which has the strongest tendency to redistribute incomes". Again, Newcomer (1935) has suggested that benefit distribution according to need is the natural corollary of taxation according to ability or capacity. It is clear, however, that equity cannot be achieved through benefit apportionment alone, tax and grant structures must also be employed. In addition, an important impediment to the use of benefit theory of redistribution is the fact that public goods are divided between the classes of national 'merit' goods, local, and personal goods as discussed in chapter 5 which limits the degree of geographical redistribution which can or should be achieved.

The benefits of public services available to any individual or firm located in a jurisdiction are composed of three elements: those derived from expenditures generated internal to that jurisdiction; those derived from expenditures by higher level governments (regional or state, central or federal); and those derived from spillovers of expenditures from other similar jurisdictions. In the last two categories there may also be spillovers in the other direction: from local jurisdictions to outside governments at higher or similar levels. If these various benefit effects are put together we can construct a matrix which depicts the flows of benefits in relation to any specific jurisdiction. Such a matrix is shown in table 9.1. This matrix represents a very simple form of the income accounts developed in chapter 4. In this case the accounts show the benefits flowing between jurisdictions. Jurisdictions at the same level of the specified jurisdiction are differentiated from higher level governments in order to emphasize the difference between competitive benefit flows and shared benefit flows. This is an important distinction since competitive benefit flows between jurisdictions at the same level of government are total losses or gains to the local jurisdiction considered, while shared benefit flows to higher level governments represent the contribution by all lower level governments to the

Table 9.1 Benefit matrix specified with reference to a given local jurisdiction

	Benefits from			
Benefits to	Specified jurisdiction	Higher level governments	Same level governments	Total benefits gained
specified jurisdiction	benefits generated and used	benefits from higher level government expenditure (national goods)	spillover	local benefits
higher level governments	contribution to higher level government (national minimum standards)	benefits to all within larger community (national merit goods)	contribution to higher level government (national minimum standards)	higher level government benefits
similar level governments	spillover to other jurisdictions	benefits from higher level to other areas	benefits generated and used internal to other areas	benefits in other jurisdictions

overall higher level or national good. This latter element of shared benefits is placed along the central row of the matrix and represents the contribution of each local government to minimum standards of service provision which have considered should be available to everyone within the higher level jurisdiction (state, region or nation); so-called 'merit goods'. Such benefits normally relate to such goods as defence, monetary policy, law, and standards.

This chapter seeks to explore the elements of geographical impurity in public goods and the related benefit distribution question concerning each element in the benefit matrix. It must be re-emphasized at the start, however, than an equitable distribution of benefits cannot be judged in isolation, it required a measure of benefit incidence against needs, costs and burdens as developed in the previous chapters. For the present, however, we consider only the geographical elements of access to direct benefits of public goods. In section 9.2, the categories of benefits are examined, and in section 9.3, the effects of tapering and benefit spillover are explored. In section 9.4 the measurement and incidence of benefits is discussed, and in section 9.5 are considered strategies which can be pursued by political jurisdictions in inducing non-jointness, exclusion or rejection as part of a policy of fiscal prudence and interjurisdictional competition.

9.2 Categories of benefits

There are two major approaches by which benefits may be measured: on a cost basis, and on a welfare basis. The cost basis makes the assumption that the benefits of a given service equal their cost (or are at least a linear proportion of their cost). If this assumption holds strictly, then total consumer benefits equal the total cost of providing the service. Herein lies the difficulty of the cost basis. Generally, it might be hoped that total benefits are greater than total cost, i.e. that a public service generates considerable joint benefits to a society which are greater than its cost. In fact as we have seen in the discussion of needs in chapter 5, it is this jointness of benefits at the geographical level which distinguishes geographical needs from individual needs. The major difficulty is that it is usually not possible to know precisely whether total benefits are greater than, less than, or equal to the cost of providing the public goods. To make a precise assessment of this equation we should first need to be able to measure those particularly unmeasurable things such as 'the public good' or 'the general welfare'. Second, we would need a measure of the economic rent and other indirect benefits received by each individual as a result of public expenditures. Third, we should need measures of all benefit spillovers between jurisdictions. And finally, we should need to know the income elasticity of demand for public service.

The welfare basis for measuring benefits of public goods also attempts to impute benefits to individuals on the basis of their cost, but weights benefits by a function expressing the marginal utility for public services of different income levels. This concept derives primarily from Adam Smith's

215

concept that benefits received are proportional to income received under the protection of the State. Hence, for different income groups, the total benefits received will not equal costs. However, there is a major difficulty in this approach which is the determination of the marginal utility of benefits at each income level. This requires not only an estimate of the preferences for each public service for each income group for both existing and new services, which would itself be difficult although not perhaps impossible, but also a means of scaling these benefits in cost terms. Herein lies the difficulty of the welfare basis. There is no unambiguous way of imputing the value of benefits to members of the community. The imputation of measurable money benefits to different income groups requires two assumptions. First, that inter-individual preferences can be aggregated and are comparable, and second, that a welfare function expressing the money value of these differences can be determined. These two assumptions of welfare economics must be generally rejected (see chapter 15). However, a number of individual analysts have employed various welfare bases in geographical and non-geographical studies of fiscal incidence, for example Maitle (1973) and Greene *et al.* (1974). Thus Maitle for example, has estimated that the income elasticity of benefits rises from 1.04 in the UK and 1.50 in the US to 3.84 in the Netherlands. These estimates demonstrate the interlinking of benefit incidence with personal preferences. Preferences for public expenditure in the UK and to a lesser extent in the US, are far more equally distributed between groups than in the Netherlands.

Whichever basis for measuring benefits is employed, we may classify public service benefits into four broad classes.

(i) *Private goods and benefits*: are available directly to individuals or locations, and allow every person or area equal access (at least in theory), e.g. government employment, government defence contracts.

(ii) *Public non-redistributive goods and benefits*: available to all on as far as possible an equal basis, e.g. police and fire protection, education, hospitals, street lighting, refuse disposal, public utilities, flood control, national defence, legal and monetary system, safety standards, and infrastructure.

(iii) *Public redistributive goods and benefits*: available directly to individuals and locations on the basis of a measure of client need: e.g. social security, welfare, and other transfer payments, industrial tax incentives.

(iv) *Geographical benefits*: available to all individuals within a given jurisdiction, sometimes on the basis of need, but not meaningfully divisible between individuals: e.g. urban renewal, water, sewerage, utilities, police and fire protection, local employment policies.

The first two of these categories refer to the two classes of public good outlined in chapter 5: private and national 'merit' goods. The last two of these categories refer to the two cases of local goods.

Private benefits are derived directly from government expenditures as factor payments or services received. A major element of this expenditure is salaries to central and local government employees: to school teachers, construction workers, service employees and so forth. A second major element is composed of government contracts and expenditures mainly derived from central government directly and from nationalized industries. Defence contracts are frequently the largest single item in these direct expenditures. It is estimated that in the US although only 1.5 million people are direct federal employees, at least a further 5 million people are dependent upon the employment generated by the indirect expenditures of government contractors.

Non-redistributive benefits result from the provision of those national and 'merit' goods by which the welfare of society as a whole is increased. There are two important sub-categories of such benefits. First, those which refer to moderately pure public goods, such as national defence, the legal and monetary system, police and fire protection, street lighting, many public building works, and public utilities. In this case non-jointness and exclusion is of limited extent (although important tapering and spillover effects do occur). The provision of such goods has the longest history, from Egyptian and Classical times to the present. A second category of non-redistributive benefits occurs where even though expenditure is directed at limited groups, benefits accrue to individuals or firms to the extent that they are members of the larger society. Important cases of such benefits are education programmes and health. Such programmes benefit limited groups of people at any time, but contribute to everyone in society in terms of overall culture, welfare and productivity. It can also be argued that poor relief, and other specifically redistributive programmes fall to some extent in this class since they free society from internal dissension (see Piven and Cloward 1971). Indeed most public benefits fall ultimately into this category.

Redistributive benefits in contrast are aimed at particular individuals, groups, or locations satisfying specific criteria. Examples are welfare programmes, income supplements, social security payments and industrial tax subsidies. The US has over 1,000 such programmes of so-called categorical grants-in-aid and revenue-sharing. Most of these federal and local expenditures are directed at individuals and hence vary with type of individual living in a given area. The most important component of such flows in all western countries is transfer payments for welfare, social security and health programmes. Another significant element is the interest payments to holders of government savings and bonds. Similar grant programmes are available to individuals in other countries. In contrast to non-redistributive programmes these benefits accrue to the recipient group only, and without proportionate increase in tax burden. They generate no external spillovers to other groups. However in practice, it has frequently been true that redistributive programmes do generate external benefit spillovers for the groups which are not direct recipients. The individual benefits in this case derive through altruism, a more stable social structure, or relief of political pressure. This has, of course, led many Marxist critics to suggest that benefit programmes are aimed at the management of the poor: redistributive programmes are viewed as a strategy to maintain the status quo of a given social structure and its class relations (see Harvey 1973; Piven and Cloward 1971). However, these critics totally deny the motives of altruism and liberalism which have undoubtedly underlain many personal and spatial transfer programmes (see, for example, Gifford 1978; Moynihan 1978).

The final category of benefits, geographical benefits, differs from each of the previous categories because it is not possible to attribute such benefits directly to individuals: they correspond to the geographical needs discussed in chapter 5, and not to the sum of individual needs at any location. They possess features in common with public redistributive goods and benefits; they are available directly to individuals sometimes on the basis of need and they are often redistributive between individuals in different locations. But they differ from the sum of individual benefits in four respects. First, they possess a significant degree of externalities such that provision for one person generates benefits for other individuals at small or zero additional cost. Second, they are indivisible, usually due to technical factors; as, for example power stations, water supply systems and mass transit facilities. Third, they possess a degree of local support or 'mass identity' at the level of the local community which is expressed by local preferences, or articulated by the political process. Finally, differences in costs and environmental factors make certain groups of public goods more relevant in some areas rather than others, e.g. flood and pollution control investments, snow clearing equipment, different levels of police and fire protection, municipal car parking, and mass transit facilities. Geographical benefits may be redistributive or non-redistributive. Most of the benefits listed above are non-redistributive, but in many countries, especially in Europe, there are many important geographical redistributive programmes. For industry a wide range of regional policy tax incentives, employment subsidies, infrastructure subsidies, and interest-free loans have been used in the European regional fund, national regional policies, the US Economic Development Administration, and so forth. Important regional aid has been given in the form of countercyclical assistance in both Europe and North America, whilst many intergovernmental grant programmes are specifically designed to be geographically redistributive to jurisdictions as a whole (see chapters 11 to 13), e.g. the UK Rate Support Grant and housing development grants, Canadian Equalization Grants, US Community Development, CETA, Revenue-Sharing and urban renewal, and the German Equalization measures.

A special aspect of private, non-redistributive and geographical benefits is changes resulting from new public policies or modifications to old policies. Whilst these generate important inter-personal distribution questions, the geographical factors here are often most important. Whilst a modification of public policy is frequently made with the deliberate intention of modifying inter-personal distribution, changes to public policy may also have other distribution effects which are specifically geographical and affect levels of personal well-being, or the marketing potential and capacity for growth of industrial firms. One important example of such effects is the development of highway systems. Particularly within urban areas, considerable changes to the market value of residential and industrial property are consequent upon a public planning decision to make such a transport investment. They may produce large windfall profits to the firm which is favourably located, and produce benefits to the commuter and the general highway user. But such developments are usually accompanied by severe losses in residential market value and in environmental quality as a consequence of air and noise pollution in adjacent zones. This has led to the compensation schemes in the UK (*Land Compensation Act*). A similar effect is produced by the large windfall profits generated in increased market value of land following the development of subway and other mass transit facilities. These accrue either to the existing home owner, or in the case of undeveloped land to the landowner, who frequently may have bought the land speculating on its increased value. Examples of such changes in market values and speculation abound in the development of the 19th-century railways and streetcar trolleys in the United States and Western Europe, and in modern freeway developments. An interrelated issue is that of development of land at the urban fringe previously zoned for agricultural use. Speculation in this area has been particularly heavy such that in Britain the *Community Land Act* (1976) with associated Development Land Tax has attempted to tax the windfall profits consequent on changes in planning policies to the extent that development gains accrue to the community as a whole rather to the landowner. Development Gains Tax has also been used for this purpose.

With respect to grant programmes, it has been recognized increasingly that changes in central government policies can have severe repercussions in local areas. Thus in the US, changes to the distribution formulae of the community development block grant, which would have had severe consequences of reallocating a higher proportion of aid to central cities, have been subject to hold-harmless clauses which prevent any of the present allocation, being diminished. In the UK, the Rate Support Grant needs element is subject to a similar hold-harmless constraint which allows only 25 to 35% of 1 year's grant allocation to deviate from that of the previous year.

In most cases, where changes to the distribution of personal incomes or benefits have been consequent upon changes to public policy, compensation or taxing policies have been sought, on the one hand, to redress the deleterious effect of planning changes, and on the other hand, to recoup to the larger community the windfall gains derived from policy changes. In discussing each of the benefits and particular effects of policy changes, we encounter

219

considerable difficulties in measurement and imputation to individuals and locations. An important class of difficulties which arises is that associated with geographical tapering and spillover benefits discussed in the next section.

9.3 Benefit tapering and spillovers

In raising the issue of the geography of benefit incidence we are drawn back to the fundamental issue of what constitutes a public good. For the existence of a pure public good three conditions as discussed in chapter 2, must be satisfied: jointness, non-excludeability, and non-rejectability. When we consider the impact of geographic effects on the distribution of public benefits, each of these conditions breaks down. In fact, frequently it is the geographic effects which lead to the greatest impurities in the character of public goods. Jointness requires that once a pure public good has been supplied its benefits can be made available to all others at zero additional cost; but this requires that it does not matter where the additional individuals or firms are located. Such a condition is frequently undermined by the need to travel or migrate to obtain the supply of a given good. Non-excludeability requires that once a pure public good has been supplied its benefits cannot be withheld from others who may wish to consume it. In practice, the division of space into separate political jurisdictions creates severe economic and social barriers to access. Similarly, non-rejectability requires that a pure public good provides benefits to all, irrespective of whether they wish to consume that good. With respect especially to public bads, e.g. pollution and poor service levels, the geographical patterning of different political jurisdictions frequently requires people and firms to partake of service dis-benefits they may wish to avoid. Moreover, since different people will have different preferences for public goods they will receive different benefits from the public expenditures which are made and which they have no choice (except migration) but to support. Hence, for all three of the Musgrave–Samuelson conditions, geographical factors lead to impurities in the benefits that can be gained from public goods. Especially important are the effects of tapering over space and spillover between jurisdictions which are discussed below.

TAPERING

Tapering is a major factor which limits the possibility of attaining geographical equity in the distribution of benefits. Tapering affects the validity of both the jointness and non-excludeability conditions for pure public goods. Tapering resulting from non-jointness arises either from the supply of public services at a specific point or area which prevents full and equal access of all to that supply, or from the spatial variations in the demands for public goods which are not matched by spatial variations in their supply. Tapering resulting from exclusion is induced by the impact of travel cost or travel time on the ability of the consumer to obtain access to public goods and facilities. Hägerstrand (1975), for example, has emphasized the constraints of space on the actions of the individual: people cannot take part in more than one action at a time, every task and movement consumes time, and there are important elements of inertia rooting the present in past situations. Each of these factors serves to create non-jointness and exclusion by inducing tapering into the supply and demand for public goods.

Recognition of the effects of tapering derives originally from Lösch's (1941) concept of the market region and range of threshold of private goods, and has been extended by Tiebout (1961) to public goods. The Löschian theory is based on two fundamental concepts: the price funnel and the demand cone. These are illustrated in figure 9.1. The price funnel (figure 9.1a) represents the total cost to the consumer of obtaining a given good (public or private) as a function of two components: first, the base price at the source of supply which is equal for everyone, and may often be zero for public goods; and second, the transport cost or effort required to obtain the good by individuals or firms located at various distances away from the source of supply. It is this second component which induces exclusion and non-jointness into public good supply. This arises because, if the costs are borne by the producer of public goods, additional supply of the good requires increased transport cost to be paid. Alternatively, if the costs are borne by the consumer of public goods, then since consumers have a fixed total budget of money, time or effort, they must consume less of the public good, or gain access to it less frequently, as their distance from the source of supply increases. This leads to the concept of the demand cone (figure 9.1b) which depicts the way in which the level of demand decreases with distance away from the source of supply.

The Löschian theory encompasses the most important impacts of the generalized transport costs and the supply and demand for public goods. Tiebout (1961) adds to this theory the effect of tapering of benefit incidence. The theory of pure public goods requires that not only the access to public goods, but also the distribution of the benefits should be uniform. Goods such as national defence, legal systems, and safety standards may possess this

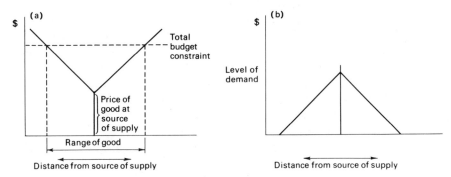

Figure 9.1 The Löschian concepts of
a   the price funnel and
b   the demand cone.

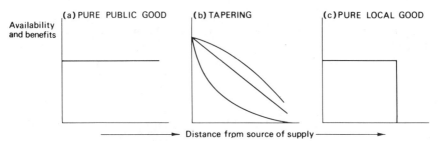

Figure 9.2 The effect of spatial tapering and range of goods inducing non-jointness with distance.

quality, but most public goods possess impurities which induce tapering in their benefits away from the source of supply (or cause spillovers as discussed later). The effect of tapering of benefits means that the total amount of a given public good is not divided equally between the resident individuals or firms served. Thus tapering of benefit incidence induces non-jointness. The spatial elements of non-jointness are depicted in figure 9.2. The theory of pure public goods requires that the availability, benefits or utility of a given good are uniform everywhere, as shown in figure 9.2a. However, typical public goods possess various taperings of benefits on availability as shown in figure 9.2b. On the basis of these differences, Lea (1978) has constructed a classification of public goods derived from their degree of impurity arising from non-jointness. He distinguishes non-spatial from spatial non-jointness and defines a category of partially joint goods where the provision of limited extra capacity or increased use of the good detracts from the quality of the service available. This classification, which should be taken as only an approximate guide, is shown in table 9.2. This allows three extreme categories of public goods to be identified. *Pure private goods* are those which are non-joint both spatially and non-spatially: both their supply, and their demand, is specific to each individual, excludes other individuals, and allows supply to other individuals only in proportion to increases in cost. *Pure public goods* are all global goods, or those to which all the Musgrave–Samuelson conditions apply. The third extreme is the important category of *pure local goods*. These are items which although spatially non-joint are joint over limited spatial extent (figure 9.2c). Perhaps the best example is a radio or television service which is available to all at no extra cost than providing for one individual, when in practice it is limited by the area of spatial coverage from each transmitting station. The supply of utilities such as gas, electricity, water and sewerage, is also in this class, although capacity limitations restrict the purity of the jointness when large increments in demand are imposed. In between these extremes is a wide range into which most public goods can be fitted.

Tapering induces inequality of access to public good supplies. A good example of such inequality is provided by the case of health care. Indeed, the

Table 9.2 Classification of public goods based on their degree of spatial and non-spatial jointness. (Partly after Lea 1978)

Non-spatial jointness	Spatial jointness		
	Joint	*Partially joint*	*Non-joint*
joint	*pure public goods (global goods)* legal system defence monetary system safety standards	education flood control weather service police hospitals fire station street lighting pollution control	*pure local goods* electricity generation gas supply radio and TV service sewerage water supply
partially joint		roads telephone service postal service refuse disposal	swimming pool park library recreation facilities
non-joint			*pure private goods* clothes food personal possessions

question of differential access to health care facilities is now usually viewed as an important part of the efficiency of medical care (Shannon and Dever 1974; Smith 1977). A good example of the inequities of access which may arise is given by Jolly and King (1966) in Uganda. As shown in figure 9.3a, outpatient and dispensary attendances per person decline with distance from the nearest hospital, and there is a very rapid decline from first-aid posts offering minimal first-aid treatment. These relationships allow 'isocare' lines to be plotted as shown in figure 9.3b. In developed countries, it is usually attempted to overcome tapering effects by providing a hierachy of facilities using the results of Lösch's analysis. For example, in Cleveland, Ohio, Shannon *et al.* (1969) found a five level hierarchy of facilities with a progressively higher degree of specialization with larger size; however, accessibility to facilities still possessed considerable inequities, although the effects of tapering were greatly reduced.

The concept of pure private, public and local goods is related to that of need and preferences as discussed in chapter 5. Need and preference for benefits of public goods are frequently related to geographical tapering, and vary significantly over space. The pure public good concept requires each individual either to have equal needs for, or place equal value on, the benefits

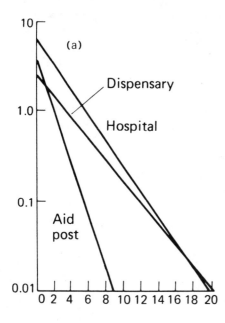

(a)

Dispensary

Hospital

Aid post

Distance of the patient's home from source of care (miles)

Figure 9.3 The effect of tapering on access to medical care in the Mityana area of Kenya.

    a General distance tapering curve for access to different facilities

    b Outpatient Isocare map

(*Source*: Jolly and King 1966, figures 6 and 7.)

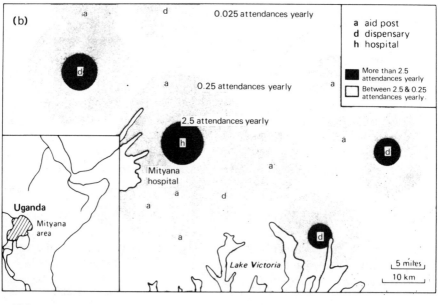

(b)

0.025 attendances yearly

a aid post
d dispensary
h hospital

■ More than 2.5 attendances yearly
□ Between 2.5 & 0.25 attendances yearly

0.25 attendances yearly

2.5 attendances yearly

Mityana hospital

Uganda

Mityana area

Lake Victoria

5 miles
10 km

of a given good. In practice, this condition seldom holds true and its effect particularly undermines the non-rejectability condition. Individuals and firms will generally need to partake to a greater or lesser extent in different public services. In the utility theory of Lindahl and Buchanan, they will derive different utilities from the same public good. Such patterns do not lend themselves to easy generalizations, but one broad indicator of need, preference or utility differences is often assumed to be income (or its related category of employment). Now it is well-known that the density of different incomes and employment groups varies spatially according to fairly predictable rules. The most well-developed empirical and theoretical generalizations are those relating to residential sites selected from land use competition within cities. The classical land use theories of Burgess (1925), Mackenzie (1926) and Alonso (1964), for example, suggest a general transition from commercial through industrial, low income residential, high income residential to industrial land uses from the centres of cities outwards. Refinements to these theories suggest the effect of sectoral transport corridors and local sub-centres of attraction within the city (Berry *et al.* 1963; Harris and Ullman 1945; Hoyt 1939). If there is any relation at all between the tapering of income or employment characteristics on the one hand, and the needs or preferences for public goods on the other, we would expect that benefits derived from a given public good by different groups would also taper resulting in both an increase of need and in utility for public services as we approach closer to the centre of cities. Although a rather simplified generalization, this relationship has underlain many of the claims that central cities are subject to exploitation by their suburbs, since it has been sometimes found that the gradient of need or utility is not being matched by a comparable gradient of expenditures and a comparable decline in revenue burden.

The interrelationship between geographical tapering of public and private costs, and of benefit incidence for public goods has stimulated a great deal of research into methods of designing arrangements for the supply of public goods which reflect the spatial inequality. These proposals concern benefit taxation and optimal districting. Benefit taxation, which is discussed above in chapters 7 and 8, concerns attempts to relate personal and local benefit incidence precisely to the personal or local revenue burden. The conclusion of that discussion was that such attempts are not only difficult, but usually undesirable. A related issue is that of optimal districting: to relate as closely as possible the political jurisdiction responsible for the supply of a public good to the area receiving the benefits from its provision, thus to govern the political choice of areal burdens by the areal extent of both political control and benefit incidence. Many mathematical algorithms are available for solving the districting problem (see, for example, Massam 1975; Scott 1971).

SPILLOVER

Spillover is perhaps the most frequent and important of the geographical effects which undermines the Musgrave–Samuelson conditions and which leads to inequalities in benefit incidence. Spillovers occur when benefits accrue to individuals or firms outside the region which bears the burden of their cost. Hence, benefit spillover is the converse of tax spillover in exporting discussed in the previous chapter, and may be an important factor in jurisdictional competition and fiscal prudence. Spillovers may affect either public goods, producing net benefits, or public bads producing public net disbenefits.

The causes of spillover are complex and result from the interplay of seven main factors. First, it is impossible, in practice, ever to achieve a one-to-one match of benefit areas and burden areas. As we have seen in chapter 6, although there may be cost-efficient sizes for many public good functions implying an optimum community size, it is usually impossible to prevent overlapping of different functions, of areas of benefits, or of burdens. In addition, it is usually necessary to simplify and aggregate zones of service provision in order to achieve administrative economy. A second, and related cause of spillover is that changes in technology, public needs and public preferences require a continuous adaptation of jurisdictional boundaries and burden incidence. It is never possible to achieve a degree of institutional adaptation required to match the rapidity of these changes and frequently there is a strong inertia induced by a historical legacy of local jurisdictions and administration which is not well suited to present demands.

A third factor is the mobility in modern society. The provision of many public goods cannot be limited just to the residents of a given community even if it were desired to do so. The provision of police protection, recreation facilities, public transportation, and especially infrastructure are cases where it is difficult to limit spillover benefits to other areas, since flows of commuters, shoppers, recreation and other uses create important spillovers. A fourth and related cause of spillover is the migration of economic and human capital. With respect to money capital, local investment in both public and private goods in one jurisdiction will generally be financed on a national capital market which allows complex gains and losses to occur between jurisdictions as local savings are used to finance investments elsewhere (see chapter 10). Labour migration gives a similar human capital flow by which the investment burdens of education, health care, welfare, manpower training and so forth, in one jurisdiction become the benefits of another jurisdiction. Conversely, migration of the less able and poor generate disbenefits (or cost spill-ins) of welfare and other services in the receiving area to the benefit of the losing area. In a free society, it is not possible, nor is it necessarily desirable, to halt these flows in the cause of equalizing benefit incidence. However, migration is usually highly selective and as we shall see in the next section, frequently jurisdictions pursue strategies which seek to maximize the benefits and minimize the disbenefits resulting from capital and labour mobility.

A fifth factor involving spillover is that of information. This is closely related to human capital mobility. The 'knowledge market' is a national and international one and investments in initial research and development in one jurisdiction will inevitably spill-out to provide benefits elsewhere. A sixth cause of spillovers is environmental factors. The very nature of many public goods and bads produce strong environmental spillovers elsewhere. Such spillovers are often public bads: the effects of air, noise and water pollution in adjacent areas (especially traffic pollution in cities), the impact of open garbage tips and sewerage disposal, and transfer of the opportunity costs of foregone reservoir sites and groundwater supply to other jurisdictions. These all represent the effects of spillover or jurisdictional interdependence induced by the effect of environmental flow. A seventh factor, which is especially important in the US, is the fragmentation and overlapping of different governments. On the one hand, fragmentation induces subsidy to poorer income tracts in proportion to the extent that higher level government taxes are progressive. On the other hand, fragmentation allows some groups to obtain the benefits and amenities of other areas at small cost.

Many studies, to be discussed in the next section, have found that considerable benefit and cost spillovers between jurisdictions occur in most countries. Generally, of course, the magnitude of these spillovers increases for smaller jurisdictions, larger total numbers of jurisdictions, and for higher degrees of fragmentation of government. The degree of spillover also varies for the category of public goods and services considered. It is not possible to reach conclusions as to the extent of spillover in any situation which are generally valid. But for US urban areas, Vincent (1971) gives a useful classification of spillover effects by expenditure category. The major factors causing benefit spillovers in the US urban areas derive from commuting, migration of human capital, and fragmentation of government. As table 9.3 shows, commuting mainly results in spillovers of highway, police, parks and other cultural facilities. Minor spillovers of health, fire and housing are also important. Migration spillovers are dominated by education, with minor health and welfare components. The effect of fragmented urban government is important for education, welfare and health. As table 9.3 shows, the total effect of these benefit spillovers also has consequences for income distribution which are especially significant for education, health and housing but also affects welfare, parks and cultural facilities.

Many authors view spillovers as one of the primary incentives for the development of mixed levels and patterns of government: the imposition by higher level governments of re-apportionment of benefits and burdens between jurisdictions; local consolidation to reduce the levels of benefit spillovers; and local level fiscal horizontal transfers (side payments) to equalize the incidence of burdens and benefits. Buchanan (1960), Musgrave and Musgrave (1976), and other authors have suggested the organization of local areas based on the range of local public good spillover effects. This suggestion is based on the concept of pure local good (discussed earlier) for which uniform benefits are available within a given limited tract, and for

227

Table 9.3 Classification of benefit spillovers in urban areas by major expenditure categories. (*Source*: Vincent 1971, table 2.1)

228

Expenditure category	Benefit spillover mechanism			Effect on income redistribution
	Community	Migration	Fragmented government	
Education	No	Yes	Yes (fiscal interdependence)	important
Highways	Yes	No	No	little
Public welfare	No	Possible (if these help make recipient more nearly self-sufficient)	Possible (if these help make recipient more nearly self-sufficient)	minor
Health and hospitals	Possible (if emergency treatment of commuters in accidents is significant)	Possible (communicable diseases reduced; reduced needs in new area)	Yes (communicable diseases reduced)	important
Police protection	Yes	No	No	little
Fire protection	Possible (however, property is probably the focal point of protection)	No	Yes (if a widespread fire which crosses boundaries is possible)	little
Sewers and sewage disposal	No	No	Yes	little
Other sanitation	Possible (includes street cleaning expenditures)	No	No	little
Parks, recreation and cultural activities	Yes (if parks are open to and used by non-residents)	No	No	minor
Housing and community redevelopment	Possible (insofar as visitors appreciate improved surroundings; but expenditures should not be affected by extent of communication)	No	No	important
General control and regulations	Possible (insofar as specific functions not charged full costs)	Possible (insofar as specific functions not charged full costs)	Possible (insofar as specific functions not charged full costs)	minor

which there are zero external benefit spillovers. For a range of pure public goods with different externality distance limits, it is possible to have a hierarchy of goods organized by a hierarchy of governments. A typical hierarchy suggested ranges upwards from purely private through local goods to national goods. The relation of spillovers to the apportionment of public expenditure functions between levels of government is discussed further in chapter 11. For the present, it is sufficient to note that however carefully the organization of public goods is undertaken, spillovers to other jurisdictions can never be totally eliminated. Their effects are quantified in the next section, and methods of overcoming these spillover effects are discussed in chapters 12 and 13.

9.4 The incidence of expenditure benefits

The assessment of benefit incidence at a geographical level (who gets what, where) involves two complex and interrelated issues: first, the measurement of expenditure benefits, and second the imputation of benefits to individuals, groups of client needs, and locations. Each of these components is discussed below.

MEASUREMENT OF EXPENDITURE BENEFITS

Expenditure benefits fall into two categories, those which are directly imputable to individuals (public distributive and non-redistributive benefits), and those which are imputable only to locations (geographical benefits).

In the measurement of individual expenditure benefits a major problem is differentiation of the quality and quantity of service available. A useful classification of benefit measures is given by Ridley and Simon (1947) and by Davies (1968) which is amended here to give benefits in four groups:

(i) *Measures of resource allocated*: (1) *Expenditure flows.* (a) *Total expenditure* allocated on current or capital accounts: total expenditure benefits per person, or (b) *net expenditure* after deductions of charges and tax levies: e.g. expenditure benefits minus tax and charge burdens per person. (2) *Physical flows*: manpower and equipment levels: numbers of teachers, child care officers, policemen, busses, refuse disposal trucks, etc.

(ii) *Measures of extensiveness of service*: proportion of population (or proportion of eligible population) who receive service: e.g. numbers of eligible children in education, numbers of eligibles in receipt of personal social services, number of prisoners or child care cases in receipt of minimum care standards, numbers of home nurse visits, units of public housing provided.

(iii) *Measures of intensity of provision*: resources allocated to recipient (inputs per client): e.g. expenditure per case, workers per case, staff per resident, teacher/pupil ratio.

(iv) *Measures of quality of provisions*: (outputs per client) standards of benefits received: e.g. examination passes per school or per candidate;

229

residents of poor houses, children in foster homes, ratio of home-helps to old people's homes, etc.

Most attention has usually been concentrated on the first category of total or net expenditure flows per person. Expenditure, manpower, and population data are usually readily available and the expenditure and physical flow ratios can be easily calculated. However, such measures do not take account of differences in the size of eligible population served (extensiveness), nor of the level of provision to eligible population (intensity), nor of quality of service differences. Moreover, the above scheme must be amended to take account, firstly, of differences in government responsibilities which affect the degree to which differences in flows, extensiveness, intensity and quality can be modified, and secondly, of the effect of local choices of revenue sources. In addition, differences in local preferences and political imperatives will induce jurisdictions to spend more or less on public goods, irrespective of the level of needs; what Hicks and Hicks (1945) termed the difference between the 'big spenders' and the 'stinters' among jurisdictions. The use of service charges rather than general tax sources, for example, will affect the level of provision and take-up of services, deflate the level of service usage, and hence the number of clients per category recognized in comparison with jurisdictions using tax sources.

In the case of assessment of extensiveness, intensity, and quality, the measurement of benefits received is further complicated by the importance of considerable elements of judgement. For example, with quality indicators, a judgement is required on the merits of small houses as opposed to high-rise apartments, or foster homes as opposed to children's homes, or home-helps rather than old people's homes, or examination passes rather than more general educational criteria. A tacit assumption is built into most intensity measures that more workers, or higher levels of expenditure per client, means higher quality. Where such judgements enter they reflect not only prejudices on the part of the researcher, but can also vary considerably in usage between jurisdictions. Jurisdictional variation can reflect real differences in local preferences, or may result from local administrative prejudices, differences in local policy paradigms, differences in political imperatives between areas, and variable cost factors. Hence, the measures of benefit are usually not strictly comparable between jurisdictions.

Measurement of levels of benefits is further complicated by the fact that even if the benefit measures are comparable between areas, they are not easy to relate to each other. For example, how can we differentiate a jurisdiction with high extensiveness but low intensity of service, such that most of eligible population is in receipt of some benefits, from a jurisdiction with low extensiveness but high intensity, such that only a few of eligible population receive benefits but the service benefits are of extremely high quality? Such variation is common in that some jurisdictions seek to ration demand for public goods by quality, whilst others use quantity limitation and waiting lists.

230

Still another category of jurisdiction may offer low extensiveness and high intensity by employment of user charges, and hence rationing demand by price. There is no simple solution to the problem of determining which of these jurisdictions is giving the 'best' distribution of public good benefits. As Davies (1968, p. 303) notes: "Evaluative studies are more difficult than it may at first appear because measures of different aspects of standards and provision – and sometimes different measures of other service aspects – are not highly correlated with one another even in relatively simple services".

The measurement of benefits directly imputable to locations again raises the difficulty of interplay of the levels of expenditures and physical flows with quantity and quality of service levels. Similar criteria to those developed in the ensuing paragraphs can be applied also to geographical benefits which cannot be imputed directly to individuals. However, at the geographical level, an additional component of benefits arises: that relating to the impact of expenditures on total local incomes. This issue is discussed more fully in chapter 14; here it is sufficient to note that the net level of local benefits will depend on the ability of the local economy to absorb expenditure flows. This depends in turn on the nature of local income multipliers. Benefit impacts may either remain mostly inside the local economy, or spill over and leak mostly outside. This depends on the nature, size and ability of local industry, commerce and retailing to absorb the expenditure spin-off. The local income benefits generated will also depend upon the extent to which local resources are already fully employed when fiscal transfers are received. When the local economy has reached a full employment ceiling, salaries to public employees, central government contracts, and other intergovernmental transfers will create price and wage inflation pressures in the local economy, and serve to encourage further local economic growth which in the long term will lead to cumulative imbalance and exacerbate the inequalities which most grant and transfer programmes attempt to reduce. In the US, for example, there have been many claims that federal expenditures have been the primary basis for economic growth in the West Coast and Gulf South-West. Thus Moynihan (1978) has claimed that the federal government "is intentionally deflating the economy of New York in order to sustain expansion elsewhere" by grant programmes. Again, in France, central government defence expenditures have underwritten the growth of Toulouse and elsewhere. When the local economy is operating at less than full employment, then the multiplier benefits of the expenditures will be high when the expenditure draws on under-used or unused resources, but will again leak away, cause inflation, or lead to locally imbalanced growth if the sectors affected are already fully employed.

IMPUTATION OF BENEFIT INCIDENCE

It is clear that the imputation of benefits deriving from the provision of public goods is rendered especially complex by the geographical features of tapering and spillover. Moreover, it has been noted frequently that the benefit element of fiscal incidence has been greatly neglected in comparison with the elements of revenue incidence. As a consequence there have been relatively few studies of the geography of expenditure incidence. However a number of significant studies have been made and these are briefly reviewed below in three categories: first, those studies which have analysed benefit incidence at national level by income group; second, those studies which have displayed regional and local benefit incidence, but for aggregate local populations; finally, there are those studies which have examined benefit incidence both

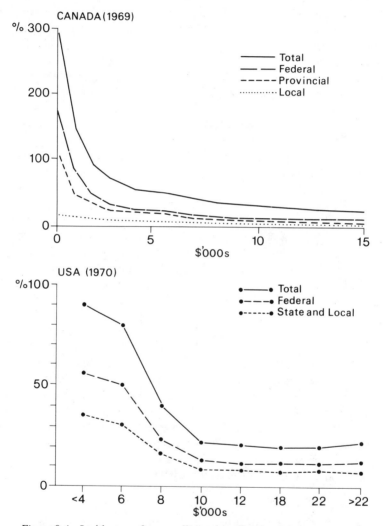

Figure 9.4 Incidence of expenditure benefits by income group in Canada, 1969, and the USA, 1970. (*Source: Canada*: Gillespie 1976; *USA*: Musgrave *et al.* 1974.)

geographically and between income and other social groups. It should be noted at the outset that no studies have yet been made at national level of the geographical distribution of expenditure benefits taking account of inter-group receipts of benefits by those in different client need groups. Nor have the measures of extensiveness, intensity and quality of the public services been widely adopted.

STUDIES OF BENEFIT INCIDENCE BY INCOME GROUPS

There has been considerable interest in the assessment of the incidence of expenditure benefits by income group and this has often been linked with studies of tax burdens (see, for example, Adler and Schlesinger 1951; Barna 1945; Conrad 1954; Gillespie 1965; Musgrave *et al.* 1974; Tucker 1953). The aim of such tax burden and benefit incidence studies is to assess the final balance of benefits and burdens in relation to need as discussed in chapter 14. It might be expected that since many expenditure programmes are deliberately redistributive (e.g. social services and transfer payments), then expenditures would be *regressive* with income, i.e. they should be higher for lower incomes. Estimates of expenditure incidence by income groups for Canada and the USA are shown in figure 9.4 and in each case confirm that a general decline with income takes place in the level of benefits for public goods. Moreover, benefit redistribution is usually higher for federal rather than intermediate or local level government. The form of benefit incidence also varies significantly for different public goods between expenditure programmes. Table 9.4, for example, shows that for the US, social security, the veterans' fund, and agricultural payments are most redistributive at federal level, and highways, education, social security and health are most redistributive at State and local levels.

STUDIES OF BENEFIT INCIDENCE BY REGIONS

The national studies of benefit incidence by income group reviewed above give no indication of geographical variation in benefits. On the other hand, many studies of geographical benefit incidence give no disaggregation by income group. A large number of studies have been made of the influence of national expenditure policies on the incidence of benefits between regions and local units of most western countries. Maps of the variation of *per capita* expenditure incidence as a percentage of GDP are shown in figure 9.5 for the EEC. These maps display considerable variation in levels of *per capita* expenditures, but although there is some relation of those areas with high expenditure incidence to those which would normally be agreed to be 'problem regions', there are many other elements affecting the pattern of benefit incidence. As we shall see in chapter 14, there is only a very approximate relationship of regional expenditure levels in these countries to need, i.e. expenditure is only partly regressive with variations in geographical incomes. Once again significant variations occur between expenditure pro-

Table 9.4 Expenditure benefits as a percentage of income for the US in 1960 at federal, State and local level. (*Source*: Gillespie 1965, tables 5 and 6.)

Governmental expenditure	Family money income brackets							
	Under $2,000	$2,000–$2,999	$3,000–$3,999	$4,000–$4,999	$5,000–$7,499	$7,500–$9,999	$10,000 and Over	Total
(1) FEDERAL								
1. Highways	—	—	—	—	—	—	—	—
2. Education	0.2	0.3	.02	0.1	0.1	0.1	0.1	0.1
3. Social security	118.9	26.9	12.3	3.8	1.1	0.8	0.2	3.9
4. Veterans	21.5	5.6	3.8	2.1	1.4	0.7	0.3	1.4
5. Agriculture	3.6	2.5	1.0	0.3	0.2	0.3	0.3	0.4
6. Health	1.9	0.8	0.3	0.2	0.1	0.1	—	0.2
7. Housing	1.0	0.5	0.2	0.1	—	0.0	0.0	—
8. Miscellaneous	10.9	4.4	2.5	1.9	1.1	0.6	0.4	1.1
(2) STATE AND LOCAL								
1. Highways	7.0	6.8	4.4	4.4	2.5	1.8	0.8	2.1
2. Education	23.6	13.0	11.0	7.6	5.4	3.3	1.8	4.5
3. Social security	44.1	12.6	1.7	0.2	—	0.0	0.0	1.1
4. Veterans	0.4	0.1	0.1	—	0.1	0.1	0.1	0.1
5. Agriculture	0.7	0.7	0.4	0.2	0.1	0.5	0.1	1.3
6. Health	26.9	9.9	2.1	1.6	0.9	0.0	0.0	0.2
7. Housing	3.5	1.9	0.7	0.2	—	0.0	0.0	0.2
8. Miscellaneous	17.1	5.6	3.1	2.0	1.2	0.7	0.4	1.3

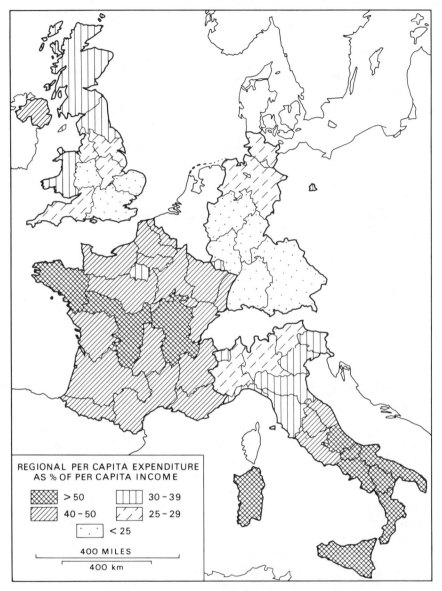

Figure 9.5 Per capita expenditure incidence of spatially differentiated expenditures as a percentage of GDP in the EEC. (Data derived from EEC 1977.)

grammes with transport, highways, infrastructure and public works and industrial and employment expenditure being the most redistributive.

With respect to the US, considerable controversy and political debate has always surrounded the allocation of federal funds to various regions. Most recently disparities in expenditure incidence have been noted between the

235

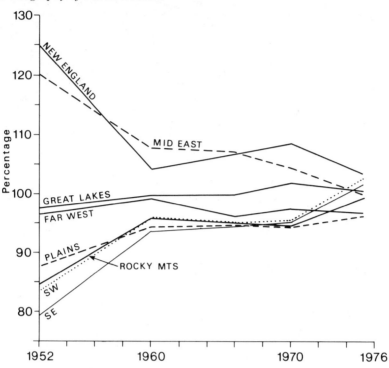

Figure 9.6 Federal government expenditures as a percentage of personal income in the US, 1952–76. (*Source*: US ACIR 1978c.)

'sun-belt' of the South and Gulf States, and the 'frost-belt' of the Eastern, New England and Mid-Western States. The most significant expenditure components are in federal employment, defence contracts, public works, and highways. As figure 9.6 shows, a considerable divergence in benefit incidence between regions of the US occurred in the 1960s, which is now narrowing, but still gives considerably higher expenditure in the 'sun-belt' States (further discussion of this result is given by Bennett 1980). Similarly in education expenditures in the US and in Canada, Coons *et al.* (1970) and Sharples (1975) respectively have found that State and provincial variation in the expenditure benefits have persisted since the 1930s and are strongly related to local incomes. Attempts to reduce these have been of only limited success. Again, in the UK, DHSS (1976) have noted the persistence and increasing disparities of health service benefits between hospital board regions.

Studies which have attempted to determine benefit incidence between different jurisdictions in terms of needs, rather than income groups, are relatively few. One major set of studies for the UK is that by Davies (1968) and Davies *et al.* (1971a,b) who has used family care, housing conditions, and social conditions indices of needs. Much work in the US has been directed at benefit incidence related to 'fiscal distress' or 'urban conditions' measures of

236

need (Bradbury 1978; Dommel *et al.* 1978; Gramlich 1976; Nathan and Adams 1976). In each case it would be expected that as the level of need rises, then the level of service expenditures, and the quality, intensity and extensiveness of the services should also rise. Davies (1968, chapters 7 to 9) found that the extensiveness of the service provision was most highly correlated with need for UK data for 1949/52, 1956/59 and 1961/62, i.e. that the number of social service cases for old age and children, and in education, rose as the level of need increased. But Davies' studies give little evidence of any relationship between quality of benefits and level of needs, as measured by staff per client need, or expenditure per client need. For various analyses of the UK Rate Support Grant, Jackman and Sellars (1978) have pointed out the poor matching of expenditure benefits to measured needs, and similar conclusions have been drawn by Jenkins and Rose (1976) and Rose (1978) for London. Similar results also obtain for the US studies. In the Nathan and Dommel (1977) study, for example, an urban hardship index was used which was based on the levels of poverty, city age, and population growth or decline, to determine the degree to which total federal grants to cities met these

Table 9.5 Urban hardship and federal aid in the US 1978. (*Source:* Nathan and Dommel 1977.) Urban conditions index is weighted sum of: % population changed 1960–70; % housing units built prior to 1939; and % of persons with incomes below poverty line. City–suburb disparity index is weighted sum of 6 factors: % unemployment, % population under 18 and over 64; % adult population with less than high school education; average *per capita* income; % housing units exceeding one person per room; % of families below 125% of low income level

(1)	*(2)*	*(3)*	*(4)*	*(5)* Total federal grants per capita $	*(6)* Stimulus package per capita $	*(7)* % increase in total grants 1975–78
City	*Region*	*Urban conditions index*	*City– suburb disparity index*			
St Louis	NC	351	231	17.5	46.3	248
Newark	NE	321	422	23.7	42.1	400
Buffalo	NE	292	189	28.8	60.0	154
Cleveland	NE	291	331	16.9	53.5	131
Boston	NE	257	198	17.3	43.9	81
Baltimore	NE	224	256	28.5	87.6	68
Philadelphia	NE	216	205	26.2	68.1	151
Chicago	NC	201	245	19.8	58.5	145
Detroit	NC	201	210	21.6	74.1	87
Atlanta	S	118	226	22.9	42.4	53
Denver	W	106	143	18.1	52.2	30
Los Angeles	W	74	105	22.1	42.9	162
Dallas	S	38	97	6.7	27.1	74
Houston	S	36	93	15.5	43.5	88
Phoenix	W	19	85	47.1	73.3	94

measured needs. As shown in table 9.5, those cities with high needs tend to be concentrated in the north and east of the United States, and are also generally those cities with the highest suburban–central city disparities. Total federal aid to cities is based heavily on geographical transfers by categorical grants, HUD programmes, Revenue-Sharing, CETA, public service employment (CETA Titles II and VI), local public works, mass transport and welfare programmes. These expenditures are shown in column 5 of table 9.5, whilst column 6 shows those elements of column 5 which derive from grants which have been aimed at more closely meeting central city needs (the so-called 'fiscal stimulus package' of public service employment, local public works and countercyclical revenue-sharing). The table shows that although total grants are only patchy in meeting urban needs as measured by the hardship index, the stimulus package has been more successfully concentrated in the areas of most extreme need, and the main increases in federal aid have been in the most needy areas. But the total distribution of funds is still far from closely in accordance to total needs. Further discussion of these programmes is given in chapter 13.

STUDIES OF BENEFIT INCIDENCE BY INCOME GROUP OR
CLIENT GROUP AND REGION

There have been very few studies of benefit incidence which permit simultaneous assessment of incidence by geographical location and by social or income group. Those studies which are available refer to expenditure incidence between groups and jurisdictions at a fairly local level, usually within cities. As such they are discussed at length in chapter 14 as one facet of general assessment of fiscal incidence, and discussion is restricted here purely to the benefit element in the incidence equation.

The major study which has developed simultaneous assessment of geographical and income group expenditure incidence is that by Greene *et al.* (1974). This study more than any other accords with the accounts basis sought in this book and gives a geographical division of incidence into three areas used in table 8.7, of the District of Columbia, Maryland and Virginia. Hence it represents almost a State level study, but where the State interactions are dominated by a single metropolitan area, Greene *et al.* used both the cost and welfare bases (see p. 215) for determining benefit incidence, and then compared results. For each expenditure category they construct a matrix of geographical and income group benefit spillovers and then sum across rows and down columns to obtain estimates of net benefit incidence (see Greene *et al.* 1974, tables 5.16 and 5.17). The distribution of spatial and individual incidence between expenditure categories is shown in figure 9.7. The total incidence pattern of the cost basis (imputing benefits of cost) shows a strong regressive feature of benefit incidence in each area. This regression in favour of the poor is important in all expenditure programmes. When the welfare basis which takes into account different marginal utilities for income is calculated, some important differences emerge. Expenditures are still very largely redistributive to the poor, but at higher incomes are much more proportional than regressive with income than the cost bases would suggest. Thus, when the utility of income is taken into account the level of redistribution is much less. These differences in bases are most marked for education, police, fire, health and 'all other' expenditures, and are least marked, as might be expected, for welfare expenditures.

When we look at the total flow of benefit spillovers between jurisdictions these are seen to be in all cases very high: constituting 3.9 and 19.7% of all benefits on the respective cost and welfare bases. The welfare basis is considerably larger because of the high marginal utility with income of free benefits which spillover from other areas. To some extent the effect of benefit spillover is somewhat self-cancelling, but as table 9.6 of net flows shows, a considerable net imbalance of benefit spillovers does indeed obtain between the District of Columbia giving substantial net benefits to Maryland and Virginia, with Maryland giving a small percentage of benefit spillover to Virginia. Further discussion of the Greene *et al.* study is given in chapter 14. For the present it should be noted that this study represents the only major piece of research to date which allows the assessment of the income incidence of central city burdens. As such, and as a study of the US capital city, with certain important individualities, these results should not be regarded as necessarily typical of other central city areas.

The geography of benefit incidence is clearly complex and requires tracing of the effects of spillover to final individual expenditure receipt. No account has been taken in the studies surveyed in this section of the effects of tapering which represent a further component of benefit variation inducing geographical inequities in benefit incidence. There are only a small number of studies which have attempted to estimate spatial incidence of benefits, but there is no doubt that a great increase in this area of research will follow in many countries. However, the assessment of incidence of the benefits of public

Table 9.6 Net benefit flows in the Washington metropolitan area on the costs basis, welfare basis in brackets ($000). (Data derived from Greene *et al.* 1974)

To	From		
	D.C.	*Maryland*	*Virginia*
D.C.	477,048	− 12,823	− 8050
	(425,767)	(− 71,751)	(− 49,142)
Maryland	12,823	422,974	1,720
	(71,751)	(401,590)	(− 4788)
Virginia	8,050	1,720	237,725
	(49,142)	(4,788)	(217,875)

COST BASIS

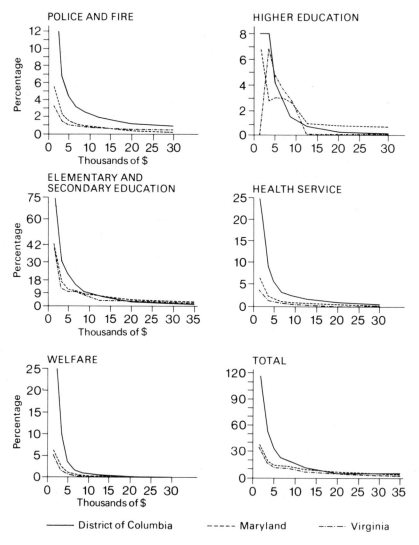

POLICE AND FIRE

HIGHER EDUCATION

ELEMENTARY AND
SECONDARY EDUCATION

HEALTH SERVICE

WELFARE

TOTAL

——— District of Columbia   ----- Maryland   —·—·— Virginia

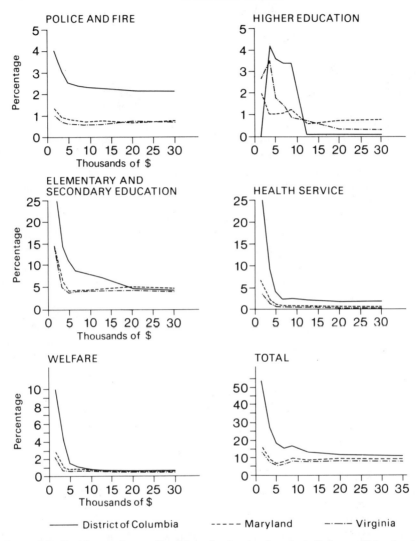

Figure 9.7 Incidence of expenditure benefits for the three jurisdictions of Maryland, Virginia, and Washington, DC, by income group. (*Source*: redrawn from Greene *et al.* 1974, figures 5.1–5.10, 5.13 and 5.14.)

goods is only one element in the final assessment of the equity of public finance. To the consideration of benefit incidence must be added the geography of expenditure need, and the relation of need and benefit to the geography of revenue burden, ability and effort. This allows the assessment of the final form of fiscal incidence and a conclusion to be drawn as to the geographical equity of the public fisc. This task is undertaken in the following

241

chapters. For the present, the next section discusses the important strategies of jurisdictional exclusion which affect the incidence of benefits.

9.5 Strategies of fiscal prudence

Frequently the breakdown of the Musgrave–Samuelson conditions for a pure public good gives rise to benefit gains and advantages to one user as against another. The classic case is that of spillovers for which benefits are obtained at less than their true cost. Such features may arise inadvertently in any system of public finance and it is probably not possible to design a system in which benefits and burdens are totally equalized (nor is it necessarily desirable that they should be). However, in many cases, individual and jurisdictional strategies of competition and fiscal prudence have been followed, the aim of which has been to enhance local benefits and to induce spillover of burdens on to others.

In following such prudent strategies, five main instruments are employed. First, there are those which relate to the second Musgrave–Samuelson condition and result in deliberate exclusion. Second, there are strategies of political lobbying, log-rolling and pork-barrelling, which are aimed at inducing non-jointness, exclusion and rejection (see chapter 15). Third, there are gerrymandering and districting strategies to induce exclusion, rejection, and non-jointness as discussed above. Fourth, there is the use of discriminatory taxation policies. Finally, there are 'do nothing' strategies of passing on public bads especially of environmental pollution as cost spillovers onto other areas.

Exclusion strategies are the most important category of strategies of fiscal prudence. They are aimed at deliberate restriction of interpersonal access to benefits. Major instruments of such policy are land use and zoning controls, building codes, and local charges. Perhaps the major aspect of exclusion relates to the use of zoning, building codes and other land use controls. In the UK, since 1947, this has been operated through the Town and Country Planning Acts, whilst in the US, since the 1916 New York City building codes, local action has been more important. In the US exclusion through zoning is operated whenever the invasion by one form of land use is anticipated to generate diseconomies for existing land uses. Frequently such zoning has been used in the US to prevent the access of lower and lower–middle income groups, and large families to higher income areas, or to prevent industrial invasion (especially of gas stations) into residential tracts. In the UK, zoning has been less frequently and explicitly used as a mechanism for social exclusion partly as a result of a much more consolidated pattern of local government, and partly as a result of a statutory obligation placed on local authorities by the Town and Country Planning Acts to produce local plans. Each of these plans should conform to criteria of good land use planning and is subject to external approval at central government level. However, the criteria of good land use planning normally place great emphasis on segregating industrial, commercial, and residential tracts, and also emphasize the maintenance of the social structure of residential neighbourhoods. Hence in practice, UK land use planning has important exclusionary effects, although a higher degree of local consolidation prevents these practices taking on the more extreme aspects which characterize the United States.

It is possible to distinguish two economic motives for zoning (Mills and Oates 1975). First, fiscal zoning is designed to attract high income groups and industry and ensures that new entrants to a community pay at least their share, but preferably greater than their share of the public budget. Second, public good zoning is designed to exclude certain social groups by the use of large building lot sizes and so forth. These two interrelated motives add a social element to fiscal prudence. Such situations have been set into the context of general external economies and diseconomies by Bish and Nourse (1975), as summarized in table 9.7. Of the six possible cases, zoning is employed in cases 5 and 6 to exclude the diseconomies of invading alternative land uses. In some cases tracts may choose to forego external economies but this will have fiscal effects. If a residential tract chooses to prohibit commercial, industrial and multi-family uses, this will undoubtedly affect the costs and burdens of providing services to the residential area. Whilst many richer suburbs may find this desirable and tolerable, exclusion in poor suburbs may have considerable impact on squeezing out middle incomes in favour of higher incomes.

In both the US and UK such zoning is intended to restrict private use for the greater public welfare. These aims are summarized well in the District of Columbia Act of 1938 (52 Stat. 797 amended 1942, Act 56, Stat. 122) which is typical of US East Coast city zoning regulations. It has been more successful than many Acts in preventing developers creating non-conforming uses through its Article 75 of 1969. The aims of the Act are wide: "to promote the

Table 9.7 Typology of externality effects leading to zoning in cases 5 and 6. (*After* Bish and Nourse 1975, chapter 9, and Curry 1979)

Type of externality	Example
(1) (+ +) Mutual external economies	Retail location adjacent to leading tradesmen; residential location of high income homes on adjacent plots: 'bandwagon' effect
(2) (− −) Mutual external diseconomies	
(3) (00) Neutral effects	Independent locational decisions, e.g. of hospitals and fire station.
(4) (+ 0) External economies for one user	Restaurant location adjacent to industry or a university.
(5) (+ −) External economies matched by external diseconomies	Residential location of low income homes in high income areas
(6) (0 −) Neutral effects matched by external diseconomies	Industrial location in residential area.

health, safety, morals, commerce, order, prosperity, or general welfare . . . and its planning and orderly development" (DLI, DC 1966, p. 69). This is achieved by restrictions on the "location, height, bulk, number of storeys, and size of buildings and other structure, the percentage of lot that may be occupied, the size of yards, courts, and other open spaces, the density of population and use of buildings, structures and land for trade, industry residence, recreation, public activities or other purposes". These regulations are operated by a zoning commission which in accordance with their comprehensive plan has very broad goals: "to lessen congestion on the streets, to secure safety from fire, panic, and other dangers, to promote health and the general welfare, and provide adequate light and air, to prevent the undue concentration of population and the overcrowding of land, and to promote such distribution of population and the uses of land as would tend to create conditions favourable to health, safety, transportation, prosperity, protection of property, civic activity, and recreational, educational, and cultural opportunities, and as would tend to further economy and efficiency in the supply of public services" (DLI, DC 1966, p. 69).

The major problem of zoning is that, despite its laudatory aims, it tends to increase markedly the degree of social and spatial segregation in any area. Because of their generally greater homogeneity, suburbs in the US have a greater chance of passing zoning ordinances than do the larger more heterogenous central cities. As a result, the suburbs tend to maintain a highly segregated class structure, whilst the cities must absorb all the rejected elements from the suburbs. Although this is an explicit spatial and social phenomenon in the US, there is much to suggest that in the UK more covert political lobbying and the difficulties of defining exclusionary zones for the cities creates similar but less marked effects. In the US restrictive zoning to exclude poorer groups has been declared unconstitutional in the Hawkins v. Town of Shaw legal decision (*Federal Supplement*, 1162, 1969, p. 302). Such so-called 'snob zoning' entails the use of large lot sizes, minimum square footage, building codes designed to increase construction costs, single family dwellings, and apartments with only one bedroom (to exclude young children and thus reduce education costs). Although such snob zoning is now illegal, in practice it seems that this decision has had little effect other than preventing the more obvious and extreme cases of exclusion.

9.6 Conclusion: equity and imbalances in benefit incidence

Consideration of benefit incidence, as discussed in this chapter, has frequently given rise to questions about equity. In each case variation in benefit incidence can be ascribed to various forms of breakdown in the Musgrave–Samuelson conditions for a pure public good. Methods by which jurisdictions seek to enhance their benefits at the expense of other jurisdictions are also important. Questions of equity have already been raised in the discussion of taxes, needs, and costs, in previous chapters. To reach a final conclusion on the equity of benefits, burdens, needs and costs, we need to be able to put each of these elements together in an equation which allows the determination of the ultimate question of fiscal incidence. This is accomplished in chapter 14. It can already be seen, however, that the problems raised by the inequities in benefit incidence lead us to a very complex set of issues for which there are a large number of possible policy responses. These range from the 'do nothing' alternative, through benefit taxation, re-districting, political consolidation, to complex grant programmes, fiscal transfers and equalization payments. These policy solutions are discussed in chapters 11 to 13. In the next chapter are considered the specific impacts on benefit incidence deriving from the capital as opposed to the current account of the public fisc.

10

The capital burden

"Economy is going without something you do not want in case you should, some day, want something you probably won't want."

Antony Hope, *The Dolly Dialogues*

10.1 Current and capital accounts

Capital finance is not distinct from the issues of need, cost, revenue burden and benefit incidence discussed in earlier chapters. However, it does raise some important new issues which require separate treatment. Capital finance particularly focuses on issues which are longer term, involve different generations of people, and affect differences in regional growth rates and performances.

Capital finance, as opposed to current account finance, arises in three main situations, two of which are legitimate, and the third of which is dubious and often illegal. First, capital finance is an important component of stabilization policy used for short-term borrowing to even out fluctuations in revenue. Sources of revenue often vary seasonally because of the consumption patterns of industry and individuals, or seasonal patterns of tax schedules. Sources of revenue also fluctuate during the economic cycle and the capital element forms an important component in Keynesian deficit finance to spread the load of fiscal burdens. A second form of capital finance is its use for the finance of capital of projects particularly those concerned with creating economic growth. Such projects are those where a significant amount of resources are tied up or sunk into a particular set of stocks, infrastructure, buildings, or utilities. Frequently these are the projects concerned with long term growth and the creation of significant new capital. Capital finance then allows the burdens of this investment to be spread over a period of years and an important issue which then arises is the equalization of the burdens of capital repayments with the flow of benefits from the investment. The third form of capital finance, which is usually rather dubious in motive and frequently forbidden by law, is the funding of current account public expenditure using loans, securities and other forms of capital finance. It is this form of capital finance which has been responsible for the fiscal crisis of some major US cities, especially New York. Such cities are characterized by a large borrowing requirement to fund an increasing current account deficit which, as a largely fixed and uncontrollable expenditure, leads to a cycle in which ever-rising

246

leads to a more detailed discussion of the nature of city fiscal crises. Section 10.4 explores those issues in the incidence of capital burdens which differ from current account revenue burdens as discussed in chapters 7 and 8; and finally, section 10.5 briefly discusses major forms of public capital institutions.

10.2 Capital formation and regional balance

The level of capital formation has three important consequences: first it affects the level of present consumption which is possible; second, it controls the level of capital assets passed on to future generations; and finally, it is usually spatially differentiated to a high degree, and hence underlies patterns of regional disparity. Attention is concentrated here on the level of capital formation and geographical differentiation.

CAPITAL FORMATION

Capital formation concerns increases in the productive capacity of the economy. For the public fisc this may involve either physical stocks (capital goods such as buildings, infrastructure, utilities and transport equipment) or human capital (characteristics of the population such as health, education and training). It is normal to exclude from physical stocks, consumer durables, military durables, and renewable natural resources such as sunshine and rain, but dwellings and raw materials are normally included (Kuznets 1961, 1973). In Kuznets' capital accounts for the US, human capital is also excluded: capital is defined as the stock of elements intended for use in producing goods and income, and which can be legally disposed of. However, in the present discussion human capital is included together with elements of political and social capital. It is certainly difficult in the public sector to differentiate between goods which do or do not contribute to the long-term increases in productive capacity but it is equally certain that many elements of public expenditure are orientated towards political and social harmony which is a necessary condition for capital formation.

A number of general theories have been proposed to describe the evolution over time of the rate of capital accumulation. For example, Keynes (1936) hypothesized that the propensity both to invest in public capital goods and to save, increased with income, although there would be important variations between groups of people. This hypothesis has been confirmed in a number of analyses, For example, the analysis of 101 countries by Chenery and Syrquin (1975), shown in figure 10.1, demonstrates that investment, savings, levels of government revenue, and investment in education, all rise with income, whilst non-public consumption declines with income. This, of course, is related to Wagner's law discussed in chapter 2.

REGIONAL BALANCE

The Keynesian hypothesis of increasing savings and public expenditure with income has important geographical implications. If there are important

current account deficits lead to increased borrowing requirement
increasing interest rates.

Despite the distinction made here between current and capi
funding, in practice for the public fisc these two sets of account:
kept totally distinct. In private sector commercial accounting prac
expenditure is depreciated over the useful life of the asset con
amortization period), and a fair indication of the actual annual cos
is obtained (including the consumption of assets each year) al
calculation of annual profits and losses. In the private sector, the
between current and capital expenditure also enables the total
working capital employed in the business to be calculated, togetl
rates of return. Moreover, both profit and loss, and rate of return c
as indices of commerical well-being. For the public fisc, howev
expenditure includes expenditure on the same types of asset as in
sector, but in addition a large part of public fixed capital
expenditure on non-traded assets which do not yield a quantifiable
return. Hence there is no revenue to set against costs, and so
loss or rates of return are therefore not applicable. For example,
purchase of existing capital stock adds nothing to the capital sto
economy as a whole, it merely changes its ownership. In additio
ments are concerned with social and political objectives as well as
ones. Such goals as education, literacy, health, redistribution of inc
environmental protection, whilst they have economic impact, ar
captured in terms of costs alone. Because of this difficulty of dividi
from capital finance in the public sector, it has sometimes been cla
the distinction is not important, either in the choice between tax:
borrowing, or in the choice between long- and short-term financing.
is claimed in the UK for example, that "The balance between tax:
borrowing, and the choice of method and term of borrowing, is deter
the government's overall assessment of the position of the economy a
best available combination of monetary and fiscal policies" (UK
1978, p. 2). Whilst there are certainly considerable problems in s
current and capital accounts in the public sector, as we shall s
subsequent discussion, there are two main difficulties which result
making as clear as possible a distinction. First, if carried to exces
combined with a lack of growth in total taxable assets, it can lead to
worsening crisis such as that characterizing some US cities. Second,
distributional effects are induced by long and short-term expenditu
affects the distribution of benefits between generations and between l

This chapter is concerned with four main issues. First, the relation
the rate of capital formation, the level of income, and public expenditu
is discussed in section 10.2 and leads to a discussion of differences in
capital formation and incomes between regions. In section 10.3, the c
tial needs and costs of capital in different locations are examined, ;

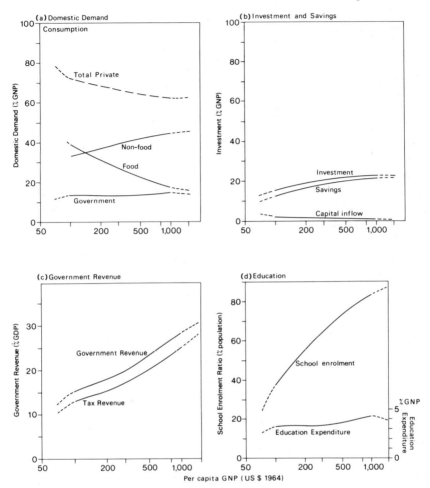

Figure 10.1 Relation of investment, savings, government activity, education and consumption to GNP in 101 countries. (*Source*: Chenery and Syrquin 1975, figure 1-4.)

differences in regional incomes, under the Keynesian theory there should be comparable differences in levels of saving and levels of public expenditures. A number of analyses confirm this to be the case. The important question is, however: if savings levels differ between regions, do the subsequent levels of public capital expenditure and investment tend to concentrate in high income or low income regions? If savings and investment are both highest in high income regions, then the capital market is disequilibrating of regional growth rates: differences in *per capita* incomes and capital stocks will steadily increase. If, however, savings accumulated in the high income regions are subsequently invested in low income regions, then the capital market is

249

equilibrating. The accepted economic argument of neoclassical models is that equilibrating capital flows do occur between the high and low income regions, but most empirical analyses of capital flows show the reverse to be true; that investments remain in the high income regions.

Empirical analyses of regional patterns of savings and investment incidence are few in number, mainly because of the difficulties in obtaining data. However, for the US, a number of studies do exist. For the *public sector* there have been a series of studies to measure the relative needs and costs of capital investment in various locations, and special agencies such as the EDA in the US, and the Public Works and Loan Board in the UK, have been set up to assess capital bids against need. These issues are discussed further in the next section. For the *private sector*, Hartland (1950), analysing US Federal Reserve Bank data for 1929–39, found that the New England region gained from other regions an average net annual receipt of investment over savings of $200m. For California, Grebler (1962) found that much of the recent growth in housing has been underwritten by massive investments derived from other States through the Federal Home Loan Bank, Veterans Administration, and other institutions. In the first major national level analysis in the US, Romans (1965) found that for 1953 data there was a massive outflow of investment from savers in the North-East and Mid-West to new investment opportunities in the South and West of the US. Estimates of these flows are given in table 10.1, and these show that the Mid-East and New England Regions were contributing $241 and $235 *per capita*, respectively, to other regions, whilst the South-West and South-East, respectively, were receiving benefits of $287 and $269 from savers in other regions.

The evidence of these analyses tends to indicate that capital flows are moderately equibrating: favouring the investment opportunities in the North-

Table 10.1 Regional incomes and capital exports in the US in 1953 (*Source:* Romans 1965, table 15)

Region	Regional income ($ per head)	Total net capital exports ($ per head)
Far West	2103	69
Mid-East	2076	241
Great Lakes	2053	38
New England	1958	235
Rocky Mountains	1667	− 255
Plains	1614	− 49
South-West	1529	− 287
South-East	1237	− 269
Continental US average	1788	− 10

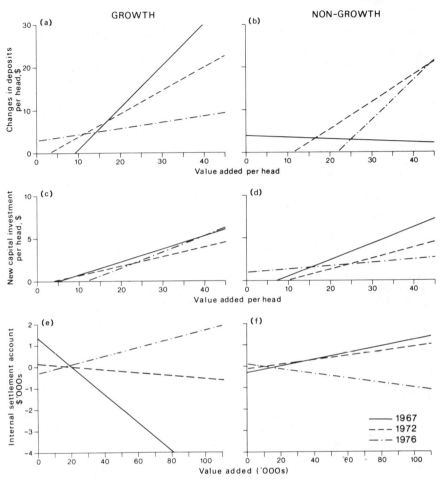

Figure 10.2 Relation of savings and capital flows in US growth and non-growth areas for 1976, 1972 and 1967. (*Source*: Bennett 1980; data derived from *US Census of Manufactures*; FDIC *Bank Operating Statistics*; and Federal Reserve Bank *Internal Settlement Account*.)

East in the 1930s, and favouring the new opportunities in the West, and South-East in the 1950s. However, more recent analysis suggests that continued flows of investment from high income savers in the North-East to the South-West and West, is tending to exacerbate the problems of regional decline in the North-East. The results of analysing changes in US commercial bank deposits, new industrial investment, and fiscal transfers between Federal Reserve Bank regions, are summarized in figure 10.2. From this it can be seen that those States which have experienced recent rapid growth in employment (mainly in the West, South-West, South-East and Plains) have contributed progressively less in savings as a proportion of value added, and have received

251

progressively more capital investment, whilst those States with low rates of growth of employment (mainly in the Mid-West, North-East and North) have produced progressively more savings as a proportion of value added, and received progressively less new capital investment. Hence, when differences in growth rates are taken into account, it is becoming increasingly clear that the continued growth of the 'sun-belt' is at the expense of decline in the 'frost-belt', and hence, of equilibrium in growth of incomes overall.

The growing awareness of these developments has occasioned increasing concern with capital institutions and the best way in which the public interest, in equalizing levels of regional incomes, can be introduced into the workings of the capital market. Various public capital institutions which can achieve this task are discussed further in section 10.5.

10.3 Capital needs, costs, and urban fiscal crises

Usually the rate of capital formation, economic growth and cyclical sensitivity differ between regions. In addition, the speed of ageing of capital stocks, the age of existing investment, and other sunk costs also differ spatially. Finally, there is also significant geographical variation in the costs of servicing capital, raising loans, and of creating new capital stocks. Each of these factors stimulates the consideration of geographical differences in capital needs and costs, and this in turn leads to a consideration of the urban fiscal crisis in terms of its specific aspects which arise on the capital account.

CAPITAL NEEDS

The major problem in assessing capital needs is one of definition. Capital accounts can be introduced into each of the accounting approaches discussed in chapter 4, but the treatment of capital elements is always difficult. Goldsmith and Lipsey (1963), for example, pose four questions of definition: (i) what is the scope of tangible and intangible assets and liabilities to be included in the account? Are human capital stocks, in terms of health, education and training, to be included together with durables, stocks and claims? (ii) How are stocks, assets and liabilities to be grouped between tangibles and intangibles? (iii) How are assets to be valued? Should a common stable price level be used, and should book value, original costs to the owner, original costs to the first person to acquire the asset, redemption value, replacement value, market value, or capitalized net income value be adopted? (iv) How should interregional debts and assets be treated? They cancel out at the level of the national economy (except for foreign transactions), but differ considerably at the level of regions or local jurisdictions, and will differ greatly depending upon the geographical unit adopted.

Capital needs differ from current needs in three main respects. First, although evaluation of the equality of services is an important issue on the current account, on the capital account it is pre-eminent. Service qualities of teacher/pupil ratios, hospital beds per head of population, firemen or policemen per head, public housing in relation to waiting lists, and so forth, give a good indication of current service qualities, but take account neither of sunk costs effects deriving from the age of the stock, nor of the costs of improving and modifying it. The age of a school, hospital, house or infrastructure is a major component affecting present service qualities and hence relative needs for capital. Second, because capital elements are relatively immobile, many capital needs can result from the bad location of a facility relative to current demand, rather than the lack of the facility. Whereas current account services can often be reallocated to other areas, a hospital, school or police station cannot be shifted. Hence capital needs, more than current needs are rooted in the past and in geographical location, and thus require particularly good forecasts of likely levels of needs in the future. Third, capital needs are 'lumpy' in that a major programme usually requires a substantial investment: the needs cannot usually be as easily financed by a small scale increment to existing service levels as can needs on the current account.

There are two main approaches to assessing capital needs. First, one based on direct valuation of capital stocks and replacement costs. Second, one based on indexes of debt burden and liquidity. The stock valuation approach is the one most commonly used by special purpose governments and in particular sector programmes. For example, in the UK, the DHSS (1976) have attempted to assess capital needs for hospitals at bed-replacement cost, written down by weighting factors appropriate to the age of each jurisdiction's hospital stock. The depreciation term differs for each jurisdiction depending on the proportion of hospital floor space in various periods of building. The capital needs are assessed by weighting the population in each jurisdiction in five need categories by the national level of capital spending on each type of need. This procedure is shown in table 10.2 for the 14 English Regional Health Authorities. With the capital needs of each jurisdiction assessed, the stock value for 1977 for all regions can be divided by the capital needs of the total national population. This gives a 'target' level of capital provision in each area which would result if the present capital assets were distributed uniformly in relation to need. The level of present capital assets in each region can than be compared with this target, as shown in figure 10.3. This figure also shows the level of equalization required to allow capital expenditure between 1976/77 and 1986/87 to bring assets in line with capital needs. A full equalization is not achieved over the 10 years because of differences in the age and amortization periods of existing capital stocks, and because of the effects of floor and ceiling limits to the degree of reapportionment, but capital resources are much more closely related to needs than at the outset of the period.

The second method of assessing capital needs, based on indexes of debt

Table 10.2 Weights applied to population levels in UK in 1981 Regional Hospital Administration regions which are used for determining capital allocations and assessing targets of stock evaluations. (*Source*: UK DHSS 1976, table D4)

| Region | Crude | 1981 *projected population* (1971-based) 000s | | | | | |
| | | *Weighted to reflect capital need for services for* | | | | | |
		Non-psychiatric in-patients	All day- and out-patients	Psychiatric in-patients	Community health	Ambulances	Aggregated Weighted population
Northern	3,172.7	3,253.7	3,472.1	3,131.7	3,341.9	3,475.5	3,276.0
Yorkshire	3,576.1	3,775.1	3,779.8	3,592.4	3,783.4	3,773.7	3,749.8
Trent	4,661.4	4,563.9	4,697.7	4,535.2	4,726.7	4,754.6	4,593.9
East Anglian	1,897.5	1,831.4	1,714.6	1,913.9	1,720.7	1,716.3	1,817.1
NW Thames	3,584.0	3,379.1	3,440.5	3,588.1	3,443.1	3,385.0	3,422.4
NE Thames	3,873.6	3,738.6	3,747.1	3,843.2	3,762.3	3,737.3	3,756.5
SE Thames	3,748.4	3,881.7	3,588.3	3,867.1	3,633.1	3,559.9	3,815.1
SW Thames	2,917.7	3,091.6	2,953.2	3,183.1	2,939.1	2,787.5	3,068.3
Wessex	2,815.9	2,802.4	2,583.2	2,952.9	2,576.7	2,548.2	2,772.8
Oxford	2,403.4	2,078.0	2,122.3	2,261.9	2,145.8	2,161.7	2,117.6
South Western	3,250.0	3,235.3	2,963.7	3,299.0	2,955.5	3,102.0	3,184.9
West Midlands	5,341.8	5,048.5	5,422.8	5,149.7	5,457.0	5,475.8	5,152.7
Mersey	2,542.8	2,633.2	2,832.8	2,465.2	2,825.5	2,849.4	2,654.5
North Western	4,145.6	4,618.8	4,612.8	4,147.5	4,620.1	4,604.0	4,549.3
England	47,930.9	47,930.9	47,930.9	47,930.9	47,930.9	47,930.9	47,930.9

Estimated national proportional capital spending on each service:

		62.6%	12.9%	14.5%	7.7%	2.3%	100%

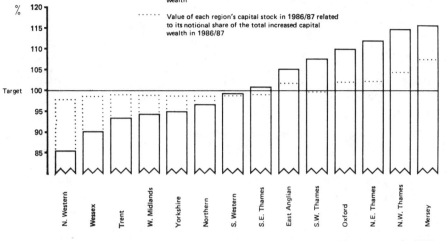

Figure 10.3 Levels of capital stock and required levels of capital investment in UK Regional Hospital Administration Areas to achieve equalization. (*Source:* UK DHSS 1976, figure D3.)

burden and liquidity, is most relevant to jurisdictions of mixed, multi-purpose governments. Such indexes are measures of the financial needs of government as a whole, rather than specific sector programmes. A range of capital need measures have been proposed, and the three most important of these are given below.

(i) *Cumulative budget deficits.* Because of the need for capital borrowing to even out short-term fluctuations in revenues, cumulative budget deficits are usually employed, instead of single year deficits, to measure capital needs for borrowing. In a study of 30 US cities in 1975, Dearborn (1977) found that the cities with the largest three year deficits were concentrated in either declining or growing areas.

(ii) *Liquidity (cash reserves).* These represent the assets in hand which enable jurisdictions to withstand fluctuations in revenue sources or expenditure needs. In Dearborn's (1977) analysis, growing cities had the highest liquidity, whilst declining cities had the lowest liquidity. Two measures often used as indexes of liquidity are as follows:

liquidity index:

$$\left[\begin{array}{l} \text{cost of} \\ \text{services not} \\ \text{earmarked as} \\ \text{sinking or} \\ \text{bond funds} \end{array} \quad - \quad \begin{array}{l} \text{short-term} \\ \text{debt out-} \\ \text{standing for} \\ \text{period} \end{array} \right] \Bigg/ \left[\begin{array}{l} \text{period} \\ \text{operating} \\ \text{expenditure} \end{array} \right]$$

255

current account balance index:

$$\frac{\left[\begin{array}{l}\text{total tax revenue}\\\text{plus user charges}\end{array}\right] \quad - \quad (A + B + C + D)}{(A + B + C + D)}$$

where A = general expenditure except capital outlay; B = expenditure on services yielding user charges; C = long-term debt retired over period; D = contributions to pensions, etc.

(iii) *Debt burden.* An important measure of capital needs is the level of total debt outstanding, standardized by the level of local revenue collections:

$$\left(\begin{array}{l}\text{long-term debt}\\\text{retired over}\\\text{period}\end{array} + \begin{array}{l}\text{interest}\\\text{payments}\end{array} + \begin{array}{l}\text{short-}\\\text{term debt}\\\text{outstanding}\\\text{for period}\end{array}\right) \Big/ \left(\begin{array}{l}\text{locally}\\\text{raised}\\\text{revenue}\end{array}\right)$$

This standardization eliminates the effects of different responsibilities between jurisdictions. As shown in table 13.18, used in the discussion on needs assessment on the current account, this index gives the greatest needs in Southern US cities where extensive interest repayments are required to service capital investment in the recent growth of infrastructure and facilities.

CAPITAL COSTS

Together with variation in the geography of capital needs, there are significant variations in the costs of funding capital investments in different locations. Just as the assessment of current account needs must be supplemented by their costing, so in the capital account needs must also be costed. The major determinant of differences in capital costs is the effect of different interest rates. These in turn reflect differences in the level of risk assessed by lenders of capital, and the opportunity costs foregone on other possible investments. Hence, interest rates vary spatially depending upon the credit-worthiness of the projects and the local governments involved. For example, in 1975 when the crisis in New York City finances was at its height, that city was forced to pay 11% interest on new bond issues, whilst other areas such as Florida were able to market bond issues at less than half that rate (Reischauer 1974).

A second factor is that of the perception of holders of capital. Some jurisdictions are more visible, better known, or have wider entry into the capital market. Generally this level of knowledge and perception of invest- ment opportunities varies directly with the size of the jurisdiction. Hence, interest rates and the availability of risk capital are particularly biased against small towns and rural areas which are more remote from the industrial and urban sources of capital (Lipton 1976). For example, in an examination of the credit-worthiness of US cities, Carleton and Lerner (1969) found that population size was a very significant determinant of interest rates to jurisdictions, together with the level of outstanding debt in relation to their tax base, the average tax collection rate, and the type of jurisdiction (whether or not a school district). For the larger cities, the level of debt was the single largest determinant of interest rates.

A third factor which affects the costs of capital is the general influence of external economic factors. Interest rates to public sector borrowers will be high when large demands for risk capital for industry are being made, or where the general level of public debt is large. In addition, periods of high inflation rates tend to cheapen the costs of capital in the short-term since interest rates tend to lag significantly behind the rate of inflation. However, with declining rates of inflation, high interest rates greatly increase the costs of debt.

URBAN FISCAL CRISES

Urban fiscal crises are frequently the result of problems connected with the capital account. They are frequently characterized by a resource-need gap in which personal and public mortgage debt is very high and increasing, where capital increasingly seeks alternative investments to those of public bonds, and where public interest rates escalate in relation to those in the private sector. The result is a large amount of expenditure concerned with merely servicing the legacy of debt from previous years. This situation can arise from two chief causes. First, the inappropriate (or illegal) use of the capital account to fund current expenditure, and second, the inappropriate apportionment of fiscal functions between governments.

The use of the capital account to fund current expenditure is probably adopted by all governments all the time. As noted in the introduction to this chapter, in the public sector it is not possible to delimit, in any simple fashion, the current and capital accounts. Moreover, many capital projects require ancillary current account finance, and vice versa. However, a considerable number of governments, especially those in the severest fiscal distress, have undertaken loan finance of current expenditures on a massive scale. This has partly arisen from the incompetence or political expediency of the mayors and councillors involved, but also results from the joint impact of inflation and rapidly rising service demands which has made it very difficult for the revenues of many governments to keep pace.

The problems of loan finance of current expenditure are nowhere better evidenced than in New York City, but New York, although more advanced along the road of fiscal crisis, is not distinct from many other US cities, or those in many of the older industrial areas of other western countries. In New York continuous loan finance of current account deficits was employed at least from 1960–1 to 1975. As shown in table 10.3, some $480m per year of capital finance was being used in 1973–4 for current spending. This is probably an understatement: first, because of deliberate misclassification of

Table 10.3 Revenue, expenditure and debt in New York City 1960–1974 ($m at current prices). (*Source:* US Bureau of Census, *City Government Finances.* Washington D. C.: Government Printing Office.)

Date	Revenue	Current expenditures plus debt retirement	Current account surplus	Capital expenditures	Net borrowing
1960	2,769.6	2,726.5	43.1	528.3	485.2
1961	2,901.0	2,948.2	− 47.2	542.0	589.2
1962	3,119.5	3,170.0	− 50.5	582.0	632.5
1963	3,408.4	3,459.0	− 50.6	667.4	718.0
1964	3,688.8	3,788.5	− 99.7	657.6	757.3
1965	3,961.1	4,015.4	− 54.3	657.7	712.0
1966	4,367.5	4,537.0	− 169.5	561.3	730.8
1967	5,174.8	5,176.0	− 1.2	554.8	556.0
1968	6,085.8	6,144.1	− 58.3	658.0	716.3
1969	6,864.7	6,945.6	− 80.9	698.3	779.2
1970	7,233.9	7,775.4	− 541.5	797.0	1,338.5
1971	8,274.8	9,053.9	− 779.1	1,135.1	1,914.2
1972	9,501.5	10,119.6	− 618.1	1,192.9	1,811.0
1973	10,774.9	10,807.2	− 32.3	1,371.5	1,403.8
1974	11,291.5	11,779.1	− 487.6	1,709.6	2,197.2

expenditure (The Municipal Assistance Corporation, MAC, estimated this disguised element at an additional $700m); and second, because pension schemes were underfunded by an estimated $200m. Hence the total deficit was closer to $1400m per year in 1973–4.

The second major cause of the urban fiscal crisis from the point of view of the capital account has been the inappropriate attack on needs at different levels of government. Often local governments have been involved in significant programmes to renew or develop infrastructure to stimulate growth. Frequently they have also been obliged to play a significant role in stabilization by funding welfare programmes and other countercyclical measures. Again, many local governments, especially in the US, have been involved in large redistribution programmes employing progressive local taxes and undertaking ambitious anti-poverty programmes which have often exacerbated fiscal migration and the flight to the suburbs. In each case the inappropriate use of local capital finance for local needs has been a major element in the resulting fiscal crises.

Where local stabilization is needed, a form of external aid is required, such as countercyclical revenue-sharing grants, implemented in the US since 1976. Where local welfare programmes are required, these should again be funded by higher level governments. In the case of New York City, many of the difficulties have resulted from too large an expenditure on welfare and medicaid mandated by federal or State governments. In addition, in-

Table 10.4 Comparison of revenue and expenditure of New York City with other large US cities. The regression analysis results control for population size, density, income level, federal and State grants, and dummy variables for region and government structure. (*Source:* Gramlich 1977, table 5)

	New York City	Mean of 27 largest US cities excluding NYC, D.C. and Honolulu	Regression predictions of hypothetical New York City
Normal revenue	962.1	580.5	681.1
Normal expenditure	493.0	273.6	372.0
'Marginal functions' expenditure	325.9	39.5	97.8
School expenditure	207.0	200.8	213.3
Current account balance	− 63.8	66.6	− 2.0

appropriate federal categorical grants requiring local matching (see chapter 12) have encouraged the use of local funds in marginal areas. This was combined in New York up to 1975 with over-ambitious local social welfare programmes aimed at substantial subsidies in public higher education, hospitals, pensions, mass transit facilities, and public housing. Such programmes are 'marginal' to city finances in the US, and elsewhere in that country they are not provided at all, they are funded by grants or user charges, are financed by special tax districts, or are provided by higher level governments at State or County level. The growth of these 'marginal' functions can be accounted for by the particular spirit of New York liberalism, but excessive public demands and union pressure also figure high. 53% of New York City expenditures were in such programmes in 1974, and over 1960–74 there was a 11.1% per year growth rate in these functions, as against 8 to 10% growth in other public functions. These circumstances have been compared by Gramlich (1977) to other US cities as shown in table 10.4. It must be admitted, of course, that New York is not an average large city. It has a specific racial mix, size, density, employment structure, metropolitan functions, high *per capita* incomes, and a specific age of development. However, the results of a regression analysis by Gramlich, shown in table 10.4, controlling for these factors demonstrates that New York still has a larger current account deficit, a larger level of spending on normal functions, and a much larger level of spending on 'marginal' functions, than other large US cities.

10.4 The incidence of capital burdens and benefits

For the capital account a similar analysis can be carried out of who bears the fiscal burdens, as for the current account. In addition to the intergroup and spatial comparisons of burdens, however, the capital account requires measurement of the shifting of burdens through time between different generations of people. Hence, there are three components of burden transfer that need to be considered: (i) shifting between socio-economic groups and sectors; (ii) geographical exporting between jurisdictions; and (iii) temporal shifting between generations. Moreover, burden transfer on the capital account cannot be considered independently of burden transfer on the current account. Hence, taxation and user charges must be considered together with the effect of loan finance. The following discussion tackles this problem from two points of view: first, one in which total resources are assumed to be fixed; and second, where resources may be considered to vary.

FIXED TOTAL RESOURCES

In the case of an isolated economy with a fixed total stock of resources, a user charge or tax has the effect of reducing levels of consumption and private investment. If this revenue is used not for investment but to finance current spending, then taxation reduces the level of capital stock available in the future. Alternatively, if tax revenues are used for capital investment, then consumption foregone by present generations represents a transfer of burdens from the future generations, who benefit from the capital facility, to the present generation. In the case of loan finance which is used to finance present consumption, there is a transfer of burdens to future generations to the benefit of present generations If, however, the loans are used to finance capital investment in facilities, then there is a burden sharing between present and future generations.

The degree to which debt burden can or cannot be passed between generations is a contentious issue. The classical economic view, due to Ricardo and to Pigou, is that loan finance as opposed to current finance is not a relevant distinction. What is important instead is the degree to which earlier generations forego consumption in order to pass on a larger capital stock. Hence, in this argument, the extent of burden transfer is proportional to the reduction in rate of saving by present generations. An alternative view is that of Bowen *et al.* (1960) which states that debt need not be financed by reductions in consumption in earlier generations, but instead by consumption reductions in later generations in order to finance the earlier excess expenditure. A third view, of Buchanan (1950), contends that burdens are transferred only to the extent that freedom of choice, or other criteria, are valued less highly than the level of consumption as a measure of well-being. However, table 10.5 makes it clear that it is the interplay of both the means of finance, and the use of finance which is important. Four possible cases are shown in this table. Although a simplification, this table allows two conclusions as to the degree of fiscal equity between generations to be drawn (Musgrave and Musgrave 1976). First, current consumption expenditure should be financed by current taxation or charges. Second, capital equipment with a significant lifespan should be financed by loans, securities, or bonds. Only if these two conditions are satisfied is it possible for the current level of net benefits to equal the current level of net burdens. However, even with these

Table 10.5 Benefit and burden transfer between generations depending upon the form of finance (current or capital) and its use (consumption or investment)

	Finance	
Useage	*Current finance tax or charge*	*Capital finance loan*
Consumption expenditure	Benefits: present Burdens: present	Benefits: present Burdens: present and future
Investment in facilities and stock	Benefits: present and future Burdens: present	Benefits: present and future Burdens: present and future

two conditions, it still has to be decided how benefit and burden are measured and assigned to each generation. Musgrave and Musgrave argue that the period and scale of repayment of loans should be so phased as to place a burden each year which is proportional to the level of benefits received each year, with the debt totally repaid at the time the facility is used up or must be replaced.

TOTAL RESOURCES NOT FIXED

The previous discussion has assumed that the total level of resources available within an area is fixed and that this area is an isolated economy. The major new element which enters when resources are more realistically assumed to be variable, is that of spatial flows of public finance: at the international level by foreign borrowing, and at the interjurisdictional level by intergovernmental transfers. With such flexibility, present consumption need not postpone capital building; and similarly, increase of the capital stock need not limit present consumption.

The sharing of investment over wider populations is the solution to the capital finance problem usually adopted when investments are very large. For example, the British New Towns are financed by borrowing from central government which is repaid out of rent income from land and buildings over a period of 60 years. But because the early years see more repayments than income, an additional loan is used to cover this period, thus increasing total repayment costs. The increase in total costs resulting from this phasing of repayments is larger, the slower is the rate of growth of population, since this controls the rate of increase of incomes from rents.

GROWTH, RENEWAL AND MIGRATION

The problem of phasing investments is most important where either major new capital stock is required, or where any major replacement and renewal of stock is necessary. It is in this context that the issue of burden transfer between generations chiefly arises. Major examples are in the fields of development finance concerned with funding the extensive infrastructure necessary to support economic growth, or in urban renewal where extensive new investment is required to refurbish or replace existing but outdated stock. The problem of phasing does not arise in those simpler cases where there is a continuous and unchanging stream of investments, constant population levels, and unchanging interest rates, since then the current, past and future levels of burdens will be identical.

For the specific case of growth-stimulated needs for heavy capital investment, different rates of growth place very different capital finance burdens on local populations. For any given rate of growth the most efficient investment plan will be that which allows the largest size of plant (to obtain economies of scale) consistent with the level of demand (size of population or industry needs) anticipated over the lifetime of the project. Hence a difficult decision has to be made as to the expected rate of growth of population and rate of change of technology. For investment in fixed facilities and infrastructure, a rapid rate of growth and economies of scale favours large and frequent increments in investment. For slower rates of growth, the population reaches the size for attaining economies of scale in plant size slower than the rate of ageing of the plant, and hence this must be accommodated by making smaller investments undertaken less frequently (see figure 10.4). Moreover, there may be different threshold sizes for different public goods and this requires phasing of public capital investment in line with growth rates. Figure 10.5, for example, shows cases of different forms of phased capital investment at two different growth rates for New Towns in South-East England. The major problem which particularly affects these New Towns is that slow growth rates may require some public services to be put off for long periods, and this may risk failure of the entire investment project. Another difficulty is the degree to which different investments can be phased. Figure 10.6 shows the actual

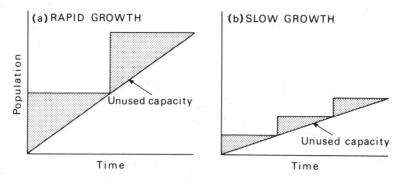

Figure 10.4   Relation of phasing of capital investments to rate of growth in demand.

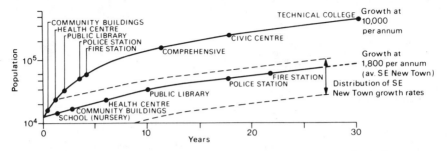

Figure 10.5 Different forms of phasing of capital investment depending upon different growth rates in new towns in South-East England in relation to population size. (*Source:* Thring 1976, figure 3.7.3)

annual costs of sewerage, site development, roads, and total costs per person for four British New Towns. Although variable for each town depending upon the size and adequacy of the existing infrastructure, sewerage and site development costs, both display very high initial costs per head, 150 to 200% above the settled mean to which they fall after 10 years. The same is true of road costs in the case of Stevenage. In each case it is difficult to phase these costs to the same degree that it is possible to phase the costs of housing or labour intensive public service provision.

A further difficulty for phasing and sharing of investment burdens is created by migration. This presents two dilemmas for equalizing fiscal burdens. First, population migration represents the movement of human capital for which the investment in education and training of one set of taxpayers confers benefits to other jurisdictions receiving the trained and educated personnel. Second, migration of industry represents the movement of physical and financial capital which shifts capital access, benefits, knowledge and stocks from one jurisdiction to another. In both cases such flows are often self-cancelling, but where some areas are marked net losers or gainers the effect can be very significant. Indeed it has been a major problem of the inner city and poorer rural areas, as noted in chapter 4, that they have suffered the net loss of the younger, more able, and higher income groups, and have not attracted the more rapidly growing firms. Hence the movement of the residential or commercial tax base has eroded the opportunity to equalize burdens across generations.

An additional difficulty resulting from migration is the problem this presents for apportioning burdens for long-term capital finance. With a static population and industry, generations are connected together by 'inheritance': it becomes meaningful to equalize the burdens of loan finance over different generations in respect to the level of benefit received. But where migration occurs, people and firms can move from one jurisdiction to another to escape the burdens of loan finance. If burdens were everywhere proportional to benefits received, such a migration decision would merely represent the

263

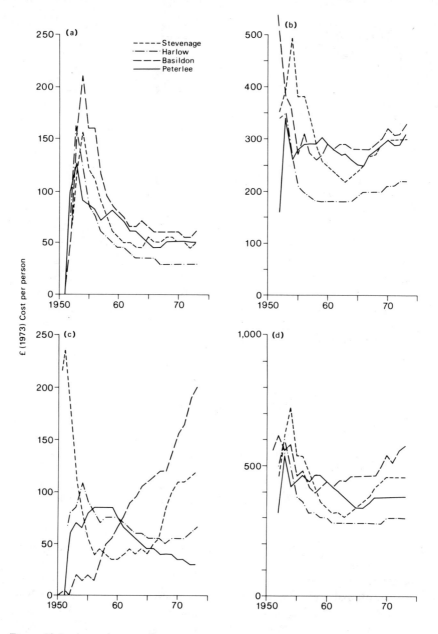

Figure 10.6 Annual costs of
a sewerage
b site development costs
c road costs, and
d total costs for four British New Towns, 1950–75.
(*Source*: Thring 1976; from Peiser 1973.)

exchange of greater or lesser benefits at a level of burden proportional to costs, and there would be no burden transfer as such. But usually it is not possible to equalize totally the levels of burdens and benefits at any time (especially where redistribution programmes are being implemented). Hence a migration decision over space will usually lead to a level of burden transfer.

10.5 Public capital institutions

There are various forms of capital finance available to jurisdictions, but generally these can be grouped into five classes: (i) securities and bonds; (ii) direct commercial loans; (iii) intergovernmental loans; (iv) information and co-ordination devices; and (v) development banks. Securities and bonds issued by governments are a major form of capital finance. For the US capital market in 1973–4, State and local government sectors accounted for a major component of the securities market: 20% of the source of such funds, and 42% of their final use (US Congress 1975). For direct loans, federal agencies account for only 6% of the source of funds and a very small share of their final use. In the US, UK and most countries, the degree to which governments can enter the open loan market is very limited, and the extent to which securities can be sold is also severely restricted. Often in the US the largest impediment to floating a bond issue is the need for a vote of local electors to support the issue; because of the implication of raised taxes, rejection of bond issues is frequent, even where important investments are required. In other countries the extent of bond issues is subject to a large measure of central control imposed to limit the expansion of liquidity in the economy as a whole as one facet of monetary policy.

Intergovernmental loans are an important element in capital finance in most countries. In the US this is controlled within individual departmental programmes, loans acting rather like categorical grants in some cases. In the UK, loans are controlled by the Public Works and Loan Board with certain 'block grants' loans in 'key sectors' (see p. 358). Loan finance has also been a major component of regional policy in many countries. For example, in the US, the major components of EDA funds have been loans and public works construction. In the UK, regional policy incentives to industry have tended to concentrate on accelerated depreciation allowances, tax holidays and other loan subsidies to migrating firms. In many countries, especially the US, a major element of subsidy for loans is tax exemption on the interest paid to purchasers of municipal bonds. This attracts substantial funds to the local sector, but since its benefits are concentrated on the relatively highly taxed individuals and banks, this subsidy effect can be highly fiscally perverse (see ACIR 1970). Intergovernmental loans are discussed in more detail in the context of intergovernmental transfers in chapters 12 and 13.

Information and co-ordination devices have been found especially useful for small jurisdictions, and for backward regions. For example, to overcome difficulties in obtaining finance in small towns and rural areas, a number of US

States have implemented local preferential loan schemes and information centres. For example, North Carolina has set up a local government commission to approve and market bond issues, to co-ordinate, and to act as a lender of last resort. Again, Vermont has established a State controlled Bond Bank allowing smaller borrowers to take advantage of the lower interest rates available to larger borrowers. In the UK two regional development associations in the North-West, and Yorkshire and Humberside have been very successful in providing investment advice, and at national level the Location of Offices Bureau has acted as an information medium, with the National Enterprise Board giving direct capital aid. The Italian Cassa del Mezzorgiorno, and other institutions in Europe, perform similar tasks.

A related mechanism is the regional development bank. It has become increasingly recognized in the US that most intergovernmental aid has attacked the short-term rather than long-term problems. Aid has been directed at either supporting current account operating budgets (as in the case of CETA and counter-cyclical revenue-sharing), or short-term capital projects (as with local public works programmes). Aid has not significantly helped rehabilitation and repair of streets, schools, libraries, port facilities, and transport or other infrastructure. To a limited extent the rapid rise in aid to the older cities has improved the credit rating of these cities, but many of the major problems are still left untackled.

The advantages of the development bank proposal are that first, it would produce credit for larger projects where it would otherwise be unavailable, especially where there was a low rate of return, or mainly social rather than economic benefits. Secondly, there could be greater emphasis on better maintenance and reconditioning of existing facilities. Thirdly, it could provide a more stable source of finance for capital projects than grant programmes which have had an unfavourable climate of uncertainty following cancellation of the HUD urban renewal programmes. Finally, a development bank could focus more effectively than private credit facilities on the problems of creating a better long-term social economy. With impending oil and gas shortages, the long-term interests of society may well be better served by investment on existing sites taking advantage of sunk costs, but private facilities are more open to the shorter term gains to be made from urban sprawl and movement to new sites.

An urban bank proposal was the centrepiece of the Carter administration's proposals for an urban policy (*Washington Post* March 21, 1977), and it has also found strong support in the Senate and elsewhere. However, against its supposed advantages many commentators have argued that although a development bank may aid small and marginal firms, it will not have any significant effect on large-scale developments since most large firms experience no difficulty in raising credit. In particular, a bank provides insufficient incentive to the redirection of investments to the most distressed rural and urban areas (Sunquist 1978). Other difficulties are the inability of the smaller and more needy areas to implement the right organization to take advantage of a bank, the lack of real ability to target, and lack of attack on the real problems which result from the form of the tax system (especially its incentives to home-ownership as against renting, and new building as against renovation). Finally, the aims of, for example, Senator Harrington, that a development bank should be able to equalize across regions the rate of return on investments, seem over-optimistic.

10.6 Conclusion

Many of the issues of the capital account discussed in this chapter are not distinct from those of the incidence of needs, costs, burdens and benefits discussed in earlier chapters. The three issues of major additional concern with the capital account are its role in stabilization, growth, and burden transfer between generations. Additionally, the fiscal crisis of many US cities shows many components specific to the difficulties of management of the capital account. Certainly for each of the issues discussed, no simple conclusion can be drawn. There are three specific and pervasive dilemmas.

First, the diversion of local finance from current spending to forward raising of loans may achieve the stabilization goal of fiscal policy, but undermines the goal of growth (although this argument will not necessarily hold when the public sector is investing in productive industry, as with nationalized industries). Second, the counter-growth effects of local loans can be circumvented by raising loans outside of the jurisdiction. This is the method most commonly used for development finance, and is essential for overcoming the fiscal problems of US cities, e.g. by development banks; but it inevitably reduces local independence. A third dilemma is that, however the loans are raised, there is a need to balance the debt burden and benefits received between different generations. In the case of a large project, such as a hospital, highway or school, for example, finance by local current taxation alone requires the present generation to bear the total burden, whilst future generations gain considerable benefits with no tax burden. Because of this effect, Musgrave and Musgrave (1976) argue that a major aim of local borrowing and taxation should be to tax each year in accordance with the current year of benefits received from the investment so that the debt is repaid by the time that the facility is used up. But the problem, recognized by Musgrave, is that equality between generations (of benefit and burden, and of capital and loan finance) is extremely difficult to achieve in a local economy because of both its 'openness', and because of the mobility of its population. These issues are discussed further in Part 3 of this book, where they form a major component of intergovernmental fiscal relations and co-ordination.

Part 3

Intergovernmental fiscal relations

11

Government structure and public finance

"Constitutions are intended to preserve practical and substantial rights, not to maintain theories."

Justice Holmes.

11.1 Constitutions, governments and fiscal power

The structure of Government within a country has crucial impact on the geography of public finance. It determines the spatial division of revenue capacity and expenditure benefits; and within any jurisdiction, the balance of revenue burdens, fiscal effort and fiscal incidence. Localized, centralized and mixed government structures each lead to markedly inequitable treatment of individuals and firms on the basis solely of location, either as a result of fiscal inequity or of mechanisms of cumulative imbalance and the considerable imperfections of the market discussed in chapter 4. In this chapter, the arguments in favour of various constitutional structures are discussed together with criteria for partitioning revenue sources and expenditure functions between different levels of government. This leads to consideration of the political elements of government consolidation and constitutional reform. In chapters 12 and 13 these considerations are expanded by a more detailed consideration of one aspect of financial relationships between governments: the need to balance local revenue capacity and local expenditure responsibility by intergovernmental fiscal co-ordination through grants, tax credits, revenue-sharing and other programmes.

Few countries have developed without some degree at least of division of responsibilities between various levels of Government. Two very general structures of multi-level government have evolved: two-level and three-level systems. The two-level system is characteristic of smaller and more centralized states. The three-level structure is more characteristic of federal states, although by no means restricted to federations. In this case there is a central level, an intermediate level, and usually a complex set of local level governments which, in many countries especially the United States, may itself be split into a further series of levels. This gives the federal, State and local structures of the United States, and the intermediate level governments of the Australian States, Canadian Provinces, German *Länder*, and Swiss Cantons. The structure of government in a range of 25 countries is shown in table 11.1. The wide variety of multi-level government is evident with most local units

271

Table 11.1 Numbers of government units at different levels in 25 countries. (*Source:* Humes and Martin 1961; with some updating)

Country	Local units	Intermediate units	
(1) English speaking			
UK	455	County	65
		Region	11
Australia	960	County	34
		State	6
South Africa		Province	4
Canada	4017	County	114
		Province	10
USA	34381	County	3049
		State	50
(2) North European			
Sweden	1037	Province	25
Finland	548	Province	12
Norway	744	Province	20
Denmark	1386	District	25
Iceland	228	District	21
(3) Central and North-West Europe			
Germany	24199	District	418
		Länder	9
Austria	4035	Länder	9
Switzerland	3101	Canton	25
Netherlands	994	Province	11
Belgium	2669	District	26
		Province	9
Luxemburg	126	—	—
(4) Eastern Europe			
USSR	51699	District	3980
		Province	142
Poland	8915	District	21
		Province	17
Bulgaria	990	Province	30
Yugoslavia	1479	District	107
(5) Southern Europe			
France	37791	District	311
		Department	90
Italy	7810	Province	92
		Region	4
Greece	5960	District	146
		Province	50
Spain	9212	Province	50
Portugal	303	District	18
		Province	11

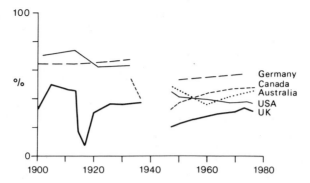

Figure 11.1 The share of local plus State or Province expenditure as a percentage of total public expenditure in five western countries. (*Sources:* Vile 1973; Peacock and Wiseman 1961; *Stateman's Yearbook.*)

being of less than 4,000 population, and most intermediate level governments being of 50 to 200,000 population. Whilst all local and State level governments in federal countries are elected, the intermediate level of government in non-federal countries is often appointed or only indirectly elected. The lack of direct representation at this regional level has been a frequent cause of concern, and has provided a major impetus to many movements for separatism, devolution, and autonomy.

In such a wide variety of government structures, the division of re-sponsibilites between central, intermediate, and local level governments is often very complex, and the centre of interest here is the division of responsibilities of revenue and expenditure functions. This is often rather independent of specific constitutional arrangements. For example, the changing share of expenditures by local and intermediate governments in a number of western countries, shown in Figure 11.1 and table 11.2, exhibits a

Table 11.2 Public expenditure as a percentage of GDP at market prices in eight countries, by level of government. (*Source*: EEC 1977, vol. II, p. 128)

Country	Date	All levels of government	Central	State or region
Australia	1972/3	27.9	22.5	5.4
Canada	1971/2	38.5	19.3	19.2
France	1972	38.3	35.4	2.9
Germany	1971	41.1	24.7	16.4
Italy	1972	41.1	35.7	5.4
UK	1972	41.5	33.9	7.6
USA	1971/72	37.6	22.8	14.8
Switzerland	1973	39.8	23.6	16.2

273

Table 11.3   Distribution of tax collection between levels of government.
(Sources: EEC 1977; Gillespie 1976; Local Government in Sweden 1978)

Country	Date	Tax revenue		
		Central	Intermediate	Local
Australia	1973–4	79.7	20.2	
Belgium	1974	92.8	—	7.2
			33.7	12.6
Canada	1969	53.7		29.6
Denmark	1974	70.4	—	
France	1974	93.5	—	6.5
Germany	1973	53.1	33.7	13.2
Ireland	1974	90.4	—	9.6
Italy	1974	94.3	—	5.7
Luxemburg	1974	84.6	—	15.4
Netherlands	1974	97.6	—	2.4
Sweden	1976	70.4	29.6	
Switzerland	1972	41.0	34.0	25.0
UK	1974	87.3	—	12.7
USA	1971–2	54.4	22.7	18.9

distinct convergence of the role of lower level governments towards about 40% of the total public expenditure, or 16 to 20% of GDP, in federal states, and up to about 35% of expenditure, or 5 to 7% of GDP, in centralized states. Germany is one of the major exceptional cases because of the relative recency of its present constitutional arrangement, deriving from the *Basic Law* of 1949. Sweden is a second major exception having undertaken an important constitutional re-apportionment of power in favour of local communities through the shift of upper secondary schooling responsibility in the late 1960s, the Municipal Administration Act of 1977, and the New Constitution of 1975. In all cases, however, the local and intermediate levels of government are very significant in terms of their total role in public expenditure.

The distribution of revenue functions between levels of government shows a remarkably similar pattern of apportionment of total revenue-raising capacity in different countries despite their markedly different constitutions. In those countries for which data are provided in table 11.3, only in Switzerland, Sweden, Germany, and Canada does the central government share of revenues drop to 50% or below. In most states, the central share of revenues is 80 to 90% of the total resources. The distribution of these revenue shares between different sources is shown in table 11.4. The major local tax in most countries is the property tax, which is often supplemented by personal income tax, sales, alcohol, licence fees, and other specialist taxes. Many of these taxes may be shared with central government (see chapter 12).

Turning to the distribution of expenditure functions between different levels of government, remarkable similarities between different countries are

Table 11.4 Revenue sources available to local and intermediate governments; tax revenues only (excludes user charges and intergovernmental transfers except those credited and shared which are attributed to point of receipt). (*Sources*: EEC 1977; UK Committee of Enquiry on Local Government Finance 1976; Local Government in Sweden)

Revenue source	% share of tax at local and intermediate levels						
	Aus.	*Canada*	*Germany*	*Sweden*	*Switzerland*	*UK*	*USA*
Property tax	100	100	100	0	100	100	100
Personal income		29	57	13.1	92.1	0	13.8
Corporate income	0	23	65	0	83.5	0	12.1
General sales and VAT	0	40	35	0	0	0	100
Alcohol	100	100	100	0	0	0	25.6
Tobacco	0	0	0	0	0	0	57.6
Motor licences	100	100	100	0	100	0	100
Death, gifts, capital gains	69	51	0	0	97	0	19.2
Employment and payroll	100	0	100	0	0	0	
Customs and excise	0	0	0	0	0	0	0
Gasoline	0	100	0	0	0	0	63.6

again evident. As shown in table 11.5, defence is uniformly a national level function, whilst public welfare, health, environment, transport, and commerce, are usually split between national and intermediate levels of State, Province, Canton or *Länder*. Other services, such as education, police, fire, and housing, show concentrations mainly at local level, or are split between local and intermediate levels. Some more minor functions such as administration, research and statistical services show no general pattern of concentration at any particular level. As shown in table 11.5 the total distribution of expenditures exhibits a distinct difference in the relative role of local government in centralized states where it constitutes only 10 to 35% of total public expenditure, and in federal states, where combined local and intermediate level expenditures constitutes 50 to 60% of total public expenditure.

It is evident from comparison of the expenditure functions of table 11.5 with the revenue sources of table 11.3, that there is a marked difference in the apportionment of revenue-raising capacity and expenditure responsibility between different levels of government in all countries. This necessitates a complex mechanism of intergovernmental transfers which is the subject of chapters 12 and 13. Two of these mechanisms of tax credits and revenue-sharing have already been taken into account in table 11.3.

The changing distribution of revenue and expenditure functions between different levels of government shown in figure 11.1 conveys an impression of static or only slowly changing government organization. This is far from the truth. In many countries the evolution of revenue and expenditure

Table 11.5 Distribution of expenditure functions between levels of government. (*After* Pommerehne 1977; all countries except Canada for 1971; Canada 1968)

Function	Country	% public expenditure				
		Central	State	Local	Total (%)	
National defence and international relations	Canada	100	—	—	8.2	Primarily national
	France	100	—	—	17.1	
	Germany	99.9	0.1	—	12.1	
	Switzerland	90.6	6.1	3.2	11.8	
	UK	100	—	—	14.0	
	USA	100	—	—	22.4	
Public welfare and health	Canada	55.6	41.1	3.3	30.4	Primarily national and intermediate
	France	91.1	8.9	—	40.5	
	Germany	54.0	18.4	27.6	25.1	
	Switzerland	32.2	48.3	19.5	20.8	
	UK	84.4	15.6	—	37.6	
	USA	31.2	42.6	26.2	14.6	
Environment resources and primary industries	Canada	63.7	36.3	—	4.6	
	France	76.3	23.7	—	4.5	
	Germany	40.6	20.8	38.6	13.2	
	Switzerland	44.9	21.0	34.1	9.8	
	UK	81.1	—	18.9	3.4	
	USA	78.1	17.1	4.2	4.0	
Transport and communications	Canada	25.3	55.7	18.9	9.8	
	France	81.8	18.2	—	3.5	
	Germany	44.0	25.6	30.4	8.6	
	Switzerland	42.7	30.5	26.8	15.0	
	UK	40.1	—	59.9	5.0	
	USA	20.4	57.1	22.5	7.2	

276

Category	Country	Primarily local and intermediate				All levels
Education	Canada	12.3	43.0		44.8	20.2
	France	94.5		5.5		15.7
	Germany	12.5	64.0		23.5	16.2
	Switzerland	15.0	45.9		39.0	22.1
	UK	18.1			81.9	14.9
	USA	12.7	38.9		48.4	24.9
Police, law, fire and prisons	Canada	22.5	35.4		42.1	4.6
	France	92.8		7.2		3.0
	Germany	6.2	77.5		16.3	4.0
	Switzerland	11.3	57.4		31.3	5.1
	UK	20.5			79.5	3.1
	USA	5.9	22.6		71.5	2.2
Housing subsidies and mortgage support	Canada	78.2	in other			
	France		49.1	21.8		2.5
	Germany	10.8			40.1	2.1
	Switzerland		in other			
	UK	24.7			75.3	4.6
	USA	24.7			75.3	4.6
General government administration research and statistical services	Canada	52.3	24.6		23.1	5.7
	France	60.8		39.2		10.9
	Germany	22.2	38.3		39.5	5.6
	Switzerland	22.3	35.7		42.0	7.5
	UK	49.3			50.7	2.8
	USA	40.3	27.6		32.1	1.0
Miscellaneous expenditures	Canada	66.0	21.5		12.5	9.1
	France	89.9		10.1		2.3
	Germany	39.1	53.3		7.6	9.6
	Switzerland	48.1	7.8		51.0	2.2
	UK	87.3			12.7	3.2
	USA	53.3	15.6		31.1	15.1
Total expenditure	Canada	47.5	34.9		17.6	100
	France	88.6		11.4		100
	Germany	43.7	32.2		24.0	100
	Switzerland	35.9	35.0		29.1	100
	UK	65.0			35.0	100
	USA	49.2	24.6		26.2	100

responsibilities has been accompanied by, or has been the result of, important changes in the organization of local and intermediate levels of government, and in the constitutional arrangements within each State. Perhaps the most marked change has been in the consolidation and dissolution of school and special purpose districts in the US which has resulted in a reduction in the total number of governments in that country from 155,000 in 1942 to 80,000 in 1978. Other important changes have occurred with the reorganization of local government in England and Wales in 1974 and in Scotland in 1976; the new German Constitution of 1949; the new Swedish Constitution of 1975, the evolving special arrangements with Quebec in Canada, and other administrative and constitutional changes in other countries. In some cases these changes have been reorganizations to rationalize an existing financial or political arrangement; in other cases such as in Sweden, Canada and Britain, the reforms have been instituted with specific political or economic motives. In the Swedish case this is the result of a positive desire to shift decision-making power closer to the people, and in Canada it has been an attempt to hold the Federation together while satisfying demands for the greater autonomy of Quebec. In Britain the aim has been to consolidate journey-to-work areas and to achieve the greater administrative and economic efficiency of larger scale units, but more recently economic arguments have been submerged beneath political and cultural imperatives for greater devolution to a regional level of government. With the focus of governmental and institutional structure, therefore, we are brought back to the themes recurrent in earlier chapters of this book; the balance of revenue capacity, burdens and effort on the one hand, and expenditure needs, costs, benefits and fiscal incidence on the other. These together determine, in a mixed structure of government, the degree of fiscal equity and inequity operating in any country.

11.2 Centralized, localized, multi-level public finance

The organization of government is particularly important in its effects on the allocation of public finance; what is provided, where, at what cost. There are four general structures of government organization; localized, centralized, federal and devolved. A completely localized government is responsible for all but a few public functions and retains these within the smallest possible groups of people. In contrast, totally centralized government retains all powers within a single unitary government. In practice neither of these forms is completely achieved, and most countries are governed by mixtures of centralized and localized systems as either federal or devolved forms (see, for example, Humes and Martin 1961). The federal principle theoretically divides sovereignty between the central and local level according to the function or public good involved; whilst devolved governments have limited discretionary powers in either the legislative, executive, judicial or administrative areas, (or any combination of these) but with ultimate responsibility for all functions retained at the central level. There are various strengths and weaknesses to each of these forms of government which are summarized below.

One of the strongest arguments for localized government is that it promotes local unity, and a sense of community, neighbourhood, and self-reliance. Local control encourages the altruism and moral sense of values which are quickly lost in larger economic units. Thomas Jefferson saw the local unit as an idealistic form of government, whilst both Adam Smith and Marx saw larger economic organizations leading to impersonality and a degree of alienation. Finer (1934, p. 335) describes local self-government as the means of achieving this local identity or community interest; "They tend most strongly . . . to destroy purely selfish impulses; to make every man feel that he lives for others as well as for himself". It must be questioned, however, to what extent this concept of sense of community is applicable at the scale at which modern local government is normally organized.

A second major argument for local self-government stresses the ability of smaller and more local governments to adjust more closely to geographical variations of local needs and preferences. This point of view has been advocated especially by modern proponents of the schools of collective action and revealed preferences (for example, Buchanan, Tulloch, Tiebout, Bish, Ostrom), since localization allows the introduction of a degree of choice into the provision of public groups, or the market mechanism. But the idea is derived from Locke and Aristotle. The contention is that each community has specific 'local needs', which (as argued in chapter 5) are the aggregate needs of the people living in a locality. These result from its specific location, physical, social, and economic structure, its age and stage of development, and historical and cultural factors. Geographical localization in the organization and provision of public goods affords a greater awareness of costs and allows a closer matching both of services to needs and preferences, and of benefits to costs. This is often referred to as achieving a high elasticity of local government to geographical and individual differences, as opposed to a low elasticity of centralized government. This fact is closely related to the concept of local community, Finer (1934, p. 3) stating for example that, "localities . . . feel that they, at any rate, differ from the abstract average of humanity legislated for by the central government, and claim discretion to apply its uniform rules in a way more closely fitting their real needs and their own ideas of themselves". Again, Laski (1919, p. 75) states that the facts of local individual and economic variation geographically refuse reduction to uniformity, and this theme is repeated in a wide variety of North American and European writings (see Barrington 1975; Studenski and Mort 1941).

A third argument for localized government is frequently held to be its promotion of freedom, democracy and responsible government. Political power is diffused and closeness to local feeling affords relevant government;

government which is easy both to control and to participate in. Such government helps to promote individual cultural life and hence promotes a richer national culture. Much of this argument undoubtedly derives from Alexis de Tocqueville who saw local and federal institutions as necessary checks on centralized control and the 'tyranny of the majority': "Local assemblies of citizens constitute the strength of free nations. Town meetings are to liberty what primary schools are to science; they bring it within the peoples' reach; they teach men how to use and to enjoy it. A nation may establish a system of free government but without the spirit of municipal institutions it cannot have the spirit of liberty" (de Tocqueville 1966, p. 62). Similarly, Cole (1921, pp. 33–4) states that "if we want public opinion to influence government, we are most likely to secure this by a wide distribution of government which will enable public pressure, backed by a real social consciousness of those exerting it, to be applied at the maximum number of points at which it can be made effective". Certainly since the 19th century the role of local self-determination in diffusing power and securing liberty is a pervasive American and European theme.

A fourth argument advanced for localized government is the encouragement it gives for innovation and experimentation with new government organizations, or public finance provisions. Such experiments are held to be 'safer' than national level experiments since they are less costly, mistakes can be much more easily absorbed, and it is easier to return to a status quo or seek a new alternative, since the outside force of the state can limit the extent of inequitable or detrimental experimentation. Certainly in the US, the experimentation of Wisconsin and other States with revenue-sharing was influential in the adoption of this form of fiscal equalization at national level. Similarly, Florida State innovations in measuring fiscal needs in education seem likely to act as archetypes for other State actions and general federal legislation. Less recently, such experimentation has been responsible for the introduction of the income tax (first used in Wisconsin), the executive budget, proportional representation, the unicameral legislature, the Oklahoma guarantees of bank deposits, and central purchasing (Studenski and Mort 1941) all of which preceded federal innovations. Again, the UK Scottish use of local tax capacity measures (rateable values) preceded their use in equalization grants for the UK as a whole.

Increased political stability represents a fifth argument in favour of localized government. It is claimed that class conflicts are not as focused at local level, and certainly the diffusion of power between a multiplicity of jurisdictions precludes easy domination by extreme groups. Du Breuil (1919, p. 84), echoing Charles Fourier's concept of the phalanx, credited the fall of the Ancien Regime in France to excessive decentralization: "In order to put an end to the 'Pharisaism' of the sophisticated self-appointed ruling classes, in order to establish a harmonious society, it is necessary to create harmony in the initial cell or in the commune".

A sixth and related factor is the promotion of national unity and security. This is the result of both the supposed greater harmony of interests achievable at local level, and the fostering of collective action possible in local communities. As Michailov (1927, p. 24) observes "Local self-government does not destroy, but on the contrary it organizes the unity of the nation". A final argument for localized government is that it lightens the load of national and higher level governments, overcoming what Lamennais terms "apoplexy at the centre". That is, strong local government leaves national government to deal with truly national issues, and regional government with truly regional issues: a geographical or hierarchical division of labour is fostered within bureaucracy.

Against the supposed benefits of localized or decentralized government must be set five major shortcomings: (1) it can give extreme inequity in service standards and fiscal burdens; (2) it results in inefficient economic organization; (3) it fosters local autocratic rule; (4) it breeds narrow parochialism and sectionalist competition; (5) it produces inertia and rigidity. Inequity in services and fiscal burdens is perhaps the major inadequacy of extreme decentralization. The smaller the jurisdiction, the narrower its resource base, and the more uniform the local social group. Whilst this produces benefits in according government organization more closely to demands and preferences, it can also foster exclusionary policies such as zoning and tends to lead to often violent disparities in fiscal capacities and levels of public services between jurisdictions. Economic inefficiency results in the duplication of equipment, services equipment and offices, and the inability to attain economies of scale, or to attract good personnel. Extreme autocratic rule results from the ability of limited and petty cliques to control local decision making. This latter feature is frequently related to the length of time an individual has been in a community. This has led to admirable local 'notables' who exert influences for good, but can frequently lead to 'petty jobbery' and local elites. Narrow parochialism and sectionalism can be fostered by extreme decentralization such that, instead of the local sense of community reinforcing national unity and contentment, it instead breeds competition and resentment between jurisdictions, as discussed in chapter 4. This characterizes the early constitution of the United States after 1776, and can be seen to characterize some of its present attributes in the fragmented government of metropolitan areas. When combined with inertia and rigidity, this results in locally narrow outlooks engendered by vested interests in local issues, jobs and roles.

CENTRALIZED GOVERNMENTS

The major argument for strong central control is its ability to act as an external force, or *force majeur*, to limit local fiscal disparity. For a totally localized system, imbalance in fiscal need and fiscal ability cannot be overcome from within. There is an important distinction to be made between those needs, benefits and burdens based on national minimum standards and merit groups which should be equalized, and those needs deriving from difference in preferences which should not be equalized. Central control usually has superior and more flexible sources of finance and can use these resources to equalize social, economic, and educational opportunities; it can also aid lagging regions and attack localized pockets of poverty, and it can overcome the detrimental effects, noted in chapter 4, of inter-jurisdictional competition and exclusionary policies. These factors provided the primary motivation for the *Federalist* writers' (Hamilton, Madison and Jay) proposition of a federal alternative. As Chevillard (1862, p. 207) notes, "Centralization is a check upon parochial jealousies, local paralysing dissensions, the waste and extravagance of dishonest and inefficient individuals". Again, Adam Smith (1776, p. 945) argues that central control delivers local areas "from the rancorous and virulent factions which are inseparable from small democracies". Other commentators (Maxwell 1946; Tarlton 1965) have argued that centralized government is crucial in areas in which there is a diversity and asymmetrical pattern of social and economic power: only central control can limit the dominance and exploitation of unequal social groups and areas.

A second advantage of centralized government is the extent to which it promotes efficiency and economy. There are many technical factors of public goods, to be discussed more fully in section 11.4, which suggest that certain goods, such as defence, foreign relations, law, standards, money supply, and so forth, are collective to a whole country, and are better organized nationally. Again, functions such as radio and television regulation, pollution, and commerce, where spillovers are involved, cannot be handled within the geographical limits of local jurisdictions. Technical efficiency also relates to economies of scale in organization of public groups, including the greater capacity of central governments to attract higher quality personnel, achieve functional specialization in their administrative technology of service provision, and gain greater access to wider sources of information. It can coordinate geographical, social and economic features, and can express the 'national interest'.

This last feature, of expressing the national interest, is related to a further argument for centralized government, that of stimulating and maintaining national unity. This can involve coercion, or purchase of compliance (e.g. by revenue-sharing and grants) of local areas or individuals with broad national aims; aims greater in extent than individual or geographically localized interests of single jurisdictions. Especially in the areas of basic human and civil rights, and in major welfare and poverty programmes, central governments usually have a greater willingness to undertake expenditures. Perhaps the primary example of this is the New Deal and T.V.A. in the United States which were able to overcome local domination by elites which were detrimental to the economic base of the local areas of the whole. As Mill (1861, p. 358) notes: "The localities may be allowed to mismanage their own interests, but not to prejudice those of others, nor violate those principles of justice between one person and another of which it is the duty of the State to maintain the rigid observance".

The promotion of equity, efficiency and unity, as detailed in these previous three factors, is related to the general features of apportionment of the functions of public finance detailed by Musgrave (1959). Under this apportionment, as discussed in chapter 3, the fiscal role of central government is concerned with income and other redistribution policies, economic stabilization, and stimulation of economic growth. Only the function of allocation, affecting changes in the prices of services, is reserved for local action. Whilst the contention of this book is that Musgrave's rigid distinction of functions between levels cannot be totally followed, it must nevertheless be accepted that a large role of redistribution must rest with national government. This is due to the progressive taxation available at national level and the fact that local jurisdictions have no incentive or no capacity to undertake reapportionment. Similarly, macroeconomic management for stabilization or growth requires a high degree of central control of the money supply and balance of payments. These then constitute strong motives for the establishment of central control. Moreover, although it is contended strongly in this book that an important measure of distribution of stabilization and growth policy must be areally based, it is true that a large amount of this geographical variation is better organized centrally than locally. With respect particularly to the equalization issue, it is not usually within the capacity of local jurisdiction to overcome the traps of declining economies, nor to stimulate growth, nor to act counter-cyclically to economic trends.

Of course, extreme centralization also has its shortcomings. Perhaps most important of these is the tendency to facilitate totalitarian domination. Such was the fear of de Tocqueville, and of Madison, Hamilton and Jay which lead them to propose the federal alternative of mutual checks and balances at central and local levels. And such has perhaps been the realization in the USSR. In addition, it can be argued that extreme centralization leads to congestion to central work-loads and the inability to be sensitive to local needs and geographical variation: the phenomenon termed by Lamennais (1848) "apoplexy at the centre, and anaemia at the periphery". It also results in imposed uniformity and hence inefficiency in the face of geographically variable needs and demands. These effects can then in turn be argued to lead to weakening of democracy, weakening of national unity, destruction of local interest and responsibility, and inefficiency. The combination of these factors then leads to bitterness and resentment against the centralized governments. This bitterness often reflects disparities of needs, benefits and burdens which go unnoticed or undetected in central government and, in the extreme cases, finally erupts into demands for local autonomy, for devolution, and even for a complete separation of sovereignty. Behind many contemporary movements for such separation can be seen the local revolt against centrally imposed

283

uniformity which has often been focused, or has been seen, as cultural suppression: of Quebecois in Canada, of the Welsh and Scots in the UK, and the Catalans and Basques in Spain.

MIXED PATTERNS OF GOVERNMENT

Both central and local control possess important advantages, but in practice, government structures have rarely been evolved which have given overwhelming prominence to one form as against the other; instead, various mixed, central–local, or federal and devolved structures have developed. As Mill (1848, p. 357) notes, there must be a balance in efficiency, knowledge and political control:

> 'The authority which is most conversant with principle should be supreme over principles, whilst that which is most competent in detail should have the detail left to it. The principal business of the central authority should be to give instruction, and of the local authority to apply it. Power may be localized, but knowledge, to be most useful, most be centralized. . . . To every branch of local administration which affects the general interest there should be a central organ. . . (to) bring the experience acquired in one locality to the knowledge of another where it is wanted'.

Mixtures of central, local and federal structures, multi-level government, are the way of organizing responsibility on the basis of what Livingstone (1956) and Dikshit (1975) term 'regionally grouped diversities': a unity combined with a sense of locality and its differences of resources, environment, culture, economy, and society.

The primary issue is one of government balance: some authors have tried to resolve this in terms of the functions which should be performed by different levels of government. But, with a few exceptions, most services concern all levels of government. Similarly, the division of public finance functions of allocation, distribution, stabilization, and growth cannot be reserved exclusively to any one level of government. Generally, a State will evolve a significant level of centralization the smaller the size of its population, the smaller it is in area, the lower its income, the lower its degree of economic development, the lower its degree of urbanization, the more diverse its population, the more unequal its distribution of incomes, regional product, and opportunity for advancement, the lower its degree of tolerance, and the lower the extent of its legal and constitutional contraints (Lee 1976; Oates 1972; Pommerehne 1977; Pryor 1967). Especially where there are differences in language (India, Belgium, Canada), religion (India, Canada, Ireland), race (Czechoslovakia), or culture, the multi-level alternative is essential. In many cases, especially with respect to achieving fiscal equity, a benevolent decentralized but unitary state, emphasizing extensive grant and other fiscal transfers, offers the best opportunity to improve the lot of the poorer areas. As Shoup (1969, p. 633) notes, the poorer areas "are better off than they would be under a decentralized system with no grants-in-aid. The bitterness of the impoverished areas in the unitary system may finally erupt into a demand that the system be decentralized centrally . . . with national taxes being levied at lower rates in poorer areas, and with government purchases of goods and services being channelled disproportionately into those areas". Within any country, then, the issues which are determined by constitutional, administrative and fiscal shifts are the balancing of needs and resources in different locations, based on funding the right mix of different levels of government control, and hence achieving a system of public finance which is adequately efficient, produces a tolerable degree of social equalization, is capable of accurate stabilization and smoothing of the economic cycle, and is robust in its effect on national and geographical components of economic growth. In the next sections this problem of balance is tackled through its separate components of revenue and expenditure apportionment to different levels of government.

11.3 The apportionment of revenue responsibility

The division of revenue responsibility between governments determines who pays what, as a function of where they live. In most countries, as has already been seen in table 11.3, the share of revenue sources at each level of government favours a heavy concentration at central level, usually about 80 to 90% of the revenues raised. Of those countries tabulated, only in Switzerland does the level of local revenue raising exceed this at central level. As well as being relatively minor, as table 11.3 demonstrates, local revenues, with the exception of the United States, are usually limited to a very small number of sources. The revenue patterns evolved in these various countries raise two distinct issues. First, how should revenue responsibility be distributed between different levels of government? Especially crucial is the issue of how important and separate should these sources be. Second, how should revenue responsibilities be apportioned for different revenue sources?

SEPARATION OF REVENUE SOURCES BETWEEN LEVELS
OF GOVERNMENT

This concept seems to derive from Adam Smith, who related revenue separation to the concept of local goods and local benefits discussed in chapters 5 and 9; "those publick works which are of such a nature that . . . the conveniency is nearly confined to some particular place or district, are always better maintained by a local or provisional revenue, under the management of a local or provisional administration, than by the general revenue of the State" (Smith 1776, pp. 730–1). Hence separation is closely linked to the Benefit Theory of apportioning tax burdens; local benefits are paid for by local revenue; general or national benefits (merit goods) by national revenue. This is an attractive theory as it encourages consumption to be self-limiting since the price rules of the market are introduced relating the supply of benefits to revenues paid. But separation of revenues is an important, emotive issue. In Britain a central feature of the Scottish demand for devolution has been the acquisition of a revenue source independent of the Westminster Government; a demand which has not yet been satisfied. Again in the Layfield Report (UK Committee of Inquiry into Local Government Finance, 1976) it was concluded that a degree of revenue separation is crucial to the preservation of local authority, autonomy, and accountability; but this can only be achieved by providing British local government with a new tax source in addition to the already over-used local property tax. The new source recommended, a local income tax, has not yet been accepted.

The advantages of separation are its reinforcement of both local autonomy and accountability; hence it is strongly related to the localist model. Independent revenues are free from tax competition between levels of government for the same source. They are also free from tax overlapping and multiple taxation which makes it unclear to the taxpayer to whom a particular tax is being paid, and what benefits derive from which tax burden. Hence, it is much easier to achieve a fiscal balance at each level of government, local expenditures match revenue burdens, and accountability and political responsibility are kept close together. It is also claimed that separation of taxes makes them easier to administer, allows a clear consensus of interest to be identified in the apportionment of each tax, and permits incorporation of better local knowledge into assessment especially of property taxes (Newcomer 1917).

The separation theory can, however, be objected to on a number of grounds. First, tax overlapping and multiple taxation can be overcome by other means than separation. Especially important are the use of tax deductions and credits, as discussed in chapter 12. Second, the claims of easier administration, identity of clearer consensus of interest, and better assessment, are somewhat dubious and depend very much on the methods of organization adopted at each government level. Third, separation can be extremely wasteful since it leads to duplication of administrative organization in each local jurisdiction. Fourth, the revenue sources most likely to be assigned at local level are usually not adequate to fund all local needs and hence some dependence on other levels of government is always necessary. Fifth, total independence and autonomy is never achievable because of the needs for intergovernmental fiscal transfers to overcome fiscal imbalance and to achieve fiscal equalization. Finally, complete separation of revenues is impossible and undesirable since there is a continually changing pattern of needs at both national and local levels, and the yields of different taxes at different levels change with long and short term economic conditions. Hence complete separation may encourage fiscally perverse effects at local level counteracting macroeconomic stabilization policy.

In practice, therefore, most countries have evolved a mixture of separate,

Table 11.6 Tax sharing, overlapping and separation in seven Western countries for 1970–74. (Sources: EEC 1977, ch. 16; Swedish Budget, 1978/79; UK Committee of Enquiry on Local Government Finance 1976)

Revenue source	Country	Revenues % shared		% overlapping		Separate to which level
		Central	State–local	Central	State–local	
Property tax	Australia	—	—	—	—	state–local
	Canada	—	—	—	—	state–local
	Germany	—	—	—	—	state–local
	Sweden	—	—	—	—	state–local
	Switzerland	—	—	—	—	state–local
	USA	—	—	—	—	state–local
	UK	—	—	—	—	local
Personal income tax	Australia	—	—	—	—	—
	Canada	—	—	71	29	—
	Germany	43	57	—	—	—
	Sweden	—	—	52	48	—
	Switzerland	—	—	7.9	92.1	—
	USA	—	—	86.2	13.8	—
	UK	—	—	—	—	central
Corporate income tax	Australia	—	—	—	—	central
	Canada	—	—	77	23	—
	Germany[1]	{20, 50}	{80, 50}	—	—	—
	Sweden	—	—	—	—	central
	Switzerland	—	—	16.5	83.5	—
	USA	—	—	87.9	12.1	—
	UK	—	—	—	—	central

(Table 11.6 Continued)

Revenue source	Country	Revenues % shared		% overlapping		Separate to which level
		Central	State–local	Central	State–local	
General Sales tax and VAT	Australia	—	—	—	—	central
	Canada	65	35	60	40	—
	Germany	—	—	—	—	central
	Sweden	—	—	—	—	central
	Switzerland	—	—	—	—	state–local
	USA	—	—	—	—	central
	UK	—	—	—	—	central
Alcohol, gambling, stamp duty and utility	Australia	—	—	—	—	state–local
	Canada	—	—	—	—	state–local
	Germany	—	—	—	—	mainly central
	Sweden	94	6	—	—	central
	Switzerland	80	20	—	—	—
	USA	—	—	74.4	—	central
	UK	—	—	—	25.6	central
Tobacco	Australia	—	—	—	—	central
	Canada	—	—	—	—	central
	Germany	—	—	—	—	central
	Sweden	—	—	—	—	central
	Switzerland	—	—	—	—	central
	USA	—	—	—	—	central
	UK	—	—	—	—	central
Death, gifts, capital gains succession	Australia	—	—	31	62	—
	Canada	—	—	49	51	—
	Germany	—	—	—	—	central
	Sweden	—	—	—	—	central
	Switzerland	—	—	3	97	—
	USA	—	—	80.8	19.2	—
	UK	—	—	—	—	central

Tax base	Country					Level
Employment and payroll tax	Australia	—	—	—	—	state–local
	Canada	—	—	—	—	state–local
	Germany	—	—	—	—	central
	Sweden	—	—	—	—	
	Switzerland	—	—	—	—	
	USA	—	—	—	—	
	UK	—	—	—	—	central
Motor fuel	Australia	—	—	—	—	state–local
	Canada	—	—	—	—	central
	Germany	—	—	—	—	central
	Sweden	—	—	—	—	central
	Switzerland	—	—	—	—	
	USA	36.4	—	—	—	central
	UK	63.6	—	—	—	central
						state–local
Total all taxes	Australia			52.1	3.4	20.5 · central
	Canada			24.0	19.9	9.0 · central
	Germany	39.2	31.9	23.2	55.4	— · state–local
	Sweden			21.4	47.8	30.2 · 10.1
	Switzerland	6.1	0.7	5.1	13.6	1.3 · 28.8
	USA			56.3	87.3	28.8 · central
	UK				12.7	state–local

[1] upper figure for Germany refers to local business taxes.

shared, and overlapping revenue sources. *Tax sharing* occurs when revenues are collected at one level, and then are made available to other levels of government on a fairly stable or guaranteed basis (see chapter 12). *Tax overlapping* occurs when two levels of government independently compete to tap the same revenue source, often with different rates, tax bases, allowances, and methods of assessment. Table 11.6 details the extent to which different revenue sources are subject to separation, sharing, or overlapping in seven Western countries. This shows that property tax, alcohol, tobacco, motor licences, employment and payroll taxes, and customs and excise, are predominantly separated revenue sources, whilst personal and corporate income tax, and death, gifts and estate duty are normally shared or overlapping tax sources. The extent of revenue sharing, overlapping and separation varies greatly between countries, with centralized states such as Britain retaining a very large proportion of revenues at the centre, centralized federations such as the United States having considerable overlapping at central and State-local revenues, and decentralized federations such as Australia, Canada, Germany and Switzerland, having a complex pattern of tax sharing and overlapping. Undoubtedly, some revenue sources are better administered at one level of government than at another. Various principles govern the choice of local revenue sources. The features of each major tax source are discussed below.

Property tax is employed at the lowest level of government and also at some intermediate levels. It is never used at national level. However, the English-speaking world gives it more emphasis than do the Continental countries. It undoubtedly has strong advantages in being cheap and easy to administer, with a very high yield; it allows easy definition of the tax base, and relates local taxation to services that result from the distribution of property (e.g. street lighting and cleaning, police and fire protection). Indeed, the property tax has been recognized as the fundamental means of relating revenue burdens to geographical distribution of benefits since the famous Elizabethan decision in Jeffrey's case. However, there are a number of important disadvantages to the property tax at local level. First, it is unpopular and assessment procedures are often arbitrary. For example, Adam Smith (1776, p. 836) recognized that "a land tax assessed according to a general survey or valuation, how equal soever it may be at first, must, in the course of a moderate period of time, become unequal. To prevent its becoming so would require the continual and painful attention of government to all variations in the State". Equalization of property tax rates, if achieved, can also be disadvantageous since poorer groups and land users are priced out of certain areas. This is detrimental to poor income groups and also undermines rural and farming interests on the urban fringe or in dormitory satellites. Second, visible property is not related very closely to ability to pay, nor does size of property necessarily accord with the use of local services. Third, because housing froms a large portion of family expenditure for low income families, property tax is regressive (see page 157) and thus works against policies of redistribution. Netzer (1974) for example shows that US State and local property tax as a percentage of income in 1970 was an average of 9% for low incomes, and only 3.7% for higher income groups. Fourth, there are incentives in many countries, particularly in the US and UK, for local jurisdictions to under-assess local values since this will result in a larger central government subsidy in many grant programmes. Fifth, discrimination in assessments between types of property (commercial and domestic) can considerably distort land use patterns in undesirable ways. Finally, where the tax is exacted on improvements to real estate, it also acts as a disincentive to the improvement of property.

Personal income tax is an important local revenue source in many countries, but although favourably evaluated for possible use in the UK (see *UK Royal Commission on the Constitution* 1973) it is unlikely to be implemented. The advantages of this tax are its elasticity, easy administration, and its clear relationship to the main index of tax paying ability, namely income. However, it has major disadvantages at local level. Because income tax is the major revenue source of most national governments, its use at local level presents problems of competition for the same tax base. Because of the effect of fiscal migration, there is little possibility of using the progressive element for redistribution at local level, and hence the major instrument of income redistribution is undermined by extensive local use. Moreover, it is very often difficult to determine incomes at local level; for example, should personal income be taxed at the domicile or at the place of employment? Where it is used, the local area over which it is levied is large and it is usually administered by tax credits or revenue-sharing.

Corporate income taxes and the closely related taxes on employment payrolls are not usually employed at local level in any Western country except Germany. They have many of the same advantages and disadvantages as personal income taxes, but four additional problems arise. First, as noted in chapter 8 (see page 191), it is difficult to apportion burdens to different jurisdictions, and when apportionment is undertaken using different assessment formulae, this can result in multiple taxation, i.e. taxes levied on greater than 100% of total income. Second, such taxes may lead to undesirable barriers to inter-area trade. Third, local corporate income tax has very little relation to services consumed. Fourth, businesses, more than any other bearers of tax burdens, are liable to tax in a large number of different jurisdictions, and hence are subject to high costs of compliance, i.e. a different tax administration procedure is required by the firm for its operations in each jurisdiction. Haig (1935) estimated the differential costs of federal and State level corporate income taxes in the US in 1934 at 4.7 and 9.5% respectively of taxes paid (and fourteen companies reported costs at greater than 40% of taxes paid). Moreover, these costs rose greatly when operations were carried out in more than one State; from 3.5% for one-State businesses, to 10.5% of taxes paid for multi-State businesses.

Sales tax is employed most fully at the local level in the US. Such taxes have the general advantage that they meet with the least resistance; they are usually the least unpopular of taxes. They are also large revenue raisers at low rates, are fairly stable (elasticity about 1.0), are related to measures of tax ability based on expenditure, and allow a measure of individual consumer sovereignty. The two main disadvantages are the strong regressive element of sales tax with respect to income, and its encouragement to purchasing out of the local area. For example, Levin (1966) estimated that a 4% sales tax in New York City in 1965 diverted 25% of retail sales to those suburbs where there was no sales tax. Thus the capacity for autonomous setting of local sales tax rates is limited, but this impact is lessened if all local governments are using sales taxes.

The remaining tax sources, severance tax, motor licences, and estate tax can be used effectively at local level, and are used in a number of countries. They have also been suggested for local use in the UK. Severance tax has provided a considerable source of revenue in resource-rich areas of the US, such as Louisiana and Texas. Oil revenue taxes have also been suggested for a devolved government in Scotland. Such taxes have the advantage to the local jurisdiction of exporting most of the tax burden out of the local area, a factor important in the 'frost-belt'–'sun-belt' controversy in the United States. Certainly, any producer tax on a fixed local resource is very flexible, administratively cheap, and high yielding, provided the resource is not close to the margin of production. For motor licence fees there are some advantages of tying the local revenues to local usage of road facilities, although these will never be totally equivalent. For estate taxes, there are advantages deriving from its relation to ability measured by wealth (hence it is redistributive) and also its use of a large tax base. However, there is usually strong competition with central government for this source, and some geographical migration will be encouraged by a high degree of variation in the rates of estate taxes.

User charges, the final set of revenue sources, have the advantages of bringing mechanisms of the market into play (thus identifying demand and rationing output), clearly identifying beneficiaries, and overcoming many of the problems of benefits spillover (see chapter 9). However, they are not a universal solution to revenue raising problems. User charges are appropriate only when the service is divisible, and when the benefits go mainly to the payer. They are extremely inappropriate when the public service is aimed at the poor or is redistributive, where there is a pure public good (e.g. defence, environmental protection or public safety), or where there are general as well as individual benefits (as with education, libraries and transport). Charges can also encourage inefficient under-use of public facilities. The 1953 increase in subway fares in New York City from 10 cents to 15 cents, for example, lost the Subway System 120 million rides per year, mainly in peak travelling periods, thus increasing road congestion (Fitch 1964). Despite these problems, user charges are readily administered at local level and are widely used for public services. In most countries the services which are usually financed in whole or in part by charges are public transport, the utilities of gas, water and electricity, public legal fees, interest on housing purchase loans, and public housing rents.

Four conclusions can be drawn from the discussion of the paragraphs above. First, certain taxes must be reserved to central level, at least for administrative purposes. These usually include corporate income tax, redistributive elements of personal income tax, gifts tax, and any heavy burdens placed on sales tax. Second, the most appropriate local taxes are usually property tax, user charges, severance tax (where possible), with limited use also made of personal income, sales and estate taxes. A third conclusion is that major attempts to achieve redistribution through taxation must be placed on central government revenue sources. Finally, alternatives to separation of revenues can achieve many of the desired benefits of geographical variability or even local autonomy. The important cases of sharing of national taxes, geographical differentiation of national tax policies, and intergovernmental grants are discussed in later chapters.

11.4 The apportionment of expenditure functions

The division of responsibilities for different expenditure functions between governments determines the degree of local political control over who receives what benefit as a function of where they live. Hence many of the issues of the nature of public goods, local and merit needs, and apportionment of expenditure benefits discussed in chapters 5, 6 and 9, are again raised. As shown in table 11.5, there is a remarkable degree of similarity in apportionment of functions in different countries irrespective of the different patterns of revenue raising adopted. It is also possible to recognize in this table a hierarchy of functions associated with the hierarchies of governments: with defence organized at national level; health, welfare, environment, transport, and commerce, primarily organized at regional level; and education, police, fire and housing, primarily organized at local level. Various theoretical approaches to the determination of the most appropriate apportionment of functions to different levels of government have evolved, and the five most important of these are discussed below; a sense of community, technical efficiency, economic efficiency, preference structures, and administrative constraints.

SENSE OF COMMUNITY

The 'sense of community' is an important overall constraint on the organization of public goods, especially those programmes orientated towards redistribution as it focuses at both local and higher levels of government. The 'sense of community', Thomas Jefferson's 'ward democracy', is a form of collective conscience which leads people to want to improve the lot of groups of individuals, or geographical areas, by pro-

293

grammes of income redistribution, re-housing, urban renewal, retraining, minimum wages, social security, health care, or education. This collective conscience itself requires a pattern of history, geographic inertia, economic conditions, and previous distribution of public goods which have given rise to a collective cultural identity and allegiance or loyalty. Often the smaller the size of the unit considered, the greater is this collective loyalty and sense of communal values. Indeed, both Adam Smith and Marx saw the ideal sense of communal values only retained in primitive societies of small scale. The collective conscience or sense of community may be the result of jointly held moral philosophy, of fear of violent upsurges by the deprived, or of concern to reflect a good image of national solidarity or well-being abroad. In fact, both Rousseau and Marx argued that distribution programmes are solely aimed to appease deprived minority groups and keep the dominating or ruling economic elite in power. But in Marxist and in liberal writings there is a pervasive belief that smaller communities allow the better development of community values.

These views have led to many proposals for the apportionment of expenditure functions to levels at which particular community ties become evident. Thus, at one extreme, public finance functions can be organized on very wide geographical bases if they reflect loosely held, infrequently used, but widely supported preferences for particular forms of government (liberal/democratic versus totalitarian organizations), for ethnic or cultural distribution (racialism and nationalism), or for social and economic organizations (market, mixed or command economies). International alliances, economic groupings and organizations such as the UN reflect a cohesion stretched to extremes of commitment and degree of support. At the other extreme, public goods such as police, education and housing, impinge on the daily lives of most people, are recurrent or continuous needs, and relate to very strongly held political, economic or cultural ethics. Charles Fourier (Office of the London Phalanx 1841) erected this hierarchy of community sense into a so-called Phalanstery;

> 'each branch of industry [in which one can include public goods] is undertaken by a distinct corporation of men, women and children, who enrol themselves voluntarily, from a natural taste and preference of vocation, and this voluntary corporation of industry is termed a '*series*' .... In a phalansterian community. .... Each series or corporation being sub-divided into a scale of minor groups, or companies, a spirit of harmonic emulation is engendered between contiguous groups, analogous to the dissonancies of contiguous notes in a chromatic scale of musical sounds' (*op. cit.* pp. 76–77, 78).

Fourier's theory of social harmony, although based heavily on community sense, also invokes elements of the preference and economic theories discussed below.

294

A technically efficient criterion for apportionment of expenditure functions involves the determination of the level of government at which the output of services can be produced at least cost in relation to economies of scale and distribution. This leads to ideas about optimum community size and density as discussed in chapter 6. Technical efficiency is most important where economies of scale are most significant (as in power generation, water and sewerage systems), or where distribution costs compose a large proportion of total service costs. This latter factor has led to a large theory of optimal districting (Johnston and Taylor 1978), organization of bus and transport services for schooling (Massam 1975; Scott 1971) delimitation of police and fire protection districts, and general optimal districting problems. However, these mathematical solutions have rarely been totally feasible in practice due to political, preferential and other constraints. They represent more broad indicia rather than rigid criteria for apportioning expenditure functions.

Each function performed by governments has a different technically efficient size of population or area served. Moreover, each function is usually a composite of a group of sub-functions each of which also has different technically efficient sizes. In addition, there are seldom sharp discontinuities in the cost curve function. This suggests that it will not usually be possible to find hierarchical clusterings of functions which accord precisely with different levels of government. In many instances, it must also be recognized that the level of government which provides a given service need not accord with the area in which consumption occurs. There are usually important spillovers and externalities which require intergovernmental agreements to overcome allocation problems. Moreover, technical efficiency is a rather static criterion which allows only slow adjustments of institutions where technological changes induce shifts in economies of scale and distribution. However, it continues to indicate important general constraints on the economic and political organization of services which have high distribution costs.

ECONOMIC EFFICIENCY

The economic efficiency criterion for allocation of expenditure functions involves the technical issues of economies of scale and distribution discussed above, but also raises three subsidiary features; first, the practicalities of apportionment of the public finance functions of allocation, distribution, stabilization, discussed in chapter 3; second, the extent of externalities and spillovers which determine the degree of 'publicness' of a public good or expenditure function; third, the price elasticity of demand for goods. With respect to the first of these features, the classical theory of public finance (see Musgrave 1959; Oates 1972) apportions the functions of distribution, stabilization and growth to national level government, and the allocation function to local level, with some allocation and perhaps minor components of growth and distribution policies at regional level. Whilst these general lines of delimitation are appropriate, as the discussion in chapter 3 has emphasized, the assignment of function in decentralized or federal countries may deviate substantially from this pattern. In such countries, decentralization of central powers, combined with co-ordination of local and regional governments, allows a considerable degree of variation in tax rates, distribution policies, and growth incentives. This can accord local services and fiscal functions more closely with variation in local preferences and levels of demand, and hence encourage greater economic efficiency.

With respect to the second feature of economic efficiency, the degree of

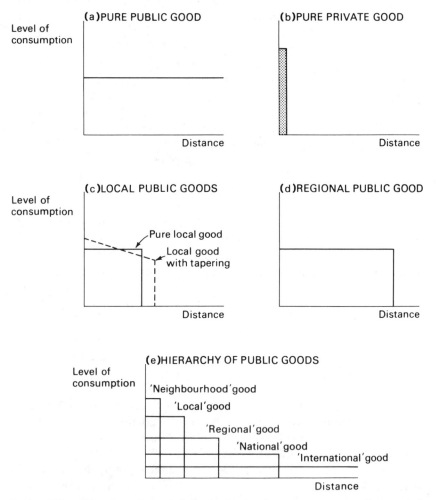

Figure 11.2 Allocation of goods between levels of government according to their degree of publicness.

externality and 'publicness' of social goods, we are drawn back to the technical hypothesis for the definition of public goods discussed in chapter 2: the allocation of goods to levels of government, and between public and private organizations, depending upon the extent to which the goods possess the three technical attributes of jointness, non-excludability and non-rejectability (see page 12). According to the degree to which a good possesses these attributes, we may rank goods from an extreme of 'purity', where a good possesses total externality (the same benefits are consumed by all, equally, and at equal cost) which is provided by a national government or international organization (as shown in figure 11.2a), to total privacy for a good which is provided by no government (as shown in figure 11.2b). Local, regional, and other forms of public goods, as shown in figure 11.2c and d, are found between these two extremes where the degree of jointness has a defined spatial extent. Hence, the economic efficiency criterion gives rise to a hierarchical apportionment of public goods according to their degree of externality as shown in figure 11.2e. Although such divisions are far from hard and fast, as the discussion in chapter 9 emphasizes, there is a remarkable degree of relationship between the amount of joint externality of many goods and their spatial range. This arises from technical practice, such as those discussed above for education, fire, police, sewerage, water and streetlighting; from supply constraints, in the case of education, police and fire; and from political and community factors which relate to the degree of socialization or group identity of people (see, for example, Breton 1965; Forte 1977; Head 1973; Musgrave and Musgrave 1976).

The third element of the economic efficiency argument, that of the price elasticity of demand for a good, apportions goods between the public and private sectors, and between government levels of the public sector, so as to allow a minimum distortion to the economically efficient allocation of economic resources. The normal demand for a private good, as shown in figure 11.3a, induces a steady decline in consumption with an increase in price. However, the consumption of many goods is inelastic to price. Where other criteria dictate that such goods should be provided publicly, the completely inelastic good is assigned to the national or international level as a merit good (figure 11.3b). Where the price of a good exhibits a degree of decreasing

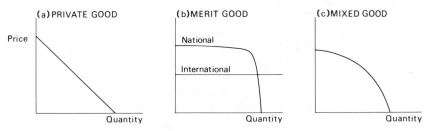

Figure 11.3 Demand curves for private, merit and mixed goods.

marginal production cost with size of a producing unit, and/or external economies (figure 11.3c), then Brownlee (1961) argues that it should be provided publicly, but that the level of government to which it is assigned will depend upon the degree of its externality and extent of its marginal savings. This last argument is based on a situation in which it is desirable for the public sector to organize a service because it can only be run efficiently as a monopoly. Examples of such services are postal deliveries, telecommunications, radio and television, law, highways, railways, many utilities, and water supply, which are either better organized locally, or regionally or nationally. They can also often be run on a private basis, but must then be subject to a degree of local or national regulation to prevent monopolistic exploitation. When run on a public basis they are usually financed by user charges.

PREFERENCE STRUCTURES

Preference structures underpin a fourth theoretical approach to apportionment of expenditure functions which is closely related to both the sense of community and to economic efficiency. This approach relies upon two components. The first of these is a basic decentralization theorem deriving from the public choice school, especially of Bish and Ostrom, that smaller communities give a better accordance with preferences, a higher chance of consensus, minimize frustration, and reduce the need for regulatory control. Hence, preferences form a major component of what Rothenberg (1970) terms forces of homogenization. The second component is the benefits to be gained from collusion and collective action when there are joint externalities and spillovers. Indeed, much of the preference school literature is based upon a wider interpretation of the externality and spillover effects so important in the economic efficiency approach. Authors such as Buchanan (1970), Breton (1965), Tullock (1969), Bish (1971), Ostrom (1973), Breton and Scott (1976), and Buchanan and Tullock (1969) have proposed that an optimal pattern of government can be based on determining, for each public good and service, the point at which the external cost resulting from collective provision of goods exceeds the external benefit to the individual. This so-called 'calculus of consent' can then be made the basis for allocation of functions between levels of government in which preferences are derived from the relative costs of involvement or non-involvement in collective decision-making. Figure 11.4 shows typical graphs of cost and benefit hypothesized by Buchanan and Tullock to characterize the provision of public goods in groups of different sizes (N). The external cost curve (figure 11.4a) depicts how the costs to the individual resulting from the action of others decline as the group size increases, i.e. the group expands to the point at which no costs are external. The decision costs, depicted in figure 11.4b, increase as the size of the group increases. This is the result of four factors; first the need for larger bureaucracies; second, more expensive consultation and participation pro-

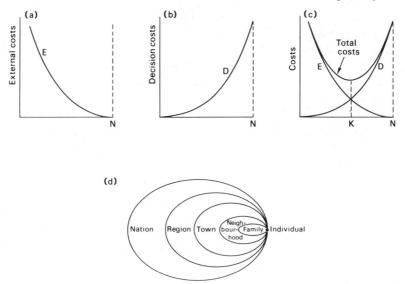

Figure 11.4 Cost curves for decision-making in groups of various sizes N. (After Buchanan and Tullock 1969.)

cesses; third, the costs to individuals from agreeing to decisions which are individually inappropriate in order to obtain gains elsewhere; and fourth, the cost resulting from lack of control over larger government. Although these cost curves will differ with different goods, the combination of these two cost curves (figure 11.4c) allows the determination of an optimal group size for organization of each public good. The optimum size is given as that point at which the costs of participation in public provision exactly equal the cost of non-participation. By combining these cost curves of various goods, Buchanan and Tullock predict that a set of groupings of goods emerges which gives individual, neighbourhood, town, regional, and national goods as shown in figure 11.4d. Hence, the hierarchy of group preferences, reflected through costs, determines a hierarchical apportionment of public goods as a form of 'optimal constitution'. A related criterion for delimitation of administrative functions is given by Davies (1976) who suggests that responsibility should be divided according to the policy paradigm under which bureaucrats are working; central policy directives should be centrally funded, local directives locally funded, and so forth: "authorities should receive grant support for virtually inescapable expenditure made as a consequence of central government policies" (Davies 1976). Such expenditures are usually those associated with national goods as discussed earlier.

Unfortunately the calculus of consent approach has at least five important drawbacks. First, it considers each government in isolation and does not incorporate the effects of competition and exclusion which may be operated by jurisdictions. Second, it assumes that a particular bundle of public services

299

is fixed for ever and leads to a once and for all layout of jurisdictions. In practice, governments must continually adjust to changing technology and demands for public services. Third, the optimum government system in terms of preferences will not usually accord with that resulting from either technical efficiency or economic efficiency criteria. Fourth, there is no reason to expect that the spillover effects from different services will be identical, nor will they usually be subject to a discontinuity which allows an hierarchical arrangement based on clusters of government functions. Finally, Bird and Hartle (1972) note that the social optimum, to which the public choice arguments of Buchanan and Breton lead, is subject to the same unrealistic assumptions and drawbacks as welfare economics; the optimum which is sought is defined with respect to the present distribution of real income, requires perfect knowledge by all actors, relies on a single set of values against which to judge optimality, and hence requires a determinate set of preferences (welfare function) which is shared without conflict by the majority of residents in any area (see chapter 15).

ADMINISTRATIVE CONSTRAINTS

The final approach to apportionment of functions between levels of government is altogether less theoretical and more practical, drawing in particular

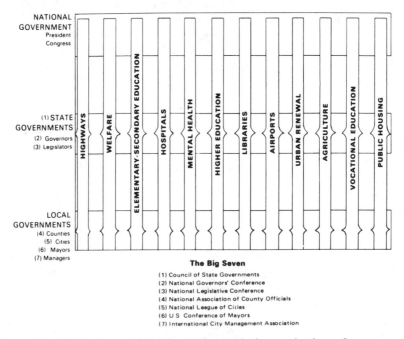

Figure 11.5 'Picket fence' federalism: the vertical organization of government administration based upon the purpose principle. Based on the discussion of Sandford (1967) and Wright (1974). (*Source*: US ACIR 1976.)

from the literature of public administration and political science. This places emphasis on the lines of vertical authority between levels of government, on horizontal co-operation between governments at the same level, and of the creation of other such cross-linkages as may be necessary. The basic assignment of functions between levels of government is a task of appropriate departmentalization which involves one or more of the following principles.

(i) *Service principle*: this involves a separate administrative department for each group of people or problem, e.g. a Ministry for the old, unemployed, a Bureau of Indian Affairs, and so forth.

(ii) *Purpose principle*: (termed by Sandford 1967 and Wright 1974 'picket fence' federalism, shown in figure 11.5). A separate administrative department is defined for each expenditure function. This is the usual governmental department structure in the UK and elsewhere.

(iii) *Process principle*: different administrative departments are defined for each type of expenditure of skill, e.g. engineers, architects, and other departments in local authorities. This is the normal method of division of labour and breakdown of decision making in industrial companies.

(iv) *Areal principle*: (so-called 'layer-cake' federalism shown in figure 11.6c). Administrative departments are evolved for each territorial unit with total devolution to lower geographical levels. Self (1972, p. 57), notes that this does not usually solve the departmentalization problems, and functions must still be allocated at the new spatial level.

Various mixtures of these four principles result in a number of other forms as shown in figure 11.6.

It is now recognized that no single method of departmentalization of government will be successful, and the 'layer-cake', 'picket fence', and other approaches of figures 11.5 and 11.6 give way to extremely complex structures. The 'marble-cake' or 'cafeteria' approach, advocated originally by Grodzins (1966), calls for area, client-group, or functional fragmentation of government as required: 'a little chaos' is a good thing. This has the benefit of allowing each service to operate at its efficient scale in accord with preferences. It has three main drawbacks. First, a high variety of local districts and fragmented control increases the cost of co-ordinating decisions and allows no economies of scale in administration at any level. Second, highly fragmented government increases fiscal disparities by fracturing economic and geographical space into very different areas of expenditure needs and revenue capacity. Third, the marble cake structure would greatly confuse financial arrangements, lead to immense overlapping and competition for tax bases, and confuse rather than clarify the lines of accountability. At the other extreme, the 'layer-cake' or 'package approach', gives a single multi-purpose government for each local area which administers all functions. This has the advantages of easier co-ordination, reduction in operating costs, and more obvious public divisibility and accountability. However, it has the major drawbacks of being relatively unadaptable to needs for changed boundaries,

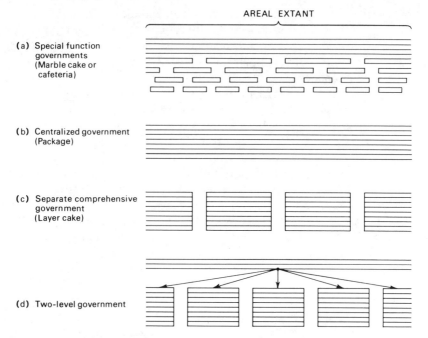

Figure 11.6 Various forms of government organization which combine purpose functions and spatial functions. The vertical divisions represent purpose functions and the horizontal divisions spatial areas. (After US ACIR 1976.)

tends to ignore small scale variation of needs, demands, and preferences within local units, induces a uniformity of taxation irrespective of variation in local fiscal ability, and often becomes uneconomically large and unresponsive.

In practice, administrative structures that have evolved in most countries contain elements of many approaches to government apportionment of expenditure functions shifting emphasis more to the evolutionary or incrementalist approach of Lindblom (1968) rather than *a priori* design of institutions. A mixture of strongly developed vertical and horizontal structures is usually present, but with a strong development also of co-operative federalism, intergovernmental fiscal transfers (either vertical or horizontal) and some degree of hierarchical organization (see, for example, Seidman 1975). The problem with such complex government organization is to organize the co-ordination between the various departments and various levels of government. This co-ordination task has been the subject of much research since the seminal writings of Fayol (1925), Gulick and Urwick (1937), and Friend and Jessop (1969), involving the forging of formal and informal linkages within, what Stringer (1967) terms, multi-organizations. Such linkages provide for the flow of information, commands, and responsibility.

CHOICE OF ORGANIZATIONAL STRUCTURE

Each of the five approaches to apportionment of expenditure functions discussed above is important in different cases, but none serve completely to specify an ideal form of organization in any instance. Economic and technical efficiency suggest a strong development of regional level functions; functions with elements of distribution, stabilization and growth require a strong development of national government; whilst political constraints, local knowledge, and variation in needs of preferences suggest a strong level of local government. In practice also, the assignment of expenditure responsibilities is not the only method of overcoming the effects of spillovers or confused preference structures. An important alternative approach is suggested by Pigou (1928): tax and grant transfers between governments to offset benefit and costs spillovers. In theory, at least, this concept has been used by Pauly (1970) and Sandler (1975) to suggest a method of optimal local finance using fees. A final suggestion of Coons *et al.* (1970) is a 'power equalizing' approach in which revenue functions are assessed over jurisdictions of wide extent (State, province, *Länder*, or national governments), whilst the size of budget of any expenditure function is decided locally. This keeps decisions locally based, but eliminates fiscal incentives to migration. It again throws emphasis on intergovernmental fiscal co-ordination and transfer. A related alternative suggested by Netzer (1974) is a proportional expenditure system which allocates to each government, and to each level of government, expenditure burdens proportional to the degree of neighbourhood, local, regional, and national responsibilities. This calls into attention the interplay of national minimum standards and the questions of local, intermediate, and national level needs discussed in chapter 5. These suggestions are discussed in the context of intergovernmental transfers in more detail in chapters 12 and 13.

11.5 Modifications to jurisdictions and responsibilities

Institutional frameworks are not rigid entities. As the famous quotation from Justice Holmes at the start of this chapter emphasizes, the division of revenue and expenditure functions between levels of government should not be a Shibboleth to the past, nor to a particular economic or political theory. Most important, constitutional relations must evolve and adjust to new technological and social influences. These influences result in two inducements to modify existing constitutional and governmental structures. First, there are changes to the needs and the technology of providing services which require adjustment to the powers available at each level of government. Second, changes in social and cultural identity require adjustments to governmental responsibility, and to physical burdens and benefits. These two sets of changes call into question the fiscal structure of government and place pressures upon it to evolve to satisfy new demands and criteria.

CHANGES IN DEMAND AND TECHNOLOGY

Constitutional and jurisdictional structures tend to be relatively static; while the population and industry within a jurisdiction changes, their demands for services change (quantitatively and qualitatively), their fiscal ability is modified, and behaviour patterns evolve. The stimuli to such modifications are mainly changes in technology, especially in transport, communications, factory construction, location, and building conventions. The earliest urban developments of railway settlements and street-car suburbs have been replaced by a settlement structure atuned to the motor car. Peoples' residences have become divorced from their workplaces, areas of shopping, schooling, cultural activities and recreation. Similarly, the location of industry has been freed from central city locations. Suburban industrial developments on estates, out-of-town shopping centres and hypermarkets, drive-in banks, and other commercial developments have grown and flourished far from the central cities. This process of suburbanization of residences and industry has led to changes in revenue bases and expenditure demands in different jurisdictions and, where the new larger scale economic activity in these evolving metropolitan and megalopolitan areas has not been matched by either co-ordination or consolidation of the different jurisdictions, severe imbalances in fiscal incidence have resulted. Similarly, new locations have emerged to replace the desirability of the old. Freeway intersections, the entrances to suburban beltways, the greater emphasis on trucking and air-freight, and the development of communications media diminishing the role of face-to-face contact, have all accelerated the decline of central cities. Attractive environments with large gardens, home ownership, and desirable climates for retirement or living, have all enhanced suburban development and regional shifts in favour of areas such as the US 'sun-belt' or West Coast. Changes in factory building technology from multistorey to single storey structures, changes in the technology of residential service provision, based in the US on the water pump and septic tank, in the economics of mass housing, the feasibility of high-rise developments, and the invention of the elevator. All these factors have contributed to the shift in population and the splitting of the locations of residence, workplace, and other activities.

Changes of location and in economic dependence which are not matched by modification of government institutions naturally given rise to difficulties. As the discussions in chapters 4 and 14 show, the migration of tax bases and changes to relative expenditure burdens creates severe fiscal imbalances and patterns of possible fiscal exploitation. Technological developments in the means of providing services modify the costs of supply and change the population thresholds necessary to support them. Each of these factors provide important inducements to modify existing jurisdictional responsibility.

COMMUNITY IDENTITY

A major problem in many contemporary societies is that the sense of community which forms such an important component of the collective identity necessary to support allegiance or loyalty to a given scheme of public finance is not in accord with the existing national, regional, or local political unit. This may be especially marked when countries have undergone progressive centralization of finances in order to achieve a greater degree of social equality of regional development. For example, in the UK, Spain, the Netherlands, Canada, and many other countries, there has been increasing resistance to redistribution programmes which seem to aid groups or areas which are irrevelant or meaningless to the areas that must make the major sacrifices and bear the main burden of costs. To sustain significant redistribution policies there must be a sense not only of identity, but of common economic and social linkage. Otherwise, separatist developments may be more meaningful. Alternatively, even with a strong sense of national identity, groups may feel that it is local identity which is stronger and wish to separate off to find an independent path of economic and social development, even if this can be achieved only at higher cost or lower standard of general welfare. This has undoubtedly underlain the strong Quebec and Basque separatist movements, and the less well-developed Friesland, Scottish, Welsh and English region devolution movements.

The importance of geographic area in the organization of public goods has long been underemphasized, but as long ago as 1830, John Quincy Adams in his presidential address to the US suggested that it was geographical divisions of opinion, rooted in the soil, climate and modes of domestic life, which were the strongest, the most permanent, and the most dangerous. In this sense, as Bertrand de Jouvenal recognizes, inappropriate organization of government undermines the *social ties* of community. This has been the contention in the US, in Spain, and in the English regions, although the present constitutional structure does not allow the adequate relation of functions to the area of political concerns. Thus, in the US, metropolitan goods tend to be organized by State governments, and in England and Wales regional goods are organized at county level, and in many countries such functions are not allocated at all.

CHANGES TO FISCAL STRUCTURE

Under the influence of changing demands, innovations in technology, and shifts in the values and cultural identity of society, various adjustments to government structure and its fiscal responsibilities can be undertaken;

(1) *Changes to government structure*
(i) Consolidation of government and changes to boundaries
(ii) Decentralization of government
(iii) Multi-tier government
(iv) Marketplace government; create new governments.
(2) *Changes to fiscal responsibility*
(i) Reassign revenue responsibilities or sources

(ii) Reassign expenditure functions

(iii) Adjust mechanisms of intergovernmental fiscal transfers and co-ordination.

Consolidation of government has been stimulated in many countries by the general climate of opinion in the 1960s in favour of increased centralism (for example, in the writings of Banfield 1970; Brunn 1974; Drucker 1969; Moynihan 1969; Sunquist and Davis 1969). This reform tradition places precedence of the 'public interest' over the individual interest, increased governmental efficiency, economies of scale, equalization of service levels and fiscal burdens, and a greater simplicity of citizen participation and control. Decentralization, on the other hand, suggests a return of greater powers to local level, in accord with Jefferson's 'ward democracy', and as implemented in the 1975 Swedish constitutional reforms. In practice, most developments have been in favour of increased two- or three-tier government with the upper levels giving the benefits of consolidation and the lower levels giving the benefits of decentralization to smaller scales. This has been the form of local government reform instituted in the UK and in Sweden, and has been advocated in the United States (e.g. by CED 1966, 1970). The fourth approach of the marketplace model suggests that institutions and governments should be allowed to evolve, rather then attempt to fit a particular formula to structural diversities. In this case, the creation of *ad hoc* bodies, or special purpose governments, is welcomed, even if these may be relatively undemocratic. The consolidation argument rests on four criteria which it is deemed administrative areas should satisfy (Jackson and Bergman 1973);

(i) A jurisdiction should cover the area associated with any function.

(ii) A jurisdiction should be sufficient in extent to include an adequate resource base for local budgeting needs.

(iii) The organization of government should facilitate intergovernmental co-operation.

(iv) Effective participation and control of government should be assured.

Three main arguments for modifying the size of a jurisdiction have been adduced. First, functional arguments suggest that enlargement of jurisdictions allows them to support a greater range of functions by crossing thresholds in population, tax base, or work load, or through the influence of economies of scale. Second, economic arguments suggest that larger units can internalize externality spillovers. Third, consolidation arguments suggest that larger units can overcome the excesses of local exclusion, migration of tax bases, and fiscal imbalance by taking all inter-linked areas into one government administration. It is the first two of these arguments which have been most frequently favoured, and underlie the reform of local government in England (Honey 1976; Redcliffe-Maud and Wood 1976; Robson 1968). But in the suggested reforms of local government in the US, it is the third argument, based on fiscal imbalance, which has been given most prominence.

The threshold size for a jurisdiction, as discussed in chapter 6, differs for different functions, but for composite common multi-purpose governments, a general cut-off of about 250,000 population has been used where these governments are responsible for personal social services and a degree of co-ordinative planning. In the UK, the Redcliffe-Maud and Labour Party proposals for local government reform deviated from this threshold for five counties and four metropolitan districts. These cases were either of jurisdictions with growing populations or where exceptionally low density rural population was present. The Conservative Government proposals for re-organization enacted in the 1972 *Local Government Act* held to the 250,000 threshold in all counties, but deviated in the metropolitan districts which were predominantly Labour-controlled.

Internalization of externality spillovers, especially of commuting, was also used as an important argument for local government reform in England (Robson 1968). However, analysis of the number of 'mis-allocated' jurisdictions in the various reform proposals by Honey (1976), as shown in table 11.7, demonstrates that the final reorganization implemented was far from satisfactory. In this table, a District is misallocated if it, and its main commuting destinations, are assigned to different counties (the higher level governments). Journey-to-work data of the 1971 Census for England's 110 Metropolitan Economic Labour Areas are used to divide the commuting areas into an inner and an outer ring with, respectively, at least 15%, and less than 15%, of the workforce commuting to the major commuting destination. Of the various proposals discussed, those by Senior (1969) and the Labour Party misallocated the smallest number of districts, whilst the Conservative Party's proposals, and the final Act, did by far the least to encourage internalization of external commuting spillovers. The dominance of metropolitan areas by a Labour Party control explains these differences; it is clear that the Conservative Government weighed internalization of externalities lightly, and preferred instead to separate urban and suburban interests. Similar

Table 11.7 Misallocated Metropolitan Districts in England's 110 Metropolitan Economic Labour Areas. Number of misallocated Districts with percentage of total districts in brackets. (*After* Honey 1976, table 2; *Sources: UK Royal Commission on Local Government in England*, 1966–69, 1969; *Local Government in England* 1971)

Reorganization proposal	Metropolitan ring > 15% commuting	Outer ring < 15% commuting	Total
Redcliffe- Maud Commission	18 (.03)	95 (.24)	113 (.12)
Derek Senior	9 (.02)	29 (.07)	38 (.04)
Labour Party	10 (.02)	88 (.22)	98 (.11)
Conservative White Paper	45 (.09)	92 (.23)	137 (.15)
Local Government Bill	53 (.10)	96 (.24)	149 (.16)
Local Government Act	55 (.11)	102 (.26)	157 (.17)

considerations have also weight in the consolidation arguments regarding the fragmented government in the US.

Jurisdictional reform and consolidation can be achieved through a wide range of different reform procedures. These can be briefly summarized as follows (see Chinitz 1964; Lineberry 1971; US ACIR 1962, 1969):

(1) *Annexation.* Addition of territory to existing jurisdictions. This is often a limited practicability because of the need, in many countries, for the agreement of the annexed areas. This has proved feasible in the Southern US, e.g. in Nashville, in order to avoid black control of cities; or to add population, as in Houston.

(2) *Combine powers of existing governments.* E.g. District–County consolidation in the UK, City–County, County–County, or metropolitan federation in the US. This is often very practical, e.g. the case of metro-Toronto, and leads to a two- or three-tier solution.

(3) *Regional councils.* Co-ordinate and link decision areas, e.g. the Economic Planning Councils in the UK, *ad hoc* co-ordinative bodies such as the UK Regional Water Boards, and Regional Hospital Authorities. This may be effective but confuses the democratic basis.

(4) *Voluntary co-ordinative councils.* Associations of Districts, Counties, Cities, Model Cities, London Boroughs, Associations, etc. This can be effective, but usually offers only forums for discussion.

(5) *Partnership and other intergovernmental agreements.* Voluntary or obligatory linking of local jurisdictions for special purposes, e.g. UK inner city partnerships in Liverpool, Birmingham, Manchester–Salford, and the London areas of Docklands and Lambeth; in the US often based on joint sales of services between jurisdictions.

(6) *Extra-territorial powers.* Constitutional settlement to give power to one jurisdiction to regulate specific activities outside, but adjacent to, its boundaries; e.g. health, refuse disposal, water supply, pollution. Used for the Los Angeles Metropolitan Water Authority supply, and extensively for refuse disposal, but rarely for zoning, planning or areas of real conflict.

(7) *Create new forms of government.* Total government reform as in the UK or Sweden, or creation of special districts for special services, e.g. water supply, housing, sewerage, airports; used in the United States in Seattle Metropolitan Municipal Corporation, the Port of New York Authority, San Francisco BART, Washington D.C. Metrobus, and the Massachusetts Metropolitan District Commission for water supply, sewerage and some highways and parks in the Boston area. This is often very efficient but is usually undemocratic.

(8) *Transfer of powers to higher level government.* E.g. to States in US as in the case of California and New Jersey water supply, or to federal or central governments. Important in the US urban renewal programmes, busing in education, mass transit, community development, and revenue-sharing programmes.

Two main objections can be raised to the consolidation movement. First, the greater the extent of consolidation, the greater is the degree to which locally governed divergent tastes and interest are subordinated to the unifying force of an increasingly distant political majority. Secondly, consolidation undertaken under the stimulus of efficiency may be quite inappropriate when members of the local community place a high value upon autonomy; there is no reason why they should not choose an 'inefficient' solution which preserves their local independence. As stated by Chinitz (1964, p. 49), "we have the right to elect seemingly 'inefficient' ways of doing things. If a man prefers to take a taxi rather than ride the subway, he can't be said to prefer an inefficient mode of transport. Likewise a community may recognise the cost of maintaining its independence but yet be perfectly willing to bear it".

As a result of these arguments, a series of counter-attacks have been made against the consolidation movement, especially by Ostrom *et al.* (1961), Ostrom (1969), Greene (1970), Rothenberg (1970), and Bish (1971). These authors emphasize the importance of the benefits of what Ostrom terms a 'polycentric political system'. As summarized by Bish and Ostrom (1973, p. 65) this states that "Balkanization in American local government is largely an illusion created by ways of thinking which associate chaos with over-lapping jurisdictions and fragmentation of authority. Federal systems of government necessarily involve overlapping jurisdictions. Separation of powers necessarily involves fragmentation of authority". Hence fragmented local government is argued not only to be a natural result of the federal system, but necessary to its survival. "The success of the American system of public enterprise has been based upon the assumption that a diversity of independent interest can reach agreeable solutions over the long run" (Ostrom 1969, p. 40). Such arguments certainly find support, adduced by many of these writers, in de Tocqueville's *Democracy in America* (1966, pp. 95–6) since he argues that "uniformity, permanence of design, the minute arrangement of details, and the perfection of administration and administrative systems must not be sought for. . . ; what we find is the presence of a power which, if it is somewhat wild, is at least robust, and an existence checkered with accident, indeed, but full of animation". In addition to these arguments, it must also be admitted that small areas are not necessarily inefficient, that uniform service provision everywhere is not necessarily a desirable goal, and that efficiency in terms of economies of scale has often been overemphasized.

However, the arguments supporting inefficiency must be treated carefully. As we have seen in the discussion of inter-jurisdictional competition (p. 62), the impact of the 'States dilemma' means that the overall public good of the larger society may be sacrificed to local sectionalist and pre-emptive interest. Economies of scale in local services may be sacrificed, spillovers of pollutants may be encouraged, and most important, severe disparities in fiscal effort and services may result, not from variable preferences, but from the variable segregation of the rich and the poor. As summarized by Chinitz (1964, pp. 49–50); "What we cannot condone is the situation in which the costs to society at large are not adequately reflected in the prices confronted by the individual or the community making its choice to maintain 'efficiency' and independence". Finally, it must be recalled that other mechanisms of fiscal transfers, external taxing and charging policies also exist which are discussed in chapters 12 and 13. These offer alternatives to consolidation as means of overcoming the problems of fragmented government and draw us towards a second approach to changing fiscal responsibility: by making available to local governments new sources of revenue, or re-assigning old ones. Most countries have followed this course of modifying fiscal responsibilities and this has been particularly encouraged in the US by Pechman (1971).

11.6 Conclusion

The organization of levels of government, and the apportionment of revenue and expenditure functions between them, has raised a number of important issues in public finance geography. These fall into two broad classes: first, the relative emphasis to be placed on local autonomy or centralization of governments; second, the adaptation of government institutions to changing demands, to changing technology, and especially in response to the divergent calls for either greater autonomy, or greater consolidation of government. The two issues are very closely interlinked. Those who support a greater degree of autonomy also suggest that continued breakup and fragmentation of governments in accord with the revelation of preferences. Overlying these issues, however, are the dimensions of political economy discussed in chapter 2. The arguments of the market-surrogate school (p. 19), for example, lead inevitably to emphasis on autonomy to permit the operation of Tiebout fiscal migration, thus permitting the mechanism of the market to control the allocation of public goods through the process of residential migration. In this way, local jurisdictions are seen as most able to satisfy individual preferences for public goods and services. The critics of this school, however, would point to the unreality of the assumptions particularly those relating to personal and corporate mobility. Strategies such as zoning, building codes, and legal or illegal social or racial discrimination undermine the assumptions of perfect mobility and make the economically efficient solutions predicted by the Tiebout model unobtainable. Moreover, the social effects of these barriers to mobility result in the market-surrogate approach leading to violent inequities between jurisdictions, especially between city and suburb, and centre and periphery. As a consequence, it must now be accepted that the total free play of market preferences for public goods, suggested by the market-surrogate school, cannot be permitted: it should not be possible for the more able and wealthy to 'opt out' of common problems by the device of a geographical move and a political barrier. The alternative of centralized government and jurisdictional consolidation is advocated by both the scientific design and ideology–appeasement schools. Increasing consolidation of jurisdictions is advocated in order to attain increased economies of scale and greater political control over residential and industrial migration. Centralization of government allows a greater degree of geographical control which can overcome the ability of private capital to migrate to locations where it is free from any social costs. These calls for higher level government intervention result largely from the ability of such governments to achieve a better equalization of local need and capacity. Since it is the geographical differences in need of fiscal ability which are the major cause of geographical inequities, these can be overcome by assessing all jurisdictions on a uniform basis in which migration (except in the nationally) confers no benefits. This throws the emphasis on national taxation measures such as income tax to raise revenues, with assessment of local needs on a uniform basis by national or, at least, higher level government. A possible consequence, then, is of remote governments which may make very inefficient resource allocation decisions in the local context. The rationalization between these various schools of approach is no simple task and chapters 12 and 13 develop the concepts of intergovernmental transfers and co-ordination which allow the rationalization of local with wider public demands.

12

Intergovernmental fiscal co-ordination

"Governments cannot change their occupation or move to other states where conditions are better . . . . The movement of their people to other states in accordance with economic conditions does not solve their problems, but on the contrary makes them more difficult. . . . It is therefore a fundamental obligation . . . . to make it possible for a State Government in distress to function . . . whatever disabilities the people of a state may suffer."

Australian Commonwealth Grants Commission, *Second Report* (1935, p. 36)

12.1 Introduction: equalization through horizontal and vertical co-ordination

Our concern in this chapter is with how public finance can be co-ordinated in order to suppress geographical and individual inequities in countries which contain several levels of government. The theory of co-ordination methods is discussed in this chapter, whilst in chapter 13 the practical experience of co-ordination in various countries is examined.

The main aims of intergovermental co-ordination are the reduction of tax overlapping and competition between jurisdictions, and the achievement of fiscal equity by reducing disparities between revenue burdens and benefits. The aim of equalization is frequently the primary one, but equity can be defined in a variety of ways: equal public finance allocation or intergovernmental transfers to all areas, equal levels of service in all jurisdictions, equal tax burdens or effort, equal finance per unit of local need, or equalization of personal and geographical incomes by social and spatial redistribution. In this chapter, in common with the development of the argument of earlier chapters, equalization is defined as equity under the public fisc: equalization of public service benefits in the face of geographical variation in both ability to pay and preferences for public goods, and in unit costs for identical public service needs. Moreover, discussion is largely limited to equalization of those needs where there is a national as opposed to a purely local interest. Hence we seek methods of co-ordinating governments to give equal treatment to equals, but unequal treatment to unequals in relation to jurisdictional variation in ability, preferences, and needs-costs.

There are two dimensions to public finance co-ordination and equalization. First, there is the balance of local autonomy and central control, discussed in

312

the previous chapter, which requires a mixture of both forms of government: higher level governments both to balance local autonomy, and to permit true geographical equalization of benefits and burdens; and local government to articulate spatial differences in individual demands and preferences. This leads to the problem of the *vertical co-ordination* between governments at different levels. The second dimension to co-ordination is that of *horizontal co-ordination*: to so structure the interrelations between governments at the same or equivalent levels, that an equalization of burdens and benefits is possible. This element of horizontal co-ordination is especially concerned with addressing the problems of benefit spillovers and tax exporting.

There are eight main forms of vertical co-ordination in public finance, some of which may also be applied horizontally between governments at equivalent levels:

(i) *Grant programmes:* these are aimed at attacking local problems by central action and their primary motivation is often one of equalization. An assessment of local needs in specific or general categories is made, often by complex formulae, and then grants are apportioned from central or intermediate level sources to meet the spatially variable needs. If correctly organized, such programmes can achieve perfect geographical equalization. The grants are of two forms: (a) *specific or categorical grants*: these are restricted to particular categories of need, for example police, urban renewal, public works, and so forth. They are usually hypothecated in that the local jurisdiction is accountable to higher level government for the way the grant is spent: so-called '*co-operative federalism*'; (b) *general or block grants*: these are often assessed on the basis of specific needs, but are given to local areas with 'no strings': the grants are unhypothecated and can be spent for whatever purposes the local areas are legally or constitutionally empowered: so-called '*dual federalism*'. Grants, although widely used, have the disadvantage of undermining local independence, and can induce inefficient expenditure and consumption patterns by distorting the real cost of local public services. However, they are a major means of sharing resources, allow progressive taxation, and aid national stabilization policies.

(ii) *Revenue-sharing*: this is related to block grants in that higher level revenues are allocated to local level government using a series of formulae. However, revenue-sharing differs from grants in three ways: first, a proportion of higher level income is allocated to local levels on a permanent basis hence maintaining local independence; second, the proportion set aside from higher level revenues is a fixed percentage; third, there are guarantees of independence from the strings attached by higher level control, e.g. by the use of a trust fund. There are two forms of revenue-sharing: (a) *special revenue-sharing*: in which a percentage of revenues from higher level government is apportioned to the lower levels, but is limited to application for specific programmes – somewhat akin to specific grants; (b) *general revenue-sharing*: in which a percentage of higher level revenues is apportioned to lower level

313

governments with minimum strings. Both forms allow localities the advantage of the wider revenue bases and the more flexible and elastic revenues available at higher levels (such as personal and corporate income taxes, see chapter 8) but without the disadvantages of complete revenue separation and extreme local autonomy.

(iii) *Tax deductibility*: this allows the individual to deduct the local, regional, or state taxes from his income liable to tax by central government. The primary aim of this form of co-ordination is the restriction of competition for revenue sources between levels of government. It also equalizes the effect of geographical differences in tax rates and is a particularly simple way of co-ordinating revenue sources.

(iv) *Tax credits and negative income tax*: this differs from tax deductibility in reducing tax liability for either expenditures or local taxation in relation to the taxes actually paid and hence is usually more equitable.

Both deductions and credits can be used to permit allowances on a wider variety of sources of individual and local expenses than local tax payments alone: they can be used to equalize on both the revenue and on the expenditure side of the local finance account. Thus, for example, deductions or credits permitted for local differences in private school or college fees, or health care, or pension schemes, and so forth, can be used to reduce the effects of geographical differences in costs and needs of public expenditure. The complete incorporation of individual variation and local needs, costs, and burdens leads to a full negative income tax system which overcomes the co-ordination problem at an individual level.

(v) *Spatially differentiated higher level government taxes and controls*: these co-ordinative instruments are extensively used in Europe and Canada, but have not been developed in the United States. Their aim is to reduce factor costs in different locations by providing either a 'stick' of development restrictions on investments, or a 'carrot' of capital and labour subsidies to employers, thus lowering the costs of production in some areas relative to others. This can be important in overcoming the disadvantages of higher transport costs, differences in labour skills, and perceptual problems which discourage investment in lagging regions. Such incentives allow lagging regions to become competitive with rapidly growing regions, thence creating greater equality of local and regional incomes, and thus, through the impact on income produced, affecting local fiscal ability and the revenue base.

(vi) *User charges*: since these allocate charges on the basis of use and hence benefits received, they are especially appropriate for horizontal co-ordination between similar levels of government. They were originally proposed by Pigou (1947) for this prime aim of improving equity, but are limited in their applicability to those services where beneficiaries relate directly to the payers, and where redistribution questions are not involved.

(vii) *Loans*: this form of co-ordination is especially appropriate for local areas in which heavy burdens of infrastructure, new investment, or renewal of

314

old investment, is required over a relatively short period and where the local population or revenue base is relatively small. For example, when local economies experience rapid economic growth, the burdens of new investments must be borne by an existing population which is small in comparison to anticipated investment needs. Similarly, in the declining economies of more mature industrial areas, the burden of renewal of infrastructure, demolition of outdated infrastructure, and environmental improvement, is high in relation to the declining local population able to service the investments required.

(viii) *Direct intergovernmental expenditures:* the most common form of such expenditure is by central or intermediate levels of government supporting a service which has a specific local effect. In this way the wider revenue base of a country or region as a whole is used to finance local expenditure needs. Important examples are the US Federal Expenditure Programmes in the 1930s New Deal; the system of EDA Public Works Grants, and the allocation of government contracts, where possible, on the basis of local needs rather than pure economic principles. In the UK and Europe equivalent direct expenditures are utilized in regional policy, e.g. advance factories, new town expansion, environmental renewal, and also in government contracts. Such expenditures are often highly political in nature and subject to extremes of log-rolling and pork-barrelling.

In addition to these vertical and horizontal co-ordination methods, the items discussed in the previous chapter on revenue separation, consolidation of local districts, and greater centralization of control, are three more radical approaches which aim to change the structure of government or of the revenue system. However, in this chapter, discussion is restricted to the co-ordination methods listed in this section, and in the following chapter the practical experiences of intergovernmental co-ordination in various countries is given.

12.2 Intergovernmental transfers: price and equity aspects

Transfers between levels of government, by adjusting the sectoral, individual, and geographical impacts of public service benefits and burdens, affect both the price and distribution of public goods and incomes, and also affect the stabilization mechanisms that can be implemented. The classical wisdom in public finance is that such transfers, especially the two most important of grants and revenue sharing, are mainly motivated by distributional and ethical criteria, but in terms of efficiency of resource allocation they have perverse and undesirable effects which modify supply and demand and result in unrealistic pricing of public goods (Bhangava 1953; Buchanan 1950; Gramlich and Galper 1973; Musgrave 1959; Scott 1952). This wisdom has been questioned by Breton (1965) and by Tiebout (1956) who suggests that in countries which possess a degree of decentralization or federation, the optimum and efficient distribution of resources is possible only if grants exist. Breton recognizes two cases: first, where there are interjurisdictional spillovers. These can be overcome by conditional grants along the lines of the

315

Pigovian compensation principle in order to reduce the fiscal stimulus to migration. Second, where the apportionment of revenue burdens is in proportion to ability or some other non-benefit principle at national level, unconditional block grants permit public service equalization. In both cases intergovernmental grants act as a substitute for fiscal mobility by reducing interjurisdictional fiscal disparitites.

Intergovernmental fiscal transfers have three major impacts on local jurisdictions,

(1) *new public spending effects*: initiation of new services and programmes, new capital projects, or expansion of existing operations;

(2) *public service maintenance effects*: continuation of existing programmes which would otherwise be terminated, and which may also improve funding and allow use of current as opposed to loan finance;

(3) *substitution (income) effects*: tax stabilization to avoid increases that would otherwise occur, or tax reduction lightening the local fiscal burden. The degree to which transfers affect each category depends on the local ratio of fiscal capacity to fiscal burden, the elasticity of demand for services with price, and political factors. Frequently, the relation of local burden and capacity is the major determinant. For example, in the grant and revenue-sharing programmes implemented in the United States and Canada, discussed in the next chapter, the degree to which new spending is accorded greater emphasis than maintenance or income effects is frequently seen to depend on the degree of local fiscal distress: the greater the local fiscal distress, the greater the pressure there is on local tax resources, and the more likely it is that programme maintenance or tax reductions will be employed; the lower local fiscal distress, the less is the pressure on local revenue and resources, and the more likely it is that intergovernmental transfers will result in new or expanded public service programmes.

The price elasticity of demand describes the degree to which intergovernmental transfers affect the level of consumption of local public goods. Since intergovernmental transfers raise local incomes both directly and through the local multiplier, they also reduce the effective price for local public goods. This stimulates both increased private spending, and increased consumption of public goods. When the share of public goods financed by intergovernmental transfers is relatively small, and the share of private market transactions very large, the price system is not greatly distorted. But commonly transfers, especially grants and direct expenditures, are quite large. Moreover tax credits and deductions make local direct taxes 'burdenless'. As a result, market prices become heavily distorted and supply prices often do not exist because the market for public goods itself does not exist. Hence, it is often not possible to judge public good provision against yardsticks of economic efficiency, since consumption of public goods is not rationed by their real price. The precise effects of transfers on consumption will depend on the price elasticity of demand, but generally some new public spending will result from transfers to local level, i.e. grants and other transfers are not mere substitutions of higher level for lower level spending, but actually lead to more services being used. For non-categorical transfers there will usually be a greater income increase than price decrease, but the extent of each depends on the way in which local governments use the additional resources. Intergovernmental transfers and co-ordination must be seen, therefore, as a geographically variable factor affecting not only the social wage and business externalities, but also as a mechanism for both direct and indirect geographical price and income modification.

Intergovernmental transfers also have important impacts on equity; indeed such transfers are often specifically designed to enhance equity. The norm of *fiscal equity* can be defined in two ways. First, the individualist definition of equity due to Buchanan (1950) states that transfer programmes should be aimed at eliminating differences in local fiscal burdens and benefits such that all citizens, who are otherwise equal, will be treated equally under the total taxation burden, no matter where they live. Second, the geographical definition of equity states that transfers should be aimed at the equalization of the benefits from provision of public goods and services for those needs where there is a national as opposed to a purely local interest, in the face of geographical inequalities of ability to pay for public goods and in inequalities in unit cost for identical needs.

The interplay between these two definitions of equity draws us back to the pervasive issue of whether redistribution and equity are better solved at an individual or geographical level. Geographically based transfer programmes have a number of disadvantages (Bish 1971; Musgrave and Musgrave 1976; Scott 1952): grant and other transfers to resource-poor areas distort the price of labour and other factors of production and hence lead to price inefficiency; when aid is directed to poor and obsolete areas of cities this may encourage in-migration of other low income groups and hence exacerbate the problem; the maintenance of decaying urban areas and regions may discourage emigration to the zones which have new job opportunities at the urban periphery or in other regions; moreover it may keep the poor, the ethnic minorities, and the disadvantaged, in a less attractive environment. In addition, Bish argues that such policies are likely to be both inefficient and costly: for example, programmes based on the growth point concept of targeting fiscal aid are most likely to assist low income families that live in or migrate to the growing areas, but may leave untouched many families which lack mobility. Hence a preferable mode of redistribution may often be individually based programmes like negative income tax which would encourage low income families to follow employment opportunities wherever they exist by equalizing public finance effects rather than distorting them in favour of geographically disadvantaged areas.

Despite these arguments, however, there are the important factors noted in earlier chapters: that many redistribution programmes are a function of locality as much as individuals: they arise from particular concentrations of people due to local economic structure, spatial adjustment to changing technology, and differential rates of growth. Pockets of poverty or other redistribution problems are not chance geographical factors. Geographical ability and redistribution are not equivalent to their inter-personal senses: as Buchanan (1950) notes, citizens in low income States have a 'right' to fiscal transfers such that they are not disadvantaged by the operation of government itself. These are not subsidies to the poor but are mechanisms of ensuring that local resources are invariant to the variation in the local need to spend. In addition, spatial fiscal transfers may be more efficient in targeting aid in many situations. Moreover, some commentators have argued that inter-personal redistribution programmes have become so saturated in North America and Western Europe, that territorially based programmes are the only alternative available. Certainly it is not sought to argue here that geographical programmes are the only means of redistribution, nor that redistribution should not also be tackled at an individual level, but many distribution questions cannot be solved purely on a personal basis independent of place.

The intergovernmental transfer programmes which show greatest utility in achieving equalization are grants and revenue-sharing. To implement equalization mechanisms of inter-governmental transfers requires an operational definition of the concept of fiscal equity. Various definitions of fiscal equity are available (Boyle 1966; Coons *et al.* 1970; Cuciti 1976, 1978; Johnson 1947; Maxwell 1946; Musgrave 1961; Mushkin 1974; Mushkin and Cotton 1969; Reischauer 1974; US ACIR 1964). Referring back to the discussion of earlier chapters, it should be expected that it is possible to define equity with respect to local outlays, and hence to design *revenue-receipt equalization transfers*. In this case transfers are from rich to poor jurisdictions in terms of actual revenues raised. A grant based on this principle is used in Germany between locations (the *Länderfinanzausgleich*), and in Austria between federal and State governments (The *Ländeskopfquotenausgleich*).

A second approach is equity in respect of the revenue base, i.e. to design *revenue equalization transfers* which aim to equalize expenditure benefits for equal fiscal capacity, fiscal effort, or both. Such transfers are distributed to jurisdictions in inverse proportion to their fiscal capacity or in direct relation to their fiscal effort: jurisdictions with low capacity or high effort are given large transfers; and jurisdictions with high capacity or low effort are given small transfers, or are even taxed through the transfer system to redistribute resources to the poorer areas. Tax capacity transfers are emphasized in Canada, whilst tax effort is incorporated in US general revenue-sharing. Countries with little fiscal autonomy such as the UK and France, require little if any emphasis to be placed on either fiscal capacity or fiscal effort. The use of fiscal capacity measures rather than tax effort or performance implies a greater devolution of power to local levels, since governments need not then match standard efforts. Hence capacity measures tend to be used in general grants and revenue-sharing, whilst effort measures better characterize specific grants.

A third approach to fiscal equity is *unit cost/client-need equalization transfers* (need-equalization transfers). These aim at achieving uniform programme performance levels providing equal benefits for public good provision for national merit goods, and equal benefits to equal individual and client-groups, irrespective of geographical variations in unit costs in providing for needs. Such transfers are distributed to jurisdictions on the basis of geographical, individual, or client-group needs and are scaled by the magnitude of the cost of providing for needs in different jurisdictions. Hence relatively needy, high-cost jurisdictions receive large transfers, and less needy, low-cost jurisdictions receive small transfers. Some need component is used to effect fiscal transfers in most countries except Canada.

None of these three transfer mechanisms is capable of complete equalization on its own. On the one hand, revenue equalization takes no account of the expenditure element; on the other hand, need equalization of unit costs takes no account of variation in the ability to support equivalent services. Hence true equalization transfers must combine revenue, outlay and expenditure components to give a complete measure of fiscal equalization.

Various designs of transfer formulae to achieve intergovernmental fiscal equity are given in figures 12.1 to 12.3. In these figures the following symbols are used:

G_i = total *per capita* local finances (local resources and transfers) in area i with mean $\bar{G}$.

E_i = local *per capita* revenues collected = local *per capita* expenditure from own source revenues in area i with mean $\bar{E}$.

B_i = tax base *per capita* (income, capacity) in area i with mean $\bar{B}$.

T_i = intergovernmental transfers to area i (positive or negative).

N_i = *per capita* need in area i with mean $\bar{N}$.

P_i = local service performance $(E_i + T_i)/N_i$, the ratio of outlays to need in area i, with mean $\bar{P}$.

t_i = local tax rate.

t_c = transfer rate from higher level government (positive or negative).

t_s = 'standard', national, or representative tax rate for given revenue bases.

n = number of jurisdictions.

From figure 12.1 it can be seen that matching and proportional transfers allocated on the basis of fiscal ability (e.g. *per capita* incomes on the representative tax base) are not equalizing and indeed the matching grant gives more to higher income areas since these jurisdictions support a higher degree of expenditure and are better able to generate matching funds. Both of these transfer categories may contain some element of equalization if the transfer revenue is raised on a progressive basis, such as income tax. However, the various categories of true equalizing transfers can attain geographical

319

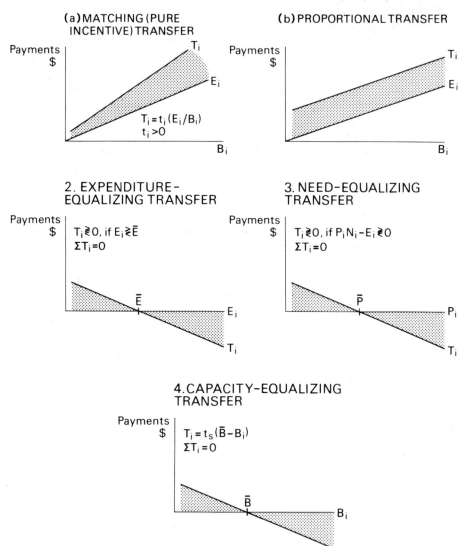

Figure 12.1 Intergovernmental transfers seeking equalization in terms of different tax bases, expenditure or needs.

redistribution even with a regressive tax base, especially in the case of redistributional transfers which exact payments from richer jurisdictions to pay to the poor. Indeed this category of equalizing transfers is equivalent to a negative income tax apportioned geographically between jurisdictions (for a discussion of NIT apportionment between individuals see section 12.5). When

320

such equalizing transfers are combined with a progressive revenue system they represent a very powerful force of personal and geographical income redistribution. Three forms of equalizing transfers are shown which re-distribute resources on the basis of respective expenditures (or outlays), needs, and revenue capacity. Expenditure equalization transfers are deficient since they give incentives to jurisdictions with high tax rates to reduce those rates and increase intergovernmental transfers in equal ratio. Need equalization transfers are deficient on the same grounds, but do take account of variable local quantities of service through the performance term P_i (the ratio of local outlays to needs). Revenue capacity equalization transfers overcome the disincentive problem by including an element related to the local tax base and local tax rates, but ignore local tax effort and local needs, and hence are inadequate in equalizing the expenditure side of the account.

The only true equalization transfers are those which seek simultaneously to equalize the revenue and expenditure sides of the local finances. Such transfers which also take into account fiscal effort are shown in figure 12.2. This is made up of two components. First, a capacity equalizing component which seeks to transfer resources to, or exact a tax from, jurisdictions equal to the

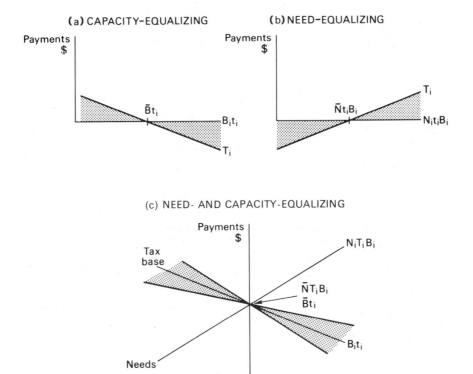

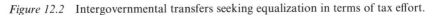

Figure 12.2 Intergovernmental transfers seeking equalization in terms of tax effort.

321

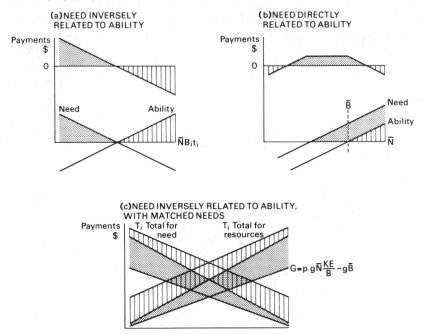

Figure 12.3 Intergovernmental transfers seeking equalization in terms of both expenditure needs and tax ability: grants stippled, taxes shaded.

difference between the revenue which would be obtained if a local tax rate were applied to the average tax base, and the revenue which is obtained from the local tax base, i.e. $(\bar{B} - B_i)t_i$ in the figure. The second component, of need equalization transfer, is similar: transfers are made, or exacted, in proportion to the difference between local needs and average needs, i.e. the $(N_i - \bar{N})t_iB_i$ term in the figure. Thus each jurisdiction obtains the same performance levels per unit cost of their expenditure. The two components, when combined, yield a joint capacity and need equalization formula displayed in the figure. It is instructive to collapse this three-dimensional graph to two dimensions by assuming a simple relation between need and ability. There is, of course, no necessary relation between need and ability, but in figure 12.3, two assumptions on need distribution are made. First, and most plausible, need is assumed inversely related to ability. Second, need is assumed directly proportional to ability. A final case, in which need is neutral to ability, is not shown. In graphical terms this reduces to the revenue equalization formulae for figure 12.1. An interesting special case of need equalizing transfers is the matched need transfer (figure 12.3c) which is capable of giving equal distribution of resources in relation to both need and ability.

In practice, completely equalizing transfers based on horizontal transfers from jurisdictions with high ability and low need to jurisdictions with low ability and high need are rarely politically feasible; indeed the German

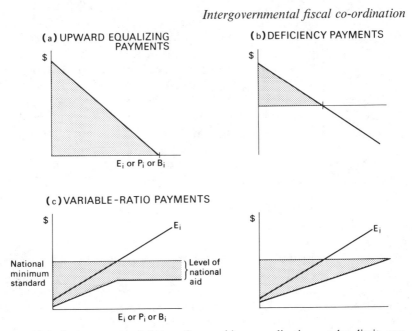

Figure 12.4 Intergovernmental transfers seeking equalization under limit constraints.

Länderfinanzausgleich is the only major example of such a horizontal transfer programme. Instead, emphasis is thrown on the vertical transfers or use is made of a number of special forms of intergovernmental transfers as shown in figure 12.4. The first of these (figure 12.4a) is upward equalizing and brings each jurisdiction up to the level of the jurisdiction with the highest ability, need or expenditure. This approach is used in Canadian equalization grants, and Australian special equalization grants. An alternative (figure 12.4b) is the deficiency payments principle used in the UK Rate Support Grant and in the Swiss Federal Direct Tax payments (*Ausgleichszahlungen*). True equalization of need, capacity, or expenditure is assessed, but transfers occur only in the form of receipts by the needy jurisdiction. In both cases, no negative transfers (taxes) are exacted from the richer or less needy jurisdictions, all payments are generated from national level revenues. A third approach (figure 12.4c) is a system of variable-ratio transfers which seek to compromise the deficiency payments principle by giving some transfers to all jurisdictions in respect of the component of local expenditures incurred in meeting nationally set minimum standards. Both the deficiency payments and variable-ratio approaches yield very imperfect or unequalizing transfers.

The form of equalizing transfers should, if possible, be independent of the policies adopted by the lower level governments. It should be clear, however, that only upward equalizing transfers possess this feature since these transfers occur independently of the strategies of lower level governments. However, these strategies possess the disadvantage that they apply the highest standard

323

to all governments and this may involve policies which are neither possible nor desired in other jurisdictions (as with revenue policies with respect to natural resource royalties in Canada and Australia). In contrast, equalization based on transfers above either an average standard, or a deficiency payment, erode incentives for local governments to involve themselves in revenue raising: if they are above the average they have every incentive to reduce tax effort, thus shifting the burden on to the wider population of the country as a whole. In practice, therefore, variable ratio grants, by combining incentive and upward equalization, often present an attractive approach, even though they cannot achieve true equalization.

12.3 Intergovernmental grants: categories and motivations

A general typology of grants and revenue-sharing has been constructed by Musgrave and Musgrave (1976) and Maxwell (1946). This is shown in table 12.1, which is based on their generality, matching requirement, and relation to need on capacity indicators. *General grants* are not tied to any specific spending programme and act as block grants which can be channelled by local governments (usually with relatively minor limitations and legal constraints) to whatever programmes they judge to be of greatest local concern or importance. General revenue-sharing in the United States and Canada, and the UK Rate Support Grant are examples of this grant category. *Selective grants* are specifically tied to limited expenditure programmes, in education, health, public infrastructure, and so forth, and are often very constrained even within these categories. Special revenue-sharing and categorical grants in the US, the UK specific grants, and many European specific grants are examples of this category. It has been frequently argued that, on the one hand, general grants are consistent with 'dual federalism' in which revenues are reassigned between levels of government, but jurisdictional competence remains unaltered, whereas on the other hand, specific grants are consistent with 'co-operative federalism' in which revenue assignment is coupled with sharing of responsibilities between government levels: a balance of national funding for

Table 12.1 Typology of grants (*After* Musgrave and Musgrave 1976)

Type of grant		Unrelated to need	Need-related
General			
	non-matching	1	5
	matching	2	6
Specific			
	non-matching	3	7
	matching	4	7

merit goods, local funding for local public goods, and so forth (Musgrave 1959; Oates 1972, 1977).

Both general and selective grants can be adjusted by matching require-ments. *Matching grants* in the US, termed conditional grants in Canada, are not extensively used in Europe, and require local government to contribute an equal or unequal proportion to the grant sum allocated by central govern-ment. *Non-matching grants* are unconditional and do not possess such requirements. The aim of matching is to induce a degree of local involvement, commitment, accountability, and responsibility for that particular expendi-ture programme. Non-matching and general, unconditional grants are more favoured in countries with a high degree of heterogeneity such as the US, Canada and Australia. Non-matching grants are also often preferred on grounds of equalization since it is easier for high-income than low-income areas to generate sufficient matching funds. On the other hand, matching and specific grants are often more applicable in smaller and unitary states with a high degree of local homogeneity in which the demands, standards, pre-ferences for services will be more similar between jurisdictions.

Grants can also be differentiated by the degree to which they are need-related. Need-related grants are allocated on the basis of a set of geographical differences in needs as defined in chapter 4, costs of servicing those needs as developed in chapter 5, and ability to pay as discussed in chapter 6, or a combination of these various elements of unit costs of needs and ability. Examples of such grants are the needs and resources elements of the UK Rate Support Grant, Canadian Equalization Grants and many US State Education Finance Grants. *Non-need-related grants* do not attempt to be equalizing and do not take geographical variations in unit costs of need or ability into account. Need assessment is a crucial element in equalization since grants affect the marginal return to expenditure in different programmes in different locations. Without need assessment and more especially, without need assessment based on the unit costs of different needs, grants set off disequilibrating forces between jurisdictions; for example by providing subsidies to higher income areas. Grants can also be distinguished as to whether they are *open* or *closed-ended*, i.e. whether transfers will finance all eligible requirements, or whether an upper limit of grant transfer has been set.

The usage of these different categories of grants derives from the motives which are similar to those in favour of strong local government discussed in chapter 11: e.g. the encouragement of local experimentation and national unity. But in more specific fiscal terms it is possible to identify nine motives which lead to the implementation of grant programmes. Of these, the primary impetus for establishment of grant programmes is usually one of equalization. Indeed this aim has been the subject of a number of state court actions in the United States (the most famous being the *Serrano v. Priest* case in California (see Coons *et al.* 1970)). Equalization may be concerned with equalizing provision for geographical variations in expenditure needs, public service costs, geographical fiscal ability and effort, or a combination of all three. In the spirit of aims of equality discussed in earlier chapters, such equalization should not be conceived as equalizing or nullifying the effect of individual or geographical differences *in toto*, but as nullifying differential effects of the benefits and burdens in the public finance system itself. Whatever the definition of equalization aimed at, it is only by mechanisms outside purely *local* fiscal conditions that it can be achieved, and grants are a major mechanism of such equalization. The primary grants used for such purposes are general block grants and general revenue-sharing allocated on the basis of need. Matching may be employed when it is sought to affect the balance of public and private choice in the local area, or where it is thought that local jurisdictions will direct the funds to other less equalizing uses. Matching is also used when equalization is aimed at single sectors only and then need-related matched grants or special revenue-sharing are often employed as in the case of the US HEW categorical grants.

A second motive for grants from higher level governments is that they can often achieve redistributional goals which are difficult to achieve in other ways. Whilst equalization aims at nullifying public finance impacts of need, cost and tax effort, redistribution aims at reallocating tax capacity or income. This draws us back to the issue of whether redistribution programmes should be solved by individually or geographically based programmes. This problem has been discussed elsewhere (pp. 40, 61) and it is only necessary here to re-state that some problems are better tackled by place-specific transfers, and others by person-specific transfers. Grants aimed at place-specific re-distribution may take many forms. When distribution problems are mainly questions of personal income and welfare, general non-matching grants or general revenue-sharing, based on assessed needs or inverse income capacity, are usually most appropriate. But when distribution problems are place-specific because of infrastructure, housing and industrial structure, special revenue-sharing or selective non-matching grants are allocated to needy areas using need indicators reflecting these problems.

A third motive for grants is that the involvement of higher level governments can stimulate the improvement of standards in local service provision: wider public finance goals are brought to bear on the management of local expenditure. This can also be related to motives for monitoring local performance of adequacy and efficiency of services. Selective matched grants are usually then employed. A fourth motive for involvement of higher level governments may be the stimulation of long-range development goals in lagging or declining local economies through renewing infrastructure, redirecting public or private investment, and improving local labour skills. Selective unmatched grants based on need would generally be employed in this case.

A fifth motive for higher level fiscal transfers is somewhat related to attempts to even out rates of economic growth and development. In a system of purely local government, there are forces of considerable magnitude which encourage under-investment. One such factor in the US is horizontal tax competition between jurisdictions for industry and business which encourages imprudent fiscal policies to attract industry. Another factor is the imprudence of local government with respect to long-term capital investment. This can arise either from domination by narrow-based local cliques, or from narrow, homogeneous but majority local views. In either case the tendency is for existing generations to put off needed capital spending and renewal, the loan servicing of which must be borne now for future needs and future generations (see chapter 10). In the US, examples abound of local capital bond issues which have failed to be enacted because of local resistance to carrying this burden of local debt. In this situation, restrictions rather than grants are often required, but selective matched grants can be usewhere local fiscal burden would otherwise be excessive.

Sixth, and related to the previous three motives, it is usually possible to define a level of national minimum standards of public services which should be available to everyone irrespective of their location. It is quite reasonable that national level government should be responsible for expenditures, through grants, for such national 'merit goods', that regional or state grants should be responsible for respective regional or state 'merit goods', and so forth. For such goods, matching non-need-related grants are normally used, which are either general or specific depending on the nature and extent of the merit goods. Occasionally, need-related grants may also be employed without matching, where there is considerable variation in local fiscal capacity. This is the approach of the United Kingdom Rate Support Grant.

A seventh motivation behind grants is as a means of intergovernmental fiscal co-operation or centralization. This can involve direction of aid towards provision of various levels of merit goods as discussed above, but also raises the questions of adequacy of local revenues, and the best apportionment of revenue sources between levels of government. Whilst most Western countries have experienced rapid expansion of services which are best organized at local levels, most of the high yielding revenue sources are usually best organized at national level (especially personal and corporate income tax). Hence to relieve the burden on local revenue sources (which are often regressive) and to provide a revenue-expenditure equalization between levels of government, it is obviously necessary to utilize some reallocation mechanism of grants or revenue-sharing. This is the primary motive for US revenue-sharing and for sharing of tax bases in Germany, Australia, Switzerland and Canada. It is also used for need-related matching grants which are general or selective depending on the extent of revenue mismatches.

An eighth, and related motive, is improved control by national governments over local fiscs in order to overcome the effects of locally perverse fiscal behaviour which runs counter to national policies of economic management.

Although the perversity factor has been over-emphasized, grants have been used to encourage local expenditures in times of recession in the US in the 1930s; more recently, in the 1970s, the US has employed an accelerated public works programme, CETA and counter-cyclical revenue-sharing grants for local government. In the UK, special development area status and job creation schemes have been used for similar purposes. Any grant programme can be used to pursue these aims, but frequently most emphasis is placed on matched and general grants. One important factor with the use of counter-cyclical grants is the difficulty of reducing or abolishing the grant with the return to better economic conditions. Thus such grants have become one important component in the displacement effect (Musgrave and Peacock 1958) noted in chapter 3.

A final, and important feature of grant programmes is their ability to limit, or to counteract, the effects of spillover of local benefits and taxes. This theory derives from Pigou (1947) and is generally referred to as the *compensation principle*. Local mechanisms for overcoming both spillover and tax exporting require co-operation between often competitive governments, or at least governments which are unconcerned with problems of other jurisdictions. In situations where equalization of benefits between jurisdictions is required to compensate for loss of benefits in other areas through spillovers, selective and matching grants can be used. In other cases, where it is sought to equalize differences in the local tax rates required to give equal levels of local service benefits, general unmatched grants are employed. The Pigou theory of the compensation principle has often been used to justify open-ended matching grants as an optimum grant procedure to overcome spillover and externalities. Break (1967), for example, shows that such grants must be categorical, with size related to spillover, with national level contributions equal to the ratio of external to total benefits, and open-ended to allow local flexibility: as Oates (1972) notes, spillovers do not stop at a particular level of service. However, the experience of practice with such grants in the US belies the theory. In that country they have been employed since 1911, thrust to importance by the Social Security Act of 1935, and now consume about 20% of all federal aid outlays mainly in Medicaid and Aid to Families with Dependent Children (AFDC). Analysis of these grants by Derthick (1975) and Beam (1978) demonstrates that they have led to underpricing of local services which has stimulated rapid expenditure growth. Moreover, the matching requirement has favoured high-income States, resulting in violent inequities in levels of service provision. They have also been extremely fiscally perverse, have been exploited by local politicians by substituting for other local expenditures, and have been characterized by extreme fraud and abuse. Hence, the use of grant payments to overcome geographical problems of benefit spillover is now somewhat clouded.

12.4 Intergovernmental revenue-sharing

Revenue-sharing and grants are both areas of vertical co-ordination between national, intermediate (State, provincial and regional), and local government. When intergovernmental grants are unconditional block grants with no strings as to application or use, grant programmes merge into general revenue-sharing. When intergovernmental grants are specific or categorical they merge into special revenue-sharing. Hence the distinction between revenue-sharing and grants rests mainly on the guaranteed flow (both in size and area) of revenue from higher to lower level governments which exists in the latter programme. This may take the form of assigning a guaranteed sum of centrally raised resources to local use. Alternatively, it may be an assignment of a specific central revenue source to local use. In each case revenue-sharing assigns to local jurisdictions a proportion of the revenue which cannot be effectively or efficiently tapped by local units. For example, personal and corporate income taxes are most efficiently collected at regional or national levels, but there is no reason to confine their use to this level of government.

The objectives of revenue-sharing are summarized well in the *Heller-Pechman Plan* proposed for the United States. This has six aims (US JEC 1967, p. 109):

(i) to strengthen the vitality, efficiency and independence of State and local government;

(ii) to relieve immediate fiscal pressures of State local finance and make their revenues more elastic to economic growth;

(iii) to increase the overall progressivity of federal, State and local taxation;

(iv) to reduce economic inequalities and fiscal disparities between State and local governments;

(v) to stimulate State-local tax effort;

(vi) to emphasize the plight of local and especially urban governments in distribution.

A major feature of these aims is that they are rooted in a belief in pluralism, decentralization, and local diversity. As Walter Heller states (US JEC 1967, p. 111) "There has to be a free flow of funds that the state and local governments can use for whatever purposes seem appropriate – that is for supporting the general structure of state and local government, for strengthening the fabric of state local government, for strengthening those functions which are not tied into matching federal grants". A second major feature of the Heller–Pechman proposal is concerned with attacking fiscal disparity at local level: aiding provision of local services on the basis of need in accordance with variable local pressures and preferences. Similar aims have been accorded to revenue-sharing in Germany, Austria, Switzerland, Canada and Australia. The emphasis of revenue-sharing is, then, like that of grants and other fiscal transfers, to achieve fiscal equity in decentralized and federal systems.

In practice revenue-sharing performs like a block grant programme but with guarantees: it is allocated from higher to lower level governments on the basis of a formula, but the total sum available for allocation is pre-set. The motivation for revenue-sharing programmes is also often similar to that of intergovernmental grants: equalization is a primary aim in the Canadian system of revenue-sharing, and is also emphasized, but to a lesser extent realized, in the United States system; equalization may also aid redistribution; revenue-sharing may also be used to meet national minimum standards, improve the adequacy and the elasticity of local finances, reduce fiscal diversity, and permit some compensation for intergovernmental spillovers. Revenue-sharing differs in motivation from grants, however, in that aims of stimulating local service provision and standards, improving developmental investment, and attaining greater central control, are less emphasized or are not obtainable. Break (1967) and US JEC (1967), for example, emphasize the importance of revenue-sharing in fostering independence and a higher degree of local autonomy whilst at the same time permitting intergovernmental co-operation.

The aims and motives of revenue-sharing have not been fully realized in any existing form of implementation. The Canadian system of revenue-sharing, implemented in 1957, places great emphasis on tax credits and equalizing grants as a means of equalization, but with revenue-sharing as a system for revenue co-ordination. Experience in the Canadian Federation suggests that revenue-sharing alone is inadequate to achieve goals of equalization and redistribution. Experience in other countries confirms this, and further discussion of revenue-sharing in the US, Canada, Germany and Australia is given in the next chapter. It is sufficient here to note that it has been a successful area of intergovernmental co-ordination, but because it favours rich over poor jurisdictions, has had to be supplemented increasingly by equalization grants which can be more directly targeted to local needs.

12.5 Intergovernmental deductibility, credits and negative income tax

Grant and revenue-sharing programmes often act as the major approaches to equalizing the operations of public finance systems, but two other approaches to co-ordination, based on tax deductibility and tax credits, are extremely useful in different contexts for solving specific co-ordination problems (Maxwell 1962).

Deductibility of local taxes from higher level assessments of tax liability is a particularly simple method of introducing vertical co-ordination of revenues, reducing revenue competition, and equalizing revenue burden across geographical areas. Deductibility permits allowances, in whole or in part, of local taxes from federal tax liability. In the US for example, both local and State personal income, death and inheritance taxes are permitted deductions. In that country deductions are allowed from corporate income tax for capital investment and this may be manipulated through accelerated depreciation allowances. Deductibility may also be combined with the more efficient central grant collection of taxes and apportionment to jurisdictions in the form of revenue raising. The total tax paid, T, is, then, $T = (Y - K - D)t$, where Y is income, K is the poverty level of exemptions, D is the deductions allowed, and t is the tax rate.

Tax credits instead of allowing removal of the proportion of expenditure or local taxation from income prior to the imposition of central taxation, permit a proportion or the whole of a given personal or corporate tax or expenditure to be subtracted from the total tax paid. The two measures differ in their effects on the marginal rate of taxation. Credits can be used at central, local or intermediate levels and can be restricted merely to credits for local taxes paid, or can apply to a wide range of expenditures on 'social goods'. Whereas deductions play an important role in US intergovernmental co-ordination, tax credits play a major role in Canadian federal–provincial co-ordination, and in West Germany. Credits for provincial, personal and corporate income taxes and estate duties in Canada are allowed against the equivalent federal taxes. This 'abatement', however, has been linked to sharing federal revenues from those sources, and is used as an alternative to revenue-sharing when the provinces wish to tax these bases themselves, as discussed in more detail in chapter 13.

Tax credits differ from deductions in their impact on equity. Deductions are allowable removals of expenditures (including local taxes) from income tax centrally *before* that central tax is exacted. Hence they have differential impact on different incomes. Expenditure of £100 on tax-deductible life insurance to an individual with small income will have the effect of removing the equivalent of £100 from taxation, but this will be a tax deduction at a much lower rate than for an individual on a much higher income (who is paying income tax at a higher marginal rate, but who is making an identical contribution to life insurance). The result of this, as shown in figure 12.5, is a system which provides least assistance to poor people, and to jurisdictions with a large percentage of poor people, and most assistance to wealthy people and wealthier jurisdictions. Hence as Maxwell (1962), Pogue (1974) and Sunley (1977) note, deductions have the effect of giving a subsidy of private costs in proportion to income. Credits, on the other hand, subtract from the final tax bill an equal or proportional amount for allowable expenditures. Hence the impact of credits on total tax paid T, is given by: $T = (Y - K)t - C$, where C is the credit and Y, K and t are defined as earlier above. This credit will be the same in terms of total money receipt whatever the marginal rate of taxation. With total credits for life insurance, as in the previous example, both high- and low-income earners receive the £100 credit. Hence, as shown in figure 12.5 credits have an equal or proportional effect on equity. It is also possible to scale allowable credits by income and make them progressive as shown in

331

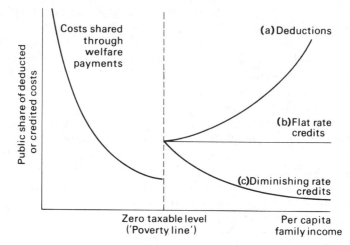

Figure 12.5 Relationship of level of tax credits or deductions to *per capita* family income. (After Pogue 1974.)

figure 12.5. From the equalization point of view, when it is desired to preserve progressivity in higher level government taxation, a credit will be preferred over a deduction. However, from the vertical co-ordination point of view, Shoup (1969) argues that a deduction is frequently favoured to a credit. Since deductibility reduces the lower level government taxes by a greater amount on higher income, this can be more effective than credits in retaining the more mobile high income residents and business.

The primary advantage of deductions and credits is that they both free local government from fear of loss of residents and businesses if they impose a tax. This encourages the expansion of local taxation areas which otherwise would be affected adversely by fiscal migration, and this has been important in the expansion of American States and Canadian provinces into the fields of estate, unemployment and personal income taxation. It allows local jurisdictions access to more flexible and progressive national revenue sources and reduces revenue overlapping both between jurisdictions and between local and higher level government. This also makes revenues more secure and progressive over-all. Credits and deductions also possess the advantages of being simple, usually much simpler than comparable grants and regulations. Moreover, they are directly targeted to individuals offsetting their service costs as a function of both individual and geographical factors. They can also be applied as negative deductions or credits (i.e. tax exactions) on individual actions which produce public dis-benefits, e.g. on pollution emissions by industrial firms. Indeed for individuals and for small firms, deductions and credits are far better than the ever-burgeoning body of regulations which seek to direct individual and economic activity, since they emphasize the role of the market and place incentives on particular patterns of behaviour. They are also less odious than the role of social security and other regulations employed to ensure fairness in grant and transfer payment apportionment.

However, there are six main disadvantages of deductions or credits. First, they induce a form of higher government involvement into new areas of action. Second, both deductions and credits erode the total tax base which ultimately requires new tax sources to be found. Third, they give incentive to individuals and employees to set up private services in competition with public ones. Fourth, deductions give aid to payers on the basis of expenditure and hence frequently favour middle and higher income groups. They also do nothing directly to effect equalization, and in the case of deductions, actually decrease equity. Fifth, there is the problem of deciding what expenditure should be allowable as credits. Life insurance and house purchase loans are almost universal allowances, but hospital and health insurance have been used in the United States since the 1940s, and education tuition fees are far less common allowances. Controversial issues are whether credit should be allowed for costs of journey-to-work, day care for children with working mothers, and the costs of solar energy installation. A final issue, related to what expenditures should be allowable, is how far deductions or credits should be permitted for private expenditures when a public service is available, e.g. in public and private education. Deductions and credits in this case could be interpreted as a subsidy to avoid the public system.

A special form of credit or deduction is *negative income tax* (NIT). This allows a range of expenditures on 'social goods' to be allowed as deductions or credits against central taxation. Such goods are those where either public service provision is used and charges result, or where the public provision would be justified by their social importance, but where private provision is used instead or in addition to public provision. Whilst deductions and credits for local taxes equalize on the revenue side, deductions for service expenses through NIT equalize on the expenditure side. Hence differences in individual and geographical benefits and costs can also be equalized.

The implementation of NIT moves individual and corporate burden assessment into the area of total income and total expenditure assessment: all fringe benefits, disbenefits, side payments, and expenditures are assessed in order to give an equitable co-ordination of local geographical and personal variation in cost, needs and burdens. The behaviour of NIT is shown in figure 12.6: separate taxation and social security (income supplements) schemes shown in figure 12.6a and b, are combined into a unified system as shown in figure 12.6c.

In general terms, NIT is somewhat related to equalizing grant payments based on total equalization (figure 12.3) except that now redistribution is directed to the individual rather than the geographical location. Thus the net tax paid or received, T, is given as $T = t(Y - K)$, where t is the tax rate, Y the income level, and K the poverty level of income. The differences of actual income and the poverty level given by the term $(Y - K)$ is frequently termed 'the

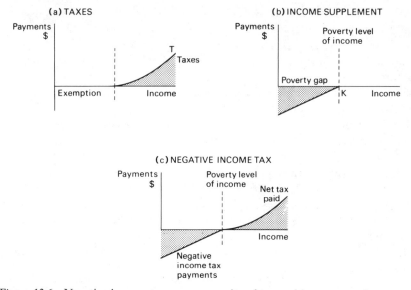

Figure 12.6   Negative income tax as a composite of tax and income supplements at given income levels.

poverty gap', but it can be either positive or negative: in the former case a tax is exacted on the individual and in the latter case a payment is made to the individual.

The major benefits of NIT are its simplicity and uniformity of treatment, its capacity to give a smooth progression of marginal taxes or benefits as individual income rises (overcoming the 'notch problem' which can act as a strong disincentive), and its ability to integrate individual and geographically variable benefits and burden into one composite and equalizing format. Moreover, it is possible to combine NIT with other specific and general transfer programmes aimed at targeting aid to specific client-groups, or to client-groups in specified locations. The *demogrant* concept, for example, directs such transfers to age groups, and *wage rates subsidies*, based on rates of pay and hours worked, direct aid on the basis of productivity and incentives (Browning 1975; Green 1967). But any properly structured form of transfer of benefits by taxation meets the general aims of directing aid to needs on an individual and geographical basis.

Despite its simplicity and other benefits, a number of technical problems arise in implementation of NIT (OECD 1974): how is the family unit defined, what is the size of allowances and credits to be allowed, and how progressive should each be; how is income defined; finally, how are differences in costs and burdens between individuals and locations to be assessed. In addition, NIT can severely undermine national management of stabilization and growth since flexibility in adjustment of taxation is limited. Its usefulness is also affected by national incentives and attitudes to welfare payments, and by

334

the relative role of income tax and of welfare payments in the national finances. It is understandable, for example, that NIT should have been discussed with more vigour in the UK, which possesses internationally high levels of both income tax and welfare benefits requiring integration (UK Government 1972), than in France or in North America.

12.6 Geographically differentiated taxes, direct expenditures, loans, and user charges

A variety of other horizontal and vertical intergovernmental co-ordination devices is available in addition to the grants, revenue-sharing, deductions, and credits discussed above. The most important categories are geographically differentiated taxes, direct higher level government expenditures, loans, and user charges. Each of these categories is discussed below.

SPATIALLY DIFFERENTIATED HIGHER LEVEL GOVERNMENT
TAXES AND CONTROLS

These are a special case of tax credits and deductability where differential, corporate or personal income tax rates are charged by central or intermediate level of governments as a function of spatial location. Although advocated by some writers in the United States (see, for example, Sunquist and Davis 1969), this mechanism has been primarily used in Canada and Europe. It is coordinative in that local variations in location costs, expenditure burdens, and revenue bases can be evened out by tax rates which reflect variations in burden, costs and in revenues raised. There are four categories of such policies:

(i) *corporate income tax adjustments*: accelerated depreciation allowances, tax reduction, grants, etc

(ii) *labour subsidies*: used extensively only in Britain from 1968 to 1976, a tax repayment to employers in depressed areas for each employee in manufacturing. Aimed at inducing a regional devaluation in labour costs (Kaldor 1970), it also had the effect of encouraging inefficient use of labour;

(iii) *labour mobility allowances*: used extensively in France and Germany, and to some extent in all of Western Europe, these are removal and retraining allowances encouraging labour mobility from lagging to growing regions;

(iv) *development restrictions*: Land use and development controls imposing limits on development in some locations rather than others, e.g. IDC and ODP controls in the UK, further discussion of these methods is given in chapter 14.

DIRECT INTERGOVERNMENTAL EXPENDITURES

These can be a means of co-ordination when, like preferential loans, expenditures are made in areas of high expenditure need using the wider and more progressive tax base available at national or intermediate level. They also have advantage of improving central control of stabilization and reducing local fiscal peversity. A prime example of such programmes in the

United States is the Roosevelt New Deal and the TVA. Subsequent areally based authorities directing public works resources preferentially to specific problem locations in the United States have been administered by various urban renewal authorities, the EDA and by various River Basin Commissions. The change in extent of these areas from 1966 to 1977 is shown in figure 12.7. As can be seen from this figure, a major problem with the

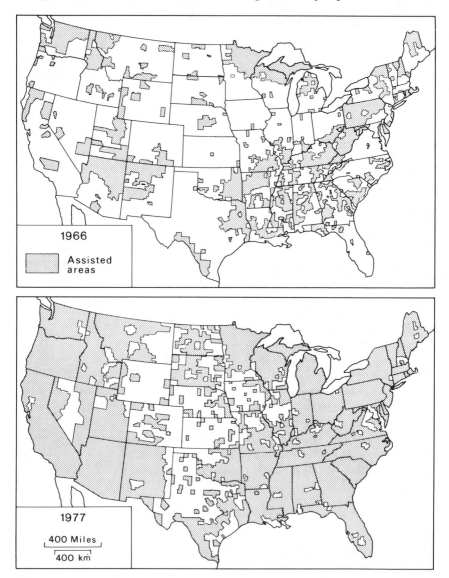

Figure 12.7 Areas qualifying for assistance from the US Economic Development Administration in 1966 and 1977. (*Source:* US EDA *Annual Reports.*)

programme has been the way in which the eligible areas have been increased so that now the degree of direct targeting of expenditures has become greatly reduced.

USER CHARGES

These are a highly co-ordinative device since they directly relate services received to the bearer of the revenue burden. They are particularly favoured for achieving horizontal co-ordination. User charges cannot be employed, however, for redistribution programmes and for expenditures where a large amount of shifting of fiscal incidence would be undesirable. Hence they are not a complete co-ordination device. There are three co-ordinative roles of user charges. First, for individual use, charges allocate burdens to areas of benefit irrespective of the location of purchase and use. Second, government purchases of services from other types or levels of government promotes both vertical and horizontal co-ordination which is particularly important in overcoming intergovernmental spillovers of benefits and exporting of tax burdens. This is a case of Pigou's (1947) compensation principle. A third co-ordinative effect is the use of special service districts exacting special tax or user charges on the basis of user benefits. Such special districts are a major feature of US local government, where in 1972 there were 23,000 such special service districts performing 18 major categories of single services, and a number of multiple service categories as well. The services range from sanitation through fire, police, sewerage, water, and utilities, to flood control and conservation. In the UK Regional Water Authorities and utility districts for gas, electricity and telephones are the only major counterparts.

LOANS

Loans can be obtained at local level in two ways: from floating bond issues, and from higher level governments. Loans raised from selling local and municipal bonds and securities are very successful when the local economy is rapidly growing or fiscally healthy, but are most difficult to raise when the local economy is in most need, e.g. when subject to declining local tax base and heavy needs for infrastructure and environmental renewal, or when beset by severest fiscal distress (see chapter 10). Loans derived from higher level governments are not subject to these limitations, and they are co-ordinative, in allowing the equalization of needs for capital finance despite differential ability to raise that capital. Such loans can be accomplished in two ways. First, by preferential rules for local bond issues, e.g. the tax-free exemptions for interest on municipal bonds granted in the US. Second, there may be specific capital equalization schemes. This is linked with spatially differentiated tax structures, and with direct higher level government expenditures, discussed above. Such schemes may take the form of higher level government underwriting of local credit, as in the case of State and federal aid to New York City in the 1970s. Alternatively, the higher level government can act as a lender of last resort to those jurisdictions unable to borrow at reasonable rates elsewhere. This approach has also underlain proposals for urban and rural development banks particularly in the United States. In many cases there are also sets of general capital aid programmes to localities which are not predicated on fiscal distress. These programmes are often not oriented specifically towards co-ordination or equalization, but are instead allocating capital finance on a project-by-project basis as in the UK Public Works and Loan Board.

12.7 Conclusion

The primary aim of this chapter has been to describe methods of inter-governmental co-ordination which aim to improve the equality in the distribution of public service benefits in relation to need, and of the distribution of revenue burdens in relation to ability to bear them. Fiscal transfers between levels of government, as we have seen in chapter 4, are essential to the attainment of goals of equity in federal and decentralized systems, they are a means of reducing interjurisdictional spillovers, and they are crucial in their impacts on total incomes and cycles of local poverty and growth. Whilst this chapter has discussed the theory of such transfers, the next chapter will discuss the experience of a variety of intergovernmental transfer programmes in a range of Western countries.

13

Fiscal co-ordination in practice

German Labour Representative: "I've never been down a mine, so you'll have to explain this to me. You say that you buy the carbide, but the miners buy the lamps?"

Company Manager: "That is correct."

Representative: "I see. I suppose you have an office above the mine where the miners work."

Manager: "Of course."

Representative: "And in the office, you supply the carbide, but the clerks have to buy their own lamps?"

Manager: "Certainly not. In the office we use electric lights."

Representative: "Oh, I see. You supply the electricity, but the clerks have to buy their bulbs and fixtures."

Quoted from American arbitration tribunal by W.A.R. Leys, 1952,
Ethics for Policy Decisions.

13.1 Fiscal co-ordination in a range of Western economies

The practice of fiscal co-ordination between levels and types of governments, like that of wage bargaining quoted above, is often arbitrary. However, the analysis of different fiscal co-ordination practices in different countries is the only means of providing comparative information on the effects, performance, and properties of different co-ordination procedures. Such international comparisons are complex since revenue and expenditure mixes are not independent of local social, economic, political and environmental factors. Moreover, the development of the revenue system, equalization procedures, and apportionment of responsibilities between levels of government usually results from a complex history. Equalization in particular usually involves a very slow but steady evolution in which rich economic groups and locations have been induced to make progressively higher contributions to the public fisc, often in exchange for other political and economic trade-offs. Hence in different countries, different imperatives for change in public finance allocation exist, and distinctions in culture and political backgrounds make different financial arrangements more necessary or acceptable.

The analysis of intergovernmental fiscal co-ordination in different countries can be approached from two points of view: first, by examining how each transfer procedure is operated in a range of instances; second, by examining the balance of mix of fiscal transfers in countries offering different economic,

339

Table 13.1 Transfer programmes as a percentage of total public expenditure in nine Western economies. Direct comparisons should be treated with care. The total includes minor programmes not detailed separately.

| Country | No. of regions and date | % total public expenditure | | Shared revenue reallocated | Federal collection of local taxes | Tax deductions and credit | Spatially differentiated higher level taxes[26] | Horizontal transfers | Total transfer as% of local expenditure[20] |
| | | Grants | | | | | | | |
		Specific	General						
Australia[15, 27]	6 1977/8	9.9[27]	0.1[4]	14.9[6]	√[21]	—	7.5	—	40.1
Canada[15]	10 1973/4	9.9[1]	3.1[5]	5.9[7]	√[22]	5.9[12]	4.8	—	31.5
USA[15]	48 1973/4	7.5	2.0	1.2[8]	—	—	26.0	—	19.0
UK[15, 19]	1976	2.1[2]	14.5	—	√[23]	—	27.2[13]	—	47.7
Switzerland[15]	25 1972	minor	minor	2.1[9]	√[24]	—	N/A	—	10.0
Germany[18]	10 1973	5.5	1.6	3.4[10]	—	—	23.4	5.8[14]	10.7
France[15]	21 1974	4.4[3]	—	6.4[11]	—	—	44.5	—	20.0
Denmark[16]	1977	15.0	6.5	—	√[25]	—	N/A	—	21.5
Sweden[17]	1976	6.6	1.2	—	—	—	N/A	—	12.4

Notes and Sources:
(1) Alternative estimates are 14 to 16%, see Carter (1971).
(2) Specific and supplementary grants (police, housing, etc.).
(3) French infrastructure and social assistance grants.
(4) Financial Assistance, Special Revenue Assistance and Special Equalization Grants.
(5) Equalization grants.
(6) Income tax sharing from 1976.
(7) Canadian revenue-sharing *and* tax credits.
(8) General revenue-sharing.
(9) Direct tax on corporate and individual incomes, and capital gains.
(10) VAT total entering into transfers.

(11) French **VRTS** payroll sharing.

(12) as in note 7.

(13) Alternative estimate of SPN (1976) is 4.6%.

(14) German *Länderfinanzausgleich*.

(15) Source: EEC (1977) vol II.

(16) Source: Lotz (1978).

(17) Source: Ministry of Local Government, Stockholm (1978), and statement of the Swedish Budget (1978/79).

(18) EEC (1977), and Reissart (1978).

(19) Layfield report (*UK Committee of Enquiry on Local Government Finance* 1976).

(20) From Pommerehne (1977), excludes revenue-sharing and loans.

(21) Income tax.

(22) Income, corporation and estate duty taxes.

(23) Swiss anticipatory tax, military service exemptions tax, and stamp duty amounting to 1.98% of public expenditure.

(24) Income, industry and trade tax, corporation tax.

(25) Income tax.

(26) Defined by notes 6 to 12 of table 13.2.

(27) Commonwealth Government of Australia (1978).

political and constitutional traditions. The former approach loses the important interplay and trade-off between the use of one transfer device rather than another, whilst the latter approach loses direct comparative emphasis. In this chapter each approach is used to some extent. In the present introductory section, direct comparisons of intergovernmental co-ordination are drawn from a range of Western countries. Then in the following sections, fiscal co-ordination practised in various countries (the UK, Canada, Germany, the US, and Australia) is examined in order to emphasize the balance and mix of different central, intermediate, and local level patterns of transfers and revenue or expenditure responsibility.

The relative emphasis placed on different transfer programmes in nine Western countries is shown in table 13.1. Direct comparisons in this table should be treated with some care: some double counting is present (e.g. of tax credits and revenue-sharing in the case of Canada); some of the figures are approximate; there is a lack of data availability in some countries; there are differences in definitions and statistical procedures for rendering information; and the data refer to single years. Despite these difficulties, however, the broad pattern of transfer programmes is correct and shows four major features. First, and most striking, there is little uniformity in the transfer schemes adopted indicating the importance of local historical, political and cultural practice. There is only a small degree of support for the existence of any *general* mechanisms of intergovernmental transfers. Second, constitutional factors have some effect on the transfer programmes adopted. Transfers form a greater proportion of local finances in unitary countries, especially France and Italy, but are also significant in the Australian and Canadian Federations. In addition, the transfers in unitary countries are heavily biased towards direct

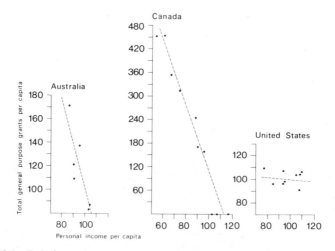

Figure 13.1 Relation of general purpose grants to regional *per capita* income. (*Source*: EEC 1977.)

central expenditure, although grant programmes (especially in the UK) are also significant. Third, transfers in federal countries are highly varied with grants, revenue-sharing, tax deductions or credits, and direct expenditures all playing important roles in different countries. Finally, revenue co-ordination involving central collection of local taxes with no transfers, is widely employed, but limited in application to federal countries.

The wide differences in transfer programmes which aim at achieving a measure of central–local co-ordination in governmental finances will have markedly different effects on the allocation, distribution, stabilization and growth functions of public finance. With respect to these functions, however, there is little comparative research from which it is possible to draw general conclusions. For stabilization and growth effects, we leave discussion until chapter 14 where intergovernmental transfer programmes are examined within the context of total fiscal incidence and regional balance. For allocation aspects we are dependent upon the results of a number of research studies on specific programmes undertaken mainly in the US (Gramlich and Galper 1973; Musgrave and Musgrave 1976). These results show that in the US general block grants and revenue-sharing tend to lead to a wide range of substitution effects (see p. 375) of tax reduction or stabilization which has important impacts on income and hence the local multiplier. Specific grants and direct expenditures, on the other hand, have important price effects. The cost of a specific public good or service funded is reduced to local consumers which encourages greater use and hence a further increase in local public expenditure need. But the extent of these effects depends, as noted in chapter 12, on the local price elasticity of demand, the ratio of transfer funding to total cost, and the extent to which the transfers are open- or closed-ended.

Turning to the impact of different transfer programmes on the distribution of public finance between individuals and locations, a great deal more international comparative data are available. Here, the redistributional effects of transfer programmes are compared using two approaches below. First, graphic and statistical comparisons are made of major transfer programmes in different countries. Second, redistribution measures are used to provide comparative redistribution statistics. The results reported below draw heavily on the important report by the EEC (EEC 1977) which has made the first major step in the area of international comparisons of local finance programmes and co-ordinative devices.

Figures 13.1 to 13.3 give graphical comparisons of the respective re-distribution effects of general purpose grants, specific purpose grants and direct intergovernmental expenditures in a range of countries. Each of these figures is a plot of the respective geographical transfer payments received against the personal *per capita* incomes of each jurisdiction. The figures aim to reveal the degree to which the grant is equalizing with respect to fiscal capacity as measured by *per capita* incomes, and thus corresponds to the hypothetical forms of equalization grants given in figures 12.1 to 12.4 with which they may

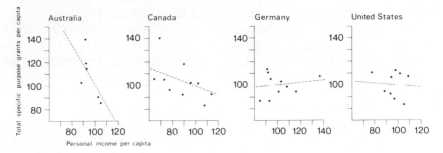

Figure 13.2 Relation of specific purpose grants to regional *per capita* income. (*Source:* EEC 1977.)

be compared. Other measures of fiscal capacity can be used, but *per capita* income provides a simple and readily available tool in international comparisons. Similarly, these transfer programmes can also be evaluated against need, but since appropriate need measures would differ considerably between programmes, no attempt is made here to evaluate need equalization, despite its importance.

In the figures, the slope of the regression lines on each graph, when expressed in standardized units, provides a comparative measure of the elasticity of each transfer programme with income. A negative slope indicates a redistributive (equalizing) transfer programme, a positive slope indicates a transfer programme which is proportional to income and is not equalizing.

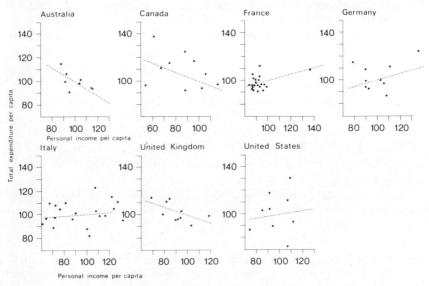

Figure 13.3 Relation of regionally relevant direct expenditures to regional *per capita* incomes. (*Source:* EEC 1977.)

344

Table 13.2 Elasticity of government transfers with regional personal *per capita* income. (*Sources:* EEC 1977; except for UK which is estimated from data in SPN 1976.)

| Country | Date | Elasticity measures with respect to personal per capita incomes within each region | | | |
		General grants	Specific grants	Revenue-sharing	Direct expenditures
France	1970	—	− 0.11[4]	0.94[5]	0.27[6]
UK	1964/76			—	− 0.32[7]
Italy	1973	—	—	—	0.28[8]
Germany	1973	− 7.39[1]	0.10	—	0.26[9]
Australia	1973/4	− 3.62[2]	− 1.68	—	− 0.59[10]
Canada	1973	− 8.39[3]	− 0.36	—	− 0.39[11]
USA	1974/5	—	− 0.68	− 0.59	0.02[12]

Notes:
[1] German supplementary grants.
[2] Australian Financial Assistance, Special Revenue Assistance and Special Grants.
[3] Equalization grants only.
[4] Weighted average of French infrastructure and operating grants.
[5] French VRTS.
[6] French current and capital expenditure and social security.
[7] UK current and capital expenditure and agricultural subsidies.
[8] Italian social security, public enterprises, wages, salaries and capital.
[9] German direct federal consumption and social security.
[10] Australian social security.
[11] Canadian social security.
[12] US direct expenditures and transfers by federal government excluding military contracts.

The elasticity estimates of these slopes are given in table 13.2. A number of general conclusions can be drawn from figures 13.1 to 13.4. General purpose grants are, on the whole, highly regressive with income and hence strongly equalizing. The major exception is the UK where the equalization possible in the Rate Support Grant needs and resources elements is heavily restricted by hold-harmless provisions. Specific grants are also equalizing, but are generally less regressive with income. For revenue-sharing and direct intergovernmental expenditures, there is not the same degree of generality. Revenue-sharing in France and Canada is more or less proportional to income, and this is to be expected since most programmes are aimed at merely apportioning central funds for use by lower level governments. In Germany and the US a more explicit redistribution policy has underlain implementation of revenue-sharing, although the effect on redistribution in the US is fairly mild. Direct intergovernmental expenditures, although variable, have usually fairly mild effects on distribution. The most significant redistribution is obtained in Australia, Canada, and the UK, whilst the countries which run strongest counter to redistribution are Italy and Germany. In the case of Germany this is largely offset by grants and revenue-sharing, but in the case of Italy, which

Table 13.3 Degree of redistribution between regions in seven countries. (*Source:* EEC 1977, p. 127.) Germany excludes Berlin

Country	No. of regions	Date	Change in Gini coefficient of per capita income inequality (average of government transfers)		Redistribution power of government transfers	
(1) Unitary states						
France	21	1969/70	52 ⎫		54 ⎫	
UK	10	1964	31 ⎬	42	36 ⎬	46
Italy	20	1973	44 ⎭		47 ⎭	
(2) Federal states						
Germany	10	1970/73	39 ⎫		29 ⎫	
Australia	6	1971/74	53 ⎬	36	53 ⎬	35
Canada	10	1969/74	28 ⎥		32 ⎥	
USA	48	1969/74	23 ⎭		28 ⎭	
Average				39		40

has no substantial transfer programmes in any other sector, intergovernmental expenditures are clearly highly unequalizing.

A number of comparative statistics which describe the differences in degree of equalization and redistribution in transfer programmes in different countries are available. The two most important of these are, first, a weighted measure of change-in-Gini-coefficient, and second, an unweighted measure of the redistribution power ratio (EEC 1977, ch. 5). Both measures are discussed in appendix 1.

The overall redistributive effects of all major intergovernmental transfers traced in the 1977 EEC study using these two measures are shown in table 13.3. From this table it can be seen that the data given by the Gini coefficient and redistributive power ratio are broadly comparable. The higher each statistic measures, the higher is the degree of redistribution due to transfers. A high degree of variability exists between the degree of redistribution achieved in each country for which data are tabulated, with the lowest levels of redistribution of central level transfers in the US, Germany, and Canada, and the highest levels of redistributive transfers in Australia, France and Italy. The differences in the magnitude of these transfers reflects three factors. First, there is a small degree of relationship to whether a country is federal or unitary in constitutional structure, with unitary states having a slightly higher level of redistributive transfers. Second, there are differences in the degree of variation in *per capita* incomes. Referring back to figures 13.1 to 13.3 it can be seen that high levels of redistribution reflect to some extent high interjurisdictional variability in *per capita* incomes (as in Italy and Australia) and low levels of

Table 13.4 Redistribution measures of revenue and expenditure in eight Western countries. (Source: EEC 1977, pp. 130–32)

Country		No. of regions	Date	Revenues	Direct expenditures	Expenditures			Redistribution measure
						General grants and revenue–sharing	Specific grants	Total	
Unitary states	France	21	1969–70	18.5		32.6		51.1	Gini Coefficient
	UK	10	1964	–1.6		36.0		36.2	
	Italy	20	1973	0.2		48.4		46.8	
Average of unitary states				6.4		39.4		45.8	
Federal states	Germany	11	1970–3	0.8	17.3	9.4	1.4	28.9	
	Australia	6	1971–4	2.7	11.8	27.1	11.2	52.8	
	Canada	10	1969–4	2.4	6.7	15.4	7.2	31.7	
	USA	48	1969–4	8.5	12.1	1.0	6.2	27.8	
	Switzerland	25	1967	–1.2	23.2	–	–	22.0	
Average of federations				3.5	12.4	13.3	6.2	35.3	
Unitary states	France	21	1969–70	20.7		31.7		52.4	Redistribution Ratio
	UK	10	1964	–1.8		32.9		31.1	
	Italy	20	1973	–1.8		45.3		43.5	
Average of unitary states				5.4		36.9		42.3	
Federal states	Germany	11	1970–3	–3.0	25.4	14.5	2.0	38.9	
	Australia	6	1971–4	9.4	9.0	20.4	14.2	53.0	
	Canada	10	1969–4	2.6	5.1	13.0	7.7	28.4	
	USA	48	1969–4	6.6	9.9	0.6	3.8	20.9	
	Switzerland	25	1967	0.7	10.3	–	–	9.6	
Average of federations				4.0	13.0	12.1	6.7	35.8	

distribution reflect low variability in jurisdiction or *per capita* income (as in the UK and Germany). Third, there are differences in the relative magnitude of central, and State or local finances. Referring to table 11.2 it can be seen that redistributive transfers are lower in those countries in which state and local expenditure levels are relatively high (e.g. Canada, US and Germany) and they are higher in those countries where state and local expenditure levels are relatively low (e.g. France, the UK and Italy). These differences to some extent reflect back to differences in constitutional structure.

Turning to the redistributive power in different transfer programmes, table 13.4 shows the Gini coefficients and redistributive power ratios for a range of countries and the transfer categories of revenue-sharing, general grants, specific grants, and direct expenditures. The redistributional impact of revenue raising through spatially progressive taxes has no relation to constitutional structure: it is highest in France, Australia, Canada and the US, and lowest in the UK, Italy and Germany. On the expenditure side, however, differences in redistributional effect reflect the same three factors as for the aggregate data: constitutional differences, differences in regional variability of *per capita* incomes, and differences in the balance of central and local expenditure. Direct expenditures and general purpose grants are usually the most redistributive; this reflects support from central salaries, social security support with its concentration in regions with low *per capita* incomes, and conscious aims of redistribution as in the needs or inverse capacity measure of the UK Rate Support Grant, French VRTS, US Revenue-Sharing, and German and Canadian Equalization Grants. It can be expected that specific grants play a more minor role in equalization since they often attack very limited expenditure programmes which are not very amenable to spatial manipulation, e.g. police protection, transport grants, education, health, and welfare.

With these general comparative data in mind, the rest of this chapter is concerned with examining in detail five examples of fiscal co-ordination in practice. The UK is examined first in section 13.2 as a case of a centralized State with relatively simple intergovernmental relations in which fiscal co-ordination consists of mainly specific and general purpose grants, plus loans and regulatory controls. This is followed in section 13.3 by discussion of the Canadian case in which a fairly classical federal structure has emerged with strong provincial power, weak local government, and only reserve or balancing powers at federal level. In sections 13.4, 13.5 and 13.6 three more complex federations are examined for the respective cases of the US, Germany and Australia. In each of these cases a wide variety of revenue-sharing, credits, grants and horizontal transfers is present. Because of the different historical, cultural, political and constitutional character of each country, the examples discussed are in no sense typical, but they do give indications of the different intergovernmental arrangements in centralized and federal states.

13.2   Fiscal co-ordination in the United Kingdom

The UK is a centralized state in which local and regional authorities possess devolved rather than federal powers. As de Smith (1971, p. 409) notes, the relationship is a partnership, but "between the rider and the horse". Hence, ultimate power rests finally in Westminster. The motives for such central control have been five-fold: improvements in local management efficiency, keeping the national budget and public expenditure in balance, maintaining central demand management of the economy as a whole, equalizing regional growth rates, and achieving national policies of minimum standards. Despite these features, however, there is a considerable measure of autonomy for the two levels of local authorities (Counties and Districts). In fact, there is no central control of levels of local expenditure or of allocation between spending programmes, although dependence on central government transfers and directives reduces this independence in practice. The fiscal arrangement between these various levels of government has a very long history, but in its present form derives from the *Local Government Act* (1972) implementing in 1974 a consolidated and new form of local government. There are also a number of unelected special purpose governments for administration of water, health, public utilities, etc. Despite its recency, however, there has been considerable criticism of the local government structure which, together with the lack of a regional tier in England, is likely to lead to further demands for changes. At present, there is a four-fold structure of local government. First, in rural areas, the District is subordinate to the County level which has the most power and liaises directly with the Westminster government. Second, in urban metropolitan areas, the Metropolitan Counties are subordinate to the Districts. Third, in London there is a separate arrangement in which there is a more equal division of power between the Districts (London boroughs) and the County level of the Greater London Council (GLC). Fourth, in Scotland, Regions replace the County level with the major functions, whilst three islands have total region plus district power. The various Metropolitan and non-Metropolitan Counties are shown in figure 13.4. The relative magnitude of revenue-raising and expenditure at each level is shown in table 13.5 together with the general expenditure categories for which each level of government is responsible. In Scotland and Wales it was proposed that devolution would lead to the government structure being supplemented by a Regional Assembly which would receive the total allocation of grants given to local authorities in that region, but could make reallocations, especially in the areas of environment and transport. This structure, rejected by referendum in 1979, may be implemented at some future date.

The sources of revenue at local level are very restricted in comparison to federal countries. Only the property tax (the rates), and user charges, are

Figure 13.4 Metropolitan and non-Metropolitan counties in England and Wales, and Scottish regions since local government reorganization in 1974.

Table 13.5 Division of fiscal responsibilities between local authorities in Great Britain, 1976. (*Source: UK Committee of Enquiry into Local Government Finance* 1976)

| Level of government and major functions (1976) | Revenue (%) | | | | Expenditure (% of total local expenditure) | Division of expenditure between tiers (%) |
	General grants	Specific grants	Property tax domestic	commercial		
ENGLAND AND WALES						
Metropolitan Counties (6) (Housing, transport, fire, police, refuse disposal consumer protection)	33	23	26	28	4	20
Metropolitan Districts (36) (Education, personal social services, housing, refuse collection, environment)	67	1	13	19	16	80
Non-Metropolitan Counties (47) (Education, personal social services, transport, police, fire, refuse disposal)	61	7	14	18	42.5	85
Non-Metropolitan Districts (333) (Housing, public transport, refuse collection)	41	6	24	29	7.5	15
GLC (1) (Arts, libraries, fire, refuse, transport)	9	16	22	53	9	45
London Boroughs (33) (Education, environment, housing, police, social services)	59	3	11	27	11	55
SCOTLAND						
Regions (9) (Education, transport, roads, police, fire, water, social work)	67	5	12	16	8.5	85
Districts (53) (and Islands) (3) (Youth employment, housing, environment, refuse)	50	3	21	26	1.5	15
Total number of jurisdictions	522					

available at local level and must be supplemented by local bond issues and intergovernmental grants; a proposal for a local income tax in the Layfield Report (*UK Committee of Enquiry into Local Government Finance* 1976) having been rejected. At present there is no finance at regional level, but central grants have been awarded (*Lord President of the Council* 1977); proposals for autonomous regional finance, or precepts on local authorities (*UK Royal Commission on the Constitution* 1973), have always been rejected. Despite their small revenue base, local authorities are responsible for about a quarter of UK public expenditure, especially in the sectors of education, housing, environmental services, police, social services, roads, and transport. The strong dependence of the property tax derives from a long history beginning with the special levies of the 13th century, formalized by the *Elizabethan Poor Law* of 1597 and the *Poor Relief Act* (1601) (Cannan 1912), enlarged by rapid growth of special levies of the 19th century, and finally codified in the *Rating and Valuation Act* (1925) and *Local Government Act* (1929). Its dominance in England has undoubtedly been responsible for its institution in other English-speaking countries.

Fiscal co-ordination in the UK involves four mechanisms: specific grants, general grants, capital loans and transfers, and regulations. Of these, general grants are the major component of transfers and have grown to an increasing importance; from 34% of total local authority income in 1949, to 45% in 1974. The Local Property Tax yields a further 28% of local income, and user charges and other income the final 27% (in 1974). The structure of the allocation procedure of specific and general grants (the Rate Support Grant) between the various levels of government is shown in figure 13.5.

Specific grants were initiated in 1835 for the prison service, increased rapidly in the 19th century and up to the 1950s, but since then have steadily declined in relative importance. They constitute about 10% of total grants, and about 6% of total local finance (in 1978). The main use of such grants at present is for finance of police (60% of specific grants, covering 50% of local police expenditure) and housing. There are other minor components for parks, land reclamation, pollution control, and so forth. The housing grants are the major category and the most complex. They are composed of four main elements. First, public housing improvement grants are allocated through regional offices of the Westminster Department of the Environment to local authorities which make bids; some preferential intra-regional allocations are made by the regional offices based on crude measures of need. Second, grants to private home owners are in part mandatory and in part discretionary. The level of grants available depends on local authority definition of General Improvement Areas, Housing Action Areas, and Priority Neighbourhoods, the order of which accords with increasing aid. Housing subsidies are a third component in housing grants designed to encourage local house building. They have five components based on the past levels of support, cost per dwelling, and the definition of housing stress areas. The

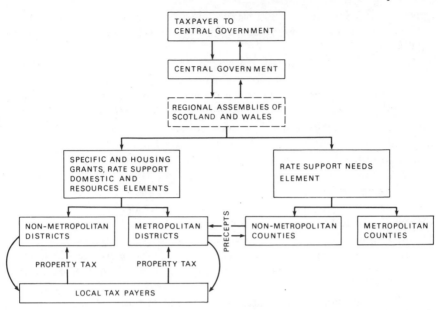

Figure 13.5 Flows of general and specific grants and taxes between levels of government in England and Wales (including proposed regional assemblies).

fourth component of housing slum clearance subsidies attempts to direct specific aid to locations in need, whilst the final component, an expanding town subsidy, directs aids to growth areas amounting to a 78% subsidy.

General grant transfers were instituted in the form of 'assigned revenues' in 1888 which were consolidated into general exchequer contribution block grants in the *Local Government Act* (1929). Their aim was to relieve the pressure of burdens on local productive industry and individuals. These block grants were distributed using a formula which attempted to equalize between rich and poor local authorities on the basis of the number of children, differences in property tax paid, numbers of unemployed, and population density. This early provision was supplemented by specific aids to the unemployed in the *Unemployment Act* (1938), and to depressed areas in the *Special Areas Act* (1934), and in subsequent regional policy legislation (see chapter 14). The form of the present block grants transfers derives from the 1929 Act as modified by the *Local Government Act* (1948) which established an Exchequer Equalization Grant. The grant payable under this legislation was calculated as the ratio of local expenditure to the national average *per capita* tax base, multiplied by the difference of the jurisdiction's *per capita* tax from the national average. The *per capita* term was calculated using weighted population, which counted children under 15 twice, and allowed for geographical variation in population density (Williams 1958–9). This was modified to become a Rate Deficiency Grant in 1958, which then became the

353

present Rate Support Grant in 1966. Each of these grants made some attempt to equalize between geographical variation in jurisdictional need and tax capacity.

The Rate Support Grant, in the period since the 1974 reorganization of local government, consists of three elements: domestic, needs, and resources. The total size of the Rate Support Grant derives from subtracting from the total central finance assigned to local authorities (excluding housing subsidies and mandatory higher education student grants) the levels of specific grants and grants for national parks. (i) The *domestic element*, about 15% of the total, instituted in the *Local Government Act* (1966) is a subsidy to domestic rate payers as against non-domestic (commercial) ratepayers which reduces the rate of residential property tax. The subsidy has stood at $18\frac{1}{2}$p per £ of assessed property value in England and 36p in Wales since 1974. (ii) The *needs element* is the largest component (about 60%) of the Rate Support Grant. It attempts to achieve equalization between jurisdictions on the basis of their differing expenditure needs using a needs formula to determine allocation. The formula used has varied considerably over the period since 1974 and the various 'need indicators' which have been employed are shown in table 5.2, where the definition of need has been analysed in more detail. The most significant indicators are the numbers of people in various levels of education or requiring social services, but other interesting components are indicators which seek to allow for geographical variations in the costs of living (wage rates), for rural–urban differences (population density), and for levels of unemployment. The need indicators used in any year are largely decided at a political level in discussions between the Westminster government represented by the Secretary of State for the Environment, and the various Local Authority Associations (Association of County Councils, Association of District Councils, Association of Metropolitan Authorities, National Association of Local Councils, and the London Boroughs Association). The weights used to relate the size of need indicator in any jurisdiction to the level of grant received are determined by a multiple regression analysis in which the dependent variable is last year's local expenditure, and the independent variables are last year's indicators of need, i.e.

$$Y_i(t) \quad = \quad a \quad + \quad b_1 \quad X_{1i}(t) \quad + \ldots + b_n \quad X_{ni}(t).$$

$Y_i(t)$ public expenditure in jurisdiction i at time t	a intercept	b_1 first need coefficient	$X_{1i}(t)$ first need indicator in jurisdiction i at time t	b_n nth need coefficient	$X_{ni}(t)$. nth need indicator in jurisdiction i

The weights are then applied to the distribution of the fixed sum set aside by the Westminster government for needs. In addition, the needs formula has since 1974 been subject to a 60 to 70% hold-harmless provision which restricts

354

the allocations to jurisdictions each year to be at least equal to 60 or 70% of last year's allocations. Clearly, then, little true equalization of expenditure needs has been achieved. (iii) The *resources element* (about 25% of the total general grant) is an attempt to achieve an equalization between jurisdictions on the basis of their variable tax capacity. The local capacity is measured by the total *per capita* property tax base (*per capita* rate values). This is then compared with the national *standard rateable value per head* defined by the Westminster government. A resource element grant is paid only to those jurisdictions falling below this standard, and hence this grant element is a form of *deficiency payment* (see figure 12.4). Tax capacities vary a great deal in the UK; measured in terms of rateable value per head, they vary from £43 in Rhondda to £35,000 in the City of London for commercial tax payers, and from £23 in Rhondda to £220 in Westminster for domestic ratepayers. In addition, the distribution of Rate Support Grant within London is made under a similar but different arrangement (Jenkins and Rose 1976) which includes horizontal transfers between jurisdictions within the GLC (the London Equalization Scheme).

The distribution of the Rate Support Grant between local authorities has become a complicated and politically vexed issue. Various studies have pointed to the influence of the controlling political party of Westminster (Cripps and Godley 1976), allocations favouring rural areas with a Conservative government, and urban areas with a Labour one. Whether from this feature or not, changes to the formula for the needs element of the grant since 1974 have resulted in a very significant shift from rural to Metropolitan areas under a Labour administration (see Jackman and Gibson 1978; Jackman and Sellars 1977, Table 2). Figure 13.6 shows the general relation of Rate

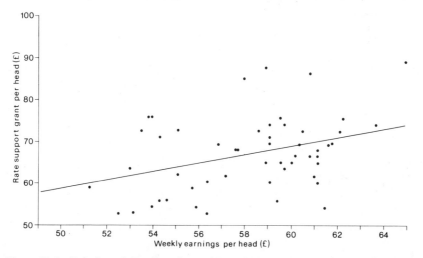

Figure 13.6 Relation of the allocations of Rate Support Grant to local tax capacity (*per capita* rateable value) in 1975.

Support Grant allocations to variations in local tax capacity (local personal wages). The allocation is a near proportional one, or even slightly regressive with geographical variation and incomes; a pattern which corresponds to the form of individual incidence of local property tax shown in figure 8.4. Various studies have been made of the incidence of the Rate Support Grant and its relationship to local need. Most of these have been critical of the present method of allocation (Jackman and Sellars 1977, 1978; Jenkins and Rose 1976; Rose 1978). A typical set of conclusions has been drawn from the North West region of Britain by SPNW (1972, 1973). The general relation of measured need indicators to allocation of Rate Support Grant in each local government and is shown in table 13.6. In their study, SPNW regroup local jurisdictions into four categories reflecting relative need measured in terms most apposite to an older industrial area such as the Manchester–Liverpool conurbation. Especially important are factors such as level of smoke, noise and water pollution, the amount of derelict land, the proportion of households with multiple occupancy or without exclusive access to basic amenities such as kitchen, bathroom and toilet. For each of these 'needs' the North West scored as one of the worst of the UK regions. The relation of local tax capacity, local expenditure, and central grants to these needs is shown in table 13.6. Local property tax capacity is generally lower for the more needy areas (the category C and D jurisdictions) and expenditures from local taxes generally 20 to 30% higher, as measured by the index of local fiscal pressure (column 3 in table 13.6). Whilst central grants permit a higher level of local expenditure to be supported in the more needy jurisdiction (column 4), the level of grants is only slightly equalizing with respect to need (column 5), with the result that the much higher local expenditure *per capita* in the more needy jurisdictions is supported largely by higher levels of local taxation.

The major criticisms of the present Rate Support Grant which derive from this and other studies are that: it takes insufficient account of the differences in real needs or preferences in different areas as opposed to minimum standards; there are a number of crucial statistical inadequacies in the estimation of the needs formula and in the provision of various data; the formula is over sensitive to population age structure; it perpetuates past trends through the hold-harmless provision, and thus encourages poverty traps and cumulative cycles of growth and decline; it takes insufficient account of non-population-based needs (e.g. environmental renewal as in the example of the North West discussed above); and it is not truly equalizing, because of the operation of the deficiency payments principle.

Capital loans and transfers to local authorities have been subject to a greater degree of regulation and control by the central government than current expenditure, mainly in order to facilitate central management of the economy (Cross 1967; de Smith 1971; Gladden 1972; Griffith 1966). Nevertheless, over the period since the 1946 *Borrowing (Control and*

Table 13.6 Relation of Rate Support Grant to environmental need in four categories of local jurisdictions in North West England in 1973. (Source: SPNW 1973)

Jurisdictions in category of need		(1) Local tax capacity (per capita rateable value)	(2) Local expenditure per capita from local taxes	(3) Local fiscal pressure (2)/(1)	(4) Local expenditure per capita from central grants	(5) Central grant as % of total local expenditure	(6) Total local expenditure per capita
Least needy	A	56.67	36.52	0.64	36.45	49	72.96
	B	40.40	31.46	0.78	48.48	61	79.18
	C	35.00	31.79	0.91	61.76	67	93.55
Most needy	D	40.90	38.30	0.94	52.46	58	90.80
England and Wales average		47.50	40.07	0.85	44.87	—	84.93

Guarantees) Act, the importance of central government as a lender to local authorities has declined, with increasing amounts of capital finance being raised by independent bond issues, and even in the early 1970s, by a substantial number of loans on the international finance market. There are three components of central–local capital transfer relations. First, for a number of services (education, transport, roads, etc.) the central government directly controls capital expenditure on a project-by-project basis within each ministry. Second, loan sanctions are required for central government to permit the raising of loans even of moderate size. This sanction is frequently used as a means of making local jurisdictions conform to central policies but is mainly aimed at achieving control of the level of debt formation in the economy as a whole. Finally, the central government limits access to the capital market through the Public Works and Loan Board, and in other cases restricts the issuing of local bonds by regulating their terms and timing. Since 1971 some increase in freedom of local capital finance has been permitted (Department of Environment, Circulars 2/70 and 66/71). General consent to the raising of loans is guaranteed for four types of schemes (I) key sector schemes; in education, principal roads, police, social services, housing mortgages, derelict land reclamation, and coastal protection, (II) land acquisition for education, principal roads, and social services, (III) improvements to housing and slum clearance, (IV) locally determined schemes; libraries, recreation areas, etc. A national total sum is set aside for category (IV) and local schemes are derived from this by administrative decision. In the other categories, departmental approval in each category is still required and the increase in freedom of local action on loans has been much less than hoped for or promised. Indeed since 1976, freedom of local action has been significantly reduced by the central limits set on local house building (Department of Environment Circular 80/76) and by the monitoring of local authorities imposed by the short-lived *Community Land Act* (1976).

Because of the more restricted autonomy of local and regional authorities in centralized states, the use of regulatory devices is more important than in federal countries. Final responsibility in any spending sector under the UK constitution and legal framework rests with the appropriate minister in the Westminster government (Cross 1977; de Smith 1971) and this has stimulated a plethora of directives on minimum standards, or forms of services. Regulatory controls operate through departmental circulars, statutory authorities in town planning and other areas, and impose either central ministerial directive or the requirement for consent to a number of activities. In addition there are powers of central inspection in education, police, fire and the local accounts; powers with relation to local default; powers to reject local by-laws; and powers to compel preparation of plans and proposals in town planning, education and other services. The precise degree to which central government can compel performance of given functions at local level is confused and is still an evolving area of law (UK Central Policy Review Staff 1977), especially with respect to local conformity with national guidelines of reorganization of education. But it is characteristic of the constitution of a centralized state such as Britain, that the degree of local autonomy will always be fairly restricted when issues of real fiscal or political conflict arise.

13.3 Fiscal co-ordination in Canada

The constitution of Canada is based on a federation of ten Provinces, the special provision for North-West Territory, a federal government in Ottawa, and a set of urban local governments. Of these levels of government, the Provinces shown in figure 13.7 are very powerful (more powerful than the States of the United States), the local level is less important fiscally than in most other Western countries, and fiscal inter-relationships occur mainly as federal–Provincial or Provincial–local interactions. There is little by-passing of the Provincial level as in the case of other federations (especially Germany, the US, and Australia). The Provinces have the major role of initiating and providing public services with the federal (Dominion) government re-sponsible for a balancing role. The relative importance of revenue-raising, grants and other transfers at each level of government is shown in table 13.7. This shows a number of features: the general importance of the provinces in revenue-raising and expenditure; the importance of transfers to local and especially Provincial governments; a shift in transfers from specific toward general equalization grants; and an increase in the role of revenue-sharing and tax credits. The particular importance of the three components of revenue-sharing and tax credits, equalization grants, and specific grants is discussed in

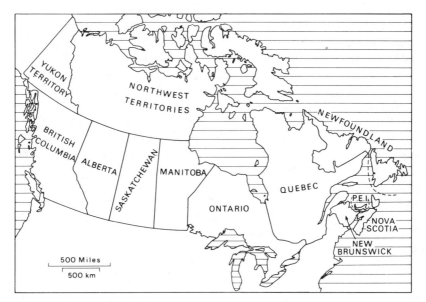

Figure 13.7 The Provinces of Canada.

359

Table 13.7 Proportion of revenue, expenditure and transfers at each level of government in Canada in 1975, with 1966 in brackets. (*Source:* Statistics Canada, *Federal Government Finance*, Ottawa.)

	Level of government					
	Federal		Province		Local (municipal)	
Revenue raised (%)	(69)	52	(18)	33	(13)	15
Expenditure (%)	(47)		(25)		(26)	
Major transfers (as % of transfers at each level)						
revenue-sharing	—			42.7	—	
tax credits (included in revenue-sharing)	—			13.0	—	
specific grants	—		(32.0)	26.1	(2.0)	1.0
general grants	—		(15.8)	22.8	(1.3)	0.6

turn below. Particularly interesting features are the operation of revenue-sharing and the equalization grants.

The *Canadian revenue-sharing system* is complex and contains elements in addition to a straightforward apportionment of the federal tax base to the Provinces. There are three components. First, there is a direct apportionment of specific federal revenues to the Provinces on a Provincial yield basis. Second, this item can be adjusted to constitute, instead of revenue-sharing, a tax credit (abatement) allowing the Provinces to raise the tax themselves at the federal apportioned rate, or above. Third, a set of equalization block grants is used to bring each Province's *per capita* yield from a bundle of 'standard taxes' up to the level of yield in the two highest revenue yielding Provinces (Ontario and British Columbia). Recently, this classification has been extended to include Alberta, so that only seven out of the ten Canadian Provinces are eligible for this third component of equalizing grant. Hence, revenue-sharing in the Canadian federation is a composite of true revenue-sharing, tax credits and equalization grants. Since it is designed as a unified programme, it is treated as such below. It is distinguished from the US revenue-sharing system by the fixed guarantees of federal tax base, the use of credit *and* equalizing grants, and the granting to Provincial and not local governments. Good discussions of the Canadian system are available in Carter (1971), US ACIR (1971), Rubinoff (1973) and Canadian Tax Foundation (1976).

Canadian revenue-sharing was initiated in 1957, but was foreshadowed in earlier discussions. In 1940 the Rowell-Sirois Report (*Royal Commission on Dominion–Provincial Relations*, 1940) stated the need for National

Adjustment Grants aimed at an equalization of revenues and needs:

> 'to make it possible for every province to provide for its people services of average Canadian standards and . . . (to) alleviate distress and shameful conditions which now weaken national unity and handicap many Canadians. They are the concrete expression of the Commission's conception of a federal system which will both preserve a healthy local autonomy and build a stronger and more unified nation' (Rowell-Sirois Commission 1940 p. 125).

These aims were incorporated into a form of revenue-sharing in the *Dominion–Provincial Tax Agreement Act* (1942), but this was delayed by the Second World War, with most Provincial revenues pre-empted to the federal government as tax rental agreements.

The *Federal–Provincial Tax Sharing Act* (1956) covering the financial years 1957–62 finally enacted a revenue-sharing formula. Revenue-sharing was combined with tax credit and equalizing grants. Credits were based on a 10–9–50 principle; each Province received an allotment of federal taxes or a credit in proportion to 10% of the personal income tax collected in that Province (excluding Old Age Security Tax), 9% of corporate income tax which was attributable to the Province, 50% of the succession (inheritance) duty attributable to the Province. Moreover, the formula was fully equalizing in that the key jurisdiction was defined as the average of the Provinces with the two highest *per capita* tax yields (British Columbia and Ontario). The revenue-sharing aid was an unconditional no strings payments which in most cases was treated as a tax credit (abatement) by the Provinces seeking to raise taxes to that level and receiving a one-to-one offset from the federal government. Finally, the equalizing grant component allocated to each Province provided payments in inverse proportion to the Provincial capacity to raise revenues from three standard taxes (personal and corporate income tax, and succession duty).

This initial revenue-sharing Act was subject to three main criticisms. First, there was a hold-harmless clause from the tax rental agreements over the previous 1942–57 period. Second, the tax bases used for revenue-sharing did not take into wide enough account the variety of revenue sources used in the Provinces. Third, there was no attempt to incorporate needs equalization; the revenue-sharing formula was only concerned with revenue equalization.

Only the second of these criticisms has been overcome by subsequent legislation. *The Federal–Provincial Arrangements Act* (1961), covering the years 1962–7, maintained the hold-harmless provision (as a stabilization payment which has been maintained ever since), increased the levels of credits allowed, and added to the revenue sources taken into account 50% of the tax yields from natural resource severance tax, and other revenues. This latter is a particularly important component for revenues in the plains Provinces, where forestry, gas and oil revenues as a percentage of total revenues comprise 40%

in Alberta, 50% in Saskatchewan, and 10% in British Columbia in 1963–4. To overcome fluctuations in this source of revenue, to which it is particularly vulnerable, the 50% allowance is based on a 3-year average of Provincial receipts.

In the *Federal–Provincial Fiscal Arrangements Act* (1967) covering the period 1967–72, the credits allowable for personal income tax reached 28% for corporate income tax 10%, and for estate tax 75% (as a mixture of credits and shared revenues depending upon the Province concerned). Two major changes to the revenue-sharing credit component were made. First, a grant was added equivalent to 50% of the Provincial cost of post-secondary education. This was part of a programme to adjust the federal grant structure for university and secondary education and shifted Canadian revenue-sharing more into the area of functional grant programmes; it also made a step towards a full geographical negative income tax structure. Second, a major change in revenue-sharing was improvement to the treatment of the revenue base in the equalization grants. These were switched from the 'standard taxes' of personal and corporate income tax, and succession (estate) duty to a representative tax system. This used 16 revenue sources comprising almost all tax sources and represents, to date, the only major implementation of the representative tax system approach to practical measurement of revenue capacity in distribution formulae. The sources used in the representative tax base are personal and corporate income tax, succession duty and estate tax, general sales tax, motor fuel tax, motor vehicle revenues, alcohol duties and taxes, natural resource levies and royalties, and water power rentals.

For each of the 16 revenue sources, a national basis is calculated; the total Provincial revenues from that source are then divided by the national base to give a national average Provincial revenue rate; this rate is then applied to the tax base in each Province, and then divided by the Province's population which gives the Provincial revenue of the national average rate. The difference between this yield and the national average *per capita* yield is the entitlement of each Province to federal equalization from that source. This term will be positive when the Provincial *per capita* yield is less than the national average, but negative when the Province has a higher *per capita* yield than the national average for that revenue source. In subsequent amendments, the major changes to revenue-sharing and credits have been the introduction of credits for personal income tax, residential property tax paid, and a shift from sharing to credits for estate gift taxes, with the federal government withdrawing from these fields. Also the range of corporate income tax credits has been extended.

In the 1972 *Federal–Provincial Fiscal Arrangements Act*, covering 1972–77, the representative tax base has been extended to 19 taxes by the addition of health insurance premiums, racetrack taxes and the Provincial share of income tax on power utilities. Subsequent amendments added municipal taxes imposed on local school purposes (1973), raising the bundle of representative taxes to 20 (see table 13.9). The post-secondary education component was also maintained. One important feature of the Canadian revenue-sharing arrangements has been the provision for any Province to opt out of the scheme. Opting out allows eligibility for separate federal grants or credits broadly equivalent to those available in the revenue-sharing programme, but independent of it. Instituted under pressure from Quebec, that Province has been the only user of the arrangement which has applied to hospital insurance, common welfare and unemployment assistance, vocational education, and health. The aim has been to maintain a degree of independence of Quebec from interdependence with, or comparison against, the other Provinces. However, there is no reduction in the federal controls and opting out does not free that Province from the standards of service provision required by the federal government, nor are funding requirements reduced. It has, however, gone some way to satisfy the demands of Quebec for separate public finance accounting, independent of the other Provinces.

The total revenue-sharing, credit, and equalization payments to each of the provinces are shown in table 13.8. In 1975–76 these payments amounted to $ 1929.5 million, of which the opting out component of Quebec amounted to $155.6 million. The largest single component is tax credits and sharing in respect of personal income tax. Together with corporate income tax, this accounts for 60% with federal transfers under the Act. The table also shows that, for those Provinces eligible for equalization grants, this component represents the largest single source of revenue. The 20 categories of revenue built into this grant component are expanded in table 13.9, from which it can be seen that the original 'standard taxes' (personal and corporate income tax, and general sales tax) are usually the most significant portions, with oil and gas revenues very significant in some Provinces. Note also that some negative elements arise for those Provinces in which the Provincial *per capita* revenue yield is greater than the national average, and this contribution is subtracted from the entitlement, thus performing as a true equalization grant (see figure 12.4).

The major strength of the Canadian revenue-sharing system is that it has been highly equalizing. It has paid equalizing grants only to low-capacity Provinces, equalization has been to the level of the provinces with the highest revenue capacities, equalization entitlements have been subtracted from Provinces as well as added, and capacity measures have been developed using the desirable features of the representative tax system. The further strength of the Canadian approach is that it has tied Provincial revenues to the automatic (and relatively elastic) rises in both national taxes and Provincial revenue rates and bases. This flexibility can also result in decline of revenues, of course, but guarantee of a minimum grant base has been given by the federal government in all cases.

There are a number of criticisms of the Canadian system, however. A major weakness is that local government is ignored. Differences in local government revenue-raising ability within Provinces are ignored, as are variations in the

Table 13.8 Transfers to Canadian Provinces under *Federal—Provincial Arrangements Act* for 1975–76 ($000s). (*Source*: Canadian Tax Foundation 1976)

Payments	Nfld.	P.E.I.	N.S.	N.B.	Que.	Ont.	Man.	Sask.	Alta.	B.C.	Total
(1) Equalization	194,427	47,800	254,736	205,146	992,067	—	132,460	102,871	—	—	1,929,507
(2) Individual income tax collected	74,288	13,452	144,446	107,578	—	2,070,114	239,405	178,856	298,426	598,898	3,725,463
(3) Corporation income tax collected	17,170	2,447	23,287	19,978	—	—	60,356	50,351	257,931	227,544	659,064
(4) Share of income tax on certain public utilities	2,008	576	—	—	3,047	11,959	1,072	29	14,758	1,742	35,191
(5) Statutory subsides	9,708	659	2,174	1,774	3,484	5,504	2,156	2,100	3,132	2,117	33,808
(6) Adjustments for prior years	n/a	n/a	n/a	n/a	n/a	—	n/a	n/a	—	—	60,000
(7) Adjustments in opting out compensation	—	—	—	—	155,600	—	—	—	—	—	155,600
(8) Payments under part IV	n/a	n/a	n/a	n/a	n/a	n/a	n/a	n/a	n/a	n/a	340,000
(9) Payments under part V	309	4	236	313	3,763	5,602	665	185	1,204	1,759	14,040
(10) Total payments	297,910	64,938	424,879	334,789	1,158,961	2,093,179	436,114	334,392	575,451	832,060	6,952,673
Post-secondary education											
(11) Value of tax abatements included in above, lines 2 and 3											
(12) 4.357% of individual income tax	8,092	1,628	16,347	11,294	161,270	295,721	24,543	19,482	50,009	85,554	673,940
(13) 1% of corporate income tax base	1,321	245	2,329	1,998	29,757	58,091	4,643	4,196	23,448	17,503	143,531
(14) Additional cash transfer	5,460	1,270	18,850	6,790	254,050	157,510	17,310	14,900	40,740	5,940	522,820
(15) Total value of post-secondary education assistance	14,873	3,143	37,526	20,082	445,077	511,322	46,496	38,578	114,197	108,997	1,340,291
(16) Individual income tax rate %	40.0	36.0	38.5	41.5	34.0	30.5	42.5	40.0	26.0	30.5	
Amount	74,288	13,452	144,446	107,578	1,258,478	2,070,114	239,405	178,856	298,426	598,898	4,983,941
(17) Corporation income tax rate %	13	10	13	10	12	12	13	12	11	13	
Amount	17,170	2,447	23,287	19,978	357,079	697,095	60,356	50,351	257,931	227,554	1,713,238
(18) Rebates, credits and reductions from corporate income tax	—	—	—	—	—	—	—	—	63,000	22,900	85,900

Table 13.9 Estimated equalization payments by revenue source in representative tax base 1975-76 ($000s). (Source: Canadian Tax Foundation 1976)

	Nfld.	P.E.I.	N.S.	N.B.	Que.	Man.	Sask.	Total seven Recipient Provinces
Equalization entitlements								
(1) Personal income taxes	65,844	15,235	64,388	69,957	176,608	45,239	61,998	499,269
(2) Corporation income taxes	25,803	6,275	36,689	26,433	81,411	18,522	31,225	226,358
(3) General and sales taxes	21,302	5,557	25,796	14,721	123,711	7,012	12,144	210,243
(4) Motive fuel taxes	8,793	597	6,496	2,381	18,030	666	− 174	36,789
(5) Motor vehicle licencing revenues	3,567	242	2,635	966	7,314	270	− 71	14,923
(6) Alcoholic beverages revenues	5,496	4	2,122	7,062	59,187	− 4,752	− 1,741	67,378
(7) Hospital and medical care insurance	4,129	841	2,061	2,908	23,155	293	3,298	36,685
(8) Succession duties and gift taxes	3,509	578	2,464	3,255	785	2,713	2,919	16,223
(9) Race track taxes	1,639	62	1,531	1,402	1,318	1,736	2,328	10,016
(10) Forestry revenues	−1,187	1,189	6,497	−2,835	11,988	6,075	3,853	25,580
(11) Crown oil revenues	16,700	3,613	24,988	20,509	188,058	29,731	−47,081	236,518
(12) Freehold oil revenues	880	190	1,317	1,081	9,912	202	− 3,933	9,649
(13) Crown gas revenues	7,606	1,646	11,381	9,342	85,651	14,101	9,681	139,408
(14) Freehold gas revenues	193	42	289	236	2,176	358	226	3,520
(15) Sales of Crown leases and reservations on oil and natural gas lands	2,426	526	3,639	2,987	27,390	4,509	28	41,505
(16) Other oil and gas revenues	1,684	364	2,520	2,068	18,966	3,034	− 2,795	25,841
(17) Metallic and non-metallic mineral revenues	− 11,906		10,994	2,451	33,973	− 17,168	6,173	14,132
(18) Water power rentals	− 3,583	169	1,051	561	−4,113	− 748	822	− 5,839
(19) Miscellaneous provincial taxes	7,578	1,594	3,790	7,231	23,027	3,759	6,615	58,594
(20) Miscellaneous provincial revenues	9,074	1,909	10,526	8,659	27,575	4,502	7,921	70,166
(21) Payments by federal government (a) share of income tax on public utilities	366	77	424	349	1,112	181	319	2,828
(b) payments under part V	201	14	− 66	221	950	164	239	1,723
(22) School purpose taxes	24,313	5,115	28,202	23,201	73,883	12,061	21,223	187,998
(23) Total equalization entitlements	194,427	47,800	254,736	205,146	992,067	132,460	102,871	1,929,507

local government shares of public service functions within Provinces. Different Provincial/local ratios of revenues and expenditures in different Provinces have different consequences especially in urbanized Provinces. Two Provinces with similar revenue capacity will receive the same grants irrespective of differences in the share of public responsibilities and expenditures. In addition, there is no account taken of the differences in range, quantity or quality of public services provided in each Province; that is, there are no specific cost or need measurements. To some extent the need variation is incorporated in the post-secondary education component, and in the 1973 amendment to the 1972 Act, in which the equalization formula was broadened to include municipal taxes imposed for school purposes (Bill C–233), but in an examination of this provision, Maxwell and Carter (1974) conclude that although school taxes are large and important, the use of this single local revenue is not equalizing and gives an inconsistent basis for need assessment. Carter (1971) argues, however, that need equalization is not required or possible in the Canadian system. First, such equalization would require conditional grants, which is at variance with the aims of revenue-sharing. Second, he argues that since revenue inequality is the major source of inequality in Canadian Provincial finances need equalization is not important. Moreover, he claims that variation in needs which do occur is quite consistent with the premise that a degree of local variation in service demands and preferences is necessary. Finally, Carter argues that need and cost equalization is too difficult to define. It is difficult totally to sustain these arguments. It is certainly true, in fact, that need equalization is best approached through conditional (specific) grants, but needs can also be attacked through general grants. Moreover, variations in unit costs of needs in Canada do not seem in most commentators' opinions to be less than other countries, and there are now available useful and practical methods of assessing expenditure need (see chapter 5).

One interesting feature of the Canadian system is the capacity it gives Provinces to compete successfully with each other by pursuing particular revenue strategies (see chapter 4). Courchene and Beavis (1973), for example, have calculated Provincial revenue strategies which result in increased receipts from equalization grants. Examples of such strategies are for Alberta or Nova Scotia to increase sales tax, or for Ontario to increase corporate income tax. Similarly, changes in tax base calculated for Nova Scotia and Quebec sales tax, or British Columbia personal income tax, can often be detrimental to the size of federal receipts in the Province concerned, i.e. as the tax base increases it raises more finance locally and hence reduces equalization payments.

Canadian specific grants originated in 1912 with grants to Provinces to provide agricultural education. This was followed in 1919 by a series of programmes aiding vocational training, Provincial roads, reduction in venereal disease, and instruction of Provincial employment officers. The 1927 *Old Age Pensions Act* initiated the first social welfare programme, followed in

Table 13.10   Grants to Provinces and municipalities 1966 to 1974 ($000s). (*Source:* Statistics Canada, from Canadian Tax Foundation 1976)

	1966	1973	1974
a) Payments to Provinces			
Unconditional grants	466.0	1,985.2	2,361.7
Conditional grants			
Hospital insurance	373.7	957.1	1,062.2
Medicare	—	629.3	676.2
Other health	45.7	43.8	39.1
Welfare	209.2	491.8	525.8
Education	160.1	77.5	99.0
Transportation	99.4	40.1	47.1
Natural resources and regional			
development	42.0	81.9	109.8
Other grants	9.9	106.1	138.2
Total conditional grants	939.9	2,427.6	2,697.4
Total payments to Provinces	1,405.9	4,412.8	5,059.1
b) Payments to municipalities			
Unconditional grants	39.4	60.5	63.9
Conditional grants	58.8	88.6	101.0
Total payments to municipalities	98.3	149.1	164.9
c) Payments to territories			
Statutory subsidies	5.7	75.5	85.3
Conditional grants	3.1	11.1	10.8
Total payments to territories	8.8	86.6	96.1
Total federal payments	1,513.0	4,648.5	5,320.1

1937 by blind persons allowances and in 1948 by a comprehensive *National Health Program*. Rapid expansion of grants occurred in the 1950s and 60s with a two-fold increase over the ten years 1956–66 as summarized in table 13.11. Important programmes are the 1950 *Trans-Canada Highway* and welfare programmes for the old in 1952, disabled in 1954, and unemployed in 1955. These were lumped together in the *Canada Assistance Plan* in 1966. Specific regional aid, although implicitly given in many grant programmes, was formerly initiated through the *Agricultural Rehabilitation and Development Act* (1951) and reinforced by the *Fund for Rural Economic Development* in 1966. Medicare aid was introduced in 1968. The relative importance of these grants has increased steadily being about 2% of federal revenue in 1948 rising to 16% in late 1960s, but declining to about 13% in the early 1970s (Carter 1971).

The range of Canadian grants closely resembles, but is much smaller than, that in the US and covers agriculture, social welfare, health, education, recreation, highways, ports and airports, and regional development (see table 13.10). The largest components, as in the US, are hospital insurance and medicare, and welfare. Education has declined in importance in the grant programmes since the post-secondary funding has become involved in revenue-sharing. Traditionally these grants have been higher in the Atlantic Provinces where they provide 30 to 40% of local revenues, than in Quebec or Ontario where they provide only 15 to 20% of revenues. The Prairies and West are in between with grants providing 20 to 25% of local revenues.

The hospital insurance programme is an open-ended specific grant which places great emphasis on unit cost criteria: allocations determined from 25% of the national average *per capita* cost of hospital care, plus 25% of the Provinces average *per capita* cost multiplied by the number of medically insured people in the Province (which covers almost the entire population). Although equalizing on unit costs, this grant programme has been criticized for not equalizing on fiscal capacity (Carter 1971). Quebec has also opted for alternative funding arrangements since 1965. Medical care is also funded by open-ended specific grants which are allocated to each Province on the basis of 50% of national average *per capita* cost of medical aid multiplied by the number of insured individuals in the Province. Hence it also equalizes costs rather than capacity. Welfare under the *Canada Assistance Plan* has, since 1965, allocated grants to Provinces on the basis of 50% of the cost of shared financial assistance for social assistance, welfare and child care, but determined by the rate of assistance set in each Province, with Quebec opting out.

The division of specific grant expenditure between Provinces is shown in table 13.11. This table brings out three main features. First, unconditional equalization grants from the revenue-sharing programme form over 30% of the total federal grants. Second, the grants to Provinces account for 97% of all grants, grants to local governments being only $163 million or 3% of the total. A third feature of table 13.11 is the difference in the relative magnitudes of different grant programmes to different Provinces. Apart from the uniform importance of medical care, hospital insurance and welfare, the Atlantic Provinces are very significantly aided by development, transport and agriculture and natural resources; the Western States rely heavily on natural resource grants; and Quebec relies heavily on development grants.

The Canadian conditional grants have come under considerable criticism, probably more so than in other countries. This criticism suggests that the categorization is inadequately defined and supervised, that they have been used as temporary rather than permanent features of intergovernmental coordination, that programmes have been initiated or modified without consultation, that there have been payment delays, and that they have required too high a degree of local matching funds, and have been inadequately supervised with no aid for administration or staffing (Carter 1971). Some authorities, such as Maxwell (1946), have argued that such grants for Canada are not inherently bad, but should be improved in administration. Others, notably Smiley (1967), have argued that the grants are inappropriate to the

Table 13.11 Specific and general grants to Provinces 1973–74 $000s. (*Source*: Canadian Tax Foundation 1976)

	Nfld.	P.E.I.	N.S.	N.B.	Que.	Ont.	Man.	Sask.	Alta.	B.C.	Total
(a) Payments to Provinces											
Total unconditional equalization grants	168,502	36,202	191,257	149,354	824,908	42,779	129,980	168,804	14,880	6,595	1,733,261
Conditional grants											
Hospital insurance	34,561	6,911	53,245	43,252	—	530,048	73,925	60,212	119,764	140,276	1,062,194
Medicare	16,710	3,547	24,832	20,064	185,385	243,341	31,185	27,712	52,700	70,697	676,173
Other health	9,850	21	77	463	11,069	10,712	1,996	1,343	3,453	165	39,149
Welfare	26,497	5,214	28,226	31,223	118	218,108	39,639	36,202	56,132	84,454	525,813
Post-secondary education	5,443	916	22,486	7,317	196,070	153,637	17,699	13,820	54,670	13,083	485,141
Other education	194	223	807	6,56?	61,698	24,103	2,096	735	984	1,576	98,977
Agriculture	1,866	15,860	4,064	9,288	41,120	7,994	6,435	8,668	10,450	2,635	108,380
Natural resources	5,263	1,330	2,071	7,552	340	661	1,216	15,737	122,087	7,629	163,886
Supervision and development of regions and localities	12,475	2	3,552	13,30?	55,245	—	1,445	780	2,407	35	89,244
Recreation and culture	70	87	86	8?	—	90	477	—	—	—	895
Transportation and communications	11,005	480	10,509	13,505	9,743	97	—	—	529	1,192	47,064
Other	1,287	113	323	802	16,786	5,028	344	378	1,625	2,250	28,926
Total	125,221	34,704	150,278	153,419	577,574	1,193,819	176,447	165,587	424,801	323,992	3,325,842
(b) Payments to municipalities											
Grants in lieu of taxes	418	156	5,145	2	14,754	28,439	4,255	1,722	3,523	5,001	63,415
Conditional grants	4,277	962	4,690	2,930	27,477	29,621	4,593	1,621	6,025	18,332	100,528
Total	4,695	1,118	9,835	2,932	42,231	58,060	8,848	3,343	9,548	23,333	163,943
Total federal payments	298,418	72,024	351,370	305,705	1,444,713	1,294,658	315,275	337,734	449,229	353,920	5,320,132ᶜ

nature of the Canadian federation with its highly developed Provincial independence and autonomy.

Despite a number of inadequacies, the Canadian system of revenue-sharing and conditional grants has been highly successful by international standards. For revenue-sharing, the aims of providing flexible and elastic sources of revenue to Provincial governments have been fulfilled, and it has produced a high degree of equalization of public finance burdens and benefits. Equalization grants and revenue-sharing have required Ontario to become what Burns terms the "benevolent 'milch cow' of the Canadian federation" (US JEC 1967, p. 440), but this has been accepted with reasonable equanimity by this province. The pressures on the Canadian federation which may cause its break-up are undoubtedly stimulating these measures and it would be unwise at this stage to speculate whether the considerable degree of fiscal equalization achieved in Canada, and the special treatment in Quebec in particular, will be sufficient to keep the Canadian federation intact.

13.4 Fiscal co-ordination in the United States

The fiscal structure of the United States is relatively centralized for a federal country, some 50 to 60% of revenues being raised and expended at the federal level. The fiscal structure is complex since between the State and federal government there is no specific assignment of revenues in the 1788 Constitution (except for reserving customs duties and excise to the federal level), nor are expenditure functions clearly delimited. At a local level, there is no uniform structure, and each State has a variable degree of centralization or decentralization of revenue and expenditure function depending on the form of the State's Constitution and subsequent evolution. Traditionally, the States were the dominant raisers of revenue and providers of public service benefits up to the 1930s, with the federal level accounting for 36% of public expenditure and local governments for only 11%. This balance changed markedly with the 1930s depression and the assumption of many new federal responsibilities under the Roosevelt New Deal. The federal role expanded again in the World War II years of the 1940s, during the Vietnam War of the 1960s and, in accordance with the displacement effect of wartime expenditures hypothesized by Peacock and Wiseman (1959) discussed earlier (p. 24), these higher levels of federal expenditure became absorbed either by new social programmes, or by increases in intergovernmental transfers from the federal government. Revenue-sharing was one important programme absorbing finance at the end of the Vietnam War, for example.

In line with the complex structure of the United States government, fiscal co-ordination is an extremely complex mixture of revenue-sharing, tax credits, general and specific grants, direct federal expenditures, and other minor programmes. In a system of complex programmes involving 50 States, the District of Columbia, some 80,000 local, city, county, school district, and other general specific purpose governments, it is difficult to make generali-

Table 13.12 Division of revenues and expenditures between levels of government in the US 1975, with 1957 in brackets for revenues, and 1964 in brackets for expenditures and transfers. (*Source:* US ACIR, Significant features of fiscal federalism 1976; US ACIR 1978, Vols. 1 to 3)

	Level of government					
	Federal		*State*		*Local*	
Revenues raised (%)	(69.6)	55.3	(14.6)	24.2	(15.8)	20.6
Expenditure (%)	(48.3)	59.0	(24.3)	22.5	(27.4)	18.5
Transfers (as % of all transfers)						
revenue-sharing	—		(0)	4.1	(0)	8.4
general grants	—			(0.5)	10	
specific grants	—			(99.5)	76	

zations. The general split of revenues, expenditures, and transfers between these levels of government is shown for 1975 in table 13.12. This shows the dominance of revenue-raising at federal level, but a shift of revenue-raising from federal to State and local levels. For expenditures, however, the contrary trend is present with the federal level taking a much increased role especially in comparison with the local level. Transfers form a significant proportion of State and local finance and have shifted from specific towards general grants and revenue-sharing programmes. A basic feature of US fiscal co-ordination has been heavy use of formula-based transfers, where various measures of fiscal capacity and effort have been employed to target aid to poorer urban areas and the rural South, away from the high capacity areas of the North-East and Mid-West. Recently, considerable changes to capacity and regional growth rates have encouraged redirection of more of this aid by formula to favour the North-East. Because of this and other complexities in the US system, attention here is restricted to those revenue-sharing, tax credit, and grant transfers which together account for over 90% of all co-ordination measures. More detailed discussion of the US government system can be obtained in Maxwell and Aronson (1977), or Musgrave and Musgrave (1976), or by reference to the US *Census of Governments*, and ACIR Annual Reports, *Significant Features of Fiscal Federalism*.

Revenue-sharing in the US is a relatively recent innovation enacted in the *State and Local Finance Act* (1972) and renewed for a further three and three-quarter years in the *State and Local Fiscal Assistance Amendments* (1976). Early precedents for revenue-sharing date from Andrew Jackson's *Surplus Distribution Act* (1836), in the organization of TVA fiscal measures, and in FHA payments to localities for waiving property taxes in federally aided slum-clearance and low-rent housing development, but these have had little effect on the final revenue-sharing legislation. More important were the 1946

Wisconsin and 1971 Minnesota State revenue-sharing arrangements, the Laird Bill of 1958, Javits Bill of 1965, proposals by Walter Heller, the Douglas Commission, ACIR and Senators Reuss and Humphrey, the Pechman Task Force set up in 1964 resulting in the famous Heller–Pechman Plan, and the congressional sub-committee report *Revenue-Sharing and its Alternatives* (US JEC 1967). Features consistently emphasized in these proposals, especially the Heller–Pechman, were the permanence of revenue-sharing, entitlement by formula *as of right*, that funds should be additional to existing grants, without strings, to local as well as State governments, using population as a primary formula element, with allowance for redistribution to poor areas and incorporating measures of tax effort.

Many of these features were enacted in the final legislation in 1972. Population levels and tax effort are incorporated into the formulae, there is a strong emphasis on pass-through to local governments, and the revenues are given largely without strings. However, the revenue-sharing Act was not intended as a permanent feature, and nor have the trust fund and proportional tax base concepts been implemented. In practice, however, it would seem that revenue-sharing has become a permanent feature in the US government system since the political consequences of withdrawal of the programme would now be very severe.

The *formula* used in the 1972 Act is complex and involves a five-step procedure: (I) allocation from federal government to the State, (II) split of allocation from States, between State and local government, (III) allocation of local shares among counties, (IV) allocation of county shares to local jurisdictions, (V) the imposition of minimum and maximum restrictions on final allotments. The allocation procedure in each stage is summarized in table 13.13. At the first stage, of federal–State allotment, the use of two formulae represents a political compromise reflecting the pork-barrel nature of US congressional politics. The House formula tends to equalize between levels of population and favours the densely populated urban states of the North East from where the bulk of House representation is drawn. The Senate formula, on the other hand, tends to equalize between States and is more favourable to rural and low-income areas, reflecting the emphasis on equal representation in the Senate. Allocation at lower levels tends to emphasize spatial equality, using the Senate formula, rather than needs equalization. The constraints entering at the lower level are also significant, affecting about \$350 million or 7% in 1974.

The 1976 Amendment to the revenue-sharing Act incorporated no important changes to the formula, but there were significant administrative changes. The political history of the Amendments is well documented by Nathan and Adams (1976). The only important formula change was the elimination of any guarantee to add annual increments to the total revenue-sharing funds distributed. Administrative changes involve, first, the requirement for accounting and auditing the programme at local level to permit more ready

Table 13.13   US Revenue-sharing formulae of 1972

1. *Federal–State allocation:* The largest allocation of
   A. *House of Representatives formula:*

Factor	weight
(i) Total State population as % of US total	0.2201
(ii) State population × relative income (from Senate formula item 3)	0.2201
(iii) State urbanized population (population in cities over 50,000)	0.2201
(iv) State tax effort (from Senate formula item 2) × State and local tax revenue as % of US total	0.1698
(v) 15% of State personal income tax plus 1 to 6% of federal income tax liability of resident population as % of US total	0.1698
	1.0000

   B. *Senate formula:*

Factor   weight
(i) Total State population as % of US total   0.3333

(ii) State tax effort = (state + local tax revenue)
$$\frac{\text{(state + local tax revenue)}}{\text{(personal income of State's resident population)}}$$ 0.3333

as % of US total   1.000

(iii) State relative income = (national average *per capita* income)
$$\frac{\text{(national average \emph{per capita} income)}}{\text{(State \emph{per capita} income)}}$$ 0.3333

as % of US total.   1.0000

(N.B. Alaska and Hawaii receive a wage-adjusted supplement to the House formula).

2. *Division of State and Local allotment:*
   (i) State government   0.3333
   (ii) Local governments   0.3333

3. *State–County allocation:*
   Senate formula B is used substituting County for State data and weighting in the same way.
   Subject to constraints:
   (i) No jurisdiction can receive more than 50% of non-school taxes and intergovernmental receipts.
   (ii) No jurisdiction can receive *per capita* more that 145% of State's *per capita* amount for distribution.
   (iii) No jurisdiction can receive less than 20% of State's *per capita* amount for distribution.

4. *County–Local allocation:*
   (i) Indian tribes and Alaskan settlements: share equal to proportion of county population.
   (ii) Other areas: allocation in proportion to non-school tax revenue raised by each township, county and municipal government.
   (iii) Within units, allocation according to State–County allocation.
   (iv) Plus constraint that no share can be less than $200 in toal.

5. *Reallocation of funds withheld due to constraints:*
   Reallocation according to the above formulae until no money is left.

tracing of the impact and use of the funds, second, the requirement for special political hearings on the use of the revenue-sharing funds, and third, the elimination of any matching requirements. A later development in 1976 was the implementation of counter-cyclical revenue-sharing. This was distributed on the general revenue-sharing formula, but only for those areas where unemployment exceeded 4.5% in the previous calendar quarter. This has attacked the problems of specific pockets of poverty and need as envisaged in the Heller–Pechman plan, but has been limited in duration from 1976 to 1979.

The impact of revenue-sharing has been examined in a number of studies at a general and a local level; in fact it is probably true to say that no single intergovernmental transfer programme has stimulated a greater amount of research. The most comprehensive studies have been those by Caputo and Cole (1974), the Michigan–NSF Study (Justen 1976), the Brookings Monitoring Study (Nathan *et al.* 1976, 1977), and other studies by Reischauer (1976), Caputo (1975), and Caputo and Cole (1976). The findings of these studies are summarized in detail below as they evidence the most highly developed research on intergovernmental transfers to date. The impact of revenue-sharing can be studied in three areas: first, the use of the funds; second, the broad relations to fiscal need, capacity and effort; and third, the incidence of allocations between different governments.

The general use of funds is summarized in table 13.14 which shows that law

Table 13.14 Use of general revenue-sharing funds in the US in 1973 and 1974 by city type. (*Source:* Caputo and Cole 1976)

	1973 survey		1974 survey	
	Central (N = 137)	Suburban (N = 75)	Central (N = 137)	Suburban (N = 71)
Expenditure category	%	%	%	%
Law enforcement	10.9	11.9	15.0	19.7
Fire prevention	12.6	6.1	16.4	13.3
Building and code enforcement	1.4	.8	.8	.6
Environmental protection	12.6	12.7	13.8	11.7
Transit systems	2.6	.5	2.8	3.3
Street and road repair	11.8	10.7	14.0	9.4
Social services	1.4	2.0	2.6	3.4
Health	1.7	.2	2.7	3.0
Parks and recreation	5.8	9.9	8.9	14.8
Building renovation	3.4	4.6	3.4	2.7
Libraries	1.6	1.0	1.7	3.1
Municipal salaries	3.8	4.7	1.6	.3
Other	11.9	15.7	13.5	8.2
Undetermined	18.5	19.2	2.8	6.5
Total	100.0	100.0	100.0	100.0

enforcement, fire protection, environmental protection, street and road repair, and parks and recreation account for the largest categories of usage; and for these categories, law enforcement, and parks and recreation are more favoured in suburbs, whilst fire protection, environmental protection and street and road repair are more favoured in central cities. An important area of political debate has been concerned with the degree to which revenue-sharing has stimulated new programmes or has maintained old public programmes. Revenue-sharing funds strictly cannot be spent on programmes for which other federal aid is available, but in practice the fungibility of grants allows them to be diverted to different uses with no easy means of tracing them. However, table 13.15 shows that revenue-sharing has stimulated an increase in local spending which would otherwise not have occurred. This accounts for about one half of the funds at local level, and one third at State

Table 13.15   Allocation of revenue-sharing funds in a sample of jurisdictions by type of fiscal effect (*Source:* Nathan and Adams 1977, Table 2.1)

Programme	1974	1975	Average of 1974 and 1975
Local governments			
New spending	**56.2**	**45.9**	**51.8**
New capital	45.2	34.5	41.4
Expanded operations	10.5	10.6	9.6
Increased pay and benefits	0.5	0.8	0.8
Substitutions	**43.9**	**52.4**	**47.0**
Programmme maintenance	12.8	14.6	13.5
Restoration of federal aid	0.4	1.1	0.8
Tax reduction	3.8	5.0	4.4
Tax stabilization	14.1	18.3	15.3
Avoidance of borrowing	9.6	7.7	8.8
Increased fund balance	2.8	3.4	3.0
Substitution not categorized	0.4	2.3	1.2
State governments			
New spending	**35.7**	**39.6**	**37.3**
New capital	21.1	21.0	21.0
Expanded operations	12.1	13.2	13.8
Increased pay and benefits	0.0	5.4	1.2
New spending not categorized	2.5	0.0	1.3
Substitutions	**64.3**	**58.2**	**62.5**
Programme maintenance	15.3	0.0	6.7
Restoration of federal aid	3.0	13.3	7.8
Tax reduction	13.2	12.0	12.2
Tax stabilization	0.0	12.5	7.6
Avoidance of borrowing	3.3	2.5	4.0
Increased fund balance	4.5	5.4	4.6
Substitution not categorized	25.0	12.5	19.6

375

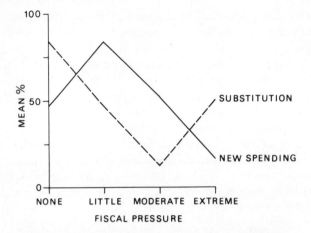

Figure 13.8 Use of revenue-sharing funds, 1973, in relation to fiscal pressure. (Data derived from Nathan *et al.* 1976, p. 229.)

level. The major proportion of this spending has been involved in capital projects for which the initial 5-year guarantee of fund availability was important, since many governments were reluctant to initiate new service programmes which they might not be able to maintain (Nathan *et al.* 1976). Of the funds which were used as substitutions for other sources, the major components at the local level have been tax stabilization (the main user being New York City), and programme maintenance (usually a major user, e.g. Massachusetts used all revenue-sharing funds in this way). At State level, the main impacts have been restitution of federal aid for terminated grant programmes, tax reduction (restricted in legal extent possible), and the stabilization of revenues (used especially in States which are fiscally distressed). The general relation of new spending and substitution to fiscal pressure is shown in figure 13.8. Substitution is favoured under intense fiscal pressure, as might be expected, in order to stabilize tax burdens. Within these general trends, considerable variation in type of spending occurs with city size, as shown in table 13.15. There is considerable difference in use of funds between the wealthy small suburban governments and less wealthy large central city governments.

The distribution of revenue-sharing can also be examined for its equalizing impacts in relation to fiscal need, capacity, and effort. These effects are displayed graphically for capacity and effort in figure 13.9, and for need in figure 13.10. The revenue-sharing formula given in table 13.14 takes account of need through the factors of total population, inverse income, extent of urbanization and fiscal pressure. Population-based needs are taken into account in the *per capita* rendering of most of the formula elements. Inverse income amounts to the same measure as capacity shown in figure 13.9, and the

376

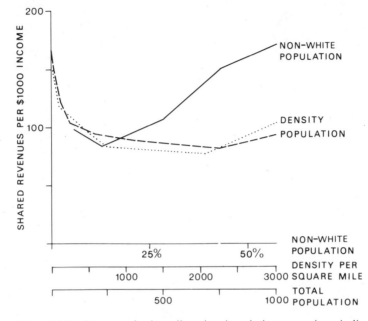

Figure 13.9 Revenue-sharing allocation in relation to various indicators of need. (Data derived from Nathan *et al.* 1976, table 5.8.)

revenue-sharing allocations are quite satisfactorily need-related. The relation of revenue-sharing funds to urbanization as a measure of need is not as clear, and if anything is neutral or inversely related to this need criterion. When we turn to fiscal pressure, Nathan *et al.* (1977) have undertaken a detailed analysis which demonstrates that although the majority of revenue-sharing funds end up as public goods, a substantial element leaks into the private sector as reduced prices, tax reductions, and revenue stabilization. Moreover, the largest private leakages are often in the areas with the greatest fiscal pressure (Nathan *et al.* 1977). This should be viewed as a general beneficial aspect of revenue-sharing; since this programme is the only major form of federal aid which is not derived from use of the local tax base, it has important implications for breaking the poverty cycle deriving from the Tiebout Model, i.e. reduced tax rates reduce the fiscal stimulus to migration. In another study by Glickman (1977) it has been estimated that for the Philadelphia region every 10% increase in revenue-sharing funds results in a 6% increase in gross domestic product of the area offset by a 3.5% increase in federal taxes, but a 3% increase in employment and personal income.

Turning to fiscal capacity and effort it can be seen that revenue-sharing has overall had the desirable effect of giving allocation in inverse proportion to *per capita* incomes as a measure of capacity, and in direct proportion to tax effort. Nathan *et al.* (1976) demonstrate that the allocations also favour capacity

377

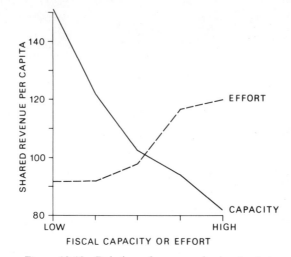

Figure 13.10   Relation of revenue-sharing funds to tax effort and fiscal capacity.
Capacity: 1970–1 own source State and general revenue.
Effort: ratio of 1970–1 taxes to 1970 personal income.
(Data derived from Nathan *et al.* 1976, tables 4.10 and 4.11.)

as measure by *per capita* income, but argue, as many other writers have done, that revenue-sharing is not effecting the degree of equalization of capacity and effort required. This is largely the result of the political compromise in the two formulae used. The result is a very narrow range of differences in allocations between areas, i.e. the programme is a very diffuse and badly targeted one. The range is from only 0.9% to 3.1% of State expenditures, with an average of 2%.

The incidence of revenue-sharing between different governments has tended to favour large cities, but only modestly. In every case in the sample by Nathan and Adams (1977) of 25 large cities, the revenue-sharing allocations to central cities was a larger proportion of revenue than the rest of SMSAs. Hence revenue-sharing has narrowed central city–suburban fiscal disparities, but the shift has been small, only 2 to 4% of local tax revenues. It would be much larger if the 145% ceiling on allocations were removed (table 13.13 *q.v.*). With respect to density, local income, and percentage of blacks, the impact of revenue-sharing has been quite marked at local level. As figure 13.10 shows, revenue-sharing has had the favourable features of rising with density and number of blacks, and this reflects an important influence at the local level of the inverse *per capita* income factor.

The major advantages of revenue-sharing are that, since revenue is raised centrally, it guarantees a geographical uniformity of tax rates with respect to those revenues. Moreover, it can be highly equalizing with appropriate choice of distribution criteria. In addition revenue-sharing does not encourage local level governments to impose taxes on the basis that they can be shifted to the rest of the country, as grant deductibility and credits can do; nor is it possible for local areas to opt out of taxation. In the case of the US 1972 and 1976 Acts, these advantages have been realized and many of the hopes of the Heller-Pechman plan have been obtained. As the various studies summarized above show, the local level of government has been strengthened, fiscal disparities have been reduced, fiscal pressures have been relieved, local service expenditures have been increased or stabilized, some measure of greater progression has been introduced in to the US system of taxation to the extent of the progression of the US income tax, and some particularly needy areas of poverty in both rural and urban areas have been aided, especially in black-dominated jurisdictions.

However, the programmes have not achieved all their hopes. With respect to the formula, the measure of fiscal capacity used, *per capita* incomes, is inappropriate at State level since it does not reflect the diversity of revenue sources used, whilst for local governments, which raise most of their revenue from property taxes, it is quite irrelevant (Manvel 1971). The measure of fiscal effort adopted takes account of only taxation and ignores user charges and loans which are highly variable between jurisdictions and are very significant in some. Thus the effort indicator fails to measure the extent of true burdens, and also fails to control for three factors; first, the extent to which jurisdictions choose to support a higher level of services; second, the quality differences in local services; third, the extent of local services, i.e. different local governments are involved in providing essentially different bundles of public goods. Hence, the use of raw effort measures in assessment of need may be merely subsidizing inefficiency in jurisdictions that choose a higher level of service provision (Break 1967). In addition, the local–State division of allotment (step 2 in table 13.13) ignores the variation in revenue needs and resources between States. If this factor were taken into account it would raise considerably the allocation to city governments in urbanized States, e.g. from 66.6% to 73.4% in California, 74.5% in New Jersey and 75% in New York. There also seems to be no clear logic underlying the use of County level allocations. Schmid *et al.* (1975) demonstrate that considerable simplification would result from eliminating this step (step 3 in table 13.14) for local allotments. An additional set of criticisms of the formula relate to the floors and ceilings which set the maximum and minimum constraints (Nathan and Adams 1976, 1977). These affect 11,000 or about a third of local governments, and further 1100 receive no revenue at all. The 165% ceiling is particularly important in limiting the allocations to urban areas; whilst the 20% floor, although of minor influence, consistently penalizes small and marginal governments. Finally, revenue-sharing may have induced increased inefficiency, encouraging what has been termed "the hazy injection of miscellaneous moneys" (Nathan *et al.* 1977, p. 279). Certainly the revenue-sharing funds directed to many of the very small New England counties and Mid-Western towns may fall into this category where revenue-sharing has been unnecessary to local needs, and has been wastefully employed.

It is perhaps still too early to pass final judgement on the importance of these effects, but it would certainly seem that revenue-sharing has strengthened rather than weakened US local government. It has emphasized local action, two-thirds of revenue going directly to this level, and has been responsible for the receipt by many governments of their first federal funds. As such it has allowed direct federal participation in a number of local policy areas, and has thus in many ways circumvented the Constitution. Hence, Nathan and Adams (1976) conclude that the general effect has been to reduce intergovernmental tax competition, to encourage intergovernmental co-operation in public service delivery, and to strengthen small town, county and municipal governments of less than 2,500 population. Hence, it has aided decentralization and is, for many local governments, now a central element of fiscal co-ordination.

General and specific grants have become increasingly important in US fiscal co-ordination increasing from 1 to over 16% of State and local revenues over the 70 years up to 1976. Traditionally these grants have been special purpose 'categoricals' administered mainly through the Department of Health, Education and Welfare: so-called HEW Grants. In recent years, however, especially since 1972, there has been a steady increase in general purpose 'block-grants'. There are currently about 500 different special and general purpose grant programmes the number being reduced significantly by amalgamation in recent year. The origin of these grants dates from the one-off land and cash payments derived from the 1785 *Articles of Federation*. The format of rural grants was begun by the *Morrill Act* of 1862 and *Hatch Act* of 1887. Up until 1911, these grants were aimed mainly at education (the Land-Grant Colleges) and agriculture, but at that date the *Weeks Act* offered federal assistance to fire protection of forested areas. This was followed by other programmes aimed at funding other public goods: the 1916 *Federal Aid to Roads Act*, became the major grant programme of that time; the *Smith–Hughes Act* of 1917 assisted the payment of teachers' salaries; and other Acts followed concerned with rehabilitating industrial injuries, and with maternal and child health.

A major impetus was given to grants by the 1930s depression. Whilst much of the assistance was concerned with road and other construction programmes (a major example being TVA), this period was influential in reducing the demands for local matching, and increasing the magnitude of welfare grants. The latter increased 100-fold from 1930–34, and culminated in the *Social Security Act* of 1935 giving grant aid to localities for the dependent children (AFDC Program), for the old and blind, and from 1950, for permanently and totally disabled. Although there was a brief reduction in the magnitude of grant programmes over the period of the Second World War, the period since 1952 has seen a steady growth in federal aid to State and local governments, with a very rapid quickening for the period since 1965. Important grant programmes in this period were Public Assistance for Highway Construction in the 1950s; Medicaid linked to the AFDC Program from 1965; the *Economic Opportunity Act* (1964) for education of the poor; and the creation of the Economic Development Administration in 1964, directing capital aid to public works in centres of high unemployment. The period since 1965 has also seen the emergence of general block grants and a large number of grants with very few strings attached. Apart from revenue-sharing, the *Housing and Community Development Act* (1974) created the CDBG, the *Comprehensive Employment and Training Act* (CETA 1976) subsidized local public employment, the *Urban Mass Transit Administration* (1976) aimed at improving urban transport, and the *Emergency Public Works Program* of the EDA (1976) has given aid to areas on the basis of employment problems, and this has been followed by the 1976–77 *Countercyclical Revenue-Sharing Program* (Schultze *et al.* 1971).

Table 13.16 lists US specific grants by functional programme and shows the heavy concentration of these grants in commerce, transport, education,

Table 13.16 Federal grants to State and local governments in 1975; the last two columns exclude general purpose grants. (*Sources:* ACIR, *Significant Features of Fiscal Federalism* 1976–77, and ACIR 1977)

Programme	$m	% of total grants	formula based (%)	Matching (%)
(1) Specific grants				
National defence	74	0.1	20.0	100.0
Agriculture	404	0.8	50.0	62.5
Natural resources, environment and energy	2,479	5.0	12.7	90.9
Commerce and transport	5,872	11.8	43.1	82.3
Community and regional development	3,335	6.7	0.0	70.6
Education, training, unemployment and social services	11,638	23.4	33.9	41.7
Health	8,810	17.7	8.4	60.6
Income security	9,279	18.7	50.0	36.4
Veterans' benefits	32	0.06	50.0	100.0
Law and justice	725	1.4	23.1	61.5
General government	105	0.2	0	100.0
(2) General purpose grants and revenue-sharing	6,971	14.0	—	—
Total	49,723	100	33.0	61.5

Table 13.17 General grants to State and local governments in the 1977 fiscal year (*Source:* ACIR 1977b)

Programme	$m	% of general grants total	% of total grants
(1) General purpose grants			
General revenue-sharing	6,776	33.8	9.3
Countercyclical revenue-sharing, TVA and special assistance	3,156	15.7	4.3
(2) 'Broad-based' block grants			
Community Development block grant (CDBG)	2,250	11.2	3.1
Comprehensive health	104	0.5	0.0
Comprehensive employment training (CETA)	2,792	13.9	3.8
Social service	2,713	13.5	3.7
Criminal justice	486	2.4	0.7
School aid for federally impacted areas	791	3.9	1.1
Local public works	987	4.9	1.4
Total	20,055	100	27.7

health, income security, and social service sectors. Of these grants, a large percentage have matching requirements, relatively low matching required only in education, income, security and social services. In addition, a significant proportion of these grants are allocated by general formulae rather than through individual jurisdictional bids on a project basis. Formula allocation is especially important in agriculture, commerce and transport, education and social services, income security, and veteran benefits. Generally those areas with the lowest level of matching place the greater reliance on allocation formulae. Comparable data for general block grants and revenue-sharing are given in table 13.17. These grants, however, are almost uniformly based on formulae for allocation and do not require matching. The major elements which enter the allocation formulae of the major general and specific grants are usually population, unemployment rates, and *per capita* income, and are the major need indicators adopted, with poverty and over-crowded housing entering the relatively recent CDBG.

In a study of five major US grant programmes, Cuciti (1978) found a variable relation to needs measured at city level as summarized in table 13.18. Needs in this study derive from the three indicators of social, economic, and fiscal need discussed in chapter 5 (p. 101) and are standardized by the following formula:

$$\text{Need of city } (i) = \frac{N_i - N_{\min}}{N_{\max} - N_{\min}}$$

Table 13.18 Relation of five US grant programmes to measures of need (discussed in chapter 5, p. 109). (*Source*: Cuciti 1978; Congressional Budget Office Analysis, Tables 16, 18, 21, 23, 25). Data relate to the 1977 fiscal year.

	Number of cities	General revenue-sharing to city government	General revenue-sharing to city and overlying County government	Antirecession fiscal assistance to city government	Antirecession fiscal assistance to city government and overlying county government	CETA Title I (block grant)	CETA Title II (public service employment)	CETA Title VI (public service employment)	Local public works grants per capita	1977 actual distribution	1977 distribution if based solely on hold-harmless considerations	1977 distribution if based solely on 1974 Act formula only	Estimated 1980 distribution based on dual formula and no hold-harmless
Social need													
All cities	39	21.60	27.83	5.96	7.18	9.74	1.99	8.28	28.71	27.86	25.53	18.78	35.63
High	10	24.71	30.85	9.26	10.39	12.86	2.34	10.06	35.45	29.90	27.85	22.85	44.85
Medium	19	21.25	28.23	5.49	7.03	8.85	1.94	7.74	28.01	28.71	27.14	18.11	34.61
Low	10	19.18	24.06	3.55	4.24	8.30	1.74	7.53	23.28	24.22	20.42	15.99	28.33
Economic need													
All cities	45	21.10	27.51	5.94	7.24	9.75	2.02	8.18	29.99	27.81	25.11	18.72	34.76
High	10	25.75	30.53	9.27	10.58	11.63	2.15	9.45	40.56	29.70	27.78	20.59	49.78
Medium	25	21.10	28.69	5.88	7.29	10.18	2.18	8.64	31.54	29.42	27.91	18.85	34.93
Low	10	16.44	21.52	2.76	3.78	6.81	1.47	5.75	15.56	21.89	15.44	16.55	19.31
Fiscal need													
All cities	38	21.25	27.72	6.46	7.88	10.07	2.09	8.41	32.43	28.66	26.23	18.84	35.93
High	10	28.29	31.55	9.65	10.64	11.70	2.05	8.75	42.03	33.89	31.96	21.27	44.11
Medium	18	21.74	28.62	6.54	8.06	10.38	2.19	8.43	31.25	30.62	28.18	20.04	37.93
Low	10	14.33	22.27	3.13	4.80	7.87	1.96	8.00	24.96	19.90	16.98	14.24	24.14

where N_i is the need indicator for city i, and N_{max} and N_{min} are the respective national maximum and minimum values of all city needs. For the anti-recession fiscal assistance package and local public works programme, the distribution of grants is fairly closely related to all three measures of need; but the three other programmes show a less clear relation. For general revenue-sharing, the direct payments to cities are only slightly higher for the more needy cities; for CETA grants, targeting to need is more effective in the case of Title I (concerned with manpower block grants), than for public service employment Titles II and III. Each is more closely related to social than fiscal or economic need. Finally, the CDBG is very poorly targeted to needy cities. As Cuciti and other have noted, however, this arises mainly from the hold-harmless provisions. If these provisions were removed, the allocation to most cities would be smaller, but much better matched to need, especially social need, as shown in table 13.18.

A major effect of federal grant programmes since about 1960 has been to direct aid to concentrations of poverty especially in cities. Apart from the *Model Cities Program*, few of these grants are aimed solely at poverty or cities, and it is argued by some commentators that insignificant aid to cities has resulted (e.g. Downs 1978). But many grants, in aiding education, the environment, and community development, do directly help cities. A major feature of the last 20 years has been, first, a major shift in federal grant programmes from apportioning grants to States, to apportioning grants directly to city and local government instead. This has the benefit of better targeting aid to localities overcoming State level pork-barrelling. The percentage of federal payments to local as opposed to State level governments increased from 9.2% in 1960 to 12.6% in 1968, to 18.2% in 1972 and 28.3% in 1974. The major influences here are the impact of revenue-sharing in 1972, and block grants appropriations for the Community Development Acts in 1978. A second feature has been a shift from project grants to block grants (Nathan and Dommel 1977). This has had a diffusional, spreading effect: whereas project grants, which are allocated on the basis of individually approved projects, can be targeted to various specific and local beneficiaries, formula grants are automatic and treat all localities identically that have the same social or economic indicators. This has had good features in that small suburban and city governments have benefited which have previously received no aid or little aid. But there have also been serious detrimental effects; large cities with severe hardships have received less in relative terms, many governments lacking real need have been aided, and the targeting in relation to the severity of need has been lost. The formula has been more popular, in many ways, because of the relative strength of Congress in contrast to weak Presidential administrations since 1972. The politics of the computer printout, so extensively referred to over this period, have come to dominate most Congressional votes on grant programmes (see chapter 15). Hence to succeed, a formula must give something to each, or to most Congressional Districts.

The US system of fiscal co-ordination is interesting because of its complexity, the political forces that have shaped it, and the immense amount of research that has been invested in monitoring and studying it. However, it is probably one of the less successful national programmes of co-ordination. Real equalization of expenditure need and revenue capacity is achieved in only a few programmes. Generally the influence of Congressional pork-barrelling has diffused the impacts of many important programmes, and the excessive fragmentation of government, with jealously guarded local and bureaucratic autonomy, has prevented the achievement of co-ordinated development or tackling of fiscal issues, especially within urban areas. This has resulted in a number of important legal battles under the State Constitutions, especially noteworthy being those with respect to inequalities in educational provision in the *Serrano v. Priest* legal case (Coons *et al.* 1970). Probably in no other country are the benefits and faults of excessively localized and fragmented government better developed.

13.5 Fiscal co-ordination in the Federal Republic of Germany

The present arrangements for fiscal co-ordination in West Germany derive from the new German constitution established in the 1949 *Basic Law* (*Grundgesetz*). They possess a number of unique features. Legislative, tax assessment, tax rates, and tax allocation functions of the public fisc are reserved to the federal level, whilst administrative and expenditure functions are reserved to the State level or *Länder*. The *Länder* have a large number of important tax sources (especially wealth and estate duty). The local authorities (*Gemeinden*) rely on sharing taxes with the *Länder* and had no taxes of their own until 1956, when they were given exclusive rights to the property tax (*Realsteuern*), businesses and trade tax (*Gewerhesteuer*), and excise. The *Gewerhesteuer* became the most important of these components in the 1960s. Unfortunately the emphasis on business tax at the local level resulted in a high degree of interjurisdictional competition and a large extent of pro-cyclical (perverse) variation in local expenditures (Reissart 1978; Timm 1969). Hence from 1970 onwards 40% of local business taxes were reallocated to the *Länder* in exchange for 14% of the federal–*Länder* personal income tax. However, taxes constitute only about 30% of local revenues, the rest coming from mainly intergovernmental transfers and borrowing. The division of revenues between the various levels of government is summarized in table 13.19.

At the level of the *Länder* (shown in figure 13.11) considerable participation is allowed in federal functions through their voting powers in the *Bundesrat*, but their major powers are in administration of public infrastructure, and with public planning and expenditure. A level of fiscal co-ordination between *Länder* was instituted in the *Basic Law* deriving from the almost unique institution of horizontal transfers under the *Länderfinanzausgleich*. With the rapid expansion in the demand for public goods since 1949, the *Länder* have come to play an increasingly important part in the German federation such

Table 13.19 Division of revenue sources between levels of government in West Germany in 1976. (*Source: Statistisches Jahrbuch*, Statistisches Bundesamt, Wiesbaden, 1977)

Revenue sources as percentage of all revenues

Revenue	%	Revenue	%
(1) Bund		*(3) Gemeinden*	
Customs	1.3	Land tax	1.8
Stocks transfer	0.1	Business profits	
		and capital	7.5
Insurance and stamp duty	0.5	Payroll	1.2
Tobacco, coffee, spirits,		Property tax	
sparkling wine, sugar	5.7	supplement	0.3
Oil	7.1	Other	0.2
Other	0.4		———
	———	Total Gemeinden taxes	11.0
Total Bund taxes	15.3		
(2) Länder		*(4) Shared taxes*	
Property tax	1.4	Personal income tax	29.5
Inheritance	0.2	Gifts	11.6
Ground rent	0.3	Capital transfer	0.9
Motor vehicle	2.2	Business profits and	
		imports	22.5
Racing, lotteries,			
fire control	0.4		———
Beer	0.5	Total shared taxes	68.7
	———		
Total Länder taxes	5.0		

that since the institution of the *Finanzverfassungsgesetz* arrangement of 1955, most taxes are shared between the *Bund, Länder*, and *Gemeinden*. Specific purpose grants to the *Länder* were initiated in the early 1950s mainly for low-cost housing, regional policy, agriculture development, and university construction with transport investment added in 1967. However, the increasing importance of these grants has led to three criticisms. First, it was felt by the 1960s that these grants violated the *Basic Law* by infringing the independence of the *Länder* in their expenditure functions. Second, these grants possess considerable incentives for the *Länder* to manipulate tax yields and increase the dependence of the poorer regions (Rheinland–Pfalz, Niedersachsen, Schleswig–Holstein and Saarland) on the richer regions (Hamburg, Bremen, Hessen and Baden–Württemberg). Finally, Knott (1977) has argued that the federal grants have increased the already high level of pro-cyclical, and hence fiscally perverse, behaviour of German local finance. This is mainly due to the heavy concentration of local expenditures and local grants in the construction sector. Moreover, variations between *Länder* indicate the surprising result that the richer and larger *Länder* pursue more

Figure 13.11 West Germany: the *Länder* and Berlin.

pro-cyclical policies than the poorer *Länder*. To counteract these tendencies the *Troeger-Kommission*, reporting in 1966 (*Kommission für die Finanzreform* 1966), recommended, first, that block grants should be instituted for 'joint· tasks', defined by constitutional amendments to the *Basic Law* as exceptions

387

Table 13.20   Percentage of each revenue source allocated to each level of government in German revenue-sharing

Revenue source	% revenue to each level of government		
	Bund	Länder	Gemeinden
Personal income tax	43	43	14
Corporate income tax	50	50	—
Business taxes	60.5	19.75	19.75
VAT 1973	35	65	—
1974	37	63	—
1975	31.75	68.75	—
1976	31	69	—

to the federal separation of powers; and second, that specific grants should be continued in more limited form and their purpose made clearer. These proposals were implemented from 1971 onwards following the 1969 *Finance Act* (Reissart 1978; Scharpf *et al.* 1976), and have been confirmed in the report of the *Enquete-Kommission* (1976). Hence, today intergovernmental relations and fiscal co-ordination in Germany have become extremely complex with a range of co-ordinative arrangements larger than in most other countries. Each major category of these is discussed in turn below.

Tax base-sharing between *Bund* and *Länder* is an important component of co-ordination and involves four main revenue sources: personal income tax, corporate income tax, business taxes and VAT. Personal income tax and business taxes on industry and trade are shared between all three levels of government (*Bund, Länder* and *Gemeinden* being allocated to the *Länder* on the basis of residence of the payer for income tax, and the location of the Head Office for business taxes. The percentage available to each level of government is shown in table 13.20. Only the VAT is redistributed on an equalization formula, each of the other taxes is apportioned on a basis which reflects as closely as possible the areas from which the revenues are raised. The *Länder* have always been staunch defenders of this principle and this has lead to some adjustments of the personal and corporate income taxes since 1970. However, a shortage of revenues by *Gemeinden* in the late 1960s resulted in the need for guarantees of 14% of personal income tax in the 1949 *Finance Act*. The VAT has been reapportioned between *Länder* since the 1969 *Finance Act* in two components. First, each *Land* receives 35% of the total *Länder* allocation on the basis of its population. Then a second element gives supplementary shares to the poorer *Länder* to give them at least 92% of the average VAT contribution. The apportionment of revenue *per capita* between the *Länder* as a percentage of the *Länder* average can be seen in table 13.21, where column 1 shows the *per capita* tax revenues before VAT redistribution, and column 2 the *per capita* tax revenue after VAT redistribution. The *Länder* in receipt of the redistributed VAT revenues are italicized. This results in a considerable

Table 13.21 Fiscal co-ordination between German *Länder* in 1973 with *Länder* receiving transfers italicized. (*Source*: EEC 1977, pp. 157, 164, 172)

Land	% Länder average			
	Per capita tax revenue before VAT redistribution and equalization (includes Land share of Joint taxes and own taxes)	*Per capita tax revenue after VAT redistribution*	*Per capita tax revenue after VAT distribution and inter-Länder equalization (Länderfinanzgleich)*	*Per capita tax revenue after VAT distribution, equalization and supplementary grants (Ergänzungsweisungen)*
Hamburg	164.3	147.9	132.4	132.4
Bremen	123.0	116.0	*124.0*	124.0
Hessen	110.7	106.6	101.2	101.2
Baden–Württemberg	109.0	105.3	100.0	100.0
Nordrhein–Westfalen	104.7	102.0	100.3	100.3
Bayern	94.5	95.8	97.0	97.9
Rheinland–Pfalz	86.4	89.0	95.0	97.5
Niedersachsen	81.0	88.1	95.8	98.1
Schleswig–Holstein	77.3	88.1	96.9	99.5
Saarland	72.2	88.1	*101.7*	*104.0*
Federal average	100	100	100	100

increase in revenue receipts for the three poorest *Länder* (Niedersachsen, Schleswig–Holstein and Saarland).

Additional reallocative tax base-sharing is operated under a horizontal transfer scheme between the *Länder* under the *Länderfinanzausgleich*. This set of horizontal transfers represent a fiscal co-ordination practice which is almost unique to West Germany. This set of transfers raises revenues in the poorer regions to 95% of the federal average. It is much less important than VAT in achieving equalization and is determined using a complex formula with three elements of tax capacity, equalization indicators, and a transfer weighting. The formula is given by:

$$\frac{\text{size of}}{\text{transfer}} = \left(\frac{\text{Land tax}}{\text{capacity}} - \frac{\text{Land equalization}}{\text{indicator}} \right) \times \frac{\text{Land transfer}}{\text{weighting}}$$

Tax capacity is measured as the sum of the *Land* and *Gemeinden* revenues. For the *Land* this is the share of the joint taxes (personal and corporate income tax, VAT and trade levies) and of its own taxes (estate duty, wealth tax, car tax, alcohol, betting, and gaming taxes). For the *Gemeinden*, capacity is determined as 50% of the share of income, real estate and trade tax on profits and capital, minus trade tax levies. In addition, each locality has its capacity reduced on a flat rate for university, port amenity costs, and other national 'merit' goods. The *equalization indicator* is given by the difference in the sum of *Land* and *Gemeinden per capita* average tax revenues from those of the federal *per capita* average, multiplied by a variable weighting made up of three components:

(i) *Population size element*:

Population sizes	weighting
0–5,000	1.0
5,001–20,000	1.1
20,001–100,000	1.15
100,001–500,000	1.2
500,001–1 million	1.25
over 1 million	1.3

(ii) *City–State element*
(Hamburg and Bremen)   1.35

(iii) *Density element*
Density *(persons/km²)*

1,500–2,000	1.02
2,001–3,000	1.04
over 3,000	1.06

These elements are a crude attempt to measure *Länder* needs and correspond approximately to a similar indicators in the UK Rate Support Grant. The final component of the *transfer weighting* adjusts the magnitude of the fiscal transfers by the percentage difference of the capacity and equalization components as follows:

Percentage difference (*capacity — equalization*)	Weighting
— 92	1.0
— 92 to 100	0.375
100 to 102	0
102 to 110	— 0.7
over 110	— 1.0

Thus *Länder* with very high needs and low tax capacity receive a full assessment of the *Länderfinanzausgleich*, this is moderated to become 0.375 of the need-capacity difference for less needy areas, and from *Länder* with very high capacity in relation to need a fiscal transfer is exacted. Thus, this transfer programme gives a form of full equalization transfer, as shown in figure 12.4; and, as shown in column 3 of table 13.21, achieves a considerable degree of financial equalization between *Länder*.

A final component of block grant *Bund–Länder* transfers is the system of supplementary grants or *Ergänzungszweisungen*. Since 1972, this has been a fixed grant for *Länder*, which between 1974 and 1976 amounted to 1.5% of total VAT revenue. It has become an increasing proportion of the equalization element growing from 8% of equalization in 1970 to 39% in 1974. As shown in column 4 on table 13.21, it is responsible for raising the equalization rate to 97.5% of the *per capita Länder* average. Five *Länder* are in receipt of the grant (Bayern 21.8%; Niedersachsen 36.9%; Rheinland–Pfalz 20.6%; Saarland 5.8%; Schleswig–Holstein 14.9%).

Specific grants in Germany are used for a large variety of programmes none of which are of large magnitude, but the overall impact of these grants is significant, amounting to about 24% of local income since 1963. The distribution of specific grants between *Länder* by a programme as shown in table 13.22 from which it can be seen that education, transport, and housing amount to the largest components. These grants are reallocated between *Länder* partly as general block grants (45%), and partly as specific grants especially for capital investment (55%). The formula for distribution of these grants uses various indicators of needs and capacity (Deutscher Städtetag 1973; Gerhardt 1976). The grants consist of five groups. First, the *Gemeinschaftsaufgaben* (or 'common tasks'), introduced in 1969 following the Troeger Report, and used to finance national merit goods such as university, aid to lagging regions, agricultural investment, and coastal protection. Second, there is limited federal funding and co-ordination in education and research. Third, there are restitutions for federal delegated functions (*Bundesauftragsverwaltung* and *Geldleistungsgetze*) where *Länder* undertake military administration, airport and road construction, give student grants, and housing and savings subsidies on behalf of the federal government.

Table 13.22 Specific grants in Germany: Dm *per capita* allocation to *Länder* by programme in 1973 (*Source*: Reissart 1978b, table 6)

Land	Health	Education	Transport	Housing	Regional and other structural policies	Sub-total	CDP 1973
Baden–Württemberg	14.8	42.9	29.1	47.1	25.2	159.1	15,280
Bayern	15.6	38.9	29.5	45.3	40.7	170.0	14,260
Berlin	22.9	48.2	44.8	41.4	6.8	164.1	16,498
Bremen	16.4	56.0	23.2	45.1	10.9	151.6	19,823
Hamburg	18.8	52.9	54.0	40.9	6.8	173.4	25,496
Hessen	16.2	42.3	44.1	40.3	22.8	165.7	15,651
Niedersachsen	15.9	38.5	28.2	43.7	57.1	183.4	12,596
Nordrhein–Westfalen	15.0	50.2	36.7	38.5	12.7	153.1	15,221
Rheinland–Pfalz	17.0	26.8	21.1	41.1	34.6	140.6	14,045
Saarland	20.6	28.7	17.0	32.3	41.3	139.9	13,243
Schleswig–Holstein	14.8	19.4	15.9	44.7	83.6	178.4	12,215
Total Dm *per capita*	15.9	42.1	32.4	42.3	29.9	162.6	14,951
Total Dm millions	984	2,609	2,010	2,620	1,853	10,076	

Fourth, there are federal grants-in-aid for investment (*Finanzhilfen*) to achieve short-term stabilization and long-term growth: mainly in local transport, urban development, housing and hospitals. Finally, there are various miscellaneous grants. As can be seen from the table, the greatest range of grant payments obtain in the cases of transport and regional policies, and these in fact are the main sources of equalization in specific grants.

Despite the complexity of tax-sharing and equalization arrangements, considerable difficulties are still present in the poorer regions. Since the *Länderfinanzausgleich* is based on capacity measures rather than revenue burdens, effort or more general measures of need, the fiscal co-ordination system has been insufficient to achieve total equality under the public fisc (Hunter 1972; Rothweiler 1972; Spahn 1977). Grants-in-aid (*Finanzhilfen*) and other specific grants have eased the situation in selected areas, but the problems of fiscal inequity remain. The *Gemeinschaftsaufgaben* has had a particular significance in helping to overcome some of these problems; it has been an important force in the depressed area policy for regions (see chapter 14) and, through the institution of planning boards has encouraged *Bund* and *Länder* co-operation. The *Bund* and *Länder* have been forced to work together in planning commissions, and the unanimity voting pattern more usual in inter-*Länder* commissions has been eroded. However, the *Länder* have been brought under greater regulatory control giving greater national uniformity in the standards of some important services, but at the expense of a loss in regional autonomy (Kisker 1971). This has stimulated further constitutional amendments bringing a larger number of functions into joint rather than sole *Länder* control (Johnson 1973; Reissart 1978; Scharpf *et al.* 1978). The 'common-task' grants have given an important stimulus to vertical financial and administrative co-ordination in Germany. However, some commentators (Reissart 1978; Scharpf *et al.* 1976) have argued that since all joint-task decisions require the support of both federal government and a majority of *Länder*, the decisions have tended to become over complicated and bureaucratic (Marnitz 1974), and have avoided real problem-solving in favour of the consensus requirements of short-term non-selective and non-targeted aid; a pattern similar to the pork-barrel politics of the US. Despite these problems, it is clear that the financial arrangements in Germany since the Troeger Report have allowed a very useful degree of intergovernmental co-ordination, which has eliminated what Reissart (1978, p. 15) terms the 'ruinous competition' between jurisdictions characteristic of the 1950–1970 period. Indeed, the *Enquete-Kommission* Report of 1976 has supported the value of the present system although suggesting that further 'organic evolution' is required.

13.6 Fiscal co-ordination in Australia

The Australian Federation was first established in 1901 along the lines of the US model, with the States retaining the major powers. It is constituted as a Commonwealth of six States, Northern Territory, which is en route to

Figure 13.12   Australia: the States, the Northern Territory and the Capital Territory.

eventual statehood, and the Australia Capital Territory (ACT) of Canberra. These are shown in figure 13.12. Within the States there are a variety of local government units, 890 in number, the structure of which differs between the States (especially in terms of the assessment procedure for the primary local revenue source of the property tax); and indeed the structure also differs within each state. However, the structure broadly reflects the English local government system pre-1972, with cities, municipalities, towns, boroughs and Civic/District Councils, plus an increasing range of *ad hoc* special purpose governments (Bowman 1976). Whilst the States have the primary constitutional powers in most major expenditure functions, the Local Authorities, especially those in the cities, have assumed a new status since 1973 and have acquired an important role in both revenue receipt and expenditure functions. In 1973 increased aid was channelled directly to local governments from the Grants Commission as part of the Labour government's policy under Whitlam of attempting to reduce the power of the State governments. Whitlam saw the States either as slow, incapable or unwilling to shoulder important responsibilities, or, because of the growth of *ad hoc* State bodies, as taking too dominant a role in government removing democratic control from the local level (Whitlam 1974). Since 1976, the New Federalism policy of the Liberal government under Fraser has sought to diffuse governmental decision making powers. This has led to a re-emphasized role for the States but retaining emphasis in the local level by a pass-through of grants from the Commonwealth Grants Commission and sharing a percentage of the federal personal income tax at local level. On the one hand, the post-1976 period can be argued to have had a fundamental effect on federal–State relations, with the Fraser government trying to impose more responsibility on the States especially for social programmes. On the other hand, it can be argued that the Fraser government has 'passed the buck' for many programmes without reducing the level of federal taxes or giving sufficient new revenue sources to the States.

As in the US, many difficulties have arisen from the profusion and variety of local political units in metropolitan areas which have zoned and taxed in order to exclude poorer groups. Recently, co-ordination between local governments has been encouraged by tax-sharing incentives with the Commonwealth government, but the effect has usually been limited in practice because of the individualism of the local units.

The primary fiscal problems of the Australian Federation have been two-fold. First, to overcome local level fiscal competition between local government units, additional co-operation has been fostered by the Whitlam grant policy of creating regional commissions (see, for example, DURD 1974; Logan *et al.* 1975; Task force Report 1975), but again the effects have been fairly limited. The second problem has been to balance the expenditure needs and fiscal capacity of the less and more populated States. On the one hand, the less populated States, have high expenditure need deriving from the low density and sparsity of their population, especially as this affects the provision of roads and distribution services such as electricity. On the other hand, the less populated States usually have lower *per capita* incomes than the more populated States of NSW and Victoria. In addition, there have been the special fiscal needs of the Northern Territory and ACT which have been catered for by direct grants from the Commonwealth government, with ACT often considered to have been very well provided for at national expense.

Within this federal structure the Commonwealth government has, since 1942, retained most of the revenue-raising powers, leaving only 20 to 30% at State and Local level. However, most of the expenditure functions have been administered at a State and a few at Local Authority level. Hence, there has evolved a complex set of intergovernmental transfer programmes. However, since 1973 there has been an important shift in the revenue powers from Commonwealth to State and Local level consequent upon tax-sharing arrangements of the personal income tax. This has had two major impacts: first, to raise the share of revenue and resources available at State and Local levels, thus reducing the need for grant-based transfers (although these are still very significant); and second, to throw more emphasis on the Local level by creating the first set of specific Commonwealth–Local Authority transfers with a mandated pass through the State level to local governments. As a result, the Australian Federation is in a state of transition from the financial point of view. Hence much of the discussion below must be preliminary and encompasses both the pre- and post-1976 period. General grants, specific grants and tax-sharing arrangements have been developed, and each of these is discussed in turn below, together with the mechanics of capital finance. More detailed discussion of Australian intergovernmental fiscal relations is given in the *Annual Reports* of the Commonwealth Grants Commission from 1934 onwards, in the Commonwealth Government of Australia annual budget statement *Payment to or for the States*, and in Dawson (1973), Head (1967), May (1971), Mathews (1974b), Mathews and Jay (1972), Maxwell (1967) and Spahn (1973).

General grants. In Australia general grants derive initially from attempts to allocate portions of the federal customs and excise revenue and of 'surplus revenue'. However, from 1910–11 these payments have been supplemented by *Special Assistance Grants* to the poorer States (which included at various times Queensland, W. Australia, Tasmania and S. Australia) and from 1934–5 these grants have been disbursed under the recommendation of the Commonwealth Grants Commision. From 1942 until 1958–9 *Tax Reimbursement Grants* were paid to the States as compensation for the loss of the revenue source of personal income tax during the Second World War; and from 1958–9 until 1976–77 these grants were replaced by *Financial Assistance Grants*. In addition, *Special Revenue Assistance Grants* have been paid on an *ad hoc* basis where compensation for special needs has been requested. Hence, over the period since 1942 up to 1976–77, Australian general grants have fallen into three categories: Special Assistance Grants, Financial Assistance Grants and Special Revenue Assistance Grants. Each of these is discussed in turn below (further details may be found in Dawson 1973; Head 1967, Mathews 1975; and Maxwell 1974).

(i) Special Assistance Grants, although instituted in 1910–11, attained significance with the establishment of the *Commonwealth Grants Commission Act* (1933). They are payments to a limited number of poorer States to compensate for differences in both fiscal capacity and expenditure need. As such, they possess more in common with the UK RSG than intergovernmental transfers in North America or Germany. *Total capacity* is measured on a representative tax system composed of eight main revenue sources which the States control (probate and estate duties, land tax, stamp duty, alcohol, gambling, payroll, corporation payments, and land revenue and mining royalties). However, the fiscal capacity index is supplemented by measurement of revenue yield at standard tax efforts (set equal to the average of the more populated States but by convention limited in practice to NSW and Victoria). Hence, at an international level it is one of the few transfer schemes to combine assessment of both capacity and effort. *Expenditure need* is measured mainly with respect to revenue requirements in the Social Services (since these constitute the major expenditure functions of Australian State Governments). The expenditure in each Social Service field is estimated as the difference of (a) the costs of each State's social services operated at the average of the wealthy States, from (b) the cost in the wealthy States. As such, it is designed to compensate for sizes of client groups, differences in service costs, differences in administration and debt charge, and variation in the mix of private and public provision. In the case of both the measures of fiscal capacity and expenditure need, comparison with NSW and Victoria has been resented, particularly because it has led to strings being attached to programmes such that revenue expenditure patterns *have to match* those in the two more populated States. As a result, States have frequently preferred other grant programmes. The Grants Commission formula for equalization between State governments is an interesting one because of its inclusion of capacity, effort and fiscal need. Indeed Australia has been one of the first countries to implement tax effort indices in grant programmes (see Grant Commission annual reports, 7th 1940; 19th 1942). The formula is also of increasing significance because of its use in other grant programmes, especially tax sharing with local governments, to be discussed below. The grant allocation *per capita* is given by the following formula (Mathews 1972a, 1975);

$$T_i = \left(D_i - \frac{D_s}{P_s} P_i \right) + \left(E_i - P_i \frac{E_s}{B_s} \frac{B_i}{P_i} \right) + \left(P_i \frac{N_s}{P_s} (1 + \gamma) - N_i \right)$$

where D = budget deficit, P = population, E = revenue from State taxes, B = tax base, E/B = tax severity (fiscal effort), B/P = *per capita* revenue capacity, N = recurrent expenditure (need), γ = additional % cost of services in State i relative to standard States s. T is the level of grant allocated, and the subscript s refers to the "standard" wealthy States (NSW, Q and Victoria up to 1958–9, NSW and Victoria 1958–9 onwards). The grant is composed of three elements: first, the differential budget; second, relative tax severity; and third, differences in expenditure levels or need. Despite its benefits, the formula is undermined by the inclusion of the budget component. As a result of this factor, tax severity is reduced almost to a measure of tax capacity alone, whilst expenditure need registers only total cost differences; quality factors are ignored.

The size of the Special Equalization Grants is minor over-all, but they have been very significant for the poorer States, especially Tasmania. Moreover, since the grants equalize only for the residual after allowance in their distribution for other federal grant transfers, they are important in increasing the level of equalization, and their significance would have increased if other transfers had been less equalizing. The relative size of the special grants can be seen from column 3 of table 13.23. From this it can be seen that the significance of the grants has declined in recent years, with Queensland now

Table 13.23 Australian general grants *per capita* (A$) in 1976–77, with 1971–72 in brackets. (*Source: Payments to or for the States* 1979–80)

State	(1) Financial Assistance Grant		(2) Special Revenue Assistance Grant		(3) Special Equalization Grant		(4) Total Grants	
NSW	228	(99)	—	(7.71)	—	—	228	(107)
Victoria	222	(99)	—	(3.85)	—	—	222	(102)
Queensland	306	(125)	—	(4.65)	12.5	(4.9)	319	(135)
S. Australia	337	(134)	—	(5.01)	—	(10.1)	337	(149)
W. Australia	364	(163)	—	(5.75)	—	—	364	(169)
Tasmania	452	(178)	—	(6.41)	—	(24.6)	452	(209)
Total	267.	(114)	—	(5.73)	12.5	(2.4)	269	(122)

the only claimant. Tasmania withdrew from the scheme in 1974–75 in a complex deal involving a larger general grant and the transfer of the State railways to the federal government. S. Australia withdrew in 1975–76.

A significance feature of the Special Equalization Grants programme has been the role of the Commonwealth Grant Commission. This is a three-man body set up by Parliament since 1933, but independent of the federal government. Its influence has been enormous, both because of its relative freedom from abuses, and because of the quality of its members over the years (see Commonwealth Grants Commission *Annual Reports*; Else-Mitchell 1974). It has, perhaps, provided a model in the international context for the objective appraisal of spending needs.

(ii) Financial Assistance Grants (FAG) have been used as an equalization programme in Australia from 1958–59 until their replacement in 1976–77 by revenue-sharing. They have constituted the major component of inter-State equalization over that period. A rather crude formula deriving from the pre-1959 Reimbursement Grants was used for their distribution. This was based on the income tax level collected from the State updated by increases in population and average wages, adjusted for density and the number of children aged 5 to 15, and a 'betterment factor' based on the level of average wages. The major difficulties arising with these grants were the infrequent updating (on a 5-year basis), inaccurate population estimates, the arbitrariness of the updating factors, and most important, the fact that their imposition precluded the States levying personal income tax. The level of the Financial Assistance Grants in 1971–72, and at their dissolution in 1976–77, is given in column 1 of table 13.23. From this it can be seen that the major beneficiaries were the four less densely populated States, with Tasmania and W. Australia receiving levels of grants respectively 30 to 40% and 60 to 70% above the *per capita* national average.

(iii) Special Revenue Assistance Grants are paid on an *ad hoc* basis on the recommendation of the Grants Commission. They are intended to offer compensation for particular expenditure needs over limited time periods, for example in 1975–76 for the transfer of the State railway system from S. Australia and Tasmania to the Commonwealth government. The grants have not been aimed at equalization in any simple or direct way: as can be seen from column 2 of table 13.23, they have declined in significance in recent years and for 1971–72 had no general relationship to the goals of equalization.

Specific grants. Probably in no other country do specific grants play a smaller and less significant role than in Australia. Although their size increased four-fold from 1960 to 1970, much greater emphasis has been placed on block transfers and revenue-sharing. Moreover, their allocation is largely on a one-off *ad hoc* basis (e.g. the Mt Lyell Mine Assistance programme). The main programmes are health, education, roads and industrial assistance. In each case allocations to the States are not made on a formula basis but are dependent instead upon a bargaining between the States and federal government largely on a project-by-project basis with some additional influence exerted by advisory commissions. These commissions may introduce formula influences, as in the case of the Australia Universities Commission which has developed needs indicators since 1959.

Most of the grants, except industrial assistance, are subject to matching which requires States to match federal funds by e.g. 25% of health capital costs, 10% of health operating costs, 65% for school education council expenditure and 50% for school education capital expenditure. For roads, matching requirements which were originally 50% are now fixed to vary as a

Table 13.24 Specific grants *per capita* in Australia 1977–78. (*Source:* Commonwealth Government of Australia 1978)

Programme	State (A$ per capita)						Total (A$m)
	NSW	Vict	Q	SA	WA	Tas	
Debt and sinking fund	2.2	2.2	2.1	3.3	2.5	5.2	2.4
Education	123.6	102.8	119.6	139.3	137.9	123.0	130.7
Hospitals and health	76.9	66.4	64.9	87.3	99.5	87.9	7.1
Social services and welfare	6.7	8.2	9.0	13.5	18.1	8.5	9.4
Housing	26.1	27.1	18.7	46.3	30.9	62.0	28.6
Environment and conservation	0.3	0.2	0.3	1.8	0.5	1.5	0.4
Transport	36.1	29.2	54.3	35.0	51.7	54.9	38.9
Water and agriculture	4.1	5.7	6.1	12.2	7.6	3.2	6.5
Other	3.9	2.1	7.5	11.5	16.9	1.5	7.6
Total (A$ per capita)	279.9	243.9	282.5	350.2	365.6	347.7	—

fraction of the rate of increase in provincial registrations of motor vehicles. The *per capita* distribution of the Australian specific grants is shown for 1977–78 in table 13.24. From this it can be seen that these grants play a particularly important role in fiscal transfers to W. Australia, Queensland S. Australia, and Tasmania for transport. Grants in respect of health, education and welfare are very broadly comparable but housing makes a significant contribution to the Tasmanian budget. Overall there is some degree of higher support for the less populated States than the more populated ones: a 5 to 35% higher level of grants *per capita*.

Revenue-sharing. In response to continuous pressure from the State governments, tax-sharing arrangements for the personal income tax were implemented in 1976–77. However, revenue-sharing in Australia, like that in the US, possesses important additional element of a New Federalism policy. A major component of this has been the implementation of transfers from Commonwealth to local government, passing through the State level (where they are hypothecated to local use), giving the local government block grants relatively free from State involvement. The revenue-sharing scheme has been implemented in two parts. Stage 1, under the *State (Personal Income Tax Sharing) Act 1976* covers the period from 1976–77, and allocates to each State a portion (33.6% in 1976–77 and 39.87% for 1978–79 onwards) of net personal income tax collections using the Financial Assistance Grant (FAG) formula until 1980–81, and replacing that grant programme. It has also absorbed a number of specific grant programmes such as Medibank. Stage 1 is subject to a complex hold-harmless provision by which a State's entitlement cannot fall below the FAG level of 1975–76, nor of the levels of FAG it would have received if revenue-sharing had not been implemented. Stage 2, implemented in the *Income Tax (Arrangements within the States) Act 1978* for 1977-78 onwards, provides that, in addition to the stage 1 arrangements, each State can increase or decrease the level of personal income tax upon its own residents, using the national assessment procedures, and with the differential levy collected by the Commonwealth Government.

The hold-harmless provision from the FAG has resulted from intense political action at the State Premiers Conference. Because of this provision and the infrequent review of the allocation procedures, many of the criticisms of the FAG allocation formula and anomalies remain, but a considerable degree of equalization between States has been achieved whilst allowing entry of the States into the personal income tax field. The Grants Commission is responsible for the assessment of the level of equalization, basing these payments on weighted population levels derived from the FAG. Where States levy income tax surcharges, the equalization payments are adjusted by the difference between (a) the yield of a given income tax surcharge in the less populous States and (b) the yield of the same surcharge if levied in NSW and Victoria. This calculation for 1978–79 is shown in table 13.25 which demonstrates the impact of the FAG formula on raising the level of

Table 13.25 Calculation of each State's share of the revenue-sharing entitlement for 1978–79. (*Source:* Commonwealth Government of Australia 1978, table 6)

State	(1) Population (000s) 31 Dec. 1978	(2) Per capita relativity (from FAG)	(3) (1) × (2)	(4) % distribution of (3)	(5) Share of 39.87% of revenue-sharing total ($m)
NSW	5029	1.02740	5167	30.5	1457.7
Victoria	3844	1.00000	3844	22.7	1090.2
Queensland	2185	1.39085	3039	18.0	844.9
S. Australia	1300	1.52676	1984	11.7	562.6
W. Australia	1239	1.66516	2062	12.2	581.4
Tasmania	416	2.00188	832	4.9	240.2
Total	14012	—	16929	100.0	4777.0

entitlement of the less populated States, especially for Tasmania, to over twice that for Victoria. In practice, because of political factors and the effects of fiscal competition, it may be expected that the level of State variation in income tax rates will be very small.

The post-1976 period of tax sharing has also been important in its impact on local government. Before 1973 there were no specific Commonwealth–Local authority transfers, although such transfers were included as a part of some other programmes (especially roads, but also nursing and disabled persons' homes, pre-school and child care, senior citizens, and airfields). This pattern was changed with the *Grants Commission Act 1973* in two ways: first, it became possible for regional groupings of local government to apply directly to the Commonwealth for financial assistance; and second, it mandated the State governments to achieve financial equality between local authorities in their State for those grant programmes which were provided to States for the use of local authorities or regional groupings of local authorities. Grants allocated by the Grants Commission in 1974–75 for this task totalled A$56m, and were given as block grants to the States for transmission to local governments. This procedure was modified by the *Commonwealth Grants Commission Act 1976* (see Bowman 1976; Mathews 1974). The main changes were first, that the Commonwealth Grant Commission has passed to the State the responsibility for recommending the amount to be paid to regional groupings; second, under the new tax-sharing arrangements of 1976, local government is to participate by receiving a proportion (1.52% 1976–77 until 1978–79, and 2% thereafter) of the personal income tax collection of the previous year, with allocation between local governments within each State on the basis of the recommendations of newly formed State Grants Commissions. The intrastate allocations are decided in two stages. Stage one

Table 13.26 Allocation of Commonwealth grants to local authorities:
distribution of pass-through at State level. (*Source:* Commonwealth
Government of Australia 1978, tables 62 and 63)

State	Commonwealth grants to Local Authorities in 1977–8 (A$000)	Distribution of grants between States (%)	Per capita grants (A$)
NSW	60.341	36.4977	12.1
Victoria	42,078	25.4513	11.1
Queensland	27,875	16.8606	12.9
S. Australia	14,220	8.6010	11.1
W. Australia	15,524	9.3897	12.8
Tasmania	5,290	3.1997	12.8
Total	165,328	100.0000	11.9

allocates a minimum of 30% to local authorities on the basis of their
population, population density, and other *ad hoc* factors. The remaining
element is allocated in stage two in proportion to the expenditure needs of
different Local Authorities or regions, thus recalling the Special Grant
programme to the State discussed earlier. The distribution of this assistance to
Local governments has introduced an important new feature into Australian
federation and in 1978–79 constituted a direct pass through from the
Commonwealth to the States of A$180m. As shown in table 13.26 this favours
the more populated States in absolute terms, but slightly favours the less
densely populated States in terms of *per capita* allocations.

Revenue-sharing in Australia under Fraser's Liberal government has thus
tended to emphasize 'co-operative federation', giving more resources to each
level of government and reducing the control by the States, rather than the
'organic federalism' favouring central control initiated by the Whitlam
Labour Government. It has also been linked with the emergence of new
institutions: the States Grants Commissions, and an Advisory Council on
International Government Relations modelled on the US ACIR.

Capital finance falls into two groups: one for State governments, and a
second for large authorities within States. The State governments are funded
within programme areas allocated by the *Loan Council* and can take the form
of direct borrowings, interest-free capital grants, and security as lender of last
resort. Large authorities within each State are also allocated loans by the Loan
Council, but the loans are distributed within the State by the State
government. Such capital grants have placed particular emphasis on infrastructure finance. In each case the Commonwealth has decided on the
programme areas within which capital loans are available, and has been
responsible for raising the loans. The share of each State or large authority is
then determined within each programme by the Loan Council. Since 1978 the

Table 13.27 Capital finance in Australia (A$000) in 1977–78. (*Source:* Commonwealth Government of Australia 1978, table 9 and 10)

State	Borrowings	Capital grants = ⅓ of each State's programme	% of total	Large authorities	% of all large authority grants
NSW	308,978	154,489	32.3	443,127	37.5
Vict	240,142	120,071	25.1	357,612	31.7
Qus	126,740	63,370	13.3	239,651	18.5
S. Australia	124,569	62,284	13.0	53,110	4.7
W. Australia	88,446	44,223	9.3	69,309	4.7
Tasmania	66,992	33,496	7.0	32,191	2.9
Total	955,867	447,933	100.0	1,195,000	100.0

role of the Loan Council has become particularly crucial because of the general shortage of capital funds. The distribution of such grants and general borrowings is shown in table 13.27. From this it can be seen that each grant programme favours the more populated as opposed to the less populated States.

13.7 Conclusion

This chapter has been concerned with examining how intergovernmental fiscal co-ordination has evolved in a range of Western countries. The more general discussion in the Introduction, and the five case studies of the UK, Canada, the United States, Germany, and Australia demonstrate the complexity of intergovernmental relations and the impossibility of representing these structures as typical, or of describing them in a few words. However, a few generalizations are possible. First, in most countries a fairly wide range of formal and informal fiscal arrangements are employed. There is plurality of co-ordination programmes rather than reliance on single instruments. Second, no grants, except the equalization grants in Canada, have used the more complex measures of fiscal capacity based on the representative tax system discussed in chapter 7. Most grants still use inverse *per capita* personal income as the capacity measure. Third, few of the grants are aimed at achieving complete uniformity of public services; the closest approximation to such an objective is usually in highway and public utility programmes. Fourth, the measurement of needs is by no means a simple task, nor one which has reached a degree of agreement in most countries. In those countries where need indicators have been developed, they are still subject to a high degree of criticism and disagreement. Fifth, the extent of equalization in most grants programmes is still very limited. This is due to both the imposition of hold-harmless provisions, as in the UK, United States, and Canada, and to the diffusion of aid by political manoeuvres such as pork-barrelling, especially in the United State Congressional proceedings. Finally, where a high degree of equalization has been achieved, as can be claimed with reasonable justification for Germany and Canada, at the respective *Länder* and provincial level (but not at local level), this has been achieved with a battery of transfer mechanisms in which revenue-sharing and equalization grants have been important components. In all countries examined, however, important and rather specific fiscal problems remain. These may be often urban problems, rural pockets of poverty, very localized needs for infrastructure investment in renewal, or inequities in economic growth and performance affecting local public and private needs and well-being.

In the face of these problems various approaches are possible. In federal countries there seems to be a need for a greater use of categorical or specific grants which are targeted to highly localized and specific geographical functional needs. This will supplement more general revenue-sharing and block grant programmes. In United States in particular, it is clear that the growth of block grants initiated in the 1930s, in attaining such great emphasis in the late 1960s and 70s, needs to be limited in the future. Second, there can be greater use of specific programmes aimed at local and urban problems. In the US, this could be a revival of the old Model Cities Program, or use of new instruments such as an urban or regional development bank. A further area is a greater emphasis on new individual distribution programmes to attack pockets of poverty and distress. Whilst greater direct federal expenditure, and urban and regional development banks are useful proposals, individual distribution programmes draw us towards tax deductions, credits, and negative income tax. In centralized countries, such as the UK, the imperative is in a different direction: towards giving greater local autonomy of funds, and towards the implementation of new sources of local revenue such as local income tax and revenue-sharing. Moreover, the demands for greater fiscal autonomy in both federal and centralized States have been linked with separatism and regional devolution. In holding together present constitutional structures and attaining stable economies, many countries are being forced to contemplate new fiscal arrangements for requiring, on the one hand, greater central control to balance needs of disadvantaged groups, lagging regions and pockets of poverty, and on the other hand, greater local fiscal autonomy in both expenditure and revenue functions. This dilemma brings us back to the central issue, of the interplay of national and individual redistribution programmes, with the programmes aimed at achieving greater local or geographical balance and fiscal autonomy. It is a dilemma which offers no single solution but for which answers are often encouraged by comparison of different fiscal and intergovernmental transfer arrangements in different countries. In chapter 14, these issues are highlighted with the consideration of total impact of the public fisc on the geographical and interpersonal incidence of the final net balance of burdens and benefits.

14

Final fiscal incidence

"The history, sociology and statistics of finance are the three pillars which alone can support a theory of public finance which is not totally divorced from reality.

Of these three pillars, financial sociology is the most important. It alone can show up the part played by the origin and composition of public revenue in the development of society as a whole and thereby in the destiny of nations and individuals alike. It depends upon social structure and upon internal and external political constellations whether taxes in kind or money taxes are preferable, whether and to what extent indirect or direct, personal taxes or taxes on objects, income and profits on land, investment, property and death taxes are to be chosen, whether the tax screw should be tightened or relieved, what groups of the population are to bear the heavier or the lighter burdens ... whether expenditure is to be reduced or revenue raised, how taxation is to be combined with economic incentives, and so on."

R. Goldscheid, 1925, *Staat*, from Musgrave, R. A.
and Peacock, A. (eds) 1961.

14.1 Fiscal incidence; the accounting problem

The previous chapters have been concerned with the individual geographical components of needs, costs, revenues, expenditures, capital components, and intergovernmental transfers which all in part determine the pattern of provision of public goods. Taken one at a time, each element has considerable complexity and difficulty of measurement, and each also raises disturbing philosophical issues. With the study of final fiscal incidence in this chapter it is attempted to put each of the individual elements together as a composite public account, and then, using this account, to reach a final conclusion on the equity of the total pattern of the public fisc in any situation; as stated in chapter 4: to determine how far like people, and like firms, are being treated alike irrespective of where they are located.

The aim of achieving fiscal equity, as stated in chapter 1 and elsewhere, is not an attempt to make everyone equal in personal attributes, but instead to cancel as far as possible the inequities in the operation of the system of public finance itself. This concerns consideration of each of the individual elements of previous chapters, but in each case combines their consideration: to determine the equity of burdens in relation to ability; the equity of expenditure benefits in relation to the unit costs of different needs; and the degree to which transfers increase or decrease overall relations to abilities and needs. As succinctly phrased by Colm (1955, p. 321) "not equality but equalisation of disproportionate inequalities".

To determine the pattern of fiscal incidence obtaining in any situation, a system of public accounts must be constructed. These can then be compared with accepted norms of equity of the public fisc. In this chapter the nature of this accounting problem is outlined in section 14.2, then in section 14.3 the equity of the public fisc at national level in a number of countries is compared. This discussion develops the methodology of fiscal incidence accounts which is then applied in section 14.4 to urban and local level studies (including the degree to which central cities can be said to be being exploited by their suburbs). Finally, in section 14.5, regional level studies are discussed within the context of total incomes in order to assess how far there are tendencies towards cumulative regional growth, decline or imbalance.

14.2 Final fiscal incidence accounts

The public finance accounts required to assess final fiscal incidence, and to conclude upon the equity of the public fisc, have already been discussed in some detail in chapter 4. The construction of such accounts can follow various routes depending upon the questions which it is sought ultimately to answer. Four approaches to such accounts can be distinguished (Musgrave 1959):

(i) specific incidence: each tax or expenditure programme is assessed individually for its distributional aspects (as discussed in chapters 7 to 9);

(ii) global incidence: the total burden or benefits of public finance are assessed for distributional aspects giving two final incidence accounts, one for burden incidence, and one for benefit incidence (as discussed in chapters 7 to 9);

(iii) budget-balance incidence: the revenue side of the public fisc is compared directly with the expenditure side, each component is weighted against respective ability or need, and final fiscal equity is assessed;

(iv) differential incidence: either the present revenue system is compared with other revenue systems supporting the same level of expenditures, *or* the present distribution of expenditure benefits is compared with other benefit distributions supported by the same level and distribution of revenue burdens.

Each of these components has significance in different circumstances, but the primary emphasis in this chapter is upon the third approach: the total benefit-burden relationship given by budget-balance accounts. The resulting set of accounts of the public fisc allow the comparison, on the one hand, of the burdens and costs of public programmes (taking account of revenue exporting), with, on the other hand, the benefits and needs of public goods (taking account of benefit spillover). Comparison of these two sets of elements then allows a conclusion to be drawn as to final fiscal incidence. We may draw up one such account for each individual, each social group, each industry, each industrial sector, or any number of permutations of the jurisdictions or regions of an economy. The final account then tells us what benefits each

Table 14.1 Final fiscal incidence accounts derived from marginal row totals of tables 4.1 and 4.2.

	Jurisdictions (N)			
	1 *Income* *groups*	*2* *Income* *groups*	. . . . . .	*N* *Income* *groups*
Total expenditure benefits				
Total revenue burdens				
Final fiscal incidence (benefits minus burdens)				

individual or region is receiving in relation to what is paid and to what is needed.

Budget-balance accounts can be derived from the constructions given in table 4.1 and 4.2. The marginal totals of each of these matrices of fiscal flows gives two sets of accounts: one for the total benefits and total revenue burdens in each jurisdiction; and a second for the total benefit spillovers and revenue exports to other jurisdictions. These two sets of final flows allow the determination of two sets of final fiscal accounts: a *final fiscal incidence account* shown in table 14.1, and a *final fiscal incidence transfer account* shown in table 14.2. The final fiscal incidence account gives a measure of the ultimate effect of the public fisc on the disposable income of each income group in each jurisdiction, after taking account of spillover, revenue shifting, revenue exporting, and intergovernmental transfers. Total revenue burdens are subtracted from total expenditure benefits to give the total net gain under the public fisc, which then allows assessment of total fiscal equity.

The final fiscal incidence transfer accounts shown in table 14.2 allow determination of the extent to which the final incidence pattern is the result of geographical transfers between jurisdictions. The total export of revenue burdens from any area, taking account of tax shifting and intergovernmental

Table 14.2 Final fiscal incidence transfer accounts for geographic flows derived from marginal column totals of tables 4.1 and 4.2.

	Jurisdictions (N)			
	1 *Income* *groups*	*2* *Income* *groups*	. . . . . .	*N* *Income* *groups*
Total expenditure spillovers				
Total revenue exports				
Final fiscal transfers (spillovers minus exports)				

transfers, is subtracted from the total spillover of benefits to other jurisdictions, again taking account of intergovernmental transfers. The final estimate of the extent of transfers (spillovers minus exports) displays how far any jurisdiction is 'exploiting', or being 'exploited' by, other jurisdictions, and the degree to which it is being fiscally prudent and successful in interjurisdictional competition. This then allows assessment of the degree to which it is geographical factors of inter-area transfers which are undermining the distributional norm of fiscal equity. Both transfer and total incidence accounts can also be constructed on an industrial, or an individual basis, as well as by income groups.

The final fiscal incidence and final fiscal incidence transfer accounts can each be approached from two points of view. First, the assessment of revenue burdens can be made purely in terms of the level of final burdens as paid, and expenditure benefits can be assessed simply in terms of the costs of service provision (as assumed in table 14.1 and 14.2). This gives the so-called direct incidence, or *cost basis*, of benefit and burden assessment. Second, however, the assessment of revenue burdens can be modified, as discussed in chapter 8, to take account of the *proportion* of incomes which is set aside for revenue payment, thus giving some weighting of burdens by income levels, utility, or the *effort* (ratio of burden to ability) required to make specific revenue payments. Similarly, the assessment of expenditure benefits deriving from both direct provision and intergovernmental transfers can be modified, as discussed in chapter 9, to take account of the utility of benefits in the hands of the receiver, e.g. as measured by inverse ability, or by need: the so-called *welfare basis* of incidence assessment.

The elements of the costs and welfare bases introduce into incidence assessment a wide range of possible accounts, depending upon whether measures of revenue effort, need, or utility of income are introduced, and the degree to which different assumptions about shifting, spillover, and exporting are followed. The intricacies of the new accounting problems that arise can be appreciated from figures 14.1 and 14.2. For any single location it is generally desired, as discussed in chapters 7 and 8, that revenue burdens increase with ability as shown in figure 14.1a. Similarly, as the discussion of chapter 5 and 9 conclude, it usually desirable that expenditures increase with the level of need,

Figure 14.1   Desired partern of relation of tax burden and expenditure to ability and need.

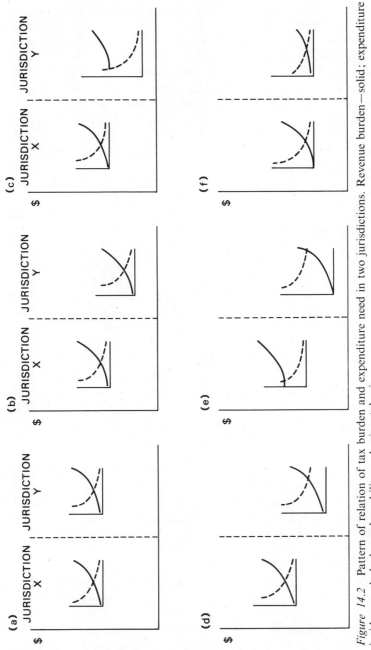

Figure 14.2 Pattern of relation of tax burden and expenditure need in two jurisdictions. Revenue burden—solid; expenditure incidence—dashed; need or ability on horizontal axis.

409

as shown in figure 14.1b. Assuming, for the sake of simplicity, that inverse *per capita* income is an adequate measure of need, then the two curves for benefit and burden incidence can be superimposed as shown in figure 14.1c. This figure reflects the generalized norms of fiscal incidence which are held in most western societies: benefits rise with need, and burdens rise with ability giving a net redistribution to the needy.

When we consider two or more jurisdictions, the questions of fiscal incidence, and the related norms of equity, become more complex. Figure 14.2 shows a number of cases in which different levels of ability and need characterize different areas. In the simplest case (fig. 14.2a) ability and need are identical in each area, and redistribution programmes can be solved adequately at national level; the geographical component is irrelevent. More commonly, however, the various other alternatives shown in the figure obtain. The gross levels of need and ability may be in balance within each jurisdiction, but differ markedly between jurisdictions, as shown in figure 14.2b. In this case each jurisdiction can solve the fiscal equity problem internally, but cannot achieve fiscal equity of like individuals in different jurisdictions; hence intergovernmental transfers are required. In the case shown in figure 14.2c another situation obtains in which ability matches need in one jurisdiction (X). so that internal redistribution can achieve equity, but in the other jurisdiction (Y) taxes are raised at the same marginal rates with income, but there will not be the same level of equity achievable as in X. The response of area Y is either to reduce the marginal rate of tax to meet expenditure needs, giving case 14.2b, or increasing the level of provision of public goods. The case shown in figure 14.2d again allows ability to match need in one jurisdiction, but in the other jurisdiction (Y), the level of *per capita* need greatly exceeds the level of *per capita* ability. This case calls for intergovernmental transfers. Cases 14.2e and f display two further instances in which, first, need and ability are both in imbalance, and second, the levels or progressivity differ in different jurisdictions. In each of these cases intergovernmental transfers are required in order to achieve equal treatment of equals in different areas.

These over-simplified examples give some indication of the complexity of simultaneously assessing the final pattern of personal and geographical fiscal incidence. Each component of benefit, need, cost, ability and burden must be assessed for each income, ability and need group, and for each spatial area. Examples of this method of assessment are developed in the next sections.

14.3 Fiscal incidence at national level

The incidence of public finance at national level has been dicussed in previous chapters in terms of two separate components. First, in chapter 8, the payment of revenues by individuals and firms has been traced to the location of final burden, taking account of the various components of forward and backward shifting of taxes, and of revenue exporting. Second, in chapter 9, the receipt of final expenditure benefits has been traced from initial expenditure incidence, via geographical spillover, to the location of received benefits. In this section these two components are combined in order to produce a total account of the public fisc and the assessment of budget-balance incidence.

Various studies of the level of net budget-balance incidence have been made for income groups at national level. Adler (1951), for example, compared 1938–39 with 1946–47 aggregate US federal, State and local level public finance to assess net benefit and redistribution effects. Tucker (1952) compares four bases for assessing net benefits by area using different criteria of need and welfare: total population, *per capita* income, *per capita* consumption, and *per capita* wealth. Gillespie (1965) and the Tax Foundation (1967) for the US, and Gillespie (1976) for Canada, measure total net incidence, and experiment with various budget and tax measures, thus allowing the assessment of the differential incidence resulting from modifications to the system of public finance.

Major studies of fiscal incidence combining each of the elements of cost and welfare bases into net fiscal incidence by income group have been made in most Western countries, and figure 14.3 shows the general pattern of incidence for three countries taking account of national, intermediate and local level transfers. In most cases the dominant pattern of burdens is one which is largely proportional to income, especially over the lower middle, middle, and upper levels of income (see chapter 8). However, the pattern of total net fiscal incidence gives a net loss from these higher income groups in favour of the very low incomes. This pattern demonstrates that substantial redistribution occurs only in favour of the very lowest income groups; elsewhere, the net balance of the public fisc is more or less neutral to income. Significant differences occur, however, between different levels of government. It is the national governments, and to a lesser extent the intermediate levels governments (States, Provinces, and *Länder*), which are responsible for the bulk of redistribution. Local governments, at the level of the city, County or *Gemeinde*, generally place a higher level of burdens on the lowest income groups, and give a net balance of incidence in favour of the higher incomes. This regressive effect of the public fisc is due in most countries to two factors: first, the dominance of taxation at the local level by the property tax; and second, the concentration of local services in the category of local merit goods (see chapter 11) which are available to all on an equal basis, e.g. police, fire, refuse disposal, street lighting, etc.

14.4 Urban and local level fiscal incidence

As in the case of national fiscal incidence, the separate components of burdens and benefits can also be combined to give final fiscal incidence accounts at local level. The number of studies which have developed this full fiscal accounting methodology have been relatively few, most studies being based not upon accounting tables in the form of tables 14.1 and 14.2, but instead

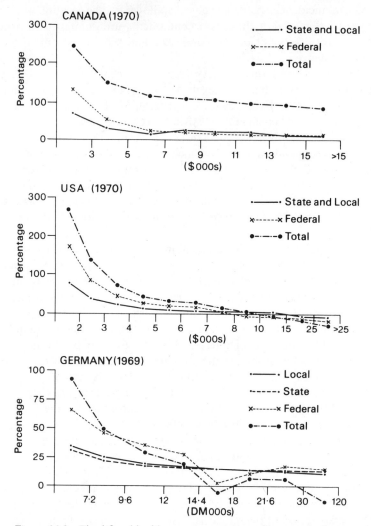

Figure 14.3 Final fiscal incidence as percentage of income in three Western countries. (*Source: Canada*: Gillespie 1976; *USA*: Reynolds and Smolensky 1974; *Germany*: Hanusch 1976.)

upon regression analysis. In the following paragraphs the limited number of detailed studies of final fiscal incidence available at urban and local level are reviewed, drawing especially from the work of Greene *et al.* (1974), and Hirsch *et al.* (1964). Because of the controversy which has surrounded the urban fiscal issue, some attention is also given to the question of central city–suburb fiscal exploitation.

The study by Greene *et al.* (1974) of Virginia, Maryland and Washington D.C., has already been reviewed in part in chapters 8 and 9 with respect to the individual accounts of revenue burdens and expenditure benefits. Here it is necessary to combine these separate incidence accounts (figures 8.7 and 9.7), and hence to construct final fiscal incidence and final fiscal incidence transfer accounts in the form of tables 14.1 and 14.2. The separate revenue and benefit accounts can be combined by using the marginal row and column totals of table 9.6. This yields two sets of accounts, one for final fiscal incidence shown in table 14.3, and one for final fiscal transfers as exports or spillovers between jurisdictions, as shown in table 14.4. In each case the accounts give the fiscal residuum resulting from subtracting benefits from burdens for each income group. From these results it is evident that all income groups and all areas receive positive benefits from the local public fisc in excess of tax payments made. This net gain is only slightly higher after taking account of the federal offset (a tax credit of the form discussed in chapter 12). On the costs basis, the benefits are greatest for the middle income groups ($3,000–10,000). A considerable difference results from moving from the cost to welfare basis accounts, however. When the different utilities of benefits to different income groups are considered, it is the higher income groups, especially those in excess of $10,000, which receive the greatest benefits. There is also variation between areas, with D.C. receiving the greatest level of benefits overall for all income groups, except the very poorest.

These accounts give an important assessment of the geographical variation in fiscal incidence for each jurisdiction taking account of intergovernmental transfers, benefit spillover and burden export. The degree to which incidence is affected by these geographical transfers is shown in table 14.4 which displays net fiscal loss or gain by each jurisdiction, i.e. net fiscal transfers by the Michigan approach to tax exporting (p. 186, *q. v.*). It is clear that D. C. is a net donor of expenditure benefits at all levels of income, but the level of transfer is particularly high from the upper income groups, especially on the welfare basis of assessment. Maryland and Virginia, on the other hand, are net receivers of geographical shifts in benefits. These benefits tend to favour middle and upper income groups, especially when the utility of benefits is taken into account on the welfare basis. At low incomes there is a near balance of gains and losses by geographical transfers, but with a tendency for there to be a loss of benefits from each State to outsiders.

More information of the nature of the geographical transfers can be gained by looking at the matrix of inter-jurisdictional gains and losses shown in tables 14.5 and 14.6. This accords with the gross fiscal transfer approach of the Wisconsin school of tax exporting studies (p.186, *q. v.*). This table shows that although D. C. is giving a high level of net benefits to both Maryland and Virginia at high income levels, at low income levels the large transfers from D. C. arise mainly from the imposition of high levels of tax burdens in other jurisdictions, especially in Maryland. Virginia makes a small net gain from Maryland, especially at high and middle income levels, mainly in the form of spillovers of benefits. There is little difference in overall conclusions to be

413

Table 14.3 Final fiscal incidence (fiscal residual) of benefits minus burdens ($000) by income group for Washington D.C., Maryland and Virginia. Final incidence in this case is derived from the results displayed in figs. 8.8 and 9.9 assuming partial forward shifting. The data are derived from the results of Greene, Neenan and Scott 1974.

		Jurisdiction									Maryland		
		D.C.											
		Incomes ($)									Incomes ($)		
		< 3,000	3,000 −3,999	4,000 −5,999	6,000 −7,499	7,500 −9,999	10,000 −14,999	15,000 −24,999	> 25,000	Total	≤ 3,000	3,000 −3,999	4,000 −5,999
Total expenditure benefits	Costs basis	120,867	33,479	71,344	52,802	72,544	72,180	42,543	18,407	484,168	22,822	7,831	19,250
	welfare basis	55,847	16,997	39,416	35,812	64,471	86,162	81,006	75,083	454,697	9,877	3,580	8,873
Total revenue burdens	before offset	7,020	2,323	6,004	5,421	8,173	12,506	16,075	15,296	72,823	5,543	1,926	5,043
	after offset	6,747	2,238	5,692	5,125	7,588	11,292	12,946	10,321	61,963	5,291	1,840	4,740
Final fiscal incidence (benefits minus burdens)	Costs before offset	5,067	31,156	65,340	47,381	64,371	59,674	26,468	3,111	411,345	17,279	5,905	14,207
	costs after offset	5,340	31,241	65,652	47,677	64,956	60,888	29,597	8,076	422,205	17,531	5,991	14,510
	welfare before offset	48,827	14,674	33,412	30,391	56,298	73,556	64,931	59,787	381,874	4,334	1,654	3,830
	welfare after offset	49,100	14,759	33,724	30,687	56,883	74,770	68,060	64,752	392,734	4,586	1,740	4,133
Final fiscal incidence per household	costs before offset	0.06	1.59	1.47	1.37	1.43	1.17	0.76	0.20	1.31	0.38	0.49	0.53
	costs after offset	0.07	.1.60	1.48	1.37	1.45	1.19	0.85	0.53	1.34	0.39	0.49	0.54
	welfare before offset	0.62	0.75	0.75	0.88	1.26	1.44	1.86	3.92	1.22	0.09	0.14	0.14
	welfare after offset	0.62	0.75	0.75	0.88	1.27	1.46	1.95	4.25	1.25	0.10	0.14	0.16

Table 14.4 Final fiscal incidence transfers ($000). Transfers of net burdens or benefits between Washington D.C., Maryland and Virginia assuming partial forward shifting of taxes. The data are derived from the results of Greene, Neenan and Scott 1974.

		Jurisdiction									Maryland	
		D.C.										
		Incomes ($)									Incomes ($)	
		≤ 3,000	3,000 −3,999	4,000 −5,999	6,000 −7,499	7,500 −9,999	10,000 −14,999	15,000 −24,999	≥ 25,000	Total	≤ 3,000	3,000 −3,999
Total expenditure benefit spillover	Costs basis	−1,421	−479	−1,105	−1,240	−3,162	−4,697	−6,124	−2,636	−20,872	927	276
	welfare basis	−276	−199	−1,471	−3,004	−8,806	−23,458	−46,089	−96,284	191,824	−8,259	−2,451
Total revenue export after offset		196	311	1,098	1,455	3,355	8,257	16,338	11,275	42,188	42	−43
Final fiscal transfer (spillover minus exports)	costs basis	−1,617	−790	−2,203	−2,695	−6,517	−12,954	−22,462	−13,911	−63,060	885	319
	welfare basis	−472	−510	·2,569	−4,459	−12,161	−43,906	−62,427	−107,559	−234,012	−8,301	−2,408
Final fiscal incidence per household	costs basis	−0.02	−0.11	−0.05	−0.08	−0.14	−0.25	−0.70	−0.91	−0.20	0.02	0.03
	welfare basis	−0.01	−0.03	−0.06	−0.13	−0.27	−0.86	−1.95	−7.05	−0.75	−0.18	−0.20

414

Virginia

Incomes ($)

6,000 -7,499	7,500 -9,999	10,000 -14,999	15,000 -24,999	≥25,000	Total	≤3,000	3,000 -3,999	4,000 -5,999	6,000 -7,499	7,500 -9,999	10,000 -14,999	15,000 -24,999	≥25,000	Total
24,967	56,660	111,746	140,892	62,246	446,418	15,008	5,931	14,260	16,382	31,906	61,069	79,368	30,013	253,940
13,204	37,226	97,523	180,497	167,209	517,992	5,518	2,575	6,953	9,716	23,512	57,990	112,185	88,404	306,856
5,816	10,827	30,234	57,262	37,703	154,358	3,362	1,238	3,317	3,728	6,604	16,846	32,586	21,944	89,630
5,438	9,876	26,746	45,247	25,105	124,285	3,207	1,180	3,111	3,492	6,045	14,975	25,616	14,539	72,167
19,151	45,833	81,512	83,630	24,543	292,064	11,646	4,693	10,943	12,654	25,302	44,223	46,782	8,069	164,310
19,529	46,784	85,000	95,645	37,141	322,133	11,801	4,751	11,149	12,890	25,861	46,094	53,752	15,474	181,773
7,388	26,399	67,289	123,235	142,104	363,134	2,156	1,337	3,636	5,988	16,908	41,144	79,599	66,460	217,226
7,766	27,350	70,777	135,250	142,104	393,707	2,311	1,395	3,842	6,224	17,467	43,015	86,569	73,865	234,689
0.74	0.96	0.87	1.17	0.66	0.75	0.39	0.48	0.49	0.59	0.72	0.74	0.65	0.29	0.59
0.75	0.98	1.09	0.97	0.99	0.83	0.41	0.49	0.49	0.60	0.74	0.77	0.75	0.56	0.66
0.28	0.55	0.72	1.26	3.81	0.94	0.07	0.14	0.16	0.28	0.48	0.69	1.11	2.40	0.79
0.30	0.57	0.76	1.38	3.81	1.02	0.08	0.14	0.17	0.29	0.49	0.72	1.21	2.67	0.85

Virginia

Incomes ($)

4,000 -5,999	6,000 -7,499	7,500 -9,999	10,000 -14,999	15,000 -24,999	≥25,000	Total	≤3,000	3,000 -3,999	4,000 -5,999	6,000 -7,499	7,500 -9,999	10,000 -14,999	15,000 -24,999	≥25,999	Total
493	549	1,402	2,907	4,557	1,259	11,104	499	205	615	694	1,762	1,794	2,830	1,379	9,772
-2,065	1,197	4,328	14,182	24,616	20,629	55,871	-4,164	-1,542	-876	1,453	4,048	8,946	21,008	16,825	45,726
25	245	1,045	5,060	9,369	6,533	24,329	-118	-175	-630	-764	-1,449	-3,017	-6,971	-4,746	-17,865
468	304	357	-2,693	-4,812	-5,274	-13,225	617	380	1,245	1,458	3,211	4,811	9,801	6,125	27,637
-2,090	952	3,283	8,582	15,247	14,096	29,542	-4,046	-1,367	-246	2,217	5,497	11,963	27,979	21,571	63,568
0.02	0.01	0.01	-0.03	-0.05	-0.14	-0.03	0.02	0.04	0.06	0.07	0.06	0.14	0.14	0.22	0.10
-0.08	0.04	0.07	0.09	0.16	0.38	0.08	-0.14	-0.14	-0.01	0.10	0.16	0.20	0.39	0.78	0.23

Table 14.5 Net fiscal flows (fiscal residuals) between jurisdictions, from Greene et al. (1974, table 7.6 and other results). Costs basis, before federal offset, with partial forward shifting.

To	Incomes ($)	From ($000) D.C. total	D.C. per h/h	Maryland total	Maryland per h/h	Virginia total	Virginia per h/h
D.C.	< 3,000	—	—	−446	−5.64	−314	−3.97
	3,000–3,999	—	—	−188	−9.65	−104	−5.35
	4,000–5,999			−599	−13.48	−355	−7.98
	6,000–7,499			−566	−16.38	−339	−9.82
	7,500–9,999			−811	−18.11	−547	−12.22
	10,000–14,999			−1,545	−30.27	−849	−16.64
	15,000–24,999			−2,430	−70.27	−1,514	−43.41
	> 25,000			−2,332	−152.99	−1,493	−97.94
	Total			−8,940	−28.47	−5,518	−11.20
Maryland	< 3,000	401	8.59	—	—	−133	−2.94
	3,000–3,999	−59	−4.89	—	—	−67	−5.51
	4,000–5,999	−539	−20.33			−260	−9.79
	6,000–7,499	−656	−25.26			−242	−13.17
	7,500–9,999	−1,007	−21.08			−785	−16.41
	10,000–14,999	−3,824	−41.02			−1,920	−20.59
	15,000–24,999	−9,603	−97.80			−5,528	−56.35
	> 25,000	−9,069	−243.40			−4,454	−119.53
	Total	−24,358	−63.07			−10.‚ 8	−26.45
Virginia	< 3,000	81	2.81	−104	−3.56	—	—
	3,000–3,999	−68	−7.01	−17	−1.75	—	—
	4,000–5,999	−416	−18.51	−34	−1.51		
	6,000–7,499	−505	−23.69	−33	−1.55		
	7,500–9,999	−634	−18.13	−1,014	−28.96		
	10,000–14,999	−2,815	−47.33	−1,142	−19.19		
	15,000–24,999	−7,466	−104.49	−3,421	−47.87		
	> 25,000	−6,503	−235.20	−3,575	−129.28		
	Total	−18,328	−66.32	−8,441	−30.54		

Table 14.6 Net fiscal transfers (fiscal residuals) between jurisdictions, based on results in Greene et al. (1974). Welfare basis, after federal offset, partial forward shifting.

To	From ($000)						Incomes
	D.C.		*Maryland*		*Virginia*		
	total	per h/h	total	per h/h	total	per h/h	
D.C.	—	—	−679	−8.57	−344	−4.35	<3,000
			−279	−13.78	−120	−6.14	3,000–3,999
			−339	−7.54	−97	−2.18	4,000–5,999
			173	5.01	188	5.46	6,000–7,499
			692	15.46	470	10.49	7,500–9,999
			1,831	35.87	1,221	23.92	10,000–14,999
			2,294	65.78	1,212	34.77	15,000–24,999
			3,323	217.96	1,460	95.77	>25,000
			7,026	22.37	3,991	12.71	Total
Maryland	−584	−12.94	—	—	−210	−4.65	<3,000
	−300	−24.78			−55	−4.53	3,000–3,999
	−107	−4.06			−25	−0.94	4,000–5,999
	1,051	40.48			257	9.89	6,000–7,499
	3,838	80.28			830	17.36	7,500–9,999
	11,490	123.26			3,020	32.40	10,000–14,999
	19,999	203.88			4,910	50.05	15,000–24,999
	19,204	515.42			4,817	129.28	>25,000
	54,592	141.36			13,553	35.09	Total
Virginia	−359	−12.33	−194	−6.65	—	—	<3,000
	−201	−20.66	−75	−7.70			3,000–3,999
	43	1.93	35	1.55			4,000–5,999
	911	42.71	359	16.83			6,000–7,499
	2,874	82.12	1,168	33.36			7,500–9,999
	6,793	114.22	3,496	58.77			10,000–14,999
	13,258	185.53	7,073	98.98			15,000–24,999
	11,806	426.96	6,602	238.75			>25,000
	35,127	127.11	18,484	66.88			Total

drawn from either the costs (table 14.5) or welfare basis (table 14.6).

From the evidence of these various results there is certainly some degree of indication of a fiscal exploitation of D. C. as a central city which is exporting a large volume of expenditure benefits, and importing considerable revenue burdens, but the level of aggregation of the analysis and the special character of the Washington metropolitan area, at this stage, preclude erecting this conclusion to one of generality characterizing all central cities.

The second study to be discussed here, by Hirsch *et al.* (1964), concerns a more restricted analysis of the incidence and geographical transfer of property tax, income tax, sales tax and other minor tax burdens, and public education benefits, for the Missouri School District of Clayton. This is a seminal study of geographical fiscal incidence, but does not give a break-down of incidence by income group. The set of geographical areas considered in this analysis consists of the Clayton School District, the rest of St Louis County, the City of St Louis, the rest of St Louis SMSA, the rest of the State of Missouri, and the rest of the USA.

Since the revenue exporting and benefit spillover occurs from only one area relative to all other areas, the final fiscal incidence accounting and transfer tables can be simplified, and indeed combined into one set of accounts, as shown in table 14.7. This table is interpreted as follows. Along the top row, the net revenue export from Clayton is compared with the net benefit spillover from Clayton; the subtraction of benefit from burden gives the net export of fiscal incidence, which in all cases, except to the rest of the US, is a net loss of benefits to Clayton. Down the left column, the net revenue export from other areas to Clayton is compared with the spillover of benefits to Clayton; the subtraction of benefit from burden again giving the net export of fiscal incidence, which in all cases is a net loss of other areas to Clayton. The comparison of net benefit spill-in to Clayton with net benefit spill-out from Clayton (the left column minus the top row) gives the net fiscal transfers, shown in the diagonal entries. In all cases, except with the rest of St Louis County, there is a net gain by Clayton from other areas, especially from the rest of the State of Missouri and from the rest of the US. These patterns result mainly from the shifting of property tax burdens by the corporate sector, the reapportionment of State income tax receipts, journey-to-work flows, and the migration of human capital.

Any assessment of fiscal incidence by geographical area permits evaluation of the way in which jurisdictions are likely to behave in competition. Hirsch *et al.* (1964) suggest for Clayton School District that this behaviour can be assessed by using a series of benefit–cost ratios of relative spillover. These represent division of the revenue cost terms (upper figure in the tables) by the expenditure benefit terms (lower figure in the table) for each entry; and these yield the new matrix shown in table 14.8. When the ratio is greater than 1 along the top row, the jurisdiction loses in competition if it raises the level of its education expenditure; however, if the ratio is greater than one down the left column, the jurisdiction gains in competition from the increase in education expenditures elsewhere. The ratio of the row to the column cost–benefit ratios gives the ratio of change in benefits to Clayton and other areas which result from each other's expenditure actions. When these ratios are greater than 1, as is the case for almost all of the diagonal entries in table 14.8, Clayton makes a net gain in competition from raising its own education expenditure, or from other areas raising their expenditures. If anything, the Hirsch *et al.* study seems to confirm a small-scale transfer of fiscal resources to the suburban Clayton School District from St Louis City and SMSA, indicating again a possible suburban exploitation. It is useful now, however, to look at the city–suburb exploitation hypothesis in more detail.

The origin of central city fiscal problems is usually ascribed to three factors: first, their character as havens for the poor and disadvantaged who make heavy demands on the revenue base; second, the historical legacy of ageing structures, congestion, inefficient organization, and diseconomies of scale which place heavy demands on both the revenue and capital accounts for renewal; third, the fragmentation of urban government causing fiscal imbalance of spillovers and benefits. It is the third of these features which concerns fiscal exploitation. The spillover effect most frequently cited is that of commuters who are able to exploit central cities by imposing revenue costs without bearing the associated revenue burdens. In addition, population migration represents a second spillover, through suburbanization of the younger and more highly trained. A third form of spillover results from differential fiscal effects on different income groups. Each of these three spillovers is discussed in turn below.

COMMUTER SPILLOVERS

The spillover of the benefits of central city expenditures to suburban residents who commute to cities for work, recreation and shopping, is the centrepiece of the so-called 'central city exploitation thesis'. In addition, there may be increased costs to be borne by central city taxpayers as a consequence of these flows. Both features have encouraged the development of city payroll and other 'commuter taxes' to offset these benefit spillovers (US ACIR 1970). Various tests of the exploitation thesis have been made. Hawley (1957) analysing 76 US cities in 1940, Brazer (1959) analysing 1953 data for 40 US cities, and Margolis (1961) using the 36 largest Metropolitan areas of the US in 1957, each concluded that central city expenditures were higher per head, but both Brazer and Margolis suggest that this is only partial confirmation of exploitation since central cities gain in property values, sales expenditures, and other benefits from non-residents. Brazer (1959) makes the particularly important observation that there is no *a priori* reason why *per capita* expenditures should not differ greatly, it is only the additional costs of suburban residents which are of significance, and these are more difficult to determine. Other studies draw rather inconclusive results. For example,

Table 14.7 Fiscal residual, or final fiscal incidence account for Clayton School District, Missouri. Flows in $000s to other areas. In each case the upper figure shows the net benefit resulting from revenue exporting, and the lower figure the net benefit spillover. The subtraction of net benefits from net burdens gives final fiscal incidence, and the diagonal terms give the net geographical transfer from Clayton School District. (*Source:* Hirsch *et al.* 1964, fig. 17)

	Clayton School District	Rest of St Louis County	City of St Louis	Rest of SMSA	Rest of Missouri	Rest of USA	Total spillout	Total education costs and benefits
Clayton School District	2,979 / −1,647 / 1,332	24 / −568 / −544	21 / −84 / −63	7 / −57 / −50	44 / −115 / −71	738 / −409 / 329	834 / −1,233 / −399	3,813 / −2,880 / 933
Rest of St Louis County	38 / −574 / −536	8						
City of St Louis	29 / −481 / −452		−389					
Rest of SMSA	18 / −245 / −227			−177				

Rest of Missouri	86		
	−1,031		
	−945	−874	
Rest of USA	1,353		
	2,037		
	−684	−1,013	
Total spillin	1,524		
	−4,368		
	−2,844	−2,445	
Total education costs and benefits for all areas	4,503		
	−6,015		
	−1,512	−2,445	

Table 14.8 Benefit–cost ratios of relative spillovers for Clayton School District. (Derived form data in Hirsch *et al.* 1964)

	Clayton School District	Rest of St Louis County	City of St Louis	Rest of SMSA	Rest of Missouri	Rest of USA	Total spill-out	Total for Clayton
Clayton School District	1.81	0.04	0.25	0.12	0.38	1.80	0.68	1.32
Rest of St Louis County	0.07	0.57						
City of St Louis	0.06		4.17					
Rest of SMSA	0.07			1.71				
Rest of Missouri	0.08				4.75			
Rest of USA	0.06					2.73		
Total spillover	0.35						1.93	
Total all areas	0.75							1.63

Banovetz (1965), Davies (1965), Kee (1977), Haskell and Leshinski (1969), and Vincent (1971), find no general relation of exploitation between city and suburbs. Relatively few studies, for example those of Neenan (1970) and of Greene *et al.* (1974), have concluded that suburbs do indeed make a net gain at the expense of the central cities; and each of these studies requires the weighting of a particular welfare basis to be accepted in adducing the magnitude of benefits. Certainly, as yet, no final conclusion can be drawn as to the validity of the exploitation thesis, and more detailed research for a large range of cities is required.

MIGRATION SPILLOVER

Migration represents the shift of human capital, together with its variable attributes of age, sex, education, and health, from one area to another. Such shifts may represent gains to the public fisc when the migration is of the fit, able and well-educated, but is a burden when the migration results in an increased proportion of the poor, young families, the aged, or the unhealthy and disabled. These shifts often affect central and older cities to a greater extent than other areas. Hirsch (1971) argues that central cities have traditionally performed the function of acculturizing immigrants to urban life, and this produces large benefits to the community as a whole. The burden of this function has continued, but many of the jobs traditionally offering employment to the acculturizing groups have been either eliminated by automation and changes in consumer demand, or have shifted to the suburbs. Moreover, those new jobs which have been created in central cities have been predominantly white collar and highly skilled. Estimates of the resulting changes in fiscal burdens have been relatively few, but Wertheimer (1970), Sjaastad (1962), Crowley (1968), and the study by Hirsch *et al.* (1964) discussed above, have all found that large cost spill-ins to central cities follow selective migration, but the magnitude of costs varies greatly between areas. A major dilemma of such studies is how far their results should be used to measure the magnitude of compensation that central cities should receive (e.g. through intergovernmental transfer programmes) for bearing the burden of a larger-than-average proportion of the very needy.

FISCAL SPILLOVER

Such spillovers are static and do not result, like migration and commuting, from the movement of people. They have two main components (Hirsch 1971). First, to the extent that general taxation is progressive, the poorer income groups of central cities receive a subsidy from higher level governments, and hence from other areas. This has been verified for the Clayton School District of St Louis (Hirsch *et al.* 1964) where the estimate of net spill-out of benefits is about \$2.3m. A second component occurs when a higher level government performs a function for only a few lower level governments, the larger area subsidizes the expenditure in the other areas.

Shoup and Rossett (1971) give an example of such cost spill-outs for law enforcement in Los Angeles County. In Europe, regional policy gives similar spatially selective tax and expenditure incidence at regional level.

14.5 'Total incomes' and regional industrial policy

Most of the preceding discussion has been concerned with fiscal incidence by income groups. In this section the discussion is extended to that of the effect of the public fisc on industrial performance, regional incomes, and regional balance of payments.

REGIONAL INDUSTRIAL POLICY

Each industry has different locational attributes. Hence changes in the structure of the national economy, and indeed of the world economy, lead to changes in the geographical pattern of industrial growth and performance which affect employment, wages, and the local public fisc, as shown in figure 3.2. Because of imperfections in the market and historical causes, growth begins and proceeds at different paces in different areas. This process has usually led to the emergence of two distinct set of regions: first, those where economic growth has become progressively concentrated giving high levels of population and incomes; second, those regions which have systematically lagged in terms of economic growth, and where population, income and employment levels have remained static, have increased only slowly, or have decreased. The pattern of such differences in incomes is often linked to distance from the centres of more vigorous growth leading to the emergence of a distinct centre–periphery fracture. Centre–periphery disparities are often further heightened by increasing agglomeration economies, and domination of the capital markets and of the political process (Lipton 1976; Tarrow 1977).

Many countries, especially those in Europe, have been concerned to redress this progressive imbalance in regional economic performance and have implemented a range of regional policies. In the growing regions these have been aimed at, first, limiting the competition for land and congestion upon it, and second, at controlling the level of public investment, e.g. in transport, water and sewerage provision. In the lagging regions, on the other hand, contrary policies have been followed to stimulate employment growth, to encourage renewal of urban and transport infrastructure, and to stimulate new industrial investment by preferential subsidies and tax concessions.

In the UK, which possesses one of the oldest set of such policies, *Special Areas* legislation was enacted in 1934, which was followed by the *Distribution of Industry Acts* of 1945 and 1949, the *New Towns Act* of 1946, the *Town and Country Planning Act* of 1947, and various subsequent developments and amendments, the most important of which have been the development of spatially differentiated tax incentives to industry from 1963 (Brown 1972; Manners 1972; McCrone 1969). In Germany, various special areas of distress have been defined in rather *ad hoc* fashion, but these have been co-ordinated since 1951 into emergency areas (*Notstandsgebeite*). To these have been added a zonal border area abutting East Germany (*Zonenrandgebeite*) in 1953. In 1960 increased co-operation was sought between the *Bund* and *Länder*, and in 1969 a new Act co-ordinated the two levels of policies (*Gesetz über die Gemeinschaffsaufgabe 'Verhesserung der regionalen Wirtschaftsstruktur'*). This Act has sought a more powerful regional policy especially with respect to growth points (Casper 1978). In Italy regional policy has been concerned above all with the disparities of North and South, and has become most effective with the establishment of a special development agency, *Casa per il Mezzorgiorno* from 1950 onwards. This has been reinforced by subsidized loans *Mediocredito*, the preferential location of state industry, and other incentives (Ronzani 1978). In France since 1957 discretionary incentives and capital grants have been given to *Départements* in 'critical zones' to overcome the dominance of Paris (Astrong 1975; Durand 1974; Hull 1978; Jalon 1967). Holland, Belgium, the Scandinavian countries, Spain, Portugal and Ireland all have similar policies. Moreover, since 1975, aid has been available to selected lagging regions in the EEC from the Community's *Regional Development Fund*. The areas eligible for this aid are shown in figure 14.4.

In North America, the US depressed areas measures date from the New Deal of the 1930s, were reviewed in 1952, but more substantial and permanent aid began only with the Appalachian Regional Development Program and the Title V Commissions under the Economic Development Administration in 1965. The areas eligible for aid from these commissions has subsequently been extended to include most of the US, and they have been supplemented by River Basin Commissions oriented towards more specific programmes (see figure 12.7). In the early 1970s a fillip was given to national and regional policy by the Nixon *New Federalism* and the 1972 *Report on National Growth*, but this, like the 1978 Carter urban proposals and White House Conference on Balanced National Growth, has been slow to have any concrete impacts (Derthick 1974; King and Clark 1978; Sunquist 1978). In Canada, a more European style of regional policy has been followed favouring the Atlantic Provinces and seeking to reduce the imbalance of incomes which are very much higher in Ontario and British Columbia than the rest of the country.

Our specific concern here is with how far various regional policy elements of public finance have affected externalities to the firm, and the extent to which they have achieved a better balance of regional growth rates, employment and income levels. The instruments of regional policy can be classified into three groups:

(i) *regional fiscal policy*: tax incentives, accelerated depreciation allowances, tax subsidies to output, and general fiscal policies aimed at benefiting specific regions;

(ii) *regional expenditure policy*: free or subsidized factory building, infrastructure investment, differential transfer payments, manipulation of

425

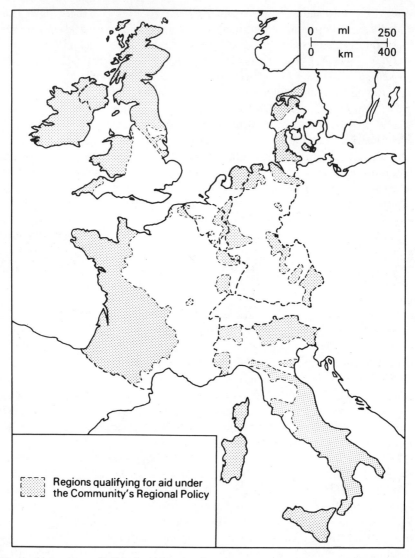

Figure 14.4   Areas eligible for aid under the EEC Regional Development Fund, 1975.

government employment, preferential award of government contracts;

(iii) *regional price policy*: reduction in the costs of capital and land inputs, capital grants, contributions to share capital, interest rate subsidies; changes to costs of labour inputs, by subsidies; subsidies to utility charges; changes to mobility of factor inputs by regulatory controls of industrial and office expansion, removal and retraining allowances for labour.

Regional fiscal policy has been very widely applied and concerns tax manipulation to aid lagging regions. The impact of such tax effects has to be assessed over the lifetime of the project. Discounted cash flow techniques must be used to evaluate the rate of return on investment.

Regional expenditure policy concerns the reorientation of the public current and capital accounts towards balancing of supply and demand within each region. The general outcome of such a policy is that a budget deficit on the public account is run in the economically lagging regions, and a budget surplus is maintained in the more prosperous regions: thus the effects of excessive demand and cumulative imbalance are 'creamed off' to aid the deficient demand or excess supply of factors in other regions. This policy has normally been concerned with the particular problem of excess labour supply, and hence has frequently been based upon unemployment indices. However, the degree to which expenditure policy can be followed on a spatially differentiated basis is severely limited by the large proportion of government activity which is oriented towards inflexible social needs: for education, social services, police, fire, water, and so forth. There is very little capacity to reorientate such expenditures towards encouragement of local growth. One important component of this policy has, however, been the preferential investment in nationalized industry, or in government contracts. In Italy, for example, 80% of new nationalized industry must be located in the South. In the UK, much civil service employment has been decentralized to aid lagging regions, and in France such policies have also affected the aerospace and energy industries. Direct public works expenditures have been favoured in the US (US ACIR 1971; Chinitz 1978; Schmidt 1977). A related form of direct investment has been the use by the British and French of New Towns aimed at producing 'counter magnets'. The preferential award of contracts have been the scene of bitter sectionalist rivalry in the US, where pork-barrel tactics are often highly significant (see chapter 15), but preferential award of contracts have been suggested and used in the European countries, e.g. Britain (Labour Party 1970).

Regional price policy concerns the manipulation of the costs of factor inputs to reduce their relative costs in lagging regions. Such policies obviously overlap with both fiscal and expenditure policy, but concern price effects which do not arise from taxation. Particularly heated debate has concerned whether such price subsidies should aid capital or labour inputs. On theoretical grounds, Borts (1966) has argued that a wage subsidy is always preferable to a capital subsidy since it yields a higher social rate of return, but this relies on assumptions of inelastic labour supply and elastic capital supply. As Stilwell (1972) notes, the opposite assumptions yield opposite conclusions. Stilwell argues, in contrast, that the effect of capital subsidies depends on the form of the production function, but labour subsidies always tend to increase employment. Hence labour subsidies generally produce more certain results than capital subsidies, but may have adverse effects on the capital/labour ratio, productivity, and entrepreneurial risk-taking. For example, the UK

427

Regional Employment Premium used from 1966 to 1976, and advocated by Kaldor (1970) on the grounds that it operated as a regional devaluation of the costs of production, certainly lead to much overmanning and inefficiency (UK House of Commons 1973). A further form of price policy, the encouragement of factor mobility, has again led to heated debate on the relative merits of moving 'work to the workers' or 'workers to the work'; i.e. encouraging capital rather than labour mobility. A major aim of such policies has been to remove the market imperfections which lead to regional imbalance noted in chapter 4: to reduce the degree of centralized wage bargaining and minimum wages, to increase the level of information on job availability and investment needs, and to speed the process of technological diffusion of new production practices.

TOTAL INCOMES AND THE REGIONAL BALANCE OF PAYMENTS

Whilst the studies of fiscal incidence discussed earlier in this chapter have been concerned with the direct effects of the public fisc on personal incomes, public finance also has major impacts on the externalities of firms and on the geography of growth, stabilization and price which determine what is often termed 'total incomes'. The assessment of total income involves the measurement of local gross income (Gross Regional Product, or GRP). Since jurisdictions and regions within countries are extremely 'open' economies with many inputs of the public fisc leaking away to other regions, and producing many complex feedbacks, the total impact of public finance can be assessed only by determining the effect of the public fisc net of other flows. This requires a full inter-regional input–output matrix of the inter-regional trade multipliers as sketched in chapter 4, which can then be used to assess overall local income multipliers (see Archibald 1967; Perloff *et al.* 1960; Reiner 1965; Steele 1969).

Having assessed total local or regional incomes, it is possible to compare disparities in income levels and assess how far the total incidence of the public fisc bears on each region: are the flows under the public fisc in aggregate equalizing or unequalizing with respect to total regional incomes? In order to answer this question, we need not only a measure of regional income, but also a measure of the rate of divergence in the growth of incomes. This latter is provided by measurement of the regional balance of payments. A region is in balance of payments surplus when it sells a greater value of products to other regions than the value of those it imports, when it receives a net gain by transfers under the public fisc from higher level government grants, transfer payments, tax exports and benefit spill-ins, or when it has a surplus of local savings over local investment needs. A region is in balance of payments deficit when it imports a greater value of products than the value it exports, when it makes net losses under the public fisc from transfers through higher level governments, tax imports, and benefit spill-outs, or when it has a deficit of savings to fund local investment needs.

428

A major problem implicit in all policies which aim at counteracting balance of payments disequilibria, however, is the effect of such policies on overall growth rates in the national economy undertaking equalization. Direct subsidies from prosperous to lagging regions, through horizontal or vertical transfers discussed in chapters 12 and 13, tend to aid the lagging regions by reducing regional incomes elsewhere. Preferable policies are those which do not directly penalize the more prosperous regions and impair overall growth rates but attempt to equalize all regions up to the level of incomes of the most prosperous regions. This is very difficult to achieve, however.

The problems in policies which directly or indirectly penalize the prosperous regions are two-fold. First, these policies may have adverse effects on incentives and profits, and hence reduce investment and growth in the more prosperous regions making them less economically sound. Second, regional transfer policies allow the fruits of economic growth in the prosperous regions to become recycled into less productive and efficient investments in other regions, and this can reduce the overall rate of growth and efficiency of the national economy, thus affecting adversely a country implementing regional redistributive policies in comparison with one which allows economic growth to proceed in the most productive locations. It has been frequently argued that both these problems have affected the UK economy and are, in part, responsible for its poor growth performance in the 1960s and 1970s, (see, for example, Holmans 1964). For the US, regional *per capita* incomes have converged steadily over this century (see figure 9.6). The high *per capita* incomes of the North-East, West and Middle Atlantic have been increasingly matched by the growth of incomes of the South-East, South-West and Plains regions. This convergence has been linked to two factors: first the reallocation of federal aid to Southern States; and second, the strong natural growth forces in the South based on energy resources. Because of the emerging reversal of the pattern of regional dominance, considerable controversy has surrounded the allocation of federal funds (see chapter 15 where the pork-barrel effects are discussed in more detail). Pennsylvania Governor J. Shapp, for example, has referred to federal aid policies which have "moved poverty from the rural South northwards . . . (such that) the cancer of Appalachia will spread from Maine to Minnesota". The controversy over federal funds has been dubbed by *Business Week* (1976) a 'second war between the States', a conflict of the 'sun-belt' and the 'frost-belt' over the pork-barrel of federal funds (see US ACIR 1978; Bennett 1980).

The importance of the public fisc for regional growth has been established in a number of studies, for example Campbell (1965), Sacks (1965), US ACIR (1978). However, the relation of the public fisc to regional balance of payments has received rather less attention. The methodology of Ohlin (1933) and Romans (1965) in constructing such accounts has been used recently by EEC (1977) to generate comparative regional balance of payments accounts for Europe. These results are shown in figure 14.5. Although not comparable

429

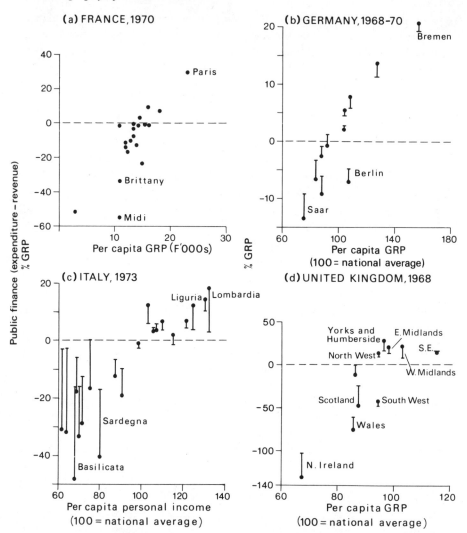

Figure 14.5 Relation of public expenditure flows (bar) and trade balance (dot), both as a percentage of GRP, to regional income (GRP) for four European countries. (*Source: France, Germany and Italy*: EEC 1977; *UK*: Woodward 1970, SPN 1976, and EEC 1977.)

in detail between countries, these data do show that, in those countries examined, the public finances are generally equalizing between regional incomes but, except for Italy, the degree of equalization is fairly small. The level of general equalizing payments which are supported are shown for selected regions in table 14.9. In the four countries examined, the balance of payments deficits for the poorer regions varies from 7% to 22% of GRP, with two exceptional cases, of Calabria and Basilicata, with levels of deficits of 26%

Table 14.9 The relation between flows of public finance aggregate transfers and regional balance of payments in four European countries. (*Source:* EEC 1977, p. 135)

	Public finance inflow (+) or outflow (−) as a % of GRP	Balance of payments current account surplus (+) or deficit (−) as a % of GRP	Public finance flows as % of balance of payments
Relatively poor regions or States			
Germany (average 1968–70)			
Niedersachsen	+ 3.4	− 6.5	52
Schleswig–Holstein	+ 6.0	− 9.8	61
Saarland	+ 9.0	− 13.6	66
France (1972)			
Bretagne	+ 11.0	− 15.0	73
UK (1964)			
Wales	+ 7.8	− 12.1	64
Scotland	+ 6.1	− 7.8	78
N. Ireland	+ 16.1	− 21.7	74
Italy (average 1971–73)			
Umbria	+ 7.8	− 17.4	45
Abruzzi	+ 14.8	− 14.8	100
Basilicata	+ 28.0	− 42.3	66
Calabria	+ 23.5	− 25.8	91
Unweighted average (excl. Basilicata + Calabria)	+ 9.1	− 13.2	69
Relatively rich regions or States			
Germany (average 1968–70)			
Baden–Württemberg	− 5.9	+ 7.9	75
Nordrhein–Westfalen	− 4.5	+ 5.2	87
Hessen	− 2.9	+ 2.2	132
UK (1964)			
South East	− 4.8	+ 2.4	200
West Midlands	− 2.9	+ 3.2	91
Italy (average 1971–73)			
Piemonte	− 7.4	+ 10.9	68
Lombardia	− 11.1	+ 15.3	73
Liguria	− 4.4	+ 12.6	35
Unweighted average	− 5.5	+ 7.5	73

and 42%, respectively. Balance of payments surpluses, on the other hand, range from 2% to 15% of GRP. The public finance inflow into balance of payments deficit regions is 3 to 16% of GRP, with an average of 9%, which rates much less than the average deficit of 13%. The outflow of public finance transfers from balance of payments surplus regions is 3 to 11%, with an average of 6%, which is less than the average surplus of 8%. Hence, although nearly 70% of current account balance of payments deficits in these four European countries is matched by equalizing transfers under the public fisc, considerable imbalances remain in each country.

Certainly regional transfer policies aimed at achieving a balance of total incomes, no less than other equalizing programmes of public finance, are extremely sensitive politically and involve a delicate balancing of the level of aid needed against the problems of erosion of incentives and economic efficiency.

14.6 Conclusion

The assessment of fiscal incidence and fiscal equity is a complex question to which completely satisfactory answers are difficult to obtain. A completely equitable system of public finance requires, first, the assessment of the level of benefits of each individual for each public service in each location. This alone requires quantification of the particularly unquantifiable effects of tapering, spillover and differential utility for benefits with income. A second requirement for assessment of incidence is that of measuring the total tax burden that each individual bears in relation to both his needs and to the ability he possesses to bear burdens. Whilst simple in theory, this problem becomes immensely complex when a complicated pattern of national taxation has evolved, where a different combination of revenues has been used at each of several levels of government, and where tax exporting plays a significant role. Further complexity is added by the interplay of such factors as interpersonal and interspatial variation in the pattern of fiscal needs, and in the costs of providing goods in different locations.

Despite these complexities, the example studies of fiscal incidence reviewed all too briefly in this chapter bring us to one conclusion: in many countries the present methods of organizing public finance are far from equitable in their total effects. Although many of the results of these studies are extremely tentative, in what is a rapidly evolving area of methodology, they do allow us to conclude that important inequities in the treatment of firms, individuals and locations are arising from the effect of geographical and other factors.

15

Fiscal politics

"Pity would be no more
If we do not make somebody poor;
And mercy no more could be
If all were as happy as we."

William Blake, The Human Abstract.

15.1 Introduction

Fiscal politics concerns the issue of *who decides* on the nature and distribution of the public fisc. We have seen at many stages of the discussion in previous chapters that unique and optimal solutions are of little relevance in the organization of public finance. What matters instead are decisions on what constitutes need, which wants will be satisfied, what burden of costs is tolerable, how tax burdens are distributed between people and between locations, who receives benefits in what quantity, who is excluded and who is allowed access to services, how are capital repayments to be phased, at what level of government are decisions to be made, and how is reallocation and equalization between levels of government to be organized. Although each of these questions can be assessed objectively, there is, in the final analysis, no economic or social optimum. Instead, we are returned to the questions raised in chapter 2: that the organization of public finance relies ultimately upon political decisions. In this chapter we are concerned with how individual preferences are translated into such final decisions at an administrative and political level, the role of party and other lobbies, and the geographical relation between representative structures and the receipt of benefits. In each case, the concern is to explore the political elements in determining who gets what fiscal benefits as a function of where they are located.

For some writers the public fisc derives from the individual who, acting as a consumer-voter, shapes the public sector through demand and supply, articulated through institutions. This is the argument of the public choice or market-surrogate schools, as exemplified especially in the Swedish work of Lindahl. For other writers, the concept of the consumer-voter is unrealistic, and instead the nature of representative government is emphasized together with the form of electoral support, constituency districts, and log-rolling to obtain votes. This is the argument of the economic theory of democracy, of for example Schumpeter, Dahl, and Downs, by which politicians compete to maximize votes. A third approach to fiscal politics rejects any belief in democratic control of public decisions, and instead views politicians as cynically following policies to retain power. Decisions are 'pork-barrelled' to buy support, and electoral districts are 'gerrymandered' in order to avoid electoral defeat. Finally, some commentators, e.g. Beer (1976) and Davies (1968), reject that even politicians retain much control over the nature of the public economy. Politicians may act to maintain electoral success, but their actions and any changes in the party in power are largely voided by the continuity of a professional bureaucracy that administers public goods and services according to its own policy paradigm.

Our response to these approaches depends upon our philosophical stance. As idealists we might not expect the public interest to be definable by individual preferences or by the vagaries of the political process, and we might judge that the need for public goods is best determined by the expert opinion of a professional bureaucracy (see p. 88). The technocrat is then the modern equivalent of Plato's philosopher ruler. However, as democratic idealists we would be disturbed by the frequent irrelevance of individual preferences to the politician and to the bureaucrat.

In this chapter, section 15.2 examines the predictions of the public choice school and the concept of the consumer-voter. Section 15.3 examines the way in which voters' preferences become translated into the programme packages of representative government the success of which depends upon trading with others' preferences through 'log-rolling'. In section 15.4, the influences of political bias and 'pork-barrel' politics are examined, and finally in section 15.5 deficiencies in the political system resulting from unequal representation are introduced.

15.2 The consumer-voter

The individual choice approach to fiscal politics of the Swedish and 'public choice' schools takes as its base the consumer-voter. The individual is assumed to have a preference pattern which is capable of ranking alternative public services, public versus private services, different revenue and expenditure patterns, and alternative distributional criteria. It is further assumed that each individual enters into a bargaining process with others from which a particular pattern of public goods and their finance emerges. Such bargaining is based on face-to-face contact and discussion and is possible only in villages and small communities. It harks back to the Jeffersonian ideal of 'ward democracy', the Schumacher concept of 'small is beautiful', and is embodied in the public choice literature, discussed in chapter 11, of Buchanan, Tullock, Olson, Bish, and Ostrom.

The logic of this public choice school is that it is the same individuals who are demanding both public and private goods. Hence, from the price point of view, both public and private goods may be treated similarly. But public goods are not concerned solely with price. Instead, it is argued, especially by Buchanan (1967), that price must be combined with consideration of institutions, organizations, and voting. Then, from a postulated political structure, it will be possible both to predict the public economy which results, and to derive the form of institutions from a particular form of exchange. Hence, when groups become too large for direct bargaining to be feasible, it is assumed that individual preferences are translated through voting to a representative government in which parties, representatives, or policies cover a composite bundle of preferences. The individual then votes for that bundle of preferences which accord most closely with his own individual preferences. Various voting systems may be used in order to achieve this expression of preferences: simple majority, plurality voting, transferable votes, or point voting. In each case, however, it is assumed that individual preferences are related, through votes, to the final form of the public fisc. A related phenomenon is often described as the politics of *Concertation*: the range of actions by which modern organizations endeavour to feed into their decisions an adequate amount of participation and information from major individual interests. Hence, like Beer's politics of collectivism or Dahl's politics of bargaining, the French concept of concertation recognizes the need for involvement in, and legitimation of, decisions; but it is assumed that this participation is a more committed and formal process than mere consultation (Coombs 1974). It involves direct account of the opinions of interest groups and the reconciling of them in final policy.

In each case it is assumed that individual votes are translated into group preferences and then into final policy. For it to be valid for this process to be achieved, two axioms must be satisfied:

(1) *comparability of alternatives*: this yields an order of preference such that A is preferred to B, and this preference is stable over a reasonably long period of time;

(2) *transitivity of alternatives*: if A is preferred to B, and B to C, then A is preferred to C.

If these two axioms are satisfied, then it should be possible to aggregate the preferences of individuals together in order to achieve a single preference function for a group as a whole. This has been the aim of welfare economics and utility theory which both attempt to determine a unique social welfare function for society as a whole. It also underlies the collective action or public choice school of public finance: that individuals come together in service clubs where they articulate similar preferences.

However, the agreement between individuals to achieve common ends in the provision of public goods and services is subject to a number of severe restrictions which arise from the implications of an impossibility theorem due to Arrow (1951). Arrow demonstrated if the two axioms of ordering the individual's preferences (the comparability and transitivity of alternatives), discussed above, are subject to certain weak conditions, then no aggregation of an individual's preference functions exists that can produce uniquely ranked aggregate social preference functions. Figure 15.1 illustrates this difficulty for a set of five individuals who each rank their preferences for five

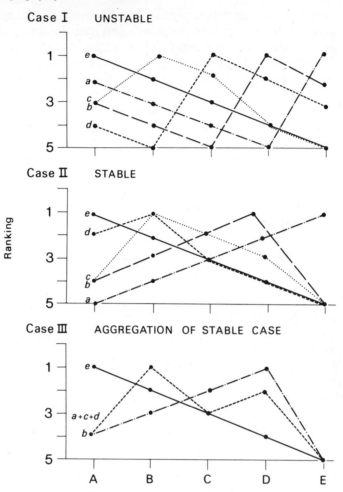

Figure 15.1 Three cases of preference rankings by five individuals (a,b,c,d,e) among five possible alternative policies (A, B, C, D, E).

alternative policies (A, B, C, D, E). In the first case there is no majority preference possible: if any single policy is put to the vote there are always three people who prefer other policies; no stable majority is possible. In the second case in the figure, a stable majority is possible: B is preferred to C, to D, to A, and finally to E. The majority is stable in this case because each individual preference pattern is *single peaked*, and Black (1958) proves this as a general result. It is this second case in figure 15.1 which is assumed to obtain in all the public choice literature: that multi-peaked preferences, and high support for two or more extreme cases is not possible. Hence, this school argues that the unstable case is unlikely in practice. Even if it does occur it is then argued that socialization reduces the range of options available and increases the degree

436

of agreement upon them. Alternatively, non-majority voting systems can be adopted. For example, point voting allows a shift from ranked to cardinal preferences for which stable solutions are obtainable even in the first case of figure 15.1. This result has been used in welfare economics, for example by Goodman and Markowitz (1952), to yield social utility functions.

The case of extreme, diametrically opposite, or multi-peaked preferences would be an insignificant special case if it were not for the fact that it arises quite frequently in practice. Musgrave and Musgrave (1976) argue that the form of the preference function depends on the type of choice being considered. Where preferences for the size of the public fisc are concerned, and there are no economies of scale, the range of expenditure functions is very small and costs are spread equally amongst all individuals. Then preferences are usually single peaked. Where taxation is progressive, multi-peaked preferences will result if the rate of progression is not constant, since tax shares change direction for different income groups as the budget expands. Again, changes in direction may differ at different time periods and general conclusions are difficult. Where several expenditure functions are involved, multi-peaked preferences will be common for qualitative and quantitative differences in the same services, or between different services. Even if individual preferences are single peaked and give unique ordering of preferences for public goods, it is frequently true that group aggregations of preferences may not give unique rankings. Margolis (1961), for example, argues that multi-peaked preferences are the rule rather than the exception in US metropolitan areas where small tracts with nearly homogeneous socio-economic characteristics maintain a close identity of preferences which are diametrically opposed to those of other areas. This is partly a result of the economic sources of social segregation in cities, and partly the result of a further paradox in voting, as shown in the third case in figure 15.1, where individuals a, c and d are aggregated together in one government unit. If each government has only one vote, the stable preferences of Case II in the figure are turned into an unstable pattern, even though the individual preference orderings allowed a stable majority. This pattern occurs frequently in urban areas, especially those in the US. Since a city is a single economic entity, common public benefits, common organizational structures, economies of scale, and other joint elements are sacrificed to fragmented government which may be further exacerbated by the practising of exclusionary policy. Wright (1975), for example, contrasts the breadth of views that are expressed at federal, State, and local level in the US where, as shown in figure 15.2, the local view is often quite broad, but does not take in the range of issues explored at State or federal level. As we have already seen in chapter 11, this stimulates exploration of the possibilities of mixed, central–local forms of government.

In addition to the problems of multi-peaked or incommensurable preferences, there are a variety of reasons why, in different circumstances, the final levels of public services will be distorted away from individual preference

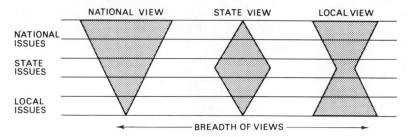

| NATIONAL VIEW | STATE VIEW | LOCAL VIEW |

NATIONAL ISSUES

STATE ISSUES

LOCAL ISSUES

← BREADTH OF VIEWS →

Figure 15.2   Relationship of the breadth of view on any issue to level of government.

patterns. Musgrave and Musgrave (1976) identify two hypotheses which lead to systematic under- and over-expansion of public services in relation to preferences. *Under-expansion* results from four main features. First, as noted first by Pigou (1947), many public goods yield public benefits in excess of their private costs. Since individuals tend to equate their direct costs with benefits, they fail to take account of the larger public good, and hence vote or support a smaller supply of services than would otherwise be the case. Second, because of the diffuse relationship of taxation to benefits, taxpayers may vote for tax cuts without thinking of the effect this will have on the level of public services that can be provided. Proposals for tax cuts are frequently registered through industrial and union lobbies, whilst in the US, tax cutting by referendum, since the 1978 California Proposition 13, has become a popular means of reducing burdens in many States, with little or no thought given to the consequences for benefit levels. The chief argument of Howard Jarvis, the California proposer of Proposition 13, being that government had 'fat' which could be removed with no effect on service levels. Third, Galbraith (1958) argues that advertising in the private sector has a differential effect in enhancing demand for private as opposed to public goods. However, the two sectors are not independent since demand created in the private sector frequently creates larger demands in the public sector as well, e.g. purchase of electrical appliances requires greater investment in generation facilities; purchase of automobiles requires more highways; and so forth. A fourth stimulus to under-expansion is the more visible and direct relation of benefits to cost. Taxation has frequently, and rightly, only a diffuse relationship to benefits received, whereas expenditure on a particular good yields immediate and obvious benefits. Hence taxes are frequently unpopular and their expansion is resisted.

On the other hand, seven major motives for *over-expansion* have also been identified. First, Buchanan and Tullock (1969, chapter 10) argue that majority voting tends to produce an oversupply of services. Since most services benefit particular subgroups, whilst tax burdens are borne by a larger or by other groups, potential recipients supporting a particular service will be obtaining additional benefits at less than their marginal costs. As stated by Wicksell (1934, in Musgrave and Peacock 1958, p. 87):

' . . . it is easy for capable but unprincipled politicians to exploit the party constellations of the day for the purpose of swelling public expenditure far beyond the amount corresponding to the collective interests of the people. Then the parties win in turn but in the end they all lose; it is like a game of roulette where the players win and lose in turn but the money finally ends up with the bank.'

A second cause of expansion is that individuals are frequently in favour of expanding services whilst being unaware of the cost implications. This may arise from assuming that someone else will bear the costs, or from the inability to make the essentially political decisions which are required in choosing, under a fixed budget, between particular types and levels of benefit. This is often more marked with less visible taxes such as indirect taxes (sales tax, for example). A third cause of over-expansion has been Keynesian stabilization policy. Whilst deficit financing has been readily expanded to absorb deficient demands in times of recession, few governments have been able fully to reduce these levels of spending in times of boom. A special form of this expansion had been influenced by a fourth factor deriving from the displacement effect of wartime finance. The resources absorbed by the public sector during such periods have never been fully returned after the cessation of wartime expenditure needs (see p. 24). A fifth cause of over-expansion has been inflation and fiscal drag. With inflation of incomes and prices, tax receipts from income, sales, severance and many other taxes rise without any conscious decision by government, usually at a rate faster than that of the underlying rate of inflation. It is unusual that all of these 'windfall' revenues are returned to the taxpayer. Over-expansion can also result from a sixth factor, the political infeasibility of direct redistribution policy. Where direct fiscal transfers between people, or horizontal transfers between jurisdictions, are precluded, general transfers are often implemented in which large numbers of people or jurisdictions receive aid, but the poorer receive more. Particularly with intergovernmental grant programmes, the dilution of aid between large numbers of jurisdictions or people has already been noted in chapters 12 and 13, and this causes excessive and wasteful public expenditure by targeting aid at the less needy as well as the really needy. This is exacerbated through the politics of concertation (see p.435) where local organizations act as pressure groups, e.g. the UK Association of County Councils, or the US National Governors Conference. This has often been responsible for the increase of block over specific purpose grants. Finally, Tarschys (1975) and Beer (1976) have argued that over-expansion results from the role of the bureaucrats and politicians which, as a producer interest, act as very powerful lobbies for the increase of services and hence of the public sector, both at the expense of the individual voter, and at the expense of the private sector. This has, as Brittan (1975) notes for the UK, raised the expectations of voters, and led to a functional specialization in a professional–bureaucratic elite divorced from public opinion.

15.3 Representative government and log-rolling

Because of the limited range of applicability of individual preference and voting models, most analysts prefer to work with models which abandon the assumption that individuals participate directly in public decisions as consumer-voters. Instead, the more realistic assumption is made that most decisions are delegated to representatives who are elected as members of political parties. According to the analysis of Dahl (1956), Downs (1956, 1967), Schumpeter (1943), and others, such politicians then compete with one another to maximize their number of votes and so stay in power. Hence the political system functions to maintain a party or coalition in office. This is achieved by following those combined programmes, or manifestos of party policy, which are in accord with the preferences of most of the electorate. The voting paradox of Arrow and Margolis is then overcome since, on the one hand, combined packages limit the range of choices available, whilst on the other hand, coalitions between parties combine voters with compatible views on a set of issues. The successful politician or party is, then, one that can find winning combinations of policies to maximize votes, and adapt these policies as the preferences of voters change. A special case of such policies is that of log-rolling in which winning coalitions are built by trading votes between different groups of supporters. By this device, it is possible for programmes to succeed where otherwise they would fail, by linking with other programmes and trading votes to support them.

An extensive theory of log-rolling has been derived by Barry (1965, chs. 14, 15). He argues that, at one extreme, when a winning coalition forms, its period of survival is strictly limited, since a consistent coalition leads to a permanently excluded minority which can only succeed in furthering its policies by civil war. The alternative, at the other extreme, of a new coalition forming on each issue, is equally unlikely, since support is lost by everyone being excluded for part of the time. Barry argues that the reality of coalition building sees a result midway between these two extremes in which minorities are never deprived of some share of public benefit, but a fairly consistent core coalition dominates decision making with log-rolling for new support to allow it to win on specific issues. The result for public finance is that there is some expenditure on all services, groups, and regions, and that services are maintained at a minimum standard which is politically acceptable to most interests. Thus, log-rolling is essentially the outcome of taking a long run view:

> 'Where the pursuit of maximum short run gain makes everyone lose compared with some "reasonable" solution, it naturally becomes a matter of self-interest to aim at the "reasonable" solution provided everyone else does likewise, . . . each party . . . wants as much as he can get and there is no way in which the several parties can reach an agreement unless the bare notions of rationality and self-interest are somehow supplemented'.

(Barry 1965, p.255). Thus, Barry argues that log-rolling yields what can be termed the 'obvious' solution; its reasonableness in terms of the more diffuse concept of the 'public interest' arising merely from the way in which coalitions form.

The degree of importance of log-rolling depends on the form of government in power. In some countries, such as Britain up to 1974, Austria, and recently in France, ready-made majorities have been available for most of the legislation programmes of the government in power. In other countries, especially the US, Germany, Canada, Belgium, Italy, and the Netherlands, and also to a lesser extent in Britain since about 1974, coalitions must be built anew for each issue. For example, in the US, the history of the Depressed Area Bills, leading to the 1961 Area Redevelopment Act, is documented by Davidson (1966), and that of revenue-sharing by Dommel (1974). However, the degree of importance of log-rolling does not depend solely on relative numbers of representatives of each party. The true bargaining power of a party derives from the complexity of coalition building between preferences within, as well as between, parties. Shapley and Shubik (1954) present what is now a classic analysis of the measurement of party power in voting situations (see also Riker and Ordeshook 1973), and recently Johnston (1977) and Johnston and Hunt (1977) have used a simplified index for measuring the distribution of power in various European institutions. Others have approached coalition building through game theory and analysis based on the combinatorial enumeration of the voting preferences of each representative (Banzhaf 1968; Brams 1975; Brams and Riker 1972).

A number of attempts have been made to relate the final outcomes of decisions and the preferences of the representatives concerned. For example, Rice (1928), Barry (1965), and Arnold (1977) argue that if individual representatives have well-defined goals (ranging from political survival, through altruism and local interest, to ideology) then the degree to which the final outcomes of decisions reflects individual preferences can be used to infer how influential each individual has been. Three general strategies can be identified: those for achieving general benefits, those directed at local benefits, and log-rolling. For example, Arnold found that military programmes had wide support and hence were only slightly influenced by committee membership in the US Congress. For water and sewerage programmes, however, there was little strong interest or preference, and a strategy was followed on Congressional committees of widening the number of areas eligible despite the original aim of helping growing communities. Again, for model cities, the areas receiving benefits were significantly widened. This effect is typical of many US federal grant and aid programmes in which the area of geographical eligibility has been diffused by use in the allocation of formal surrogate variables which target aid to 'urban problems', 'economically depressed areas', or 'educationally disadvantaged' districts, but which are wide enough to include enough other jurisdictions for winning coalitions to be constructed.

441

This issue also draws us towards the pork-barrel politics discussed in the next section.

15.4 Political bias in finance allocation: the pork-barrel

It is a logical consequence of economic theories of politics such as those of Schumpeter and Downs, that politicians should seek to enhance their competitiveness to retain office by use of the public fisc. Selective disbursement of expenditure benefits, and adjustments to the incidence of revenue burdens, can critically influence voting patterns and electoral support. At an individual level this involves selective use of what Coleman (1974) terms 'political money' in order to win the allegiance of voters. At the geographical level competitiveness can be enhanced by dividing up grant and expenditure programmes between areas. It is this latter phenomenon which is frequently termed the pork-barrel: the chopping up of expenditure programmes, especially those involving intergovernmental grants, in order to appease political interest, or to *buy* votes for coalition building and log-rolling. In practice, therefore, the distinction between log-rolling and pork-barrelling tends to be one of the degree to which selfish interest is involved.

Generally the extent of pork-barrelling will be larger, the greater is the degree of unanimity required to pass a given piece of legislation. Frequently the form of pork-barrelling is distinctive to the level of government in which it takes place. For example, Brunn (1974) has suggested that ministerial appointments within the US administration are used by the executive (President) to buy political support in major States. In the UK, the success of the two Secretaries of State for Scotland and Wales in obtaining additional public expenditure for those two regions prior to devolution is also well-known. At the level of the legislature, pork-barrel politics are nowhere better developed than in the US Congress where membership of Congressional committees is usually viewed as providing the most effective access to political money. A third level of concern is political bias in administration. Although the civil service administration in all countries acts out the decisions of ministers in supposedly unbiased fashion, considerable bias can enter, especially where departments become increasingly dominated by a professional elite with its own policy paradigm. Although the administrative area is probably the least politically biased in most countries, it nevertheless divorces decisions both from individual preferences and from politicians. At the level of intermediate and local governments, considerable pork-barrelling can occur. Shoup (1969, p.633) sees the decentralization of government to State and local units as the major way in which pork-barrelling is revealed:

> 'What the decentralized state does is to bring into the open the struggle between those who want to optimize on the basis of the existing distribution of disposable income, including government free services in that income, and those who want to see that distribution made more nearly equal. This struggle is far less discernible in the unitary state, since

the presumption in such a state is that all taxes shall be geographically uniform and all free services shall be at the same level everywhere. This state of affairs does not of course prevent most households in some areas from being poorer than most households in certain other areas.'

For example, revenue-sharing was enacted in the US only when funds were allocated to States as well as local governments, thus 'buying' the support of the State representatives for this programme. At local level, pork-barrelling is frequently most notable in the award of building contracts and the selective relaxation of land use development controls in both Britain and the US. The local level also impinges on the central level, both in terms of how far given central programmes are implemented or achieve their desired aims, and what level of resources local governments receive.

At an aggregate level, many studies have found a close relation between the distribution of public finance and the political colour of the party concerned. One major problem in such studies has been that of differentiating political factors from social, economic and fiscal ones, and some studies have produced rather inconclusive results. As a result many writers have concluded that party colour alone is less significant than two other factors: first, the time a particular party has been in office, and second, the relationship between the party at one level of government and that at the other levels of government. Thus, Brunn and Hoffman (1969) and Johnston (1978) have found a close relation of State to US federal politics to be important. For example, electorally 'safe' and marginal States receive more aid than those in which opposition parties sit. This pattern of aid is confirmed in British experience of the allocation of the Rate Support Grant, with grants tipping in favour of urban areas under a Labour Government, and in favour of rural areas under a Conservative one (see Alt 1971; Boaden 1971; Jackman and Sellars 1978). Substantiating this idea, figure 15.3 shows the relation between the level of Rate Support Grant allocated and party colour. In contrast, in both the Oliver and Stanyer (1969) and the Nicolson and Topham (1971) studies of Britain, political factors were found of only minor significance in explaining expenditure levels compared with socio-economic ones. However, it is often the time that a party has been in office and the use made of funds rather than its colour and total expenditure which is most important. Newton and Sharpe (1976), for example, suggest the following typology:

Local Government	*Central Government*	
	Labour	*Conservative*
Labour	High local expenditure	Medium local expenditure
Conservative	Medium local expenditure	Low local expenditure

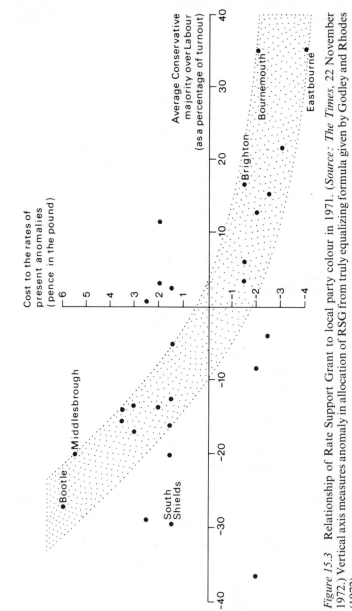

Figure 15.3 Relationship of Rate Support Grant to local party colour in 1971. (*Source: The Times*, 22 November 1972.) Vertical axis measures anomaly in allocation of RSG from truly equalizing formula given by Godley and Rhodes (1972).

Again, changing business conditions have been found to be an important influence by Kramer (1971), Stigler (1972), and Bloom and Price (1975): it seems that voters apportion credit or blame for economic conditions on the government in power and vote accordingly.

A major example of the effect of political lobbying and pork-barrelling is that of the conflict between the 'sun-belt' states of the South and West of the US, and those of the 'frost-belt' in the North, North-East and Mid-West United States. During the 1975–77 period the frost-belt/sun-belt conflict became a particularly heated issue, as registered in Congressional proceedings, the Conference of Governors, and other fora. *Business Week* (1976, p. 92) dubbed this, "the second war between the States (which) will take the form of political and economic manoeuvre. But the conflict can be nonetheless bitter and divisive because it will be a struggle for income, jobs, people and capital". Two influential *National Journal* (1976, 1977) studies entitled *The North's Loss is the South's Gain*, and *The Sunbelt Fights Back*, thrust this concern to attention. Other more popular studies such as Phillips' *The Emerging Republican Majority* (1969), Kirkpatrick Sale's *Power Shift* (1975), and Dent's *The Prodigal South Returns to Power* (1978) held that the shift in Congressional and Presidential influential was moving very markedly in favour of the Southern States. The 1976 Governors' Conference was particularly important in registering this conflict. Pennsylvania Governor J. Shapp, for example, charged that the North-East States had been a victim of "planned neglect", that the Nixon and Ford administrations had followed policies which had "moved poverty from the rural South northward", the result of which will be that "the cancer of Applachia will spread from Maine to Minnesota . . . we will continue to lose our industrial base and population . . . we will suffer further tragic urban decay until the process becomes virtually irreversible" (quoted in *National Journal* 1976, pp. 1695–6).

These perceived problems became, and continue to be, focused on bipartisan regional lobbies at all levels of US Government: in the Senate, the House, and in the States. Indeed the expansion of Washington offices by regional, State and local interests has been one of the fastest growing sectors of the Washington economy. In the Senate, a bipartisan coalition has been chaired by Senator Howard Metzebaum (Democrat, Ohio). In the House, research has been funded by the Council for North-East Economic Action, and coalitions have grown out of the New England Congressional Caucus founded in 1972. The North-East–Mid-West Economic Advancement Coalition, with 204 House members, was founded in 1976, with prominent members being Michael Harrington (Democrat, Massachusetts), Frank Horton (Republican, New York) and James Oberstron (Democrat, Minnesota). At State level, the Coalition of North-East Governors (CONEG), created in 1976, has also been influential. In the sun-belt, the Southern Growth Policies Board founded in 1971, the TVA, and the Western Governors' Conference have fought back resolutely and successfully.

445

Examples of the effects of these lobbies have been the success of the North-East US in the 1975 Congress Bill S 1009 aimed at obtaining annual statistics of population and federal spending to aid lobbying, the massive expansion of the Economic Development Administration areas for special public works assistance, joint attacks on defence and aerospace contracts, and the Defense Department policy statement of 1952 that defence contracts should be accepted preferentially from depressed areas provided the bids were not more than 10% higher than the lowest bid elsewhere. Representative Harrington even mooted a legal suit against the Economic Development Administration on the grounds that they were not giving equal treatment to the Northern States.

The greatest impact of the US Congressional lobbies has probably been in effecting changes to intergovernmental grant distribution formulae. As pointed out by *US News and World Report* (1977, p. 40): "A basic weapon in their arsenal is the computer printout . . . to show each (Congressman) how his district would fair under proposed changes in aid distribution formulas. Members now vote by printout. It is a tool of the trade". The general aim of the frost-belt interests has been to include greater weight on such 'need' factors as cost of living, local tax effort, fiscal distress, urban indicators, and the removal of the high level of federal transfer payments in the North-East from *per capita* income indicators of tax capacity. In the South and West the emphasis has been on such factors as *per capita* income to aid the rural South, development costs to aid the West, or on economic efficiency. As a result, it has become almost impossible to achieve effective targeting of aid programmes to the locations in the severest of need: grants are diluted, and in the true sense of the pork-barrel, no one ends up with useful aid. The effect of these lobbies can be seen in general revenue-sharing in the compromise between the House formula, favouring the urban locations, and the Senate formula, favouring the rural areas (see chapter 13, p.373). Similarly, the two formulae of the Community Development Block Grant favour the South with emphasis on population, poverty, and house overcrowding, and favour the North with emphasis on age of housing. Notable lobbying successes for the North have been accorded in this area. Important examples are in the addition of a cost of living factor to the Food Stamp programme in 1977, the addition of an unemployment factor to local public works projects, the inclusion of population decline and revenue decline Titles II and VI counter-cyclical revenue-sharing aiding northern cities, the aid to railways in the Boston–New York–Washington corridor in the 1976 *Railroad Revitalization and Regulatory Reform Act* (90, Stat. 31) and finally in the structure of the aid allocation in Public Works Employment (CETA, Titles II and VI). In contrast, the attempts to close the gap in energy prices between the North and South have failed. Issues which remain to be resolved are tax reforms encouraging renewal of housing, aid to educationally disadvantaged areas, and the form of poverty programmes.

An important means of affecting the allocation of federal expenditure grants in the US is membership of Congressional committees. Since the committees of the US Congress are very influential in decision making, members seek seats on these committees relevant to their district interests. This results in over-representation of those constituencies which have a big stake in such decisions, so that members can exert disproportionate influence on the receipt of public benefits in their area. A number of studies have confirmed the general importance of this factor. For example, Niskanen (1971) and Goss (1972) confirm the importance of membership of relevant committees on military contracts (although not all contracts are explicable by the membership variable). Similar results were found by Ferejohn (1974) and Rundquist and Ferejohn (1976) for urban renewal, river and harbour expenditures, and wastes treatment construction, by Brunn (1975) for defence contracts, by Wohlenberg (1976) for AFDC programmes, by Arnold (1977) for military employment, Model Cities grants, and water and sewerage grants, and by Johnston (1977, 1978) for 15 departmental expenditure programmes. Johnston also found that membership of the House Legislative Committee was more significant than membership of the Appropriations Committee, whilst in the Senate this conclusion was reversed.

The pork-barrel is probably nowhere better developed than in the US, but similar features affect all countries, where additional arguments such as 'autonomy' or 'local rights' are used to gain bargaining power. The general results of the diffusion of aid away from the most needy, and significant over-expansion of the public fisc, are common in Europe, Australia, and elsewhere.

15.5 Unequal representation

The economic model of politics which underlies the explanation of log-rolling, pork-barrelling, and other effects of fiscal politics, can be expanded to encompass the effects of imperfectly competitive systems. This results in unequal bargaining power between jurisdictions and representatives. Smith (1776, p.945) noted one example of this as the unequal power of the centre and the periphery of a nation:

> 'In all great countries which are united under a uniform government, the spirit of party commonly prevails less in the remoter provinces than in the centre of the empire. The distance of those provinces from the capital, from the principal seat of the great scramble of faction and ambition, makes them enter less into the views of any of the contending parties . . .'

More recently, it has become clear in both the US and EEC, that the concentration of electors in the industrial areas has enabled them to draw special attention for their problems involving aid for regional policy and transport subsidies, whilst rural areas and less populated urban centres have tended to be the losers in the contest for funds unless they are 'marginal' constituencies. Again, the decisions of any devolved Scottish Assembly would be likely to be permanently dominated by the interests of the heavily populated Scottish Central Valley. Had devolution been enacted for Scotland, this would have accounted for the maintenance of the Westminster-controlled Highlands and Islands Development Board, and for the vote by the Shetland Islands to retain a level of autonomy under the Westminster government.

At the local level, many inner city areas have resisted policies which would contribute to regeneration and renewal because this would change the nature of employment and residential structures of their areas and erode long-held party dominance. For example, in London's Docklands, the Labour-controlled Local Boroughs have resisted the invasion of offices and middle income social groups, and the construction of the Jubilee Line subway system, which would contribute to the regeneration of the area, but which would change the balance of the electorate towards the Conservative Party.

Imperfect competition within the political system is frequently the result of the party system itself. Parties are dominated by a discipline which limits their degree of responsiveness to local preferences. Moreover, each party tends to fight for the centre ground, thus neglecting smaller scale interests; some electoral systems, particularly the simple majority system, exclude minorities to an extent which other systems such as proportional representation, would not; political campaigns are costly and are not usually fought by parties with equal financial resources; electoral districts are sometimes manipulated to give unequal weight to votes by gerrymandering; political support may be linked to other factors such as bias in the media; and the political system and the media may be manipulated, as Marx and others have suggested, by a party to retain office. Finally, as Commons (1940) and Olson (1965) note, other groups, ranging from protest groups, conservation groups, societies, and even the church, all have influences on the selection of representatives and on voting.

A major deficiency in the translation of voting preferences into policy concerns the degree to which elected politicians may not be truly representative of the preferences of the constituents because of bias in electoral districts. Where log-rolling results from preferences being expressable only for combined packages, electoral bias results in preferences, expressed through votes, carrying different weights. It has usually been the fundamental tenet of democracy that one man has one vote which is of equal weight to all other votes: as Mill states, "one man, one vote; one vote, one value". However, two factors militate against this principle holding in all cases. First, many countries practice only limited franchise: voting is restricted by age, sex, property tenure, or other characteristics. For example, the residents of Washington D. C. only obtained general franchise in 1980 in Congressional elections. Second, and most important, where geographically delimited constituencies are used as the basis of representation, election results can be biased, inadvertently or deliberately, so that the proportion of representatives of a particular party elected does not equal the proportion of votes cast for that party. This latter electoral bias results from a spatial mismatch of the boundaries of constituency districts with the distribution of voters of various opinions.

Where constituencies are deliberately designed to favour one party as against others, the process is termed gerrymandering. Such strategies can be developed by three routes. First, if the districts are allowed to vary greatly in size, and hence in numbers of voters, and one party's strength is concentrated in the smaller districts, then that party needs a smaller number of total votes to gain more seats. This is the main reason for bias in favour of US Democrats, and UK Conservatives, whose support is often drawn from the smaller rural constituencies. For example, Eichen (1975) has examined the degree of variation in the size of population in Congressional Districts in the US. In 1964 the range of variation was very large, only five States had a maximum variation in District population of less than 10%. After the redistricting of 1970 and a series of important court decisions in the 1960s, of which the *Wesbury v. Saunders* decision (376, US., 1964) was perhaps the most significant, the greatest variation of District population averages within States was 5.9% for Hawaii. Again in the proposals for elections to the European parliament (see, for example, UK Government 1976), Taylor and Johnston (1978b) find widely inequitable representation of population in which the smaller countries, such as Luxembourg, Ireland, Denmark, Belgium and the Netherlands, are over-represented, and the large countries, such as Germany, France, Italy and the UK, are under-represented.

A second factor in electoral bias is the placement of boundary lines. If, as in many urban areas, patterns of voting are very sharply delimited in geographical space, it is possible to draw district boundary lines to include a minority of voters for one party with a majority of voters for another party in a majority of districts. This feature alone is sufficient to assure a party of winning more seats and is significant in the US (Eichen 1975) and other countries (Taylor and Johnston 1978a). A third factor in electoral bias applies to two-stage voting. For example, in the US Presidential elections, the voters in smaller States have a greater influence in determining the Electoral College votes for a given seat, but because the number of Electoral College votes available to each State is determined by each State's population, larger States have a greater influence on the final result. Thus, for example, Banzhaf (1968) estimates that the New York voter has 3.312 times as much power as the District of Columbia voter in the choice of President.

Whilst districting can be used as a deliberate strategy (akin to fiscal prudence and exclusion) to gain greater public benefits or reduced public costs by shifting the balance of representation and control, frequently various objective methods of districting have been adopted in order to ensure as equal a representation as possible. Three main approaches have been followed: legal, mathematical, and functional. The legalistic approach to districting by the UK Boundary Commission and similar bodies in other countries, primarily attempts to achieve an equity of votes across space (Chisholm 1976). Most of the emphasis of this work has been on equity of the population of electorate, but considerations of compactness and contiguity of the boundaries are also important.

The mathematical approach to districting attempts to combine the criteria for equal value of votes, with contiguity and compactness, as an objective function which it is sought to maximize. Such procedures derive from research on service distribution and catchment area delimitation (Massam 1975; Scott 1971) and are usually termed location-allocation problems. A recent review is that by Taylor and Johnston (1978a), and prominent contributions are those by Cox *et al.* (1973) Weaver and Hess (1963), and Mills (1967).

Frequently, attempts have been made to combine optimal districting of electoral boundaries with optimal service districts as a functional approach to boundary determination. Indeed this is necessary if a meaningful relation is to be established between representatives and the public goods for which they make policies. A large number of examples of applications of mathematical optimization to service area delimitation have been proposed: by Yeates (1963) and Brown and Ferguson (1978) for school districts, Gould and Leinbach (1966) for hospitals. Hogg (1969) for fire stations, Drake *et al.* (1972) for emergency services, Coyle and Martin (1969) for refuse collection, and by Mills (1967) and Goodchild and Massam (1969) for electricity administration areas. The functional approach also owes its origin to early writings on the existence of 'natural' geographical regions. For example, Vidal de la Blache (1911), Dickinson (1976), and others have argued that there is a fundamental tie between the features of human and physical geography which gives rise to natural cultural, and hence political, units. This conception of the sense of community has now perhaps most relevence to the close social homogeneity of neighbourhoods in cities, which have little relation to the physical features of the land.

15.6 Conclusion

The issues of fiscal politics may fire the researcher with new enthusiasm for the intricacies and complexities of public finance. Alternatively, they may fill the researcher with despair that the objective goals of equity, need and ability are never satisfied. As realists we should not be surprised by such a dilemma: we accept that we cannot objectively define issues such as equity or the public interest, and hence the results of this chapter are proof of our irrationality in attempting to do so. Hence we would reject the tenets of the public choice school, and its concept of the consumer-voter, as a means of deriving the form of the public fisc. However, as idealists, we must be disappointed at the extent to which individual preferences and more objective criteria of social distribution and economic efficiency become submerged beneath political expediency or technocratic professionalism. From the discussion of fiscal politics that has been presented here, it must be concluded that although political issues raise new and important complexities to attention, these new issues should not distract us from the more central concerns of public finance geography: to explore the variations in needs, costs, burdens and benefits across space, and to use this information as an approximate guide to decisions on the best form of intergovernmental transfers and other distributional problems. As will be recalled from the concluding discussion of chapter 2, many of these issues in the geography of public finance have remained obscured, and much of the data necessary to validate hypotheses of geographical distribution have been left uncollected. With the acquisition of new data the issues of fiscal politics will be better revealed, as well as the extent of true needs, costs, burdens and benefits, and this should lead to means of improving both the equity and efficiency of resource allocation in the public economy.

16

The geography of public finance

"You have got a marketplace where there is suburbia, the rural areas that are competing with the inner cities for industry, for people, for tax base, and all the other goodies that make the thing go .... You are at war with each other in the marketplace."

Congressman Richard Kelly, US Congress, Impact of the Federal Budget on Cities 1977, p. 158.

"Men's lives are surely . . . the important phenomena in society, the things of beauty or at least of interest. Consumption is merely the means of supporting their lives. To the social philosopher interested in human beings it must seem absurd that one should be so passionately interested in equalising among these lives supplies of the 'stuff', on the grounds that absorbing the stuff is the stuff of life."

Bertrand de Jouvenal 1951 , The Ethics of Redistribution

16.1 Pervasive dilemmas

This book has been concerned with the financial relations of areas, governments, individuals, and firms. As such it has emphasized the materialist side of social relations rather than the wider issues raised by Bertrand de Jouvenal and other humanist writers. The emphasis in the discussion of equity, in particular, has been concerned only with equity of incomes, of wealth, or of in-kind benefits: wider issues of social equity have been excluded. Similarly, any concern with the way in which income or wealth is used has been largely eliminated from consideration. This emphasis has been deliberate. Following Tawney, it has been deemed impossible, and undesirable, to seek to achieve an equity between people in all their attributes. We seek only equity in the fiscal system itself.

Indeed it is not the role of the State to accomplish any greater task. A concern with the distribution of income or wealth does not pretend that other wider issues are not of equal importance, but emphasizes instead the practical issues of determining criteria which have merit in measuring an individual's, or a location's, ability to contribute to the public fisc. Apportionment of tax burdens and benefits according to such gross measures of ability as income, wealth or expenditure is probably the only approach that can be used at a practical level to achieve equity of fiscal incidence. Nevertheless, such criteria of fiscal incidence are not without considerable difficulties in interpretation.

The recent evolution of public finance, especially through the 1960s and 1970s, has seen the emergence of an increasing number of difficulties. On the one hand, economic problems have become increasingly acute: there has been continued and increasingly high inflation and unemployment so that previously unacceptable levels of both indicia have now become commonplace; economic recessions have become long, and recovery uncertain; there have been continuing and increasing disparities of wealth between the developed and less developed countries, and between regions in all countries; and doubts have been growing as to whether economic growth can be sustained in the face of declining supplies of natural resources, increasing pollution, and diminishing potential for increases in growth of output by capital investment. On the other hand, the demands placed on governments have become increasingly great. First, the reforms of the 1930s, 1940s and 1950s, which created the 'welfare state' in Western societies, are now accepted as commonplace and people have looked to further improvements to basic services. This has been especially marked where services are highly income-elastic, as with health care, education, utilities, etc. Whilst it is believed that the State has banished poverty, continual improvements are sought. Second, new value positions have replaced the previous acceptance that economic growth of output and higher incomes are sufficient to create general satisfaction within society. Prosperity is now taken for granted as a necessary condition for satisfaction, but has been supplanted as the major aim by additional goals of environmental protection, improved quality of life, quality of work, or social equality. This has resulted in increased resistance to what is seen as the enslavement by work, greater emphasis on leisure, education and cultural facilities, and resistance to 'progress' and technological development (especially notable in protest movements resisting nuclear power technology, oil, coal and gas exploitation, freeway developments, and aerospace investments). Many Western societies have been progressively influenced by the Calvinist ethic: it is better for the land to produce a little less and for the people to lead better lives. A third cause of increased demands has been increasing resistance to informal and formal structures within society. This has been expressed in calls for legal reform, the break-up of government bureaucracy, greater participation in planning, greater worker control in industry, distaste for managerial and bureaucratic structures, and demands for greater local autonomy and geographical variation in government organization. Finally, demands on the State have increased by the greater emphasis on equity, fairness and distribution which has led to the need to justify projects and policies to society as a whole: to demonstrate their social utility. This has led to the proliferation of impact statements, cost–benefit analyses, extensive planning enquiries, and a log-jamming expansion of further bureaucracy. Apart from engendering further resentment of government and increasing the remoteness of decisions from people, such bureaucracies have frequently led to a redistribution of power from the individual to the State, to the creation of new technocratic elites, and to a more total dependence of individuals upon the State. Most significantly, this transfer of functions to the State has left the

453

individual and private institutions with diminished responsibilities. As de Jouvenal has noted, the family is eroded since education, welfare and other elements are no longer its functions; the individual is left with income sufficient only for personal support and for 'pocket money'; and the incentives for personal advancement, improvement of families, maintaining of the environment, or contributing to the arts or sciences, are all lost. The State, through its increasing effect on the size of the social wage and industrial externalities, has assumed these roles, and the responsibilities are often willingly shed.

Public finance has been caught, then, between the two conflicting forces of the smaller rate of growth in total economic resources, and an increasing demand placed upon those resources. As the 'national cake' has grown more slowly, and these demands have been satisfied, the role of the public sector has steadily increased such that in some countries (notably in the UK and Sweden), public resources now account for as much as 60% of total national resources. The increasing share of national income directly consumed by the public sector, or at least passing through public hands, creates further complications. The aims and goals of the public sector are very different from those of the traditional investor or entrepreneur: they are not the goals of economic efficiency, or of long-term growth and appreciation of capital; instead, they are predominantly short-term expenditures on services to people, or the short-term expedients of political survival through pork-barrelling. True, there will be long-term investments in buildings, infrastructure and manpower training, but in most modern economies current spending far outweighs capital spending, and the latter is usually the first to be cut in times of recession. In addition, much of the stock of private investment is going increasingly into the hands of institutional investors (banks, insurance companies) where once again the shorter term needs of paying pensions and benefits predominate over longer term capital building. In the UK for example, about three-quarters of the equity investment is controlled by public or institutional investors, and most of this is not oriented towards the goal of economic growth, i.e. is not concerned with increasing the size of the 'national cake'. In a very real sense, then, Western society has evolved to a position of wanting its 'cake' in all ways: maximum public goods, with minimum public interference, and the smallest possible fiscal burdens.

16.2 Implications

Within these general trends the geography of public finance is emerging as an increasing focus of attention. As argued throughout the preceding chapters, it does not divert attention from individual and corporate questions of allocation or distribution, but instead adds to these an additional concern with aggregate regional and jurisdictional imbalances which affect the public fisc. It has been argued in earlier chapters that a large number of factors undermine the treatment of fiscal questions as purely ones of national or of individual concern. Locations have unequal access to natural resources and to markets; changes in technology, institutional barriers, increasing indivisibilities of units of production, and imperfect information, each lead to variable patterns of economic investment and evolution over time. In addition, the effects of tapering and spillover, together with fragmented and mixed levels of government, lead to few goods possessing the ideal conditions characterizing pure public goods. Moreover, preferences and the demands of the market work to increase, rather than diminish, the level of economic inequality; and if anything, preferences are tending to shift towards greater fragmentation of government and increased autonomy free of the control of central bureaucrats.

The geographical focus for public finance has led to a large number of questions being raised at various points in earlier chapters: the degree to which the need for spatial price variation stimulates a centralist or localist model of resource allocation, and the degree to which distribution, stabilization and growth policies should be uniform or spatially differentiated. These questions draw attention to further issues such as the degree to which place-specific needs, costs, abilities, and benefits exist; the extent of the spatial relation of revenue burdens to revenue ability, tax effort and tax severity; and the degree of accord of benefit incidence with geographically variable needs. The pervasive issue of equity underlying each of these issues raises further questions concerning the measurement of client group as opposed to individual needs, the extent of exclusion and competition induced by fiscal prudence and the State's and Samaritan's dilemmas. This further draws us towards the so-called fiscal crisis of local governments, especially those of central cities and rural communities which are affected by adverse fiscal migration and the high costs of renewing 'sunk' capital.

Each of these questions concerns the degree to which the public fisc should be oriented, on the one hand, towards places and governments, and on the other hand, towards people and firms. It is the conclusion of this book that each approach, both person-oriented and place-oriented, must be considered. Inevitably, the relative emphasis on place as opposed to person depends upon an appropriate balance being struck in different circumstances. What is clear is that apportionment of both tax and expenditure functions requires a mixed pattern of individual and geographical distribution and allocation programmes, and this in turn stimulates a mixed pattern of central, local and intermediate levels of government. Such multi-level governments in turn stimulate the need for, first, a variable pattern of separated, shared and overlapping tax and expenditure functions; second, a complex set of transfer programmes up, down and across the governmental hierarchy based on mixtures of grants, deductions, credits, shared revenues, shared expenditures, and centrally organized spatially differentiated expenditures; and finally, improved co-ordination, horizontal transfers, and, under some circumstances, consolidation of local governments. In this way, the various problems of accountability, autonomy, freedom from local sectional interest, the national interest, and fiscally stable government can all be solved; final fiscal incidence can be equalized as far as possible; and the excesses of log-rolling and pork-barrelling reduced to a minimum.

Despite these conclusions, the answers to the questions which arise in the geography of public finance are not altogether clear, nor is sufficient empirical evidence yet available to yield unambiguous answers. What is apparent is that considerable research is required in order that the questions which relate to the geographical allocation of resources can be answered in addition to those concerned with specific individual or industrial issues. The whole stance of this book is that solutions to the economic, social, and political problems created by differences in wealth and income can be found only in methods of public finance which take geographical factors explicitly into account. They cannot be solved, as some writers have suggested, solely by attempts to equalize fiscal incidence between individuals since, if there is any progression at all in incomes, inequities will still emerge at the spatial level, merely because the rich choose to live together, or the poor have no choice but to live together. Moreover, these inequities will emerge with or without a pattern of jurisdictional partitioning based on local governments. Although it can be argued that there should be no objection to spatial inequalities which merely express the agreed level of income progressivity in society as a whole, it is becoming increasingly clear that place-specific and government-specific needs cannot be solved by national redistribution policies alone, that the geographical focus is crucial to the tackling of many needs, and that to ignore such problems as special cases ignores also the cumulative impact of inequities on total incomes and regional imbalance. If this book helps to stimulate research in some of these areas, then it will have achieved its major goals.

Appendix

Measures of spatial distribution

Two measures which are used for assessing the equality of spatial distibution of the public fisc in chapters 11 and 12 are reviewed here: first, a weighted measure of change in Gini coefficient, and second, the unweighted measure of the redistributive power ratio. (further discussion is given by EEC 1977, chapter 5).

THE CHANGE IN GINI COEFFICIENT

This is used in classical analysis of interpersonal income distribution. It measures the ratio of jurisdictional inequality indicated by the Gini coefficient for personal income as modified by intergovernmental transfers or other analysed fiscal effects to the Gini coefficient unmodified by transfers. The Gini coefficient for *unmodified income* is given by:

$$g = \tfrac{1}{2} \sum_{i=1}^{n} \sum_{j=1}^{n} p_i p_j |d_i - d_j|$$

where p_i is the population in the ith jurisdiction, d_i is the *per capita* income differential of jurisdiction i from the national average, and n is the number of jurisdictions considered. The d_i term is defined by $(y_i/p_i - d)$, where y_i is the total unmodified personal income of people in jurisdiction i, and d is the national average *per capita* income, which is set equal to 1. The Gini coefficient for *modified income* g^m is given analogously as:

$$g^m = \tfrac{1}{2} \sum_{i=1}^{n} \sum_{j=1}^{n} p_i p_j |d_i^m - d_j^m|$$

where y_i^m is the proportion of personal *per capita* income affected by the financial programme considered, or the change in tax burdens which result, i.e. $d_i^m = (y_i^m/p_i - d)$. The value of the Gini coefficient varies between zero, for exact equality in the effect of the public fisc on revenue burdens, and 1, when the effect of the public fisc on burdens is concentrated in one region. The final measure, of income redistribution induced by the public fisc, is given as the percentage ratio of the modified and unmodified Gini coefficients, i.e.

$$g^m/g \times 100 = G$$

Where G is the change in Gini coefficient.

THE REDISTRIBUTIVE POWER RATIO

This has been proposed by Horst Rechenbach (EEC 1977, ch. 5) and gauges the average extent to which jurisdictional income differentials are reduced by given transfer programmes or revenue raising patterns. This measure r is given by:

$$r = (\sum_{i=1}^{n} d_i^2 r_i)/(\sum_{i=1}^{n} d_i^2)$$

$$r_i = (d_i - d_i^m)/d_i$$

and each symbol is defined as before, with r_i equal to the proportional reduction in jurisdictional incomes resulting from transfers or revenue burdens. Thus, this measure gives the reduction in each jurisdiction's income differences from the national average ($d_i^m = y_i^m/p_i - d$) as a percentage of local unmodified income. Each of these jurisdictional modified income differences is then weighted by squares of the unmodified income differences. Although

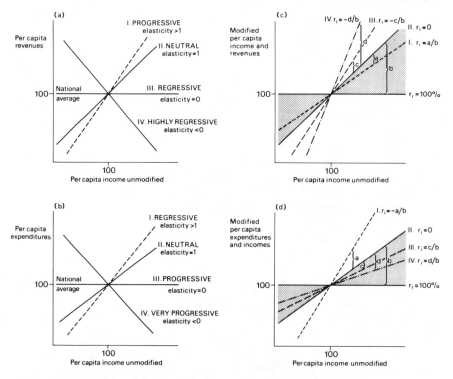

Appendix 1 Modification of public finance distribution by new programmes and relation of redistribution power ratio to revenue and expenditure elasticity.
  a Cases of revenue elasticity
  b Cases of expenditure elasticity
  c Redistribution power for different revenue elasticities
  d Redistribution powers for different expenditure elasticities
Shaded area is zone in which redistribution is in favour of higher income jurisdictions.
(After EEC 1977, Chapter 5, chart 1, p. 142.)

complex, this measure has the simple property that it is directly related to the income elasticity of the intergovernmental revenue burden. Hence a transfer or revenue burden which has neutral (proportional) relation to income, has an elasticity of 1, and will have a redistributive power ratio of zero: a transfer or burden which is progressive will have a positive ratio (indicating a lack of redistribution of benefits): and a regressive transfer will have a negative ratio (indicating larger redistributive benefits to the lower income areas). This relationship can be seen from Appendix figure 1. On the left-hand side of the figure, a and b show the relation of revenue-raising and expenditure incidence to jurisdictional *per capita* incomes before the effect of transfers is taken into account. The slope of the relationship is equal to the unmodified revenue or expenditure elasticity with income. On the right-hand side of the figure, c and d show the modification of *per capita* incomes induced by transfers or other fiscal effects, on both the revenue and expenditure accounts. The shaded areas correspond to programmes which induce modification in favour of redistribution to lower income areas. These are programmes with income elasticity of revenues greater than 1 and an income elasticity of expenditure of less than 1.

A major difficulty affecting both redistribution measures is the determination of the modified *per capita* income of each jurisdiction. Modified income should include the effects of both revenue and expenditures on income levels. This requires the revenue burden and the expenditure benefits to be assessed for each jurisdiction, and hence relies heavily on the tax shifting and exporting studies discussed in chapters 7 and 8. The change in Gini coefficient allows for differences in absolute magnitudes of transfers, by incorporating population weights, but the redistribution power ratio has the two advantages of, first, allowing direct comparison between jurisdictions, and second, permitting programmes to be aggregated or disaggregated (i.e. the measure is strictly additive).

Bibliography

ABEL-SMITH, B. and TITMUSS, R. M. (1956) *The cost of the national health service in England and Wales*. Cambridge: University Press.

ADAMS, C. (1977) untitled, unpublished mimeo. Brookings Institution, Washington D. C.

ADAMS, H. C. (1898) *The Science of Finance: An investigation of public expenditure and public revenues*. New York: Henry Holt.

ADAMS, R. F. (1965) On the variation in the consumption of public services. *Review of Economics and Statistics* **47**, 400–5.

ADLER, J. H. (1951) The fiscal system. The distribution of income and public welfare. In Poole K. (ed.) *Fiscal policies and the American Economy*. New York: Prentice-Hall.

AKIN, J. H. (1973) Fiscal capacity and the estimation method of the ACIR. *National Tax Journal* **26**, 275–92.

ALBERS, W. (1964) Finanzzuweisungen und Standortverteilung. *Schriften des Vereins für Socialpolitik Gesellschaft für Wirtschafts- und Sozialwissenschaften*, N. F. **32**, 253–86.

ALONSO, W. (1964) *Location and Land Use*. Cambridge, Mass.: Harvard University Press.

ALT, J. E. (1971) Some social and political correlates of county borough expenditures. *British Journal of Political Science* **1**, 49–60.

AMERICAN LIBRARY ASSOCIATION (1967) *Minimum standards for public library systems*. Chicago: American Library Association.

ANDERSON, P. (1974) *Lineages of the Absolutist State*. London: New Left Books.

ARCHIBALD, G. C. (1967) Regional multiplier effects in the U. K. *Oxford Economic Papers* **19**, 22–45.

ARNOLD, R. D. (1977) *Congressmen, bureaucrats, and constituency benefits: the politics of geographic allocation*. Unpublished Ph.D., Faculty of the Graduate School, Yale.

ARONSON, J. R. and KING, A. E., undated, *Evidence on the extent of the state and local government fiscal crises outside New York*. Unpublished mimeo, Lehigh University.

ARONSON, J. R. and SCHWARTZ, E. (1973) Financing public goods and the distribution of population in a system of local governments. *National Tax Journal* **26**, 137–59.

ARROW, K. J. (1951) *Social choice and individual values*, New Haven, Conn.: Yale University Press. 124pp.

ASHFORD, D. E. (1974) The effects of central finance of the British local government system. *British Journal of Political Science* **4**, 305–22.

ASTRONG, P. (1975) Le dévelopement régional et l'aménagement des territoires. In Pagé, D. (ed.) *Profil Economique de la France*. Paris: La Documentation Française.

AULD, D. A. L. and COOK, G. C. A. (1972) Suburban-Central City exploitation thesis: A comment. *National Tax Journal* **25**, 597.

AUTEN, G. E. (1972a) *The Measurement of local public expenditure needs*. Unpublished Ph.D. University of Michigan.

Bibliography

AUTEN, G. E. (1972b) *An approach to measuring local public expenditure needs.* National Tax Association—Tax Institute of America Proceedings pp. 283–302.
AUTEN, G. E. (1974) The distribution of revenue-sharing funds and local public expenditure needs. *Public Finance Quarterly* **2**, 352–75.

BAHL, R. W. (1971) Measuring the creditworthiness of state and local governments. *Proceedings National Tax Association,* 600–22.
BALOPOULOS, E. R. (1967) *Fiscal policy models of the British Economy.* Amsterdam: North Holland.
BANFIELD, E. C. (1970) *The unheavenly city: the nature and future of our urban crisis.* Boston: Little Brown.
BANOVETZ, J. M. (1965) *Government cost burdens and service benefits in the Twin Cities Metropolitan Area.* Minneapolis: University of Minnesota, Public administration Center.
BANZHAF, J. G. (1968) One man, 3.312 votes: a mathematical analysis of the electoral colleges. *Villanova Law Review* **14**, 304–32.
BARLOW, I. M. (1978) *Intermunicipal variations in expenditures for two public services in the Montreal Metropolitan area.* Presented at Conference of Association of American Geographers, New Orleans.
BARNA, T. (1945) *Redistribution of incomes through public finance in 1937.* Oxford: Clarendon Press.
BARRINGTON, T. J. (1975) *From big to local government: The road to decentralisation.* Dublin: Institute of Public Administration. 238pp.
BARRY, B. (1965) *Political Argument.* London: Routledge and Kegan Paul. 364pp.
BEAM, D. R. (1978) *Economic theory as policy prescription: pessimistic findings on 'optimising' governments.* Presented at Conference of American Political Science Association, New York.
BEER, S. H. (1976) The adoption of German revenue sharing: a case study in public politics. *Public Policy* **24**, 127–95.
BEIL, D., HUSSMAN, E. and SCHNYDER, S. (1972) Zur regionalen einkommensverteilung in der europäischen Wirtschaftsgemeinschaft. *Die Weltwirtschaft* **1**, 64–78.
BENNETT, R. J. (1975) Dynamic systems modelling of the North west region. *Environment and Planning* **7**, 525–38, 539–66, 617–36, 887–98.
BENNETT, R. J. (1979) *Spatial time series: Analysis, forecasting and control.* London: Pion. 674pp.
BENNETT, R. J. (1980) Interregional flows of savings in the United States.
BENTHAM, J. (1952) *Economic Writings.* STROK, W. (ed.) London: Royal Economic Society.
BERRY, B. J. L., SIMMONS, J. W. and TENNANT, R. J. (1963) Urban population densities: structure and change. *Geographical Review* **53**, 389–405.
BHAGWATI, J. (1958) International trade and economic expansion. *American Economic Review* **48**, 941–53.
BHANGAVA, R. R. (1953) Theory of federal finance. *Economic Journal* **63**, 84–97.
BIRD, R. M. and HARTLE, D. G. (1972) The design of governments. In BIRD, R. M. and HEAD, J. G. (eds.) *Modern Fiscal Issues.* Toronto: Tortonto University Press. 351pp.
BIRD, R. M. and HEAD, J. G. (eds.) (1972) *Modern Fiscal Issues: Essays in Honor of Carl Shoup.* Toronto: University Press. 351pp.
BISH, R. L. (1971) *The public economy of metropolitan areas.* Chicago: Markham. 176pp.
BISH, R. L. and NOURSE, H. O. (1975) *Urban economics and political analysis.* New York: McGraw-Hill.

461

Bibliography

BISH, R. L. and OSTROM, V. (1973) *Understanding Urban government*. Washington D. C.: American Enterprise Institute.

BLACK, D. (1958) On the rationale of group decision making. *Journal of Political Economy* **56**, 23–34.

BLOOM, H. S. and PRICE, H. D. (1975) Voter response to short-run economic conditions: the asymmetric effect of prosperity and depression. *American Political Science Review* **69**, 1240–54.

BLOUGH, J. R. (1935) Equalisation methods from the distribution of federal relief funds. *Social Service Review* **9**, 423–44.

BOADEN, N. (1971) *Urban policy making*. Cambridge: University Press.

BOELAERT, R. (1970) Political fragmentation and inequality of fiscal capacity in the Milwaukee SMSA. *National Tax Journal* **23**, 83–8.

BOIS-GUILLEBENT, P. (1840) *Le Détail de la France, la cause de la diminution de ses biens et la facilité du remède*. Paris.

BORTS, G. H. (1966) Criteria for the evaluation of regional development programmes. In HIRSCH, W. Z. (ed.) *Regional Accounts for policy decisions*. Baltimore: Johns Hopkins Press.

BOULDING, K. E. (1966) The concept of need in health services. *Millbank Memorial Fund Quarterly* **44**, 126–36.

BOWEN, W. G. DAVIS, R. G. and KNOPF, D. H. (1960) The public debt: A burden on future generations? *American Economic Review* **50**, 701–6.

BOWMAN, M. (1974) Tax exportability, intergovernmental aid and school finance reform. *National Tax Journal* **27**, 163–73.

BOWMAN, M. (1976) *Local government in the Australian States*. Urban paper, Department of the Environment and community development. Canberra: Australian Government Publishing Service.

BOYLE, L. (1966) *Equalisation and the future of local government finance*. Edinburgh: Oliver and Boyd. 142pp.

BRADBURY, K. E. (1978) *The fiscal distress of cities*. Washington D. C.: Brookings Institution, mimeo.

BRADFORD, D. F., MALT, R. A. and OATES, W. E. (1969) The rising cost of local public services: some evidence and reflections. *National Tax Journal* **22**, 185–202.

BRADSHAW, J. (1972) A taxonomy of social need. In McLachlan, G. (ed.) *Portfolio for health*. London: Oxford University Press.

BRAMS, S. J. (1975) *Game theory and politics*. New York: Free Press.

BRAMS, S. J. and RIKER, W. H. (1972) Models of coalition formation in voting bodies. In Hendon, J. F. and Bernd, J. L. (eds.) *Mathematical application in Political science 6*. Charlottesville: Virginia University Press.

BRAZER, H. E. (1959) *City expenditures in the United States*. New York: National Bureau of Economic Research.

BRAZER, H. E. (1964) Some fiscal implications of metropolitanism, In Chinitz, B. (ed.) *City and Suburb: The economics of Metropolitan growth*. New Jersey: Prentice-Hall.

BREAK, G. (1967) *Intergovernmental fiscal relations in the United States*. Washington D. C.: Brookings Institution.

BRECHLING, F. (1967) Trends and cycles in British regional unemployment. *Oxford Economic Papers* **19**, 1–21.

BRETON, A. (1965) A theory of government grants. *Canadian Journal of Economics and Political Science* **31**, 175–87.

BRETON, A. and SCOTT, A. (1976) The assignment problem in federal structures. In Feldstein, M. S. and Inman, R. P. (eds.) *The Economics of Public Finance*. London: Macmillan, for Institute of Economic Affairs.

BREUIL, L. du (1919) *L'Idée Régionaliste sous la Revolution*. Paris: Marcel Alcan.

BRITTAN, S. (1975) the economic contradictions of democracy, *British Journal of Political Science* **5**, 129–59.

BROOKFIELD, H. (1975) *Interdependent development*, London: Methuen.

BROWN, A. J. (1972) *A framework for regional economics in the United Kingdom*. Cambridge: University Press.

BROWN, P. J. B. and FERGUSON, S. S. (1978) To close or not to close–an educational question: towards a method for evaluating primary school closure strategies for the inner city areas. Proceedings of PTRC Seminar, '*Policy analysis for urban and regional planning*'. London.

BROWNING, E. K. (1975) *Redistribution and the welfare system*. Washington D. C.: American Enterprise Institute. 131pp.

BROWNLEE, O. H. (1960) *Estimated distribution of Minnesota taxes and public expenditure benefits*. Minneapolis: University of Minnesota Press. 45pp.

BROWNLEE, O. H. (1961) User Prices vs taxes. In National Bureau of Economic Research, *Public Finances; Needs, Sources and Utilization*. New Jersey: Princeton University Press.

BRUNN, S. D. (1974) *Geography and politics in America*. New York: Harper and Row.

BRUNN, S. D. (1975) Vietnam war defense contracts and the House Armed Services Committee. *The East Lakes Geographer* **10**, 19–32.

BRUNN, S. D. and HOFFMAN, W. L. (1969) *Federal grants-in-aid to States: A statistical and Cartographical analysis*. Presented at the Association American Geographers Conference, Washington D. C.

BUCHANAN, J. M. (1950) Federalism and fiscal equity. *American Economic Review* **40**, 583–97.

BUCHANAN, J. M. (1952) Federal grants and resource allocation, *Journal of political economy* **60**, 208–17.

BUCHANAN, J. M. (1960) *Fiscal theory and political economy*. Chapel Hill: North Carolina University Press.

BUCHANAN, J. M. (1965) An economic theory of clubs, *Economica* **32**, 1–14.

BUCHANAN, J. M. (1967) *The demand and supply of public goods*. Chicago: Rand McNally.

BUCHANAN, J. M. (1970) Notes for an economic theory of socialism, *Public Choice* **10**, 1–14.

BUCHANAN, J. M. (1971) Principles of urban fiscal strategy, *Public Choice* **11**, 1–16.

BUCHANAN, J. M. (1975) The Samaritan's dilemma. In Phelps, E. S. (ed.) *Altruism, morality, and economic theory*. New York: Russell Sage Foundation. 232pp.

BUCHANAN, J. M. and TOLLISON, R. D. (eds.) (1972) *Theory of public choice: political applications of economics*. Ann Arbor: Michigan University Press.

BUCHANAN, J. M. and TULLOCK, G. (1969) *The calculus of consent*, Ann Arbor: University of Michigan Press. 361pp.

BUNCE, H. (1976) *An evaluation of the Community development block grant formula*. Washington D. C.: US Department of Housing and Urban Development.

BURGESS, E. (1925) *The growth of the city*. Chicago: University Press.

BUSINESS WEEK, (1976) *Special report: The second war between the States*. 17 May, 92–114.

CAMERON, G. and WINGO, L. (eds.) (1973) *Cities, Regions and public policy*. Edinburgh: Oliver and Boyd.

CAMPAIGN FOR THE NORTH (1978) *Up north! How to unshackle a forgotten people*. Temperton P. (ed.) Hebden Bridge: Campaign for the North.

CAMPBELL, A. K. (1965) State and local taxes, expenditures and economic development, In *State and local taxes on Business*. Princeton: Tax Institute of America. 352pp.

CANADIAN TAX FOUNDATION (1976) *The national Finances 1975–76: An analysis of the revenues and expenditures of the government in Canada*, Toronto: Canadian Tax foundation. 256pp.

CANNAN, E. (1972) *History of local rates in England*, 2nd ed. London: King and Son. 215pp.

CAPUTO, D. A. (ed.) (1975) General revenue sharing and federalism. Special Issue of the *Annals of the American Academy of Political and Social Science*. Philadelphia.

CAPUTO, D. A. and COLE, R. L. (eds.) (1976) *Revenue sharing: methodological approaches and problems*. Lexington, Mass.: D. C. Heath.

CARLETON, W. T. and LERNER, F. M. (1969) Statistical credit scoring of municipal bonds. *Journal of Money Credit and Banking* **1**, 750–64.

CARNARD, N. F. (1801) *Principes d'économique politique*. Paris: F. Buisson.

CARNEY, J., HUDSON, R., IVE, G. and LEWIS, J. (1976) Regional underdevelopment in Late Capitalism: a study of North East England. In Masser, I. (ed.), London Papers in Regional Science 6. *Theory and practice in regional Science*. London: Pion. pp. 11–29.

CARTER, G. E. (1971) *Canadian conditional grants since World War II*. Toronto: Canadian Tax Foundation. 130pp.

CARVER, T. N. (1895) The ethical basis of distribution and its application to taxation. *The Annals of the American Academy of Political and Social Science* **13**, 79–99.

CASPER, U. (1978) *Background notes to regional incentives in the Federal Republic of Germany*. Paper at IIM conference Racine Wisconsin.

CASTELLS, M. (1976) *The urban question*. London: Arnold.

CHENERY, H. and SYRQUIN, M. (1975) *Patterns of development 1950–1970*. London: Oxford University Press, for the World Bank. 234pp.

CHEVILLARD, J. (1862) *Etudes d'Administration*. Paris: Durand.

CHINITZ, B. (ed.) (1964) *City and suburb: the economics of metropolitan growth*. New Jersey: Prentice-Hall.

CHINITZ, B. (1978) *Title V Regional Commissions: An evaluation*. Binghamton: State University of New York, Center for Social Analysis.

CHISHOLM, M. D. I. (1976) Academics and government, In Coppock, J. T. and Sewell, W. R. D. (eds.) *Spatial dimensions of public policy*. Oxford: Pergamon. 271pp.

CHISM, L. L. (1936) *The economic ability of the States to finance public schools*. New York: American Management Association.

CLARK, C., WILSON, F. and BRADLEY, J. (1969) Industrial location and economic potential in Western Europe. *Regional Studies* **3**, 197–212.

CLARK, D. (1969) *Fiscal need and revenue equalisation grants*. Toronto: Canadian Tax Foundation.

COATES, B. E., JOHNSTON, R. J. and KNOX, P. L. (1977) *Geography and inequality*. Oxford: Oxford University Press. 292pp.

COLE, G. D. H. (1921) *The future of local government*. London: Cassell.

COLE, R. L. and CAPUTO, D. A. (1974) *Urban politics and decentralisation: The case of general revenue sharing*. Lexington, Mass.: D. C. Heath. 180pp.

COLEMAN, J. S. (1970) Foreward. In Coons, J. E., Clune, W. H. and Sugarman, S. D. (eds.) *Private wealth and public education*. Cambridge, Mass.: Belknap and Harvard University Press.

COLEMAN, J. S. (1974) Political money. *American political Science Review* **64**, 1074–87.

COLM, G. (1955) *Essays in public finance and fiscal policy*. London: Oxford University Press.

COMMONS, J. R. (1940) *Economics of collective action.* New York: Macmillan.

COMMONWEALTH GOVERNMENT OF AUSTRALIA (1978) *Payments to or for the States, The Northern Territory and Local Government Authorities 1978–79.* Canberra: Australian Government Publishing Service. 1978–79 Budget paper No. 7. 197pp.

COMMONWEALTH GRANTS COMMISSION, various dates, *Annual Report.* Canberra: Commonwealth of Australia Printing Office.

CONRAD, A. (1954) On the calculation of tax burdens. *Economica* **22**, 342–8.

COOMBS, D. (1974) 'Concertation' in the nation state and in the European Community. In Ionescu, G. (ed.) *Between Sovereignty and integration.* London: Croom Helm. 192pp.

COONS, J. E., CLUNE. W. H. and SUGARMAN, S. D. (1970) *Private wealth and public education.* Cambridge Mass.: Belknap and Harvard University Press. 520pp.

CORNELL, F. G. (1936) *A measure of taxpaying ability of local administrative units.* Columbia, New York: Teachers College.

COURCHENE, T. J. and BEAVIS, D. A. (1973) Federal-provincial tax equalisation: an evaluation. *Canadian Journal of Economics* **6**, 483–502.

COX, K. R., (1973) *Conflict, power and politics in the city: A geographic view.* New York: McGraw-Hill.

COX, K. R., REYNOLDS, D. R. and ROKKEN, S. (1973) *Locational approaches to power and conflict.* New York: Wiley.

COYLE, R. G. and MARTIN, M. J. C. (1969) Case study: the cost minimisation of refuse collection operations. *Operations Research Quarterly* **20**, 43–56.

CRIPPS, F. and GODLEY, W. (1976) *Local government finance and its reform.* Cambridge: University Department of Applied Economics.

CROSS, C. A. (1967) *Principles of local government law.* London: Sweet and Maxwell.

CROSS, C. A. (1977) The local government system. In Griffith, J. A. (ed.) *From Policy to Administration, Essays in Honour of W. A. Robson.* London: Allen and Unwin.

CROWLEY, R. W. (1968)*Internal migration: A case study of costs imposed on cities in the United States.* Unpublished Ph.D., Duke University.

CUBBERLY, E. P. (1905) *School funds and their apportionment.* Columbia, New York: Bureau of Public Teachers College.

CUCITI, P. L. (1976) *The distribution of grants to local governments: equalisation in the American Policy.* Presented at American Political Science Association Conference, Chicago.

CUCITI, P. L. (1978) *City Need and the responsiveness of federal grants programs.* Washington D. C.: US Congress, Committee on Banking, Finance and Urban Affairs, subcommittee on the city.

CULYER, A. J. (ed.) (1974) *Economic policies and social goals: aspects of public choice.* London: Martin Robertson.

CULYER, A. J., LAVERS, R. J. and WILLIAMS, A. (1972) Health indicators. In Shonfield A. and Shaw, S. (eds.) *Social Indicators and social policy.* London: Heinemann.

CURRAN, D. J. (1973) *Metropolitan financing: The Milwaukee experience 1920–1970.* Madison: Wisconsin University Press. 166pp.

CURRY, L. (1979) Demand in the spatial economy I. Homo deterministicus: *Geographia Polonica* **42** 185–212.

CZMANSKI, S. (1966) *Regional income and product accounts of North-Eastern Nova Scotia.* Dalhousie, New Brunswick: Dalhousie University, Institute of Public Affairs.

CZMANSKI, S. (1973) *Regional and interregional social accounting.* Lexington Mass.: D. C. Heath. 204pp.

465

Bibliography

DAHL, R. A. (1956) *A preface to democratic theory.* Chicago: University of Chicago Press.

DALTON, H. (1936) *Principles of public finance*, 3rd ed. London: University of London Press.

DANZIGER, J. N. (1974) *Budget-making and expenditure variations in English County Boroughs.* Unpublished Ph.D., Stanford University, California.

DAVIDSON, R. H. (1966) *Coalition-building for depressed areas bills: 1955–1965.* Indianapolis: Bobbs-Merrill. Inter-university case program No. 103.

DAVIES, B. (1968) *Social needs and resources in local services.* London: Joseph.

DAVIES, B. (1974) Personal social services. In Maunder W. F. (ed,) *Review of UK Statistical Sources*, Vol. 1. London: Heinemann.

DAVIES, B. (1975) On local expenditures and a 'Standard level of service'. Submission to UK Committee of Enquiry into Local Government Finance. Canterbury: University of Kent.

DAVIES, B., BARTON, A. J., MCMILLAN, I. S. and WILLIAMSON, V. K. (1971a) *Variations in services for the aged.* London: Bell.

DAVIES, B., BARTON, A. J. and MCMILLAN, I. S. (1971b) *Variations in childrens' services among British urban authorities.* London: Bell.

DAVIES, D. (1965) Financing urban functions and services. *Law and contemporary problems* **30**, 127–61.

DAVIS, O. H. and WHINSTON, A. B. (1961) The economics of urban renewal. *Law and Contemporary Problems* **26**, 105–17.

DAWSON, D. (1973) *Revenue and equalisation in Australia, Canada, West Germany and the USA.* London: HMSO, Royal Commission on the Constitution, Research Paper 9. 94pp.

DAWSON, D. A. (1972) Economies of scale in the Ontario public secondary schools. *Canadian Journal of Economics* **5**, 306–9.

DEARBORN, P. M. (1977) *Elements of municipal financial analysis; four parts.* Boston: First Boston Corporation.

DENT, H. S. (1978) *The Prodigal South Returns to Power.* New York: Wiley. 308pp.

DERTHICK, M. (1974) *Between State and nation.* Washington D. C.: Brookings Institution.

DERTHICK, M. (1975) *Uncontrollable spending for social service grants.* Washington D. C.: Brookings Institution.

DEUTSCHER STÄDLETAG (1973) *Kommunaler finanzausgleich in der Bundesländern.* Köln: Deutscher Städtetag.

DICKINSON, R. E. (1976) *The regional concept: The Anglo-American leaders.* London: Routledge and Kegan Paul.

DIKSHIT, R. D. (1975) *The political geography of federalism: an inquiry into origins and stability.* Delhi: Macmillan.

DLI, D. C. (1966) *Zoning regulations of the District of Columbia: 1966 edition.* Washington D. C.: Department of Licences and Inspections.

DOMMEL, P. (1974) *The politics of revenue sharing.* Bloomington: Indiana University Press. 205pp.

DOMMEL, P. and JAFFE, J. M. (1978) *Report on the allocation of Community development funds to small cities.* Washington D. C.: Brookings Institution.

DOMMEL, P., NATHAN, R., LIEBSCHUTZ, S. F., WRIGHTSON, M. T. and associates (1978) *Decentralising community development.* Washington D. C.: Brookings Institution.

DOWNING, P. B. (1969a) Extension of sewer services at the urban fringe. *Land Economics* **45**, 103–11.

466

DOWNING, P. B. (1969b) *The economics of sewerage disposal*. New York: Praeger.

DOWNS, A. (1956) *An economic theory of democracy*. New York: Harper and Row.

DOWNS, A. (1967) *Inside bureaucracy*. Boston: Little Brown.

DOWNS, A. (1978) Urban policy. In Pechman, J. A. (ed.) *Setting national priorities: The 1979 Budget*. Washington D. C.: Brookings Institution.

DRAKE, A. W., KEENEY, R. L. and MORSE, P. M. (1972) *Analysis of public systems*. Cambridge, Mass.: MIT Press.

DROR, Y. (1971) *Design for policy science*, New York: Elsevier.

DRUCKER, P. F. (1969) *The age of Discontinuity*. London: Pan. 369pp.

DSPSE, (1976) *Development of the Strategic Plan for the South East*. Report of the Resources Group, London, Joint Planning Team, Department of the Environment. 48pp and 3 annexes.

DURAND, P. (1974) *Industrie et régions*. Paris: La documentation Française.

DURD (1974) *A National Program for Urban and Regional Development*. Canberra: Australian Printing Service, Department of Urban and Regional Development.

ECKER-RACZ, L. L. (1970) *The politics and economics of State-local finance*. New Jersey: Prentice-Hall. 242pp.

ECKSTEIN, O. (1961) A survey of the theory of public expenditure criteria. In National Bureau of Economic Research, *Public Finances; Needs, Sources and Utilization*. New Jersey: Princeton University Press.

ECKSTEIN, O. (1973) *Public finance*, 3rd ed. New Jersey: Prentice-Hall. 132pp.

ECSC (1953) *Report on the problems raised by the different turnover tax system applied within the Common Market* (Tinbergen Report). Amsterdam: European Coal and Steel Community.

EDGEWORTH, F. Y. (1897) The pure theory of taxation. *Economic Journal* 7, 46–70, 226–38, 550–71.

EEC (1963) *Report of the fiscal and financial committee* (Neumark Report). Amsterdam: EEC committee on tax harmonisation.

EEC (1977) *Report of the study group on the role of public finance in European Integration*, Vols. 1 and 2 Brussels: Commission of the European Communities, Directorate-General for Economic and Financial Affairs.

EICHEN, M. (1975) *Wishes, dreams and lies: Congressional redistricting after the 1970 census in Ohio, Massachusetts and New York*. Unpublished Ph.D., Ohio State University.

ELLICKSON, B. (1973) A generalisation of the pure theory of public goods. *American Economic Review* 63, 417–32.

ELSE-MITCHELL, R. (1974) The Australian Grants Commission, *Journal of Constitutional and Parliamentary Studies* 8, 560–72.

ENQUETE-KOMMISSION VERFASSUNGSREFORM (1976) *Schlusshericht der Enquete-Kommission Verfassungsreform*. Bonn: Bundestags-Druchsache, 7/5924.

EULAU, H. and MARCH, J. G. (eds.) (1969) *Political Science*. New Jersey: Prentice-Hall.

FABRICANT, S. (1952) *The trend of government activity in the United States since 1900*. New York: National Bureau of Economic Research. 267pp.

FAYOL, H. (1925) *L'Administration industrielle et générale-prévoyance, organisation, fondement, coordination contrôle*. Bulletin de la société de l'industrie minérale. Paris: Dunod.

THE FEDERALIST (1788) Papers of Hamilton, A., Madison, J. and Jay, J. in Wright, B. F. (ed.) Cambridge Mass.: Harvard University Press and Belknap. 572pp.

Bibliography

FEREJOHN, J. A. (1974) *Pork-barrel politics: Rivers and harbours legislation 1947–1968.* California: Stanford University Press. 288pp.
FINER, H. (1934) *English Local Government.* Columbia: University Press.
FISHER, G. W. (1961) Interstate variation in State-local government expenditure. *National Tax Journal* 17, 57–74.
FITCH, L. C. (1964) Metropolitan financial problems. In Chinitz, B. (ed.) *City and Surburb: The economics of metropolitan Growth.* New Jersey: Prentice-Hall.
FITZGERALD, R. (1977) *Human needs and politics.* Oxford: Pergamon. 278pp.
FORTE, F. (1977) Principles for the assignment of public economic functions in a setting of multi-layer government. In *Report of the study group on the role of public finance in European integration,* Vol. 2. Brussels: EEC.
FOURIER, C. (1851) *The passions of the human soul and their influence on society and civilisation* Vols. 1 and 2. London: Hippolyte Bailliere. 404pp. and 463pp.
FRANK, G. (1973) *Capitalism and underdevelopment in Latin America: Historical studies of Chile and Brazil.* London: Monthly Review Press.
FRIED, R. C. (1972) *Comparative urban performance.* Los Angeles: UCLA. European Urban Research paper 1.
FRIEDMAN, M. (1962) *Capitalism and freedom.* Chicago: University Press.
FRIEND, J. K. and JESSOP, N. (1969) *Local government and strategic choice: An operational research approach to the processes of public planning.* London: Tavistock. 296pp.

GALBRAITH, J. K. (1958) *The Affluent Society.* London: Hamish Hamilton. 288pp.
GALBRAITH, J. K. (1973) *Economics and the public purpose.* London: Deutsch. 334pp.
GARLAND, G. A. WEDDLE, B. R. (1974) Sharing solid waste collection costs. *National Cities* 12, 2.
GERHARDT, K. (1976) *Der Kommunale Finanzausgleich in Baden-Württemberg.* Stuttgart: Kohlhammer.
GERIG, D. S. and MUSHKIN, S. J. (1938) Variable grants: A study of the methods and feasibility of varying percentage federal grants-in-aid to State. Washington D. C.: Department of HEW.
GIFFORD, B. R. (1978) New York City: The political economy of cosmopolitan liberalism. *Harvard Political Review* 36, 169–200.
GILLESPIE, W. I. (1965) Effect of public expenditure on the distribution of income. In Musgrave R. A. (ed.) *Essays in Fiscal Federalism.* Washington D. C.: Brookings Institution.
GILLESPIE, W. I. (1975) *The redistribution of income in Canada. An analysis of the incidence of taxes and public expenditures in the Canadian economy.* Ottawa: Carleton University Department of Economics.
GILLESPIE, W. I. (1976) On the redistribution of income in Canada. *Canadian Tax Journal* 24, 419–50.
GLADDEN, E. N. (1972) *Central government administration.* London: Staples Press.
GLDP (1968) *Greater London Development Plan.* London: Greater London Council.
GLICKMAN, N. J. (1977) *Econometric analysis of regional systems: explorations in model building and policy analysis.* New York: Academic Press. 210pp.
GODLEY, W. and RHODES, J. (1972) *The rate support grant system.* Cambridge, England: Department of Applied Economics.
GODLEY, W. and RHODES, J. (1973) The Rate Support Grant System, In *Local Government Finance,* Proceedings of Institute of Fiscal studies Conference, London. 141pp.
GOLDSMITH, R. W. (ed.) (1973) *Institutional investors and corporate stock: A background study.* Washington D. C.: District of Columbia University Press.

GOLDSMITH, R. W., BRADY, D. S. and MENDENAUSEN, H. (1956) *A Study of savings in the United States. Vol III: Special studies.* New Jersey: Princeton University Press. 476pp.

GOLDSMITH, R. W. and LIPSEY, R. E. (1963) *Studies in the National Balance sheet of the United States, Vol I.* New Jersey: Princeton University Press. 433pp.

GOODCHILD, M. F. and MASSAM, B. H. (1969) Some least-cost models of spatial administrative districts. *Geografiska Annaler* **52**, 86–94.

GOODMAN, L. A. and MARKOWITZ, H. (1952) *Social welfare functions based on individual voting.* Chicago: Cowles Commission.

GOSS, C. F. (1972) Military committee membership and defense-related benefits in the House of Representatives. *Western Political Science Quarterly* **25**, 215–33.

GOULD, P. R. and LEINBACH, T. R. (1966) An approach to the geographical assignment of hospital services. *Tijschrift vor Economie und Social Geographie* **57**, 203–6.

GRAMLICH, E. M. (1976) The New York city fiscal crisis: What happened and what is to be done? *American Economic Review* **66**, 415–29.

GRAMLICH, E. M. and GALPER, H. (1973) State and local fiscal behaviour and federal grant policy. *Brookings Papers on Economic Activity* **1**, 15–65.

GRAMSCI, A. (1975) *Marcismo e litteratura.* Rome: Edotori Riuniti.

GREBLER, L. (1962) California's dependence on capital imports for mortgage investment. *California Management Review* **5**, 3, 47–54.

GREEN, C. (1967) *Negative taxes and the poverty problem.* Washington D. C.: Brookings Institution. 210pp.

GREENE, K. V. (1970) Some institutional considerations in federal–state fiscal relations. *Public Choice* **9**. 1–18.

GREENE, K. V., NEENAN, W. B. and SCOTT, C. D. (1974) *Fiscal interactions in a metropolitan area.* Lexington, Mass.: D. C. Heath. 263pp.

GRIFFITH, J. A. G. (1966) *Central departments and local authorities.* London: Allen and Unwin. 574pp.

GRODZINS, M. (1966) *The American system.* New York: Rand McNally.

GROVES, H. M. (1964) *Financing Government,* 6th edn. New York: Holt, Rinehart and Winston. 692pp.

GROVES, H. M. (1974) *Tax philosophers: two hundred years of thought in Great Britain and the United States.* Madison: Wisconsin University Press.

GROVES, H. M. and BISH, R. L. (1973) *Financing government,* 7th edn. New York: Holt, Rinehart and Winston.

GROVES, H. M. and KNIGHT, W. D. (co-chairmen) (1959) *Wisconsin State and local tax burden: impact, incidence and tax revision alternatives.* Madison: Tax Committee, University of Wisconsin.

GULICK, L. H. and URWICK, L. (1937) *Papers on the Science of Administration.* New York: Institute of Public Administration. 195pp.

GUPTA, S. P. and HUTTON, J. P. (1968) *Economies of scale in local government services.* London: HMSO, Royal Commission on Local Government in England, Research Study No. 3.

HÄGERSTRAND, T. (1975) Space, time and human conditions. In Karlquist, A. Lunquist, L. and Snickars, F. (eds.) *Dynamic allocation of urban space.* Farnborough: Saxon House D. C. Heath. 383pp.

HAGGETT, P. (1971) Leads and lags in interregional systems: a study of the cyclic fluctuations in the south west economy. In Chisholm, M. and Manners, G. (eds.) *Spatial Policy Problems of the British Economy.* Cambridge: University Press.

HAIG, R. M. (1935) The cost to business concerns of compliance with tax laws. *The Management Review* **24**, 328–30.

469

Bibliography

HALL, J. K. (1938) The incidence of federal social security payroll taxes. *Quarterly Journal of Economics* **53**, 38–63.

HALSTEAD, K. (1978) *Tax wealth in fifty States*. Washington D. C.: National Institute of Education.

HANSEN, A. H. and PERLOFF, H. S. (1944) *State and local finance in the national economy*. New York: Norton. 310pp.

HANSEN, B. (1969) *Fiscal policies in seven countries 1955–65*. Paris: OECD.

HANSEN, N. M. (1965) The structure and determinants of local public investment expenditures. *Review of Economics and Statistics* **47**, 150–62.

HANSEN, N. M. (1970) *Rural poverty and the urban crisis: a strategy for regional development*. Bloomington: Indiana University Press. 352pp.

HANSON, E. J. (1961) *Fiscal needs of the Canadian Provinces*. Toronto: Canadian Tax Foundation. 230pp.

HANSON, N. W. (1966) Economy of scale as a cost factor in financing public schools. *National Tax Journal* **17**, 70–83.

HANUSCH, H. (1976) *Personale Verteilung Oeffentlicher Leistungen*. Göttingen: Vandenhoek and Ruprecht.

HARRIS, C. D. and ULLMANN, E. L. (1945) The nature of cities. *Annals American Academy of Political and Social Science* **242**, 1–17.

HARRIS, W. T. (1905) Some conditions which cause variation in the rate of school expenditures in different localities. *Proceedings of the National Education Association*, Chicago. University of Chicago Press.

HARROD, R. F. (1948) *Towards a dynamic economy*. London: Macmillan.

HARTLAND, P. C. (1950) *Balance of interregional payments of New England*. Providence Rhode Is.: Brown University Press. 125pp.

HARVARD REGIONAL PLANNING DEPARTMENT (1955) *The cost of municipal services in residential areas*. Washington D. C.: US Housing and House Finance Agency.

HARVEY, D. (1973) *Social Justice in the City*. London: Arnold.

HASKELL, M. A. and LESHINSKI, S. (1969) Fiscal influences on residential choice: A study of the New York region. *Quarterly review of Economics and Business* **9**, 47–56.

HAWLEY, A. H. (1957) Metropolitan population and muncipal government expenditures in central cities. In Hatt, P. K. and Reiss, E. J. (eds.) *Cities and Society*. Glencoe: Free Press.

HAYEK, F. A. (1944) *The road to serfdom*. London: Routledge and Kegan Paul. 184pp.

HEAD, J. G. (1967) Financial equality in a federation: A study of the Commonwealth Grants Commission in Australia. *Finanzarchiv* **26**, 214–31.

HEAD, J. G. (1973) Public goods and multi-level government. In David, W. L. (ed.) *Public finance, planning and economic development: essays in honour of Ursula Hicks*. London: Macmillan. 349pp.

HECHTER, M. (1975) *Internal colonialism: The Celtic fringe in British National development, 1536–1966*. London: Routledge and Kegan Paul. 361pp.

HENDERSON, J. M. (1968) Local government expenditures: a social welfare analysis. *Review of Economics and Statistics* **50**, 156–63.

HENDRICK, R. L. and FRIEDMAN, D. G. (1966) Potential impacts of storm modification on the insurance industry. In Sewell, W. R. D. (ed.) *Human dimensions of weather modification*. Chicago: Department of Geography Research Paper 105.

HEPPLE, L. W. (1975) Spectral techniques and the study of interregional business cycles. In Peel, R., Haggett, P. and Chisholm, M. (eds.) *Processes in Physical and Human Geography*. London: Butterworths.

KEGAN, L. R. and RONINGEN, G. P. (1968) The outlook for State and local finance. In US Committee for Economic Development, *Fiscal Issues in the future of federalism.* Washington D. C.: Government Printing Office. 283pp.

KEYNES, J. K. M. (1926) *The end of laissez-faire.* London: L. and V. Woolf.

KEYNES, J. K. M. (1936) *The general theory of employment, interest and money.* London: Macmillan. 403pp.

KIESLING, H. J. (1966) Measuring a local government service: a study of school districts in New York State. *Review of Economics and Statistics* **48**, 139–54.

KING, G. (1804) *Natural and political observations and conclusions upon the state and condition of England 1696.* London: J. J. Stockdale.

KING, L. J., CASSETTI, E. and JEFFREY, D. (1969) Economic impulses in regional system of cities: a study of spatial interactions. *Regional Studies* **3**, 213–18.

KING, L. J. and CLARK, G. L. (1978) Government policy and regional development. *Progress in Human Geography* **2**, 1–16.

KISKER, G. (1971) *Kooperation im Bundesstaat.* Tübingen: Mohr/Siebeck.

KNOTT, J. H. (1977) *Accomodating purposes: fiscal and budgetary policy in West Germany.* Unpublished Ph.D., Michigan State University.

KOMMISSION FÜR DIE FINANZREFORM (1966) *Gutachen über die Finanzreform in der Bundesrepublik Deutschland.* Stuttgart: Kahlhammer.

KORNAI, J. (1967) *Mathematical planning of structural decisions.* Amsterdam: North Holland.

KRAMER, G. H. (1971) Short-run fluctuations in US voting behavior. *American Political Science Review* **65**, 131–43.

KUZNETS, S. (1961) *Capital in the American economy: its formation and financing.* New Jersey: Princeton University Press. 664pp.

KUZNETS, S. (1973) *Population, capital and growth: selected essays.* New York: Norton. 342pp.

LABOUR PARTY (1970) *Report of the study group on regional planning policy.* London: Transport House.

LAMMENAIS, H. F. R. de (1848) *Project de Constitution de la République Française.* Paris: Bureau du Peuple Constituant.

LASKI, H.J. (1919) *Authority in the modern state.* New Haven, Conn.: Yale University Press.

LAVER, M. (1976) Exit, voice and loyalty revisited: the strategic production and consumption of public and private goods. *British Journal of Political Science* **6**, 463–82.

LEA, A. C. (1978) *Interjurisdictional spillovers and efficient public good provision.* Association of American Geographers Conference, New Orleans.

LEE, R. (1976) Public finance and the urban economy: some comments on spatial reformism. *Antipode* **8**, 44–50.

LENIN, V. I. (1960) *Selected Works*, Vols. 1 to 3. Moscow: Foreign Languages Press.

LERNER, A. P. (1946) *The Economics of Control.* New York: Macmillan. 428pp.

LEVEBVRE, H. (1972) *La pensée marxiste et la ville.* Paris: Anthropos.

LEVIN, M. B. (1966) *The alienated voter: Politics in Boston.* New York: Holt, Rinehart and Winston.

LINDAHL, E. (1919) Just taxation: A positive solution. In Musgrave R. A. and Peacock A. T. (eds.) (1958) *Classics in the theory of public Finance.* London: Macmillan.

LINDBLOM, C. (1968) *The intelligence of democracy.* London: Collier-Macmillan. 352pp.

LINEBERRY, R. L. (1971) Crisis in urban government. In Lineberry, R. L. and

Bibliography

Sharkanski, I. (eds.) *Urban politics and public policy.* New York: Harper and Row.

LIPTON, M. (1976) *Why poor people stay poor: Urban bias in world development.* London: Temple Smith.

LIVINGSTONE, W. S. (1956) *Federalism and constitutional change.* London: Oxford University Press.

Local Government in England (1971) Conservative government white paper Cmnd 4584. London: HMSO.

Local Government in Sweden (1978) Stockholm: Ministry of Local Government. 64pp.

LOGAN, M. I., MAHER, C. A. MCKAY, J. and HUMPHREYS, J. S. (1975) *Urban and Regional Australia: Analysis and Policy Issues.* Melbourne: Sorrett.

LOJKINE, J. (1977) L'analyse marxiste de l'état. *International Journal of Urban and Regional Research* **1**, 19–23.

LOMAX, K. S. (1951) Cost curves for gas supply. *Bulletin Oxford Institute of Statistics* **13**, 243–6.

LONDON DOCKLANDS JOINT PLANNING TEAM (1976) *London Docklands a Strategic Plan.* London: HMSO.

LORD PRESIDENT OF THE COUNCIL (1977) *Devolution: financing the devolved services,* Cmnd 6890. London: HMSO. 23pp.

LÖSCH, A. (1941) *The economics of location,* translated 1951. New York: Wiley.

LOTZ, J. R. (1978) *Social need equalisation in the distribution of general grants to local governments: The Danish Case.* Copenhagen, unpublished mimeo.

LUDLOW, W. H. (1953) Urban densities and their costs. In Woodbury, C. (ed.) *Urban redevelopment problems and practices.* Chicago: University Press.

LUXEMBURG, R. (1913) *Die Akkumulation des Kapitals; ein Beitrag zur ökonomischen Erklärung des Imperialismus.* Berlin: P. Singer.

LYNN, J. H. (1968) *Comparing provincial revenue yields: the tax indicator approach.* Toronto: Canadian Tax Foundation. 80pp.

MAIR, D. (1975) *Report on the rating of non-domestic subjects.* Committee of Enquiry into Local Government Finance, Appendix. Edinburgh: Department of Economics, Heriot Watt University.

MAITLE, S. (1973) Public goods and income distribution: Some further results. *Econometrica* **41**, 561–8.

MANNERS, G. (1964) *The Geography of Energy.* London: Hutchinson.

MANNERS, G. (ed.) (1972) *Regional Development in Britain.* London: Wiley. 448pp.

MANVEL, A. (1971) Differences in fiscal capacity and effort: their significance for a federal revenue sharing system. *National Tax Journal* **24**, 193–204.

MARCH, J. G. and SIMON, H. (1961) *Organizations.* London: Wiley. 262pp.

MARGOLIS, J. (1957) Municipal fiscal structure in a Metropolitan region. *Journal of Political Economy* **65**, 225–36.

MARGOLIS, J. (1961) Metropolitan finance problems: territories, functions and growth. In National Bureau of Economic Research, *Public Finance: Needs, sources and utilisation.* New Jersey: Princeton University Press.

MARGOLIS, J. (1968) The demand for urban public services. In Perloff, H. S. and Wingo, L. (eds.) *Issues in Urban Economics.* Baltimore: Johns Hopkins University Press.

MARNITZ, S. (1974) *Die Gemeinschaftsaufgahen de Ant 91a G G als Versuch einer verfassungsrechtlichen Institutionalisierung der Bundestaatlichen Kooperation.* Berlin: Duncker and Humblot.

MARSHALL, A. (1920) *Principles of Economics,* 8th edn. London: Macmillan. 731pp.

MARX, K. (1875) Critique of the Gotha Program. In Tucker, R. G. (ed.) (1972) *The Marx-Engels Reader.* New York: W. Norton.

MARX, K. (1888) Theses on Feuerbach. In *Selected works of K. Marx and F. Engels.* London: Lawrence and Wishart.

MARX, K. (1967) *Capital*, Vols. 1 to 3. Moscow: Foreign Languages Press.

MASSAM, B. (1975) *Location and space in social administration.* London: Arnold. 192pp.

MATHEWS, R. (1974a) Fiscal equalisation in local government. *The Economic Record* **50**, 329–45.

MATHEWS, R. (ed.) (1974b) *Intergovernmental relations in Australia.* Sydney: Angus and Robertson.

MATHEWS, R. (1975) Fiscal equalisation in Australia: the methodology of the Grants Commission. *Finanzarchiv, New Series* **34**, 66–85.

MATHEWS, R. and JAY, W. R. C. (1972) *Federal finance: intergovernmental relations in Australia since federation.* Melbourne: Helson.

MAUNDER, W. J. (1970) *The value of the weather.* London: Methuen. 388pp.

MAXWELL, J. A. (1946) *The fiscal impact of federalism in the United States.* Cambridge, Mass.: Harvard University Press.

MAXWELL, J. A. (1952) *Federal grants and the business cycle.* New York: National Bureau of Economic Research. 122pp.

MAXWELL, J. A. (1958) Countercyclical role of state and local governments *National Tax Journal* **11**, 371–8.

MAXWELL, J. A. (1962) *Tax credits and intergovernmental fiscal relations.* Washington D. C.: Brookings Institution.

MAXWELL, J. A. (1967) *Commonwealth-State financial relations in Australia.* Melbourne: University Press.

MAXWELL, J. A. (1974) Federal grants in Canada, Australia and the United States. *Publius* **4**, 63–75.

MAXWELL, J. A. and ARONSON, J. R. (1977) *Financing State and local governments.* Washington D. C.: Brookings Institution.

MAXWELL, J. A. and CARTER, G. E. (1974) Equalizing Local Government Revenues. *Canadian Tax Journal* **22**, 397–405.

MAXWELL SCHOOL (1975) *The fiscal implications of inflation: A study of six local governments.* Syracuse: Maxwell School of Public Finance, Syracuse University.

MAY, R. J. (1971) *Financing the small States in Australian federalism.* Melbourne: Oxford University Press.

MCCLURE, C. E. (1967) The interstate exporting of State and local taxes: Estimates for 1962. *National Tax Journal* **20**, 49–77.

MCCRONE, G. A. (1969) *Regional Policy in Britain.* London: Allen and Unwin.

MICHAILOV, A. (1927) Tzentralizatsia i Decentralizatsia Mestnovo Upravlenia. *Kommunalnaya Entziklopedia.* Moscow.

MIESZKOWSKI, P. (1969) Tax incidence theory: the effects of taxes on the distribution of income. *Journal of Economic Literature* **7**, 1103–24.

MILL, J. S. (1848) *Principles of political economy.* People's edition (1865) in *Collected Works*, 17 vols. London: Routledge and Kegan Paul.

MILL, J. S. (1861) *Considerations on representative government.* London: Parker, Son and Bourn.

MILLER, D. (1976) *Social Justice.* Oxford: Clarendon Press. 367pp.

MILLS, C. A. (1942) *Climate makes man.* New York: Harper. 320pp.

MILLS, G. (1967) The determination of local government electoral boundaries. *Operations Research Quarterly* **18**, 243–55.

MILLS, E. S. and OATES, W. E. (1975) *Fiscal zoning and land use controls.* Farnborough: Saxon House/D. C. Heath.

MINER, J. (1963) *Social and economic factors in spending on education.* New York: McGraw-Hill.

Bibliography

MONTESQUIEU, M. de (1777) *Complete works*. London: T. Evans.
MORGAN, W. D. (1974) An alternative measure of fiscal capacity. *National Tax Journal* 27, 361–5.
MORT, P. R. (1936) *Federal support for public education*. New York: Columbia University Press.
MOSELEY, M. J. (1974) *Growth centres in spatial planning*. Oxford: Pergamon.
MOYNIHAN, D. P. (1969) *Maximum feasible misunderstanding*. New York: Free Press.
MOYNIHAN, D. P. (1978) The politics and economics of regional growth. *The Public Interest* 51, 3–21.
MULLER, T. (1976) *Growing and declining urban areas: a fiscal comparison*. Washington D. C.: Urban Institute. 121pp.
MUSGRAVE, R. A. (1959) *Theory of public finance*. New York. McGraw-Hill.
MUSGRAVE, R. A. (1961) Approaches to a fiscal theory of political federalism. In National Bureau of Economic Research, *Public Finances: Needs, sources and utilisation*. New Jersey: Princeton University Press.
MUSGRAVE, R. A. (1969) *Fiscal Systems*, New Haven: Yale University Press. 397pp.
MUSGRAVE, R. A., CARROLL, J. J., COOK, L. D. and FRAME, L. (1951) Distribution of tax payments by income groups: a case study for 1948. *National Tax Journal* 4, 1–53.
MUSGRAVE, R. A., CASE, K. E. and LEONARD, H. (1974) The distribution of fiscal burdens and benefits. *Public Finance Quarterly* 2, 259–311.
MUSGRAVE, R. A. and DAICOFF, D. W. (1958) Who pays the Michigan taxes? In Brazer, H. E. (ed.) *Michigan Tax Study: Staff papers*. Lansing: Michigan joint research team.
MUSGRAVE, R. A. and FRAME, L. (1952) Rejoinder to Dr Tucker. *National Tax Journal* 5, 15–35.
MUSGRAVE, R. A. and MUSGRAVE, P. B. (1976) *Public Finance in theory and practice*. Tokyo: McGraw-Hill. 778pp.
MUSGRAVE, R. A. and PEACOCK, A. (1958) *Classics in the theory of public finance*. London: Macmillan.
MUSGRAVE, R. A. and POLINSKY, A. (1970) Revenue sharing–a critical view. In *Financing State and Local governments*. Boston: Federal Reserve Bank of Boston.
MUSGRAVE, R. A. and RICHMAN, P. D. (1964) Allocation aspects, domestic and international. *In The Role of direct and indirect taxes in the federal revenue system*. New Jersey: Princeton University Press.
MUSHKIN, S. (1974) *Services to People, Part 1 State and National urban strategies; Part 2 State aids for human services in a federal System*. Washington D. C.: Georgetown University Public Services Laboratory.
MUSHKIN, S. and COTTON, J. F. (1969) *Functional federalism*. Washington D. C.: George Washington University Press.
MUSHKIN, S., and CROWTHER, B. (1954) *Federal taxes and the measurement of state capacity*. Washington D. C.: Public Health Service. Division of Public Health Methods.
MUSHKIN, S. and LUPO, J. C. (1967) Project '70: Projecting the State–local sector. *Review of Economics and Statistics* 69, 237–50.
MUTH, R. F (1975) *Urban economic problems*. New York: Harper and Row. 402pp.
MYRDAL, G. (1944) *The American dilemma: the Negro problem and modern democracy*. New York: Harper and Row.
MYRDAL, G. (1953) *The political element in the development of economic theory*. London: Routledge and Kegan Paul. 248pp.
MYRDAL, G. (1958) *Economic Theory and underdevelopment*. London: Methuen.

476

NATHAN, R. P. and ADAMS, C. F. (1976) Understanding central city hardship. *Political Science Quarterly* **91**, 47–62.

NATHAN, R. P. and ADAMS, C. F. (1977) *Revenue sharing: the second round.* Washington D. C.: Brookings Institution. 268pp.

NATHAN, R. P. and DOMMEL, P. (1977) The cities. In Pechman, J. A. (ed.) *Setting National Priorities: The 1978 Budget.* Washington D. C.: Brookings Institution. 443pp.

NATHAN, R. P., MANVEL, A. D., and CALKINS, S. E. (1976) *Monitoring revenue sharing.* Washington D. C.: Brookings Institution. 394pp.

National Journal (1976) *Federal spending: The north's loss is the Sunbelt's gain.* Havemann, J. and Stanfield, R. L. 26 June, 878–91.

National Journal (1977) *A year later, the Frostbelt strikes back.* Havemann, J. and Stanfield, R. L., 2 July, 1028–37.

NATIONAL TAX ASSOCIATION (1933, 1934) Second report on a plan of a model system of State and local taxation. *Proceedings National Tax Association.*

NBER (1939) *Conference on research in income and wealth*, Vol III. New York: National Bureau of Economic Research. 500pp.

NBER (1961) *Public finances: Needs, sources and utilisation.* New Jersey: Princeton University Press.

NEDC (1971) *Investment appraisal.* London: HMSO and National Economic Development Office. 30pp.

NEENAN, W. B. (1970) Suburban–central city exploitation thesis: one city's fate. *National Tax Journal* **23**, 119–29.

NEENAN, W. B. (1972) *The political economy of urban areas.* Chicago: Markham.

NERLOVE, M. (1961) *Returns to scale in electricity supply.* Stanford University, California, Institute for Mathematical Studies in the Social Sciences.

NETZER, D. (1966) *The economics of the Property tax.* Washington D. C.: Brookings Institution.

NETZER, D. (1968) Federal, State and local finance in a metropolitan context. In Perloff, H. S. and Wingo, L. (eds.) *Issues in Urban Economics.* Baltimore: Johns Hopkins University Press.

NETZER, D. (1974) *Economics and urban problems: diagnosis and prescriptions.* New York: Basic Books. 275pp.

NEW YORK, STATE COMMISSION (1973) *The Fleischmann Report on the quality, cost and financing of elementary and secondary education in New York State*, Vols. 1 to 3. New York: Viking.

NEWCOMER, M. (1917) Separation of state and local revenues in the United States. *Columbia University Studies in History, Economics and Public Law.* **76**, 295pp.

NEWCOMER, M. (1935) *An index of the taxpaying ability of state and local government.* New York: Columbia University Press for Bureau of Public Teachers College.

NEWCOMER, M. (1937) Estimate of the tax burden on different income classes. In Twentienth Century Fund, *Studies in Current Tax Problems*, New York: Bureau of Public Teachers College.

NEWMAN, M. (1972) *Political economy of Appalachia.* Lexington, Mass.: D. C. Heath.

NEWMAN, M. (1978) *Whither multi-state regional commissions.* Paper presented at Annual Meeting of Regional Science Association. Department of Economics, Pennsylvania State University.

NEWTON, K. and SHARPE, L. J. (1976) *Service output in local government: some reflections and proposals*, Mimeo. Oxford: Nuffield College.

NICHOLSON, R. J. and TOPHAM, N. (1971) The determinants of investments in housing by local authorities: an econometric approach. *Journal Royal Statistical: Society A* **134**, 273–303.

Bibliography

NICHOLSON, R. J. and TOPHAM, N. (1972) Investment decisions and the size of local authorities, *Policy and Politics* **1**, 23–44.

NISKANEN, W. A. (1971) *Bureaucracy and representative government.* Chicago: Aldine-Atherton.

NORTH, D. C. (1955) Location theory and regional economic growth. *Journal of Political Economy* **43**, 243–58.

NORTHERN REGIONAL STRATEGY (1976) Public expenditure in the Northern Regions and other British regions 1969/70–1973/74. Technical report 12. Newcastle upon Tyne: NRS Planning Team.

NORTON, J. K. (1926) The ability of the States to support education. Washington D. C.: National Education Association.

NORTON, J. K. and NORTON, M. A. (1937) Wealth, children and education. Columbia, New York: Teachers College Press.

NURSKE, R. (1961) *Patterns of trade and development.* Oxford: University Press.

OATES, W. E. (1968) The theory of public finance in a federal system. *Canadian Journal of Economics* **1**, 37–54.

OATES, W. E. (1969) The effects of property taxes and local public spending on property values: An empirical study of tax capitalization and the Tiebout hypothesis. *Journal of Political Economy* **77**, 957–71.

OATES, W. E. (1972) *Fiscal Federalism,* New York: Harcourt Brace Jovanovich.256pp.

OATES, W. E. (ed.) (1977) *The political economy of fiscal federalism.* Lexington, Mass: D. C. Heath. 355pp.

O'CONNOR, J. (1973) *The fiscal crisis of the state.* New York: St Martins Press.

OECD (1962) *Forecasting educational needs for economic and social development.* Paris: OECD. 113pp.

OECD (1974) *Negative income tax: an approach to the coordination of taxation and social welfare policies.* Paris: OECD. 56pp.

OFFICE OF THE LONDON PHALANX (1841) *Charles Fourier theory of attractive industry and the moral harmony of passions.* London: Office of the London Phalanx. 120pp.

OHLIN, B. (1933) *Interregional and international trade.* Cambridge, Mass.: Harvard University Press.

OLIVER, F. R. and STANYER, J. (1969) Some aspects of the financial behaviour of county boroughs, *Public administration* **47**, 169–84.

OLSON, M. (1965) *The logic of collective action.* Cambridge, Mass.: Harvard University Press.

OLSON, M. (1969) The principle of 'fiscal equivalence': The division of responsibilities between different levels of government, *American Economic Review* **59**, 479–87.

ORSHANSKY, M. (1963) *Children of the poor.* Washington D. C.: Social Services Administration, Bulletin.

ORSHANSKY, M. (1965) *Counting the poor: another look at the poverty profile.* Washington D. C.: Social Services Administration, Bulletin.

OSTROM, V. (1969) Operational federalism: Organisation of public services in the American federal system. *Public Choice* **7**, 1–17.

OSTROM, V. (1973) *The intellectual crisis in American public administration.* Montgomery: Alabana University Press.

OSTROM, V., TIEBOUT, C. M. and WARREN, R. (1961) The organisation of government in metropolitan areas: A theoretical enquiry. *American Political Science Review* **40**, 831–42.

PARETO, V. F. D. (1966) *Sociological writings,* London: Routledge.

PAULY, M. V. (1970) Optimality, public goods and local governments: a general theoretical analysis. *Journal of Political Economy* **78**, 572–85.

478

PEACOCK, A. T. and WISEMAN, J. (1961) *The growth of public expenditure in the United Kingdom.* London: Princeton University Press.

PECHMAN, J. A. (1971) Fiscal federalism in the 1970's. *National Tax Journal* **24**, 281–90.

PECHMAN, J. A. (1973) *International trends in the distribution of tax burdens: implications for tax policy.* London: Institute for Fiscal Studies.

PECHMAN, J. A. (ed.) (1977) *Comprehensive Income taxation.* Washington D. C.: Brookings Institution.

PECHMAN, J.A. and OKNER, B.A. (1974) *Who bears the tax burden?* Washington D.C.: Brookings Institution.

PEISER, R. (1973) *New town infrastructure costs.* Cambridge: University Department of Land Economy working paper.

PERLOFF, H. S., DUNN, E. S., LAMPARD, E. E. and MUTH, R. F. (1960) *Regions, Resources and Economic Growth.* Baltimore: Johns Hopkins University Press.

PERROUX, F. (1955) Note sur la notion de 'pôle' de croissance. *Economie Appliquée* **8** (1-2), 307–20.

PETERSON, G. E. (1976) Finance, In Gorham, W. and Glazer, N. (eds.) *The Urban Predicament.* Washington D. C.: Urban Institute.

PETERSON, G. E. (1977) *Federal tax policy and urban development.* Washington D. C.: Urban Institute.

PETTY, W. (1687) *Five essays in political arithmetick*, London: Mark Pardoe.

PHARES, D. (1973) State–local tax equity. Lexington, Mass.: D. C. Heath. 185pp.

PHELPS, E. S. (ed.) (1965) *Private wants and public needs: issues surrounding the size and scope of government expenditure.* New York: Norton. 178pp.

PHILLIPS, C. F. (1969) *The economics of regulation: theory and practice in the transport and public utility industries.* Homewood: R. D. Irwin. 774pp.

PHILLIPS, K. (1969) *The Emerging Republican Majority.* New Rochelle, New York: Arlington House.

PIGOU, A. C. (1928) *Study in Public Finance.* London: Macmillan.

PIGOU, A. C. (1947) *A study in public finance*, 3rd edn. London: Macmillan.

PIVEN, F.F. and CLOWARD, R. A. (1971) *Regulating the poor: the functions of public welfare.* New York: Pantheon-Random House. 389pp.

POGUE, T. F. (1974) Deductions vs. credits: A comment. *National Tax Journal* **27**, 659–62.

POGUE, T. (1976) Tax exporting and the measurement of fiscal capacity. *Proceedings National Tax Association Conference*, 79–89.

POLLAKOWSKI, H. O. (1973) The effects of property taxes and local public spending on property values: A comment and further results. *Journal Political Economy* **81**, 994–1003.

POMMEREHNE, W. W. (1977) Quantitative aspects of federalism: a study of six countries. In Oates W. E. (ed.) *The political economy of fiscal federalism.* Lexington, Mass.: D. C. Heath.

POULANTZAS, N. (1975) *Political power and social classes.* London: New Left Books.

PRAYOR, F. L. (1967) Elements of a positive theory of public expenditures. *Finanzarchiv* **26**, 405–30.

PUBLIUS (1977) Special issue: Federalism in Australia, **7** (3).

RAFUSE, K. (1965) Cyclical behaviour of State–local finances. In Musgrave, R. A. (ed.) *Essays in Fiscal federalism.* Washington D. C.: Brookings Institution.

RAMSEY, D. D. (1972) Suburban–Central city exploitation thesis: Comment. *National Tax Journal* **25**, 602.

REAL ESTATE RESEARCH CORPORATION (1974) *The costs of sprawl*, Vols. 1 & 2. Washington D. C.: Council on Environmental Quality, Department of Housing and Urban Development, and Environmental Protection Agency.

479

Bibliography

RECHTENWALD, H. C. (1971) *Tax incidence and income redistribution.* Detroit: Wayne State University Press.

REDCLIFFE-MAUD, J. P. and WOOD, B. (1976) *English local government reformed.* London: Oxford University Press.

REINER, T. (1965) Sub-national and national planning: decision criteria. *Papers, Regional Science Association,* 107–136.

REISCHAUER, R. D. (1974) *Rich governments–Poor governments: determining the fiscal capacity and revenue requirements of State and local government.* Washington D. C.: Brookings Institution.

REISCHAUER, R. D. (1976) General revenue sharing – The program's incentives. In Oates, W. E. (ed.) *Financing the New Federalism: Revenue sharing, conditional grants and taxation.*: Baltimore: RFF and Johns Hopkins Press.

REISSART, B. (1978a) Responsibility sharing and joint tasks in West German federalism. In Spahn, P. B. (ed.) *Principles of Federal Policy Coordination in the Federal Republic of Germany: Basic Issues and annotated legislation.* Canberra: ANU Centre for Research on Federal Fiscal Relations.

REISSART, B. (1978b) *Federal and state grants to local governments: some descriptive material on the West German case.* Berlin: International Institute of Management, Wissenschaftszentrum, paper IIM/78–1. 37pp.

RESCHER, N. (1966) *Distributive justice: A constructive critique of utilitarian theory of distribution.* Indianapolis: Bobbs-Merrill.

REYNOLDS, M. and SMOLENSKY, E. (1976) *Public expenditures, taxes, and the distribution of income: The United States, 1950, 1961, 1970.* New York: Academic Press. 139pp.

REYNOLDS, T. J. (1935) *Costs of administering the various state and local taxes.* New York: Twentieth Century Fund.

RICARDO, D. (1817) *On the principles of political economy and taxation.* London: Macmillan.

RICE, S. A. (1928) *Quantitative methods in politics.* New York: Russell and Russell. 331pp.

RICHARDSON, H. W. (1969) *Urban and Regional Economics.* London: Weidenfeld and Nicholson.

RICHARDSON, H. W. (1973) *The economics of urban size.* Farnborough: Saxon House D. C. Heath.

RIDLEY, C. and SIMON, H. (1974) *Measuring municipal activity.* Chicago: International City Managers Association.

RIKER, W. H. (1962) *The theory of Political Coalitions.* New Haven, Yale University Press.

RIKER, W. H. and ORDESHOOK, P. (1973) *An introduction to positive political theory.* New Jersey: Prentice-Hall.

RITSCHL, H. (1931) *Gemeinwirtschaft und Kapitalistiche Marketwirtschaft zur erkenntris der duolistischen Wirtschaftsungnung.* Tübergen: J. C. B. Mohr.

ROBBINS, L. (1952) *The theory of economic policy.* London: Macmillan.

ROBINSON, J. (1969) *Economic Philosophy.* London: Pitman.

ROBINSON, T. R. and COURCHENE, T. J. (1969) Fiscal federalism and economic stability: an examination of multi-level public finances in Canada, 1952–1965. *Canadian Journal of Economics* 2, 165–89.

ROBSON, W. A. (1968) *Local government in crisis.* London: Allen and Unwin.

ROMANS, T. T. (1965) *Capital exports and growth among US regions.* Middletown, Conn.: Wesleyian University Press. 230pp.

RONZANI, S. (1978) *Background notes to regional incentives in Italy.* Paper at IIM conference, Racine, Wisconsin.

ROSE, M. (1978) *Needs element, rate equalisation and London's inner urban areas.* Mimeo, Greater London Council.

ROSS, J. P. and BURKHEAD, J. (1974) *Productivity in the local government sector.* Lexington, Mass.: DC. Heath.

ROTHENBERG, J. (1970) Local decentralisation and the theory of optimal government. In Margolis, J. (ed.) *The Analysis of Public Output:* Princeton, N. J.: University Press.

ROTHWEILER, R. L. (1972) Revenue sharing in the Federal Republic of Germany. *Publius* **2** (1) 4–25.

ROUSSEAU, J. J. (1765) The constitutional project in Corsica. In Watkins, F. (ed.) *Rousseau: political writings.* London: Nelson. 320pp.

ROUSSEAU, J. J. (1772) Considerations on the government of Poland. In Watkins, F. (ed.) *Rousseau: political writings.* London: Nelson. 320pp.

ROYAL COMMISSION ON DOMINION-PROVINCIAL RELATIONS (1940) (Rowell-Sirois Report) Ottawa: Queen's Printer.

RUBINOFF, A. S. (1973) New and emerging fiscal arrangements in the Canadian federation. *Proceedings of 67th National Tax Association Conference.* Washington D. C.: Tax Institute of America.

RUNQUIST, B. S. and FEREJOHN, J. A. (1976) Observations on a Distributive theory of policy making: two American expenditure programs compared. In Liske, C. Lock, W. and McCamat, J. (eds.) *Comparative Public Policy.* New York: Wiley.

SACKS, S. (1961) *Financing government in a metropolitan area: the Cleveland experience.* Glencoe: Free Press.

SACKS, S. (1965) State and local finances and economic development. In *State and local taxes on Business.* New Jersey: Princeton, Tax Institute of America. 352pp.

SALATHIEL, D. (1975) *Local authority expenditure per head variations with population decline per head.* London: Department of Environment Finance and local government grants working group.

SALE, K. (1975) *Power shift: the rise of the Southern Rim and its challenge to the Eastern establishment.* New York: Random House. 362pp.

SAMUELSON, P. A. (1954) The pure theory of public expenditure, *Review of Economics and Statistics* **36**, 387–9.

SANDFORD, T. (1967) *Storm over the states.* Chicago: McGraw-Hill.

SANDLER, T. (1975) Pareto optimality, pure public goods, impure public goods and mulitregional spillovers. *Scottish Journal of Political Economy* **22**, 25–38.

SANT, M. (1973) *The geography of business cycles: A case study of economic fluctuations in East Anglia 1951–1968.* LSE Geographical papers 5. London: London School of Economics.

SAX, E. (1924) Die wertungstheorie der Steur. *Zeitschridt für Volkswirtschaft und Sozialpolitik, New Series,* **4**.

SAY, J. B. (1855) *A treatise on political economy.* Philadelphia: Lippincott.

SCHARPF, F. W., REISSART, B. and SCHNABEL, F. (1976) *Politikverflechtung Theorie und Empirik der Kooperativen Föderalismus in der Bundesrepublik.* Kronberg: Scriptor.

SCHARPF, F. W., REISSART, B., and SCHNABEL, F. (1978) Policy effectiveness and conflict avoidance in intergovernmental policy formation. In Harf, K. and Scharpf, F. W. (eds.) *Intergovernmental Policy making.* London: Sage.

SCHMANDT, H. J. (1961) *The municipal incorporation trend 1950–1960.* Madison: Wisconsin University Press.

SCHMID, G., LIPINSKI, H. and PALMER, M. (1975) *An alternative to general revenue sharing: a needs-based allocation formula.* Menlo Park, California: Institute for the Future.

SCHMIDT, R. E. (1977) *Regional development commissions: An alternative federal intervention strategy.* Washington D. C.: Urban Institute, WR, 2–0090–10–2.

SCHNENNER, R. W. (1973) The determinants of municipal employee wages. *Review of Economics and Statistics* **55**, 83–90.

SCHULTZE, C. D., FRIED, E. R., RIVLIN, A. M. and TEETERS, N. H. (1971) *Setting national priorities: The 1972 Budget.* Washington D. C.: Brookings Institution. 336pp.

SCHUMPETER, J. A. (1943) *Capitalism, Socialism and democracy.* New York: Allen and Unwin.

SCOTT, A. D. (1952) Federal grants and resource allocation. *Journal of Political Economy* **60**, 534–8.

SCOTT, A. D. (1964) The economic goals of federal finance. *Public Finance* **19**, 241–88.

SCOTT, A. J. (1971) *Combinatorial programming, spatial analysis and planning.* London: Methuen. 204pp.

SEIDMAN, H. (1975) *Politics, position and power: the dynamics of federal organisation,* 2nd edn. London: Oxford University Press. 354pp.

SELF, P. (1972) *Administrative theories and politics: an enquiry into the structure and processes of modern government.* London: Allen and Unwin. 308pp.

SELIGMAN, E. R. A. (1913) *Essays in taxation.* New York: Columbia University Press.

SELIGMAN, E. R. A. (1927) *The shifting and incidence of taxation,* 5th edn. New York: Columbia University Press.. 431pp.

SENIOR, D. (1969) *Report of the Royal Commission on Local Government in England,* Vol. II. London: HMSO.

SHANNON, G. W., BASHSHUR, R. L. and METZNER, C. A. (1969) The concept of distance as a factor in accessibility and utilization of health care. *Medical Care Review* **26**, 143–61.

SHANNON, G. W. and DEVER, G. E. A. (1974) *The geography of health care.* New York: McGraw-Hill.

SHAPLEY, L. S. and SHUBIK, M. (1954) A method for evaluating the distribution of power in a committee system. *American Political Science Review* **48**, 787–92.

SHARPLES, B. (1975) Provincial disparities in educational expenditures. *Canadian Tax Journal* **23**, 383–93.

SHOUP, C. S. (1964) Standards for distributing a free governmental service: crime protection, *Public finance* **19**, 383–92.

SHOUP, C. S. (1969) *Public Finance.* Chicago: Aldine. 660pp.

SHOUP, C. S., SHINBERG, B. L. and VICKREY, W. (1935) A comparison of aggregate burden of federal income tax and state income tax in eleven selected States. In *Studies in Current Tax Problems.* New York: Twentieth Century Fund, 303pp.

SHOUP, D. C. and ROSSETT, A. (1971) Fiscal exploitation by overlapping government, In Hirsch, W. Z., Vincent, P. E., Terrell, H. S. and Shoup, D. C., *Fiscal pressures on the central city.* New York: Praeger.

SJAASTAD, L. (1962) The costs and returns of human migration. *J. Political Economy, Supplement* **70**, 80–93.

SMILEY, D. V. (1967) *The Canadian Political nationality.* Toronto: Methuen.

SMITH, A. (1776) *An inquiry into the nature and causes of the wealth of nations.* In Campbell, R. H. Skinner A. S. and Todd, W. B. (eds.) (1976) Oxford: Clarendon Press.

SMITH, D. M. (1977) *Human Geography; A welfare approach.* London: Arnold.

SMITH, S. de (1971) *Constitutional and administrative law.* Harmondsworth: Penguin 712pp.

SNYDER, W. W. (1970a) Measuring economic stabilisation. *American Economic Review* **60**, 924–33.

SNYDER, W. W. (1970b) Measuring the effects of German budget policies 1955–1965. *Weltwirtschaftliches Archiv* **104**, 302–24.

SNYDER, W. W. (1973) Are the budgets of state and local governments destabilising? A six country comparison. *European Economic Review* **4**, 197–203.

SPAHN, P. B. (1977) The pattern of State and local taxation in the Federal Republic of Germany. In Mathews R. L. (ed.) *State and local taxation.* Canberra: Australian National University Press.

SPAHN, P. B. (ed.) (1978) *Principles of federal policy coordination in the Federal Republic of Germany: Basic issues and annotated legislation.* Canberra: ANU Centre for Research on Federal Financial Relations.

SPAHN, R. N. (1973) *Public administration in Australia,* 3rd edn. Sydney: Government Printer.

SPEK, J. E. (1972) On the economic analysis of health and medical care in a Swedish health district. In Hauser M. H. (ed.) *The Economics of medical care.* London: Allen and Unwin.

SPN (1976) *Strategic plan for the Northern region.* London: HMSO.

SPNW (1972) *The urban environment.* Strategic Plan for the North West, Manchester. London: HMSO.

SPNW (1973) *Strategic plan for the North West region,* London: HMSO.

STEELE, D. B. (1969) Regional Multipliers in Great Britain. *Oxford economic papers* **21**, 269–92.

STEIN, L. von (1885) *Lehrbuch der Finanzwissenschaft,* 5th edn. Leipzig: O. Wigard.

STIGLER, G. (1945) The cost of subsistence. *Journal of Farm Economics* **27**, 303–14.

STIGLER, G. J. (1972) General economic conditions and national elections. *Public Choice* **13**, 91–101.

STILWELL, F. J. B. (1972) *Regional economic policy.* London: Macmillan.

STOLPER, W. F. and TIEBOUT, C. M. (1978) The balance of payments of a small area as an analytical tool. In Funck R. and Parr, J. B. (eds.) *The analysis of regional structure: essays in honour of August Lösch.* London: Pion.

STONE, P. A. (1961) Social accounts at the regional level: A survey. In *Regional Economic Planning: Techniques and analysis.* Paris: OECD.

STONE, P. A. (1963) *Housing, town development, land and costs.* London: The Estates Gazette.

STONE, P. A. (1970a) *Urban development in Britain–standards, costs and resources 1964–2004,* vol. 1: *Population trends and housing.* Cambridge: University Press.

STONE, P. A. (1970b) *Some economic restraints on building and town development.* London: Butterworths.

STONE, P. A. (1973a) The economics of the form and organisation of cities. In Cameron, G. and Wingo, L. (eds.) *Cities, Regions and public policy.* Edinburgh: Oliver and Boyd.

STONE, P. A. (1973b) *The structure, size and cost of urban settlements.* Cambridge: University Press.

STRAYER, G. and HAIG, R. M. (1925) *The financing of education in the State of New York.* New York: Educational Finance Inquiry.

STRINGER, J. (1967) Operational research for multiorganisations. *Operational Research Quarterly* **18**, 105–20.

STUDENSKI, P. (1935) Chapters in Public Finance. In Spahn, W. E. (ed.) *Economic Principles and Problems.* New York; Farrar and Rinehart.

Bibliography

STUDENSKI, P. (1943) *Measurement of variations in State economic and fiscal capacity.* Washington D. C.: Social Security Board Memorandum No. 50.

STUDENSKI, P. and MORT, P. R. (1941) *Centralised vs. decentralised government in relation to democracy.* Columbia University, Bureau of publications, Teachers College. 69pp.

SUGG, A. L. (1967) Economic aspects of hurricanes. *Monthly weather Review* **95**, 143–6.

SUNDELSON, J. W. and MUSHKIN, S. (1944) *The measurment of State and local tax effort.* Washington D. C.: Social Security Board Memorandum No. 58.

SUNLEY, E. M. (1977) The choice between deductions and credits. *National Tax Journal* **30**, 243–7.

SUNQUIST, J. L. (1978) *Regional growth policy in the United States.* Presented at IIM conference, Racine, Wisconsin.

SUNQUIST, J. L. and DAVIS, D. W. (1969) *Making federalism work: A study of program coordination at the community level.* Washington D. C.: Brookings Institution. 293pp.

SVIMEZ, A. (1967) *Ricenca sui costa d'insediamento.* Quoted in EFTA, 1968, Regional policy in the European Free Trade Area, London.

A six country comparison. *European Economic Review* **4**, 197–213.

TARASOV, H. (1942) *Who pays the taxes?* Washington D. C.: Temporary National Economic Committee. Monograph No. 3.

TARLTON, C. D. (1965) Symmetry and assymetry as elements of federalism, *Journal of Politics* **27**, 861–74.

TARROW, S. (1977) *Between centre and periphery: grass roots politicians in Italy and France.* New Haven: Yale University Press. 272pp.

TARSCHYS, D. (1975) The growth of public expenditure: nine models of explanation. *Scandinavian Political Studies* **10**, 9–31.

TASK FORCES REPORT (1975) *A regional basis for Australian government administration.* Report to the Royal Commission on Australian Government Administration, Vols. 1 and 2. Canberra: Government Publishing Service.

TAWNEY, R. H. (1952) Equality, 4th edn. London: Allen and Unwin. 285pp.

TAX FOUNDATION (1966) *Fiscal outlook for State and local governments to 1975.* New York: Tax Foundation Inc.

TAX FOUNDATION (1967) *Tax burdens and benefits of government expenditures by income class, 1961 and 1965.* New York: Tax Foundation Inc.

TAYLOR, J. A. (ed.) (1970) *Weather economics.* Oxford: Pergamon.

TAYLOR, P. J. and JOHNSTON, R. J. (1978) Population distributions and political power in the European parliament. *Regional Studies* **12**, 61–8.

THOMPSON, W. (1965) *A preface to urban economics.* Baltimore: the Johns Hopkins University Press.

THRALL, G. (1974) Two studies in taxation: VAT and spatially invariant tax. Ohio State University Department of Geography, Mimeograph.

THRING, J. B. (1975) *Residential service systems.* Unpublished Ph.D. University of Cambridge.

THRING, J. B. (1976) *Variations in development costs.* Annex 7 of Resource issues report, DSPSE, Strategy for the South east: 1976 Review. London: Department of the Environment.

THUROW, L. (1973) Towards a definition of economic justice. *The Public Interest* **31**, 65–7.

TIEBOUT, C. M. (1956) A pure theory of local expenditures. *Journal of Political Economy* **64**, 416–24.

TIEBOUT, C. M. (1961) An economic theory of fiscal decentralisation. In National Bureau of Economic Research, *Public Finances: Needs, sources and utilisation.* New Jersey: Princeton University Press.

TIMM, H. (1974) Finanzpolitische Autonomie untergeordneter Gebietskörpenschafteb (Gemeinden) und Standortverteilung. Ein Beitrag zur ökonomischen Beurteilung des Finanzausgleichs. *Schiften des Vereins für Socialpolitik Gesellschaft für Wirtschafts-und Sozialwissenschaften, N. F.* **32**, 9–60.

TIMM, H. (1969) Gemeindefinanzpolitik in der Wachstumszyklen, *Finanzarchiv* **28**, 441–8.

TNEC (1938-39) Assessment of tax incidence. Monographs 1 and 2. Washington D. C.: Temporary National Economic Committee.

TOCQUEVILLE, A. de (1966) *Democracy in America.* New York: Wiley.

TOWNSEND, C. B. (1960) *The economics of waste water treatment.* London: Institute of Civil Engineers, paper 6424.

TUCKER, R. S. (1951) Distribution of tax burdens in 1948. *National Tax Journal* **4**, 269–85.

TUCKER, R. S. (1952) Rebuttal, *National Tax Journal* **5**, 36–8.

TUCKER, R. S. (1953) The distribution of government burdens and benefits. *American Economic Review* **43**, 518–43.

TULLOCK, G. (1969) Federalism: problems of scale, *Public Choice* **6**, 19–29.

UK, Committee of Enquiry into local government finance (1976) Chairman F. Layfield. London: HMSO.

UK, Central Policy Review Staff (1977) *Relations between central government and local authorities.* London: HMSO.

UK, DHSS (1976) *Sharing resources for health in England.* London HMSO, Report of Resource Allocation Working Party.

UK, DOE (1975a) *Harmood Street Area, Report of ministerial working party*, London: Department of the Environment.

UK, DOE (1975b) *Housing cost yardstick, circular 61/75.* London: Department of the Environment.

UK GOVERNMENT (1971) *The future shape of local government finances.* Green paper, Cmnd 4741. London: HMSO.

UK GOVERNMENT (1972) *Proposals for a tax-credit system.* London: HMSO, Cmnd 5116. 34pp.

UK GOVERNMENT (1976) *Direct elections to the European Assembly*, Green paper. London: HMSO.

UK HOUSE OF COMMONS (1973) *Regional development incentives: Report*, House of Commons Expenditure Committee. London: HMSO.

UK Royal Commission on the Constitution (1973) Report, Vols. 1 and 2. Cmnd. 5460. London: HMSO.

UK Royal Commission on Local Government In England (1968a) *Local authority services and the characteristics of administrative areas.* London: HMSO, Research Paper 5.

UK Royal Commission on Local Government in England (1968b) *Performance and size of local education authorities.* London: HMSO, Research Paper 4.

UK Royal Commission on Local Government in England 1966–69 (1969) Cmnd 4040. London: HMSO.

UK TREASURY (1978) Capital and Current expenditure. *Economic Progress Report* **104**, 1–3. London: UK Treasury.

US ACIR (1962a) *Measures of state and local fiscal capacity and tax effort*, Report M-

16. Washington D. C: US Advisory Commission on Intergovernmental Relations.

US ACIR (1962b) *Alternative approaches to metropolitan reorganisation in metropolitan areas.* Report A-11. Washington D. C.: US Advisory Commission on Intergovernmental Relations.

US ACIR (1964) *The role of equalisation in federal grants.* Report A-19. Washington D. C.: US Advisory Commission on Intergovernmental Relations.

US ACIR (1965) *Metropolitan social and economic disparities: implications for intergovernmental relations in central cities and suburbs.* Report A-25. Washington D. C.: US advisory Commission on Intergovernmental Relations.

US ACIR (1967) *State-local taxation and industrial location.* Report A-30. Washington D. C.: US Advisory Commission on Intergovernmental Relations.

US ACIR (1968) *Fiscal balance in the American federal system. Vol 2. Metropolitan fiscal disparities.* Report A-31. Washington D. C.: US Advisory Commission on Intergovernmental Relations.

US ACIR (1969) *Urban America and the federal system.* Report M-47. Washington D. C.: US Advisory Commission on Intergovernmental Relations.

US ACIR (1970) *The commuter and the municipal income tax* Report M-51. Washington D. C.: US Advisory Commission on Intergovernmental Relations.

US ACIR (1971a) *In search of balance – Canada's intergovernmental experience.* Report M-68. Washington D. C.: US Advisory Commission on Intergovernmental Relations.

US ACIR (1971b) *Measuring the fiscal capacity and effort of state and local areas.* Report M-58. Washington D. C.: US Advisory Commission on Intergovernmental Relations.

US ACIR (1976) *Improving Urban America: a challenge to federalism.* Report M-107. Washington D. C.: US Advisory Commission on Intergovernmental Relations.

US ACIR (1977a) *Community Development: the workings of a federal block grant.* Report A-57. Washington D. C.: US Advisory Commission on Intergovernmental Relations.

US ACIR (1977b) *Categorical grants: their role and design.* Report A-52. Washington D. C.: US Advisory Commission on Intergovernmental Relations.

US ACIR (1977c) *Measuring the fiscal 'blood pressure' of the States – 1964–1975.* Report M-111. Washington D. C.: US Advisory Commission on Intergovernmental Relations.

US ACIR (1978a) *Significant features of fiscal federalism 1977–8.* Washington D. C.: US Advisory Commission on Intergovernmental Relations.

US ACIR (1978b) Frostbelt and sunbelt: convergence over time. *Intergovernmental perspective* **4**, 8–15. Washington D. C.: US Advisory Commission on Intergovernmental Relations.

US ACIR (1978c) *Regional Growth Study.* Washington D. C.: US Advisory Commission on Intergovernmental Relations.

US CBO (1977) *Troubled local economies and the distribution of tax dollars.* Washington D. C.: Congressional Budget Office.

US CED (1966) *Modernizing local government.* New York: Committee for Economic Development.

US CED (1970) *Reshaping government in metropolitan areas.* New York: Committee for Economic Development.

US COMPTROLLER GENERAL (1972) *Study of health facilities construction costs.* Report to US 92nd Congress, 2nd session. Washington D. C.: GPO, 888pp.

US Congress (1975) *The US market for securities,* subcommittee on Economic Progress. Washington D. C.: GPO.

US CRS (1977) *Selected essays on patterns of regional change: the changes, the federal role, and the federal response.* Washington D. C.: GPO, US Library of Congress, Congressional Research Service.

US DOT (1972) *The 1972 National Highway needs report.* House document 92–266. Washington D. C.: Department of Transportation.

US GAO (1977) *Changing patterns of federal aid to state and local governments 1969–75.* Washington D. C.: General Accounting Office. 64pp.

US HEW (1976) *The measure of poverty.* Washington D. C.: Department of Health, Education and Welfare.

US HUD (1978) *A new partnership to conserve America's communities: A national urban policy.* Washington D. C.: Department of Housing and Urban Development.

US JEC (1967) *Revenue sharing and its alternatives: What future for fiscal federalism?* US Congress, 90th congress, 1st session, Hearings before the subcommittee on economic policy. Washington D. C.: GPO, Joint Economic Committee.

US JEC (1975) *Credit flows and interest costs.* Washington D. C.: Joint Economic Committee, Subcommittee on Economic Progress.

US NEWS AND WORLD REPORT (1977) *Special report: The pork-barrel war between the States.* 5 December, 39–41.

US TREASURY (1943) *Federal, state and local government fiscal relations.* 78th. Congress, 1st session Document 69, 23 June. Washington D. C.: GPO. 595pp.

US TREASURY (1978) *Report on the fiscal impact of the economic stimulus package on 48 large urban governments.* Washington D. C.: Office of State and Local Finance, US Treasury.

VAUBAN, S. (1707) *Testament politique ... dans lequel ce seigneur donne les moyens d'augmenter considerablement les revenues de la couronne, par l'establishment d'une dixine royale . . .* Vols. 1 and 2. Paris.

VERRI, P. (1771) Meditozione sulla Economia Politica. In Custodi P. (ed.) 1804–5, *Scitori Classica Italiani di Economia Politica, Parte Moderna,* Vols. 15–17. Milan: G. G. Destefaris, 41 vols.

VIDAL DE LA BLACHE, P. (1911) *Les genres de vie dans la géographie humaine. Annales de Géographie* **20**, 193–212, 289–304.

VILE, M. J. C. (1973) *Federalism in the United States, Canada and Australia.* Research Paper No. 2, Royal Commission on the Constitution. London: HMSO.

VINCENT, P. E. (1971) The fiscal impact of commuters. In Hirsch, W. Z. Vincent, P. E. Terrell, H. S. Shoup D. C., and Rosett, A. (eds.) *Fiscal Pressure on the central city.* New York: Praeger.

VINING, R. (1945) Regional variations in cyclical flucatuations viewed as a frequency distribution. *Econometrica* **13**, 183–213.

VOSEL, J. H. (1974) *Police stations: planning and specifications.* Seattle: University of Washington, Bureau of Governmental Research and Services, Report 128.

WAGNER, A (1890) *Finanzwissenschaft.* Leipzig: C. F. Winter.

WARNTZ, W. (1956) *Macrogeography of income fronts.* Philadephia: Regional Science Association.

WEAVER, J. B. and HESS, S. W. (1963) A procedure for non-partisan districting: development of computer techniques. *Yale Law Journal* **73**, 288–308.

WEBER, A. (1909) *Über den Standart der Industrien.* Tübingen: 256pp.

WEICHER, J. C. (1972) Determinaints of central city expenditures: some overlooked factors and problems. *National Tax Journal* **23**, 379–96.

WEISSBROD, R. (1976) *Diffusion of relative wage inflation in South east Pennsylvania.*

Bibliography

Evanston, Ill.: Northwestern University Press. Studies in Geography 23.

WERTHEIMER, R. (1970) *The monetary rewards of migration within the United States.* Washington D. C.: Urban Institute.

WHEATON, W. L. and SCHUSSHEIM. M. (1956) *The cost of municipal services in residential areas.* Washington D. C.: GPO.

WHITLAM, E. G. (1974) The future of Australian federalism—A labour view. In Mathews, R. L. (ed.) *Intergovernmental relations in Australia.* Sydney: Angus and Robertson.

WICKSELL, K. (1896) *Finanztheoretische Undersuchunge und das Steurwesen Schwedens.* Jena.

WICKSELL, K. (1934) *Föresläsningar i nationalekonomie.* London: G. Routledge.

WIESER, F. F. von (1898) *Handwönterbuch der Staatwissenschaften.* Jena.

WILLIAMS, A (1958–9) The finance of local government in England and Wales since 1948, 3 parts. *National Tax Journal* **11**, 302–13; **12**, 1–21. 127–50.

WILLIAMS, A. (1974) 'Need' as a demand concept (with special reference to health). In Culyer A. J. (ed.) *Economic policies and Social goals: aspects of public choice.* London: Martin Robertson.

WOHLENBERG, E. H. (1976) Interstate variation in AFDC programmes, *Economic Geography* **52**, 254–66.

WOOD, C. M., LEE, N., LUKER, J. A. and SAUNDERS, P. J. W. (1974) *The Geography of pollution: a study of greater Manchester.* Manchester: University Press.

WOOD, R. C. (1961) *1400 Governments.* Cambridge, Mass.: Harvard University Press.

WOODWARD, V. H. (1970) *Regional social accounts for the United Kingdom.* Cambridge: University Press.

WRIGHT, D. S. (1975) Revenue sharing and structural features of American federalism. In Caputo D. A. (ed.) *General Revenue sharing and federalism.* Annals of the American Academy of Political and Social Science, Philadelphia.

WRIGHT, G. (1974) The political economy of New Deal spending: An econometric analysis. *Review of Economics and Statistics* **56**, 30–8.

YEATES, M. (1963) Hinterland delimitation—a distance minimizing approach. *Professional Geographer* **15**, 7–10.

ZEGEL, F. H. (1967) Meteorology—firing back on hail. *Time* 13 October, 73.

Index